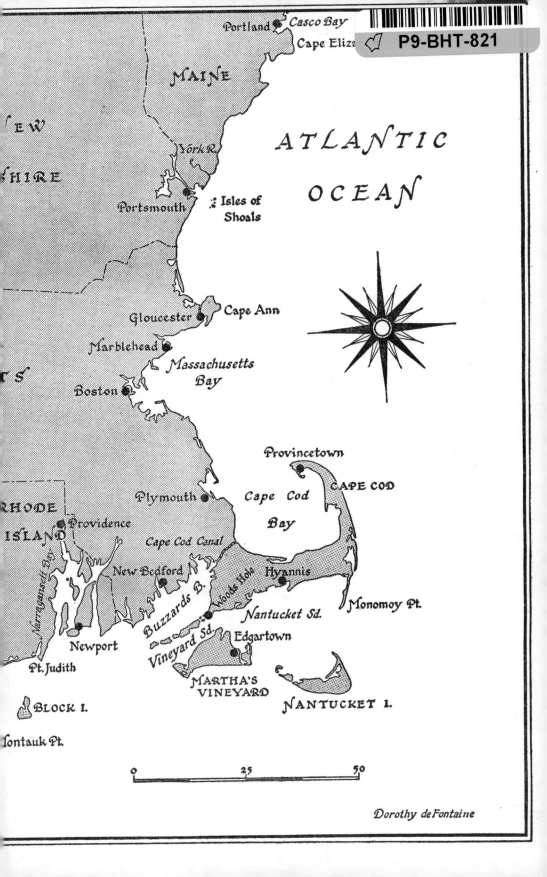

Portland • Casco Bay
Cape Eliza—

MAINE

ATLANTIC

OCEAN

York R.

Portsmouth •   ∴ Isles of
                  Shoals

Gloucester •   Cape Ann

Marblehead •   Massachusetts
                  Bay

Boston •

Provincetown

Plymouth •   Cape Cod   CAPE COD
                  Bay

RHODE
ISLAND   • Providence   Cape Cod Canal

New Bedford •   Woods Hole Hyannis •

                  Buzzards B.   Monomoy Pt.

                  Vineyard Sd.   Nantucket Sd.

Newport •   Edgartown •

Pt. Judith

                  MARTHA'S
                  VINEYARD   NANTUCKET I.

• BLOCK I.

Montauk Pt.

0   25   50

Dorothy de Fontaine

A CRUISING GUIDE TO THE

NEW ENGLAND COAST

Including the Hudson River, Long Island Sound,

and

the Coast of New Brunswick

OTHER DODD, MEAD CRUISING GUIDES

A Cruising Guide to the Chesapeake
A Cruising Guide to the Southern Coast

A Cruising Guide

TO THE

NEW ENGLAND COAST

INCLUDING THE HUDSON RIVER,
LONG ISLAND SOUND, AND
THE COAST OF NEW BRUNSWICK

By

ROGER F. DUNCAN

AND

JOHN P. WARE

⚓

WITH ILLUSTRATIONS AND CHARTS

⚓

1972 EDITION
WITH 1975 REVISIONS

NEW YORK

Dodd, Mead & Company

The poem "Offshore" from *Weathers and Edges*
by Philip Booth, copyright © 1963 by Philip Booth,
reprinted by permission of The Viking Press, Inc.

The quotation from *The Wind in the Willows*
by Kenneth Grahame, copyright 1933, reprinted with
permission of Charles Scribner's Sons, New York.

Selections from *Carter's Coast of New England,* reprinted by
permission of New Hampshire Publishing
Company, Somersworth, N.H.

Fourth Printing

ISBN: 0-396-05599-0
LIBRARY OF CONGRESS CATALOG CARD NUMBER: 78-39650
PRINTED IN THE UNITED STATES OF AMERICA
BY VAIL-BALLOU PRESS, INC., BINGHAMTON, N. Y.

This book is dedicated with respect
and affection to
ROBERT F. DUNCAN
and to the late
FESSENDEN S. BLANCHARD,

who first conceived the idea of this
Guide and established its character,
inspiring in thousands of sailors a
love of the coast and its people.

Foreword

The purpose of this *Guide* is to contribute to the safety and enjoyment of the cruising man. In no way is it intended to supersede such necessary aids as the *U.S. Coast Pilot,* National Ocean Survey charts, or tables of tides and currents. We have tried to supplement them by adding information of navigational importance where we can and also by supplying information they do not include about facilities ashore. Also, we hope to make the coast more interesting by adding such notes from history, tradition, and folklore as will give character and color to what otherwise might be mere harbors, capes, and islands.

We have visited personally at some time almost every harbor described in this book and have supplemented our experience from books and magazines. More importantly, we have been assisted by literally hundreds of yachtsmen, fishermen, town officials, and local residents. We have made strenuous efforts to be accurate, but we warn readers that **the information contained herein cannot be guaranteed and must be used with caution. Charts reproduced as illustrations are not for navigational purposes but are printed through the cooperation of the National Ocean Survey as aids to following the text.**

In some cases we have mentioned names of specific people or businesses because we believed this information to be of value to the cruising man. In doing so, we intend no slight whatever to those left unmentioned. This *Guide* is not intended as an advertising medium and has never been permitted to be used in that way.

The continued value of the book depends heavily on the cooperation of its readers. Because each edition is necessarily to a large extent a subjective work, limited by the experiences and judgments of the authors, we urge cruising men to contribute to future editions and revisions any information and reflections that will improve the *Guide.*

The astute reader will note that a few harbors of a remote and secluded nature have been omitted, in the spirit of Descartes, who wrote in the introduction to his *Geometry:*

"I hope that posterity will judge me kindly, not only for those things which I have included; but also for those which I have purposely omitted that others may share in the joy of discovery."

ROGER F. DUNCAN
Box 66
East Boothbay, Maine 04544

The Origin and History of
A Cruising Guide to the New England Coast

Robert F. Duncan, an experienced cruising man familiar with the harbors of Massachusetts and Maine, prepared for his eastward-bound friend, Fessenden S. Blanchard, "Notes on Cruising Down East" in July, 1934, Mr. Blanchard added to these notes in the course of his cruise from Woods Hole to Penobscot Bay. In the following winters the experiences of other members of the Coastwise Cruising Club of Scarsdale, New York, were added and the notes expanded to cover harbors from Larchmont, New York, to Eastport, Maine.

On May 1, 1936, a mimeographed edition of 169 pages was prepared and circulated among fellow cruising men, who contributed further information. In 1937 a printed edition of 1500 copies was published by David Kemp. A second edition, revised and enlarged, was published in 1938.

In 1946, a third edition was published by Dodd, Mead & Company, with Mr. Blanchard as co-author; and the range of the book was extended to include the Hudson and the Saint John rivers. After the fourth edition, Mr. Duncan turned over the management of the enterprise to his son, Roger F. Duncan, who produced the fifth edition in 1961 with the invaluable help of Mr. Blanchard and his son-in-law, John P. Ware. After the death of Mr. Blanchard, Mr. Ware became co-author, writing the chapters on the Hudson River, Long Island Sound, Narragansett Bay, and the west side of Buzzards Bay. His knowledge of printing and publishing has helped materially in maintaining the quality of the book through the sixth edition, published in 1967.

With this, the seventh edition of the *Guide,* published thirty-eight years after the original "Notes on Cruising Down East," we reflect changes of a character and magnitude unforseen in those days. Yet we have tried to maintain the same respect for accuracy and completeness and the same enthusiasm for cruising that inspired the original authors and the first editions.

Roger F. Duncan,
John P. Ware

Acknowledgments

The authors acknowledge with thanks the generous contributions of a great many people to this book. Especially significant was the help of Hartley Lord, who re-explored most of the Portsmouth to Cape Elizabeth area; Edward A. Myers, who wrote the section on the Damariscotta River; Donald Lewis, who furnished the report on the Penobscot River; Farnham Butler, who checked up on the Mt. Desert area; Edward Hartshorn, who supplied important material on Canadian ports; and Hugh G. Williams, whose broad knowledge of the coast and eager personal support have been invaluable. Mrs. Robert C. Duncan, Mrs. Stephen Winship, and Mrs. Elizabeth Swan were most helpful in preparing the manuscript. My wife, Mary C. Duncan, was foredeck hand on numerous cruises and has borne with an author's idiosyncracies most charitably.

Special gratitude is also extended to Virginia Ewalt, assistant to the publicity director, and Edward Watson, Harbor Master, who updated the information on Mystic Seaport; to Gerard Boardman of the South Street Seaport Museum; Arthur Woldt of the New York State Department of Environmental Conservation; Philip M. DeGaetano, Division of Pure Waters, New York State Department of Environmental Conservation; Dominick J. Pirone and Barbara Harry of the Hudson River Sloop Restoration, Inc.; Freeman Rolfe, Harbor Master of Essex, Connecticut; and to George S. Fox, public information manager of Northeast Utilities, for contributing the section on Millstone Point, Connecticut.

Finally, we offer our appreciation to the following correspondents, friends, and acquaintances who in one way or another have contributed to the accuracy and the interest of this volume:

Gordon Abbott
Blaise Alfano
Bruce Angus
Keno Bailey
Walton Baker
Malcolm Barter
Charles Bartlett
Chris and Warren Bayreuther
Alan Bemis
Mary C. Blanchard
Peter Burckmyer

John Bogart
Philip Booth
Rev. Neal Bousfield
Robert H. Boyle
Ted Brown
Charles Bruno
Robert Butman
Robert Chase
Mr. and Mrs. Dean Conger
Purcell Corbett
Mr. and Mrs. Alfred Curtis

Leverett Davis
F. Spaulding Dunbar
Donald Duncan
Robert C. Duncan
Robert F. Duncan
Prof. Jacqueline Evans
Thomas Flint
John Winsor Frost
Eugene Gardner
Tom Haley
John Hallowell
Jay Hanna
Clark Hill
Robert Hinckley
Harris Huey
Charles Ingalls
John Jenkins
Howland Jones
Prof. John Kingsbury
Orin Leach
"Shorty" Lesch
Andrew Lindsay
William Locke
Mr. and Mrs. George Lockwood
Oscar Look
Robert Love
Richard Lovejoy
Clifton Lund
David Lusty
Herbert Macaulay
George Morrill
Mr. and Mrs. Herbert Mattlage
James Nemiah
Paul Neustadt
Jarvis Newman
Ed Noessel
Robert Peacock
William Pendleton

Frank Perkins
Fred Potter
Mortimer Pratt
Thomas Reeves
Mr. and Mrs. Constantine Rhodes
Robert Richardson
John Riesman
Thomas Ring
Mr. and Mrs. Albert Roberts
William Robinson
Edward Ryerson
Harold Sims
S.B. Smith
M.B. Sprague
Thomas Stetson
William Stiles
Tim Sturtevant
Hank Van Beever
J. Hallowell Vaughan
Edward Wadsworth
Edward Ware
Henry Ware
Jennifer Ware
Leslie Ware
Molly Ware
Moses Ware
John Watson, Jr.
Peter Webster
Kenneth Weeks, Jr.
Pete Welles
Samuel Whinery
Joel White
Robert White
Charles Willauer
Stephen Winship
James Wright
Alvin Zink

Contents

Part One: INTRODUCTORY

Part Two: HARBORS

Whitehall, N.Y., to the Headwaters of the St. John River, N.B.

Contents

Illustrations

The Rat said nothing, but stooped and unfastened a rope and hauled on it; then lightly stepped into a little boat which the Mole had not observed. It was painted blue outside and white within, and was just the size for two animals; and the Mole's whole heart went out to it at once, even though he did not yet fully understand its uses.

The Rat sculled smartly across and made fast. Then he held up his forepaw as the Mole stepped gingerly down. "Lean on that!" he said. "Now then, step lively!" and the Mole to his surprise and rapture found himself actually seated in the stern of a real boat.

"This has been a wonderful day!" said he, as the Rat shoved off and took to the sculls again. "Do you know, I've never been in a boat before in all my life."

"What?" cried the Rat, open-mouthed. "Never been in a—you—never—well I—what have you been doing, then?"

"Is it so nice as all that?" asked the Mole shyly, though he was quite prepared to believe it as he leant back in his seat and surveyed the cushions, the oars, the rowlocks, and all the fascinating fittings, and felt the boat sway lightly under him.

"Nice? It's the *only* thing," said the Water Rat solemnly as he leant for ward for his stroke. "Believe me, my young friend, there is *nothing*—absolutely nothing—half so much worth doing as simply messing about in boats. Simply messing," he went on dreamily, "messing—about—in—boats; messing—"

"Look ahead, Rat!" cried the Mole suddenly.

It was too late. The boat struck the bank full tilt. The dreamer, the joyous oarsman, lay on his back at the bottom of the boat, his heels in the air.

"—about in boats—or *with* boats," the Rat went on composedly, picking himself up with a pleasant laugh. "In or out of 'em, it doesn't matter. Nothing seems really to matter, that's the charm of it. Whether you get away, or whether you don't; whether you arrive at your destination or whether you reach somewhere else, or whether you never get anywhere at all, you're always busy, and you never do anything in particular; and when you've done it there's always something else to do, and you can do it if you like, but you'd much better not. Look here! If you've really nothing else on hand this morning, supposing we drop down the river together, and have a long day of it?"

The Mole waggled his toes from sheer happiness, spread his chest with a sigh of full contentment, and leaned back blissfully into the soft cushions. "*What* a day I'm having!" he said. "Let us start at once!"

The Wind in the Willows—by Kenneth Grahame

OFFSHORE

The bay was anchor, sky,
and island: a land's end
sail, and the world tidal,
that day of blue and boat.

The island swam in the wind
all noon, a seal until
the sun furled down. Orion
loomed, that night, from unfathomed

tides; the flooding sky
was Baltic with thick stars.
On watch for whatever catch,
we coursed that open sea

as if by stars sailed off
the chart; we crewed with Arc-
turus, Vega, Polaris,
tacking into the dark.

PHILIP BOOTH

What I wanted in this poem were highly com-
pressed images, images stressed—almost like standing rigging—toward the surreal quality of a perfect
cruising day. The images aren't specifically local-
ized; they mean to distill the almost abstract
essense of heading through islands—say Penobscot
Bay islands—and *out:* to that further perfection
where navigational stars have a specific reality of
their own.

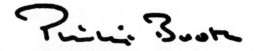

PART ONE

INTRODUCTORY

Important Notes

1. The **United States government charts** from which sections are reproduced in this book are for illustrations of the text only, and are not to be used for navigation purposes.

2. The **use of the charts** for illustration of the text is by courtesy of the National Ocean Survey.

3. "B.Y." indicated on the charts refers to a boatyard; "Y.C." to a yacht club; "B.C." to a boat club.

4. **Prices** given for dockage, etc., are the prices in effect at the time of writing and are subject to change.

5. **Distances** are in nautical miles (approximately 6 nautical miles equals 7 statute miles).

CHAPTER I

Introduction to the Coast

Fortunate indeed is the man or woman, boy or girl, who can cruise the waters covered by this volume. Nowhere else in the United States are greater and more lovely contrasts to be found so close together. Spread on the table before you the upper half of a U.S. Coast Geodetic Survey chart 1000. Within a few hundred miles lie the protected waters of the Hudson River, the lively racing activities of Long Island Sound, the sport fishing grounds from Montauk to Cape Cod, the sand dunes of the Cape. From the Cape it is but a day's sail to rocky Cape Ann and an overnight run to the Maine Coast, where granite islands form sheltered and uninhabited harbors. The gray and tide-churned waters of the Bay of Fundy run over the Reversing Falls at Saint John into the placid Saint John River, where channels are said to be marked by black cows grazing to port and red cows to starboard.

Along this coast the strong and colorful traditions of our seagoing ancestors were firmly established. High-pooped, square-ended seventeenth century vessels cautiously sailed up the rivers and explored the sounds, commanded by Hudson, Gosnold, Waymouth, Captain John Smith, and "merry brown Champlain, the King's geographer." Fishermen, whalers, coasters, clippers, and the fast, tough frigates of 1812 sailed these seas. The first steamers ploughed these waters and the giant North Atlantic liners of the early twentieth century moved grandly down New York Harbor, hailed by the arching jets of fireboats. Naval vessels and convoys of two world wars are still remembered by cruising men today, and you may see an atomic submarine off New London. Most of us now are just summertime sailors, but the long seas rolling into Penobscot Bay come out of the same Atlantic that Champlain sailed, and the same northeaster that sends us running for shelter drove *Mayflower* into Provincetown.

The old charts showed in the margins vignettes of the coast from off shore, little steel engravings showing church steeples rising from wooded hills or a lighthouse on the end of a point to help the mariner recognize the landmarks of a harbor entrance. A few sketches from different parts of the coast may help to suggest which regions the yachtsman may choose to explore.

3

The Hudson River flows between low, rounded mountains forested with hardwoods and rising quite sharply from the water. Along the edge of the stream runs a road and a railroad. A tug with several barges in tow comes down the middle, taking advantage of the current. Against the shore a little beacon on the end of a breakwater signals an anchorage in the mouth of a creek out of the tide. A power cruiser spreads a wide "V" on the smooth surface. Perhaps *Clearwater,* the replica of an old Hudson River sloop, rounds a distant headland, her enormous mainsail using all of the light air she can catch.

Shift the scene to Long Island Sound on a July Sunday. There must be over a hundred sailing craft in sight. Here is a class of Stars racing, everyone keyed up, getting every bit out of the boat and alert to the tactics of the competition. Over on the Connecticut shore a cruising ketch slides along before the gentle westerly, her crew sunning on top of the cabin house, the helmsman with the tiller in one hand and a cool can in the other. Ahead is an ocean racing yawl—you have seen her picture in *Yachting*—exercising the crew. A great yellow-and-blue spinnaker blossoms ahead of her. The low line of the Connecticut shore is hazy with smoke, but the harbors are clearly marked by white lighthouses or beacons and by throngs of anchored yachts. The Long Island shore looks much the same, but our contemplation of it is distracted by an airplane gliding in toward LaGuardia and then by a gleaming power cruiser, all white enamel, gold leaf, and varnish. From a flying bridge shaded by a striped awning, two men in swimming trunks wave down at us. If we put into one of the harbors tonight, we will find moorings crowded closely together, and at the marina, tiers of boats in finger piers.

Passing inside of Block Island in a fresh southerly we feel the heave of the open Atlantic and see around us fishermen with pulpits manned for the sight of a fin or with baits on long outriggers, the fisherman lounging in the fighting chair. Yonder is a party boat from Montauk, anchored and rolling heavily in the tide while the customers catch ground fish or mackerel. Passing a commercial dragger, perhaps we are lucky enough to see off Newport a great crowd of sails, dominated by the tall spars of 12-meter Cup Defenders. Milling about watching are schooners, little sloops with outboards, cruisers, steamers crowded with sightseers, even a seagoing automobile complete with horn and windshield wiper! After the race, the whole fleet will run up into Newport, filling Brenton's Cove, lining the wharves, and thronging Newport's bars and restaurants.

With East Chop astern, we find a very different scene. Last night we lay in Hadley Harbor, lucky to find a quiet berth. Some who came too late had to lie outside. We shot through Woods Hole this morning and with a fair wind and 2 knots of tide, we are running down Nantucket

Sound for the Cross Rip horn buoy. The water is a light greenish color, for it is shallow here. The sea is short and choppy, the wind quite fresh all of a sudden. There is no land in sight, although we aren't far from the low shore. Cape Poge Light is a pencil on the southern horizon, and several water towers on the south shore of Cape Cod show above the skyline to port. As it breezes up rapidly, we overtake a small sloop lugging a Genoa jib too big for the breeze, burying her bow, yawing wildly and leaving a wide wake. Coming toward us is a power cruiser leaping half out of the water on almost every sea, being driven hard against the steepening chop. Astern, a steamer bound for Nantucket is overtaking us, her high decks crowded with vacationers. We have called ahead for a slip in the Nantucket Marina. The old whaling town is profoundly changed but in many ways we will find much to remind us of the early days. The cobbled streets lead up the hill past the whale-oil mansions of Coffins and Macys and Starbucks, and on across the bleak moors and barren beaches the whalemen knew.

Far to port are the sandy little harbors of the south shore, protected by jetties and constantly dredged—crowded, quiet little places, the shores teeming with refugees from metropolitan heat and humidity.

Look again and see us off Plymouth, north of Cape Cod. The water is dark green and much colder. The shore is a long yellow ribbon of sand, backed by yellow dunes sparsely grown over with grass. Astern is the high hill of Manomet. Abeam is Gurnet Point with the light on top, and just visible behind it is the dark cylinder of Duxbury Pier Light. The low hills inland are quite distant, but on Captains Hill in Duxbury is the unmistakeable Pilgrim Monument. Far off to starboard another Pilgrim Monument rises over the dunes of Provincetown. We are running under power, for it is calm and, short of Scituate, nearly 15 miles ahead, there is no harbor fit for a vessel of our draft. Inshore is a fleet of small powerboats fishing. One of them, a light aluminum outboard, circles us. Like an advertisement in a magazine, a girl in a bikini waves. Astern are several power cruisers drumming steadily up the shore for the suburban ports of Cohasset and Hingham. Ahead lies a sloop becalmed, rolling in the uneven wash, her skipper preferring to sail all night rather than use the power. The air is vibrant with internal combustion.

Off Cape Ann we see the Marblehead racing fleet, and late in the afternoon the procession of heavy draggers heading for Gloucester after several days' fishing. A steamer out of Boston passes astern on a course for Cape Sable and European ports. Inshore are the first high rocky shores we have seen, with elaborate summer homes at intervals along the cliffs. Thacher's Island with its tall twin towers keeps us clear of the wicked ledges ahead, now gently washing in the easy swell. A whale may startle us here with his hoarse blow and the majestic roll of back and fin. Fifteen feet high go the flukes and he sounds, leaving only a slick in the water and our incredulous eyes and quickened pulse.

Eastward we sail, past miles of exposed beach, here and there speckled with summer cottages or broken by river mouths. At Isles of Shoals, the first uncrowded offshore harbor, we spend the night, scarcely aware of the easy offshore swell.

The next day we are into Casco Bay; and with the fair southwest breeze astern we find a new world of islands and ledges between long points of mainland until the Maine fog shuts down, cold and gray. Our world is a circle, two waves wide. We listen carefully for the distant roll of surf. We hear Halfway Rock bleating regularly astern and far ahead the diaphone on Seguin—otherwise only the swash of water along the lee side. The navigator, alert for pot buoys to judge the tide, watches the fathometer, listens to the peeping of the R.D.F., keeps an eye on clock and compass. The radar reflector swings in the rigging and drops of fog-dew patter on deck. But with the powerful fog horns on Seguin and the Cuckolds, with bells, whistles, and bold shore to run for, there is no need for worry. Snug anchorages lie ahead.

Across Penobscot Bay we catch a brisk northwester. The Camden Hills stand sharply behind us. The water is cold and a bright blue-green, whitecaps and dark puffs rushing across it. A lobster fisherman hauling a trap waves as we rush by, our lee rail awash. In Deer Island Thorofare we thread our way among islands wooded to the water's edge and fragrant with the sun on raspberry, sweetfern, wild rose, and spruce. Crossing Jericho Bay we meet the three-masted schooner *Victory Chimes* close hauled and leaning to the puffs. We count fifteen sails, some running east with us for Mt. Desert, others beating up for Eggemoggin, and three working up under Isle au Haut. A motor yacht slashes by, throwing clean spray from her bow and dragging a turbid wake, which only for a moment interrupts the rhythm of our running. A gull swings under our stern and an eider duck hustles her fleet of ducklings off Long Ledge. As the wind eases late in the afternoon, we have a wide choice of harbors. We can run up Blue Hill Bay toward Prettymarsh and tuck in under Western Mountain for the night. Ahead is Swan's Island with a quiet spruce-ringed anchorage at Buckle Harbor. Or we can go down to Burnt Coat, where we will find a store, and a telephone, and a wharf where we can buy gas and lobsters. Or we can press on for Mt. Desert, where we will arrive after dark, the mountains black against the sky and the harbors starred with anchor lights.

East of Mt. Desert the character of the coast changes again. Off Petit Manan, everything is far away. To the westward is the low profile of Mt.

Desert. Schoodic, left astern two hours ago, shows blue already. Petit Manan lighthouse abeam is a lonesome shaft, gray and forbidding above the bleak dwelling, the shore behind it scarcely showing in the distance. Far up Narraguagus Bay is Cape Split and the white spot of Nash Island light. Ahead the great cliffs of Crumple Island, Great Wass Island, and Mistake Island have not yet risen above the horizon. The tide is running hard as we pass the bell, and the sea is lumpy and irregular. It is a bare and lonely spot with not a lobsterman or yacht anywhere in sight. Porpoises roll and a guillemot skitters off, the white patches on his wings flashing. But we are by 'Tit Manan, and a libation to the gods of wind and tide is due. They have favored us thus far, but they may test us at any time.

From the blue Passamaquoddy we are shot out through Letite Passage on a swirling tide into the icy gray Bay of Fundy and a mighty tidal stream funneling up toward Saint John. A puffin may burst out of water nearby and splash into flight. To port are cliffs, flat-topped and sheer, with the rolling hills of New Brunswick behind them. Harbors are few and exposed, protected by massive government wharves. Few yachtsmen ever see this coast, usually shrouded in fog.

But if we make it through busy Saint John Harbor and up the Reversing Falls, we find the hospitable Canadian yachtsmen sailing the long reaches of the river in clear, warm sunshine. Salmon roll, the water is clean enough to swim in, and even, in places, clean enough to drink. Pleasant farms, gentle hills, green islands grazed by cows and sheep make this a paradise after the fog and chill outside.

Start where you will. Go as far as you want and as fast. Run off shore from one big lighthouse and fog signal to another or work your way among the islands, anchoring in quiet coves, yarning with fishermen, or visiting country stores. Sail with the racing fraternity from yacht club to marina or fish the rips and ledges. The coast is to be enjoyed by each in his own way and at his own pace. By virtue of no authority whatsoever, the authors welcome you to the coast and hope that this *Guide* will add to the safety and pleasure of your cruise.

CHAPTER II

General Conditions,
Suggestions, and Advice
to the Eastward-bound Mariner

1. Weather. I have often asked a fisherman about the safety of some harbor or the advisability of an offshore run and been told, "Take *summertime,* they ain't nothin' to hurt ye." In relation to winter weather, this is true. Nevertheless, a few observations on coastal summer weather may be helpful.

Throughout the whole coastal area covered by this book, the prevailing summer wind is southwest. This is due partly to the presence of a large high-pressure area between the Azores and Bermuda and partly to the effect of the heated land close to water cooled by a branch of the Labrador Current.

In midsummer, day after day will repeat the following pattern: In the morning it will be warm and quiet. Not a ripple will break the surface. The sky will be cloudless or thinly veiled with high cirrus. Later in the morning, as the land heats up, small, puffy clouds will appear over the land. Soon zephyrs from south or even southeast will come in, hauling soon to south-southwest or southwest. Then on the glassy water will appear cat's-paws and the ripples of the daily southwester. The southwester may come at any time from shortly after dawn until noon, often coming earlier when the flood tide makes in the morning. Meteorologists deny the connection between wind and tide, but the writers are backed by local fishermen in believing that a phenomenon so frequently observed has some foundation. The arrival of this breeze is often dramatic. You may lie becalmed, sweltering in the heat, and slow roll for an hour. Then in the space of five minutes the sails fill, the temperature drops comfortably, and you are under way doing 3 or 4 knots with the calm forgotten. Close astern may be another vessel still becalmed. This breeze may increase to as much as 25 knots in some places. Buzzards Bay is notorious for its vigorous afternoon southwesters which, with a strong ebb tide, can become dangerous for small craft and "high charged" power boats.

Many cruising men have noticed that contrary to what we might expect, the southwest wind is stronger under the lee of an island or point and is likely to have a bit more westerly in it than offshore. Conversely, off a point or close to windward of the land the breeze is sometimes quite feeble.

The late Dr. Charles F. Brooks of the Blue Hill Observatory in Milton explained the phenomenon thus. The southwest wind as it blows over the open sea has vertical stability. That is, it is flowing like a great river of air with the air on the bottom staying on the bottom. This lower air is somewhat slowed by friction with the water, so the upper air is traveling considerably faster. When this air approaches an island warmed by the sun, the rising currents of warm air and the interference of the land itself stir up the air, and the speed of the upper air is imparted to the whole mass. Hence Massachusetts Bay, Ipswich Bay, upper Penobscot Bay, and the northeast side of Mt. Desert and Isle au Haut are renowned as having plenty of wind even when it is much quieter offshore. It is often better to beat to the westward through the Maine islands, where one finds a good breeze and smooth water, than it is to slat about offshore in a light air.

As the sun drops in the afternoon and the land cools, the breeze moderates. Sometimes it just quits, cut off as though someone had turned a celestial switch. The evening is likely to be calm, although sometimes the land may cool enough to produce a light northerly drawing down a harbor. By dawn, conditions will have become stable again and the pattern may repeat itself.

This schedule, however, may be interrupted by a cyclonic disturbance. This is often heralded by a murky afternoon and the southwester continuing into the evening. When this happens, the next day is usually showery and sometimes is followed by a northwester.

These northwest days are the ones we wait for all winter. Usually the early morning will be crystal-clear, with a gentle northerly breeze increasing in dark little puffs. As the sun gets up and the day develops, the breeze increases. By noontime it may be blowing a reefing breeze, with the puffs rushing out to sea, dark green and silvery. Still there are no clouds, and houses ten miles away still stand out sharply. As one runs offshore, the puffs become more moderate and the wind steadies. The presence of cumulus clouds over the land usually indicates that the breeze will moderate and even shift to the southwest or west-southwest later in the day. However, toward sunset the northerly will often reassert itself and provide a fine chance to make a harbor well to the westward. These are great days to travel, especially for the westward-bound vessel. Such a vessel should ease sheets and stand offshore to make all the westing and southing possible if the glass is rising rapidly. Otherwise it is well to hang under the shore, where there is more wind and where it is likely to last longer.

One cruising skipper turned his crew out and got under way before breakfast when he awoke at dawn in Camden Harbor and saw an easterly breeze and a clear sky. "A bird's nest in the grass" he termed it as he made long legs of it to the westward. Occasionally during the summer these dry easterlies come in and are indeed a gift to the westward-bound skipper. Later in the day the sky usually clouds up, visibility shortens, and the day may end in rain or fog, but 40 or 50 miles of beating up toward Boston may have been saved.

Fog. The coast from Cape Elizabeth to Saint John is subject in the summer to thick and lasting fogs. The table on page 201 of the 1960 *Coast Pilot I,* which gives hours of fog signal operation, indicates that fogs are more frequent the farther east one goes, and that in general July is the worst month. Petit Manan holds the record with 252 hours. When you consider, however, that July has 744 hours, your chances of clear weather at any particular time, even in July, are about two to one in your favor.

If one understands the cause of fog, its vagaries are more easily understood. Imagine a warm southerly wind blowing across the ocean far offshore on a sunny day. The surface water is relatively warm and the air near the surface becomes saturated with moisture. As this air approaches the coast, it passes over water that has been stirred up by the tide and hence is colder. The saturated air is cooled, the moisture condenses, and it is "thick o' fog."

Sometimes fog shuts down without warning, but the experienced skipper can often forecast it. If the weather has been southerly and hazy for twenty-four hours and the wind comes in south or a little east, fog is likely. If one can "see his breath" in the middle of the afternoon, it is evidence of mounting humidity and the likelihood of fog before night. Often distant land will disappear in thickening haze that conceals the approach of a real fog bank, choking thick. Once the writer had the fog drop on him all at once. It had been a quiet, hazy day. We had floated across Petit Manan Bar and were off Nash Island bound up for Cape Split before a light southerly. Visibility was about 5 miles and we could see Petit Manan Light clearly. A band of fog appeared over Jordan's Delight and in less than ten minutes we could not see 100 feet.

Fog has several peculiarities that the thoughtful skipper can use to his advantage. As it is produced by a drop in surface temperature, one can expect it to shut down at night and be thick in the morning. If the sun is shining through it, the fog will often burn off as the morning advances, giving way first in the passages to leeward of large islands and hanging over the cold water in the middle of the bays. If the southerly breeze comes in early, it may pack in again, but the chances of getting a "scale-up" toward noon are good.

In planning the day's run, try to make a bold shore on the lee side of an island. The warming and drying effect of the land will give you a better chance to "make." Avoid the weather side of the land. It will be thicker than tar out there. If you must make an offshore run, get well offshore and run for the horns, light vessels, and big whistles. Plan to get in well before dark. Fog and dark make a combination in which it is scarcely sensible to move among the islands and ledges inshore.

Fog seems to do strange things to sound. Never count on picking up a whistle or bell when it is to leeward of you. Also "dead spots" seem to form, and the vigorous bellow of a horn 10 miles away may be inaudible within 3 miles of the station yet may nearly blow you off the deck within 2 miles. (See further discussion of fog under Penobscot Bay, Chapter XI.)

Thunderstorms. These storms in eastern New England are seldom severe offshore and always provide adequate warning. Occasionally, however, a really heavy one will cause considerable damage. Long Island Sound and Salem Bay are renowned "hot spots" for thunderstorms.

A thunderstorm first shows as a thunderhead, a heavy, towering, cumulus cloud with a dark base. If it is north of northwest, it will usually pass over the land, but the ones to the west or west-northwest will probably come aboard.

As the cloud builds up, the top flattens and becomes anvil-shaped. The bottom is blue-black. As it approaches, flickers and grumbles come out of it and a veil of rain appears. The cautious skipper will shorten sail, be sure he has sea room to leeward, and jog along. If the clouds are not violently agitated, probably there is only a capful of wind, a dash of rain, and some thunder and lightning. But the dangerous ones will be boiling inside. There will be a hard roll of white cloud across the front that forms an arch. Tie up all canvas when you see this, and prepare to take what comes. A white line of wind and rain rushes across the water out of the northwest and you are on your own. These squalls can blow really hard for a short time.

Usually you will soon see light under the clouds, a rainbow will appear in the east, the sky will blow clear, and it may come off a lovely northwest evening.

Hurricanes. Occasionally a tropical hurricane will leave the usual course and run north along the New England coast. This happens seldom, but when it does, the results are so devastating that it is only good judgment to be prepared. The unannounced hurricane of September 21, 1938, dealt New England's seacoast a heavy blow indeed, wrecking boats and houses, flooding cities, and even depositing an oceangoing steamer on the bridge at New London. Again in 1944 and twice in 1954 hurricanes came through this area, the latter pair, Carol and Edna, nearly wiping out the Portland Yacht Club fleet. Hurricane Donna, in 1960, was so well advertised that much less damage was done.

The earliest warning of the approach of one of these storms, quixotically named after girls, is the radio. The Weather Bureau keeps constant watch on their formation and progress and even flies aircraft through them to explore their vitals.

The presence of a hurricane off Puerto Rico, Florida, or even Carolina need give the skipper no cause for alarm. A great percentage of them swing eastward off Hatteras. But if the lady reaches New Jersey, it is well to seek a landlocked anchorage and look to one's ground tackle.

These storms do not conform to many hard-and-fast rules, but the section in *The American Practical Navigator* about cyclonic storms and the section in the *Coast Pilot I* are well worth reading and studying closely. In the writer's experience, these storms are heralded by oppressive weather, often with light easterlies and very clear atmosphere. A heavy roll makes in from the southeast as the sky thickens. The storm itself begins with rain squalls and increasing wind. If the storm center is to pass out to sea, the wind will work easterly and northerly into the northwest. If the storm is to pass inland, the wind will work the other way and may increase beyond belief. A sheltered anchorage, good anchors, plenty of scope, and an engine that can be run slowly in the gusts to take some of the strain off the anchors are necessary. Avoid anchoring close to other vessels, especially if they are large or unattended. Against a dragging barge, little you can do is of any help. Seldom do these storms last six hours, and few well-prepared and skillfully handled vessels are lost, so one need not despair. Nevertheless, a hurricane is a severe test of boat and crew, even if one is anchored in a good harbor.

2. Tides. The moon, assisted by the sun at new and full moon, picks up a wave and carries it westward along the shore from the Bay of Fundy. High water is one-half to one hour before the moon crosses the meridian. The water, released by each previous wave, runs east to join the next one coming, so the tidal current, in general, runs *east on the flood and west on the ebb*. This rule is subject to many exceptions caused by configurations of land. For instance, the tide ebbing out of Blue Hill Bay runs east across Bass Harbor Bar. There seems to be a constant westerly set of current off Two Bush at the entrance to Penobscot Bay, and the tide seems to set almost northwest into Saco Bay on both ebb and flood. (See notes in the text under these places.)

In general, the farther east one goes, the higher the tide rises and the more vigorous the current. The exceptions to this generality are so many that one need call attention only to Hell Gate in the East River, The Race in Long Island Sound, and Cape Cod Canal, by way of illustration. But these are "tide holes," and the generality still stands.

West of Cape Elizabeth the tidal current nearly parallels the course of the coastwise cruiser, but on the Maine coast the tide sets in and out of the bays, running nearly across one's course. The current is strong enough to make a considerable difference to a sailing yacht or slow auxiliary. The writer's experience has been that for the bays west of Schoodic Point about one-quarter mile should be allowed for tide for every hour one will be in the current. At the full strength of a moon tide, however, this will not be enough. Watch the tide running by lobster buoys and remember that your first guess at the velocity of the current should be divided in half. Most people overestimate the speeds of both wind and tide.

The draggers and sardiners move so fast that they make very little if any allowance for tide.

If you keep a record in your log book of the time of high water and the way the tide sets at different times and places relative to it, you will doubtless become badly confused because you will find through the years considerable inconsistency in your evidence. Tides are often influenced by winds, a tide running against the wind often turning early and one running to leeward turning late. In some places the tide works around in a circle, running east, for instance, at three hours before high water but east-southeast an hour later and perhaps south at low-water slack. This seems to be the situation in Jericho Bay. The writer started across one foggy day and allowed for a flood tide we supposed to be running north into Eggemoggin Reach and Blue Hill Bay. Between Egg Rock and Long Ledge the tide must have been running east, for we sailed across Potato Ledge and made Shabby Island far to the south. Careful observation, good luck, and a habit of hedging every bet with log, lead, and lookout —these you need for successful thick weather navigation anywhere on the New England coast.

3. Navigating Equipment. *Compass and clock.* The first and single most important instrument to be provided is a first-class compass in good condition. It should be permanently mounted in a solid binnacle where it is easily read from the wheel and where it can be used to take bearings. Secondly, it must be properly compensated and frequently checked in clear weather. Not only must iron and steel be kept away from it, but instruments like light meters and transistor radios must be kept away from it, for they have powerful little magnets in them.

Almost as important as the compass is a clock firmly mounted where it is visible from chart table and wheel. In the fog, your runs are made in terms of time at a known—or estimated—speed. Obviously you must use the same timepiece at all times. When you run out your time, don't just keep going in the hope something will turn up. Stop and listen, take a sounding, or make a square.

Charts. An old and reliable friend of the writer was anchored in Rockland Harbor one foggy morning, cleaning up after breakfast and waiting for the fog to scale up, when he heard the motors of a power cruiser approaching. Presently a large varnished and be-chromed cruiser churned out of the fog, threw both motors into reverse, and came to a stop close by. The owner, clad picturesquely in a yachting cap and uniform, appeared from the wheel house and hailed.

"Hey, which way to Bar Harbor?"

Somewhat startled by the apparition and by the question, he was tempted to reply "First left," but instead invited the "captain" aboard. As the visitor squeezed down the hatch, the down-easter unrolled chart 1203 on the bunk.

"Say," ejaculated the motorboater. "That's a swell map. Where do you get those? And what's all the numbers?"

It appeared later that he had come up from Marblehead in his new boat navigating from the map in a railroad timetable.

If you have not been born with this kind of luck, you will need charts.

The United States Coast and Geodetic Survey publishes these, and they are obtainable in many ports along the shore. (See the Appendix to *Coast Pilot I.*) Every vessel should carry a small-scale chart of the whole coast, such as 70 or 1106, the complete 1200 series on a 1/80,000 scale, and the complete 300 or 200 series on a 1/40,000 scale for the area to be covered. In addition there are numerous charts of harbors or small areas that are most helpful. All these are listed in the Appendix to the *Coast Pilot.*

The navigator should realize, however, that while charts are available in most major harbors on the coast, by mid-season the stores are likely to be sold out of the one chart you need. A good plan is to make up a list from the *Coast Pilot* and get your charts all at once, early in the spring, from The Hammond Map Store, 10 East 41st St., New York, or from

Robert E. White Instruments, Commercial Wharf, Boston. Both will respond to mail or telephone orders.

Publications. The U.S. coast and Geodetic Survey, now renamed National Ocean Survey, prints the *U.S. Coast Pilot*. Formerly revised at five-year intervals, it is now kept on computer tape and republished each year in paperback. Originally written for large vessels, it has been adapted to include information for coastwise yachtsmen. It is almost indispensable for a great deal of factual information not included in this *Guide*. The first three chapters and the Appendix provide an excellent source of general information on the coast.

Eldridge Tide and Pilot Book contains tide tables for many places on the coast and is particularly valuable for the current tables on Buzzards Bay, Nantucket and Vineyard sounds, Block Island Sound, and the Race. It also contains information on radio direction-finder stations and weather broadcasts, as well as a number of interesting and useful articles. It is published by Robert E. White, Commercial Wharf, Boston.

The Light and Buoy List is published by the National Ocean Survey and lists every light and buoy on the coast. It gives characteristics, appearance, fog signal and radio signal of each light, and the location of each buoy relative to the shoal it marks. This volume is a necessary supplement to the chart.

Tide and Current Tables may be useful but are not really necessary if you have Eldridge. If you are going into Canadian waters, get the necessary charts and pilot books from the Department of Mines and Transport, Ottawa, Canada. See the introduction to the chapter on the Coast of New Brunswick.

Log Book. In the writer's opinion the log book, while not a publication exactly, is a very important part of cruising equipment. Don't use these expensive canvas-covered yacht logs ruled in columns for engine revolutions and gas consumption. Get a hard-bound law-student's notebook. Use it to keep a record of course and distance. In the fog, especially, you should write down the exact time of departure, your best guess at speed, course, and estimated time of arrival. As you go along, include depths, bearings of horns and bells, sounds of surf or gulls, and anything that might be of help. If you miss your mark, stop, listen, and review the run. Then make a square, still keeping careful account and stopping to listen at every corner. When you finally get straightened out, go back and re-plot your courses to find out where you went wrong.

The log book should be used to enter names of people, places, vessels, and facts that you want to remember. If the record is kept up to date, it serves also as a legal document, should a "regrettable incident" arise.

Most importantly, though, the log is a journal of one of the good times in your life. Make it detailed. Describe what you see and tell how you feel about it. Put in what people did and said. Enjoy writing it; you will enjoy reading it.

4. Electronic Equipment. For centuries men have sailed the New England coast without the aid of electronics, and some people still do. Nevertheless, there are a few relatively inexpensive aids that may be of great help.

The fathometer is the first of these. The instrument saves the picturesque but cold, wet, and slow operation of sounding with a lead. The fathometer is especially useful in fog navigation. The chart indicates contour lines at 18, 30, 60, and 120 feet. One can follow one of these with the fathometer, often right into a harbor. In Maine especially, ends of points make off a long way under water. And on the back of Cape Cod the bottom slopes evenly off the beach. You can often locate your position from the depth.

It is not as useful in shallow water as one might think, for it gives the depth under the boat only and gives no hint of what is ahead.

A radio-direction finder is a useful instrument, if not so precise as the most expensive radar and Loran machines. You can use it to "home in" on a station, but remember in approaching a lightship that you may be on a converging course with a 100,000-ton tanker. Be alert to sounds from astern as well as from both sides. For a station abeam, R.D.F. is less accurate. To get the most out of it, be sure it is firmly mounted and then calibrate it on a clear day from a known source, thus compensating for any "bending" of the radio impulses due to local conditions aboard. *Eldridge* gives the frequencies of the RDF stations and so does the *Light List*. If not dead accurate, at least the machine gives a useful indication.

A radiotelephone is carried by many yachts. By 1975 at least, all yachts with radiotelephone will have to use VHF and abandon current FM frequencies. Already forty-six VHF stations that connect with telephone lines are being established. In 1971 station KQU-620 on channel 26, 161.900 MH, was established at Camden and is effective from Portland almost to the Canadian border. Weather reports are broadcast continuously on 162.55 MH or 162.40 MH. Also WWV, the time-signal station, will broadcast reports of hurricanes and major storms between the sixteenth and the seventeenth minute after every hour on 2.5; 5; 10; 15; and 25 KH. Of course many commercial stations carry weather reports too, but these change frequently. *Eldridge* usually has an up-to-date listing.

Now that the Coast Guard no longer patrols the beaches or watches from towers, almost the only effective way to call for help is by radiotelephone, to which the Coast Guard listens attentively. In the event of severe illness or accident, a radiotelephone could be the difference between a diasaster and an adventure.

5. Safety Equipment. Anyone taking command of a vessel is responsible for the safety of those aboard. This is a legal and a moral obligation sanctioned by long tradition. The skipper, before he drops the mooring, should be sure that he has the required government equipment, consisting of a life preserver for each person aboard, adequate fire extinguishers, bell, horn, and proper running lights in working order. The provident skipper will add an efficient bilge pump, at least two good anchors with 200 feet of anchor rode for each, a complete first aid kit and a copy of Dr. Paul Sheldon's *First Aid Afloat,* a ring buoy or horseshoe buoy carried loosely on deck with a strobe light attached, and a tall pole weighted to float upright. A pole in the water is much easier to see from the yacht than a man, and the man too can see the pole and perhaps make his way to it to await rescue. The yacht should be provided with a dinghy and a quickly inflatable rescue raft big enough to accommodate all hands. Next to fire, the greatest danger to a cruising yacht is a steamer. In a locker handy to the helmsman should be a powerful electric light that will bring the mate out on the bridge of a tanker at a range of a mile. Some yachts carry strobe lights at the masthead. It may not be legal, but it may save your life. Flares are also useful steamer scarers. Probably the best defense in all weather, however, is a good radar reflector. Some skippers keep one aloft at all times. One can be improvised by hanging up a pie plate or frying pan, but one composed of three planes intersecting at right angles is better.

Seldom is a well-equipped cruising boat lost, and seldom are yachtsmen injured. Compared to driving a car, sailing is the epitome of safety. Nevertheless, accidents do happen at sea; and if the proper equipment is on hand, serious loss or injury may be averted.

6. Pollution. The major issues on this topic are enormously important and affect the entire population of the world. Jacques Cousteau, who ought to know, gives the oceans only forty years to live. If life in the ocean is seriously damaged, yachting won't be a problem. In this volume we cannot hope to deal with the major issues of pollution, but we might consider what yachtsmen can do to keep their own environment clean and improve coastal conditions as much as possible.

In the last five years considerable progress has been made in cleaning up the waters on which we sail. In the old days, you could throw overboard a paper bag or a paper plate, knowing that in half an hour it would disintegrate. Now, however, with the wide use of plastics, most things you throw overboard will float forever. Most of us know this, and while we have been distressed to see plastic-foam drinking cups floating jauntily thirty miles offshore and beer cans bobbing in the Fundy tide rips, in general there is nothing like the mess afloat there used to be. The trash cans ashore are stuffed and running over. Two little boys came alongside one night in a skiff and offered to carry ashore our garbage and sold us some of their mother's blueberry tarts instead of asking payment, in an effort to make cleanliness both attractive and profitable.

However, the problem of sewage has become more serious. In crowded harbors and especially in marinas the problem can reach disgusting proportions. The machinery of the federal government is moving in majestic fashion to produce an anti-pollution code that will be acceptable to all States and enforceable therein. New York State and a number of towns in Connecticut and Massachusetts have made laws but find them difficult to administer because of lack of pump-out stations. A list of those now available appears in Appendix C. These problems are being solved, but as we go to press, there is no clear and universal solution. In the next few years, however, prepare to construct either a holding tank or a disinfecting system.

More serious than sewage is the problem of municipal and industrial pollution, including the dangers of oil from tankers and refineries.

As far as Maine is concerned, the root of the pollution problem goes far deeper than the question of oil or no oil. Maine—eastern Maine in particular—is a disaster area. There is almost no productive work available. Some go lobstering or clamming. Some cut pulp. There are a few summer people but not many, for Washington County is a long way from centers of population. There is a little subsistence farming and there are a few retired people with independent incomes. But there is not enough work to support the small population. Therefore oil or anything else that will bring in jobs and money is attractive. The man who can find a clean industry that can be operated economically in eastern Maine will deserve undying thanks.

Until such a solution is found, about all the yachtsman can do to save the coast is to cooperate with the organizations that are defending it against polluters. The Machias project is dead, the Sears Island project expired in hearing, and Portland is now embattled. Both moral and financial help are badly needed.

7. Conservation. Various groups, including Friends of Nature, the Audubon Society, and the Nature Conservancy in particular, are raising money by subscription to buy and preserve wild areas of the coast. It is not our purpose to list these places, for the list would be out of date in a month. Rather, we call on all those who love the coast to do three things:

First, whenever you land, especially on an island, be sure to leave nothing there but your footprints. Be especially careful with fire. The soil on some islands is composed of rotted vegetation built slowly through centuries. The soil is thin, and in late summer it dries out right down to the bed rock. In this condition it is inflammable. A fire that gets into the soil will smolder, flaring up perhaps when the wind fans it, and will in a week reduce the island to an ash heap. Build any fire below high-water mark and be certain it is out.

Secondly, be careful of wildlife. The ecological balances are very delicately adjusted. To walk through a meadow where terns are nesting may destroy some eggs and chicks, however careful you are, and also may drive mothers away from the nests either permanently or for so long as to damage the young. Petrels nest in holes. Tread on the ground over the hole and you may cave it in. Rats will multiply rapidly and wipe out a bird colony. Your pet dog, glad of a run ashore, may do serious damage to sheep or small animals.

Lastly, consider devoting 10 percent of your fitting-out bills to one of the organizations mentioned above.

Those interested in a nationwide analysis of conservation problems and progress on their solution should read *Islands of America,* published by the U.S. Department of the Interior, Bureau of Outdoor Recreation, Washington, D.C. 20240.

The Authors' Prejudices. Should anyone have the hardihood to read this book through, he will doubtless become aware of some of the writers' prejudices. Even with the best intentions, it is impossible to comment helpfully on so many places without occasionally making judgments with which others disagree. We admit to preferring sail to power and have made various comments about prevailing winds that power boat men may find irrelevant. However, we hold no hard feelings toward those who prefer to motor and indeed have noted places which they may find uncomfortable or even dangerous and other places accessible to them alone.

Perhaps our most violent prejudice we would do well to air at once. We are strongly prejudiced in favor of the people who live in coastal communities the year round. The towns are theirs. They pay the taxes, provide the facilities, do the work. Yachtsmen are at best uninvited guests and should behave themselves accordingly. The local people, I suppose, are "natives" in that we all are natives of some town, but we should not speak of them as if they lived in grass huts. Local people, in this standardized age, still have a characteristic manner of speech, still use colloquial-isms that we consider picturesque, still dress in a way different from ours. Nevertheless, they are not living isolated lives in a part of the world little known to city people. They listen to the same radio programs, see the same TV shows, hear the same weather reports, go to the same movies that yachtsmen do. They also deposit their money in the same banks and own shares of the same stocks. In some cases they are far ahead of their visitors.

I am reminded of the story about the city man who accosted a resident of Cape Cod and asked him the way to West Dennis. The old gentleman eyed the young city man thoughtfully, pondered a moment, and admitted that he didn't know the way to West Dennis. The city man said, patroniz-ingly,

"You don't get around much, do you, Grampa?"

"Well," answered the old gentleman, "I've been to Hong Kong, Singa-pore, and Manila, but I never had any reason to go to West Dennis."

One proud moment in the life of one writer came when a Maine lady said, "You aren't a summer fellow; you're a local resident who goes away winters."

Most of these people, at least the ones who make their living afloat, have poured more salt-water out of their boots than we have ever sailed over. They know what is dangerous, and their advice is worth taking. Al-though you may not know it, they are watching out for one another and for you. If you ever get into trouble, you may be amazed at how fast help comes. My father and I in a skiff were run down by a seiner. Before the seiner could circle back to us, a lobsterman was alongside helping us out of the water. If a fisherman gives you advice, take it and thank him. If he helps you in a difficult crisis, thank him and offer him a drink in the cockpit; and if he has spent time, gasoline, or gear in your behalf, you can offer to pay for it. You can pay most effectively, however, with your affection and respect.

One more piece of gratuitous and prejudiced advice will conclude this introductory chapter. Don't ruin a cruise by hurrying. Early starts can be delightful. Anchoring by starlight can be magical. But to start early and run late, using the engine whenever the wind drops or hauls ahead, can be grueling. You will ruin your own disposition and your crew's. Vary your activities. Get in early and take a walk ashore. Anchor and try the codfish, or dig a bucket of clams at low water. If the breeze falls off, ghost along for a while, or lie becalmed for a while. You will appreciate the breeze when it comes in. If you find it thick or raining when you put your head out the hatch in the morning, pull it in again and lay over for a half a day or a day. Read a book or play cards or go up to the store and see who's there. Those who like to cook can profitably be encouraged.

On a cruise with my son and my new daughter-in-law I nearly ruined her cruising life by running all day in the fog from Cutler outside Moose Peak and up to Trafton's Island. It was no fun, there was no need of it, and had the lady been anything less than saintly, she never would have gone to sea again. Don't let it happen to you.

PART TWO

HARBORS

WHITEHALL, N.Y., TO THE HEADWATERS OF THE
SAINT JOHN RIVER, N.B.

CHAPTER III

The Hudson River
and the Passage from Long Island Sound

Introduction to the Hudson

The fiords of Norway are a long way off. The Hudson River is at the back door of Long Island Sound. It is only 18 miles to the Hudson from City Island by way of the East and Harlem Rivers, through Hell Gate. And don't let the name of that gate discourage you from leaving the Sound by the back door. Because, if it does, you will miss one of the most beautiful river cruises on the Atlantic Coast, perhaps *the* most beautiful.

From the point where the Harlem River enters the Hudson (which is 12 miles above the Battery) to the Federal Dam and Lock at Troy, New York, is a distance of about 120 nautical miles. From the Battery at the south end of Manhattan to what is generally called the head of navigation on the Hudson, it is 132 miles. But for cruising yachts who want to explore further, perhaps go to lovely Lake Champlain, the Troy Lock is not the head of navigation but the beginning of a further cruise of 54 miles to Whitehall at the foot of Lake Champlain. Beckoning further, above Lake Champlain, is the Richelieu River leading into the St. Lawrence; but that is another story. Still another story is a cruise along the Mohawk River and the subsequent canals, westward from the Hudson starting just above Troy at Waterford. This leads to lakes Ontario and Erie, and our chapter is about the Hudson River.

While, except in the vicinity of Albany, almost all of the Hudson River is attractive, the most beautiful part, in our opinion, is below Catskill, which is 85 miles north of the Harlem River and 97 miles from the Battery. But include Catskill in this, for Catskill Creek is our favorite port on the entire Hudson. The parts of the Hudson which are most impressive are: (1) *along Manhattan Island,* where the grandeur is man-made; (2) *along the Palisades,* which begin in New Jersey, opposite New York City, and continue a short distance north of the New York State line; and (3) most beautiful of all, the section of the river that lies *between Stony Point* (where there is a first-class yacht basin at Grassy Point, 22½ miles above the Harlem River) *and Newburgh,* 41 miles above the

Harlem. Along this last stretch of 18½ miles are such famous landmarks as Bear Mountain (1305 feet) and St. Anthony's Nose (900 feet) on the other side; the United States Military Academy at West Point, part of it perched on a high cliff; Storm King Mountain (1355 feet), and Bull Hill (1425 feet), on the east shore, less well known but higher.

If you can't make the whole Hudson trip, go as far as Newburgh anyway; but we'd hate to have you miss Catskill, where the steep hills are reflected in the still water. It is only 85 miles above the Harlem, as we noted. We shan't soon forget a night spent there in October, 1954, with our boat lying quietly at the dock and the moon reflected on the glassy water. This was the time of year when the banks of the Hudson were of red, yellow, and gold, as well as green, adding a new beauty to the scene, as we went "Cruising down the river on a Sunday afternoon."

Through James Fenimore Cooper's writings, we can receive an impression of what a Hudson River cruise was all about more than 150 years ago:

In 1803, the celebrated river we were navigating, though it had all the natural features it possesses today [1844], was by no means the same picture of moving life. The steamboat did not appear on its surface until four years later. . . . In that day, the passenger did not hurry on board . . . he passed his morning saying adieu, and when he repaired to the vessel it was with gentlemanlike leisure, often to pass hours on board previously to sailing. . . . There was no jostling of each other . . . no impertinence manifested, no swearing about missing the eastern or southern boats, or Schenectady, or Saratoga, or Boston trains, on account of a screw being loose. . . . On the contrary, wine and fruit were provided, as if the travellers intended to enjoy themselves; and a journey in that day was a *festa*. . . . The vessel usually got aground once at least, and frequently several times a trip; and often a day or two were thus delightfully lost, giving the stranger an opportunity of visiting the surrounding country.

The Hudson River rises in *Tear of the Clouds,* a small lake in the Adirondack Mountains, in the northeastern section of New York State. It flows in a general southerly direction and empties into New York Bay, about 300 miles from its source. Most of it is deep, though there are some shoals to avoid. Navigation is not at all difficult, for the river is extremely well buoyed. While tide water extends to Albany, the river is generally fresh above Poughkeepsie. The mean range of tide is 4½ feet at the Battery, 3½ feet at Yonkers, 2¾ feet at West Point, 4 feet at Hudson, and 4½ feet at Albany. Currents for different parts of the river are given in the Current Tables and range from 0.6 knot average velocity at strength of current to 2.0, the strongest currents being in the lower Hudson off Manhattan (where it runs 1.9 to 2 knots) and at Catskill and vicinity (1.8). Around the entrance to Spuyten Duyvil and the Harlem River currents are swift and erratic. Numerous fish traps are planted each spring in the lower Hudson, usually from about the middle of March to the middle of May, during the seasonal running of shad to the spawning grounds in the upper Hudson. In general, the traps extend from one-fourth to two-thirds the distance across the river from the west side of the channel to the New Jersey shore. The outer ends of the stakes are usually marked by flags, during the day, or by lanterns at night.*

"From the point of its southward turn into the old glacial channel the Hudson flows through a gorge within an old valley. The floor of the gorge from almost as far north as Albany to its mouth lies below the level of the sea, creating a fiord or estuary where the fresh waters are ever subject to the invasion of salty ocean tides. . . . For thousands of years the great stream ran, constantly lowering its level and digging one of the deepest canyons the world has ever known. From a shallow beginning, as scientists have discovered by soundings, the floor of the gorge dropped steeply until in some places it reached a depth of 3600 feet, a thousand feet deeper than the Royal Gorge of the Colorado. Had there been human life then, a traveler in a boat on the Hudson might have looked up to the blue sky between walls more than two miles high." ** But the sea came back and buried the canyon.

Once many great private estates lined the Hudson. Some still do, but now a considerable number of them have been taken over by various institutions: Catholic colleges and monasteries, Protestant organizations, museums, sanitaria, schools, etc.

There have been many changes since Giovanni da Verrazano, Florentine explorer, wrote to his employer, Francis I of France, in July 1524: "We have found," he said, "a pleasant place below steep little hills. And from those hills a mighty deep-mouthed river ran into the sea." Eighty-five years later, on September 2, 1609, an English sea captain, employed by the Dutch East India Company to find the Northwest Passage to China, sailed his *Half Moon* into the river that bears his name and came to anchor near the mouth.

There are many good docks or sheltered anchorages in the 132 miles of the Hudson River from the Battery to the Troy Lock. In the pages that follow we have described the ones that we consider the most important,

---

* Data in this paragraph from the *Coast Pilot*.
** From *The Hudson*, by Carl Carmer, in "The Rivers of America" series (Rinehart & Co., Inc.)—a very interesting book for those who cruise the Hudson.

thirty-one in all to Troy. We don't pretend to have covered all of them, and even if we did, we should soon be out of date, for new ones are constantly being developed, as the Hudson becomes more and more popular among cruising yachtsmen. Evidence of this rising popularity is presented in a recent letter from the Director of Canal Operations, New York Department of Public Works. "Your impression that pleasure boat traffic on the canal system has increased markedly in recent years is correct. The number of pleasure boat permits for canal passage has grown from 6128 in 1960 to 10,026 in 1965."

Here is a table of the distances in nautical miles, most of them upriver from the point where the Harlem River joins the Hudson. Distances are given to a spot on the Hudson opposite each port. It may take ½ mile to a mile or so to reach the dock.

	Distance Above the Battery
Seventy-ninth Street Boat Basin (east shore)	6.
Edgewater Yacht Basin (west shore)	8.5
Englewood Boat Basin (west shore, across from Harlem River)	12.
Harlem River (enters from east shore)	12.
	Distance Above Harlem River
Alpine Boat Basin (west shore)	4.
Hastings-on-Hudson (east shore, Tower Ridge Yacht Club)	7.
Tarrytown Harbor (east shore)	12.
Upper Nyack (west shore, Julius Petersen Inc., boat yard)	13.
Ossining (east shore)	16.5
Haverstraw (west shore)	20.5
Grassy Point (town Stony Point—west shore)	22.5
Montrose (east shore)	23.5
Peekskill (east shore, Peekskill Yacht Club)	26.
Fort Montgomery (west shore)	29.
Garrison (east shore)	33.
Cornwall-on-Hudson	37.5
Newburgh (west shore, Newburgh Yacht Club)	41.
New Hamburg (east shore)	46.5
Poughkeepsie (east shore)	53.5
Maritje Kill (east shore)	56.
Staatsburg, Indian Kill (east shore, Norrie Park Boat Basin)	61.5
Kingston, Rondout Creek (west shore, 2 miles to dock)	67.
Saugerties, Esopus Creek (west shore)	76.
Catskill, Catskill Creek (west shore)	85.
Athens (west shore)	89.
Coxsackie (west shore)	95.5

Schodack Creek (east shore)	99.
Coeymans (west shore)	102.
Castleton-on-Hudson (east shore)	105.5
Rensselaer (east shore, Albany Yacht Club)	112.5
Watervliet (west shore)	118.
Troy (east shore, Federal Lock)	120.

Above Tidewater Area

	From (*Federal Troy*) Lock
North Troy	2.
Lock 1. Canalized, Upper Hudson	2.5
Mechanicsville	10.
Schuylerville	24.
Fort Edwards (beginning of Champlain Barge Canal)	34.
Smith Basin	41.
Whitehall (lower end of Lake Champlain)	54.
Total—the Battery to Lake Champlain	186.

We are hoping that the fellow who asked us if there were any good stopping places on the Hudson will read the above and then study our descriptions of these ports below. But first we must get to the Hudson.

City Island to the Hudson River, N.Y.
(223, 226, 274, 745, 746, 747).

1. The Current. The important thing about the passage through the East River and its famous Hell Gate is to pick the current right. Unlike Long Island Sound, the ebb current here sets westward, the flood eastward. A good plan is to start from City Island about an hour before the ebb turns westward at Rikers Island (6 miles from City Island) and then carry the ebb through the East River and Hell Gate. From Whitestone Bridge to North Brother Island the current at mean velocity is 1½ knots. In Hell Gate, off Mill Rock, the mean velocity at strength of current is about 3½ knots for the eastward current and 4½ knots for the westward (ebb current). In the Harlem River the *north* current toward the Hudson from Hell Gate flows while the *west* or ebb current is flowing through East River and Hell Gate—and vice versa. Thus, if you carry a favorable ebb current from Long Island Sound to Hell Gate (westward), you will also carry a favorable current (northward) through the Harlem River. The northerly current in the Harlem is considered the ebb, for after passing under the bridge at Hell Gate, on its way to New York Bay,

Hudson River looking north from West Point. Storm King Mountain on left.

it swings around Ward and Randall islands into the Harlem River and later joins the ebb current on the Hudson at Spuyten Duyvil. This is an added reason for picking the current right if you are headed for the Hudson from City Island. Currents in the Harlem River range from 2.8 opposite Little Hell Gate to 1.1 in other parts.

The authors are indebted to James Gordon Gilkey, Jr., who, as an experienced Hudson River skipper, provides us here with additional information on tidal currents. His description has been approved by the Chief of Currents Section, Oceanography Division of the U.S. Department of Commerce.

Because the Hudson River between Manhattan Island and Troy, below the Federal Lock, for a distance of approximately 120 miles, is influenced both by the flow of tidal currents as well as by the downstream flow of the river, taking advantage of the current when cruising on the Hudson is a somewhat tricky business. Particularly going upstream, however, the alert cruisingman can save both time and fuel by giving a little consideration to the flow of the current.

Under ordinary summer conditions, when most pleasure cruisers will be making the trip, the downstream flow of the Hudson River, eliminating the effect of tidal action, is approximately one-half a knot. There is, of course, considerable local variation, depending upon the width of the river at a given point, the fresh water flowing into the Hudson from tributary streams, and the location of the navigation channel with respect to the channel the current of the river follows.

Because of the flow of the river current downstream the tidal current floods upstream for only a bit over five hours between slack waters, while the ebb current flows downstream for approximately seven hours. This discrepancy will puzzle a skipper the first time he travels up or down the Hudson River. Table #1 of the *Tidal Current Tables for the Atlantic Coast of North America,* published by the National Ocean Survey, gives the times of slack water and the times and velocities of maximum current for a calendar year at various points along the coast. From this Table of Daily Current Predictions, giving the time when slack water occurs at The Narrows, New York Harbor, the cruising navigator can calculate, by using Table #2 in the same publication, the difference in the time slack water occurs at thirty different points along the Hudson between the Battery and Troy Lock. For every twenty miles traveled up the Hudson, slack water occurs at approximately an hour later than downstream. This rough generalization means that slack water at the Battery comes an hour and a half later than slack water in the Narrows; at the Thruway Bridge over the Tappan Zee just below Tarrytown slack water comes two and a half hours later than at the Narrows; at Poughkeepsie it comes four and a half hours later; at Catskill about six hours later; and at Albany seven and a half hours later.

Cruising *up* the Hudson, if the time of departure can be scheduled for a couple of hours *after* the time of maximum *ebb* current, as given in Table #1 for the Narrows, and corrected in Table #2 for the point of departure on the Hudson, the current the cruiser will have to buck going upstream will diminish and after slack water will then for about five hours be in his favor before once again turning against him. The buoys marking the channel in the Hudson will quickly show whether or not his calculations are accurate. Since the ebb current flows at an average rate of 1 to 2 knots, and the average flood current flows between .8 and 1.6 knots, the advantage of going with the current is considerable. During times of spring tides (new and full moon) the velocities will be about 20 percent stronger; and at certain periods of the year (around October 15) the velocity of flood could be up to 2 knots, while the ebb might run as strong as 3 knots. The effect upon fuel consumption of such currents, obviously, becomes a significant factor in any trip up or down the Hudson River.

It frequently happens that the difference of a few hours in departure time, in cruisers moving along at a speed of about 10 knots (which is maximum speed in any case in the canals for which the trip is planned), makes the difference between bucking the current or having a favorable current for much of the day. Since there are plenty of sights to see all along the Hudson while waiting for a favorable current, and since pleasure cruising is intended to be just that, adjusting the hour of departure to take advantage of the current is a game well worth the candle, and the price of fuel.

2. Distances. From City Island, the distances toward the Hudson are about as follows:

To Rikers Island, east end	6.
To Mill Rock, Hell Gate, where Harlem River comes in	11.
Via Harlem River	
To the Harlem River entrance on the Hudson	18.
Around Manhattan Island	
To the Battery	17.
To the Harlem River entrance on the Hudson	29.

Thus, it is about eleven miles further if you go around Manhattan Island. But if you have time, it is an entrancing trip, which can also be made exciting by tides, traffic, and floating debris. Don't try it at night, when the driftwood may be invisible.

3. Bridges. Should you decide to reach the Hudson via the Harlem River, however, be advised that of the fourteen bridges that span the Harlem, separating the Bronx and Manhattan, nine have a clearance under 35 feet.

Entering the Harlem River, having passed through Hell Gate or up the East River, the first bridge you will reach is a foot bridge at 103rd Street (55 feet, fixed). After the 103rd Street Bridge come, in order, the Triborough Bridge (54 feet, fixed), Willis Avenue Bridge (25 feet, swing), Third Avenue Bridge (26 feet, swing), Park Avenue Bridge (35 feet, lift), Madison Avenue Bridge (25 feet, swing), 145th Street Bridge (25 feet, swing), Macombs Dam Bridge (30 feet, swing), Alexander Hamilton Bridge (103 feet, fixed), Washington Bridge (134 feet, fixed), the University Heights Bridge (24 feet, swing), and then arrives the Broadway Bridge, which is a lift bridge (24 feet high).

Now let Parton Keese describe the Harlem as he did in *The New York Times,* (June 23, 1968):

The Broadway Bridge operator, as all operators are required to do, keeps a record of the vessel passing through, as well as the time, and if he cannot make out the name on the hull (many times it is on the stern and impossible to see), he will shout for the skipper to tell him.

However, in this modern day, it seems archaic, somehow, for two grown persons having to shout 100 feet apart in noisy river traffic such things as My Sweetie Pie or Onomatopoeia IV, or worse, spell out the letters to these names from boat to bridge. Nevertheless, this scene is repeated for each bridge opening.

The Broadway Bridge is followed by a fixed bridge, the Henry Hudson (141 feet high), and then at last comes a railroad bridge of the swing type, only 5 feet high but usually left in an open position, as trains seldom run on its tracks.

There are three types of bridges in the metropolitan waterways system that open for tall vessels: . . . a swing bridge, which rotates on a mechanized turntable; a bascule, or draw, bridge, which breaks in the center and raises upward, and a lift bridge, which goes up like an elevator.

On the Harlem, however, there are only the swing and lift types, besides the fixed bridges that are all more than 100 feet above water level.

Bridges are governed by Federal law, and according to Paul E. Stobbe, the engineer in charge of the Harlem River bridges for the City Department of Public Works, the law states that since each skipper is the best judge of clearance, his signal—three blasts—is an order for the bridge operator to open for him.

There are exceptions, however. Because of the havoc that would be created by halting traffic during rush hours, bridges of the Harlem River will not open from 6 A.M. to 10 A.M. or from 5 P.M. to 8 P.M., weekends included, except for fire or Government vessels.

Railroad bridges also have priority. When a vessel approaches a bridge that has tracks, the bridge operator must first request a transfer of power from the Transit Authority. The T.A., of course, will not allow the bridge to open if a train is due.

Stobbe offered a piece of advice for boatowners planning a sail on the Harlem River. "Know the closing times of the bridges, naturally, but also check on the tides. It is not only stupid, but pretty embarrassing, to sail halfway down the river, get slowed by the current and then find that the rest of the bridges won't open for three or four hours."

It might even make you angrier than when you started.

4. Anchorages: *City Island to Hudson River.* After passing between Throggs Neck and Willets Point there are several places to anchor, of which we'll mention the only two we consider fairly good. However, the anchorages or docks in the Hudson may be considered better and we'd recommend keeping on if there is still daylight.

a. Flushing Bay—World's Fair Marina **(226).** As you approach College Point to port, you head in a southwesterly direction into Flushing Bay. Note that Rikers Island channel's eastern entrance is completly obstructed by a lighted runway approach at LaGuardia Field and that just beyond to the west a bridge spans across this channel from the mainland to the island. The main channel into the bay is very clearly marked, and from bell buoy 3 it is a straight run to the special anchorage and facilities at the World's Fair Marina. Here is a moderately good anchorage, though somewhat exposed to the north and distant from the main passage. There are 450 slips at 25¢ per foot for those boats using 110v electricity and 30¢ per foot for those using 220v. The minimum charge is $7.50. A courtesy car goes for local purchases during office hours. Hauling runs even on weekends and holidays. Gas, Diesel fuel, ice, water, showers, laundromat, supplies, a restaurant, and full-time mechanics are all on hand. Subways to New York run nearby but so does the noisy air traffic to and from the airport. Run by Nichols Yacht Yard, Inc., this is one of the largest permanent facilities on the East Coast and as such can probably serve you and your boat's every need.

b. East River—New York Skyports Marina (745). This marina, over-water parking garage, and seaplane base, jutting out 350 feet from the west bank of the East River at 23rd Street, is easily identified by a large blue building. Just to the north has been constructed a new school for the children of United Nations' delegates. The Dock Master, Captain Bill Barron, who is on duty from May 1 to October 31, offers gas, diesel fuel, ice water, and electricity at the slips. Since this is a popular spot that's handy to the center of Manhattan, we were advised to reserve our slip in advance by phoning MU 6-4548. Food stores are located on nearby First Avenue, and a score of fine restaurants may be found along Third Avenue. Good protection and accessibility are the major attributes of this modern facility.

c. East River—South Street Seaport (745). Although there is extensive dockage space here, *no private boats* of any size are permitted to tie up without the seaport's specific permission. This continual restoration, in the style and tradition of Williamsburg, Mystic Seaport, and other notable havens of history, is open free to the public. It is a short and most rewarding trip to its site via the Second Avenue bus or by taxi for yachtsmen moored at the New York Skyports Marina.

South Street Seaport Museum, chartered by the New York State Board of Regents in 1967, set as its goal the restoration of this area officially designated as State Historic Trust Preservation Site. The museum is now restoring five blocks of old New York waterfront in Lower Manhattan, known as the "Street of Ships." Buildings of the early 1800s still survive and are being saved in the old Fulton Fish Market area.

During the last century, South Street was a lively place, a home of packet ships, fishing schooners, clippers, and Long Island Sound steamers. It swarmed with seamen, merchants, travelers, and people bustling their way to market.

Today, six ships of the Seaport Museum are berthed at Pier 16, foot of Fulton Street: *Wavertree,* a large sailing vessel of 1885, now undergoing restoration; the first *Ambrose* lightship of 1907; *Pioneer,* a cargo schooner of 1885 still actively cruising; *Caviare,* a Gloucester fishing schooner of 1891; *Mathilda,* a steam tug of 1899; and the red-and-white Fulton ferry boat, *Major General William H. Hart.* At the time of writing, negotiations were underway to add to this historic fleet the 335-foot, four-masted bark *Moshulu,* famed as the winner of the last grain race from Australia to England, and the 338-foot Hudson River paddlewheel steamer, *Alexander Hamilton.*

Ashore there's a Seaport Bookshop and Gallery and a museum display at 16 Fulton Street. Museum hours are daily from noon to 6 P.M. Nearby Sweet's Restaurant has the distinction of being New York's oldest seafood restaurant and is open from noon to 8 P.M., Monday through Friday.

A visit to fascinating South Street Seaport is a "must" for any follower, young or old, of our American maritime heritage.

Hudson River Ports Below the Harlem River
(Going upriver, leave black buoys to port, red to starboard.)

Before cruising men embark on a trip up the Hudson, it may be wise, though regrettable, for us to warn them that this "great river of the mountains" is fast becoming a "cesspool," according to *The New York Times*. Native fishermen tell the story that a nail dropped into the river near Albany or New York City won't rust because there is no oxygen left in the water. And New York State studies prove more conclusively that there is now six times as much pollution in the Hudson as there was at the turn of the century. Gross pollution exists from New York City up to Tarrytown. From that point the river water is slightly contaminated to a point just north of Peekskill. The cleanest water to be found flows along the stretch from Peekskill to Kingston, but the rest of the Hudson is heavily polluted as it meets the Mohawk River above Troy. A Health Department doctor reports that he would not dare drink any of this water, much less swim in it. Yet these very waters afford you one of the loveliest river trips in America.

Robert H. Boyle, author of the now-classic book *The Hudson—A Natural and Unnatural History,** is "an outspoken friend of this great but manhandled river." In considering the Hudson's future, he presents these two alternatives:

The first is that of a clean and wholesome river from the Adirondacks down to the harbor; a wild unfettered stream in its forested mountain headwaters; productive tidewater from Troy south. Useful for both navigation and drinking water, the Hudson will be a river toward which millions of people can turn with pride and expectation. In recreation alone, the Hudson will be worth billions to the communities along its banks.

The second vision is not pleasant. Dammed and strangled in the Adirondacks to serve as a draw-down reservoir, the upper river trickles to the estuary. Overloaded with sewage and industrial wastes and cooked by cooling water from power plants, the lower Hudson is bereft of the

* Published in 1969 by W.W. Norton & Co.

large forms of life except for a few stray catfish or carp in isolated "zones of recovery." At night, the mountains of the Highlands thrum to the noise of pumped storage plants sucking part of the river uphill. Discovery of a dead sturgeon or a striped bass along the shore is cause for excitement and a front-page story in the *Times* on the wonder of it all. Here and there, between the transmission towers and stacks, a few breathtaking views of the valley landscape are still to be seen, if you look quickly while speeding behind a truck over a six-lane highway built on filled-in river bottom. In essence, the valley is jammed with senseless sprawl, and the river is a gutted ditch, an aquatic Appalachia, a squalid monument to greed.

The future of our "American Rhine," however, may appear to be brighter than its present waters, which Henry Hudson once found "clear, blue, and wonderful to taste." The state and federal governments, with special assigned funds, are now committed to a major effort toward reducing pollution in the Hudson. True, it will take years to clean up the river and remove many of the eyesores along its waterfront, but the Scenic Hudson Preservation Conference, the Hudson River Sloop Restoration, Inc., and other dedicated conservation groups have taken united action toward maintaining its heritage and majestic scenery.

A letter written to us in late 1971 from the public relations officer of the New York State Department of Environmental Conservation tells some of the steps being taken to clean up the river:

> Our records show 180 industrial and 125 municipal polluters for a total of 305 in the Hudson River Drainage Basin. . . . One hundred and fifty of these polluters are abated, which means they have completed construction and are operating or they have connected to an existing approved treatment plant. Another 104 have submitted plans for treatment plants. The number of plants now under construction is 45.
>
> An overall range of completion dates is difficult to determine. However, under New York's Pure Waters Program construction must begin by March 31, 1972, if a municipality is to be eligible for a Pure Waters Program grant.
>
> Forty-two comprehensive sewerage studies have been completed for municipalities in the Hudson River region.

Even an extinct type of sailboat that plied the Hudson by the hundreds during the nineteenth century has made a comeback. The Hudson River sloop with a length of 75 feet, beam of 24½ feet, an 80-foot mast with gaff rig, and 100-ton displacement, was the major workhorse for commerce between New York and Albany, making the trip in less than a day. An exact replica, designed and constructed by Hudson River Sloop Restoration, Inc., may now be seen in the form of a traveling exhibit in various ports up and down the river. The *Clearwater* promises to be just one of the many surprises in store for you as you set sail upon this unique highway of history.

1. Hudson Harbor—79th Street Boat Basin, N.Y. (east shore— 746). This is the first good yacht dock to which you come on the way up the Hudson from the Battery. Slips with 13 feet at low water, gas,* Diesel fuel, electric connections, and toilets in the house at the head of the basin are all available. Food and supplies will be delivered if you order by dock phone. At times you feel like a goldfish in a bowl, though if you want a bit more privacy, with less convenience but more roll, use an outer mooring.

Each of the 200 slips is available at 25¢ per foot with an $8.00 minimum charge. This marina also provides off-season limited dockage, but no winter moorings or showers, and is open twenty-four hours a day with a watchman on duty. Repair service, a ship's store, and snack bar complete the facilities.

This accessible basin has become very popular with boats both large and small. Such majestic diesel yachts as *Argo* and *Highlander* often dock here to the wonderment of all eyes. Perhaps it is wise to reserve space in advance of your arrival by phoning EN 2-0909. Full service is available from May 1 to October 31.

In 1971, the basin received considerable publicity as the scene of a $3.5 million hashish smuggling, undertaken by a yacht sailed all the way from Morocco by a four-man crew. Although much of the hashish was rapidly unloaded, the *Beaver* was soon impounded by the United States Customs and the culprits were seized.

2. Edgewater, N.J. (west shore—746). As you come abeam of the range lights on each side of the river, you will spot a large white building marking the location of the Richmond Marina. Water, electricity, and telephone are available, with 110 slips for boats from 14 feet to 50 feet in a fully bulkheaded area. A gas dock supplies Texaco products, ice, and complete repair service seven days a week. Traveling lifts can handle boats up to 25 tons and 55 feet in length. A snack bar, marine store with charts, and a sundeck add to the facilities here. The shore line is not very picturesque but it may afford you a panoramic view of the Manhattan skyline.

---

* "Gas" is used throughout as an abbreviation for gasoline.

3. Englewood Boat Basin, N.J. (west shore—747). This is slightly below the point where the Harlem River joins the Hudson and one of the best yacht basins on the river. Located under the shadow of the Palisades as the sun goes down in the west, the surroundings are pleasant, and a wooden breakwater supplemented by sunken barges gives good protection from the confused waters of the much-traveled Hudson. This large and well-kept yacht marina is operated by the Palisades Interstate Park Commission, which made a charge, at the time we were there, of $3.50 per night for slips and somewhat less than that for moorings. While most of the slips are rented for the season, several are reserved for transients, and there may also be vacancies while boats are away. Gas, water, ice, and electricity are provided, but supplies are available only by phoning a taxi.

Hudson River Above the Harlem River
(747, 748, 282, 283, 284).

4. Alpine Boat Basin, N.J. (west shore—747). Like the Englewood Boat Basin, this is run by the Palisades Interstate Park Commission, and has similar facilities and prices except that there is no adequate breakwater and yachts are subject to almost continuous motion. Gas, water, and electricity are available with two slips reserved for transients. We prefer the basin at Englewood, where the Palisades also rise up steeply behind in a totally uncommercial setting.

Unfortunately, the Ludlow Marine Corp., a major boatyard formerly located across the river at Yonkers, went out of business in 1971.

5. Hastings-on-Hudson, N.Y. (east shore—748). Here is the first yacht club you will reach on the way up the river. Just above some oil tanks, the battered and ancient remnants of a once-active brigantine serve as a breakwater for an oil company loading dock and also give partial protection to the float of the small, unpretentious and friendly Tower Ridge Yacht Club, opposite the bow of the old vessel. When we were there in 1971, the club was busily constructing a new stone breakwater to give it much needed protection from the north. Don't come up dockside, where there is just 2 to 3 feet at low water. Gas can be purchased here at high water, but for slip space, ice, and supplies, put in at the Hastings Marina a few hundred yards downriver. The club may have an extra mooring available.

The wooden breakwater was once the brigantine *City of Beaumont,* which carried lumber by sail during World War I and then roosted for years at a New York City pier. When Prohibition came she was renamed the *Buccaneer,* anchored off Tarrytown, where she functioned as a floating speakeasy and showboat, until the authorities interceded. The late Mayor Jimmy Walker is said to have entertained his friends there. Now her task is more prosaic and her keel rests firmly on the ground.

6. Tarrytown, N.Y. (east shore—282). With the availability of the Tappan Zee Bridge and dredging to 12 feet in its channel, Tarrytown Harbor has now become extremely convenient as a rendezvous from either side of the Hudson. Tarrytown Marina is located on a narrow point, north of a T-shaped breakwater shown on the chart. It has a $150,000 section, the westernmost walkway of which contains its own built-in breakwater. Leave red nun 6 to starboard before heading for the main dock to the north of the point. You will approach a large basin with 263 slips located offshore of the Tarrytown Boat Club. There is 4 to 5 feet of water at the slips but 6 feet at the gas dock, where the Dock Master, Harry Beckley, will assign you a slip and give you the marina's rules. They will charge you a fee of 20¢ a foot at the slips and offer ice, water, electricity, showers, marine charts, pump-out facilities, and marine supplies, and arrangements can be made for you to obtain groceries nearby. The bar and restaurant belong to the Tarrytown Boat Club; there are a theater and a hospital in the vicinity.

The Washington Irving Boat Club, which is located just to the south, is best suited for boats under 30 feet but is less comfortable due to its close proximity to the N.Y. Central Railroad.

In leaving this harbor heading north, be sure to follow closely the buoys marking the north connecting channel. You'll pass the Tarrytown Lighthouse. Constructed in 1883, it guided boats past these shores until the mid-1950s, when the completion of the Tappan Zee Bridge made it obsolete.

A short distance south of the junction of the bridge and the New York Thruway stands "one of the great houses of America—uniting in its walls the beginning and culmination of Hudson River Gothic." Here is Lyndhurst, a huge baronial castle of dazzling beauty, built in 1838 and for a time the home of Jay Gould. Visiting hours at this historic preservation are from 10 A.M. to 5 P.M. daily.

Settled as a Dutch trading post in the seventeenth century, Tarrytown was developed as farmland with the rest of the rich Hudson Valley by Dutch and English manor lords. Of historic interest in this "Sleepy Hollow" country is Philipse Castle, the seventeenth-century home of Frederick Philipse, First Lord of the Manor, who once owned most of Westchester. Recently, his old gristmill was rebuilt by Sleepy Hollow Restoration, offering visitors a good opportunity to see what a center of commerce looked like over two hundred years ago. One can also pay a visit to Sunnyside, the gabled and turreted home of Washington Irving, who peopled these slumbering hills with gnomes, trolls, and comic Dutchmen.

7. Nyack, N.Y. (west shore—282). At Upper Nyack is Julius Petersen, Inc., where visiting yachts up to 120 feet can find about everything they need: slips, gas, Diesel fuel, water, ice, marine railways, indoor and outdoor storage, a splendidly equipped marine hardware and supply store, repair men, deep water, but unfortunately no showers. There's a functional look about the place, obviously not so attractive as the new Lighthouse Yacht Center, giving one an impression of what old traditional yacht yards should resemble. However, Petersen's rates are comparatively low and they promise, "We'll guarantee you a quiet night's sleep."

Its dock is located at Upper Nyack north of the new Lighthouse Yacht Center and is easy to identify by a number of large gray boat sheds. The small Powell Boat Yard and the Nyack Boat Club are above the old ferry. The club is said to have only 3½ feet at the dock.

Next to the Nyack Boat Club has risen the newest and perhaps the most ambitious marina on the Hudson. Owned by Mr. Victor Farris, a New Jersey inventor-industrialist, the enterprise is part of a 10-acre, multi-million-dollar riverside complex known as the Lighthouse Yacht Center. Its protected basin with 7-foot depth is identified by a prominent white lighthouse formerly a four-story oil tank. When we were there in 1971, the center was in full swing and in full bloom, looking perhaps a bit more spectacular than Terra Mar at Saybrook.

The facilities here are endless. They are all itemized in a brochure that they'll hand you on your arrival. The basin accommodates 75 boats, with the usual marine repairs and supplies on tap. Pier 7 has a swimming pool, cabana, and an impressive restaurant seating 400 guests. Visiting yachtsmen using Pier 7 are credited toward their dockage fee. Of interest to the distaff side, perhaps less to their skippers, is a colorful art gallery and a boutique in the lighthouse, offering fine clothes from the fashion centers. Dress is informal, and the usual credit cards are honored. Transient rates are as follows: up to 29'6"—$7.50 minimum; 30' to 39'6"—$10.00 minimum; 40' to 49'6"—$12.50 minimum. This is the first marina we have visited that has scheduled a check-out time. It is high noon. We hope they haven't started a new trend.

Jim Downey is the manager who runs a tight ship here. By following the center's sensible rules, everybody seems to have a happier time. Reservations are suggested; phone 693-2971.

The Tappan Zee Playhouse up on Nyack's main street is only a ten-minute walk. Well-known artists such as Faye Dunaway, Eli Wallach, and

Hume Cronyn appear here from time to time in major Broadway hits. Its season runs from late June to early September.

8. Ossining, N.Y. (east shore—282). "The sunsets are out of this world," said the manager of the Shattemuc Yacht Club, as we looked westward across the panorama of mountains and hills. This club is located on the northernmost projection of land on the Ossining water front, where an L-shaped pier shows on the chart. The three-story club-house has a high projecting piazza. There are gas, water, ice, showers, and electricity—in season—at the slips, which have 6 feet at low water on both sides. Members of other recognized yacht clubs are welcome, and the club facilities include a bar, snack bar, and restaurant. You may phone Gristede's for the delivery of groceries. There are inland slips, complete hull work, and good engine work at the Westerly Marina just to the south. We regret to report that fire destroyed the clubhouse in 1973.

The club usually has spare dock space for guests. At night the signal is two white lights between one red. The take-off point for the club is from Hudson red lighted buoy 8. If coming from the north, give Tellers Point a wide berth of at least ¼ mile, as the gravel-bottomed shoal projects southward further than the chart indicates. In approaching from the south, be sure to stay well outside of the dolphins. You don't need a stout heart to climb to local stores, for the club will help you out if they possibly can.

On our most recent visit here, we were generously hosted by Commodore Don Carret and a congenial member of his afterguard, Bill Fanning. We learned of the club's growing reputation as a major sailing center on the Hudson, evidenced, in part, by the fine fleet of cruising auxiliaries and one-design racing classes tied up snugly behind a 300-foot break-water of steel barges. That day was a Hudson River scorcher; it was all we could do to keep from leaping, sailing duds and all, into the club's swimming pool. Now plans are afoot to erect a new building on the original club site.

If you look westward across the river, this spot is attractive, but it is wide open, except from the southeast to northwest, in one of the widest parts of the Hudson.

The famous Sing Sing Prison was established at Ossining in 1824 with the intention of using convict labor on marble quarries. Once a prison in which severe repression was practiced, Sing Sing has now become known for its enlightened penal practices.

9. Haverstraw, N.Y. (west shore—282). Nestled below the craggy cliffs of High Tor, Little Tor, and Pnygyp (so named because it resembles a Dutch loaf of bread) lies a little cove shown on the chart just southwest of black can 15. Hug this can close to port in heading for the flagpole of the Rockland-Bergen Boat Club. The entrance is shallow, but two poles, to be kept to starboard, will guide you by the stone breakwater. The dock master located on the port dock is on duty from 4:30 P.M. to 9 P.M. Monday through Thursday and all day the rest of the week. Except for gas and a limited number of slips, you won't find much else here. It is a pleasant spot, and yet we prefer the more manicured setting at Grassy Point.

Here it was, on September 22, 1780, that Benedict Arnold met Major John André to plot the betrayal of West Point. James Wood later discovered the modern process of making brick, establishing an industry that at one time included here forty brickyards producing over 325,000 bricks a year.

Robert H. Boyle, author of *The Hudson—A Natural and Unnatural History,* describes Haverstraw Bay's wealth of marine life in the March 1971 issue of *Audubon Magazine:*

From my point of view, Haverstraw Bay, the widest part of the Hudson—more than three miles across—is the richest exploring ground in the whole river. Changing salinities and temperatures bring an amazingly wide variety and abundance of both saltwater and freshwater life. It is the only body of water that I know of which has yielded codfish, largemouth bass, sunfish, herring, mackerel, yellow perch, sand sharks, seals, muskrats, bluefish, damselfly larvae, blue crabs, jack crevalles, needlefish, stripers, anchovies, silver hake, menhaden, Johnny darters, sea sturgeon probably up to 500 pounds, and the "endangered" short-nosed sturgeon. Biologists who have been on the bay with me have gone away flabbergasted. My main prize has been a mangrove snapper, which ranges in this hemisphere from Florida south to Brazil. It is also found on the West African coast. So far as I can determine, the mangrove snapper is now the only species of fish which has been found in both the Hudson and the Congo.

10. Grassy Point—at town of Stony Point (west shore—282). This is one of the best ports on the Hudson River and certainly the finest in the area. Its location can be spotted from the river by a prominent church spire and water tower nearby. One can enter by following a 6-foot channel about 150 feet off the shore of Grassy Point until red and black buoys are reached opposite the entrance between the breakwaters. Go in between the buoys, keeping about 10 feet away from the eastern bulkhead. Here is a dredged-out clay hole with a 20-foot depth running almost to the shore. Opposite the entrance is the attractive Minisceongo Yacht

Club, which was founded by the High Tor Sailing Fleet and whose name is derived from an Indian phrase, "winding waters."

The clubhouse was built entirely by the members "with their own hands." Visiting yachtsmen from other recognized yacht clubs may use the floats and facilities "as long as they behave themselves." Upon entering the basin, all boats should go to the gas dock. You may tie there temporarily until you are assigned a slip at $5.00 and up. The overnight slip charge for boats 31 to 40 feet in length is $6.00 and for over 40 feet the charge is $8.00. Dropping your anchor is not permitted. Water, ice, electricity, gas, showers, and a snack bar open on the weekends are all available, with food supplies delivered to you if ordered by phone. Minor repair work can be done and there is one small marine railway.

We enjoyed tremendously this snug, quiet little harbor with its friendliness and rather rustic atmosphere. We have cruised here in June and October from Newburgh through some of the most magnificent scenery on the Hudson, and the coloring along the shores left us hunting for appropriate adjectives.

For major repair work and marine supplies we suggest Grassy Point Marina next door to the east. They have 4 feet dockside. The docks at the Seaweed Boat Landing located to the north have the same depths but the approach is shoal and is wide open to the east.

The village of Stony Point, and the rocky bluff on the shore of the Hudson, bear a name familiar to American schoolboys. Be sure to visit the Stony Point Battlefield Reservation. Here, on July 16, 1779, 1200 Continentals under General "Mad" Anthony Wayne stormed and captured a fort held by British forces. In the daring charge, General Wayne was wounded and borne forward over the rampart to victory on the shoulders of his men. A story is told that during the discussion of Hudson River tactics, Washington asked Wayne if he thought he could storm Stony Point. The General replied: "I'll storm hell, sir, if you'll make the plans!" Washington looked at him meditatively for a moment, then replied: "Better try Stony Point first." On one of the highest points on the promontory is the Stony Point Museum.

The huge "mothball fleet" of 189 ships, known as the "National Defense Reserve Fleet," is no longer anchored above Stony Point. Most of these Liberty ships were mothballed from World War II to the Korean war, after the Korean war to the Suez crisis, and then again for the Vietnam war. Now they rest in some foreign port as floating warehouses or upon some rusty scrap pile to serve a newer purpose. The final sixteen ships were sold in 1971 to a Pakistani concern for $1.7 million, and the last of these slipped proudly down the Hudson towed by a tug flying the German flag.

11. Montrose, N.Y. (east shore—282). On the eastern shore opposite Stony Point Bay, Georges Island juts out into the Hudson as an unspoiled peninsula, ideal for hiking, picnicking, and nature study. The 175 acres that comprise this Westchester County-owned park have been carefully preserved for the recreation and enjoyment of boatmen and local residents. A popular launching ramp located on the peninsula's southern shore has been built to accommodate boats up to 20 feet overall and leads directly to a 60-foot-wide channel dredged to a depth of 4 feet below mean low water extending some 430 feet into the river. Do not attempt to tie up to the many buoys you will see in this area. We poked along this sylvan shore in our boat of 3-foot draft, finding the best anchorage with the most beautiful setting in the bight on the peninsula's north side. If you enjoy visiting places that are different, you will not be disappointed here. The park closes at sunset.

Almost a mile northward along the innermost part of Greens Cove lies the Montrose Marina, home of the Cortlandt Yacht Club and the Montrose Cabana Club, sheltered behind a small but prominent island. It is further identified by a line of colorful cabanas. Outer red and black cans mark the entrance to the channel 75 feet in width and dredged to 10 feet all the way into the slips, where there is 6 feet of water. Go between these cans and make for the dock after having swung around the second black can, keeping it to port.

Here you can be supplied with gas, water, electricity, slip space, and taxi service on call. The marina can handle engine repairs. A snack bar is next to one of the few swimming pools on the Hudson. Free swims are included in the dockage fee. Restaurants and a motel are nearby.

Wes Harrington, the general factotum at Montrose, has won through his good services lots of boating devotees, some of whom are regular visitors down from Canada. Slip reservations can be made in advance by phoning Peekskill 7-9540.

12. Peekskill, N.Y. (east shore—282). "Everybody is welcome" is always the greeting we receive when we stop at the Peekskill Yacht Club, founded in 1908 as the Peekskill Motorboat Club. The best way to get there is to go in from the Hudson River beacon 18, whose flashing light has been changed from red to white. In 1971, the beacon itself was red and black with its number unpainted. Leave this to port and the red nun channel buoy 2 to starboard. Round red nun 4, further in, and head for the club dock on Travis Point. The chart indicates 6½ feet in the channel, and we were informed that there is 6 feet at the dock. Enter on the north end of the barges, which form a breakwater. Unless the space is already occupied, yachts may be permitted to tie up on the north side of the dock, where they are out of the way of boats coming in for gas there, and can take lengthwise any wash that comes in from the river. Water, electricity, ice, and gas are supplied, as well as a possible mooring if the dock space is occupied.

George White, a dyed-in-the-wool native of these parts, appears to be the club's official greeter. Seated inside the attractive new clubhouse recently rebuilt on an old barge, he can spin many an enchanting yarn about the Hudson's past and present.

While the Peekskill water front is what might be expected in a good-sized commercial city, the view across the river to Dunderberg (930 feet) is pleasant. The Peekskill Motor Inn nearby is an excellent spot for meals, and shops are not far away. In ordinary quiet summer weather this port is O.K., but it is open to the river for some distance to the northwest and southwest.

To the south on Indian Point, you will note Consolidated Edison's nuclear power plant #1 with a generating capacity of 265,000 kilowatts and its power plant #2, which energizes an impressive 873,000 kilowatts. Indian Point #3, to be completed in 1972, is expected to add another 965,000 kilowatts to Con Edison's capacity to meet the future energy needs of New York and Westchester. Special guided tours of these plants are available to the public at the Nuclear Information Center from 1 P.M. to 5 P.M., Wednesday through Sunday, including most holidays. Visitors can also enjoy the scenic nature walks, picnic grounds, and lake surrounding the plants' property.

13. Fort Montgomery, N.Y. (west shore—282). Just below Bear Mountain Bridge you may observe a small anchorage basin for boats whose crews wish to enjoy all the sights and conveniences of one of New York's finest state parks. The Appalachian Nature Trail, running all the way from Lake Huron in Canada to the Cumberland Mountains of Alabama, crosses the Hudson here.

About one-fourth mile above the bridge, and near the foot of towering Bear Mountain (1305 feet), is a small unpretentious dock with concrete launching ramp close by. This is operated by the Fort Montgomery Marina, which provides adequate facilities, supplies, and a limited number of slips looking out upon an exceptionally lovely view across river to a steep, thickly wooded hill known as Anthony's Nose. Its service also includes a first-class mechanic and a restaurant with good home-style cooking. If you wish to adventure on land for a few hours to Bear Mountain State Park or to nearby West Point Military Academy, a car rental service is available. Should you prefer a motorcycle, we believe that could be arranged, since Russell Strongman, a most congenial fellow, handles both boat and Honda dealerships.

The trouble with this place for overnight is that it is too small and exposed to a strong current and heavy wake for some distance up and down the river. Freight trains rumble close by at least twice a night. In spite of these drawbacks, we enjoyed our stopover here.

14. Garrison, N.Y. (east shore—282). As you proceed north to Garrison you will behold the magnificent Gothic spectacle that is West Point rising from the west bank of the river. There is limited docking space at the academy, with reservation by permit only. However, across the river is the basin of the Garrison Landing Marina, identified by two red-lighted bulkheads. There is 13 feet at the gas dock and sufficient water in the protected basin for boats of 3-foot draft. The mean range of tide here is about 3 feet. The price for overnight dockage runs 15¢ a foot with water and electricity thrown in. An old-style country store in back of the marina may help you "replenish the larder, or pick up that item which was forgotten." Here we learned from a native fisherman that leaping carp, so often seen on the Hudson, usually designate shallow water of 2- to 3-foot depths.

The film *Hello Dolly* was shot at Garrison, since its surroundings so closely resemble the Yonkers of the 1890s. Art fans from miles around come here annually in late August to attend the colorful Garrison art festival.

If you can obtain transportation, a memorable experience may be had by a visit to nearby Boscobel, a beautiful eighteenth-century restored mansion originally built by States Morris Dyckman for his beloved wife.

Railroad buffs may be interested to learn that Garrison has restored its antique depot, where railroad tycoons used to wait for their private cars in style. It is worth-while to visit this "living museum of transportation," with the real show-stopper a perfect model of the old steam engine "West Point."

15. Cold Spring, N.Y. (east shore—282). The village of Cold Spring is included in this edition because it offers its visitors certain delights not found at any other Hudson River port. Having just passed Constitution Island, one cannot miss the sight of a picturesque bandstand and village green set behind a prominent dock. From here, the magnificent views of West Point, Cro'nest, Storm King, and Constitution Island have probably been painted and photographed more frequently than any other scenes along the Hudson Valley.

The Cold Spring Dock and Marina has facilities for shoal-draft boats to tie up for a visit, or there is a possibility of a temporary mooring at the dock already mentioned. If you can arrange to get ashore, an anchorage just off of it in deeper water can be made.

A short way up the main street, one can visit the colorful Hudson River Sloop Restoration headquarters. This is a non-profit corporation chartered by the State of New York for the purposes of education in the history and ecology of the Hudson River Valley. Through the financial support of its membership and other interested groups, it built, owns, and sails the *Clearwater,* an exact replica of a Hudson River sloop. It also conducts summertime waterfront festivals. The sloop is available to school, college, and community groups who wish to sail the river.

Next to the bandstand rises the Hudson View Hotel, the third oldest hostelry in continuous use in New York State—only the Beekman Arms in Rhinebeck and the Canoe Place Inn on Long Island antedate it. Built in 1837, it houses famous Gus's Antique Bar filled with the pungent atmosphere of a German ale house and a wild display of steins, military insignia, and weapons of the American past.

Although history doesn't record that George Washington slept at Cold Spring, it is a fact that in frequent visits to his American Revolutionary troops encamped nearby, he often drank from a local spring which gives the village its present name.

16. Cornwall-on-the-Hudson, N.Y. (west shore—282). As you proceed north to Cornwall, you will behold some impressive wonders both natural and historic. Just above West Point there is a sharp bend in the river named Worlds End with depth exceeding 150 feet. At this point, through which you should move cautiously, the colonials strung a wrought-iron chain during the Revolution to prevent British advance upriver. Then you may see from the river the old battlements of Fort Constitution peeking out from the jagged cliffs on the northwestern side of Constitution Island. Further along on the western shore rises magnificent 1400-foot Storm King Mountain, which natives years ago believed to be the haunt of hobgoblins and elves. Still looming over the horizon is the "storm over Storm Kill" with Consolidated Edison's plans to construct a $400 million pumped-storage complex on the mountain to the outraged opposition of the Scenic Hudson Preservation Conference. The conference and other environmentalists claim that the project would contaminate salt-water intrusion into the Hudson, admit thermal pollution, destroy scenery and fish life, and present grave dangers to New York City's Catskill Aqueduct.

On the western shore across from Pollepel Island, on which Bannerman's Castle rises in medieval splendor, lies the Cornwall Yacht Club, identified by a small white building flanked by a string of barges forming a very protected basin. The stern of the prominent black barge marks the entrance, which should be approached from due east. Keep the floating marker to port on entering the basin. Sound your horn as you enter and check with the steward to be assigned a slip. There is a charge of 15¢ a foot at the slips with 8-foot depth at the outer slips. Gas, water, ice, and electrical connections are all available. The warm reception we received here with its quiet anchorage makes Cornwall a recommended spot.

Bannerman, who began as a munitions dealer at the end of the Civil War, built his Rhine-type castle in 1900 as a storehouse for his supply of guns, armor, and ammunition. After his death in 1918, the arsenal was abandoned, with the business moving to Long Island. A fire raged through this castle in 1971, gutting the interior but fortunately leaving its "ramparts" intact.

17. Newburgh, N.Y. (west shore—282). At the upper end of what we consider the most spectacular passage on the Hudson is the well-equipped and hospitable Newburgh Yacht Club, where there is a basin with many slips protected by sunken barges. It is located just below the Newburgh fixed bridge, at the foot of a steep hill. The entrance to the basin is at the southern end of a line of barges. Slips are usually available for visiting yachts, and gas, Diesel fuel, water, ice, and electricity are on tap. There is an average of about 6 feet in the basin. Besides the lift, there is a marine railway and modest restaurant in the clubhouse.

While the immediate surroundings are not beautiful, this is a very convenient and well-protected place to stop, and if you have the climbing ability of a mountain goat or the cash for a taxi, you can reach some movies and good stores in the city. The Hanaford Boating Center (telephone 2771) has all sorts of marine supplies and will deliver them at the Yacht Club on call.

18. New Hamburg, N.Y. (east shore—283). To enter White's Hudson River Marina's basin from the south, turn sharply to starboard at the midchannel light marking Diamond Reef and run a course close and parallel to the barges forming the basin's southern edge. With only 4 feet of water at the basin's western side, this place is best suited for power boats under 30 feet. The owner, Mr. John White, offers marine supplies, repair work, a mobile lift, and complete dock facilities.

Although the surroundings are far from scenic and the whole place has a topsy-turvy look, there is excellent protection, especially from the north, and we were told that boats here have been safe even in storms of hurricane strength. Light sleepers beware, however. You may not appreciate the New York Central trains that rumble by only a few hundred yards away.

19. Poughkeepsie, N.Y. (east shore—283). About halfway between New York and Albany, Poughkeepsie is well known as the location of Vassar College and also for the Intercollegiate rowing championships formerly held there. Huge college letters painted on boulders and still visible are the only trace of these regattas first held in 1895.

Just above Hudson River at Highland Landing on the west shore lies the active Mariner's Harbor Marina with good dock facilities in deep water. Ice, gas, Diesel fuel, water, showers, and electricity are furnished here. The main attraction here is its nautical-looking restaurant, patio, and bar providing "gracious riverside dining." The menu specializes in sea food, with guests selecting their own lobsters from the tank. It's fairly peaceful here except for an occasional passing train and wake from the river's traffic. Mariner's Harbor has built another marina and restaurant at Eddyville, described later in this book.

Poughkeepsie's urban renewal project has forced the Poughkeepsie Yacht Club to move from its former location in the shadow of the Mid Hudson Bridge. This turn of events has been fortunate for all concerned. Now the club is enjoying a rebirth at its appealing new location on the east shore off Blunts Island one mile below Indian Kill. We were greeted by the club's Dock Master, Ed Lynk, and its Vice Commodore, Harold Krom. They told us how their members had pitched in to improve the new layout, filling in the land on which a proposed clubhouse and swimming pool will be built.

At the time of writing, the club's facilities include gas, Diesel fuel, water, electricity, ice, repair work, a launching ramp, and all the depth you'll need off its outer slips. Although it lies near the railroad and is exposed to river wake, it offers fair protection and a commanding view of the Hudson. A special anchorage area off the club's shore to the south will probably be established in the near future.

When their plans materialize, as they undoubtedly will, this will be a choice spot for a night's layover. The B-Lion National Catamaran Championship was held here in 1971.

20. Maritje Kill (east shore—283). Two miles above the Mid Hudson Bridge the mouth of Maritje Kill on the eastern shore marks the location of the Riverdale Marina and Boat Basin. Sunken barges at the basin entrance will provide you with a quieter anchorage than you will find at the Poughkeepsie Yacht Club, but the noise of the New York Central Railroad is still too close for complete comfort. There is 6 feet of water in the basin and there are facilities to handle boats up to 35 feet. The manager, Mr. Frank Richie, can offer you gas, water, ice, showers, and repair service. There is a restaurant and bar, which includes a swimming pool for limited use. Groceries can be ordered from a local grocer. We found this isolated basin, with its picnic tables and bordering trees, pleasant and friendly.

21. Indian Kill, Staatsburg (east shore—283). In our opinion, this is one of the two best overnight stopping places on the Hudson—the other being Catskill Creek. The Margaret Lewis Norrie State Park Boat Basin, dredged to a depth of 8 feet, is one of the most beautiful basins we have seen and is located at the mouth of Indian Kill, where two lights are shown on the chart a short distance north of Esopus Island. You come in between two lighted spars, red and green, on the north side of the inlet, and the dock master will show you where to tie up, giving you a docking permit. On our visit in 1971, the rate at the slips was 15¢ per foot. Water and electric current, for lights only, are included in this price, with gas and ice on tap at the outer end of the dock. At the inner end is a small store where soft drinks and snacks are served. Just to the south of the basin lies the charming Norrie Inn Restaurant, which is open from noon to midnight, welcoming overnight yachtsmen dressed in informal attire. For those who might prefer a round of golf, there is a public eighteen-hole course only a mile distant. The Port Captain, Mr. Bob Garrett, pointed out a fine concrete launching ramp and presented us with some of the regulations established and strictly enforced by the Taconic State Park Commission administering the marina. We have abbreviated them somewhat:

(1) The dock master assigns slips.
(2) Don't waste water.
(3) Unnecessary noise, loud talking, playing of musical instruments or radios between the hours of 11 P.M. and 8 A.M. are prohibited.
(4) Storage on dock is prohibited.
(5) Fitting-out or major repair work in berths is prohibited.
(6) Disposal of garbage or trash must be in receptacles provided for the purpose.
(7) Laundry shall not be exposed to public view at any time.
(8) No beer drinking is permitted in the park.
(9) Since this boat basin is run by New York, all visiting craft must be equipped with state-approved holding tanks. There are pump-out facilities here similar to those at Catskill, Hudson, and Coeymans-on-Hudson.

On all sides and across the river the surroundings and view are lovely. Some of the most lordly estates along the Hudson are within easy reach of

Indian Kill. Just to the south, one of them with its own dock is the Vanderbilt Mansion National Historic Site, commanding a magnificent view of the river. The fifty-room dwelling contains many masterpieces of Italian art and is open to the public daily. In nearby Hyde Park is the home of Franklin D. Roosevelt, another National Historic Site with many fascinating collections and relics acquired by the late President. Roosevelt's grave in the rose garden is marked by a simple and impressive white marble monument. Adjacent is the Roosevelt Library, with much material of historic interest and also some unusual gifts sent to the White House. About 1 mile north of Indian Kill at Dinsmore, you will note the Ogden Mills and Ruth Livingston Mills Memorial State Park—the 200-acre estate of the former Secretary of the Treasury. The sixty-five-room Mills mansion in French Renaissance style is open daily Monday through Friday from 10:30 A.M. to 4:00 P.M. If your boat does not draw over 3 feet, you may tie up at the gray stone boathouse located at the foot of the mansion while you pay your visit.

22. Kingston, Rondout Creek, N.Y. (west shore—283). On entering Kingston, be sure to keep the lighthouse marking the channel entrance well to starboard, since shoal water extends for considerable distance from the northern shore. Maximum speed permitted throughout the entire channel is 5 m.p.h. and the tide range is about 3½ feet. The lower part of Rondout Creek is commercial and unattractive, but about 1 mile up, where the Kingston Power Boat Association is located, it is very different. The clubhouse and dock of this friendly and active organization are well situated on the starboard or north shore. The water is deep and, at the dock, gas, water, and electricity are available. The club gives reciprocal privileges to members of other recognized clubs and, as we know from experience, visitors are sure to get a hospitable welcome. Across the creek is the substantial-looking Rondout Marine, which we can recommend should your boat, whether sail or power, require any hull or engine work. There are two basins here both providing slips—the upper one for large craft and the lower one for boats under 20 feet. Rondout's facilities include gas, Diesel fuel, water, showers, laundromats, and a marine supply store.

For a comparatively pleasant, rustic anchorage, we suggest going further up the creek to Eddyville, although it lacks some facilities; make sure to hug closely to the starboard bank on the way. You'll have good water in the marked channel as far as Anchorage Rest, located just as you reach the third bridge at Eddyville. About 500 yards beyond Gumaer Island, you will reach the Dockside Marina set forward on a small penin-

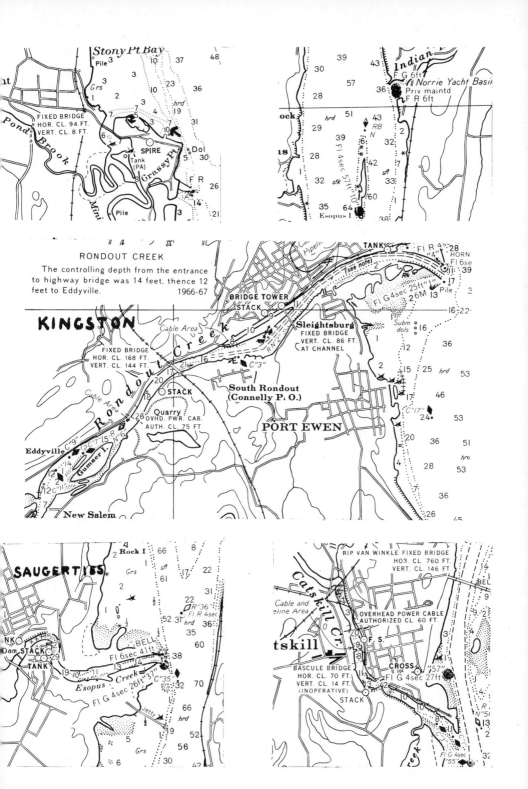

Some ports along the Hudson River. Upper left, refer to Chart 282; others, refer to Chart 283.

sula amidst a grove of willow trees. There is plenty of hospitality here but marine supplies are limited, as is engine and hull repair work. Dockside is a branch of Marina's Harbor in Highland, N.Y., both of which offer an excellent cuisine at reasonable prices. At the time of writing, this marina was being completely refurbished inside and out for the comfort and pleasure of cruising yachtsmen. Plans were afoot to dredge along the face of new docks and inside the adjacent lagoon, and to install a pump-out facility. Their services include gas, ice, water, and grocery supply. Price for space dockside runs 20¢ per foot.

The best anchorage may be found along the shore across from Dockside. Here there is 8 feet of water literally alive with bass, perch, pickerel, stripers, and carp. You may not enjoy some of the outboard noise here and the rumblings from rock excavations, but once darkness falls you will find it peaceful. If Dockside is filled, a slip might be open at Anchorage Rest beyond. There is a small general store nearby. The swimming is reported fine just below the dam, and nearby one can see the ruins of the first lock of the abandoned Delaware and Hudson Canal, on whose waters barges used to be drawn from the Pennsylvania coal mines. The mountains surrounding Eddyville have furnished much of the stone toward the construction of some of New York's highest skyscrapers.

23. Saugerties, Esopus Creek (west shore—283). This is one of the best natural anchorages on the Hudson, and boats entering the creek should stay in midchannel and not exceed a speed of 5 m.p.h. A few years ago, the channel was dredged to a depth of 12 feet as far as the Coast Guard station a short distance up on the starboard shore. Across from this station lies the white clubhouse of the Saugerties Power Boat Association. We have always enjoyed our many visits here. Electricity, ice, and water are at the slips, where there is a 10¢ per foot overnight charge. The clubhouse provides showers and a weekend bar. One small example of this club's conviviality is the special ceremony of launching any member's boat in return for two pitchers of beer to wet the whistle of the workers. We were cautioned to stay well clear of the dam situated at the head of the creek.

We put into Saugerties Marine next to the club for gas and marine supplies, then took a look at Lynch's Marina further up on the port bank. Here you'll find equally pleasant surroundings, a bit more privacy, good water, and a capability to handle larger crafts. No repair work is available at Saugerties.

Although attractive homes border the channel, some ruins of old docks are reminders that once there was a Saugerties Night Line that maintained daily passenger service to New York. Saugerties was once a haven

for the swiftest steamboats on the Hudson, such as the *Mary Powell*.
Saugerties is Dutch for "sawyer's town."

24. Catskill, Catskill Creek (west shore—283). Along the entire Hudson, this is one of our favorite spots. It was first visited by Hendrick Hudson and his crew on September 15, 1609, in his vain search for a northwest passage to the Indies. "Now," according to a Catskill native, "if the river could be cleaned up, we would have to string a velvet rope across the channel and let boats in two at a time." With a large shallow mud bank covering much of the southern part of the creek entrance, it is wise to swing wide to the east and north of black can 55 as you make your approach. Once inside, the best water is in mid-creek, keeping the channel stakes to port. Halfway up the channel you may spot to starboard the plant of the Allied Boat Co., which builds handsome fiberglass auxiliary yachts. One Allied class boat, a Seawind 30, claims to be the first fiberglass vessel to circumnavigate the world several years ago. Just beyond you can tie up at Catskill Marina nestled on the edge of the northern shore, where the hills rise steeply on both sides and are mirrored in the glassy water. The location is delightful; at the dock are telephones, gas, ice, water, and electric connections along the floats. There's a small swimming pool for the kids but no repair service for your boat. You may walk several blocks away to the churches, stores, and theater on Main Street in Catskill. Certainly it would be hard to find a more picturesque, safe, and friendly anchorage than here. The swanky Skyline Restaurant is 1½ miles away, should you feel inclined to "step out on the town."

Across the creek on the south shore is Hop-O-Nose Marina, with gas, water, ice, showers, a marine railway, cookout facilities, and the claim to be tops in engine repair work. Motel arrangements can be made for you, and transportation to town for supplies is available; people come from miles around to enjoy the restaurant's very palatable pizzas. Since Catskill is an extremely popular port of call during the summer season, it is advisable to phone ahead for slip space reservations. Speaking of making advance reservations reminds us of the conversation between two dolls at a large marina on the Hudson. As they traipsed alongside we overheard one ask the other, "Well, which boat are you sleeping on tonight, dearie?"

Once known as Catskill Landing and before then called Kaatskill by the Dutch in the days of river and turnpike transportation, this port was a busy and prosperous shipping point. "Early tavernkeepers in this community were known as 'retailers of liquid damnation.'" Catskill mountain-brewed applejack was a staple during the prohibition era, and shady characters once established hideouts in the hills. And it was at a spot near

Catskill that Rip Van Winkle is supposed to have indulged in his legendary sleep. Things are different now, for in summer many vacationists descend on Catskill and yachts come and go. But so far, nothing seems to have spoiled the quiet charm of this snug harbor, except possibly occasional lively freshets in the spring.*

25. Athens, N.Y. (west shore—283). As you approach Hudson, you will pick up the Hudson Island Lighthouse, one of the two remaining midstream lighthouses on the Hudson. The other is at Esopus Flats. Leaving the lighthouse to starboard, you will leave the main channel and pass by the town of Athens, making sure to keep well off of Middle Ground Flats. Near the mouth of Murderers Creek, approximately 1½ miles beyond Hudson Island Lighthouse, you can make out Athens Marine Center, identified by a gray stone building. This location is extremely well protected from the main channel although open to winds from the north and southwest. The owners have gone out of their way in providing visiting yachtsmen with a modest-sized marina that is spanking clean, modern, and set in peaceful surroundings. Their attractive restaurant alone offers a refreshing change. Food for your galley will be delivered to your slip on call. Don't count on having major repair work performed here, as you will find limited dock space and facilities.

26. Coxsackie, N.Y. (west shore—284). There is a good anchorage in 12 feet of water off the main channel to the west of Coxsackie Island. Stay well clear of the sandbar that stretches out from the southern tip of the island. It is well sheltered here along the former main channel except from directly south. The pretty surroundings promise you pleasant picnicking or walking tours. On the shore is the attractive Coxsackie Yacht Club, with floats, ice, water, electricity, gas, and moorings, about a third of the way above the lower end of the island. When we put in here early one morning, the club's founder, Mr. James Carroll, invited us for breakfast and told us about their special Sunday dinner at 1 P.M.—all one can eat at reasonable prices. In the summer of 1971, those dinners were still going strong. He pointed out the swimming beach just south of the clubhouse and warned us against venturing through the treacherous water behind Rattlesnake Island, where many a boat has struck sunken objects. Groceries will be delivered every day of the week; phone 731-8047. There is no charge for overnight dockage, but a "little brown jug" at the club's bar invites volunteer contributions both large and small.

Coxsackie is an Indian name meaning "hoot of an owl," and tribes

---

* From *New York*—American Guide Series (Oxford University Press).

from miles around used to gather here to make arrowheads. It is no coincidence, therefore, that the club's burgee is identified by a red arrowhead on a field of white. Now the surrounding country is one of the largest mushroom-growing centers in the world—an industry that was first developed in huge icehouses formerly supplying natural ice to New York City.

27. Schodack Creek, N.Y. (east shore—284). As you approach the entrance to Schodack Creek, you will note mid-channel light 36, marking the southern tip of Houghtaling Island. Remember that a dike connects this light with the island and keep all to port on moving up the middle of the creek. The channel is unmarked but you will be safe in following mid-channel leading to the dock and clubhouse of the private Hook Boat Club. Here you may dock or anchor in deep water in the most rural, attractive, and calm spot one can find before reaching Troy. Although we were tempted to venture further up Schodack Creek, we were advised of uncharted rocks and urged not to do so without complete local knowledge. The protection at the Hook Boat Club more than makes up for its lack of supplies and facilities.

28. Coeymans, N.Y. (west shore—284). Hug the west shore until you pick up flashing-light marker 43 marking the southernmost extension of a treacherous 1500-foot dike facing the harbor. If you do not wish to join the disreputable "Coeyman's Dike Club," be sure to leave this lighted marker 43 well to starboard, keeping off the dike at least 75 feet at all times. The five Coeyman's Dike day beacons. "A" through "E," are equipped with diamond-shaped white day marks with orange reflective borders in whose center read the words, "Danger—Submerged Jetty." As you approach Gerry Finke's Marine docks, keep inside of the line of moorings and you will arrive safely before a large pink brick building. You can tie up to floating docks undisturbed by rough water or wash kicked up by large boats plying the river channel. Although this marina is not too attractive, it can offer a cruising boat practically any service or supplies it might require. Most of the big marinas along the Hudson honor credit cards, and Gerry Finke's is no exception.

We prefer the Ravena Coeyman's Yacht Club because of its woodsy and noncommercial appeal. This club, situated just to the north of Finke's offers reciprocal privileges and similar protection but limited docking space and no gas. If you don't need supplies and you are lucky to obtain a slip, a stop here will be found enjoyable.

The Tri-City Yacht Club formerly located at Cedar Hill has moved to a new location on the west shore almost 2 miles north of Ravena Coeyman's Yacht Club and just south of the fixed highway bridge. Its entrance is marked by two upright marked poles forming a break in a low stone breakwater running north-south. Favor the starboard pole as you enter the basin with your bow on line with the top of the clubhouse roof and watch for shoaling inside the breakwater, although the basin proper has a depth of about 8 feet. The clubhouse, which one might consider chalet style but which is termed a "flustered synagogue" by some of its membership, offers showers, water, and overnight dockage, if available, to members of other recognized yacht clubs. If you must anchor, pick a spot about 50 yards above the northernmost dock, making sure not to proceed as far as the bridge. We found this new haven and the people there equally delightful.

29. Castleton-on-Hudson, N.Y. (east shore—284). Just above red nun 54 lies the progressive Castleton Boat Club and Auxiliary. There are a fine concrete launching ramp, floats with gas, ice, a picnic table, moorings, a restaurant and bar, a laundromat, showers, and a nearby grocery store. The club is housed in a small, well-located green building. Though there is a considerable stretch of open Hudson to the north and south, the river is narrow enough here to get little opportunity for waves to make up in stiff winds from the west. The wash from the passing boats may not trouble you half so much as the noise from the trains nearby.

30. Rensselaer, N.Y. (east shore—284). Here, just below the new fixed bridge to Albany at Mill Creek, is located the recently built one-story clubhouse of the Albany Yacht Club. In 1970 the club moved to its present site, making way for the bridge construction. Mr. Walsh, the Dock Master, informed us that they have gas, ice, electricity at dockside, and water. The clubhouse offers as complete facilities inside as you will find along the upper Hudson. Behind the club are many stores and eating places in the city of Rensselaer. Across the new bridge is the capital of the state, with fine hotels and shops, but with a water front to be expected of most large cities. This is a better place for shopping and meeting friends than it is for spending the night on your boat—that is, if you like quiet and good scenery.

Two blocks south of the club is restored Fort Crailo, a museum and national landmark, where the famous song *Yankee Doodle* was written in 1758. A visit here any time between 9 A.M. and 5 P.M. is well worthwhile.

31. Watervliet, N.Y. (west shore—284). The shoreline along Watervliet is almost unrecognizeable to one who has not recently cruised these waters. Gone are the Tri-City Yacht Basin and the Boating Center where we used to stop—all replaced by a new river-front highway bordering the western banks.

Troy and Watervliet are both important industrial centers, and the latter has a large arsenal. According to our historical source of information: *

The War of 1812 brought the settlement one of the largest arsenals in the United States, now the Watervliet Arsenal, and immortalized Samuel Wilson, who supplied the soldiers quartered nearby with what they called "Uncle Sam's beef," as the original "Uncle Sam."

In 1825 Mrs. Hannah Lord Montague, a Troy housewife, developed a detachable collar for men's shirts; according to tradition, she cut the dirty collars off her husband's shirts to save herself the trouble of washing the entire garment, and thereby created a new industry.

The Federal Lock, Troy (east shore—284)

Hug the east shore to avoid shoal water below the dam. You will notice a new mooring wall installed in 1970 for use by boats awaiting the opening of the lock. Proceed to the lock's entrance when the green light shows while avoiding being swept westward by the current. No permit is required for this lock, and like the other locks above, there is no charge for transit. This is the biggest lock in the system, but the lift is only 14 feet. At the time we were there the schedule called for opening the lock for pleasure craft on the hour, but should a lockage for commercial vessels be made at any other time, it is possible to follow along provided there is sufficient room.

The Canalized Hudson and the Champlain Barge Canal
("Book of Charts of New York Canals")

Above the Troy Lock, as previously noted, the "road" forks. One fork begins with the Mohawk River and leads westward through canal, river, and lake into lakes Ontario and Erie. The other fork begins as a continuation of the Hudson River—called the Canalized Hudson—and leads northward for about 34 miles. It then becomes the Champlain Barge Canal and continues northward for 20 more miles (making 54 in all) until it reaches Whitehall, at the southern end of Lake Champlain. While the westward fork is beyond the scope of this *Guide,* and involves a long trip, the northern passage offers the possibility of reaching beautiful Lake Champlain from the Troy Lock in about a day. For those who

* *New York*—American Guide Series (Oxford University Press).

want to cruise farther than Lake Champlain, there is the possibility of continuing northward by way of the Richelieu River into the St. Lawrence and thence eastward into the Gulf of St. Lawrence; then around (or through) Cape Breton; then south and west around Nova Scotia and across the Bay of Fundy to the New England Coast.

Between the Troy Lock and Lake Champlain are several stopping places that we can only mention here, with their approximate distances from the Troy Lock (in parentheses): Strunk Marine (2); Mechanicville (10); Schuylerville (24); Fort Edward, beginning of the Champlain Barge Canal (34); Smith Basin (41). There are undoubtedly other places for overnight tie up and supplies, but these are also beyond the range of our explorations for this *Guide*.

The upper Canalized Hudson is pretty and pastoral but lacking in the spectacular beauty found in the Hudson below Albany. Progress is slow on the voyage to Lake Champlain, because of the eleven locks (numbered to 12 with 10 omitted), each of which may cause delay, and also because of the speed limit between the locks: 10 miles an hour in the Canalized Hudson and 6 in the Champlain Barge Canal. The route is well marked and covered to Lake Champlain by Chart No. 180, *New York State Barge Canal System,* obtainable at a cost of $2.00 from the Lake Survey Center —National Ocean Survey, 630 Federal Building, Detroit, Michigan 48226, or through its local chart agencies. There is no official chart covering the Erie Canal from Lyons to Tonawanda, since this section is a land-cut for which charts are not necessary.

Those planning this trip should also write beforehand for a copy of the annual *Cruising Guide Book* for the New York State Barge Canal System and connecting navigable Candian lakes and rivers ($2.00). Contact Mr. Vedda Peters at 146 Sheridan St., Albany, N.Y. A few basic rules and regulations for pleasure boaters are outlined in the free pamphlet *Cruising the Canal System,* obtained by writing to the Director, Waterways Maintenance Subdivision, New York State Department of Transportation, 1220 Washington Ave., Albany, N.Y. 12226. An important leaflet entitled *Your Key to the Lock,* describing the operation of the Federal Lock and Dam at Troy is available from District Engineers, U.S. Army Engineer, District-New York, 26 Federal Plaza, New York, N.Y. 10007. There is no charge for this.

The canal is toll-free, and pleasure boats *are no longer required to obtain permits to pass the locks and lift bridges.* However, the lock permit should not be confused with boat registration, which is still required by law. Motorboats and sailboats with auxiliary power that are used principally in New York State must be registered with the Office of Parks and Recreation, Division of Marine and Recreational Vehicles, State Campus,

Bldg. #2, 1220 Washington Ave., Albany, N.Y. 12226.

Also useful and obtainable from the above address are the three "Cruise 'N Chart Kits" priced at $5.00 each. Kit No. 1 covers the Hudson River, Champlain Canal, and Lake Champlain. Kit No. 2 covers the Erie, Oswego, and Cayuga and Seneca canals. Kit No. 3 covers Lake Erie, the Welland Canal, Lake Ontario, and the St. Lawrence River. Each of these contains a complete chart book and illustrated guide.

CHAPTER IV

North Shore of Long Island Sound
Throgs Neck, New York, to New London, Connecticut

Throgs Neck, N.Y. (223). At the western end of Long Island Sound a long and narrow peninsula, known as Throgs Neck, marks the place where the sound ends and the East River begins. On the east side of this peninsula between the northern end of the Neck and Locust Point is one of the snuggest harbors on Long Island Sound—a fine overnight stopping place for cruising boats on their way to or from Manhattan or the Hudson River. The Locust Point Yacht Club, around "the corner" to starboard as one enters, is hospitable to visiting yachtsmen and will help them to find a mooring if one is available. A club burgee, one of the friendly members told us, is all the introduction needed. Ice and water are obtainable at the club during the season.

At the end of the harbor is the Locust Point Marine Service, where gas, oil, ice, water, etc., as well as small repairs, are available. From the club, buses connect with the Manhattan subway at Westchester Square.

As the chart shows, there is plenty of water inside the harbor, but one must use care in getting past several outlying rocks off Locust Point at the entrance. However, during the summer the yacht club has a pole on the outermost rock, which must be left to starboard going in.

While the harbor is apt to be crowded, it is over ¼ mile long, and it is usually possible to find room somewhere. The Throgs Neck Bridge from the Bronx to Long Island passes over the entrance between Locust Point and Throgs Neck, but all except auxiliaries with fairly tall masts will have no difficulty in getting through. Yachts inside the harbor, we were told, rode out Hurricane Donna without difficulty.

At the end of Throgs Neck is Fort Schuyler, erected over a hundred years ago, with Fort Totten on the opposite shore, to protect New York City from enemy attack from the Sound. Now it is the home of the Maritime College, part of the State University of New York. Those standing at the end of Throgs Neck on a fateful day in October, 1776, might have watched the passage of a flotilla loaded with redcoats on their way to land on the northern shore of Eastchester Bay. The British attempt to cut off the retreat of General Washington and his army from Manhattan to White Plains failed, thanks in part to a withering cross fire from Colonel John Glover and his fishermen of Marblehead.

Little Neck Bay, N.Y. (223). The fetch of water between Fort Totten on the west and the U.S. Merchant Marine Academy on Kings Point to the east forms the mouth of Little Neck Bay, where there is plenty of deep water due to recent dredging, as illustrated on the latest chart. However, as you pull up on the west shore to the docks of the Bayside Yacht Club, identified on the chart and seaward by a prominent flagpole, depths decrease to less than 4 feet at m.l.w. The club has limited facilities for transients but is nevertheless cordial in welcoming visiting yachtsmen from other recognized yacht clubs. Bayside Marina, just to the north, has gas, ice, water, and marine supplies but little space for overnighters.

In 1969, 350 acres of mud were dredged out of much of the bay to attain controlling depths of 7 feet for anchoring. Such depths can be found now in mid-channel to a point where you come abeam the southeast shore of Willett's Neck. From that point, 7 feet can be carried safely to starboard into a sector forming almost one-third of the western part of the bay. Also from that point, only about 4 feet can be carried to port into another sector forming approximately one-third of the bay's eastern part. The center line down through the bay shoals to 3- and 4-foot depths at m.l.w. At low ebb, no boat of 3-foot draft or greater should venture closer than 300 yards from the bay's shoreline. A popular anchorage for boats of fairly shoal draft is in the bight formed on the chart near Udalls Mill Pond on the eastern shore.

It is estimated that 500 recreational boats are moored in Little Neck Bay, and the figure is growing. Although there are limited facilities and it's wide open to the north, yachtsmen often use the bay as a convenient jumping-off point for cruising east or west.

City Island, N.Y. (223). City Island is New York headquarters for yacht building and repair. Rimmed from end to end with more than a dozen shipyards, it is a forest of masts and a beehive of nautical activity in the spring. The island is about a mile long, connected with the mainland by a swing bridge, and accessible to New York by bus or taxi, and subway.

No yachtsman should miss a visit to City Island; but it is not the place for a quiet, secure anchorage. The best anchorage for large boats is to the east, approximately off the middle of the island. The holding ground, however, is reported to be only fair, and the anchorage is exposed to northeasterly and southeasterly blows. In such storms, it is well to run over to the shore of Hart Island and anchor off the upper half of that island, where the holding ground is said to be good. There is also a possibility of tying up at a slip at one of the large docks that run along the eastern shore of City Island.

For boats drawing less than 7 feet, the western side of the island is preferred, though it is exposed to southerly winds. The yacht clubs are on this side and as a rule have moorings and launch service available to members of other recognized clubs. The Morris Yacht and Beach Club is on the southerly point, near the dock used by the pilots and Coast Guard.

The City Island Yacht Club is in a white building with a green roof a short distance to the north along the westerly shore. It has a long dock with shear legs, and over 6 feet of water at low tide. The club is especially popular among the sailing fraternity and maintains a few guest moorings. The Stuyvesant Yacht Club is a little farther north, and the Harlem Yacht Club, the oldest on City Island, is in a cove on the northwest side of the island.

There are also a number of good yards and marinas on the western shore, most of them catering to smaller craft and located at the northern end. Some of the popular ones on this side of the island from south to north are Sagman's Marine, Inc. (specializing in the care and sale of smaller craft—hauling, storage, repair, slips, moorings, etc.), Kretzer Boat Works (which can take care of fairly large boats, does welding and rigging work, and has been favorably known for many years), Ray's Chris-Craft, and the upcoming Thwaites Marina and Restaurant, where manager R. J. Borchers tempts yachtsmen to "stop by and watch our progress!"

On the east shore, among the leading yards are Triboro Shipyard, Minneford Yacht Yard and Marina (builders of *Intrepid* and *Constellation*), United Boat Service Corp., and Consolidated Yachts, run by W. Rodstrom.

Relatively few yachts are now built on City Island. High costs and foreign competition have taken care of that. But few ports have as much to offer in maintenance, repair, storage, marine equipment of all kinds. Be sure to call at Winsette's, 358 City Island Avenue. This used to be known as the Gadget Shop and is a unique institution with many fascinating gadgets that a yachtsman will find it difficult to resist. Charts may also be bought there. Geils & Foerst Marine Electric, about eight blocks south, are top specialists in all types of electronics.

Several leading sailmakers have their offices on City Island, including Ratsey and Lapthorn, whose reputation among yachtsmen is world-wide, Charles Ulmer, also highly regarded, and Hild Sails, who also do good work. This doesn't pretend to be a list of *all* of the good boat yards, services, and sailmakers on City Island—just a few of the ones of that we know. The mean range of tide at City Island is 7¼ feet.

The island got its name in 1761, when some early settlers devised a plan to develop the area into a booming seaport that would some day out-rival New York. Now many of the island's permanent residents, all very community-minded, but linked to the Bronx by a bridge and taxes, are more interested in keeping the island the way it is than in competing with any other place. It's so geographically isolated that one can believe the remark recently made by a native islander: "You daren't say anything to anybody about somebody here because the chances are they're somebody's cousin."

In the early summer of 1614, Captain Adriaen Block, Dutch fur trader, sailed past City Island in his 44½-foot "jacht" *Onrust* (Restless) and thus began the first cruise on Long Island Sound ever made by white men. Many thousands of yachts have followed the path of the *Onrust* and on a weekend in summer the waters to the south of that famous island are in a perpetual state of confusion from conflicting wakes.

New Rochelle, N.Y. (223). This is one of two harbors serving the New Rochelle area. The other is Echo Bay. The two do not connect. There is a well-protected anchorage in attractive surroundings inside of Glen Island to the southwest of the bascule bridge connecting Glen Island Park to the mainland. With three blasts of your horn the bridge will open promptly. Here on the northwest shore just inside the bridge is located the excellent Huguenot Yacht Club, which extends the use of its facilities to members of other recognized yacht clubs offering reciprocal privileges. In 1965 this third-oldest yacht club on the sound was swept by fire but, like a phoenix, it has sprung anew from its own ashes with a clubhouse that once belonged to Lillian Gish, over 1200 feet of new docks, and improved depths at dockside to 8 feet. There is a fine bar in the clubhouse, and a dining terrace has been built overlooking the sound. Mr. Rod Williams, a most interesting fellow we met once at the ship's store, told us that "we go out of our way to please transients." It is quite obvious that they do so. The facilities include launch service, guest moorings, water, ice, gas, and supplies when requested of the dock master. Don't tie up on the outside of the front floats; these are reserved for the club launches.

Across the channel on Glen Island is a conversation piece—the remains of John Starin's "Rhine castle" built in 1880. Starin, a shipping magnate, ran excursions from New York City to the beer garden he operated on what is now the site of the casino built by the Westchester Park Commission in 1924. The comparative prices paid for the island by Starin in 1880 and by the county in 1924 offer an interesting footnote—

from $18,000 the price jumped to $500,000.

Still further to the southwest is the large and well-equipped N.Y. Athletic Club Yacht Club and service center belonging to the famous New York Athletic Club. Members of other recognized clubs are welcome, and usually slips or moorings are available. Gas is sold here, and it is not so crowded as further to the east. Launch service and other facilities are offered at this recently enlarged marina. Beyond the N.Y.A.C. the channel is tricky and should not be attempted without a local pilot. Speed limit in the harbor is 4 knots.

While Glen Island Park is reserved for residents of Westchester County, it provides a pleasant outlook for visiting yachts anchored in the harbor. From the other side access to the heart of the City of New Rochelle is obtained by bus from the Fort Slocum Dock.

There are two main channels into New Rochelle Harbor, one between Glen and Davids islands and the other north of Davids Island. They are both well marked, but don't skip any of the buoys; there are many outlying rocks.

Besides the harbor behind Glen Island there is also a Northeast Channel behind Davenport Neck. Caution is necessary here as there are no markers inside the harbor entrance. This channel with 5-foot depth leads to the Neptune Boat Club, which has a small clubhouse to starboard, with a runway and float extending to the dredged channel. This harbor is commercial and less attractive than the one behind Glen Island. The Davenport Yacht Club, housed in a stucco building just to the south, has slips, gas, water, and ice.

If the anchorages of the Huguenot Yacht Club or the N.Y.A.C. are crowded or hot and moorings are unavailable, the best place to anchor is in the stretch of water between Goose and Glen islands. This spot offers fair protection in all but northeast storms and is apt to be cooler than inside.

First settled by Huguenot refugees in 1689, New Rochelle is said to have been the scene of George M. Cohan's *Forty-five Minutes from Broadway.*

Echo Bay, New Rochelle, N.Y. (222). This harbor behind Beaufort Point is too commercial and crowded to be appealing for an overnight stop, though it is well protected from all winds. The Queen City Marina, to starboard as one enters the inner harbor, is a convenient place for obtaining gas, water, and other facilities, including repairs, but offers a limited number of slips. Beyond is the large Municipal Marina. In 1971, this facility was completely modernized at a cost of $2.3 million, borne by New Rochelle and New York State under the Harbor and Refuge Act.

Concessions here include boat and engine repair shops, a snack bar, and a gas dock. Docking is available for 600 boats, including 145 slips for those over 18 feet overall. However, slips are usually reserved for local residents. The Harbor Master at this dock will assign a mooring if one is available. Groceries are located nearby to the south on Pelham Road.

One of these (Mooring 1A area), for large craft, is in the western part of Echo Bay inside of a line from can 5 off Duck Point to the flashing buoy off Bailey Rock. This is open from northeast to south. The other (Mooring 1B area), for smaller yachts, is northeast of a line running between nun buoys 4, 6, 8, and 10. A guest mooring is available in 6 feet of water near where the chart shows 3 feet. Other space for anchoring, which is much used, is between Beaufort Point and Echo Island to the east of the channel. This anchorage is, however, wide open to the southeast, and any wind between east and south may make it uncomfortable for a small boat.

The Harrison Island Yacht Club has its clubhouse on the south side of Harrison Island, and a shore station at Beaufort Point. Moorings are sometimes available for members of accredited yacht clubs on inquiry at the Harrison Island float, and launch service is also available.

Echo Bay is a convenient anchorage, because it is only a short distance from the center of New Rochelle, which is about thirty minutes from Grand Central station, New York. Except for shoal-draft boats, it does not provide a comfortable or safe anchorage in northeasterly to southerly winds, and is much less secure than New Rochelle or Mamaroneck harbors nearby. However, in a storm, shelter can be found in the inner harbor.

Larchmont, N.Y. (222). Like Marblehead, Massachusetts, this is one of the most important yacht racing centers on the coast; it is attractive for that reason, rather than for the excellence of its harbor. During Race Week several hundred boats are anchored off Larchmont or race from there. The harbor is protected from easterlies by a breakwater but is open from approximately southeast through south. The breakwater has a flashing red light and the harbor is easy to enter at night. The beacons on North Ledge and on Umbrella Rock are lighted by the club from May 10 to September 10.

The large and well-equipped Larchmont Yacht Club is on the westerly shore. The club float and launch service are available to members of recognized yacht clubs. Moorings are also occasionally obtainable. Anchor in the southern part of the harbor, or fairly close to the breakwater, if moorings are unavailable. There is no public gas dock in the harbor, though the yacht club supplies gas to its members at the work float. The nearest boat yards are in Rye and Mamaroneck. Several good restaurants are available on the Post Road, a short distance from the harbor.

A tour of Larchmont's clubhouse will soon reveal how highly established it has become as a hub of our yachting heritage. Interclub dinghy racing first began here in 1946. Another contribution was Larchmont's convincing demonstration that the Marconi rig was a more efficient racing rig than the old gaff. In 1917, in a series of ten informal regattas, the Marconi-rigged *Varuna* won eight out of ten races against four gaff-rigged one-design competitors in the O boat class, designed by William Gardner. The S class and the Victory class, still seen on the sound today, are said to be the two first one-design Marconi-rigged yacht classes to be built.*

Larchmont is famous for its frostbite dinghy racing carried on all winter by the yacht club, which remains active the year round. It is said that more than half of the total adult population of Larchmont commutes daily to New York.

Mamaroneck, N.Y. (222). Mamaroneck (Indian for "he assembles the people") was first settled in 1650, by English farmers. Apparently some of the neighboring cities did not always approve of what went on there later, for in 1704, Colonel Caleb Heathcote, Lord of the Manor of nearby Scarsdale, wrote as follows: ** "The most rude and heathenish country I ever saw in my life, which call themselves Christian; there being not so much as the least marks or footsteps of religion of any sort; Sundays being the only time set apart by them for all manner of vain sports and lewd diversion."

We are afraid that Mamaroneck must plead guilty, not to the absence of churches, for there are many, but to being—even on Sunday—a very active center for many sports and diversions, though neither vain nor lewd—especially yachting. Believe it or not, in this small harbor, we have located eight yacht clubs and eight boat yards, and we may have missed a few.

Mamaroneck is a splendid example of what a community can do to increase the attractiveness and value of its harbor and water front. The West Basin, formerly flats at low tide, showed a controlled depth of 6 feet in a 1970 survey, and Harbor Island (which isn't really an island) between East and West basins has been converted into an attractive park with beach facilities and a village dock. The dock is on the westerly shore of Harbor Island about halfway up the Basin, and the Harbor Master

---

* From *Long Island Sound*, by Fessenden S. Blanchard (D. Van Nostrand Co., 1958).
** Quoted in the section on Mamaroneck from *New York*—American Guide Series (Oxford University Press).

Mamaroneck Harbor from the air, looking about northwest.

will assign a guest mooring to a visiting yacht if one is available.

Mamaroneck offers much better protection from wind and sea than its neighbors, Milton Harbor at Rye, or Larchmont Harbor. There are two snug, if crowded, landlocked basins, fully protected from all directions. However, the other two harbors mentioned offer considerably more privacy, and have their own particular assets. There is also an outer harbor at Mamaroneck where many boats are moored during the summer months but which is open from southeast to southwest. During the winter, boating continues at Mamaroneck—now active in "frostbiting."

The entrance to the inner harbor is narrow and a speed-limit sign outside warns boats to slow down on entering. The place where the channels fork is marked by a red-and-black buoy. Follow the channel carefully, whichever way you go, as there are closely bordering shoals.

The West Basin is prettier and quieter than the East Basin, and not close to the Boston Post Road and its heavy traffic, as is the other basin. At the same time, however, it is less convenient to the city center with its many fine stores. An exception is the excellent Washington Arms Restaurant, which is just a long heave of the log away on the Post Road.

For overnight, we much prefer the West Basin, the best tie-up being to port halfway up the basin at the dock of the Nichols Yacht Yard (Mamaroneck branch), formerly the Orienta Marine Corp., but acquired on an outright basis by John B. Nichols, who also runs the Rye yard of the same name. There is 6 feet of water at the main dock, and gas may be obtained there as well as fresh water, electric connections, ice, and a telephone. Slips are sometimes available for visiting yachts; if not, the yard will help visitors to find a berth somewhere in the basin. The yard has good repair service, a railway and travelift, and a pump-out station. John Nichols is highly regarded by many yachtsmen, including ourselves.

At the entrance to the West Basin, on the point to port on the west side of a long narrow cove, is McMichael Yacht Yard # 7. Depths vary from 3 to 6 feet at the float at low tide and this yard is not as fully equipped as the Nichols for visiting yachts. Behind the next dock, there is on display and for sale a fine assortment of small craft, from dinghies to outboard cruisers, boat trailers and miscellaneous. This dock and yard are operated by Mamaroneck Boats and Motors and run by one of the most accommodating and competent men the writer has run across in a long time, Ted Deutermann. If you have any type of outboard that needs repair, or want to buy one, or need almost any type of small boat, they'll get it for you. Gas is sold at the M.B. and M. float, where there is 5 feet at low tide.

In 1966 the East Basin was re-dredged at a cost of $500,000, resulting in a depth of 6 feet for a midwidth of 80 feet in the East Branch channel.

The branch channel to the north of this basin now records a depth of 9 feet for a midwidth of 65 feet. At the basin's north end are gathered over half of the boat yards and yacht clubs in Mamaroneck, all crowded together. From west to east they are: the Post Road Boat Yard, Robert E. Derecktor Shipyard, Orienta Yacht Club, Shongut Yacht Yard, and McMichael Yacht Yard #1. Nearby on the Post Road is Brewers', a first-rate marine hardware emporium, sometimes open on Sundays in summer for boat supplies. There is service to be had of all kinds at Mamaroneck, where recent dredging has relieved some of its former congestion. There are first-rate boat yards here, but our advice to visiting yachtsmen is still to spend the night in the West Basin.

James Fenimore Cooper married a Mamaroneck girl in 1811 and lived in his wife's ancestral home for a while after the wedding. The original building was eventually sold at auction for $11 and then moved.

Rye (Milton Harbor), N.Y. (222). In coming from the direction of Lloyd Harbor, a tall office building in New Rochelle with a square knob on the top is a good guide for the Scotch Caps buoys and the entrance to Rye. On entering at night, it is important to give the Scotch Caps a wide berth, as the entrance is deceptive, the lighted buoy being much farther to the west than the contour of the coast would seem to require. After leaving the Scotch Caps lighted bell buoy to starboard, run toward the north until the two red range lights on the club grounds are in sight, and then run in. Note that on West Rock at the south end of the Caps, there's a day beacon considerably difficult to spot from seaward. This is privately maintained from April 1 to November 1.

The anchorage, to the west and southwest of the American Yacht Club, is fair except in a southwester, when, if desired, one can quickly run over to Mamaroneck. It is frequently rough in the harbor, and uncomfortable when the tide is against the wind. If drawing more than 5 feet, anchor in the deep water between the southern end of Hen Island and the end of Milton Point, if possible, either to the north or to the south of the gut that runs between the clubhouse point and the first of three islets forming the Scotch Caps chain. A tide rip runs through this gut, and in a storm the sea comes through. The bottom is soft, sticky mud.

Over on Hen Island, thirty-four families enjoy the isolation of Spartan island living surrounded by many species of bird and marine life. This little Shangri-La was first occupied by Indians of the Apaqquaminis tribe, whose sachem sold Rye to John Budd in 1662.

The American Yacht Club float, with gas, water, and a depth of 6 feet at low tide, is available to visitors from accredited yacht clubs, as is the club launch service, on three blasts of the horn. The club has three guest moorings with vacant moorings sometimes available; contact the launch-man. The Shenorock Yacht Club is beyond the stone town dock.

Supplies can be obtained from the Marina Delicatessen a short way down the road on Milton Point; it is open evenings and part of the time on Sunday. Other stores near there are well supplied, and prepared foods are obtainable. The White Elephant, about 1 mile from the club, is the nearest restaurant.

At the head of the harbor are two boat yards in a basin, all reached by a narrow, 1-mile-long channel marked by #5 class buoys and recently dredged to 6 feet at m.l.w. The mean range of tide here is about 7 feet. On the west fork at the northern end of the harbor is the Nichols Yacht Yard, with about 6 feet at the dock at low water. The writer has used this yard from time to time and found it very satisfactory. On the east fork is the Erbsland Boat Yard (up for sale at the time of writing), the only spot for gas and possible overnight dockage, and beyond that the Municipal Marina, open only to residents of Rye and not set up to handle transients.

The American Yacht Club is reportedly the fourth-oldest yacht club in the United States, founded in May 1883 by a small group of steam-yacht enthusiasts headed by Jay Gould. It became one of the leaders in the middle 1920s in establishing a Junior Yacht Club and instructional program that is now one of the most active on the sound. Over the years, it has hosted scores of national and regional sailing championship competitions; many of its members have distinguished themselves often in winning racing honors on Long Island Sound and in international events. *Thunderbird,* a Cal-40 owned and skippered by T. Vincent Learson, won the Newport-to-Bermuda race in 1966, sailing against a record fleet of 167 yachts.

The remarkable recovery of the American Yacht Club from a fire in July 27, 1951, which resulted in the destruction of its three-story club-house built in 1887, is a credit to the resourcefulness of its officers and the loyalty of its members. The annual Club Cruise started on the date planned, two days after the fire. The neighboring Apawamis and Sheno-rock Shore Clubs made their facilities available, so that most of the club services could continue. The first meal was served one year, to a day, after the fire, in a new and modern clubhouse. With the old flagpole still a white landmark, the present home of the American Yacht Club now looks out from Milton Point on one of the busiest scenes on Long Island Sound.

Playland, Rye, N.Y. (222). This is an artificial harbor made by two converging breakwaters at Rye Beach. The narrow entrance is open to the southeast, but the harbor offers a good shelter from all other winds. The jetty lights are operated by the Westchester County Playland Commission. Playland is a summer harbor, so if one is entering out of season, a careful check on the neighborning buoys and lights should be made in advance. There is from 6 to 10 feet of water in the anchorage at low tide, with 10 feet at the pier.

The park, which is well worth a visit as an example of the latest thing in community enterprise, is operated efficiently and like "Spotless Town" by the commission. There is an excellent beach of "imported" sand, and plenty of music, dancing, and restaurants—a complete change for people on a cruise, except possibly for the roller coasters. However, one's privacy is about equal to that of a goldfish, as in summer the beach is crowded and swimmers are apt to line the log boom nearby. Don't try to drink soup, for it may land in your lap from the waves of a passing speedboat. A beautiful 80-acre salt-water lake lying behind the amusement area offers a wildlife sanctuary that attracts bird watchers and boating enthusiasts from seven to seventy. A main attraction is the famous *Showboat,* a small replica of a Mississippi river boat, which gives its riders a twenty-minute tour of the islands. Both electric- and rowboats are rented by the hour there.

In entering at night, watch for a line of heavy log booms parallel with the beach and well out from it. The nearest boat yard is at Rye. Supplies and gas can be obtained about 4 blocks away. The Rye railroad station is about 2 miles away, reached by bus from Playland.

Playland is the largest, and one of the finest, municipally owned amusement parks in the world, with over 270 acres. If you want an evening of fun, go there.

Port Chester, N.Y. (222). The best place here for overnight anchorage or tie-up is not in the crowded and commercial Byram River, where oil barges and tankers come and go. There are two better choices: one is an anchorage (if there is room) in the deep water south of the black beacon with the flashing green light, and to the west of the main channel. Another possibility is to tie up in a slip (if one is available) in a yard the existence of which you might never suspect from looking at the chart. This is the Tide Mill Yacht Basin in the bight at the edge of Kirby Pond and behind Manursing Island. The basin there has been dredged to a depth of 6 feet and is reached by following private black and red cans marking a 6-foot dredged channel. The approach is through the charted deep water south and southwest of the black beacon mentioned earlier. This marina is identified by a prominent red dockhouse offering gas, Diesel fuel, ice, showers, telephone, slips with electrical connections, a mechanic, and various marine supplies. Groceries can be telephoned for and will be delivered. The basin is protected from all winds and seas, though a good deal may be going on there. The price for overnight tie-up was reported as 20 ¢ a foot.

The Port Chester Yacht Club is on the north shore at the entrance of the Byram River and will let you tie up at their float for a while if you want to get supplies.

Port Chester has improved its name as well as its harbor. It was once known as Saw Log Swamp and later as Saw Pit.

Byram Harbor, Port Chester, N.Y. (222). Byram Harbor is attractive mainly if the tide is high enough for boats to go into the shallow cove to the west of Huckleberry Island. Byram Park is a pretty place, and the fellows at the Byram Shore Boat Club in the cove are most hospitable. The best place to anchor is to the east of the line between Huckleberry Island and Wilson Head, but this is only for shoal-draft boats and is open from east to south.

The depth in the cove is about 3 feet at mean low water. There is a guest mooring just outside of the narrow channel to the cove, but no gas or supplies are available at the club. Check in with the Harbor Master before picking up this mooring. Slips in the cove are reserved only for local residents.

For deeper-draft craft, the best anchorage is north of Calf Islands between the tower and the flashing red-lighted buoy south of Otter Rocks. Enter between this buoy and black can 1 north of Bowers Island. A reef, bare at low water, connects the two islands. Southern Calf, owned by the Greenwich YMCA, has become, partly because of its natural charm, a favorite rendezvous spot for many local yacht club fleets, including the Westchester Power Squadron. Groups wishing to go ashore for a picnic game should first place their reservation with the YMCA officials. Another possibly quiet anchorage, except in southerlies, can be found in the bight formed by the western shore of Calf Island and the small private island to the northwest on which is located the stone tower.

Greenwich, Conn. (222). Captain Harbor, north of Great and Little Captain islands, affords fair shelter for large boats in the open area east of Field Point and the channel. Small craft should anchor across the channel west of the attractive and well-equipped Indian Harbor Yacht Club, which stands on the point to the east of the main channel, whose depth all the way to the head of the harbor is reported to be 12 feet at the time of writing. The Captain Harbor anchorage is exposed to the south and southeast, although the islands afford some protection. It is comfortable only for large yachts or in calm weather.

In bad weather the best entrance is the easterly one, as a direct course can be laid from the light on the bell to the end of the channel off Field Point. Give at least 50 yards' berth to the beacon on Hen and Chickens. From there to the yacht club the harbor is filled with boats in summer, and a visitor can pick an anchorage in the vicinity of boats about his own size. The outer or larger yachts all carry mooring lights and one should have no trouble.

In a storm, a moderate-draft boat can find a snug anchorage in Chimney Corner north of Tweed Island, though it may be crowded.

There is seldom any weather to which the inner harbor is exposed. The Indian Harbor Yacht Club float, launch service, and guest moorings are open to members of recognized yacht clubs. The dock master will assign you a mooring if one is available. Depth at the float is about 5 feet. The Greenwich Yacht & Boat Club has headquarters at Grass Island. The town dock is on the east side of Grass Island. Just above the yacht club lies the bulkhead of the Fairfield Home Oil Co., where one can find most types of supplies but no general repair work. For a change of scene, you might visit, "in boating denims or a Dior," the smart-looking Showboat Inn at the head of the harbor, where its "Showboat on the Water" serves up fine food and music. Dockage is free for those making a stay here. Or you might prefer the widely acclaimed Italian cuisine found at Manero's Restaurant halfway up the channel on the starboard shore.

Greenwich is a convenient place to meet people coming from New York, as the Indian Harbor Yacht Club is only ½ mile from the Penn Central station and ¾ mile from the post office.

The town, just north of the depot, offers excellent shops and restaurants. The country back of Greenwich, with many large estates on high land enjoying wide views of the sound, is most attractive and well worth a motor ride. It was at Greenwich that General Putnam of Revolutionary War fame escaped the British by riding down the face of a cliff.

Cos Cob or Riverside, Conn. (222). Many yachtsmen prefer this harbor to Greenwich. The buoys should be watched carefully on entering, as there are numerous rocks and shoal spots. The best anchorage is on the western side of the channel, northeast of Goose Island. The channel narrows quickly after passing Sunken Rock, and mud flats rise sharply on both sides.

The Riverside Yacht Club is one of the most attractive and hospitable clubs on the sound and is glad to welcome yachtsmen from other clubs with whom reciprocal privileges are exchanged. It is on the point to the starboard as you enter (just before reaching nun 6), and has a long pier, with 5 feet of water along its edge, reaching to the channel. Gas, water, and sometimes guest moorings are available. The club's dining room commands a splendid view.

The boat yards and marine services are concentrated along the west shore of the Mianus River above the bascule bridge that will open on signal. From Riverside to the fixed highway bridge at Mianus the controlling mid-channel depth is 6 feet at m.l.w. The facilities that have come to our attention are Palmer Point Marina (with the most facilities), Harbor Marine Center, Hansens Boat Yard, Drenckhahn Boat Basin, and the Boat Center (near the upper bridge). We especially like the looks of McMichael Yacht Yard No. 3, under the management of cooperative Karl Gleason. Some of them have slips available for overnight; some do repair work on inboards, some on outboards. They are all close together, so if you can't find what you want, try another. Harry Newman, the owner of The Boat Center, is an authority on who does what. Why not ask him?

The nearest good hotels are in Greenwich and Stamford. An excellent restaurant, the Clam Box, is on U.S. Route 1, a short walk from the above marinas.

Riverside, like Larchmont, Manhasset Bay, and other yacht clubs on Long Island Sound, has become active in frostbiting and has a large fleet of dinghies.

Greenwich Cove, Riverside, Conn. (222). Here is an attractive, cool anchorage with plenty of room, though without shore facilities or supplies for cruising yachtsmen. The swimming is first-rate. There is fairly good protection from all sides if you anchor northeast of Pelican Island; another anchorage is further up the harbor opposite Greenwich Island. The bottom is mud.

Come in toward Cove Rock and its nun, numbered 2, keeping south of the line between this buoy and the red flasher on Newfoundland Reef in order to avoid Finch Rock, marked by a privately maintained can buoy.

The Old Greenwich Boat Club has a dock with 6 feet of water just to the east of the northern tip of Greenwich Point, south of Pelican Island. The club also occupies the tower nearby, and, if our experience is any guide, is hospitable to visiting yachtsmen from other clubs.

Julius Wilensky, author of the very useful guide *Where To Go; What To Do; How To Do It on Long Island Sound,* gives us some background on this area:

The whole of Greenwich Point, Flat Neck Point, and the narrow neck north of Greenwich Point is a public park, much of it left wild. Ducks and swans are at home here. It is known locally as Tod's Point, not to

Greenwich Harbor. Indian Harbor Yacht Club is on the point near the center of the photograph, Smith Cove is on the right.

be confused with the point of the same name at the south end of River-side. The Tod family had a huge three-story Victorian mansion on the Point, which wasn't torn down until 1961. Greenwich had bought the peninsula for $550,000 early in World War II, and used the mansion to house returning veterans. The park includes an arboretum.*

Don't get caught outside the park after dark, for everything locks up at 8 P.M. We tried every password in the book to get past the guard at the front gate. One of them finally worked, and we were faced with a long trudge in pitch blackness back to our anchorage.

Stamford, Conn. (221). Thanks to considerable development and improvement in the last few years the facilities and opportunities at Stamford Harbor available to visiting yachtsmen are among the best on the sound. Along the eastern shore of the upper harbor, on the East Branch, there are now at least five boat yards and marinas, including one of the finest marinas on the coast—Yacht Haven. On Shippan Point, well up the harbor, the Stamford Yacht Club, one of the sound's leading clubs and host of the annual Vineyard Race, is very active in both the yachting and social life of the community.

Stamford Harbor is easy to enter and the channel inside the breakwaters is simple to follow. But outside of the channel there are a few rocks in inconvenient places to be avoided in looking for an anchorage. The two breakwaters have greatly improved the harbor as a place of refuge, though it is still large enough in the outer harbor for many "local" whitecaps, and boats may drag in a southwester. The Stamford Yacht Club is noted on the chart and is about halfway up Shippan Point, an attractive residential section of Stamford. In case you approach the channel in poor visibility, as we did on a recent visit, we might note that the fog signal at the west breakwater light has been changed from a siren to a horn sounding one blast for a two-second duration every twenty seconds.

For boats not wishing to land, a convenient and easy anchorage is just behind the western breakwater, east of the rocks shown on the chart. Further up the channel, a course taken from red nun 8 directly for the end of the Stamford Yacht Club dock will give at least 5 feet of depth all the way in; but don't stray from this "straight and narrow path," for there are some rocks close to the north side of the channel and on the south side, too. Near the yacht club, just south of this channel, are two small private buoys, each surmounted by a stick and marking rocks that lie between them. Yachts drawing 5 feet or less can go to the dock through the fleet

---

* From *Where To Go; What To Do; How To Do It on Long Island Sound,* by Julius M. Wilensky (Snug Harbor Publishing Co., 1968).

without following the channel to nun 8, provided they keep north of the private buoys referred to and south of the line from nun 8 to the dock.

There is a depth of about 5 feet at mean low water at the outer end of the Stamford Yacht Club dock. Gas and water are available. The club facilities, including guest moorings when not in use, are available to members of recognized yacht clubs who come there by boat. On a summer weekend the swimming pool and tennis courts are very active, while in the harbor one has to keep a watchful eye to avoid water skiers, "sailfish," as well as the many attractive yachts that make up the fleet. Supplies can be ordered at the club from the city, which is 2 or 3 miles distant.

The boat yards and marinas along the East Branch, to starboard as one enters, are as follows. Yacht Haven, which you come to first, has about everything a yachtsman could want and now ranks as the largest marina on the East Coast, even exceeding Bahia-Mar at Fort Lauderdale, Florida. It also runs a sizable yacht brokerage and chartering service. A breakwater offering good protection has been constructed from Jack Island eastward to the mainland. Dredging has taken place just above this breakwater to provide fill for the building up of the southern shore of Ware Island, permitting the formation of additional piers. There are now twelve piers with a total of about 500 slips having depths of 9 feet, and a daily rate of 15¢ for each foot with a $4.00 minimum. This includes water, electricity, and use of showers. Gas, Diesel fuel, ice, telephone, a well-equipped repair service, and marine store with charts, a laundromat, travelifts to haul up to forty tons, and even a swimming pool are among the many facilities. "Ship to Shore," on Shippan Point, will deliver liquor and groceries, and the Prime Rib Restaurant of Stamford House will send a car to pick up diners, although it might be more convenient to try the Continental cuisine at the Admiral Benbow Restaurant on Ware Island. The rule about no parties on deck after 8:30 P.M. has been enforced, and Yacht Haven can boast about its quietness after dark. It is run by the Scott-Paine Corporation.

Just beyond is a small marina, Doanes, and beyond that is the large and well-equipped Scofield Boat Yard, which hauls and repairs large yachts as well as small craft, especially sailing craft. Gas and other facilities are available. Further north is Lindstrom's Boat Yard, which hauls and repairs but does not provide slips or gas. Above Lindstrom is Shippan Shore Marina, which has gas, ice, electricity, water, does repair work, and has expanded its basin to the northeast with a depth of 6 feet.

In 1967, a new hurricane barrier was constructed across the East Branch channel between Yacht Haven and Doanes. Its 90-foot-wide gate is equipped with lights. This dike presumably gives the upper channel added protection, but boatmen along the shore have viewed the performance of the "contraption" with dubious eyes. From this point, 6½ feet can be carried to within 100 yards of the head of the channel.

The Southfield Park and Marina, located to port just beyond the entrance to the West Branch, is open only to local residents. In entering at night, note the two range lights where the channel separates. This is the wider and deeper of the two branches but it is generally less attractive. Halfway up to starboard looms the new complex belonging to Stamford Landing Marina, a subsidiary of Marina America, Inc. It is situated on land formerly occupied by the Luders Marine Construction Co., builders of the 12-meter contenders, *Weatherly* and *American Eagle*. Here you can obtain about everything but food supplies and perhaps a steak dinner. Experienced ship builders and mechanics, fiberglass craftsmen and yacht riggers—all are available the full year. The Ponus Yacht Club is just beyond on the same shore.

Express trains run between Stamford and New York City, making it a convenient place for picking up crews or reaching Manhattan.

It was a Stamford resident, Abraham Davenport, member of the Connecticut House of Representatives in 1780, whose high sense of duty enabled him to stand firm before his fellow members of the legislature during Connecticut's "Dark Day" of May 19 in that year. As the sky became darker and darker, the Solons, at the State Capital, fearing that Judgment Day had come, carried a motion to adjourn. When this motion came before the Council, Davenport rose to his feet, and spoke as follows: "I am against adjournment. The Day of Judgment is either approaching or it is not. If it is not, there is no cause for adjournment; if it is, I choose to be found doing my duty. I wish therefore that candles may be brought." *

Westcott Cove, Stamford, Conn. (221). Westcott Cove has a completely sheltered "lagoon," as it is called locally. It has a well-marked channel with a surveyed depth at mean low water of 7 feet in 1971 and a width of 100 feet. But follow the channel carefully; it is very shoal on either side, especially to port entering.

On the westerly shore of the channel is Muzzio Bros. Yacht Yard, which supplies gas and ice, and does hauling and repairs, etc. Northrop and Johnson, distributors of many fiberglass yachts, has its dock and office at Muzzio's yard. At the northwest corner of the lagoon, in Cummings Park, is the Halloween Yacht Club, which offers its facilities to yachtsmen from recognized clubs with whom reciprocal privileges are exchanged. The club, we were told, usually has a spare slip or berth for visiting yachtsmen. Tie up is fore and aft, as the harbor is too small and busy to allow swinging at anchor.

* From *Connecticut*—American Guide Series (Houghton Mifflin Co.).

The water is deep over most of the lagoon. There are several good grocery stores about ¼ mile from the club. On the point to the south of the lagoon is an excellent bathhouse. The vicinity is apt to be crowded and busy on weekends, and there is less privacy than in a larger, more isolated harbor.

Darien River, Noroton, Conn. (221). This is one of the numerous "made" harbors on Long Island Sound, located off the Noroton Yacht Club on the western shore of Long Neck Point. Be sure to keep nun 4 well to starboard in entering. About midway between this nun and the end of the yacht club pier there is a bar across the channel, as the chart indicates, but it has recently reported to have been partially eliminated. This may be troublesome, however, only at low water for most small cruising craft, though it can be rough on the bar in strong southwest to southeast winds. There are range lights at the club from Decoration Day to Labor Day. One of these is located at the end of the dock and the other stands at the right edge of the attractive clubhouse. There is 6 feet of water at dockside.

In entering, head from nun 4 to the yacht club dock. Once past the bar, there is plenty of water to the pier, where a guest mooring is sometimes obtainable. Beyond the pier also there is good water to the gut opposite Peartree Point, above which it has shoaled considerably. Not shown on the chart is some fairly deep water, reported at 10 feet, in the dredged but congested basin to the west of the pier, where it is well protected; but space may be hard to find. Large boats anchor close to Pratt Island outside buoy 4, where it is deeper, less crowded, though more open.

In 1968, a special anchorage area, as shown on the chart, was established off the southwesterly side of Long Neck Point. It begins just north of nun 2, runs northwest to the easterly and then northerly sides of Pratt Island, on over to Gorham Pond on the north, and finally returns south-southeast back to nun 2.

There is a large and impressive-looking residence at the end of Long Neck Point. Once the estate of Anson Phelps Stokes, it is now occupied by the Convent of the Sacred Heart, which took it over in 1924 and runs a notable boarding school for girls.

The Noroton Yacht Club has a large fleet of "Lightnings" and "Blue Jays," and the anchorage is often full. The weekend racing is hotly contested. The club has an outstanding reputation in yachting circles largely due to its philosophy that there is nothing more important than sailing. Its excellent junior program has produced some great sailors, such as Bob Bavier, helmsman of the winning America's Cup defender, *Constellation,* and Bill Cox, skipper of the almost-defender, *American Eagle*. In addition to his credit, Cox has the Sears Cup, International Class championships, and two Lightning National titles. And if that is not enough, there's Bob Smith, the top catamaran sailor, who challenged for the Little America's Cup, and Bob Shiels, winner of the nationals in the Tiger Cats. The ladies had their share of glory, too, when Sue Sinclair won the Women's National Championship in 1962.

The club is most hospitable to members of recognized yacht clubs and has a snack bar but no bar, and water but no gasoline. Repair facilities are available at nearby Fivemile River or at Stamford. It is about 1 mile to the village of Noroton. There is a good beach at Peartree Point, open only to local residents. However, a small pleasant beach spreads out in front of the clubhouse. This harbor is a good destination in normal summer weather and provides a most appealing natural setting.

Hay Island, Noroton, Conn. (221). North of Hay Island, on the east side of Long Neck Point, is one of the lesser known and most attractive harbors on the sound, well protected from all but strong winds from northeast to southeast, when an unpleasant roll penetrates. Shallow-draft yachts, however, can escape most of this by going south behind the island. This delightful inlet with its low rocky cliffs and lush foliage is known locally as Ziegler's Cove. How it earned the name, no one seems to know.

In entering, pick up nun 28 off Long Neck Point and then head for the exposed rock, with the (uncharted) white spindle, just east of Hay Island. Leave this close to port and head for the steep shore on Great Island. Follow this in, and anchor, preferably, near the 8-foot spot. The harbor is surrounded by private estates and no supplies or public landing facilities are available. You'll think you are in Maine until you go swimming, and then you'll be glad you aren't.

The harbor is apt to be crowded on weekends so get in early if you want to find plenty of swinging room. Fortunately, some boats come there to fish—and often do very well at it—but leave in the early evening so the overnight flotilla is reduced considerably. The writer has been there at least six or eight times and has never failed to find satisfactory anchorage. It is one of his favorite ports on the sound.

Fivemile River, Rowayton, Conn. (221). This anchorage, between Roton Point and Darien, rates high on the following counts: (1) convenience; (2) protection from all winds; (3) docks from which groceries, gasoline, ice, and water can be obtained; (4) boat yards and machine shops. The nun (Number 26) off Greens Ledge Light is a good guide to the entrance, about 1 mile distant. The entrance is well buoyed, though narrow. There is a 6-foot spot just outside the outer twin buoys.

This harbor is attractive, with perfect shelter from all winds, but crowded. Butler Island, at the left of the entrance, is wooded and high, and marked by a flagpole. There is a dredged basin on the westerly shore opposite red nun 6 beyond Butler Island. This is a possible anchorage but the crowded harbor makes a tie-up preferable.

Farther up the river are two good boat yards, the Wm. P. Jenkins Boat Yard and the Rowayton Marine Works. Both yards have gas and other services. Jenkins has a number of berths, as does the Rowayton Marina further up the river, which also has gas. There are convenient stores along the principal water-front street. Anchorage must be in line with the other boats. Above Rowayton Marina is Gene's Boat Livery. Try them for fresh lobsters, clams, blue-shell crabs, and complete fishing gear.

Fivemile River is a friendly and intimate place, and the writer has rarely been in there without finding friends along the boat-lined water front. Though there is no yacht club on the river, the clubby atmosphere makes one seem unnecessary. The Norwalk Yacht Club, however, is just across the point.

Rowayton has well been called "a delicious and crazy hodgepodge of boat yards, lobster fishermen, artists, writers, boating enthusiasts and just plain local people." *

South and East Norwalk, Conn. (221). Like Stamford, here is another case where man has stepped in to improve yachting facilities. There are now seven possible anchorages or tie-ups but the snuggest and, in our opinion, the most desirable of all is the man-made dredged harbor behind Calfpasture Point, across the river from the conspicuous stacks of the Connecticut Light and Power Company on Manrissa Island.

A number of yachtsmen have reported that the entrance channel to Norwalk through Sheffield Harbor is narrow, increasingly busy with boating traffic, and tending to shoal along its edges. The approach from the east through Cockenoe Harbor may be found less formidable, though a sharp lookout and helmsman are still required. But moving in a more or less easterly direction, as we are in this book, the seven anchorages or tie-ups are as follows:

1. *Off the Norwalk Yacht Club* in what is locally known as Wilson Cove located roughly between Noroton Point, Tavern Island, and Wilson Point. The club landing, in a new location on the east shore on Wilson Point, has 6 feet at low water, and there are club moorings usually available with tender service. Hug the eastern side of the cove as you enter. The club, organized in 1894, boasts a large fleet of good-looking

* From *The Exurbanites*, by A. C. Spectorsky (J.B. Lippincott Company, 1955).

cruising boats and is very active in dinghy and frostbite racing. Take a look at the clever dinghy dolly developed by Capt. Victor Black, the club's steward. Ice, water, and gasoline may be had at the landing. The protection is not good in a hard blow from south to west, but in normal summer weather this is a most attractive and convenient stopping place. The modern one-story clubhouse is made available to members of other recognized yacht clubs. Continuing northward following the markers lining a 6-foot-deep channel, one can reach the dock of the Wilson Cove Yacht Club, which was constructed in 1960 and offers slips for an overnight stay, gas, water, and ice. Just to the east is nestled the Wilson Cove Marina. A quieter or more secluded place than this would be hard to find.

2. Those who want to "get away from it all" can anchor off the *north shore of Sheffield Island,* where there is good holding ground. Usually the anchorage is safe in summer and the island is a good place for a picnic. The usual anchorage is off a stone pier at the northerly point of the island. However, this is open to the southwest.

3. *Between Calfpasture Point and Peach Island,* on the eastern side of the dredged channel and off the pier shown on the chart. This is exposed to the south for some distance, though partly protected by the Norwalk Islands. It is also close to the traffic along a busy channel.

4. In the *anchorage triangle above Gregory Point.* This, however, is on the edge of Norwalk River traffic, somewhat less than private, and unattractive.

5. *McMichael Yacht Yard #4* on the west side of the river just above the triangular basin. Slips, water, electricity, telephone, repairs, marine supplies, hauling, and other facilities and services are available.

6. *Rex Marine Center,* on the west side of the river just above McMichael. Here are berths for transients, a well-stocked marine store, gas, Diesel fuel, ice, water, electricity at slips, the renowned Pier Restaurant on the water front, and one of the most complete marine repair yards around. A shopping center is nearby. This boat center is run by Gardella, father of the fellow running the Cove Marina described below.

7. *Norwalk Cove Marina,* behind Calfpasture Point. This is the best of all, if you enjoy a snug anchorage and don't mind a tie-up or its cost. Just beyond black can 17 to the northeastward a sign (to be left to port) and a wooden breakwater indicate a 10-foot dredged entrance channel between Calfpasture and Gregory Point leading into a protected basin of 8- to 10-foot depths throughout with piers and slips. Black buoys indicate the port side of the channel. A gas dock is on the starboard side of the entrance and there dockage is assigned. Besides gas, Diesel fuel is available, as are ice, water, electricity, telephone, showers, a marine supply store,

launderette, and a thirty-five-ton travelift. Dockage is 20¢ a foot. We have often seen some fine-looking deep-draft auxiliaries there as well as motor cruisers. The nearby Skipper's Restaurant offers temporary free dockage to its patrons, and visiting yachtsmen can use the park swimming pool on weekdays for a small fee. There is also a miniature golf course. The small Ascension Beach Yacht Club is up on the starboard side of the basin.

All kinds of supplies are available in South Norwalk and two excellent hardware stores carry marine hardware.

On July 11, 1779, Calfpasture Point was used as a landing place for 2500 British troops carried by twenty-six vessels. Both Congregational and Episcopalian churches were burned, as well as many houses and barns. The Indians used the point as a pasture. Norwalk was formerly one of the largest trans-Atlantic oyster-shipping ports in the country.

Saugatuck, Conn. (221). Compo Beach Harbor has been dredged in the lee of Cedar Point at the east of the entrance to the Saugatuck River. Its entrance can be easily located from seaward by sighting a tall orange-and-white observation tower plotted on the chart. A correspondent contributes the following:

> The channel to the yacht basin (known as the Compo Beach Municipal Yacht Basin, run by the town) is well marked on both sides by buoys provided by the town. It has range lights for entrance after dark. To enter this harbor, do not attempt the passage from the west described in the *Coast Pilot*. The channel from Pecks Ledge Lighthouse around Cockenoe Island to the Saugatuck River is not marked, and at low tide the best draft obtainable is not more than 2 feet. Enter this harbor from the east, carrying the black can off Georges Rock and the lighted buoy off Cedar Point on your port. Just before approaching Saugatuck River nun 8, you will find the channel to the yacht basin. When entering this channel, be sure to carry this nun on your port. The channel to the harbor has a draft of 6 feet at low tide, except just off the point on the south shore of the yacht basin. Just before reaching this point, stay well to the port side of the channel, and if entering at night, carry the red and green range lights slightly to the starboard.

The 50-foot channel has been dredged to a 10-foot depth and the range lights realigned. Protection from all winds may be found in the oval basin, 400 yards long by 100 yards wide, with a depth of about 9 feet. The basin is quite congested, over 180 boats, large and small, being moored there on any Labor Day weekend. Anchoring is impossible, so it is necessary to obtain a mooring. As a rule, two guest moorings are vacant, but if they are occupied, the dock master can usually provide an alternate. A depth of 8 feet at low water can be carried to the float, where gasoline and water may be obtained. There is no overnight dockage. The dock master is on duty seven days of the week from 9 A.M. to 8 P.M. and is usually spotted in the clubhouse formerly held by the Cedar Point Yacht Club, which has now moved westward to a new location on Bluff Point. We found nearby Compo Beach active with bathers.

Former charts of this area showed Bluff Point, on the northeastern shore of Saugatuck Shores, surrounded by marshes. But the Cedar Point Yacht Club's members with inspired ingenuity changed this typography much to cruising yachtsmen's benefit. In 1966 a very impressive-looking two-story clubhouse was erected on the point south of can 15. "It's 'Cedar Point modern,'" exclaimed Rear Commodore George Morris, whose congeniality made us feel right at home. Standing on this beautiful site, we were treated to a panoramic view of the region while listening to his story of a yacht club on the move. A narrow channel, running southeast from nun 16, now cuts through the peninsula on Bluff Point and leads into a freshly dredged basin approximately 150 yards wide by 250 yards long with 10-foot depth throughout. No anchoring is permitted in the basin, but this is no drawback since the new slips are among the finest we have seen with electrical outlets. The club's facilities include gas, ice, water, showers, and a neat snack bar open daily from 11 A.M. to 6 P.M. Facing open water, a 600-foot beach invites ideal bathing. We saw a preponderance of sailboats here, since the club has a rich sailing heritage; it has hosted the National Atlantic Class Championships for several years and runs an active Junior Program. Cedar Point extends reciprocal privileges to members of other recognized clubs with the understandable request that visiting yachts please not lay over longer than twenty-four hours or discharge their heads into the basin. Pick up a copy of the club's guest rules on registering.

Further up the Saugatuck River channel on the western shore lies the Saugatuck Harbor Yacht Club's dock at the head of Duck Creek, affording a quiet and unspoiled shelter. Keep the marker in the center of the entrance to starboard coming in. As you pass the gas dock to port, pick up the range lights that will help guide you further in. The only facilities here are gas, water, ice, and electricity at the docks reported to have 8-foot depths. This club, which began with an old carriage house as its clubhouse in 1960, charges a flat fee of $6.00 for boats 30 feet and under, and $12.00 for longer craft. When leaving the creek, be sure to stand off until incoming boats have cleared the "narrows" at the entrance.

The nearest inns are 2½ miles to the north at Westport.

The channel up the Saugatuck River to the railroad bridge is now marked but subject to shoaling with a 3-foot depth at low water reported just beyond nun 26. Above the bridge the channel is not marked and strangers are advised not to attempt it. However, just above the railroad bridge on the west bank is Coastwise Marine. If you want to go there for any reason, tie up temporarily at the Yacht Basin, telephone the yard, and they will send a man to pilot you to their dock. At high tide the yard can haul out boats up to 45 feet with a draft of 6 feet.

Southport, Conn. (220). Here is another instance of a community's improving its water front to form a perfect shelter under any conditions. By means of a breakwater and dredging, the entrance to Mill River has become an appealing, fully protected, though narrow harbor with a channel width of 100 feet and a depth of 9 feet at low water.

Though the channel is marked by two flashing lights and eight can and nun buoys and appears on the chart to have a width of 100 feet with a depth of 9 feet, it is somewhat tricky. For instance, on our latest visit, we were advised by a local authority not to go too close to the outer nun buoys but to favor the black cans until the last red nun, number 10, was reached; that nun should be favored closely. Like many offshore channels with shoal water on each side, this one has a tendency to silt up at times. So enter with caution if the tide is low. We don't advise strangers to enter after dark. Watch for oyster stakes off the entrance.

The town dock is on the west side of the entrance channel near where the chart shows White Rock. Gas and water are available there or a possible tie-up or mooring. Beyond, also to port, where the harbor widens, is the well-known Pequot Yacht Club, one of the leading clubs on the sound. The club offers reciprocal privileges to members of other recognized yacht clubs and may be able to provide a mooring. It is necessary to tie up fore and aft, as the river is crowded and narrow. Launch service runs from 8 A.M. to 8 P.M.

Gasoline, ice, and water can also be procured at the club float, where there is 7 feet at low tide. Stores are within a short walking distance of the club. The Horseshoe Tavern serves good meals down at the shopping center. Pequot Inn no longer exists, and the ancient Tide Mill Inn now houses doctors' offices. Southport is one of the most delightful harbors on the Connecticut shore.

In Revolutionary times, crews were organized in Southport to protect the town from numerous Tory depredations suffered by settlements along the sound. Southport was once a famous onion-shipping point. It is part of the town of Fairfield.

On October 21, 1799, the town voted that it was willing to allow the General Assembly to grant a lottery to raise money for "Sinking the channel of Mill River harbor."

Black Rock Harbor, Bridgeport, Conn. (220). This harbor, west of Bridgeport, is easy to make both day and night, on account of the lights and buoys at the north and south of the entrance. A white tower on the sandspit to the east of the entrance is a good guide in the daytime from far out in the sound. Penfield Reef Light, now converted to automatic operation, is a sure guide to the entrance at night.

The Black Rock Yacht Club is in a white building to the west, inside of Grover Hill, where a pier is indicated on the chart. The best anchorage for all but small and shoal-draft boats is across the channel from this yacht club north of nun 8. This, however, is exposed from southeast to southwest. In a blow it is possible to run for shelter into Cedar Creek, where complete protection is available in the dredged channel.

The Black Rock Yacht Club is both an attractive social club and a yacht club. Besides its dock and yachting facilities, it has a swimming pool, tennis courts, restaurant, and a very good-looking clubhouse—all open during the summer months. Across the channel, opposite, a considerable fleet of yachts may be seen anchored or moored. An overnight mooring is available at $3.00, with launch service provided. Members of other recognized yacht clubs are welcomed by the club. Its Sunday night buffet is quite a feast and reasonably priced.

Further up the harbor on the west shore of Cedar Creek, across from Fayerweather Island and on the point where Black Rock is indicated on the chart, is the Fayerweather Yacht Club, with a large membership and open the year round. When we were there during a recent Labor Day weekend, the large barroom was active and crowded. Unlike many of the other yacht clubs visited, in this club more men of our own age were around than younger people, and the convivial aspects of the club were much in evidence among the hospitable members who were on hand. There is 5 feet of water at the dock, and the club usually has spare moorings for visitors, and provides gas, ice, and water. Visiting yachtsmen are always welcome, we were told, whether members of other clubs or not. "We aren't fussy," said one of the members. "We like to be friendly to everyone." And they certainly have been to us.

Should you happen to get caught in a blow and don't carry too deep a draft, you'll find a protected spot in Burr Creek, north of can 15. Hug the eastern shore of the creek where the water runs deepest. There is 6 feet of water at the slips. The Burr Creek Municipal Marina does not have many facilities nor is it a very pretty place but, according to the dock master, "everybody seems to find us whenever a three-day nor'easter strikes."

Black Rock is less commercial than Bridgeport Harbor and much to be preferred by yachtsmen.

Bridgeport, Conn. (220). The best anchorage is up Johnson's Creek just beyond the large gas tanks on the western point as one enters the creek. The Miamogue Yacht Club is here with increased dockage space and will advise yachtsmen as to moorings and where to get gasoline and supplies.

While this is a fully protected anchorage, it is very unattractive and commercial, with tankers coming and going nearby. Not much can be said for going up the long channel into Bridgeport. One will probably meet barges and collect much coal dust and soot. Bridgeport is useful to cruisers chiefly as a protection in a storm.

Stratford, Conn. (219). Here is another river entrance cutting into the Connecticut shore that is no place to enter at night if it can be avoided. There is a strong current in the river, and sometimes, when the wind is against an outgoing tide, a short, hard sea breaks in the channel and the buoys are dragged under. However, dredging of the channel to a 100-foot width and an approximate depth of 17 feet, at least as far north as can 29 below Popes Island, has helped to minimize the current and make river navigation easier. The mean range of tide at Stratford is 5.5 feet.

Two tall black chimneys at Devon, up the Housatonic, stand out prominently as a good guide in clear weather from far out in the sound for both Milford and the entrance of the Housatonic River. The ebb tide swirls and eddies about, so that power is a necessity.

The Pootatuck Yacht Club, in its red building with two rows of piazzas, is located west of what appears on the chart as black can 19 opposite where the river channel turns northeastward, about 2½ miles from the entrance of the river. The club sometimes has slips, and also has gas, water, ice, and usually spare moorings for visiting yachtsmen.

Just below the yacht club is Stratford Marina, formerly Fladd & Kahle's, with one hundred and forty deep-water slips and the most complete facilities around. Should you need any repair work on your boat, have it done here, since Fladd & Kahle have consolidated with the very reputable Bedells Shipyard. Even a good canvas maker is on duty. Having dredged the creek that winds around behind the 6½-acre tract, this marina is the largest complex in the Bridgeport area. In 1971, it was due for further expansion, with the announcement that it would become the "future home of Sea Port Inn & Marina" boasting 240 guest rooms, a swimming pool, and other conveniences. Meanwhile, you are within easy walking distance of a laundromat, a liquor and drug store, such fine restaurants as Fagan's and Spada's Blue Goose, and a well-stocked ships store is on the premises. A free courtesy car will take you to Steve's Market for supplies. They obviously cater to the theater-goers here.

On one of our previous trips, we stayed at the hospitable Housatonic Boat Club, which is just above nun 16 on the west shore; they offer no gas or ice, but they do have guest moorings and launch service until 8 P.M. Conveniently near the impressive American Shakespeare Theater, whose appearance exudes the very atmosphere of Elizabethan England, we decided to combine intellectual pleasures with physical ones by attending a matinee performance of *Henry V*. So if you are in the mood for sharing an unforgettable theatrical experience, "follow your spirit" and our example. For ticket information call Connecticut (203) 375-4457.

The anchorage off the Pootatuck Yacht Club is exposed to the southward and northeast for some distance along the river, and most of the nearby land is low and marshy. While the yacht facilities, stores, and other conveniences are at Stratford, the beauty of the Housatonic is up the river. If you are interested in exploring further, it is a run of about 9 miles from the yacht club, along a well-marked channel, to the head of navigation at Derby and Shelton. Beyond Culver Bar at can 31, the controlling depth in the channel is about 3 feet at m.l.w. These minimum depths are found in the channel between cans 31 and 37, and occur again along Drews Bar at nun 62. Along the shores as you approach Derby, the scenery is impressive, and hills of 200 to 300 feet in height come down to the shores.

While Adriaen Block, the Dutch fur trader, stopped at Stratford in 1614, the first settlers were English. They came there in 1639 and named it for Stratford-on-Avon. Today, it is well known for its summer Shakespearean festivals.

Milford, Conn. (219). We once visited the well-protected but crowded port of Milford on a Labor Day weekend and found this busy yachting center swarming with attractive young boys and girls who had gathered there from far and near with their "Blue Jays" for a series of races. Some of the boats were on trailers getting a final going over, others in the water or on the way in. The Milford Yacht Club was host and all the liveliness seemed to verify a club officer's comment that, "We're probably the most active sailing club on the sound." Stars, Lightnings, 210s, Thistles, Blue Jays, and 420s were teeming with youngsters aboard.

The snack bar on the club grounds was dishing out hot dogs and soft drinks, and in the harbor many good-looking cruising yachts were moored at both ends. Across the Wepawaug River above the yacht club were the docks and oyster boats of the Cedar Island Corporation, for oysters and clams have been important Milford products since the earliest days of the settlement. While now it is the Northern Oyster Company, the oyster business continues. The U.S. Fish and Wildlife Service has a laboratory at Milford to advise oyster "farmers."

We wondered what the early settlers had been doing on a similar September weekday over three hundred years earlier—perhaps building the palisades that once enclosed a square mile of the town, for the Indians were numerous and hostile. Or perhaps they were engaged in worship, for Milford was a "Church State" in which only members of the Church were allowed to vote. In the year 1640, it is said, the colonists passed the following, not unduly modest, resolution:

Voted: That the earth is the Lord's and the fullness thereof.
Voted: That the earth is given to the Saints.
Voted: That we are the Saints.*

The harbor is formed by two jetties at the mouth of the Wepawaug River, completing the protection of the anchorage from all winds. The 75-foot channel, lined by buoys with reflectors, carries about 7 feet all the way to the Milford Yacht Club on the west side of the entrance, on Burns Point to port. Members of other recognized yacht clubs who register in the clubhouse are welcomed hospitably; dock master Everett Jones will assign guest moorings and slip space if available. In 1971, Vice Commodore Charles Stokesbury, Jr., with warm congeniality, sat us down to bring our readers up-to-date on his club and the sixth-oldest town in Connecticut. Gas, water, ice, telephones, a bar, afternoon tea, and meals are all available at the club, and there are stores fairly nearby. The club runs launch service. A swimming pool has been built but is open only to members and their registered guests.

Congestion is the chief difficulty at this otherwise splendid harbor. The outgoing tide sweeps in under a bridge from the east, making it unwise to anchor behind the eastern jetty, where it is also shoal. On a warm summer day even the beach at the club is crowded. There is 8 feet at the club float at low tide. Milford is a good place to visit, but it is quieter on weekdays or nights than on weekends. The late Captain Bradley, a local authority, told us, "The ducks may wake you up if you are fool enough to feed them." And don't be foolish enough to try to anchor along the river.

The channel upriver from a point 250 yards above Burns Point has a reported depth of about 6 feet at low water all the way to the town dock

* From *Connecticut—American Guide Series* (Houghton Mifflin Co.).

(convenient to supplies) shown to port on the chart, near the end of the dredged part of the river. At the time of our visit there were 4 boat yards on the Wepawaug River, all providing slips and other facilities and thus helping to lessen the congestion in the lower river: Nichols Yacht Yard (in yellow buildings to port just below the first creek that runs among the marshes); Spencer's (housed in a barn-red building to starboard at the prominent pier a short distance further up); Wepawaug Marina (to port just below the town dock); and the Milford Harbor Marina (also to port beyond the town dock at the end of the dredged section). Although Nichols has the least amount of slip space, its salty New England atmosphere appeals to sailing yachtsmen. We were attracted by Jim Allen's larger Spencer's Marina, which, according to local authorities, renders complete and very efficient service to boats of all types and is to be generally preferred. The two marinas further upriver are a bit more congested and cater primarily to power boats.

At the turn of the century, Milford was, strangely, a center for the manufacture of straw hats. Now it's a popular and attractive summer resort with pleasantly shaded streets and lovely homes. There is a railway station on the main line of the Penn Central with express trains to New York or Boston stopping at nearby New Haven.

"On a quiet night a pleasant place to anchor if bound east or west," writes a yachtsman, "is just to the north of Charles Island. The bottom is sand and good-holding. At low water a bar connecting Charles Island with the mainland is dry, so don't anchor to the northwest of the island. This, also, is a good spot to duck into for a quick bite if the going is rugged on the sound."

Charles Island, now owned by the United Illuminating Co., is rich in historic lore and was originally purchased in 1639 by Milford settlers from Ansantawae, chief of the local Paugusset tribe, for 6 coats, 10 blankets, 1 kettle, 12 hatchets, 12 hoes, 24 knives, and 12 small mirrors. Its peaceful, rustic appearance is deceptive, for down through the years it has borne three mysterious curses, harbored the secret hiding place of two unfound treasures (one of them Captain Kidd's), and served as the proving ground for America's first submarine, *The Turtle,* which served conspicuously in an American Revolutionary naval battle. At various times in its history, it housed a mansion, hotel, factory, and a Dominican retreat, whose foundations may still be seen. If you enjoy exploring ashore, don't miss a stop here.

New Haven, Conn. (218). This harbor, the third-busiest commercial port in New England, is accordingly of little interest to yachtsmen except as a refuge or a place to obtain supplies. As the chief carrying trade of the port is coal and oil, and as New Haven is a manufacturing town, coal dust abounds. Despite three outer breakwaters, small boats usually have a restless time. The entrance, outside of which stand numerous oyster stakes, is well lighted and easy to make at night or in fog or storm.

The usual anchorage for yachts is at Morris Cove, on the east side of the harbor near its mouth. The New Haven Yacht Club has gone out of existence and there are no good facilities for yachtsmen, though the New Haven Marina on the cove's southwestern shore has a gas dock in a tiny basin behind a prominent stone jetty. Vreeland's Marine Service just to the east handles engine and hull repairs. The only drawback here is that both of these places report 2½ feet depths dockside.

The anchorage at Morris Cove is not a quiet one. A sea roll from the southwest frequently makes in by the breakwaters, and the anchorage is rough in westerly winds. A sheltered spot can be found at the head of the harbor, but the distance is so great and the environment so unattractive that few yachts go north to the wharves. Anchorages are described in the *Coast Pilot*. The harbors 5 miles to the west at Milford or to the east at Branford, Pine Orchard, or the Thimble Islands are ordinarily much to be preferred.

About the best facility in New Haven Harbor is Claud-Ann Marina, identified on the chart as two peninsulas jutting out from the southern shore of City Point just north of can 11. Make your approach passing the buoys marking the West River channel. Claud-Ann has space for over one hundred boats, most of which tie up in 10 feet of water in the basin formed between the peninsulas. Deep-draft boats usually lie outside along the bulkhead, which is completely open to the northeast. You'll find gas, ice, water, and general repair work here, but don't bank on getting any supplies. The surroundings are not overly commercial-looking, since there is a residential district to the north. Boats are widely exposed to winds from the east and south, but apparently this spot is good enough for the New Haven Harbor police, who make it their "headquarters."

In 1970, West River channel was dredged to a controlled depth of 12 feet up to the bascule bridge and thence 6 feet into the anchorage beyond. This bridge is closed during the morning and late afternoon rush hours and also at noon. Adams and Podoloff, Inc., and the City Point Yacht Club lie just above the bascule bridge, promising good protection in case of a blow. But this is a good example of a place with simply too many power boats and not enough space.

Branford, Conn. (217). Chart 217 shows a large shallow bay 4 miles east of New Haven, fully exposed to the south. But, like so many other places on the Connecticut shore, the farther in one goes, the better the anchorage for small boats.

In 1965 the 100-foot-wide channel was dredged to a depth of 9 feet from Little Mermaid all the way to the bridge at the upper end of the river. By 1970, however, the channel depth had shoaled to give a reading of 7 feet from Lovers Island to a point where the channel runs due north just beyond Bruce & Johnson's Marina. From this point, depths reduce to 5 feet to the head of navigation at the bridge with some 3-foot shoal spots along the way. The river entrance must be made under power by all except very small boats. Don't attempt it at night. If you must enter by night, we would like to advise that the flashing green light on Big Mermaid's pipe tower is difficult to pick up.

With dredging and filling, and new docks at the yacht club located on the north shore, this harbor was transformed prior to "Branford Day," which came on August 18, 1954. Now Branford has become, in its facilities for yachtsmen, one of the finest ports on Long Island Sound. Yachting activities revolve around the Branford Yacht Club, which was organized in 1909 and is now equipped with a first-class marina containing many slips. Members of recognized yacht clubs offering reciprocal privileges are welcomed there. Report when you come in to the dock master at the long new gas dock to your port. He will assign you a slip or a tie-up between mooring stakes across the channel, if one is available.

Besides gas, ice, and a telephone at the main dock, electricity and fresh water are provided at the slips. At the large piers, depths of 8 feet are available. Supplies may be purchased at a store about ¼ mile away.

Not only has the Branford Yacht Club concentrated on maintaining its fine dockage. Its clubhouse is spic-and-span and its manicured grounds with numerous picnic tables afford a splendid view of the river.

The channel, marked in part by stakes on both sides as one proceeds upriver, winds its way among the marshes. Hug these stakes closely. In the middle of the bend on the east shore, on now-filled land, is Bruce & Johnson's Marina, with slips, ice, water, gas, and Diesel fuel, a ships store, full repair work, showers, and a restaurant. This place is popular with sailing men. After rounding the bend and heading westward beyond the stakes, keep in the middle. Below some large buildings on the west shore is the Dutch Wharf Boat Yard Marina. Here are slips and moorings, a supply store, but no gas. Hauling and repair work are done here, and we saw some fine-looking yachts tied up. A package and grocery store may be found nearby.

Pier 66, just beyond the yacht club, is a developing marina run by Armand Williams, Jr., who knows the harbor like the back of his hand. Although it has limited shore facilities, Pier 66 has apparent appeal for power boats. He warned us that "boats with deep draft should not go upriver beyond Dutch Wharf no matter what the chart shows."

Branford is an attractive residential community, deservedly popular among cruising men. There are many fine old houses. Yankee traders were once very active there. When West Indies rum didn't pay, some took up slave trading and on occasions procured slaves for some very pious people. One of the pious was Reverend Ezra Stiles, president of Yale, who asked for a fine specimen and got him.*

Pine Orchard, Conn. (217). Pine Orchard is an attractive summer resort between Branford and the Thimble Islands. In making your approach at night, line up on the club's range lights marking the outer end of a breakwater. East of Brown Point and behind this breakwater there is a dredged basin with depths that vary from time to time according to the dredging. This basin inside of St. Helena Island was dredged in 1964 to a depth of 7 feet at m.l.w. On entering make a sharp turn to port just after passing the eastern end of the breakwater that marks the short channel to the basin. Stay well off of a chain of rocks that extends southward from St. Helena Island.

On the west shore of the basin is Pine Orchard Club, with a fine clubhouse, docks, tennis courts, a nine-hole golf course, a fresh-water swimming pool, dining room, and yacht facilities that include slips, guest moorings, water, ice, electric connections, gas, telephone, etc. An enthusiastic member once told us that this was the "only club on Long Island Sound that has everything." Judging from what we have seen, he wasn't far off. Guest privileges, we were told, are granted to yachtsmen who are members of recognized clubs that accord reciprocal privileges.

Anchoring in the basin is not permitted, because of limited swinging room. The club has red and blue floats for fore and aft mooring, for which it charges $4.00 per night. The inner moorings lie in 5-foot depths, and there's 7 feet further out. You'll pay 25¢ a foot at the slips, where you may be astounded by the efficiency and courtesy of the dock boys. They recommended the Pine Orchard Market, ½ mile distant, as a good source for supplies.

Large yachts can anchor outside the island but with little protection from south to east winds. Flocks of gulls on St. Helena's often scream up a storm early in the morning.

During the summer months an active group of attractive people of all ages keeps the club and nearby waters very busy.

This harbor, now dredged again to its former depths, has become one of the most appealing ports of call on the sound except in easterlies.

* From *The Yankees of Connecticut,* by W. Storrs Lee (Henry Holt & Co.).

Little Harbor, Leetes Island, Conn. (217). For yachts drawing under 4 feet here is a very pretty "little harbor," protected by jetties on both sides of the entrance of Harrison and Clark points. While no depths are given on the chart, our soundings indicated depths of 7 feet or more leading up to the entrance, 6 feet at the entrance, 5 feet just inside, and 4 feet at mean low water in most of that section of the harbor that is south and west of the point that separates the two inner branches. Most of the bottom is fairly hard, and we would expect the holding ground to be only fair. If you are so lucky as to find enough free swinging room, an anchorage here is satisfactory in ordinary summer weather, though likely to be uncomfortable in strong southerlies.

For those who don't need supplies or want to land, this is a pleasant variation from the usual, better-known anchorages, and appealing especially to those who like poking into new places. The surrounding land and docks are privately owned, so there are no landing facilities for visiting yachts, except possibly in dinghies on the beach at the head of the east fork.

Thimble Islands, Stony Creek, Conn. (217). "Like a section of the Maine Coast, drifted into Long Island Sound," the Thimbles offer a good, picturesque anchorage between Money Island and West Crib Island.*

Despite the red lines on the chart warning about cables, this anchorage is clear. It is preferable to that at Sachem Head, being larger and much better protected. But it is a difficult place to enter at night or in the fog. In the daytime a shoal boat under power can approach through the narrow passage from the east, but it is not recommended without power. The anchorage is apt to be rough in a storm or strong sou'wester, and a roll frequently comes in from the sound. We have found the most scenic spots to anchor, offering good holding ground, are either northwest of Money Island just to the south of the Cribs, or along the shore southeast of High Island.

The village of Stony Creek lies about 1 mile north of the anchorage. With caution a draft of 4 feet can be carried at low tide to the public dock, which is on the point east of Burr Island. Gas and supplies can be had here.

A supply "Islands Service" motorboat runs frequently between the islands in summer and will transport one to Stony Creek, where there is an attractive hotel, the Indian Point House, near the public landing. At one of our visists to Stony Creek, we were told by the obliging Captain

* Quotation from *Connecticut*—American Guide Series (Houghton Mifflin Co.).

Howd, the ferry skipper, that the boat leaves Stony Creek during the summer at a quarter before the hour, from 7 A.M. to 9 P.M., and will pick up passengers from yachts for the return trip if signaled or on call from the phone at the public dock on Money Island (telephone Hubbard 8-9978). The pick-up would be about on the hour, as it is a fifteen-minute trip each way. Thus, it is possible for visiting yachtsmen without power dinghies to obtain supplies or a shore meal at Stony Creek, while their boat lies at anchor among the islands. Aside from the inconvenience of obtaining supplies, the Thimble Islands afford one of the most appealing anchorages on the sound.

The Thimble Islands anchorage is a good stopping place for the first night on the way east from the various yachting centers at the western end of Long Island Sound. In good weather and during the daytime it is easy to enter and very little off the direct course eastward.

Wayne Allen Hall, in his article in *The New York Times,* presents us here with an interesting story about the Thimbles.

Named by the Stony Creek Indians for the lowly thimble berry, second cousin to the gooseberry, the Thimble Islands consist of 365 islands, 32 of them habitable, the largest being Horse Island, 17 acres, and the smallest, Dogfish Island, three-quarters of an acre.

The islands are glacial deposits of pink granite, which was quarried at the turn of the century to make sturdy foundations for the Statue of Liberty and the Brooklyn Bridge. Even the Indians discovered that the rocks made excellent arrowheads.

Captain Kidd had his observation headquarters on High Island, providing him with a semilandlocked cove, where he hid from American sloops of war. Across the narrow channel on Pot Island, he found a cavern, reachable only from under the water.

It is rumored that Kidd left a substantial amount of gold in the cavern, but to this day no one has been able to find the underwater entrance. High Island still flies the Jolly Roger, has black cottages and black motorboats and is the summer residence of a semisecret club of businessmen who call themselves the Buccaneers.

Pot Island gained fame in the 1880's when a fat men's club used the island's glacially formed potholes for a drinking rite. The club filled one pothole 30 feet deep with their punch and didn't leave the island until the hole had been drained.

Sachem Head, Conn. (217). This is a small harbor, open to the west and southwest, at the outer end of Sachem Head, with 6 to 10 feet of water at low tide. In entering, keep well off the southerly side of the point. The anchorage is difficult for strangers at night, but in the morning they will be won over by the charming scene of a rock-ribbed shoreline on which lovely residences are perched.

The Thimble Islands anchorage is less crowded, larger, and better protected. Sachem Head is highly recommended for shelter in easterlies. In northwesters it can be very unpleasant, and in hard southwesters a correspondent warns, "It is a regular saucer bowl and is apt to roll the sticks out of you."

The Sachem Head Yacht Club, with three well-marked guest moorings, maintains a well-sheltered float at the shore end of the lighted breakwater extending northwestward from the small island to the south of the entrance. A flashing red light is on the breakwater's outer end, and across the harbor below Joshua Point there's a privately maintained flashing white beacon. Consult the steward regarding moorings reserved for guests from accredited yacht clubs. After two nights of free use of club moorings, visitors are required to pay a charge of $2.00 a night, the limit on such mooring to be a total of one week. Boats should not remain at the club docks for any reason other than to load or unload. Gas and ice are not available. Snacks are served at the club.

The nearest boat yard is at Branford. The town of Guilford, where there are good restaurants and all manner of supplies can be purchased, is only three miles distant. A house built in 1639 is extant.

On Sachem Head a bloody battle of the Pequot War was fought in 1637. Tradition says that the head of an Indian, slain in combat, was placed by Uncas in the fork of a tree, where the skull remained for many years, giving the point its present name.*

Guilford, Conn. (217). This harbor acts as a delta, taking the mud silt coming down from East River and Sluice Creek. As such, it is subject to shoaling. Latest reports say that there is 4½ feet in the main channel to Sluice Creek, into which just 3½ feet can be carried at low water. Here to starboard you will find Capt'n Fred's Marine with minor repair work and the Captain's Table Restaurant available. Slips can be found to port at the Town of Guilford Marina, where there is a gas dock and a Coast Guard Auxiliary. A meal at the Old Stone House Restaurant is a must but not on Monday, when everything along the creek shuts down. Check with the dock master to pick up a town mooring up the East River in the basin, where there is just 3 feet throughout. One must moor fore-and-aft here since the 3-knot current runs strong and all channels are narrow. Jacobs Public Beach, which stretches to port at the harbor's entrance, is re-

---

* From *Connecticut*—American Guide Series (Houghton Mifflin Co.).

ported to have good clean water and looked extremely inviting to us.

Although the Guilford Yacht Club stands along the West River, we were strongly advised not to attempt this passage.

Clinton, Conn. (216). Here is another harbor whose channel has improved with dredging in 1972. This 100-foot-wide passage carries 8 feet at low water its entire length to the Cedar Island Marina. Follow the middle carefully and stay within the channel around Cedar Island until you see the Holiday Dock "Bait Shop" on the starboard shore a short distance beyond nun 16. Here you will find the town dock master, who will assign you a fore-and-aft mooring along the opposite side of the channel or will place you at the dock if space is open. Further up to starboard is the modest-looking Clinton Marine Basin with gas, water, ice, slips, all kinds of repair work and supplies nearby. We preferred the more modern and attractive Cedar Island Marina just beyond. Here you usually can find space alongside flotation slips furnished with electrical connections and given breakwater protection. Showers and a snack bar are on the premises, and motels, restaurants, and food stores are nearby. Since the Hammonasset River begins to shoal beyond these marinas, boats of deep draft are advised not to proceed further upriver without local knowledge.

Among the old dwellings in Clinton is Stanton House, built in 1789, and now a Colonial museum. In the center of the green is a monument commemorating the early years of the Collegiate School, later Yale. The first Yale students attended classes at this school until the opening of the college of Saybrook.

Duck Island Roads, Clinton, Conn. (216). To some yachtsmen (not including the writers) this is the most appealing harbor on Long Island Sound, although designated by the *Coast Pilot* as a harbor of refuge. It is formed by two long breakwaters extending north and west from Duck Island. Another breakwater to the westward offers additional protection from the southwest.

One determined yachtsman, who is obviously on our side, presents his impression of this questionable retreat:

> Who has not chilled, at least once, to the aubade of a wifely voice saying, "Goodness, I didn't thick we had anchored that close to the breakwater!" For me, this summarizes this place. Avoid it. Either your anchor drags or it fouls among the lobster pots and it's a damn tide hole. If caught here, look up the Patchogue River for a berth.

There is a strong run of tide off Kelsey Point Breakwater. When you are making Duck Island Roads from mid-sound with no direct bearings, the cottages on Hammonasset Beach and the tank to the east are helpful. An experienced cruising man writes as follows (consult chart 216 in reading these directions):

If approaching from the west at night with a slight to medium haze, and sailing fairly close in along the Connecticut shore, having left Falkner Island well astern (roughly 4 miles) and bearing about east a quarter north to gong 8 (roughly 2½ miles ahead), it is then well to know of certain confusion which has been experienced by others under similar circumstances because of the varying intensity of the lights on the three breakwaters.

As one approaches closer, with the white light appearing to be very close at hand, one should also begin to pick up the flashing (every four seconds) red light on the west end of the longer breakwater on Duck Island proper (one half of the intensity of the white light). It is then wise to note that the new, white Kelsey Point Breakwater light is probably dead ahead, mingled in the background of shore lights on Pine Orchard Beach. Don't fear that this 2½ sec. white light is past or lies well to port, but hold on, bearing off somewhat to starboard (south), and await your approach close aboard the Kelsey Point Breakwater before this white light may come to distinct view.

The danger lies in attempting to go farther inshore in the hope of running in closer to, and thus picking up, this white light, which in reality has little brilliance and is probably dead ahead clouded by the shore lights. To run in may present the danger of entering the foul waters surrounding Stone Island Reef.

Having held on, picked up the white light, and passed it close abeam on the port hand, one will find the entrance simple. Swing the bow to port (north) and run close past the red light of the longer Duck Island Breakwater to starboard.

It might be appropriate here to remind the reader that changes in aids to navigation are constantly being made on the sound as well as along our entire coast. To cite an example, Kelsey Point Breakwater Light, Branford Reef Light, and Seaflower Reef Light have all been given a new daytime appearance. They have been "changed to pipe towers and equipped with diamond-shaped daymarks divided into four diamond shapes which are colored so that the horizontal diamonds are white and the vertical diamonds are black with a white reflective border."

Good anchorage will be found in the V of the breakwater, with only fair holding ground. But don't get so near to the breakwater that you haven't plenty of room to swing and let out more scope on your anchor in case of a northwester or a northwest squall. The lights on the break-water make Duck Island Roads extremely easy of access at night, with no particular dangers. However, lobster pots sprinkled throughout the area have become an annoyance to many a skipper.

A large fleet can be accommodated, and everything is lovely if it doesn't start blowing from the northwest. There is some privacy, and the very desolateness of the place has a charm. Gas can be obtained in a dredged basin in the Patchogue River, also ice and small supplies at a nearby store. When we visited the Pilots Point Marina on the Patchogue River, we were told that boats anchored in Duck Island Roads could phone this marina (EX 9-9537) to have its staff actually deliver meals or supplies right aboard.

On the northeast end of the shorter breakwater on Duck Island proper there is a brilliant flashing (every four seconds) white light. This has four times the intensity of one of the other breakwater lights, and can under most conditions be picked up long before the flashing (every two and one-half seconds) white light on the sound end of Kelsey Point Breakwater. In midsummer this condition is aggravated by the mass of lights in the background, at Kelsey Point and along Pine Orchard Beach. This white light is well out to sea and some 2 miles nearer the approaching vessel than the aforementioned white light that flashes at four-second intervals.

There has been considerable shoaling in the last few years, and the chart at the time of writing showed depths of 6 or 7 feet, even a 5-foot spot, in the angle between the breakwaters, where 15 to 19 feet were shown in 1948.

Patchogue River, Westbrook, Conn. (216). Here is another fairly re-cently developed man-made channel and harbor, the most convenient al-ternative to Duck Island Roads. For those who prefer to anchor in the Roads for the night it is a nearby place for gassing up or obtaining ice. The channel is not wide and was reported in 1970 to have a controlling depth of only 4 feet all the way up to the highway bridge, the head of navigation. However, we learned on our last visit that re-dredging of the entire river to its former depth of 8 feet had been finally completed in late 1972. Nevertheless, be sure to stick to the "straight and narrow path" while observing the signs saying "Leave No Wake." The Pilots Point Marina is on the main channel just beyond nun 6. The first two of the three east basins shown on the chart have been dredged to 8 feet, and substantial bulkheads have been erected. The charge is $5.00 minimum, 20¢ per foot, along the slips perfectly sheltered by these bulkheads. Gas, water, ice, showers, and a ships store with charts are all available here. A travelift to haul boats up to 40 feet, a nearby market, laundromat, mechanic, and canvas-maker complete the facilities.

To the east and up on the starboard shore of the Menunketesuck River lies the attractive Duck Island Marina, with similar facilities in more pleasant surroundings, with a restaurant nearby. The only drawback is that although its river approach carries about 6 feet, there tends to be bad shoaling at its entrance off the Patchogue River channel. Proceed cautiously through this entrance, keeping the two black piles here to port and the one red stake to starboard, while favoring the port shore, not cutting it too closely. This marina, run by Bob Bantel, charges a flat rate of $5.00 at the slips, which afford good blue-shell crab hunting. The convivial Menunketesuck Yacht Club, founded in 1968, is pleasantly housed in the marina's red building.

Far up the Patchogue River you'll first come upon Holbrook Marina on the port shore, lined with small sailing craft belonging to the local residents. Just below the bridge are gas dock and slips belonging to Lawson's Marina, where there's an excellent lobster pound and a market for supplies ½ mile away. But this area is congested and not nearly as attractive as downstream.

Most of these marinas offer yachtsmen complimentary transportation to such top restaurants as The Dragon Wick and Wagon Wheel.

Connecticut River, Conn. (215, 266, 267).

Entrance: Saybrook (215). Yachtsmen with a love for exploring rivers and creeks and poking their way into fascinating byways should not miss the Connecticut River. Some of its byways between Essex and Middletown have a beauty and charm reminiscent of the Upper Hudson or the coast of Maine. While long a mecca for motorboats, the depths of some of its coves and creeks and the speed with which the drawbridges are opened make the Connecticut attractive for sailing craft also. It is not recommended, however, for boats without power, except for purposes of refuge near the entrance and with favoring tides. The Connecticut state boating law restricts speed limits to 6 m.p.h. within 100 feet of anchored boats, docks, or marinas.

We might advise those who are planning a cruise up the Quinnehtqut, the Indian term for "long tidal water," that the Connecticut River Watershed Council has updated its eighty-six-page river-guide booklet. It covers the entire 410-mile stretch of the river from Canada to Long Island Sound. Useful information on boating, fishing, and camping is provided, with particular emphasis on canoeing. In addition to the booklet, the guide "package" includes maps of the three major sections of the river. All of this may be obtained for $3.50 by writing to the Connecticut River Watershed Council, Inc., 497 Main St., P.O. Box 89, Greenfield, Mass. 01301.

Charles A. Goodwin, in his very interesting *Connecticut River Pilot* (1944), explains that, while Adriaen Block discovered the river, it was King Charles and his bishops who forced the first settlement at Saybrook. Lord Say and Lord Brook got together with Pym and decided to resist the King and to prepare in the wilderness a place of refuge for the conspirators, in case their plans miscarried.

In 1797, Timothy Dwight, president of Yale College, looked upon the land bordering the Connecticut River and wrote this description: "In its extent, it is magnificent. In its form, it is beautiful. Its banks possess uncommon elegance, almost universally handsome, with a margin entirely neat and commonly ornamented with a fine fringe of shrubs and trees." At the same time, he reported the river's water to be "remarkably pure and light . . . everywhere pure, potable, perfectly salubrious."

Now much of the water is spoiled. At the time of writing, however, plans are being considered to restore the valley through the initiative of the Bureau of Outdoor Recreation, a division of the United States Department of the Interior. A federal report recommends the creation of a 125,000-acre conservation belt from the Canadian border to Long Island Sound, consisting of a national recreation area, part state parks, and part private land to be restricted against further industrialization.

Rising in the extreme northern part of New Hampshire, 375 miles from the entrance, the Connecticut River is one of the most important rivers in New England. Hartford, 45 miles upriver, is the head of navigation for all but very shoal draft boats, except in times of high water, though the most beautiful part of the river is below Middletown. At Deep Water, 10½ miles from the sound, and above, the water is fresh. High water occurs at Hartford four and three-fourths hours after it does at the entrance at Saybrook, and low water six and one-fourth hours later. Some of the principal towns or entrances to the best anchorages are at the following distances from the Saybrook Breakwater Light:

	Nautical Miles
Saybrook Point	1.4
Essex	6.0
Hamburg Cove entrance	7.5
Selden Creek entrance	9.0
Salmon River entrance	15.0
Middletown	28.0
Wethersfield	42.0
Hartford	45.2

With 4 or 5 knots of power, there is no difficulty in entering for shelter or to explore. Any smart sailing boat can negotiate the river without power with favorable winds. Tidal current is a factor as far as Middletown, and the combination of river current and ebb tide can be strong, occasionally 3.5 knots. The mean rise and fall of tides in the Connecticut varies from 3½ feet at Saybrook to 1¾ feet at Hartford.

The entrance is clearly marked by Saybrook Light and a pair of stone jetties. The entire river is well marked by buoys, but reference to charts is essential, as the buoys are not always self-explanatory.

In entering between the jetties, watch for the sweep of the current across the entrance and note the shoals inside the jetties, particularly the one to starboard.

There has been a striking extension in the ports, marinas, and facilities along the Connecticut River in the last few years. It is now possible to find overnight dockage or anchorage to suit almost any taste or purse, from the luxury of Terra Mar to the privacy of Selden Creek or Salmon Cove, from the active sailing community at Essex to the motorboat haven in landlocked Wethersfield Cove. In discussing the many ports and tie-ups along the river, we shall "cruise" northward from Long Island Sound. We should remind those proceeding upriver to give three toots of the horn on approaching the railroad bridge.

While we have made every effort to spot the principal docks and marinas offering tie-ups or other facilities along the way, we won't guarantee that we have mentioned them all. In fact, we are sure that by the time you get there after reading this book, there will be some unmentioned new ones. But we think we have suggested enough possibilities to take care of any requirements. Where prices are given it is at the time of writing and they are, of course, subject to change.

1. *Hull Harbor Marina, Saybrook Point* (*west shore—215*). This is just below conspicuous Terra Mar. There is 6 feet of water at the docks, where gas, Diesel fuel, water, electricity, ice, crank-case service (in fifteen minutes), an emergency pump, etc., are available. We were told they give good engine service.

"We don't encourage sailboats," the dock master told us; "they don't buy much, if any, gas; but if we have space, we won't throw them out."

Shelter from all winds, except perhaps strong easterlies coming across the river, is provided by a breakwater on the south side and outlying bulkheads.

This place is simple and sticks to yachting needs only. If you want something beyond that, go next door to Terra Mar.

2. *Terra Mar Marina, Saybrook Point (west shore—215)*. This is the most luxurious marina we have visited this side of the famed Bahia Mar at Fort Lauderdale, Florida. Among the offerings are a hotel and a restaurant, a night club, the Tiki Bar, a coffee shop, clothing store, sauna baths, two swimming pools, a lounge with TV, tennis and shuffleboard facilities, ping-pong, dancing, sun-bathing, and, last but not least, a fine marina with many slips. Although 7 feet of water is reported at the slips, most deep-draft keel auxiliaries prefer to tie up at the outer dock. This is primarily a motorboat haven, and almost every yacht we saw there belonged in that class. However, it is also most convenient to auxiliaries proceeding alongshore who would like to gas up or stop for a meal.

The cost of an overnight tie-up is 35¢ a foot, with a minimum of $10.00. This includes water, electric connections, etc. The other services listed as available are: "telephone installed in your boat, lounge, showers, rest rooms, tide and weather information, charts, ice delivery, grocery delivery, garbage collection, assistance in entering and leaving your slip, mail service, watchman, fire and police protection, bottled gas, a modern marine service station with marine gas, Diesel fuel, oil, batteries, automatic washers and dryers."

The marina does not undertake repairs and mechanical service; that is left to the boat yards further upriver. A store carries marine supplies and some canned goods; it also has milk and bread.

The "Rules and Regulations of the Terra Mar Yacht Basin" are aimed at keeping the marina neat and in good order and to prevent sales solicitation by those not tenants of Terra Mar.

Yachtsmen won't see as many sailing cronies at Terra Mar as they will at Essex, but it is a paradise for motor cruising men and women who want luxury and can pay for it, who enjoy glitter and like to share in it. Even those who prefer to anchor in some hidden gunk hole will enjoy the contrast once in a while. As an ad slogan says, "You've got to see it to believe it!"

North Cove and its channel, just above Terra Mar, were dredged in 1965 to provide a new harbor of refuge for cruising yachtsmen. The channel, with a 100-foot width and reported depth of 5 feet, should be followed dead center as you run from can 15 eastward through the middle of the narrow mouth of the cove between nun 2 and can 3. Be sure to compensate for the river's strong current abeam so as to avoid being swept up on the channel's shallow edges. This popular basin has at least 5 feet of water, but the stakes marking the rectangular dredged area must be observed carefully, as the remainder of the cove, especially in the northwestern and southwestern corners, is only a foot or so deep at low water. The bottom is good for holding, the shelter excellent from all directions in a blow. There are no shore facilities, although the town, ¼ mile distant, has put in a small dock at the western end. The Village Restaurant a short walk up the street serves good food at reasonable prices. Here is a fine protected spot where you can "get away from it all."

3. Bridge Marina, Old Saybrook (*west shore—215*). This is just above the railroad bridge, where the old ferry slip was located. Gas, water, ice, and slips with electricity are available. This marina offers repair work and is fairly well protected, except from easterlies. It prefers to get power boats.

4. Saybrook Marine Service, Old Saybrook (*west shore—215*). Just above Bridge Marina and the railroad bridge, this marina caters especially to sailboats. Most of the boats stored here for the winter are sailing craft, and they come in all sizes. There is 8 feet at the dock at mean low water; gas, water, ice, and electric connections are available, and usually a slip or dock space for transients. Repair and haulage is done for good-sized boats. We liked very much what we have seen here.

5. Oak Leaf Marina, Old Saybrook (*west shore—215*). This is a small place just above the highway bridge and has 6 feet at the dock, where gas and ice are sold and repair work is done. A state launching ramp is located here.

6. Baldwin Bridge Yacht Basin, Old Saybrook (*west shore—215*). This is just beyond Oak Leaf, and 10 feet of water is available at the dock. Here we saw boats of all types, since, for total services, this is one of the best stopping places before one reaches Essex. Gas is sold and there are guest moorings and slips. Hauling and repair work is undertaken.

7. Ferry Point Marina, Old Saybrook (*west shore—215*). Unless you happen to be a native of the Connecticut or an avid reader of such cruising guides as this one, you might pass right by this charming little marina tucked away in a secluded basin on the southwestern shore of Ferry Point. The narrow dredged channel with 10 feet at m.l.w. runs south from a point just beyond some old stone piers located along the point's northern shore. On entering this channel you will pass between some piles and note a sunken barge that marks its starboard edge. Gas, Diesel fuel, water, showers, and ice are here, plus electricity at the slips, where 6 feet of water is reported at m.l.w. There is a flat fee of $4.00 for an overnight stay. Food supplies are located about 3 miles away in Old Saybrook.

Try the Howard Johnson's just a stone's throw away should you be short rations.

All is calm here. The loudest noise we heard came from the voices of the sports fishermen who were proudly comparing their day's catch.

8. Old Lyme Marina, Old Lyme (east shore—215). Sheltered behind Calves Island and in attractive surroundings, this is one of the best ports on the river. Follow the channel behind Calves Island to a first-rate dock on the east shore of the channel about halfway up to the point where the channel turns to the northwest. Nun RB is left well to port. We liked Peter Chapman, who became this marina's owner in 1971 and told us that there's a good 25 feet at dockside. Overnight dockage runs 15 ¢ per foot with a $5.00 minimum; the rate for a mooring is $4.00. Gas, Diesel fuel, ice, water, electricity, showers, all types of repair work, and even taxi service are among the facilities. The marine store is now attractively re-decorated and the whole place is kept "Bristol fashion," reflecting Chapman's active interest to offer the best in service. A shopping center with a good restaurant, drug store, A & P store, a bank, etc., are "only five minutes away."

For years we have read and heard about the glories of Lord Cove as a gunk hole beautifully sheltered beneath the steeps of Lord Hill to the north. Morten Lund records in his book *Eastward on Five Sounds* that he reached Lord Creek way across the unmarked cove without mishap using power and depth-sounder in a catamaran drawing 2½ feet. But we have been advised by Old Lyme natives that in a boat of any greater draft, it is unwise to venture beyond the cove's entrance between Goose Island and Quarry Hill. Use bow and stern anchors if you wish to lie to here.

9. Essex (west shore—215). Six miles above the entrance to the Connecticut River, this ancient town clambers up several hills above the valley and looks down on its three coves and one of the most active yachting scenes to be found on Long Island Sound. Few harbors are as popular as Essex among real cruising men, and few have as much to offer.

"On Main Street, the interesting Griswold Inn, built in 1776, well preserves the flavor of an earlier day. Visitors are provided with the 'Rules of the Tavern,' which stipulate that bed and supper may be obtained for six pence, that no more than five may sleep in one bed, that boots may not be worn in bed, and organ-grinders must sleep in the washhouse, while razor-grinders and tinkers are not taken in at all." * We can recommend

* From *Where To Retire and How*, by Fessenden S. Blanchard (Dodd, Mead & Co.).

the drinks, food, and pictures at this fascinating inn, which is only a short walk from the water front.

Sailing yachts coming to Essex often stop at the dock of the Essex Paint and Marine Co., just north of the Essex Yacht Club. While dockage space is somewhat limited, the company has a good many moorings, some of which are available to visiting yachts at a moderate fee. Slips cost more, with water and electric connections included. Charts and a wide selection of marine supplies are at hand at the dock.

The Essex Yacht Club, founded in 1933, with adjoining dinghy dock and clubhouse, provides launch service and may have a spare mooring. We heard that it is "undoubtedly the first if not the only yacht club which was founded through the inspiration of frostbite dinghy sailing." The Cruising Club of America has a station at this club, with many yachts moored there belonging to members of that famous organization of cruising men. On the other side of the E.P. and M. Co. is the fenced-in Dauntless Yacht Club, with a limited and exclusive membership, said to be better known for its social activities than for its yachting. The Pettipaug Yacht Club is now stationed upriver on the western shore facing Brockway Island. It is active in small-boat racing.

The prominent Steamboat Dock Marina has a number of slips providing electricity, water, ice, etc., and is largely patronized by power cruisers. Texaco gas and Diesel fuel are sold here. On the "Upper Deck" cocktails and meals are served, with a splendid view of the river thrown in. All shopping is located within walking distance. The Essex harbor master, Freeman Rolfe, has his boat moored at Steamboat Dock.

Northward, across the narrow channel leading to North Cove, is the attractive Colonial-style complex of the Essex Island Marina, where, according to its slogan and our experience, "it's fun in the sun and cool in the pool." For transient boats of any size, this spot is "tops" in our book. Its management appears to have anticipated· practically every visitor's need—for his boat and for his crew.

This marina is actually set on the southern tip of an island, so a ferry constantly runs guests across the 150-foot channel to the mainland. Numerous protective basins and floating docks frame the large administration building, swimming pool, repair shops, and "The Galley Locker." The daily charge for dockage runs $12.00 for boats up to 40 feet, $16.00 up to 50 feet, and $20.00 up to 60 feet. Prices include use of all facilities. They offer towing service and can "quick-haul" a boat as fast as any yard we've seen.

There are several fine boat yards in Essex. The Essex Boat Works and the Dauntless Boatyard are to port just inside the entrance channel to North Cove. They have good service but limited dock space in well-pro-

Litton Industries—Aero Service Division

Essex Harbor looking down the Connecticut River toward Long Island Sound.

tected waters. The last yard is at the southwest end of Middle Cove, which is unnamed on the chart but is the small cove between North and South Coves. It is entered through a narrow staked channel, which has a reported depth of 6 feet. Keep in the middle of the narrow part and then follow the port shore slowly. The yard here, run by the Essex Marine Railway, has some slips for motorboats and a large building for indoor storage and sales. We were much struck by the friendly and cooperative attitude of W.M. Jenks when we came up to their dock. All three boat yards do hauling and repair work.

There are many fine old houses along the shaded streets of Essex, and a second inn, the Osage, is even older than the Griswold, though less accessible to yachtsmen. Larders can be stocked in town, about three blocks from the water front.

It is reported that there are normally eight hours of ebb current at Essex and four hours of flood. Essex is a secure and most attractive anchorage though it can also be a bit uneasy on occasions when the wind blows strongly from the north or southeast, unless you are tied up at one of the boat yards.

At Essex, in 1775, Uriah Hayden constructed the *Oliver Cromwell,* the first warship of the Continental Navy. A year later he built The Old Ship Tavern, a structure still in use as the headquarters of the Dauntless Yacht Club. On April 8, 1814, British marines landed near where the Steamboat Dock now stands and burned twenty-eight local ships.

10. Hamburg Cove (east shore—215). Half a mile above Essex, opposite Brockway's Island, is the entrance to Hamburg Cove, which is practically a fiord, 1½ miles long. The entrance channel is well marked with buoys, and there is a depth of at least 7 feet, but the channel is narrow and buoys should be hugged, especially the black-and-red nun at the mouth, which should be kept to starboard on entering. The cove is a perfect anchorage, with depths averaging 17 feet except at the edges. Here is absolute quiet with only sky, smooth water, trees, and a few houses to be seen. Few who enter for the first time realize that up what looks like a deserted cove (northeast) there is a channel ending in a picturesque basin off the village of Hamburg. There is a landing in Hamburg Basin, but the basin is crowded in summer with motorboats. The channel to the basin is marked by stakes with pointers put out during the season by the Hamburg Yacht Club, located on the eastern shore of the cove, with 3 feet at its docks.

At the cove landing in the village can be found the harbor master, Mr. Donald G. Reynolds. The upper basin is largely fresh water. There is 2 or 3 feet of tide. At the Cove Landing Marina, run by Leland Rey-

Hamburg Cove, landlocked harbor on the Connecticut River. The turning
basin at the village of Hamburg is shown at upper left.

nolds, limited services are available to transients, and there's 6 feet dockside. Reynolds says that the cove's water is cleaner now than it was fifty years ago when he was here as a young lad. Supplies are available at the Cove Landing Store. Several good inns are at Old Lyme, about 5 miles away. The nearest railroad station is at Saybrook, about 8 miles away. If you have a chance, visit the state park 8 miles from the wharf. It is known as the Devil's Hop Yard.

The Lower Cove is the place to anchor for the night, in one of the most attractive anchorages anywhere. The many ball-shaped moorings here are privately owned, but perhaps a vacant one can be picked up if your conscience doesn't bother you. Shut in by wooded hills, the place can be hot, but, except in very warm weather, it is a delightful and beautiful spot.

11. Selden (or Shirley) Creek (east shore—215, 266). The entrance to Selden Creek is not impressive and does not reveal the attractiveness you discover farther up. You will find the opening on the east shore after passing the stone-walled Brockway's Landing. The entrance is in a flat, marshy area, flanked by the stumps of uprooted trees, and just upriver from a high rock cliff with two houses at its foot. Soundings by one of the authors in the spring of 1970 revealed at least 10 feet at low water in the center of the entrance, on a line running down the middle of the creek. A shoal makes out from the northern point and a smaller shoal from the south bank. There is plenty of deep water between these shoals, but it is advisable to proceed up the creek on a rising tide.

After you get inside, keep in the middle. The creek is only 50-feet wide in spots and continues for about 2 miles, with from 4 to 18 feet of water up to Selden Cove's entrance. The best anchorage for deep-draft vessels is under the first or second rock cliff almost a mile up the creek along the starboard shore. Carry a bow line to the shore and set out a stern anchor to prevent swinging across the channel here. Further up, just below the cove, you will come to two forks in the channel. Stay out of the left or western fork since it leads to a dead end and has little water in it. The right fork, giving passage to the cove, carries about 3 feet at high water, but watch out for some boulders as you enter. If you are crafty enough to get into the cove with a shallow draft boat, don't anchor there for long or you'll get hung up. On one visit on an ebbing tide, we were suprirised to see a 30-foot auxiliary sloop on her beam's end in the middle of the cove. We hailed its crew, offering assistance, to which the skipper replied nonchalantly, "We're just sitting here waiting for that old tide to shift."

The current in the creek is not strong, but anchorage fore and aft is usually necessary. The upper passage directly from the cove to the river is reported to have been nearly filled in by a hurricane.

During the Revolution, river shipping used to hide in Selden Creek from British raiding parties.

About a mile north of Selden Cove is the Rhenish castle built by the actor William Gillette, who won fame for his portrayal of Sherlock Holmes. When he died in 1937, his will specified that he hoped the executors would see that the property did not get into "the possession of some blithering saphead who has no conception of where he is or with what surrounded." He need not have had any fear, for his estate is now the beautiful Gillette Castle State Park, commanding a superb view of the Connecticut River. If you want some exercise while moored in the creek, row across the cove and walk to the park, which is open from 11 A.M to 5 P.M. every day but Monday from late May to October.

One can also reach the castle by tying up at a small landing just above the Hadlyme ferry dock on the east shore, as shown on the chart. From here, it's a steep climb straight up the hill to meet the road leading to the castle grounds about 400 yards to the north.

12. Connecticut River Marina, Chester (west shore—266). Across river from Selden Creek's northern exit lies the mouth of Chester Creek, which shows very little water according to the chart. But just to the south, Bob Garthwaite has one of the larger boating facilities on the Connecticut River with 5 feet of water at the slips. Most of your boat's needs will be filled here. Connecticut River Marina is also one of the few spots this far north that furnishes some food supplies with a restaurant. Associated with Baldwin Bridge Yacht Basin, it has twenty-four hour service, including towing service should you experience engine failure (phone 526-9076). It is wise to approach the dredged basin here by heading westward from a point in the main channel that is well north of black can 37.

13. Whalebone Creek (east shore—266). Just above Selden Creek's northern exit, this creek is a fascinating detour for boats drawing under 2½ feet, or for dinghies or canoes.

14. Middletown Yacht Club (west shore—266). On the west bank opposite the lower end of Lord Island, the Middletown Yacht Club has its well-groomed headquarters. A dredged basin with bulkheads on three sides and rows of slips provides an efficient-looking modern layout. Gas is available at a float and a clubhouse on high ground overlooks the river. Yachts not in the slips are usually moored across the river near Lord Island, off the channel, with launch service furnished. The large swimming pool is a center of activity. Members of recognized yacht clubs would do well to stop at this fine club to see if a slip or mooring is available.

15. *Goodspeed's Landing, East Haddam* (*east shore—266*). A stopover here promises a rewarding experience for anyone who is interested in American theatrical history or who enjoys fine continental cuisine.

If there's space, you can tie up at the Opera House dock just below the bridge to starboard. A short walk will take you to the center of the charming old town, where all types of supplies may be purchased.

In 1877, William Goodspeed, a shipbuilder, created the Goodspeed Opera House. It became a rousing success, but by the late 1950s it was forsaken and ready for demolition. This triggered widespread interest in Goodspeed's value to history, and the Goodspeed Opera House Foundation was formed to refurbish it. It now has an active season from mid-June to mid-September, offering the finest in Broadway drama and musicals. In 1965, it housed the first production of *Man of La Mancha*. Performances begin at 8:30 P.M. with matinees on Wednesdays at 2:30 P.M. and on Saturdays at 5 P.M.

The Gelston House, next door, is a charming Victorian establishment where one may enjoy a view of the river's rustic landscape and the culinary delights of Marius Zino, formerly with Maxim's of Paris.

16. *Salmon River* (*east shore—266*). Just above East Haddam is the entrance to Salmon River, where a good anchorage in deep water is to be found in the narrow part of the channel. But feel your way in carefully, as the entrance is subject to shoaling and, as is frequently the case with tributaries leading into larger rivers, the upriver point has a fairly long shoal, to port as you go in. A good anchorage is just opposite the first tiny creek you will meet to starboard. The latest *Coast Pilot* reports that Salmon Cove "is navigable for vessels of less than 6-foot draft as far as Scovill Landing, about 1½ miles above the entrance, and for small craft of less than 3-foot draft about 1 mile farther. Considerable grass in the channel and cove makes boat operation difficult." Based on our recent, arduous voyage upriver, we can subscribe only to the *Pilot's* last sentence. Depths recorded on the present chart are badly outdated. Beyond the aforementioned creek, the unmarked channel begins to shoal along much of its western edge to muddy, grassy depths of 2 to 3 feet, with not much more water to starboard. We advise not to proceed farther. The land is marshy along the shores, but to the east the heights rise to 300 feet or more. Just above the entrance to Salmon River, on the opposite shore of the Connecticut, is Russell's Boat Yard, where gas and repairs can be found.

The loveliest part of the Connecticut River is between Salmon River and Middletown, especially the passage through the Straits just below Middletown.

17. Portland (east [north] shore—267). The Portland Boat Works is a high-class yard catering to inboards. Gas, water, electricity, ice, telephone, hauling, repairs are all available, as well as a number of slips. Supplies are about 1 mile away, and the Boat Works will provide transportation. Just above on the same shore is Holters Yacht Yard, with similar overnight facilities.

Middletown, across the river, is the principal shopping center of Middlesex County and the home of Wesleyan University. It was once an important shipping port for the West Indies. Its name resulted from the fact that the city is about halfway between Saybrook and Hartford.

The river between Middletown and Hartford is less settled and also less beautiful than it is below, but it is nevertheless pleasant and less crowded. Except in Wethersfield Cove, the only good anchorages are in the river itself. Within the last few years the number of docks supplying gas, and in some cases, slips, has increased considerably.

18. Glastonbury Marina (east shore—267). This is the largest marina above Middletown and has several floats with slips, fine macadam launching ramps, and a large parking place, obviously for cars and empty trailers. Gas is available. The marina is just above range beacon 84 and opposite a stack.

19. Rocky Hill (west shore—267). Just below the ferry landing is a small dock with gas called Hales Landing. There is a nice anchorage in pretty surroundings across the river on the bend above the east side ferry landing.

20. South Wethersfield (267). The latest chart will show you that a new gunk hole has been formed through the western shore of the river about 2 miles south of Wethersfield Cove. It is such a concealed place that it hasn't been given a proper name, so natives call it simply "No Name Cove."

This rectangular basin, 1000 yards long and almost as wide, was dredged out in recent years to provide fill for the construction of nearby Highway 91. Its narrow entrance is difficult to spot but lies at the foot of Crow Point, across the river and just beyond range beacon 94. Hug the port shore on entering; 5 feet can be carried. Inside there is good water throughout with a bottom composed of soft ooze. You'll probably find yourself alone with no marinas to mar the natural beauty of the still water surrounded by tiny beaches, lush trees, and bushes. The cove is incomparable. Although there is no one around to tell us, it may closely resemble the Wethersfield Cove of a century or more ago.

21. Wethersfield Cove (267). This is a rather unusual, completely landlocked cove with a very narrow entrance. The shoalest point is at the entrance of the channel between the black and red privately maintained, though charted, buoys. In 1968 the centerline of the entire channel recorded a depth of 6 feet at m.l.w., and this same depth can be carried throughout most of the basin's southern portion. The tidal change is about 1½ feet, so most motor cruisers have no trouble in getting in. Keep in the middle of the entrance channel and then follow the buoys to the Wethersfield Yacht Club dock on the southwest shore. Regardless of an apparent shoal spot on the channel side of the last black buoy, follow close to these markers and you will be all right—at least, that is what we were told by a local authority.

The yacht club has gas, water, and a few supplies, and is most hospitable to members of other yacht clubs. If there is a spare mooring, the club will make it available. Its number of private aid buoys has been reduced. The harbor master at the Cove Park Anchorage on the southeastern shore may also be able to provide a mooring. The bottom is soft clay, so set your anchor well in a blow.

An excellent launching ramp is located on Cove Park's shore, and inland there are picnic tables and telephones. The old stone-and-wood building is a warehouse where traders stored their loads of fish and furs during the times of the Revolution.

Two events have taken place that have stripped this cove of much of its former appeal. Extreme water pollution, an increasing problem along the Connecticut, prohibits any swimming here. And the new fixed highway bridge, arching 38 feet over the channel, banished much natural beauty, replacing it with traffic's din.

Cruising yachts able to get in would do well to make Wethersfield Cove the end of their upriver navigation. There are no good yacht facilities in Hartford, and above Hartford the river is usually too shoal for cruiser navigation except possibly by expert pilots with local knowledge.

"The Connecticut River above Hartford," says the *Coast Pilot*, "is practically unimproved, but is navigable about 30 miles to Holyoke for boats not exceeding 3-foot draft, when the river is not low. The channel is constantly shifting. For a distance of about 10 miles above Hartford to Enfield Rapids, bars with 2½ feet at low water and many other obstructions are encountered."

Niantic River, Conn. (214). Before you approach this river, we would like to note that recently a special anchorage area off the Niantic Bay Yacht Club on the western side of Niantic Bay was assigned by the Coast Guard and appears on the latest charts. The club has guest moorings with launch service but its anchorage is wide open to winds from the east and southeast. Its basin at Crescent Beach, however, is protected on the south and east by a breakwater.

To go up the Niantic River, boats formerly had to cope with tidal currents of 2 knots or more, but with channel dredging in 1970 to a low water depth of 6 feet all the way north to Sandy Point, the flow is now less swift, and entry through the two narrow bridges at the entrance is not such a great challenge. However, it is still advisable to make this passage at slack water or against the current. There is a 2½-foot tide range here.

Although the first bridge may be open, unless a train is approaching, the second (swing) bridge is always closed and often slow to open. The first bridge opens on signal of one long blast and two short blasts of horn or whistle; the second, on sounding three short blasts. Never proceed until your signal has been acknowledged, but if you should hear two longs blasts from either bridge, back off and wait. In this event, stay within the turning basins, which have been dredged on both sides of the bridge and marked with poles on which reflectors have been placed. Between the two bridges you may come to lie along the bulkheading there.

Proceeding up the marked channel, you will note similar-looking marinas lined up in the following order: Niantic River Marina; Boats, Inc., catering only to outboards; Darrows Boatyard, with a marine railway and travelift; and Niantic Boatyard, also with a railway. The services here are rather complete and comparable but water at their docks runs only about 4 feet.

About ½ mile above these facilities, the narrow 50-foot-wide channel will lead you to the entrance to sheltered Smith Cove. Privately maintained buoys have been set out to mark the 6-foot-deep channel leading to Bayreuther Boatyard & Marina, where their slips offer 8-foot depths. Since most of Smith Cove is 3-foot deep with a mud bottom, a tie-up at Bayreuther is advised.

Chris and Warren Bayreuther, who keep their establishment "Bristol fashion," obviously cater to transients and deep-draft boats. They have about everything to suit you and your boat's needs and fancy, including excellent repair men on duty, complete supplies, a galley store, and the most polished restrooms and showers you'll ever see in any marina. Motels and a shopping center are nearby. A courtesy car is at your disposal. Yachtsmen who are between cruises often use Bayreuther as a layover preferable to New London.

The quiet cove, almost pond-like, presents the observer with a pleasant image. The water is clear, the swimming good, for all boats putting in here are not permitted to pump their heads unless equipped with a retaining tank. Fish such as flounder, stripers, and mackerel abound here and along the river.

The channel further up the river is apt to shift from time to time but is marked by privately maintained stakes that are moved to conform to the changes. Niantic River is a beautiful spot, widens into a well-sheltered lake, and offers good holding ground in about 15 feet of water south of Sandy Point's bluff.

Excellent taxi service from Niantic can take you to good restaurants in the vicinity and in Old Lyme.

Millstone Point, Conn. (214). This is an intriguing little cove on the southwest side of Millstone Point (east side of Niantic Bay). It is just south of a 375-foot-high, red-and-white banded ventilation stack located at Northeast Utilities' Millstone Nuclear Power Station. Entering, leave the lighted buoy near Little Rock to port and then beware of the 1-foot rocky shoal located at the end of the point to the west of the entrance. A portion of an old barge remains sunken, its fore-and-aft pointing in a northeast direction and blocking the harbor's entrance. Entering yachtsmen, having passed the shoal area, should stay well to port only about 25 feet off the cove's western and then northern shore in arriving at the best anchorage area to starboard along the curving beach. There is a sandy bottom here with 7-foot depth. You'll be exposed only to westerly winds sweeping across Niantic Bay. Don't tie up to the dolphin standing to the south.

The harbor is open to the public and is frequently used on weekends by yachtsmen as an overnight anchorage. Except in emergencies, however, landings on the small beach docks and headland area are not presently permitted. If this property, owned by Northeast Utilities, is developed in the future for public recreational use, signs will be posted permitting yachtsmen to trespass ashore. The power plant has been in operation since 1970; a second unit is due for completion in 1974.

Other areas of Millstone Point are open to the public, including Fox Island to the east and Bay Point to the west. Fishing in the plant's warm-water discharge near Fox Island was reported in 1971 as extremely popular and productive. Another favorite spot during the summer months is a beach picnic area and visitors' information center at Bay Point. The swimming beach is enclosed by a buoy line, but boat access to it is permitted nearby.

The U.S. Naval Underwater Sound Laboratory still occupies the big stone quarry said to be one of the oldest in southern New England. Boats are not permitted to enter here through the opening to Twotree Island Channel, where a log boom acts as a gate.

If you don't require supplies but are interested in seeing a place that's different, do stop at Millstone Harbor. But do so before sunset!

New London, Conn. (293, 359). This is one of the leading yacht centers on the sound, and provides virtually every requirement the cruising yachtsman may seek, except possibly a snug anchorage. New London Harbor, formed by the Thames River, is large and seldom quiet. But it is fairly well protected, and has all sorts of provision for cruisers.

On the west side of the lower harbor there are several yacht stations with moorings for small yachts and cruisers. These stations are open at all hours, ready to furnish all supplies. In the upper harbor is another yacht station with service available at all hours. The best small-boat anchorage is in the west side of the lower harbor. Heavy repair work is done at the Electric Boat Company and the Thames Shipyard, and small repairs will be made by a mechanic at any one of the yacht stations.

Harbor conditions are generally good except in strong southerly winds, when it is advisable to anchor in the upper harbor north of the United States Coast Guard docks on the west side 2½ miles from Southwest Ledge. These docks are distinguishable at night by a red light at the outer end.

Burr's Yacht Haven, just below the Orient Point Ferry and about 1 mile from the entrance on the western shore in Green's Harbor, is an excellent place to leave a boat or to outfit for a trip. There is 9 feet of water at low tide. Permanent moorings, in the shape of large orange, pick-up, ball buoys, are available, and good care will be taken of any boat left with the management. The moorings are obtainable at $3.00 a night and slips at 20¢ per foot. Moorings may be picked up after checking personally with the dock master. Many convenient slips with electrical connections have been built at the wharf for those who prefer to tie up there. Here you'll find "complete one-stop service." Burr's claims that, "if we haven't got it, we can get it."

Gas, Diesel fuel, electricity, ice, water, etc., are found at the dock, and up at the marine store, owned by Raymond Bergamo, you can find an ample stock of hardware, charts, and groceries. Complete engine/hull repair work is available. On the premises are showers, a laundromat, The Grogg Shoppe, and Chuck's Steak House, where informal dress is permissible. The Trade Winds Restaurant is within walking distance.

One block west of Burr's up the hill is a road on which buses run to

New London every fifteen minutes. Taxis can be ordered quickly by phone to provide transportation to the New London railroad station, where most through trains between Boston and New York stop. Ferries also run to Fishers Island and Block Island.

Just south of Burr's lies Marsters Marine Service, whose efficiency has been praised by a Corinthian yachtsman. The Thames Yacht Club is located next door. On one of our visits here, the people there couldn't have been nicer in rightfully showing off their fine new clubhouse, including immaculate showers and snack bar. Visiting yachtsmen may make use of its sandy beach and perhaps a spare mooring or two but they can obtain no gas or supplies. This active sailing club, open from 10 A.M. to 6 P.M. offers anchorage in the most attractive surroundings found on the Thames.

There is moderate protection for shoal-draft boat off the Shennecossett Yacht Club behind Pine Island on the east side of the river entrance, but there are limited supplies. Anchoring here saves making the trip up the river. This small harbor is marked by a prominent water tower of the Coast Guard station on Avery Point. Make your approach through the western passage until you reach the yacht club's dock with a reported 6-foot depth. You can find gas, ice, marine supplies, and spare moorings. W.C. Spicer Boat Livery just beyond the yacht club has gas, water, and ice, but here the water shoals rapidly to 3 feet at m.l.w.

For protection in blows, yachts sometimes go further up the river through a drawbridge into landlocked Shaw Cove on the west side of the Thames. The bridge operates for boat traffic from 5:30 A.M. to 8 P.M. Several coal wharves, however, help to make this "hurricane hole" rather unattractive.

Places of interest in New London are Connecticut College for Women, the United States Submarine Base above the railway bridge, the Coast Guard station, United States Coast Guard Academy, and the Connecticut State Pier. There are several good hotels, of which the Mohican is best known.

It is interesting, from a mooring or slip at Burr's Landing, to see the sleek, gray submarines glide by, to watch fine-looking yachts as they come and go, to share in the conversation and activities at one of the leading ports or rendezvous for cruising men on the New England coast.

Special Note on Tides. The tide runs strongly off the southern end of Bartlett Reef, near New London, and the same is true of Black Point.

The tides are strongest at the easterly end of the sound—especially east of Falkner Island. The tide is almost twice as strong outside Long Shoal —near the Cornfield lighted buoy—as inside the shoal. A correspondent reports finding an ebb tide of from 1½ to 2 knots off Cornfield, and making good time to New London from the Duck Island westerly breakwater by taking the slightly longer outside route. (See special government tide and current book on Long Island Sound tides.) Therefore, should you be riding a fair current along the 6-mile length of Long Sand Shoal and be heading up the sound, stay to the south and gain the extra lift. Bucking the current, however, run north of the shoal, where the velocity is weaker.

CHAPTER V

South Shore of Long Island Sound
Manhasset Bay to Montauk Point

Manhasset Bay and Port Washington, Long Island, N.Y. (223). Manhasset Bay, though large, is one of the best harbors on Long Island Sound. It has deep water everywhere and a good holding bottom, is easy to enter by day or night, and has plenty of good anchorage space with protection from wind or sea. There are practically no tidal currents except at the entrance, and the average rise of tide is about 6 feet.

Few, if any, harbors on the Atlantic coast have as many services and facilities to offer yachtsmen as Manhasset Bay. There are so many yacht clubs—we have counted ten—that we can mention only several of the best-known. Boat yards, marinas, marine supply shops, public and private docks, water-front restaurants greet the mariner whichever way he looks.

One of the two oldest yacht clubs on Long Island Sound, the North Shore Yacht Club, is now housed in a small white building in Manorhaven on the north shore. Organized as the New York Canoe Club in 1871, it has been going ever since and gives visitors a friendly reception, as we know from experience. The two luxurious marinas next to the club, the Capri Marina just to the west and the Riviera Marina to the east, have about everything to offer, including slips and moorings, restaurants, swimming pools, gas, water, electricity, showers, toilets, telephones, and repairs.

Behind Toms Point are several small marinas, but the real display of facilities is at Port Washington, along the eastern shore of Manhasset Bay. Here, from north to south, are three large and well-known yacht clubs: the Knickerbocker Yacht Club (1874), which held the first frostbite race, on January 2, 1932; the Manhasset Bay Yacht Club (1891), which began life on a scow with a piano and a bar and now has luxurious quarters overlooking a swimming pool and the bay; and the Port Washington Yacht Club, furthest south, with a modern clubhouse flanked by a pool with a long pier in front. Manhasset Bay Yacht Club is credited with having helped launch a new type of racing in January 1932—frostbiting. The regatta's first prize, won by Colin Ratsey, was a reported "suitably engraved gallon alcohol tin—empty." All of these clubs are hospitable to yachtsmen from other recognized clubs offering reciprocal privileges. All maintain launch service.

Among the leading boat yards and marine supply houses along the Port Washington shore, from north to south, is McMichael Yacht Yard #5 (just to the east of black can 5). The dock facilities include gas, water, electricity, and telephone. The repair work here is reputed to be among the finest, since their expert foremen have credentials from such top yards as Nevins, Wheeler, and Minneford. Next door is the impressive store of A. and R. Marshall, Inc., which has one of the most complete collections of marine supplies and charts we have seen anywhere. Should one have any money left after a visit here, it is just a few steps to the renowned Louies Shore Restaurant, equipped with its own docks. Peterson's Shipyard is close to the Manhasset Bay Yacht Club, and further to the south between that club and the Port Washington Yacht Club is the Purdy Boat Co., which has been well known for years for building, hauling, and repair. Supplies are conveniently available in many places along the Port Washington water front. Most cruising yachts tie up at one of the marinas, or anchor or moor off one of the Port Washington yacht clubs.

For supplies, one may be able to tie up temporarily at the North Hempstead Town Dock just north of McMichael's. Stores are just a block or so away.

There is little commercial traffic in Manhasset Bay, just swarms of yachts, large and small. The Coast Guard has estimated that there are now about 200,000 small craft plying Long Island Sound each summer, and at certain times one might imagine they have all gathered together in Manhasset Bay. And don't be surprised if you spot two odd-looking barges there on your next trip. One is the *Capn's Galley,* a unique type of sail-in restaurant dishing out shrimp, hamburgers, soft drinks, and ice cream. The other, the Gulfway Marine Service Barge, obviously caters to those skippers who are on the go. Manhasset, at the southern end of the bay, has some interesting old houses, such as the Onderdonk House, considered a fine example of Greek Revival architecture. It also has an active shopping center.

Glen Cove (Hempstead Harbor), Long Island, N.Y. (223). "The old order changeth, yielding place to new." Gone is the glitter from the Glen Cove yachting scene. All that is left to remind one of the famous Station 10 of the New York Yacht Club, once located just inside of the breakwater on the east shore, is a small gray building with wide overhanging eaves. The larger building, once the clubhouse where the "four hundred" of the yachting world were wont to gather, was rafted away in June, 1949, to become a fixture on the grounds of the Marine Historical Association at Mystic Seaport. This was the end of an era at Glen Cove, when palatial yachts belonging to such men as J. Pierpont Morgan and Cornelius Vanderbilt lay moored off Station 10.

Now, the site is called Glen Cove Landing and the anchorage area is known as Glen Cove Harbor. Behind the gas dock, the gray building with the paneled eaves now houses the Glen Cove City Yacht Club. You may find some room at dockside in 6 feet of water, or perhaps the dock master can let you borrow one of the private moorings for overnight. It is pretty isolated here, with added protection from the breakwater rebuilt in 1966. But this is no place to be anchored in a sou'wester! Just to the north lies the beach where Morgan used to take his morning dip after strolling down from his mansion.

Off the dock are many small sailboats and motor cruisers where once the *Corsair* lay. Most of the larger boats we found moored further up the harbor. But the best shelter from northerly winds is off the yacht club's dock behind the breakwater. It is also much cooler there on hot summer nights than it is at the landlocked Glen Cove Marina, described below.

South of Glen Cove Landing, also on the east shore, in Mosquito Cove, is the Hempstead Harbour Club. We hope that the name of the cove is not suggestive, though there are marshes nearby. The dock master says that there is 4 feet at low water at the club dock and that the club offers reciprocal privileges to members of other recognized yacht clubs. There are several guest moorings in deep water, but these are open to the northward for a considerable distance and under some conditions provide an uncomfortable anchorage. The club does not supply gas, but water and ice are obtainable. Another club, the Sea Cliff Yacht Club, is on the south side of the cove. A dredged channel, 75 feet wide with a depth of 8 feet, leads to the club's extended pier. Head almost due south in making your approach. Not only is Sea Cliff an appealing-looking club but its members seem like a spirited group. On our last visit we enjoyed watching their bricklaying party held on the club's front patio. "We have the best bar and the cheapest drinks in Glen Cove," exclaimed one busy member with trowel in hand. Other services, depending upon one's mood or the time of day, include a fine restaurant and regular launch service.

More evidence of the change at Glen Cove is obtained when one glides into the 8-foot channel of Glen Cove Creek. Located to starboard in the first basin right off the channel is the Sea Cove Marina with the usual facilities, including compass overhauling and radiotelephone repair work. Adjacent to Sea Cove is the Glen Cove Yacht Service with gas, berths, and more or less similar service. In the second basin beyond, with a mean depth of 8 feet, one may find the largest facility in Glen Cove—the Glen Cove Marina. This place may well be your best bet for the deepest water in the creek, the snuggest though perhaps the most active anchorage, and the most convenient location to stores, restaurants, and theaters. All these marinas do comparable repair work. In the summer you will not only find the creek extremely sociable but often quite hot.

The southern part of Hempstead Harbor is entered through a dredged, marked channel from the entrance at Bar Beach. The 1971 *Coast Pilot* reports that, "in 1968, the controlling depths were 4 feet to a point opposite South Glenwood Landing thence 4 feet at midchannel to a point opposite the Old Town Wharf."

At the south end of the harbor, on the east shore opposite Bar Beach, is the site of the old Fyfe Shipyard which, from its humble beginnings in 1905, came to be known as the "Tiffany" of boat yards. Here such majestic "gold-platers" as J.P. Morgan's *Corsair* and Marjorie Merriweather Post's *Sea Cloud* came to be fitted out in times gone past. Now it is out of business, perhaps having been too wedded to wood construction in the age of fiberglass. Plans are afoot at the time of writing to turn the historic yard into an arts-and-crafts center, with restaurants, marine facilities, and shops for artisans. Its proposed new name is *Fife and Drum*.

Glen Cove has exchanged much of its former glamor for modern conveniences, suited to the more modest pocketbooks of those who now use its docks and facilities.

An article by Clarence E. ("Ike") Lovejoy in *The New York Times* in the late thirties describes Glen Cove as it used to be and to some extent still is:

> The curious, gingerbread-type of building used by the N. Y. Y. C. has a history of its own. It was part of the original club station provided at Weehawken by John C. Stevens, founder and first commodore. But in 1907 the building was towed from the Hudson, up the East River, through Hell Gate and to Hempstead Harbor to be located on land made available by J.P. Morgan. . . .
>
> South of Glen Cove and the N. Y. Y. C. anchorage plenty of water is available for a night's anchorage off Bar Beach, the curious, narrow sandspit that almost—but not quite—closes the inner harbor. Bar Beach is sandy, just right for a swim, and many a yacht party up for an early Sunday breakfast has seen the congregation of some colored church on the North Shore gather here for a daybreak baptism, the preacher immersing members of his flock while standing waist-deep off the beach and the brethren and sisters singing hymns.

Passing around the point of Bar Beach and in front of Fyfe's ship-yard, yachts of medium draft may run right up to the head of naviga-tion at Roslyn and tie up along public bulkheading for a meal ashore.

Roslyn, which dates from 1636, got its present name in 1844 when William Cullen Bryant and others felt the surrounding country resem-bled Roslyn Castle in Scotland. Hempstead Harbor was first entered in 1640 by immigrants from Lynn, Massachusetts, and the first use of the necks of land now occupied by great estates and summer homes was for the common pasturage of cattle. Settlers worshiped on Sundays in stockades, assembling at the call of kettledrums from the ramparts.

Glen Cove was called Musketo (or Musceta) Cove until 1834. This word really meant to the Indians "cove of grassy flats"; but because it was confused with mosquito, the new name was wisely adopted.

The Long Island Lighting Company buildings dominate the upper harbor, which is less attractive than it is nearer the entrance. A small boat basin is located at Glenwood Landing.

Oyster Bay, Long Island, N.Y. (224). This is an attractive, well-pro-tected bay with several good anchorages. One is off the Seawanhaka Cor-inthian Yacht Club in the cove west of Plum Point, Center Island. This club, organized in 1871, is one of the two oldest yacht clubs still in busi-ness on Long Island Sound, the other being the North Shore Yacht Club of Port Washington. While the surroundings are lovely, the anchorage is inaccessible when supplies are needed, and the tide runs strongly.

"At the time of Seawanhaka's organization, the group who left the han-dling of their yachts to professional skippers and crews, the wealthier members, were in control of the New York Yacht Club. Some of the other group, the Do-it-Yourself exponents, who skippered and sailed their own boats, decided to form a new club in which the principles of amateur or 'Corinthian' racing would prevail." * Apparently, sailing with amateur crews had long been popular in England, but it was the found-ing fathers of this one-hundred-year-old club who are recognized as hav-ing introduced an entirely new system in racing to American yachting.

The Cruising Club of America, which has held many a rendezvous in Oyster Bay, usually anchors either off the south shore of Centre Island or preferably, we think, in the large bight between Cove Neck and the wharf at Oyster Bay.

In 1965 the former shoal area that ran along the southern shore of the harbor from the oyster dock west to the charted dredged canal was re-moved, thereby making the various facilities here accessible to boats of

* From *Long Island Sound,* by Fessenden S. Blanchard (D. Van Nostrand Co., Inc.).

deep draft. The first marina you will reach is Mr. Park Benjamin's Oyster Bay Yacht Service. A very agreeable fellow, he was eager to state that he can provide yachtsmen with gas, water, and ice at dockside, and that his moorings, including launch service, run $3.00 for an overnight stay. He has a good supply of marine hardware and can haul and repair boats up to 40 feet. Practically next door is the Sagamore Yacht Club, in an attractive shingled building that we enjoyed visiting. Inside you will find a restaurant and showers. Only gas and water are available at dockside, and you may have to settle for a mooring if one is available, since slip space is hard to come by anywhere in the harbor. This very tidy club offers reciprocal guest privileges to members of other recognized yacht clubs. The Town of Oyster Bay has further developed its Roosevelt Memorial Park Boat Basin, shown on the chart as just east of a prominent flagpole. Gas may be obtained here but unfortunately the docking facilities are open only to local residents. Supplies can be obtained nearby.

Jakobson's Shipyard, well and favorably known to many Long Island Sound yachtsmen, is located in the cove to the west of the flagpole. Hauling and repairs are available, and gas.

Another good anchorage with less tide than the others and good swimming is at the northerly end of the bay, west of Centre Island; but keep well away from Brickyard (Soper) Point to avoid some outlying rocks. This area has no official name of its own, but the local people often call it Morris Cove. Shoal-draft craft sometimes go through the drawbridge into Mill Neck Creek and anchor there, but the tide is strong at the bridge and the charted soundings unreliable. If curiosity gets the better of you, go in at high water but proceed with care.

Theodore Roosevelt's famous home, Sagamore Hill, is about 1½ miles from Oyster Bay Village. It is now open to the public and well worth a visit, especially by admirers of "T.R."

Cold Spring Harbor, Long Island, N.Y. (224). A hundred years ago Cold Spring Harbor was a whaling port, with a main street on which so many languages were spoken that it was called Bedlam Street. Today, so far as we know, whatever bedlam there is in the vicinity is left behind in the Sand Hole at Lloyd Point, which you pass on your way to one of the prettiest and most foolproof harbors on the sound. It has been vastly improved through recent dredging at the southern end of the channel.

It is almost impossible to get into any trouble in Cold Spring Harbor, at least in your navigating. A conspicuous lighthouse shows you the way in; once past this, there are no obstacles to avoid if you keep a reasonable distance from shore. The water front is private, lovely, and unspoiled. The only place at which gas is available is concealed from the outer harbor behind the Cold Spring Beach peninsula at the southern end of the harbor. A narrow but deep-water channel with well over 10 feet at m.l.w. was dredged in 1966 through the cut between the north end of the peninsula and an island, enabling yachts to tie up at H&M Powles Marine and obtain gas, water, ice, food supplies, repair work, etc., east of the peninsula, close to a main road. Two red cans and a black one mark the narrow channel cut off of Cold Spring Beach.

Further up to port lies the site of The Moorings, a restaurant that burned down in 1968. A good lobster or fish dinner may be savored at Joe's King Neptune nearby. Depths at their docksides show 3 feet at low water, so be wary. Good water, however, can be carried in the channel all the way to the delightful basin at the harbor's head. The Whaler's Cove Yacht Club to port offers only water and electricity at its slips but has become a popular visiting place in recent years. The best water is to be found along the eastern shore. We were advised to rent an overnight mooring from Powles and to stay within the perimeter marked by the mooring floats, since there are mud flats to the west.

The Cold Spring Harbor Beach Club, on the east shore near the head of the harbor, is the only yacht club, though it is also an attractive tennis and beach club. There is at least 9 feet at the dock. In summer, the small basin, protected by a hook of land and a jetty, is filled with small sailboats and dinghies. Here, where there's a fine fleet of Atlantics, we were first introduced to the Laser Class, a new 13-feet-10-inch sleek fun-boat designed by Bruce Kirby and more sophisticated than the Sun-Fish. Visitors from other recognized yacht clubs, we were told, are given reciprocal privileges, and several guest moorings are usually available. The club has put in a new swimming pool and runs a snack bar during the day. While the Huntington Hotel is no longer there, Anchorage Inn, about ½ mile from the club, is said to furnish good accommodations.

Yachts can find good anchorage, except in strong northwesters, almost anywhere in the harbor. The depth is almost uniformly from 15 to 18 feet and the holding ground is good, with room for plenty of scope if necessary. But it is no place to be in nor'westers, as we once found out. In winds from this direction, perhaps the best place to be found is in the bight on Cove Neck opposite Sagamore Hill, Theodore Roosevelt's famous home.

On Cold Spring Harbor's main street its Whaling Museum Society maintains a museum open three days a week during the summer. Here you'll find a fascinating collection of whaling paraphernalia, including a whale boat, old prints, scrimshaw, ship models, whaling irons, and log books. Mr. Leslie Peckham is in charge.

The "Sand Hole" at Lloyd Point, Long Island, N.Y. (224). This popular weekend harbor is inadequately charted, so the description that follows may be helpful to the few people who haven't already been there.

The "Sand Hole," or "Sand Diggers" as it is often called by Long Islanders, was dug out of the low-lying end of Lloyd Point and is not easy to recognize at a distance until perhaps you see some tall spars apparently rising out of the sand. The high land south of the Sand Hole is visible for a long distance. A cluster of dolphins marking the inner channel must be kept to starboard on entering the hole. As there is an often-submerged breakwater projecting to the north of the entrance and a bar to the south, don't enter too "careless-like."

Head into the opening, giving the breakwater to starboard a fair berth but keeping clear of the shoal, which projects a short distance a bit further out on the opposite or port shore. After that, follow the shore to port. It shelves fairly steeply most of the way, but don't get too close. Since the good water is between the sandspit and the aforementioned dolphins, be sure to keep the latter to starboard as you make your final swing into the harbor. Visiting yachts may come there to anchor but their crews are not allowed to land ashore. Don't go too close to the east shore or too far to the north. Rafting-up is forbidden.

The "Sand Hole" is popular among the weekend yachting fraternity of New York City and points east. During July and August it is apt to be crowded with motorboats of every description bearing occupants of both sexes possessed of varying musical abilities and financial resources. If you plan to spend a night there, we'd suggest avoiding midsummer weekends. It is now under the control of the New York State Park Commission and recently became a part of the Caumsett State Park, a 1426-acre tract in the center of Lloyd Neck.

No supplies or facilities of any kind are available nearer than Cold Spring Harbor. When it isn't too crowded, it is a pleasant place to anchor, though the presence of an untouchable beach can be irritating.

Lloyd Harbor, Long Island, N.Y. (224). This excellent anchorage is on the southeast side of Lloyd Neck, just west of the entrance to Huntington Bay. The most popular anchorage is in the northeast corner of the harbor, in sticky mud, behind the sandspit. The holding ground here is good.

In a strong southwesterly, anchorage off the southwest shore of the harbor is to be preferred, though it is lined with private estates.

In a dinghy one can sail westward far up the harbor to the narrow strip of land that separates Lloyd Harbor from Oyster Bay to the west.

This is one of the most isolated anchorages to be found within a similar distance of New York City. The shores are thickly wooded. There are no stores or facilities of any kind, but you can land on the east beach.

Yachtsmen who go ashore and roam over the sandspit will find genuine Texas cactus growing wild, a rarity in these latitudes.

While many more deep-water cruising yachts are to be seen there than in the "Sand Hole," the chief "out" about Lloyd Harbor is its popularity, especially on weekends. But, if you like to visit around or to watch some fine-looking yachts come and go, you will enjoy it there. And if you are from suburban New York you'll undoubtedly see some of your friends.

While under ordinary conditions this is a well-sheltered, landlocked harbor, in strong gales from the eastward at high tide the water from Huntington Bay may sweep in over the narrow point and make it extremely unpleasant. At times like these it is well to run up into Huntington Harbor close by. This is also the place to go for gas or supplies.

We recall the cooling breeze on hot summer evenings wafting down the long western channel that leads to Oyster Bay. Neither can we forget the sound of sailors singing to the crackling of a fire on a chilly autumn night, huddled around the ruins of the point's old light.

In September, 1931, Lloyd Point was the scene of one of the most baffling murder mysteries ever to confront the police of Long Island. Two still unknown pirates boarded a motor cruiser on which were cruising Benjamin Collings with his wife and a five-year-old daughter. Collings was bound and thrown overboard. His battered body was found on the beach a week later. The boat was left drifting off Lloyd Point with no one on board but the five-year-old girl. Mrs. Collings was found the next morning screaming for help in a moored boat in Oyster Bay. The mystery and motive were never solved. Some called it "the perfect crime." *

Huntington, Long Island, N.Y. (224). This is one of the best all-around harbors on Long Island and the most convenient port for gas and other supplies in the Huntington Bay area. Its major drawback is the ever-increasing congestion. The harbor is seemingly one vast fleet of wall-to-wall boats except for the narrow marked channel resembling the exit lane of a modern shopping-center complex. Speed limit in the channel is 5 m.p.h.

In entering, be prepared to find a stiff current in the narrow cut off Wincoma Point. After passing this point keep straight ahead until you have left the flashing green buoy to port. Follow the buoys southward and then east between hundreds of yachts moored on either side of the

---

* An account in some detail of the circumstances of the Collings murder mystery is contained in *Long Island Sound*, by Fessenden S. Blanchard (D. Van Nostrand Co., Inc.).

channel. A less-crowded anchorage, if you can find swinging space, may be found in the cove to starboard after having passed the lighted channel buoy inside the entrance. Around the bend on the south side of the harbor is the Wyncote Yacht Club, where gas, ice, electricity, and slips are available in 6 feet of water. Their minimum charge for dockage is $3.00. Anglers Haven, just to the east, furnishes a few berths and fishing information.

A good plan is to continue up the harbor to the hospitable Huntington Yacht Club. This club, to port just beyond nun 12, has gas, water, and ice, and offers its facilities to yachtsmen from other recognized clubs who offer reciprocal privileges. The clubhouse, built following a fire that destroyed the old one, is a most attractive modern structure, with a dining room that has a fine outlook. A marina and Olympic-size swimming pool were constructed here in 1970. James Gribben, a club official, brought us up-to-date during our last visit. Gas, Diesel fuel, ice, and water are furnished, and electrical outlets are at the thirty-one slips. Charge for dockage is 25¢ per foot, with an $8.00 minimum. There's a night watchman on hand. The club has launch service, and if you're lucky a spare mooring may be available.

Beyond, on the east shore just north of the "Old Town Dock," is the Thomas Knutson Shipbuilding Corp., which builds, hauls, stores, and repairs large yachts. For supplies we suggest that you tie up to the Town Dock for a maximum time limit of twenty minutes while you visit the nearby delicatessen. The Harbor Master can usually be found in a green building close to the dock. Further to the south lies the Ketewomoke Yacht Club, and then comes Augie's Boat Shop (in the southeast corner), with marine supplies and service. Around the corner north of the bridge is the impressive-looking Knutson Marine Center, with a marina and slips (with a $10.00 minimum overnight charge for boats up to 40 feet and $15.00 for those of greater length). This Knutson has electricity, gas, water, ice, showers, telephone, repair service, and hauling. The town-owned Mill Dam Marina just to the west is used just by local residents.

"Isn't it a bit confusing," we asked, "two Knutsons in one harbor?" Then it turned out that they were father and son, and Tillotson, who runs Augie's, is a son-in-in-law. It would seem that if you want to get anything done to your boat in Huntington, it would be a good idea to consult the Knutson family.

Beyond the bridge across the pond some fine concrete ramps and nearby parking space offer encouragement to owners of trailer-borne outboards.

The shores of the harbor are pretty and illustrate what a residential community can do with its water front. If you enjoy seeing a wide variety of boats and crowds of people of all ages having a mad whirl on the water, come to Huntington. The harbor is well protected from sea and wind, and transportation can be obtained to the town of Huntington, 2 or 3 miles away, where there are stores and a railroad station.

At Halesite in Hungtington is a monument to Nathan Hale, the noted American spy, who landed there and was captured by the British in September, 1776. On the monument are the famous words uttered by Captain Hale shortly before he died: "I only regret I have but one life to lose for my country."

Today, much of Huntington's citizenry is up in arms about the harbor's pollution, overcrowding, and too many years of neglect.

In a special article on Huntington by Richard Graf that appeared in the August, 1971, issue of *On the Sound* magazine, we note the following comment:

> "There's been an almost casual approach to the waters over the years," says Davis Haines, the youthful editor and publisher of Huntington's weekly, *The Long Islander,* founded by Walt Whitman. "Each town administration has dealt with harbor problems one at a time, as they've come up. It has all been piecemeal. Now, maybe, they'll have to move. They can't afford not to."

SPECIAL NOTE

Entrance to Northport Bay, Long Island, N.Y. (224). When entering from the west in fair weather, skirt along the row of red nuns off Lloyd Neck. Then steer southward heading just to the left of the nearest tall gray water tower that rises above the houses in the middle of the shore ahead. The flashing buoy off the tip of West Beach marks the turn to Price Bend, Northport, and Duck Island Harbor.

Price Bend, Long Island, N.Y. (224). This anchorage, open to the south for some distance, used to be a favorite rendezvous for the Cruising Club of America in May and October. The entrance between buoys along the shore to the south is easy to follow. In entering, leave can 3 to port and then swing your bow in a wide arc toward the north to avoid the charted shoals. The holding ground is rather poor and in two October rendezvous a number of Cruising Club boats dragged their anchors. The area is no longer completely deserted but there are no stores nearer than Northport. The shore is not very attractive, except for the clean, coarse sand beaches left by dredging operations on the east. These are weed-free and offer good swimming and steep shores even at low tide. This popular sandspit, on which the foundations of an old sand and gravel company may still be seen, is now open to the public under the name of Hobart Beach, established for the town of Huntington. The north and east sides of Price's Bend are private and now all built up, including the entire shoreline between the northern end of the sandspit and the southern end of the Eaton's Neck cove.

Duck Island Harbor, Eaton's Neck, Long Island, N.Y. (224). This harbor should not be confused with Duck Island Roads, 45 miles to the east on the Connecticut shore. This is a remote, unspoiled, seldom-visited, well-protected, but small and shallow anchorage on the northeast side of Northport Bay, open across the bay to the south and southwest. Note that off Winkle Point, Little Neck Point, and Duck Island Bluff, red stakes have been placed in 10 feet of water. Stay outside of these and you'll avoid grounding. In entering, go to a point about 75 feet west of the flashing red buoy off Duck Island Bluff. Then steer for the entrance, curving slightly to the west to avoid a 4-foot spot off the eastern shore. At low tide a lead is desirable.

There is 12 feet at the entrance and 8 feet a little way in, but the water shoals rapidly with a 7-foot tide range. Although the harbor is a haven for water skiers, there is little other traffic, and hence one can safely lie in mid-channel just inside the entrance.

The chief disadvantages of the harbor are difficulty in making a landing at low tide and lack of supplies. Asharoken police boats hound these waters to prevent crews from venturing ashore.

Duck Island is well suited to anyone desiring quiet and good protection.

Another popular anchorage offering shelter in northerlies is behind the bluff rimming the south shore of Duck Island. The water shoals rapidly northward here so anchor well offshore.

Northport, Long Island, N.Y. (224). Like all of the ports on Huntington Bay, this harbor is attractive. Under most conditions the shelter is fairly good, though it can be very rough there in nor'westers. The place to go, if you are a member of a recognized yacht club, is to the Northport Yacht Club, formerly called the Edgewater Yacht Club. This is at the first large pier to which you come, on your port hand, after passing Bluff Point. There you can obtain gas, water, and launch service. The club's swimming pool, bar, and restaurant are most appealing. There's 4 feet of water at the face of the dock where you can tie up for a thirty-minute limit. While guest moorings are not usually available, the dock master may be able to spot an open one for you. The Mariners Inn serves excellent meals next to the club, providing moorage and dockage for guests.

Further south, on the same shore, is the weather-beaten Seymour Boat Shops, with gas and water but no slips, and the Public Dock, with an amber light and a two-hour tie-up limit. There may be space at this dock for a twenty-four hour tie-up in 8 feet, but after 8 P.M., you'll be charged a flat rate of $10.00 for an overnight stay. Looking to the southwest, you will note that a channel, shoaling to 5 feet in spots and marked with block bouys, leads to the protected basin shown due south on the chart. Keep in mid-channel close to these bouys as you make your approach to the most elaborate facility in the harbor—Northport Boatyard & Marina. There's everything here but a restaurant, and even that is not far off. They can repair a compass, a fiberglass hull, sails, any engine, restock your galley, restock your chart library, or haul a 60-footer. Outside, the channel maintains its depth as it circles to the north around and behind the prominent low-lying island.

In 1971, rumors were flying that a new marina may be established in the old sand pit along the northeast shore of Bluff Point.

At Little Neck, or Centerport, across from the town of Northport, is the Centerport Yacht Club. This Neck used to be occupied by the Vanderbilt estate, which had its own private golf course. The tee for the first hole was on the roof of the main building. Now it is the Vanderbilt Museum, open to the public. Seventeen thousand varieties of marine and wildlife are housed there—animals, birds, fishes, shells, shields, daggers, guns—collected from many parts of the world by the adventurous William K. Vanderbilt. There are also bathtubs of solid marble and gold plumbing fixtures, reminiscent of the good old days when millionaires were millionaires and expressed themselves grandly.

Once, ships built in Northport sailed around the world. Now it is a deservedly popular and attractive center of yachting activities.

Eaton's Neck Basin, Long Island, N.Y. (224). The narrow entrance is clearly marked by buoys well south of the tip of the point, and as you make your approach, note that the jetties on either side are underwater from half to flood tide. The channel leads from the buoys northeast, parallel with the shore, into the virtually landlocked pond at the tip of Eaton Point. There is excellent shelter from all winds except south of southwest, and the water in that direction is so shoal as to be likely to break most seas.

The sandspit is subject to changes annually, and at very high water the southern end is submerged. It differs from Lloyd Point in that landing is permitted on the beach, where you'll see clusters of people grouped around tents and fires like so many nomads.

Fairchild Aerial Surveys, Inc.

Eaton Neck, with Northport and Huntington Bays. This air photo, looking southwest, shows, from left to right: the entrance to Duck Island Harbor and anchorage there; the anchorage at Price Bend and entrance to Northport Bay; anchorage at Eaton Point; and, in upper right-hand corner, Huntington River and Lloyd Harbor.

In the channel from the buoys up to an anchorage inside the western shore of the spit there is a range from 10 to 21 feet at low tide. The three entrance buoys make access to this excellent harbor under power an easy matter. The swimming is as good as this section of the sound affords. The water in the lagoon is, at least in early June, much warmer than on the outer beach. A grand place to take the children for a picnic and swim!

The most peaceful anchorage can be found in good water off the dock on the east shore just before you reach nun 8. On our last visit here, we saw a Bristol 29 anchored 100 yards south of this point go hard aground, much to the dismay of its crew. A line squall, packing up to 50-knot winds with stinging rain, later came screaming across the basin, turning it into a seething caldron. But the fleet there rode it out safely in relative protection.

As a refuge during thick weather, however, this cove is impossible for rest and relaxation because of the proximity (only a few yards away) of the Eaton Point fog signal. A new Electronic Remote Control and Communications Center installed here at the Eaton's Neck Coast Guard Station probably marks the beginning of the end of Long Island lighthouse keepers' lonely jobs. This center operates the lights, radio beacons, and fog horns of the following lighthouses: Eaton's Neck, Penfield Reef, Stratford Point, Stratford Shoal, Greens Ledge, and Great Captain's Island. And all with a mere flick of a switch! If the new system works out, similar electronic centers will be installed elsewhere. Looking backward, this station was opened in 1792 by order of President George Washington.

Asharoken Beach Sand Hole, Northport, Long Island, N.Y. (224). At various places on Long Island Sound sand and gravel companies are creating excellent harbors for their tugs and scows. One of the most interesting of these is the sand hole at the eastern end of Asharoken Beach, which rims the easterly shore of Eaton Point. It's identified as Northport Basin on the chart.

Unfortunately, the construction here of the Long Island Lighting Company's huge power plant with its trio of 610-foot stacks and prominent, bare buildings has stripped the harbor of much of its former appeal. And when we were there in 1970, the plant had erected, for transshipment purposes, an elevated mooring platform, with off-lying mooring buoys, marked by a light-and-fog signal on its western end. This is located approximately 1½ miles due north of the basin's entrance.

The entrance can be recognized from the sound by large sand cliffs, private lighted and unlighted buoys, and the tall stack of the power plant located on the basin's east shore. There is at least 12 feet in the channel. Run in parallel to the east jetty, avoiding the dangerous rock at the end of the west jetty to starboard. Once inside, be sure to keep clear of the plant's docks to port, where currents often swirl. Minimum depth throughout the area is 7 feet at m.l.w. Your best anchorage is in the small bight to starboard, well out of the main channel. At the head of the basin lies an old barge reminding one of former visits here when the Metropolitan Sand and Gravel Company used to work the pit.

It is still an intriguing place, much of its old charm lost by the installation of the power plant to meet the needs of an expanding population. The nearest source of supplies is at Northport, about 1½ miles away.

This harbor is the easternmost of a number of harbors on the "North Shore" of Long Island, from Manhasset Bay to the Asharoken Beach Sand Hole. From here eastward, the shore is far less hospitable to cruising men, with Port Jefferson, Mount Sinai, and Mattituck Inlet the only available harbors between the Asharoken Beach Sand Hole and Green port.

Port Jefferson, Long Island, N.Y. (361). Few yachtsmen who have cruised Long Island Sound have failed to visit "Port Jeff," and many of them have stopped there more than once. It is an ideal place for a yacht club cruise to rendezvous. It is large and deep enough for a good-sized fleet; it is completely landlocked; all kinds of supplies are conveniently available, together with good landing docks, railway connections to New York, and ferry connections across the sound to Bridgeport. And— another important point—except for Mount Sinai Harbor, where there are few supplies, it is the last port on the Long Island shore, as you head eastward, until Mattituck is reached 25 miles away. And Mattituck has its limitations, so that for some cruising yachts the nearest good Long Island Harbor is at Greenport, 52 miles away.

In approaching Port Jefferson from any direction, it is wise to keep offshore and watch the chart carefully, as there are outlying rocks and shoals. The entrance is narrow and there is apt to be a strong tidal current in or out. An experienced cruising man warns that:

> Sometimes a really dangerous sea makes up outside and between the jetties on an ebb tide against strong northerly or northwesterly winds. Entering under such conditions is possible, provided proper care is taken, but leaving is attended by risk. I have seen many vessels trying to leave get completely out of control between the jetties in high seas, and strongly recommend that all vessels in harbor during a strong northwester not attempt to leave until the tide floods.

For convenience to docks and supplies the best anchorage is along the eastern shore off the piers, where there is ample protection except in a hard northwester. In that eventuality one can run toward the "Sand

Hole," often called Mt. Misery Cove, just inside the harbor entrance to the east. This is protected perfectly on all sides, but is a long way from supplies. Fessenden Blanchard went in there many years ago on the brigantine *Yankee,* which drew 9 feet. To enter the Sand Hole, make southward for green flashing bell #3, leave it to port, and then head for the bluff rising from the entrance's starboard shore. Follow close along the piers south of the entrance while favoring the starboard shore until about one-third of the way in. Then you can bear off to port, anchoring in the northeastern sector of the Hole under the steep sandbank there. One must be careful in the Hole, however, for it is filling in and offers poor holding ground. Another possibility is to anchor in the lee of the outer beaches and particularly at a spot about 500 yards east of the main channel just south of the sandspit.

Although many boats like to anchor in the lee of Old Field Beach, it is wise to keep well offshore, avoiding the various shoal spots shown on the chart. The bottom here is mud. In southerlies and westerlies, a possible anchorage is off the northeast shore of Strongs Neck if one avoids the 5-foot shoal in the center of the bight. The *Coast Pilot* warns that strangers should not attempt to enter the narrow channel leading westward to Conscience Bay, for treacherous bars and rocks are there. But we are not the only ones who have enjoyed anchoring in the peaceful and pretty gunkhole just beyond the Narrows. Favor the starboard shore going through until you approach a small sandy beach close to the 2-foot mark appearing on the chart. Then swing over to mid-channel and slightly favor the port shore going in. With lovely homes and marshes surrounding us, the only nautical neighbor we had was a 40-foot sloop whose skipper must obviously know his way around these parts.

For those anchoring in the main harbor and wishing to go ashore for supplies or a good meal, the central pier marked "Bayles" in big letters and brilliantly lighted at night is the one to use. It has a gasoline station at its seaward end and provides electricity, water, ice, Diesel fuel, and showers. A fine restaurant, motel and stores are on the main street nearby. The dock, with 7 feet of water, offers twelve slips to accommodate boats up to 65 feet. Ned Bayles, who commands this station, will give you excellent service. In 1966 the Setauket Yacht Club purchased the Bayles property, including a two-story building and existing dock space. Plans for refurbishing the clubhouse and expanding services involve dredging the bulkhead area to provide more berthing space, and offering regular launch service. The Port Jefferson Marina, just to starboard, usually has room for about twenty overnight transients. The attractive brick building of the Port Jefferson Yacht Club on the west side of the harbor has a restaurant, limited dock space and guest moorings, and is accommodating to visiting yachtsmen from other clubs.

The chief trouble with "Port Jeff" is its size, making it far from snug when the wind blows from the wrong direction. And if it is blowing at all, you may find your boat "showered" with the fine rock dust kicked up by the New York Trap Rock's activity at the head of the harbor. Yet it is popular and important to yachtsmen, for it is the last port with complete facilities on the north shore of the island, sailing east, until you reach Greenport.

Setauket, Port Jefferson, Long Island, N.Y. (361). Picturesque Setauket Harbor may be reached by following a dredged 150-foot channel winding west from red nun 2 between Tinkers Point and Strongs Neck. The entrance is easily identified from Port Jefferson Harbor by the high wooded bluff that marks the northeast point on Strongs Neck. Since the harbor is quite shallow and the controlling depth through the channel is about 5 feet, boats of deep draft should not attempt to enter except at high tide and under power. There is a mean range of tide of about 6½ feet, and it is wise to keep in mid-channel away from the mud flats extending from both shores.

Once well past the shoaling at Tinkers Point and heading due south, you will have good water for ½-mile length in mid-channel until you come abeam of the Setauket Harbor Boat Basin down on the port shore. This inner, very narrow channel is poorly marked by buoys or ranges, some of them uncharted and privately maintained. One often has to wend one's way among the congested boats at their private moorings, since they actually mark the deepest water. One may have difficulty in locating sufficient swinging room in which to drop the hook.

Since dredged channels have a way of filling, we'd advise caution and a flooding tide for yachts entering this harbor for the first time. If your boat doesn't draw too much, however, Setauket is worth trying.

Once you get into the deep area south of Strongs Neck you will probably be glad you came. It is much snugger than Port Jeff and attractive. There is a small boat yard on the east shore of the shallow cove to the south, which can be reached only at high tide.

Mount Sinai, Long Island, N.Y. (361). This harbor, about 2½ miles east of Port Jefferson, is recommended for those who like an evening "away from it all," especially if you have a sailing tender or one with an outboard motor for exploring the shallow inner harbor. The channel entrance can be spotted at the easternmost end of a long high bluff running along the northern shore of Mt. Misery Point. Enter carefully midway between the short jetties, which are usually awash at high water. The one to the east normally has a flashing light on it. The dredged channel, in which the current runs up to 2 knots, has a controlling depth of 8 feet. The narrow inlet behind the sandspit to starboard has now, unfortunately, completely filled in.

Mount Sinai Harbor has undergone quite a change in the past few years due to sizable dredging throughout the northern sector of the harbor. Dredging has been completed on a 10-foot-deep channel with a constant width of 1200 feet running eastward all the way from the main entrance channel and passing south of Cedar Beach to the marshes bordering the harbor's eastern shore. Unlighted block buoys maintained by the town of Brookhaven mark this main channel. A possible anchorage, therefore, is anywhere you can find swinging room along the southern side of this dredged trough, but most yachtsmen prefer to anchor along the prominent but small spit just southeast of the harbor's entrance.

In 1964 this harbor was blessed by the establishment of a new yacht club—the Mount Sinai Yacht Club located on the southwestern point of Cedar Beach. It is proudly described by its members as a "working man's" organization, composed of real boating enthusiasts who are truck drivers, doctors, lawyers, businessmen, teachers, lobstermen, and engineers. Warren Wenberg, the club's first commodore, commented that "we bought the old barge that forms the basis of our clubhouse from the Delhart Shipyard on Staten Island for $800. It had been retired by the B & O Railroad." With perspiration and inspiration, the membership hauled it ashore, converted it into a charming clubhouse with a bar, restaurant, and fireplace, and constructed a massive concrete bulkhead out in front. We climbed "aboard" to interview the following club officers who couldn't have been nicer: George Welch, Robert Burns, and Carlo Bondi. When you stop here, you'll find gas, water, ice, perhaps some space dockside, and a few guest moorings.

"Seeing your family doctor tarring the roof alongside a truck driver is one of a hundred examples of the marvelous spirit that has made this club a success," Mr. Wenberg exclaimed. We sensed that same spirit, which we feel certain will be shared by other visiting yachtsmen.

Further up to port lies the Mount Sinai Marina, which, with its 8 floating docks, proves that power boats have at last discovered Mount Sinai. Gas, water, and electricity are all available, but the place is choked with small craft and there are no supplies. A 6-foot rise in tide is reported here.

Davis Island Boat Yard is located on the southwestern shore of the harbor, and Ralph's Fishing Station is across to the east. It is preferable to come into these places at high water. Here you may gather a few supplies,

Mattituck Inlet on the north shore of Long Island looking southward to the town's basin. Great Peconic Bay lies beyond.

but otherwise there are no facilities around for yachtsmen. The balance of the harbor is covered with shoal mud flats and marshes that are often dry at low water. The marshes make it a paradise for mosquitoes. Despite these, Mount Sinai is crowded on weekends, for the place is picturesque and away from the lights and sounds of a town, and the swimming on Cedar Beach is excellent. The land to the west is high, wooded, with many private estates.

A delightful old fisherman with a personality as salty as his looks, who did not give us his name "less the police seek me out," warnéd us to avoid the uncharted rocks that lie ½ mile off Cedar Beach.

Mattituck Inlet, Long Island, N.Y. (363). Several years ago, the federal government designated Mattituck as a "port of refuge," re-dredged the channel, and added further improvements to help make this harbor an outstanding one. It is the only available harbor on the north shore of Long Island between Port Jefferson or Mount Sinai and Greenport, making it particularly important to yachtsmen cruising Long Island Sound. More and more boats are visiting here, since it offers excellent protection should sudden storms or foul weather arise. Once you get inside, the harbor provides absolute shelter and a chance to get supplies conveniently, and it is an interesting place withal.

Mattituck's major drawback is the fact that its entire channel is continually subject to shoaling, requiring intermittent dredging. The 1971 *Coast Pilot* reports that "in March 1969, the controlling depths in the channel to the turning basin, about 1.8 miles above the entrance, were 8½ feet for a midwidth of 50 feet to the first turn in the channel, thence in 1965, 6½ feet for a width of 60 feet to the turning basin and 7 feet in the basin itself." In 1972, however, Harbor Master Tom Reeves advised us that a safer estimate of the channel's depth was 5 feet at m.l.w. throughout. The mean tide range is about 5 feet.

A flashing beacon silhouetted against the prominent tanks of the Mattituck Petroleum Corporation marks the narrow entrance to Mattituck Creek. Entering is difficult should you have a northeast wind and the 3-knot tidal current running against you. Barges use this channel and require deep water at least as far as their docks, which are just inside the entrance on the south side of the first bend in the creek. A channel with a 9-foot depth was dredged to these docks in 1966 and we were assured that this depth would be maintained.

The entrance to Mattituck Inlet is not easy to identify from some distance away, as the breakwaters, though long, are low. The best idea is to pick up black bell 3A and then head for the tower on the starboard or west jetty, which has a flashing white light. The shore is a low point of white sand and pebbles between fairly high hills and cliffs on both sides. A long break in the bluffs marks the inlet. Keep in the middle as you go in, for there are shoals inside of each jetty, especially along the port side just before the first bend.

The Mattituck Park District Marina at the head of the channel has a landing dock a short walk from the center of the village. The basin here lies in quite charming surroundings with an atmosphere one could describe as homey. On a summer weekend, it attracts as many as fifty boats resting at anchor with a dozen more at dockside, where the depths are 6 feet and the charge is 15¢ per foot, including electricity. Tom Reeves, one of the most accommodating and enthusiastic harbor masters we have met, will provide you with ice, water, showers, gas nearby, and, believe it or not, a free drive to town for supplies. Mattituck Laundromat, only a block away on Route 27A, does laundry on one-half-day delivery; no self-service. During our last visit we visited the expanding Matt-A-Mar Marina, run by Frank Nowak on the northeast side of the basin.

Frank thrives on business "progress," partly evidenced by the installation of his marina's Olympic-size swimming pool. Morton Hunt, author of the fine book *The Inland Sea,* called "a sailor's affectionate look at the people and places on Long Island Sound," visited Matt-A-Mar recently and recorded his conversation with Frank in an article appearing in the August 28, 1971, issue of *The New Yorker.* Here are some of the owner's comments:

It's still only the beginning—we'll be building a restaurant and a motel soon, and who knows what else? Most sailboats seem to like to anchor in the middle of the basin, if there's any room. Anyhow, our setup here is designed for the convenience of powerboats.

They're nice people who come here, decent people. They needed this marina, and as fast as I've built it up I keep having to add more space. Before next summer, I'll dredge over there where you see that marsh grass, and put in another twenty slips. Every year, we get bigger. It's been a great thing.

In coming up the creek, you can find a slip at the Naugles Dock a short way up on the starboard side or tie up and obtain gas and ice at the Anchor Inn bulkhead dock. Nearby, Ye Old Mill Inn (moderately expensive and old-world) provides good meals. Just above the bridge, the Mattituck Inlet Marina and Shipyard has a swimming pool, repair work, and the most complete facilities in the harbor.

The anchorage near the bridge, while convenient, is apt to be warmer and less peaceful than further downstream. A genial Mattituck native named Morrison Wines, whose personality is as appealing as his name, pointed out to us that few yachtsmen take advantage of the pleasant anchorages to be found in the several finger inlets running off of the main channel. Venture up these inlets with their 6-foot depths, keeping in mid-channel, and you will be alone and quiet. The first inlet to starboard is perhaps the choicest, but, as are the others, it is unmarked, so avoid the small island located at its entrance. Should you desire a bit more civilization, you can run all the way to the head of the creek where you will find the aforementioned basin. Mattituck claims that it is "the Village that has everything." We quite agree.

Plum Gut Harbor, Long Island, N.Y. (362). This is a scooped-out puddle, nearly landlocked, with about 15 feet in the entrance and harbor, though some shoaling has occurred. Keep midway between the jetties and head for the wharves, where yachts seeking shelter usually lie. Plum Gut Harbor and the island itself are under the supervision of the U.S. Department of Agriculture, which maintains its Animal Disease Laboratory, "the nation's only research center for the study of contagious foreign animal diseases." It may be used only with the permission of the local representative of that department, as suggested in the following tactful reply to our inquiry: "Ferry or government boats use the wharf daily. Harbor would be sought by yachtsmen only as a harbor of refuge."

A correspondent, writing about Potter Cove in Narragansett Bay, says, "The mosquitoes are bad but not as bad as at Plum Island."

It is reported that Plum Island got its name from early explorers who were enchanted by the beach plums growing along the shore. In 1659 the ruling Indian Chief of Long Island sold this island to the first European owner for a coat, a barrel of biscuits, and one hundred fishhooks.

Shelter Island and Shelter Island Sound, Long Island, N.Y. (363). Shelter Island is best known as a delightful summer resort of wooded hills, winding roads, and snug harbors, with a year 'round population of about 1200 and a summer population several times that number. It is a connecting link between the north and south flukes of eastern Long Island. With its five harbors, each providing its own special charm, the island has long been a popular rendezvous for Long Island Sound cruising men.

Though not settled by whites until 1652, Shelter Island, which the Indians called "Ahaquatawamock," had several English owners before then, from whom it successively acquired the names of "Mr. Farrett's Island" and "Mr. Goodyear's Island." In 1651 Mr. Goodyear sold the island for "1,600 pounds of good merchantable Muscavado sugar"—which has been calculated as a valuation of 1¢ an acre, based on the price of sugar at that time. About 150 years ago ships large enough to cross the ocean with a fair-sized cargo were built on Shelter Island, on a tributary of West Neck Creek.

The principal whaling ports on the Atlantic Coast were Provincetown, Nantucket, New Bedford, Fairhaven, New London, and Sag Harbor. Many young men of Shelter Island sailed from the last of these harbors. Whales have been seen or caught between Shelter Island and Greenport.

Eventually Shelter Island became a summer resort, the new era beginning in 1871, when a group of Methodists bought "Prospect" for their camp meetings. A year later a hotel went up. Now sport fishing and summer visitors, or both, are leading industries.

Just before his death in 1929, Samuel H. Groser wrote a poem about Shelter Island, called "My Playland," in which (as illustrated in the second verse) he expressed his "poignant longing":

> For the wonderful view from its headlands,
> For the clear, cool, starry nights,
> For the gorgeous hues of the sunsets,
> And the harbor with myriad lights;
> For the shady roads through the woodlands,
> For the green on the Dering side,
> For Ram Head, and White Hill, and the beaches,
> For the lap of the lazy tide.*

While we found the tide anything but lazy, to the rest of these sentiments we would add a hearty assent.

There are two ferry services to and from Shelter Island: one between Greenport and Dering Harbor on the northwest shore and one from the south shore of the island at Smith Cove to North Haven Peninsula and Sag Harbor.

In discussing the harbors on, or across from, Shelter Island, we'll first go around Shelter Island via Shelter Island Sound in a counterclockwise direction. Those who want to go further, into Great and Little Peconic Bays, will find the harbors on these bays covered in the Peconic Bays Section.

1. Greenport, Long Island, N.Y. (363). This is the leading port in the Shelter Island Sound area from the point of view of boat yards, gas docks, marine hardware, and general facilities of all kinds. But it is by no means the most beautiful, and it is noted more as a fishing headquarters than as

---

* Historical data and verse from *History of Shelter Island*, by Ralph G. Duvall, with a Supplement by Jean L. Schladermundt (Shelter Island Heights Association).

a rendezvous for yacht club fleets, though the Essex Station of the Cruising Club of America has found Stirling Basin, Greenport, a more satisfactory and protected harbor for its annual cruise than Dering.

As you approach the town, the white church spire near the northern end, and the standpipe that shows up over the center, are good landmarks. The flashing red Greenport Harbor Light, on the end of the breakwater off Youngs Point, is the most obvious guide for those entering at night.

While many boats anchor southwest of the breakwater, this anchorage is frequently very uneasy, as the sound is apt to be choppy along here and there is a considerable sweep from the southwest. The best place for the night by far is in Stirling Basin, which has been dredged to a depth of 8 feet. Since the harbor master controls anchoring in the basin, look him up for a mooring. His headquarters are indicated by a sign well up the basin to port. "Sing out for me," he told us, "when you want me. Someone will always be around who knows where I am." A 100-foot-wide channel with about 9-foot depth leads up to the head of the basin. In the western fork is situated the rather swanky Townsend Manor Marina, boasting a hotel and restaurant and offering weary crews a dip into a swimming pool or into a cocktail. Although this place can accommodate boats only up to 45 feet in length, it is sheltered, complete in its service except for repairs and supplies, and fairly close to the center of town.

By far the most impressive marina in Stirling Basin is the Stirling Harbor Shipyard & Marina, identified as a sizable boat basin in the eastern fork. Its manager, Mr. LaGrant Chapman, pointed out to us the facilities, which include a restaurant, laundromat, showers, and the gas dock also providing water and ice. Since there is 10 feet throughout the basin, boats up to 62 feet have been able to put in here. We were also informed that this marina is equipped to perform major repair work.

There are several large shipyards along the Greenport water front between Stirling Basin and the ferry slip. Greenport Yacht and Shipbuilding in this area is well equipped to do all kinds of work. Along the bight west of the ferry slip can be bought gas to suit every taste, as well as Diesel fuel.

Nearby, the town furnishes a wide variety of everything, including marine hardware, charts, and antiques and paintings in a fascinating store run by S. T. Preston & Son. Claudio's Marina at the foot of Main Street has a fine reputation among cruising yachtsmen, due in part to its restaurant specializing in ocean-fresh lobster. Mitchell's Marina & Restaurant to the west has a well-stocked fishing supply store and is convenient to a nearby market. At both these places we were told that, "You don't have to climb into any fancy dress to eat in here." So far as we know, there is no important yacht club on the Greenport water front; the nearest is across Shelter Island Sound at Dering Harbor.

Greenport has direct rail connection with New York City and is a splendid place to meet guests, fit out, leave the boat for a while, or enjoy the boaty atmosphere.

Gull Pond to the northeast between Youngs Point and Cleaves Point is a secure basin for craft drawing 3 feet or less. Although the chart shows a depth of 6 feet between the jetties, only about 3 feet can be carried over an outer bar at low water. The controlling depth throughout most of the pond is 5 feet. Part of this place's charm comes from its snugness, its lack of commercialism, and the attractive appearance of the private homes gathered along the eastern shore. Two creeks running north from the pond have been dredged to good depths for further gunk-holing. The northwest channel leading to a smaller hole is preferable to the one that stretches northward.

2. Dering Harbor, Shelter Island, N.Y. (363). If you want to see a fine-looking collection of sailing yachts, you will find them at Dering Harbor at almost any time during the summer months. They may be on a cruise of the Off Soundings Club, or perhaps on an American Yacht Club rendezvous, a Triton Association fleet, or just a lot of handsome yachts following their own inclinations. The harbor is attractive, and the Shelter Island Yacht Club, on the point to starboard of the entrance, is most hospitable to members of other recognized yacht clubs. The club-house has undergone a complete modernization, with the installation of a restaurant and bar accommodating 210 people.

The only objection to Dering Harbor is that it is very uncomfortable in northwesters. The Essex Station of the Cruising Club of America moved to Stirling Basin at Greenport for that reason. However, the protection is good with winds from all other directions, and we have stayed there many times in complete comfort, usually finding friends among the fleet, savoring the keen enjoyment that comes from watching yachts coming in to find anchorage while we are already well fixed for the night.

In entering, be sure to stay well off the northern tip of Shelter Island Heights, where shoaling to 4 feet has been reported. Depths throughout the harbor are ample, though behind the yacht club hook of land, the chart shows 4 feet, and the area is too small, anyway, to offer protection to many yachts in northwesters. The club offers six guest moorings at a $3.00 overnight charge, with launch service running from 8 A.M. to 1 A.M. on weekends.

Gas, Diesel fuel, water, ice, showers, a short meal, and supplies, including spirits, can be obtained at the head of the harbor by the town docks or at Dering Harbor Marina, located to the north of Chases Creek. The Chequit Inn is not far from Dering Harbor. The Pridwin, located on the northern shore of Jennings Point, best reached by car or by water, has its own beach and dock and serves very good food, besides providing a splendid view of the sound. Greenport is easily reached by ferry, if any of your crew want to see a movie or catch a train to New York. The ferry runs every twenty minutes, with the last trip from Greenport scheduled at 12:30 P.M.

The harbor is named for Thomas Dering, of an ancient Saxon family, who married a Shelter Island girl and took up residence there in 1760, to become a leading citizen. But if you throw a stone into a crowd on Shelter Island, you'll probably hit a Tuthill. And then you may get into trouble, for he'll probably be supervisor of the island.

3. Southold, Long Island, N.Y. (363). In checking our latest charts at the time of writing, we noted that there was 6½ feet at m.l.w. at the channel entrance to Southold, that Jockey Creek carried 6 feet for the most part down the middle, and that Town Creek showed about a foot more of depth all the way to its head. These depths are good for a width of about 75 feet except for the reported shoaling in Town Creek to 4½ feet at low water. The harbor entrance is marked not only by a prominent tower but by bulkheads and sandy beaches to both port and starboard. Uncharted red and black vertical stakes clearly identify the channel, which is rimmed by extremely shoal water. Make your approach from due east and you will not run into trouble. At the docks, just inside to starboard, the depths are not greater than in the channel. Many good-sized motor cruisers were tied up at the slips.

These docks on Founders Landing offer you the deepest water at any marina in Southold and belong to Goldsmith's Boat Shop, Inc., which provides gas, water, electricity, and telephone, besides repairs, hauling, and limited dockage. While you will have plenty of neighbors and little privacy if tied up at the dock, and the surroundings of a boat yard are not usually ideal, this place is well protected. A suitable anchorage may be found up Jockey Creek; or, as we did, run up to the head of Town Creek, which is not only a pleasant spot but extremely convenient to the town and its facilities.

The unpretentious Southold Yacht Club is on the northern tip of Paradise Point.

4. West Neck Harbor, Shelter Island, N.Y. (363). Based on our latest visit here, we have three important words of advice to yachtsmen negotiating the channel's entrance—proceed with caution! Certain natural

Shelter Island, west side. Dering Harbor, West Neck Harbor and Creek (refer to Chart 363).

changes are taking place here and there are no plans for dredging. The tidal current has become swifter and the bar marked on the chart as a 2-foot spot has extended very close to the lighted end of West Neck Point. Fortunately the clean water enables you to sight the shoaling bottom off to starboard as you enter from the southeast. Favor the light on the point, but at the same time don't hug the port shore too closely. Coming into the harbor you will pass by one red privately maintained channel marker, which should be kept close to starboard. Keep the single black marker close to your port.

After passing the inner marker, swing to port and run parallel and fairly close to Shell Beach, making sure to avoid the middle ground to starboard and noting the sign that says "anchor no closer than 400 feet offshore." After you have run along about two-thirds of the length of Shell Beach, swing northwest toward the neck marking the entrance to West Neck Creek. As you pass the neck be sure to give it a wide berth while avoiding the 4-foot spot in mid-channel just beyond. The entrance can be further identified by a flagpole ahead on the port shore and by a large harbor sign, which should be left to starboard. Having passed all of this, keep generally in the middle. The channel into West Neck Bay has been shoaling up in recent years, and our soundings in 1970 showed 6 feet at low water where 10 feet appear on the chart.

While in very hot weather it would probably be cooler in the wide part of the lower harbor or in West Neck Bay at the other end, the snuggest and prettiest anchorages are in West Neck Creek in one of the spots where it widens out. A very good place for dropping your hook is in the bight with 5-foot depth just before West Neck Creek turns to the west into West Neck Bay. Here there is a deeply shelving beach for easy landing and a road leading to a store only ¾ mile away. Further up in West Neck Bay, the best anchorages are either near the docks along the southeastern shore or to the port or starboard of the small point that juts out from the northern shore.

West Neck Harbor is one of the most attractive, unspoiled, and well-protected harbors in the entire Shelter Island-Peconic Bay area. It is unfortunate that the chart depths are so deceptive. With the prevailing tidal difference of about 2½ feet, sailing yachts drawing no more than 5 feet should have no difficulty in entering, except at low tide. Most motor cruisers will have no trouble at any time if they stick to the channel.

Supplies are obtainable at Dering Harbor a mile or so away, but if you want to cook your own clam chowder, join the clam diggers along the inside of the long sandspit.

Everett Tuthill, a long-time native and one-man chamber of commerce for the area, maintains a boat yard on the northeasterly shore of the wide part of West Neck Harbor, where yachts drawing up to 5 feet can be hauled, and gasoline and some marine supplies are available, between 7:30 A.M. and 5 P.M. on weekdays and 8 A.M. to 1 P.M. on Sundays. Privately placed stakes line the small channel to his friendly dock, where there is 3 feet at low water.

5. *Smith Cove, Shelter Island, N.Y. (363).* On southern Shelter Island, this cove offers an attractive anchorage amidst quiet surroundings reminiscent of the Coast of Maine. There is a nice beach under a fairly high bluff, and you will find that deep water runs surprisingly close to the shore. While it is open to the southeast, it is well protected in winds from other directions. A small marina named Shelter Island Marina & Fishing Station is installed on the west shore so that supplies, unobtainable heretofore, can now be secured. They can furnish gas, ice, water, marine supplies, a laundromat, showers, and slip space with electricity. Transportation to town is provided, with a market and motel nearby.

For those boats anchoring in the harbor, no trespassing along private shore-front property is permitted. The ferry to North Haven Peninsula and Sag Harbor runs from Smith Cove.

6. *Majors Harbor, Shelter Island, N.Y. (363).* About a mile southeast of Smith Cove, Majors Harbor provides the same kind of protection in northerly winds and exposure to the south. On entering the harbor from the north, one should keep well to starboard of the rocks lying off Majors Point and shown on the chart. Spread out before you appears a sandy crescent-shaped beach bordered by a colorful tree line and tall grass. The clear, clean water and smooth bottom will tempt your crew to take a swim in perfect solitude, while the romantic appearance of the land calls for a picnic or further adventures along the shore. We were tempted to do so until we noticed signs reading "Beware of dogs. No fishing, hunting or trespassing under penalty of the law."

7. *Sag Harbor, Long Island, N.Y. (363).* This harbor is well protected from all seas by the breakwater, on the western end of which stands a high skeleton tower marked by a flashing white light. There is plenty of room for anchorage behind this breakwater, but the Sag Harbor Yacht Club to the starboard—or west—of the large oil tanks (which don't add to the harbor's beauty) may just have a mooring but no launch service. Here all yachtsmen are welcomed whether or not they are affiliated with any yacht club. There is 10 feet at the outer dock and 6 feet in the slips, where gas, water, Diesel fuel, ice, and electricity are obtainable. There is a moderate charge for overnight dockage, and although there is no club restaurant, food and supplies may be purchased in the center of town nearby. An excellent launching ramp lies in the small inner basin.

From the clubhouse, we observed to the east a large, clear-span boat shed—the newest phenomenon in small boat storage. This place is aptly called Saltair Nursery, a facility of Sag Harbor Yachts, where literally hundreds of small boats can be easily "dry-landed," stacked up piggy-back fashion on racks like so many colorful cords of wood. This system serves a number of unique purposes. It is an answer to the belief that marinas and mooring areas have not been able to keep pace with the number of boats owned by Long Islanders, which is expected to double in the next decade. Indoor storage can usually double the life of a boat, and its owner, using such a "high-and-dry" marina, may use his craft year round by just picking up the phone. The Saltair technique could be the wave of the future.

Do not attempt to go into Sag Harbor after dark; there are too many outlying shoals and unlighted buoys, especially off the eastern shore of North Haven Peninsula. A particularly dangerous spot is Little Gull Island, formed by a cluster of rocks just south of lighted buoy 13. In daylight, the entrance presents no difficulties.

Sag Harbor Yachts is the only marina in the harbor available for sizable sailing craft. It has 8 feet dockside, gas and Diesel fuel, ice, water, slips, full repair work, but no showers.

The channel up into Sag Harbor Cove just west of the main harbor has been dredged to a width of 75 feet and a depth of about 8 feet, and is marked by privately maintained buoys. If you can pass under the fixed bridge with its vertical clearance of 20 feet at mean high water, you will find first to port Whalers Marina, both convenient to the center of town and the only place in the cove that performs engine repairs. Further up to port lies the red dockhouse of Baron's Marina, which carries 8 feet at its outer dock and about 4 feet in the bulkheaded basin. Baron's has the most complete facilities in Sag Harbor, including gas, water, and ice for boats up to 60 feet. For the crew there's a swimming pool, snack bar, laundromat, showers, groceries nearby, a motel, and an expensive-looking restaurant. The minimum rate here is $8.00 up to 32 feet for overnight dockage. The only real drawback at this marina is its lack of repair service.

You may wish to venture further by following the buoyed channel to the west leading you to Long Beach, where there is excellent swimming on the Noyack Bay side. Although it appears from the chart that 7 feet can be carried around Brush Neck, the deepest water has not been marked, and all we saw were a few small powerboats. Check at Baron's before taking this passage. The area up there is pleasantly surrounded by

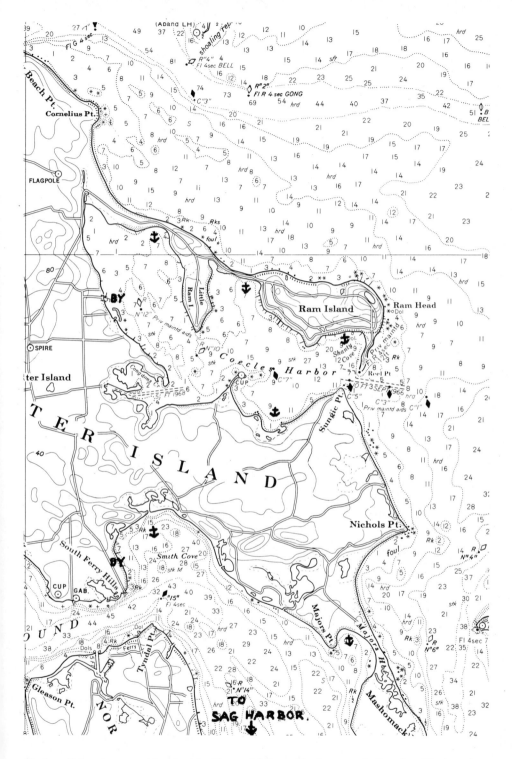

Shelter Island, east side. Smith Cove, Majors Harbor, and Coecles Harbor (refer to Chart 363).

houses tucked along the shore.

In town, a whaling museum is open to the public and some interesting old doorways can be seen. Sag Harbor came to share with New Bedford, Fair Haven, Nantucket, and New London, among a few others, the distinction of being one of America's leading whaling ports. In 1845, it had sixty-three whaling vessels. We were reminded of all this when we suddenly stumbled upon a weathered old keel alongshore the yacht club. Saltair Industries recently gave this 92-foot keel to the Mystic Seaport, where marine historians verified that the timbers belonged to the old whaleship *Thames*. The *Thames* first sailed out of Sag Harbor in 1818, ending her days as a breakwater near Conklin's Point.

8. *Coecles Harbor, Shelter Island, N.Y. (363).* In 1968 this harbor's entrance was dredged to a depth of 10 feet, offering a first-rate place for a large fleet of yachts. Previously, boats drawing anything over 6 feet were lucky to negotiate the channel, which is still tricky but well marked by privately maintained tripods, beacons, and buoys. The best plan is to head in from a point nearly perpendicular to the eastern shore of Ram Island toward black can 1 off Reel Point. Continue following the buoys until you are well beyond the entrance. Then steer dead ahead or make a broad swing to port according to where you want to go and the anchorage that offers the best protection from the prevailing wind. Coecles Harbor is large and unfavorable in northeast winds.

The most popular anchorages are as follows: (1) in the first large bight to the south of the entrance. This is very pretty and more "away from it all" than other anchorages. Be sure to clear can 5 before turning to enter this bight; (2) in the first bight to the north after entering. Here some yachts are moored and there are a number of private docks; (3) in the second or third bights to the north; (4) at the dock or on the moorings of the Shelter Island Boatyard & Marina, a division of Saltair Industries, Inc., on the upper, western shore of the harbor just beyond a small island. Keep the red nuns close to starboard in making your approach. This first-class dock, which is F-shaped, has 6 feet of water at its outer end and room for fifty boats. The manager, Gus Ciacia, showed us that his marina with its Shelter Island Boat Yard offers every necessity and convenience for boat and sailor. There are complete hauling facilities as well as full-time mechanics and carpenters capable of performing any type of repair work. Gas, Diesel fuel, water, ice, and electricity are available at the berths, and you can find showers and a laundromat. Grocery orders taken by the dock attendants before noon will be delivered at your boat in the afternoon. The marina's bus runs to town for sightseeing and dinner on a regular time schedule throughout the day. The overnight minimum charge is $5.00 for boats up to 30 feet and 15¢ for each additional foot. Pumpout facilities have been installed here.

Coecles Harbor is pretty and unspoiled by commercial activities, though too large to be snug, like West Neck Creek, for example. There is comparatively little traffic in the harbor, and particularly in the southern bight just beyond the entrance you may have the place almost to yourself.

Along the neck that connects Ram Island with the rest of Shelter Island are some huge osprey nests, perched on the tops of telegraph poles.

It can be rough at the entrance of Coecles Harbor when the wind blows strongly from often-turbulent Gardiners Bay, so use care in entering. Once inside, you can find protection from any wind by choosing the right bight.

Peconic Bays (Great and Little), Long Island, N.Y. (363)

In discussing the harbors along the two Peconic Bays, we shall again follow a counterclockwise course, as we leave Shelter Island Sound, and enter Little Peconic Bay, heading for Nassau Point. There are still no good harbors on the north shore until this point is rounded. However, those skippers whose boats are shallow draft and who are dying to discover new gunk-holes may want to poke into two dredged creeks located in the extreme northwestern end of Hog Neck Bay. There is about 6 feet of water in the channel leading into and connecting with a number of shorter finger channels inside of Corey Creek, which is shown on the chart as due east of Laughing Waters. And just to the southwest, red privately maintained stakes mark the 7-foot channel running to the tip of Indian Neck and then westward into Richmond Creek. Through all these very narrow channels, one must proceed cautiously while following the markers closely. You won't find any facilities, only enchanting surroundings. Should you decide to anchor for the night in one of the creeks, allow for the effects of current and run up your anchor light.

One of the authors will not soon forget a struggle he once had trying to bring his sloop around high and wooded Nassau Point from Hog Neck Bay, in the face of a rising easterly gale. There is a long and dangerous shoal which we first had to weather. Never did a port look better to us than the tiny private lagoon which we found in the lee of the point.

1. Cutchogue Harbor, Little Peconic Bay (363). Across Cutchogue Harbor, which as a whole is fairly open to winds from southwest to southeast, there is a "barb" of what looks like a Nassau Point "spear." This forms a shelter (known as the Horseshoe) from southerly winds and is often used for this purpose by boats drawing 6 feet or less. There are no landing facilities, except a sand beach, and no supplies. A preferred anchorage is along the inner western shore of the barb.

Nassau Point is hilly and occupied by many attractive estates, several of which have their own lagoons. Channels have been dredged into Haywater and Broadwater coves, to the north, which offer good dinghy sailing. The vicinity is full of creeks and you never can tell where you will find an unexpected harbor.

There is a 2-knot flow and 6-foot depth through the main channel leading to East and Mud creeks running to the northwest and to Haywater and Broadwater coves running to the east. Follow the middle of the channel, keeping the red stakes fairly close to starboard. As you pass the sandspit to starboard, don't cut around it sharply to the east or you'll probably run aground in shallow Haywater Cove. Rather, maintain your original course as you detour around the east shore of the large grassy island located north of the entrance.

Here you'll find yourself in the middle of a waterway labyrinth, but it is an easy matter to run due north, following the red stakes leading into Mud Creek, where we sounded 8 feet all the way up. A prettier passage is promised by following the eastward, staked channel into Broadwater Cove. Favor the port side of this channel to its head in the northwest quadrant of the cove. An anchorage here offers complete seclusion in 5 feet at m.l.w. There are slightly greater depths in the staked channel in East Creek, which unfortunately leads into a tiny, barren mud hole. With the very limited traffic running through these marshy creeks, however, one is fairly free to select the anchorage of his choice—one which will guarantee sufficient swinging room, water under one's keel, and a view that's most pleasing to the eye.

If you do not draw over 4 feet, you can make a delightful stop at Boatmen's Harbor, which has slips and general services and is located off Marsh Point at the starboard entrance to Wickham Creek. We might note here that there is bad shoaling off to port as you make your approach. The staked entrance channel is extremely narrow but deep along its middle. There's 7 feet off the marina's docks, which afford unusual peace and security.

2. New Suffolk, Little Peconic Bay (363). On the point on the west side of the entrance of Cutchogue Harbor is an intriguing little lagoon. It is known as Schoolhouse Creek and shows on the chart as a tiny "slit" in the shore, just north of the streets of New Suffolk. The entrance is close to the south of a battered wooden scow, most of which is submerged at high water, and runs between this scow and a wooden piling. The entrance is further identified by red stakes. Avoid the projecting rocks to port. Don't try it under sail, but if you have power, keep in the middle. The channel frequently fills in and then gets dredged again, so check up on dredging operations. The tide rises about 3½ feet.

Depths in the entrance channel at mean low water were reported as at least 3 to 4 feet when we returned there in 1971. A fisherman had said on our previous visit, "I draw 3½ feet, 4 when I settle down under way. I have never had any trouble getting in or out." Stick to the middle of the channel and you'll have no trouble.

Inside the entrance, the depths remain at 4 feet, and you will find on both sides of two narrow forked channels rows of slips occupied by numerous motorboats, large and small—almost all equipped for taking out fishing parties. It gives perfect protection. George Moore, one of the local fishermen, rode out the 1938 hurricane there in complete security.

In May and June nearly every slip is taken by pleasure boats, for that is the big season for flounder and weakfish. Later there are a few vacant slips. New Suffolk Shipyard, between the forks of the channel where the depth is reported as about 4 feet at its gas dock, has a few slips, is a handy source for supplies, and is well equipped to repair boats up to 40 feet, although it's closed on Mondays. Schoolhouse Creek has much of the atmosphere of a down-East fishing village. Near this basin is the site of the first submarine base in America, where the U.S.S. *Holland,* first submarine commissioned by the U.S. Navy, was based for trials between 1899 and 1905.

Just to the south of the creek entrance are two breakwaters. The one nearest to the end of the point, on the south, belongs to the town. Here's as tiny a basin as you'll find anywhere, but it affords good protection and depth. Run out both bow and stern anchors. A launching ramp can be observed ashore. Between this breakwater and the creek is another small town basin, with more than 10 feet of water, enclosed by a partly submerged breakwater and piles. You can tie up here, get gas, and, nearby, supplies, and be well protected except from strong easterlies. New Suffolk has good eating places and stores, with fishing-party signs and bait on all sides. There is a small marine railway at the breakwater.

3. *Mattituck, Great Peconic Bay* (363). On a heading west toward Mattituck, you will pass through North Race, leaving can 3 to port and nun 4 to starboard to avoid the nasty bar running all the way from this nun northward to the mainland. Readers who are fascinated by the migratory habits of animals might be interested in learning of reports that deer have been spotted crossing North Race on their way to and from Robins Island. Their familiarity with the rules of the road has yet to be determined.

Although there is at present 5 feet at low water at the entrance to James Creek, there is a 3-foot rise in tide, making this inlet a possible harbor of refuge for a small craft caught in foul weather along the northern shore of Great Peconic Bay. The creek entrance can be identified by taking a bearing on the prominent flagpole just west of the entrance or on the lighted sign of the small Mattituck Marina at night. After having left the red-marked private stakes close to starboard outside the creek, favor the port side of the channel once you're past the breakwater. You will experience very little tide rip. When you swing past the first bend to starboard, you will spot the small Mattituck Marina, situated on grassy mud banks but surrounded by some attractive private estates. Mr. Strong, the manager, offered us gas and water and advised us that boats over 30 feet should not enter this inlet because of the lack of turning and anchorage space. The upper end of the narrow channel to the west has been dredged to 5 feet where the red stakes must be kept close aboard. The best way to find a peaceful refuge here is to take a slip at the marina if one is vacant or, if you must, to anchor just beyond the marina where the channel opens up.

4. South Jamesport, Flanders Bay (363). The facilities of the South Jamesport Boat Marina make this small harbor the finest presently available in the entire western part of Great Peconic Bay. Its entrance is just west of Miamogue Point and can be detected at night by a flashing white light set out by the South Jamesport Boat Marina. Approach the channel entrance from the south running between flashing red buoy 4 and black can 5 until you reach three prominent striped stakes, which should be left closely to port. The outer stake is lighted. The channel depth is 5 feet at low water, with a 5-foot rise and fall in tide. The marina's basin further on to starboard has been dredged to a depth of about 5 feet and has accommodated yachts up to 55 feet in length. We enjoyed an evening at this friendly spot, which offers complete repair facilities, supplies, and a chance for a stroll around the nearby summer colony. The Dreamers Cove Restaurant caters to visiting yachtsmen and extends cab service to them. This is a much more practical and attractive stopover than Riverhead to the west.

The Town of Riverhead has recently dredged and bulkheaded a well-protected basin in the lower half of East Creek just ½ mile northeast of Miamogue Point. A lighted red piling stands well off the entrance to the southeast. On our last visit, we lined up with the range reflectors located at the entrance and passed between the two prominent sandspits. Stay in the middle and swing to starboard into the basin, giving the starboard shore fairly good berth. You can anchor here, tie up to the bulkheads surrounding the basin, or run in to the modest Riverhead Town Marina on the eastern shore, where overnight slips are available for $2.00 and up. Gas, water, ice, electricity, and a small store can be found here. This place is appealingly different and provides an excellent launching ramp. There's at least 6 feet of clear water in the basin. Everywhere you look there is sand, which has helped to form an unspoiled swimming beach to the east. We predict that this will become a popular spot.

5. *Aquabogue, Flanders Bay* (363). Proceeding west from lighted buoy 9, near the entrance to the Peconic River, you can pick up the red and black private stakes marking the recently dredged 7-foot channel leading into Meetinghouse Creek. Follow through the stakes, passing close to the light off the point to starboard. Halfway up the creek lie 3 black stakes, which should be kept to port. The narrow channel leads on to the modern, clean-looking Lighthouse Marina resting on the starboard shore. This is the finest overall marina to be found in Flanders Bay. Its manager, Larry Galasso, mentioned its services, which include gas, water, ice, showers, electricity, a laundromat, a minimum charge of $5.00 at the slips, complete repair work with a travelift, a well-stocked marine store, and the Poopdeck Clam Bar and Restaurant. Food supplies may be purchased at a general store located at the head of the creek. Whether you stay at the marina or anchor in the northern end of the channel, as a port of call Meetinghouse Creek is to be much preferred over busy and commercial Riverhead. Boats can even anchor in the newly dredged 7-foot channels off Terrys Creek to the west of Indian Island or up into Reeves Creek to the east, but do so with caution since markers may not be there to guide you.

6. *Riverhead, Flanders Bay* (363). This anchorage is in the Peconic River, on the west side of the large, difficult, and shoal Flanders Bay. Unless you have some strong reason for going to Riverhead, our advice is to skip it. The channel is narrow, commercial, and unattractive. There are several small boat yards. Visiting craft tie up at piles along the shore. Riverhead is a good-sized town.

7. *Red Creek Pond, Great Peconic Bay* (363). Red Creek Pond, lying to the east of Red Cedar Point, has been opened up to permit visits from boats of under 4-foot draft. Simple bush stakes mark the narrow channel, which reportedly in 1971 had a depth of about 5 feet at low water. The pond offers privacy, and except for a few attractive summer houses, it has kept its primordial charm. There are no markers within, so it is wise to anchor in or close to the end of the dredged channel halfway down along the eastern shore. We saw a number of small auxiliary sloops anchored snugly in this area. The pond's bottom is said to be mud.

8. *Shinnecock Canal Basin, Great Peconic Bay* (*363*). If you wish to find shelter for the night in the southern part of Great Peconic Bay and your boat doesn't draw over 4½ feet, go into the basin at the northerly entrance of the Shinnecock Canal. It is just to port as you enter, and you can tie up at the bulkhead, but not for more than seventy-two hours. One must obtain a permit for a longer stay. This basin, which belongs to Suffolk County, has a dock master, water, electricity, showers, and heads, and charges 10¢ per foot for overnight dockage. No swirling from the canal's current is felt here. At the basin's outer edge you'll find a rig to unstep your mast should you desire to proceed south through the canal. A fine swimming beach is located just to the north.

The mile-long canal has been dredged to a controlling depth of 5 feet above the locks and to a depth of 4½ feet below them. In 1966 it was reported that the approach to the mouth of the canal had been dredged to a depth of 10 feet.

Corrigan's Yacht Basin, which apparently caters to sports fishermen, is located on the starboard shore north of the railroad bridge. There is 8 feet of water off the slips. Gas, Diesel fuel, water, electricity, ice, marine supplies, and complete repair service can be found here. The overnight dockage charge is 15¢ a foot. Many of the marinas along the canal have courtesy cars for use in picking up supplies.

Below Corrigan's lies the Shinnecock Yacht Yard & Marina, a division of Saltair Industries, Inc. It boasts a 40-ton hoist and complete and elaborate facilities, including the only laundromat on the canal. Their charge is 25¢ a foot dockside.

If your craft is a power boat with a mast height of under 20 feet and a draft of under 4½ feet, you may go, preferably at high tide, through the Shinnecock Canal, explore the great bays along the outer Long Island shore, and poke your nose out into the Atlantic. We were told that there is some shoaling at the gates just below the first bridge where the current runs about 1½ knots. When the gates are opened to permit the flow to set south through the canal, currents can build up to a nasty 5 knots. There is no difficulty in gaining passage through the gates if one observes their lights and signals three blasts of one's horn.

The Skipper's Motel on the starboard shore below the second bridge can guarantee the whole family a quiet night ashore in attractive surroundings at reasonable prices. Patrons can tie up at the motel's docks in 4 feet of water. Natives of Shinnecock recommend Judge's Sea Food Restaurant near the second bridge as the place to go for the best in meals.

Cold Spring Pond, whose entrance lies a mile east of the canal, is now a possible harbor for boats of 3-foot draft and under. Enter between nun 2 and lighted buoy 1 while heading between the stakes and on a direct line with the center of the entrance's mouth. Be prepared to face a fairly strong current. The main channel inside runs east and then southward into a 4-foot dredged basin that resembles a key on the chart. Skippers should not enter the pond without local knowledge.

9. Sebonac Creek, Southampton, Great Peconic Bay (363). The low-lying entrance to this very appealing creek may be spotted just to the north of the famous National Golf Links of America Course, situated on rolling hills. From lighted buoy 35 approach the channel entrance lined with red and black styrofoam block buoys. The depth at the entrance in 1966 was 9 feet. A white range light rises off the sandy point to port and shortly beyond stands a red-lighted range tower in midstream. Keep this to starboard as you wend your way up the marked creek, which has shoaled to a depth of 5 feet at low water all the way in.

One-half mile in on the port side, the private Bull Head Yacht Club has a first-class dock with 4½ feet at low tide at the end of a road leading to the northeast shore of Bullhead Bay. It provides slips, moorings, fresh water and electricity, and gas, as well as rest rooms and showers housed in a fine new clubhouse. All the docks have been built and maintained by the club's hard-working membership. The best anchorage for deep-draft boats is in 7 feet of water off the northeastern shore of Ram Island facing the club docks. The town dock next to the club has 5 feet at m.l.w., but watch out for a large submerged rock lying 100 feet off its outer end and further marked by a red-and-black buoy. Phone Sid's Market for food supplies.

Bull Head's members say that their neighbor, a New York lawyer named Pincus, has the perfect commute. He flies his seaplane daily from his home on Ram Island to the East River skyport.

This is one of the best ports in the Peconic Bay area, affording excellent protection in easterly winds, a 2½ foot rise and fall in tide, and most scenic surroundings.

10. North Sea Harbor, Little Peconic Bay (363). This is another harbor that looks impossible for all but craft with drafts of under 2 or 3 feet. Yet is is better than it looks. A row of red stakes marks an outlying shoal that runs more or less parallel to the shore. Enter from the easternmost stake, which is lighted, and run west, leaving the stakes fairly close to starboard. But if you go in on a weekend, don't get too close to the port shore, for you may interfere with the casting of some fishermen. Your boat will face a rather fierce current should you try to enter this harbor at ebb tide.

While the outer channel gives a depth of 6½ feet, yachts drawing over 3 feet should not attempt this harbor, especially at low tide.

There is a bulkhead inside to port just beyond a bridge to Conscience Point. Don't go beyond here without local knowledge; there are some unmarked shoals. The small North Sea Marina can be found on the southwestern shore of the harbor, but use caution in getting here, for there are no markers inside. The bottom is soft with good holding ground.

At present, this harbor is much less appealing to us than nearby Wooley Pond, which is to be preferred in almost all respects.

In 1640, colonists from Lynn, Massachusetts, landed on Conscience Point and founded Southampton, the first English settlement in New York State.

11. Wooley Pond, Little Peconic Bay (363). This is a fascinating place on the eastern shore of Little Peconic Bay. A large and sturdy, lighted black beacon and nun 2 show the well-concealed entrance through which the tide rushes fast. Favor the red nun on entering, then try to keep in the middle of the channel while avoiding the visible shoals on either hand, one to port, which you reach first, and then one to starboard just inside. Once past the entrance and its Scylla and Charybdis, you swing sharply to starboard and follow a fairly straight channel into Wooley Pond, favoring the starboard shore and keeping close to that shore all the way around until you reach the unpretentious Little Peconic Yacht Club toward the end of the pond to starboard. There, members of recognized yacht clubs will receive a hospitable welcome.

At the extreme eastern end of the pond at the foot of the marked channel lies the Peconic Marina, with docks in 6 feet of water. There are no moorings, but slips are available as well as gas, water, ice, and supplies; a mechanic is on duty. A bar and restaurant complete the facilities.

In 1971, plans were being made to deepen the channel leading into the pond from 6 feet to 8 feet. This step should open up a very snug and scenic harbor to yachts of considerable draft, provided they stay within the markers and use care in negotiating the challenging entrance when the tide runs strong.

12. Mill Creek, Noyack Bay (363). Beating against a strong westerly on one of our cruises in Noyack Bay, we decided to make a run for protection to Mill Creek Harbor, located on its southern shore. It turned out to be a wise decision, for this well-sheltered harbor, not often used by cruising boats, continues to expand its facilities, and in 1971 dredgers were deepening its channel to 8 feet at low water. A prominent pointed radio tower standing inland is almost due south and on a line with the 100-foot channel. On entering, keep well to starboard of the black can, which marks shoaling water along the built-up sand bar. Keep between the red and black stakes until you make your sharp swing to port outside of the black can and stake located off the end of the spit. After you have rounded the spit, you will pick up ahead to starboard the large building of the Noyac Marina nestled among a string of small private homes. The hospitable owners, Ed Jacobsen and Harry Smith, can supply you with gas, water, ice, and all types of fishing gear and marine equipment, and will point out the location of the general store and Noyac Motel nearby. This marina also specializes in servicing outboards. You can tie up to the bulkhead in about 5 feet of water or pick up an overnight mooring for $3.00 with launch service provided.

Mill Creek, only 4 miles by car and 7 miles by water from Sag Harbor, still strikes us as up-and-coming. The Mill Creek Marina lies at the foot of the road along the southeastern shore of the creek. Docking facilities are here; there's a hoist to haul boats up to 30 feet. Depths are 6 feet at low water here. This is a spot that will offer you delightful snugness amidst pleasant surroundings. Mill Creek is a small fishing center, and only 2 miles away lies Jessup Neck, reputed to be the finest fishing grounds in the area, where blues, weakfish, kings, and porgies abound. This neck is a federal preserve open to landing parties for swimming and exploring.

13. Northwest Harbor, Long Island, N.Y. (363).

Heading east to Three Mile Harbor from Sag Harbor, one passes along Northwest Harbor, whose southern shore is marked by a bluff on Barcelona Point. Just to the east of this point, a navigable channel has been dredged southward through a sandbar into Northwest Creek located to the south of Cedar Point. We made our approach to the entrance almost due south from can 5. Although the channel had a reported depth at the time of 7 feet, be sure to stay in the middle and then favor the starboard shore to avoid some shoaling to port. Having passed through the cut, swing gradually to port and head for the dock front along the southern shore. Don't expect to find any facilities here, just a few small cottages and outboards. There's at least 6 feet in the anchorage area, which is open a bit to the south but otherwise well sheltered. Why we were the only sizable boat there we cannot tell, for this "secret" harbor has a quiet and natural charm hardly duplicated elsewhere on Long Island. Its lovely sandy beach and wetland to the south merely help to "gild the lily."

14. Threemile Harbor, Gardiners Bay (362). This is a first-class protected harbor that is large and deep enough for a whole yacht-club fleet. In approaching its entrance from the west, be sure to keep well off the rocks marked by a red-and-black buoy that lies 1½ miles east of the light on Cedar Point. This area is known locally as Hedges Bank.

The main channel has been dredged to a 150-foot width and to a controlling depth of 10 feet. An unlighted bell buoy lies 800 yards due north of the red-and-black buoys marking the channel entrance. Avoid the shifting bars on either side while picking up the privately maintained light to port and line of block buoys arranged to guide you in. Be very careful not to turn too soon toward the center of the harbor for an anchorage, making sure to pass well beyond the last buoy before swinging to starboard. Prepare to face up to 3-knot currents at the channel's entrance.

Most yachts will want to stop at the well-equipped Maidstone Marina when they spot its staked channel just north of the Maidstone Boat Yard on the eastern shore. These two places are not directly affiliated. An attractive modern building marks the marina's location to port just before the inner end of the channel is reached. There is about 5 feet at low water in an enclosed basin with 125 slips and 400 feet of side dockage. The Off Soundings fleet often uses Maidstone as a port of call. The charge for a slip is $4.50 minimum. Gas, water, ice, and electricity may be obtained at the dock, and for the crew there are showers, a launderette, and good food and drink served in the main building in a modern atmosphere. The Galley Shop sells groceries, and for marine supplies as well as gadgets in many appealing forms you might try the Mariner's Mart. A cookout picnic area and a special "take out" dinner plan complete the wide facilities to be found here. It has been said that "There are larger waves in the Maidstone swimming pool than in its basin in a hurricane." Motor cruisers prefer Maidstone, thereby making it quieter for sailing craft anchored in the main harbor, which is still subject to considerable sweep of wind and a local chop from several directions.

Dick Sage, the Boat Yard's director next door, caters especially to sailing craft. After all, he is an experienced sailing man himself, whose conscientiousness is reflected in his remark, "Any boat I handle here, I treat like my very own." He has slips with electricity behind a protected basin with an 8-foot depth. Launch service will shuttle you back and forth from the twenty moorings lying off the basin. Gas, Diesel fuel, water, ice, showers, a shed for dryland storage, pump-out facilities, marine supplies, and three competent repair men on duty complete his services. There's a special sociability about the place; free newspapers are handed out and the complimentary Sunday breakfast encourages the usual swapping of yarns among the various crews. Young Mr. Sage strikes us as a fellow who really cares—about the future of his harbor, his yard, and his clientele.

Yachts may also proceed up the channel to put into several small marinas along the port shore. The Shagwong Marina basin, faced by a bulkhead, has thirty-three slips in 4½ feet at low water and ample facilities situated in a natural setting. Boats belonging mostly to sports fishermen and local residents stay here. There is more water and space further up at Threemile's oldest marina, Halsey Marina. The trimmed grass lining the docks adds great appeal to this secluded spot. There is 6 feet of water in the channel leading to the cove at the southern end of the harbor, but watch out for the shoaling to port as you enter. The town dock is in the eastern fork of this cove, and to the starboard lies the dock of the Threemile Harbor Boat Yard, where there are slips supplying electricity, fresh water, and perfect shelter from all but the sound of traffic nearby. However, as this isn't one of Long Island's main roads, we doubt if this would be bothersome at night. More dockage space may be found at the East Hampton Marina, reached by entering the other fork to the west. This is one of the few places in the harbor where you can pick up food supplies conveniently. No anchoring is permitted in the cove. The town park adjoining makes the surroundings pleasant but less private than the outer harbor.

Regular seaplane service flying to New York City is now available at Threemile Harbor. If necessary, check with Dick Sage for details. While visiting Threemile, cruising people have become accustomed to picking up supplies of native clams and shellfish at Howard Lobster pound, located on the harbor's eastern shore, just below its entrance.

15. *Acabonack Harbor, Napeague Bay* (362). On our previous visit the late Captain H.R. Miller of the Devon Yacht Club had given us a guided tour of this important harbor, opened up in 1959 for cruising craft. It is the only harbor of refuge between Threemile Harbor and Montauk. The southern tip of Cape Gardner, forming a breakwater to the harbor, has been completely filled in to the mainland and a new channel cut through it due west of red nun 8. Run west from this buoy until you are able to pick out the channel cutting through the shoreline. Favor the starboard point going in, for a bar stretches out toward the channel from the southern point. Privately maintained buoys mark the channel entrance as well as the three branch channels inside. A light is affixed to the black can kept to port on entering. The channel was dredged to a depth of 4 feet at low water in 1971, but this figure is not too reliable, with the swift current tending to build up shoals at the entrance. Depths in the branch channels are 7 feet. A possible anchorage is at the end of the channel and to the southeast of the first island you meet coming in and marked on the chart. Or you can run to port or starboard for about 400 yards, hugging the western shore of Cape Gardner, and anchor in 6 feet of water. The harbor bottom is clay.

As yet there are no facilities here, but this adds to the place's natural charm. Captain Miller, as a former president of the East Hampton Baymen's Association, a conservationist group, was largely responsible for developing, yet not spoiling, this rustic area, which has few homes, picturesque marshes, and beaches lined with multicolored shells.

The friendly Devon Yacht Club, offering reciprocal guest privileges to members of other recognized yacht clubs, lies 2 miles to the southeast with 7 feet at its dock. There is good holding ground here. An exclusive restaurant is in the main clubhouse. Just to the east a wooden breakwater marks the starboard side of a 50-foot-wide, 7-foot-deep channel leading to a dredged basin with similar depth and a twenty-seven-boat capacity. This is the Devon Marina, belonging to the yacht club. Captain Blackmore, a retired New York City police captain, described the marina as supplying gas, Diesel fuel, ice, water, and electricity at the slips, where there is a flat charge of $10.00 along the basin's south side and $15.00 along its north side. Included in the dockage fee is use of the bathhouse and showers. Captain Blackmore can arrange to obtain supplies for you from Easthampton. The northeast section of the basin can be rough in storms but is still better than being at anchor outside, where a boat may become fully exposed to easterlies sweeping across the bay.

The Devon Yacht Club was founded in 1917, under the name of the Gardiner's Bay Boat Club, by a group of summer residents largely from Cincinnati.

Little may one realize that Gardiners Island, perched in the bay about 4 miles north of the Devon Yacht Club, boasts the longest ownership by a continued dynasty of any piece of land in the United States. Purchased in 1639 by Lion Gardiner from the Montauk Indians for a blanket, some trinkets, a very large dog, and a bottle of rum, it is now preserved as a naturalist's paradise by the sixteenth Lord of the Manor, Robert David Lion Gardiner. Deer and wild turkeys roam the island underbrush, hundreds of different bird species make it their home, and as many as 150 majestic ospreys nest here regularly from March to September.

Such an intriguing place may tempt you to pay a visit ashore, but don't try unless you happen to be a Gardiner—just listen to an anecdote that Mitchel Levitas spun in *The New York Times.*

Among the uninvited visitors shooed off a few years ago were several brothers Rockefeller. Jock Mackay, who has worked and lived on the island since he left Scotland in 1929, spotted the group disembarking from a boat. When he asked them to leave, recalls Mackay, the visitors identified themselves, adding that they were friends of the absent proprietor. Mackay was not moved. "I'm sorry," he said, "I don't care if your Astorbilts, you'll have to go."

A few years ago, Robert Gardiner decided to open the island on a limited basis to visitors because of his interest in helping build the scholarship trust fund of Southampton College of Long Island University. The price of a tour during the summer of 1971 was reportedly $110 per person. Lucky visitors can now observe such historic landmarks as the 1795 windmill, which still contains its original machinery; Whale Hill, commanding a view of Block Island Sound; the virgin-oak Bostwick Forest with its aged trees, many of them pre-Columbian; and the site of Captain Kidd's treasure, buried and recovered in 1699.

Approximately 3 miles east-northeast of Gardiners Island, the U.S. Navy has established a restricted anchorage area for the exclusive use of its submarines operating out of New London. It is shown on the chart as a ¾ x 2-mile rectangle. Regulations state that no vessel or person may approach or remain within 500 yards of a U.S. Navy submarine anchored in this area.

16. Napeague Harbor (362). For use by cruising men, this harbor located southeast of Gardiners Island has a number of strikes against it. Its entrance channels are unmarked, narrow, and tend to silt, and the harbor is shoal for the most part—too large to be snug. Since this port is also being used for oyster farming, local residents frown on the appearance of cruising yachts here where no facilities exist.

There are two reasons for our mentioning Napeague: It can be a possible refuge in northeasterly weather when the local bays are kicking up. Also, the entrance channels north and south of Hicks Island were dredged to tolerable depths in 1967.

Enter cautiously through the northerly channel, which at the time of writing gave a depth of 10 feet at m.l.w. Favor the eastern shore all the way in, having posted a bow lookout. Don't be tempted to head over to any moorings to the west but select an anchorage fairly close along the eastern shoreline, avoiding the three charted rocks. The low-lying dunes will not give you much protection in winds from any direction, but, once here, you may find that you've escaped the "graybeards" sweeping across from Block Island Sound.

17. Montauk (Great Pond) (362). This is primarily a great sport fishing port that caters more to fishermen than to cruising yachtsmen. But dredgings and newly constructed facilities have improved this harbor. The strong harbor currents and poor holding ground, however, still exist. In 1969, the controlling depth in the channel was 12 feet to the boat basin northwest of Star Island with a 10-foot depth reported in the basin itself. You can carry 12 feet also to the yacht basin east of the island. The channels are marked by privately maintained seasonal buoys. We were told by a Coast Guard duty officer at his station on Star Island that some yachtsmen entering the channel at night overlook the fact that the bell buoy just north of the jetties is unlighted, resulting in some near collisions.

In coming in, most water is to the west, and as you get to the southerly end of the jetties, swing away from the day beacon and over slightly to port to the channel center where there is plenty of water. Leading off to starboard just inside the jetties, a narrow 6-foot-deep marked channel runs along some small-boat marinas. Only a small area off the docks to starboard has deep water, with about 10 feet; and this is near the channel through which the 2½-knot tide sweeps. In the small bight on the western shore, facing the Coast Guard station, lies the Montauk Marine Basin with pump-out facilities, reputed to provide about the best all-round repair service. The major problem here is the congestion. Boats of under 5-feet draft can proceed from this basin southward in a recently dredged and buoyed channel running along the western shore of Star Island. Sports fishermen will find good refuge and service at Cove Marina, located to starboard at the end of this channel. Gas, ice, water, electricity at the slips, marine and fishing supplies, an ice locker for fish storage, groceries, and a fine machine shop are all here.

"Montauk is not a good place to spend the night riding at anchor," says the commodore of a leading Long Island Sound Yacht Club, who brought his sloop in there a few years ago. "The currents swirl all over the place, causing anchored yachts to swing every which way." This report is still true, but with the advent of some outstanding marinas affording boats good protection dockside, many yachtsmen prefer to tie up, keeping their anchors stowed away. Furthermore, the latest chart shows changes in hydrography from a 1971 survey by the National Ocean Survey all of which reflect improved depths for a roomier anchorage in Lake Montauk than heretofore.

From the Coast Guard station to starboard there is ample water to the Sea and Sky Portel channel, which is ⅜ mile S S E further into the harbor along its shore to port. It has been dredged to 6 feet at m.l.w. and is well marked by a row of pilings along its northern face and a bulkhead opposite. This is a modern and unique marina run by a delightful manager, Henry Mund, and serving travelers of land, sea, and air. Located on the eastern shore, the docks can accommodate twenty-four boats at an individual charge of $5.00 for overnight. The very complete facilities include water, ice, gas, electricity, a laundromat, food supplies, and air and car rental service, sailboat rentals, and the marina even arranges for horseback riding. Rooms are available and the Flying Fish Restaurant serves a good meal. The Montauk Airport is nearby but we were told by visiting yachtsmen there that they had not been disturbed by any droning aircraft during the night.

The old Montauk Yacht Club dock is directly across the harbor on the eastern shore of Star Island and is shown on the chart. Here there is plenty of water, as there is at the long town dock beyond, which was formerly in the hands of the Navy. We don't know the reasons for the demise of this beautiful club, which used to house an impressive bar and elegant restaurant. Rumor has it that the land will be used for luxury homes. One can find a fair anchorage off its docks but not southeastward. Looking to the north, one cannot help but be impressed by the titivated appearance of the Deep Sea Marina. This is a fisherman's haven, organized by the Deep Sea Club, which extends excellent service and welcomes visiting yachtsmen to its facilities, which include a bar and restaurant, showers, gas, Diesel fuel, ice, water, showers dockside, and slips in 12 feet of water, at a rate of $7.00 for boats under 30 feet and $7.50 for those 30 to 50 feet overall, including electricity for an overnight stay. There is no repair work. Manager Bob Derenberg, who has been most helpful in bringing us up-to-date on Montauk, advised that Herb's Market and White's Liquor Store will deliver supplies dockside.

If you plan to proceed to the southern part of Lake Montauk, go between the three sets of red-and-black privately maintained buoys marking the deep water. You can swing over to port into 8-foot depths only after having passed the last black can 7. A pier shown on the chart as jutting out from the shoreline southwest of Prospect Hill designates the location of the Captains Marina and Inn, one of the most unusual-looking boatels we have ever seen. It is further identified by a prominent control tower. We felt like millionaires as we approached this beautiful Norman villa recently converted from a private estate into an ego-building haven for yachtsmen. The Captain's Table Restaurant here is recommended and, as at the Deep Sea Marina, major credit cards are honored. There is 7 feet of water at the slips, with much more in the salt-water swimming pool, and about all else you could wish, save mundane repair service, hardly appropriate in such heavenly surroundings.

Taxis to the village of Montauk may be obtained by telephoning 668-

5232. There are several good sea-food restaurants at Fort Pond Bay to the west, where many fishermen moor, though it is wide open from north to west.

In its early days, as the original Montauk Indians passed from the scene, Montauk became one of America's first cattle- and sheep-ranching areas, then a whaling center, and finally a commercial fishing port near the turn of the century. Its year-round population is about 3000, which rises to about 18,000 during the summer season. It is now very much on the move toward progress.

Montauk Manor, built in the 1920s, closed in 1964 but is now being converted into a condominium. Gosman's Dock has bloomed into a clean, colorful, and charming group of boutiques and restaurants near the fishing docks. Much of Montauk's past is equally colorful.

The Star Island Casino, now the site of the Deep Sea Marina, housed illegal gambling throughout the 1920s, and well into the 1930s, when the law finally put it out of business. It was here that Mayor Jimmy Walker of New York was "pinched" in a police raid. He hung a white towel over his arm, posed briefly as a waiter, and finally fled barefoot down the dock to the sanctuary of the nearby yacht club.

One of the most tragic boating accidents in recent years off Montauk was the capsizing of the fishing boat *Pelican* on September 1, 1952. Of the sixty-four persons aboard, forty-five lost their lives.

Montauk is the last harbor to the eastward on Long Island and thus a good "jumping-off place" for Block Island, about 18 miles away, and points east. Its famous lighthouse, constructed in 1796 by order of President George Washington, is an octagonal stone tower 108 feet high, with the light 168 feet above sea level. Henry Baker was its keeper during the first quarter of the nineteenth century. His pay was $333.33 a year.

Now this old landmark is in danger of toppling into the sea below. It stood 297 feet away from the cliff when first erected but nature's inexorable erosion has brought the edge to within only 49 feet. The Coast Guard gives the lighthouse a maximum life expectancy of two more decades.

Robert Moses, former chairman of the State Council of Parks, is reported to have said: "Everyone who loves water, wind, sky, and distance, and is not chilled by bleakness, must love Montauk." *

* From *New York*—American Guide Series (Oxford University Press).

CHAPTER VI

Fishers Island to Buzzards Bay, Including Narragansett Bay

Fishers Island, N. Y. (358).

SPECIAL NOTE ON FISHERS ISLAND SOUND

All wise yachtsmen use the current whenever possible when going east or west along the shore. For that reason it is well to remember that the velocity of the currents through the Race is twice as great as through Fishers Island Sound. It may be preferable, therefore, in heading east or west, to work your way through Watch Hill Passage. Note here that in strong easterlies and westerlies cans 3 and 5 are often swept nearly underwater at times of maximum flow, although the currents in this passage run considerably weaker than at the Race. The government publication *Tidal Current Charts, Block Island Sound and Eastern Long Island Sound Including the Thames and Connecticut Rivers,* available at $1.00 at all National Ocean Survey sales agents or from the National Ocean Survey, Distribution Division (C44), Washington, D.C. 20235, shows the direction and strength of currents each hour. The 1971 revision of this portfolio is extremely useful in these waters. There have been many navigational-aid changes recently along this section of the coast, so it is necessary for yachtsmen to refer to the latest charts.

There are often fluky winds and "soft spots" off New London Harbor and west of Dumpling Island. There is an eddy on the flood, and little current, close under the west end of Fishers Island.

1. Silver Eel Pond, Fishers Island (358). This tiny harbor is no longer reserved solely for Government use. Steamers from New London dock there, instead of in West Harbor as formerly, and use a dock on the west shore. However, there is usually room for a few yachts to tie up. While the protection is very good, no gas or supplies were available when we last went in, and the place is uninviting, with Government buildings all around and cars going to and from the steamers. The entrance between the lighted docks is not easy to negotiate in westerly winds and one should be on the lookout for reported pilings that have washed into the channel. Silver Eel Pond is valuable chiefly as a convenient and safe harbor of refuge, or as a take-off point for the Race.

2. Hay Harbor, Fishers Island (358). This harbor makes a quiet mooring for motor cruisers from 34-footers down. The channel is narrow and difficult without local knowledge and not recommended for keel boats. We poked in here in a boat drawing 3 feet and experienced little difficulty, having posted a bow watch. A local authority says that with the aid of local stakes 4 feet can be taken inside, though how this is done at low water is not evident on Chart 358. Once inside, there is good water in the western part of the harbor and a dock.

The children on the island have much of their fun around Hay Harbor.

3. West Harbor, Fishers Island (358). Among cruising yachtsmen this is by far the most popular harbor on Fishers Island, and deservedly so. It is easy to enter, provided you watch the shoal to starboard, well protected except from the northeast, has good holding ground, and is altogether delightful. Although the channel has been dredged to a depth of 12 feet at the time of writing, we were told not to hug nun 14 too closely to starboard. And deep-draft boats should be especially wary of the 5-foot spot just beyond this nun that marks the end of the dredging.

Steamers from New London no longer use West Harbor, though the steamer dock is still available for tying up. Steamers now run between New London and Silver Eel Pond, as already pointed out. Gas and Diesel fuel are available in West Harbor at the West End Land Co. dock just beyond the old steamboat wharf, where slips are sometimes to be had. The Fishers Island Yacht Club, in a small white clubhouse beyond the gas dock to starboard, is hospitable to visiting yachtsmen from other recognized clubs. Water and ice can be obtained at the club and there is launch service. Sometimes the club has spare moorings available, or possibly dockage space.

In 1971, a channel leading into the shallow inner basins at the southern end of the harbor was dredged primarily for local commercial use to a width of 100 feet and controlled depth of 8 feet.

While West Harbor is open for a considerable distance to the northeast, some protection for a few of the smaller yachts can be found behind the Mobilgas dock wall or at the yacht club's inner slips. Shoal-draft motor cruisers can obtain complete shelter from all winds in the cove at the south end of the harbor.

The nearest stores are not in the main shopping center, which is a good walk away from the docks, but alongshore to the right on landing. Follow the shore road for less than ½ mile and you will find a good food store. A drug store (with New York papers) and other stores are reached by following the main road and making two left turns. A popular spot where boating people can eat, drink, and be merry is the old Pequot Inn just a short walk from the yacht club.

West Harbor is typically high-class residential, with many fine yachts permanently moored there in summer. There is plenty to do ashore, but, as in similar communities, some things may be expensive. The swimming is very good.

4. East Harbor, Fishers Island (358). There is considerable foul ground in East Harbor, but it is well marked with buoys. A good guide on entering is the prominent former Coast Guard station near South Beach which is now privately owned. The long private Fishers Island Club pier is the first one you will see to starboard. We found shoal water right off both of these docks. An excellent 18-hole golf course borders on East Harbor. The harbor is exposed to winds from northeast to northwest, but the holding ground is fairly good.

Noank, Conn. (358). This village, on the west bank of the Mystic River, has docks along the water front, with plenty of deep water. But don't get too close to nuns 8 or 10. The well-kept Noank Shipyard, located behind a protected bulkhead on the port shore just above nun 8, offers as complete service as you'll find along the river. Its overnight charge at a slip is about $4.50, and a store for supplies is nearby. A great asset of Noank is the famous Skipper's Dock, to which visitors come from miles around. Besides serving excellent food, the Dock allows guests to use its pier, which in 1971 was showing the signs of old age. The Dock allows yachts to tie up there overnight, if is room. "The steaks are terrific," said a yachtsman who stopped there for a meal. Don't worry about any need for formal attire, since the management "welcomes crews right off the decks." Mrs. A.M. Haring at the Gulf Marine Service, a short distance downriver from the Skippers Dock, sells charts and is a good source for local information. In ordinary summer weather Noank is O.K. for overnight, but it is very exposed to winds from the northeast to southeast, and is close to the much-used channel to Mystic Seaport, thus a victim to the wash of many passing boats.

Mason Island, Conn. (358). Progress has recently come to Mason Island, so far as facilities for yachtsmen are concerned. On the west shore of

Mason Island, opposite black can 23, is a fine, classy, modern marina, the Mystic River Marina, with 6 feet in the slips at low water and a reported 10 or 12 feet at the end of the gas dock. Here, besides gas and Diesel fuel, are available many slips, water, ice, electricity, showers, toilets, telephone, a laundromat, marine store, swimming pool, restaurant, a mechanic on duty, and a twenty-ton travelift.

A large packing space is an encouragement to amphibious cruisers. A glassed-in building with a long sloping roof offers an opportunity for lounging. Minimum charge for overnight dockage, we were told, is $3.00.

On the other side of the island, with less luxury and more privacy, there is an anchorage between Mason and Dodges islands off the flagstaff of the Mason Island Yacht Club, which has a pier on the east shore of Mason Island just north of Baker Island. Visiting yachtsmen from other recognized yacht clubs are welcomed at this attractive club, located on the private property of the Mason Island Company.

Ten feet can be carried 100 yards north of the flagstaff. There is excellent holding ground and plenty of room to swing, but the place is not good in a blow, as it is open to the south and has a long sweep to the north also. In northerlies, better protection can be obtained by running around Baker Island into the bight between there and Mason Point.

In entering the upper anchorage area along Mason Island's eastern shore, leave nun 6 well to starboard to avoid the rocks on the northwest. The anchorage is attractive and private.

Mystic, Conn. (358). Entering the Mystic River you see the picturesque village of Noank to port, where a floodlit church spire is a beacon after dark, and off your starboard quarter, Masons Island and the Mystic River Marina. The course is nearly due north to Mystic, at the upper end of which is the Marine Historical Association's far-famed maritime museum, Mystic Seaport. A near-perfect shelter for visiting yachtsmen amid attractive surroundings, aesthetic as well as history-laden, is offered here.

The Mystic River—Mistick, which means "great tidal river," as the Indians named it—is as fascinating in history as it is in actuality. Undoubtedly to know a little about these shores will help alleviate the sometimes frustrating delay caused by the yachtsman's necessary adherence to the two bridge schedules he must encounter.

The Penn Central railroad bridge has a flexible schedule, governed, of course, by the flow of traffic over its rails. If a train is approaching, you must wait in the river until it passes. While waiting, look just beyond the bridge to the left of the rocky promontory partially covered by foliage with a few old houses strewn about its base. This was Fort Rachel, where in 1814 a hardy band of local people successfully manned an artillery bat-

Aerial view of The Marine Historical Association's nineteenth-century maritime museum, Mystic Seaport, Mystic, Connecticut. Route I-95 is seen in background.

tery and soundly repulsed the British, who were bent to the task of the assault and sack of the town.

Concerning your passage upriver, we add the following words of caution. The speed limit throughout the river is 6 miles per hour; this limit is posted and enforced. The average river channel depth at mean low water is about 12 feet. However, there is serious shoaling in many spots, especially at the channel turns. So beware of the pitfalls of the Mystic River channel!

Once through the railroad draw, you may again have to wait, this time for the highway bridge in downtown Mystic, which has a most precise schedule: one opening each hour at fifteen minutes past the hour, from 8:15 A.M. through 7:15 P.M. At other times the bridge will open at the yachtsman's signal—one long and two short blasts of a horn or whistle. Be sure to watch this unique bridge in action. It is called a *bascule* bridge, which in French means *seesaw*.

Now look along the western bank of the river. There on Gravel Street are handsome houses built a hundred years ago or more. These were homes of some of the more affluent in the area: shipowners and builders, sea captains and merchants. On the eastern bank of the river you will soon see a large red building and a lift dock, which are part of the new Ships' Preservation Facility at Mystic Seaport, and which mark the south end of the museum grounds.

Advance reservations *must* be made for all visits to Mystic Seaport. These may be arranged by writing, or by telephoning Area Code 203-536-2631 and asking for the Harbor Master.

When you arrive at the Seaport you will be met, at least between 9:00 A.M. and 6:30 P.M., by a dock attendant. He will assist in your berthing, register you, and generally be at your service. He will deliver various folders that will help orient you, explain the museum exhibits, and answer questions relative to the shower and laundry facilities at the New York Yacht Club Station 10 Annex. He will also point the way to the Galley, the delightful Seamen's Inne, and the Seaport Stores. At the dock houses adjacent to the wharves, you will find weather information, tide tables, a list of local boat yards, and the taxi number. It is handy also to know that food markets and spirit shops are within easy walking distance of the Seaport.

Family members and those holding higher classifications of membership in the Marine Historical Association are not required to pay dockage fees for the first twenty-four hours of their visit. However, if a second night's stay is involved, the customary fee of 15¢ per foot of overall length is levied. Permission for longer visits may be granted only through the office of the director. All non-members of the association who arrive by boat (except professional crew members) must pay the regular admission charges to the Seaport grounds. All fees for dockage and admission should be paid to the dock attendant upon arrival.

Frankly, you, your family and guests will need at least one full day to see Mystic Seaport properly. Go aboard the tall ships for a keener flavor of their meaning, study the Mystic River Diorama to waft yourself back properly a hundred years to Mystic's formative days, and allow plenty of time to see the formal maritime exhibits and to observe the craft shops in action. Also share the pride and fun of the Mariners on the *Conrad* or sailing in the harbor. These young people are in residence training as part of the Seaport-sponsored educational program based on the *Joseph Conrad,* nineteenth-century training ship.

During the summer the Seaport Planetarium offers special programs for visiting yachtsmen and their guests. The *Yachtsmen's Special,* four evenings a week at 9:45 P.M., is an hour-long program of special interest to navigators. On Wednesdays at 8:30 P.M. the *Family Special* presentation in the planetarium is followed, weather permitting, by outdoor observing through telescopes.

So, by all means, head for Mystic Seaport, take heed of their cheery "Welcome Aboard," and linger a while to relax and to absorb a host of exciting activities and memories.

Stonington, Conn. (358). Stonington makes an excellent stopping place. It is well protected, except during hurricane tides, by three breakwaters, the east one 2000-feet long. In winds from south to northwest, or in no winds at all, the prettiest, quietest, and cleanest anchorage, though the least convenient for landing or supplies, is behind the second breakwater—the long one to port off the west shore. In northwesters you can carry 9 feet close to the west shore. In southwest winds, anchorage in the angle of the breakwater is to be preferred. In northerly or easterly winds good shelter can be obtained either behind the small breakwater on the east shore or in the special anchorage area well up the harbor. This last anchorage is good under ordinary conditions. The only "out" about this area is the noise from the passing trains on the main shore line of the Penn Central railroad.

In 1970, a new, less familiar sound began to come wafting across Stonington Harbor. Natives call it the "humidity horn" or, as one shellback snarled, "Everything you can lay a tongue to!" Yachtsmen, however, attempting to enter the harbor in poor visibility will probably bless the blast. It's the new foghorn established at the Stonington outer breakwater light sounding one blast every ten seconds.

The attractive Wadawanuck Yacht Club, on the northeast shore at the head of the harbor, is hospitable to visiting yachtsmen from other recognized yacht clubs with whom reciprocal privileges are exchanged. It should be understood, however, that the club is open and attended for a short season only and is without the launch services or other facilities usually available at larger clubs. The Yacht Club is affiliated with the Wadawanuck Club, which engages in athletic and social activities other than yachting.

"We have just salty boat-loving people here," exclaimed John Dodson, owner of the Dodson Boat Yard tucked away in the northeast "special anchorage area." This is the one all-service marina in the harbor of primary attraction to sailing craft. The charge is 15¢ per foot at dockside, where there is a depth of 6½ feet, and gas, Diesel fuel, water, ice, and electricity are available. Dodson can be reached for reservations by phoning 535-1507. Overnight moorings may be obtained at $2.50 with launch service. Repair work and hauling are performed, and besides the marine railway there is a lift for outboards. Necessary marine supplies and a laundromat are also on tap. Although the holding ground is mud, it is choked with eel grass, which suggests mooring rather than anchoring.

Whenever a yacht-club fleet comes into Dodson's, it often takes over, and under such circumstances, one may have difficulty in finding any space without a reservation. In that event, the Stonington Shipyard, situated on the east shore halfway up the harbor, is your best bet. You might prefer being closer to the center of the town here; the facilities and repair work are reported as quite complete and satisfactory.

Stonington has all of the facilities a yachtsman is apt to desire in the way of supplies, repairs, and communications. The Sugar & Spice Shop on Water Street specializes in rare food delicacies, the preparation of exotic box lunches, and in Stonington's Portuguese bread. The Harbor View Restaurant, farther down Water Street toward the point, is a "must" for anyone who dotes on fresh seafood and famous Stonington chowder. It's housed in an old plant that used to process whale oil from the town's large whaling fleet. Cameron's Coffee House is delightful for a light breakfast or lunch, and a well-stocked bookstore is just around the corner.

Stonington helped to make history and was once called a "nursery for seamen." Captain Edmund Fanning of Stonington served as a midshipman under John Paul Jones. When he was eighteen years old (July 15, 1798), he discovered the Fanning Islands, now an important air stop on the Pacific Ocean. During the Revolution and the War of 1812, the town was twice attacked by the British and twice successfully repelled the invaders. Some British cannon balls are now valued relics.* The town has

* Historical data from *Connecticut*—American Guide Series (Houghton Mifflin Co.).

that intangible quality called "atmosphere" and it's fun to wander through its streets, perhaps on the way to view relics of bygone days in the museum of the Stonington Historical Society at the old granite lighthouse near Stonington Point.

Watch Hill, R.I. (358). As the chart clearly shows, the anchorage at Stonington is nearer the east-west course through Fishers Island Sound than is the anchorage at Watch Hill. To reach the latter it is necessary to go a considerable distance to the north around Sandy Point and then southeast through a well-buoyed but narrow channel. For this reason, Watch Hill is a less frequent port of call for 'longshore cruisers than it deserves to be, as it is an attractive summer resort.

In entering Little Narragansett Bay on your way to Watch Hill, keep as far off Sandy Point as the buoys allow, for the shoal off the island is moving westward. Stick close to the black buoys to port. After that, follow the entrance channel carefully, as there are rocks and shoal spots in several places just off the channel. According to local yachtsmen, at least 8 feet can be carried at low water through the short channel leading into Watch Hill Cove.

There are several good docks for visiting yachts. The first to starboard that entering yachts will reach is that of the hospitable Watch Hill Yacht Club, where the usual reciprocal privileges are given to members of other recognized yacht clubs. Launch service runs here, and you may be able to pick up a spare mooring. If not, an anchorage is possible just to the west of the club's small boat fleet inside the breakwater; or run up the cove to the large public Watch Hill Docks for overnight dockage where there's gas, water, ice on order, and electricity, with a depth of 8 feet alongside. Check for space with the dock master. No lights are required at anchorages. Stores are near at hand, or can be reached by telephone. D.F. Larkin, a very active member and frequent officer of the Watch Hill Yacht Club, is a valuable authority on these and other waters. Reaves Strobel, who is at the Watch Hill Boat Yard up the Pawcatuck River, will service your boat at the yacht club; phone him at 348-8148.

The only "out" about Watch Hill is that it usually takes a terrible licking in hurricanes, for the protecting Napatree Beach is low, and hurricane-driven tides go right over it. Hurricane Carol (August 31, 1954) badly damaged the yacht clubhouse and docks.

Some improvements have been completed at Watch Hill Cove. The jetty at the western entrance is now enlarged, and dredging in the anchorage basin has given it a depth of 10 feet at m.l.w. Nevertheless, this harbor is still wide open for some distance from north to northwest. On our last visit there were seven state moorings in Watch Hill Cove.

Westerly, R.I. (358). Those who want better protection or who like to poke their way up rivers or creeks may find it interesting to go up the Pawcatuck River for all or part of the way to Westerly. On their way they will leave to starboard the Watch Hill Boat Yard headquarters on Colonel Willie Cove. To reach there, make a heading just before reaching nun 4 toward the marshy end of Graves Neck. Having passed this point fairly close aboard, swing to the southeast to pick up the yard's buoyed channel. Depths for this approach are 5 feet. A short distance further upriver lies the Avondale Boat Yard. Both of these facilities have gas, water, ice, electricity, marine supplies, and repair service. A good market for supplies may be found near the latter's docks. The Frank Hall Boat Yard a bit further up to starboard has charts, slips, and moorings, but no gas.

Still further up, across the river from Pawcatuck Rock, is the modern marina and clubhouse of the Westerly Yacht Club, with many slips, gas, water, electricity, an ample parking space, and a large fleet, chiefly of motorboats. The river bottom is mud. The anchorage just beyond nun 16 is well protected from all directions.

Further up the dredged channel is the city of Westerly, with many stores, shops, restaurants, etc. The best place for an overnight tie-up would be at the Westerly Yacht Club if there is room, and they extend the usual privileges to members of other recognized yacht clubs. We were told at the club that there is no great advantage in proceeding further upriver.

Block Island, R.I. (269, 271). Although discovered by Giovanni da Verrazano in 1524, Block Island was named for Adriaen Block, who first arrived there, nearly ninety years later, on his way to Narragansett Bay. Verrazano found the hills of the island covered with trees, most of which have long since gone, though various types of wild flowers now help to fill the aesthetic gap. The Indians called it the "Isle of Manisses" or "Little God's Island." The clay-formed Mohegan Bluffs, which remind one of the chalk cliffs of Dover, stretch along the island's southern shore, rising to more than 200 feet above sea level. They were so named when, centuries ago, the island's Manissean Indians drove a group of invading Mohegans across the moors and over these majestic bluffs to their death.

About 5 miles long and with an elevation of 211 feet, this is the first of the outlying islands encountered on the way east from Long Island Sound. Though not so attractive as Martha's Vineyard, Nantucket, and other islands further east, it is an interesting place to visit and a convenient offshore stopping point on the way to Vineyard Sound.

There are two good harbors, one on the east and one on the west side

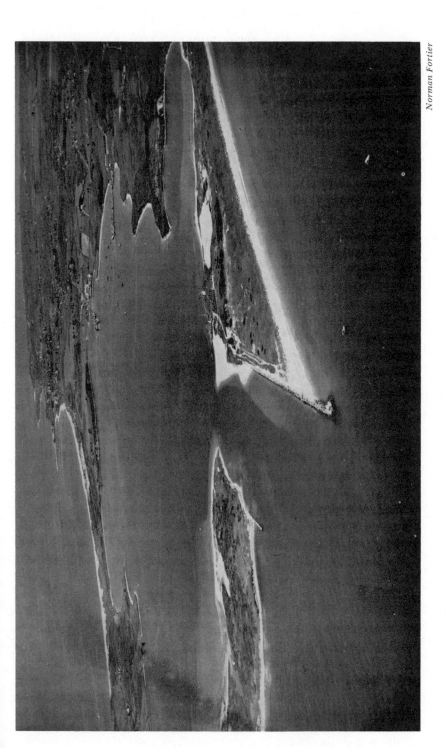

Block Island, showing Great Salt Pond, New Harbor, and the breakwaters at Old Harbor beyond at the upper left.

of the island; the latter is the harbor usually preferred by yachtsmen, as the former is small and used mainly by commercial fishermen. There is a good deal of open water between Long Island, Block Island, and the mainland, so anyone who ventures to Block Island in a small boat must be prepared to go to sea. Fogs are frequent in Block Island Sound during July and August, and the current information in Eldridge must be figured out. In 1969 the Coast and Geodetic Survey issued large-scale Chart 271 providing complete up-to-date detail for the safe navigation of busy Block Island Sound and the east entrance to Long Island Sound. It has been estimated that 500,000 recreational craft frequent this area each year.

In the vicinity of Montauk, on the ebb tide, there is a decided trend of the current to the eastward. If one is bound for Block Island, it is well to get away from the Long Island shore, so as to minimize the current and avoid the rips off Montauk. One correspondent writes: "I decided at the last moment, 5:30 P.M., to sail to Block Island in a light four-knot wind at full ebb tide. The course was east by north. I sailed northeast, and hit Salt Pond light on the nose at 10:15 P.M."

A sailing yachtsman who visited Block Island in the summer of 1954 gave us his impressions, which still ring true today:

> The island itself we found quite interesting. Despite its present dilapidated state, it has superior geographic features that could be developed someday by a Steve Hanagan or a Zeckendorf. The only thing we didn't like about Block Island is that the harbor seems to be a mecca for power boats. At the time of our visit they were tied up at the dock five and six abreast with much goings-on. I would warn anybody going there to anchor for the night to stay as far away from said dock as possible.

1. Great Salt Pond, Block Island (269). Because of two jetty lights, the fog signal on this jetty to the southwest of the entrance, and the Block Island Coast Guard station nearby, this harbor, the southern part of which is called New Harbor, is quite easy to make. In early 1972, the Corps of Engineers redredged the entrance channel to a 100-foot width and a depth of 12 feet at m.l.w. since shoaling forms off the inner jetty light. As most of the bad weather at Block Island comes from the eastern quadrant, it is to be preferred to East Harbor, though it is large and can be rough, particularly in a northeast gale. The best anchorage is off Champlin's Marina on the south shore, between it and the steamer dock, or north of the yacht dock, where there is less wash and the lee of a bluff provides some protection from the prevailing afternoon southwest winds.

In a storm, go to the snug inner harbor, readily navigable and land-locked. Proceed to the steamer dock at the east side and follow in, hugging close both to it and to the fish building. Then cut over to the 10-foot channel. This place is known as the Hog Pen or Smuggler's Cove. Payne's Dock at the ferry landing has good facilities, including slips with electricity at $5.00 minimum, gas, Diesel fuel, ice, showers, groceries, and local delicacies—clam cakes and chowder. No repair service is available here, however.

Among the facilities or supplies obtainable at Champlin's Marina are gas, Diesel fuel, water, ice, marine supplies, charts, engine repairs, showers, a salt-water swimming pool, laundromat, bicycles for hire, liquor, and basic food supplies in a shack dockside. Other supplies can be had at the village across the island to the east. Deadeye Dick's restaurant, 200 yards up the road from the steamboat dock, is well recommended for its excellent service and food, particularly its swordfish and lobsters. Ballard's Inn, over at Old Harbor, has been renovated and offers room and board the year round. Champlin runs a jitney service to and from the center of town every twenty minutes. We found Victor Filippi, the Dock Master at Champlin's, most hospitable and cooperative. He charges transients a flat rate of 30¢ per foot dockside including electricity.

The harbor is deep and the bottom close to shore shelves off steeply. Yachtsmen are warned not to forget this when anchoring and to allow for plenty of scope. Much to the dismay of their skippers and to our edification, we have watched boats here with short anchor rodes dragging into each other. In the summer of 1970, we observed a Cruising Club of America fleet safely ride out a driving gale while anchored along the shore just to the northwest of Champlin's dock. Champlin's no longer has moorings, at the time of writing. Should you spot one, pick it up at your own risk, since it has probably fallen into disrepair.

Champlin has an attractive new competitor lying just to the west of the ferry landing. The Block Island Marina, run by Bill Transue and open all year, has become a popular port of call of the Storm Trysail fleet. It doesn't boast a swimming pool, but in other respects its services are comparable to Champlin's. In addition it has a fifteen-ton lift, complete repair work, the well-stocked Windjammer Country Store, and the Oar Restaurant with cocktail lounge and overnight lodging. The rates dockside, with 10-foot depth, are $8.00 up to 30 feet; $10.00 up to 40 feet. Don't miss seeing the now-rare Block Island double-ender out in front of this marina.

For excellent surf bathing, take the dinghy to the shore east by north from Champlin's dock, ½ to ¾ miles. Then cross the road and take the path through a break in the fence to the ocean. Here is a 2-mile beach;

once practically deserted, it now has a new State of Rhode Island Pavilion picnic area. It is sometimes hard to escape "progress."

The interstate Navigation Co. (Point Judith, R.I.) operates steamers between Point Judith and Block Island, four times daily in summer, and once a day (except Sundays) in winter. It also runs daily trips in summer from Providence and Newport, arriving and departing from Old Harbor. The Nelseco Navigation Co. (New London, Conn.) operates between New London and Block Island once a day in summer. Sailing time from Point Judith is about one and one-quarter hours; from New London, two and one-quarter hours. Get in touch with these companies if you want their latest schedules. Viking Airlines runs daily flights between Block Island and Providence, and Block Island and Westerly. Montauk-Caribbean, Inc., conducts daily flights in summer between Block Island and Flushing Airport (next to LaGuardia).

Block Island offers some pleasant drives. Ask for Maizie at the steamer dock. She knows everybody and everything and has written a book about Block Island, besides driving her taxi. Her name is Mrs. Melvin Rose, and she is one of the most entertaining people we have met in our wanderings. Another authority who has written a book about Block Island is Mrs. Frederick N. Ritchie, *Block Island Lore and Legends*. There are plenty of them, as you will find out if you talk to either of these two ladies.

Great Salt Pond is a favorite rendezvous for yacht-club fleets, and you seldom find a New England cruising yachtsman who hasn't been there at least once. Ten or 11 miles off the Rhode Island Coast, it has the special type of appeal which attracts so many yachtsmen to outlying islands.

2. Block Island Harbor on East Harbor (269). This artificial harbor on the eastern shore, shown on the chart as Old Harbor, is likely to be crowded in summer. In coming in from the east in a fog, watch for the "dead spot" under the cliffs; you may not hear the fog horn at Block Island Southeast Lighthouse. A member of the Cruising Club of America lost a boat here a few years ago. "Lots of others, too," writes a correspondent.

Harbor Master Omar Littlefield brought us up-to-date on Old Harbor on our most recent visit there. We saw how the place had been improved through the 1970 installation of new bulkheading along the eastern shore of the inner basin in front of Ballard's Inn. Register at Littlefield's office at the head of the harbor. His charge for a night's layover is $6.00 for boats up to 30 feet and $8.00 for those 30 to 40 feet overall. This covers water and electricity. There are no showers, and the only restrooms are in the inn. Should you decide to anchor in the less-protected outer basin, make sure to stay clear of the ferry dock to the west.

Up until a few years ago there was a fish market on the dock at Old Harbor. A conversation was overheard there one day when a woman bought two lobsters and asked the elderly fisherman who was on duty to split them for her. As he brought his meat axe deftly right through the lobster's middle, she inquired: "Does that kill it?" "Well," he replied with typical dry Block Island understatement, "it don't help it none."

Supplies can be obtained right in the town of New Shoreham. There's a rusticated movie theater here, but if you want a picture of Block Island nightlife, try Smugglers Cove or the Block Island Inn.

Block Island was never popular as a summer resort for the very well-to-do. There are no imposing "cottages" like those to be found in Newport and on Fishers Island. There was no adequate harbor at first, so the whaling vessels didn't put in. Perhaps that's why you don't see any imposing mansions with their "captain's walks," like those found on the Vineyard. But Block Island's heyday finally arrived during the latter half of the nineteenth century, when Victorian architecture was all the rage.

The famous Ocean View Hotel was erected in 1873 and stood on that prominent knoll above Old Harbor's entrance. It had two notable features: it had the longest bar in the world (287-feet long, with one hundred bar stools), and it was the summer "White House" of President Grant. Whether there was any connection between these two facts, no one has discovered. All we know is that the bartenders wore roller skates to provide for their thirsty customers with unusual alacrity, and that this wonderful old homestead burned to the ground in 1966.

Point Judith Harbor of Refuge, R.I. (268). If you are approaching Point Judith Light from the northeast, be careful to maintain a course 2 miles off of Point Judith Neck. These offshore waters are thriving with fish traps. Anchor in the southern end of the harbor—the angle of the main breakwater—in about 4 fathoms. This is almost the only good holding ground, and here the water is usually quietest. One should be aware of the heavy kelp bottom; a sandbar is building up inside the elbow of the breakwater, so give it good berth.

Care should be taken not to anchor too far southward in the V-shaped part of the breakwater. In sudden northwest squalls at night, several boats have gone ashore on the inside of the breakwater and been completely wrecked. While the water inside the breakwater is apparently calm, the surge of the sea penetrates through the rocks, making landing on all parts of the V-shaped breakwater difficult, except in the calmest weather. Main breakwater west light has four black square daymarks.

Most yachts wisely prefer to go north toward Point Judith Pond, pass the recently improved breakwater located to starboard, and tie up or anchor in Galilee, where a Block Island Ferry dock has been built, or else go northward in the Pond for 3 or 4 miles further to the thriving city of Wakefield. There are three state moorings in Point Judith Harbor.

Galilee, R.I. (268). Most yachts cruising alongshore find a tie-up here at the public dock on the east shore, or anchor in the dredged triangular basin, where it is quieter but less convenient. The best plan is to see the accommodating Harbor Master, whose office is on the shore end of the conspicuous state pier. He will either find space for you at the pier for overnight or suggest an anchorage well out of the steamer's way. Gas is available nearby. Along the shore is a long row of commercial and sport fishing docks, and on the main road are small stores, restaurants, hot dog joints, and what have you. Don't forget to visit George's Restaurant located at the foot of the main road. It's a Mecca for seafood gourmands. You'll see a mixture of all kinds of people, from genuine fishermen to tourists in search of atmosphere or a good time. The noise pollution emitted here at dawn by fishermen, gulls, and engines shouldn't upset the early riser.

This port is a good place for shelter, but you will like it better on weekdays than on weekends unless you are very gregarious by nature. The tide is strong at times, and if you are at anchor you may do some swinging.

At Snug Harbor on the west shore of Point Judith Pond and just above Galilee is the recently expanded Snug Harbor Marina, with berths, gas, Diesel fuel, and other facilities. Nearby is the Salt Pond Marine Railway, with gas, etc. There are fine accommodations here, but once tied up at one of the slips, you are apt to get a good roll from the nearby channel traffic. Excellent quahauging is reported to be found in the pond.

Wakefield, R.I. (268). If you have time and your boat draws under 4½ feet you can follow the buoyed channel for 3 or 4 miles to the attractive city of Wakefield, where there are good shopping facilities, hotels, eating places, etc. Making this passage on a *flood* tide during our last visit, we tailed a Concordia yawl of 5'8" draft without incident. The mean range of tide is 3 feet. Consult your chart and favor the port side of the channel all the way up. Along the way, anchorage can be found in several places, one of which is Smelt Brook Cove in the northwestern part of Point Judith Pond just north of Crown Point. Stay fairly close to the port shore on entering, since a rock ledge lies along the northern mouth of the cove. Here you can lie at a quiet anchorage in about 5 feet of water lined with a gravel bottom. Another good anchorage, though exposed to the north and south, is between Gardner and Beach Islands. Between the channel's red nun 16 and black can 21 be sure to follow the buoys rather than what appears on the chart as the deeper water. A dangerous spot for strangers is what natives term "Bill's Island," a rock shelf just west of can 17. (You will find how this island got its name shortly.) Proceed cautiously throughout this area, keeping both rock and can well to port. At Wakefield's Upper Pond basin with 6 feet of water at low tide, there are several boat yards with hauling and repair facilities, and docks well equipped for landing and providing gas, water, electricity, and other facilities. This is an interesting trip and provides anchorages or tie-ups in some ways more desirable than those at the towns with the biblical names.

At Wakefield are two small yacht clubs, the Point Judith Yacht Club and the University of Rhode Island Yacht Club, both located on the west shore. During our many visits here we have become friendly with Bill Schmid, manager of the Ram Point Marina, and can vouch for his very competent engine- and electronic-repair service. We suggest you lay over here while at Wakefield, for the basin's mud bottom offers poor holding ground. You can hang on one of Bill's sixteen moorings for an overnight charge of $1.00, or take one of his ten transient slips for 10¢ a foot. This is such a popular spot that it might be wise to phone 783-4535 for an advance reservation. Ram Point's facilities are quite adequate, although you'll have to go a mile to Wakefield for supplies. Bill's wife runs the store, which is well stocked with charts and all sorts of marine gear. She caters to female customers too. The reputable Larchwood Inn and the Sweet Meadows Inn are hospitable to yachtsmen, providing transportation on call to and from Ram Point.

Narragansett Bay, R.I., and Mass. (236, 278, 353).

A well-known manufacturer of small boats tells of a yachtsman who chartered a yacht from him in Narragansett Bay for a period of three weeks during World War II, and then discovered that he couldn't take the boat out of the bay. A submarine net barred his way.

"Don't keep her any longer than you want to and we'll fix the price accordingly," said the boat manufacturer.

Three weeks passed, with nothing heard from the fellow who did the chartering until the last day.

"I could have spent a month cruising in Narragansett Bay," was his enthusiastic comment.

This well-protected, well-buoyed, well-lighted bay of many good harbors affords some delightful sailing, despite the omnipresent United States Navy. The scenery is restful and pastoral, the water is generally smooth, and the wind is usually just right. At the foot of the bay is the famous yachting (and Navy) harbor of Newport, where the Bermuda racing fleet gathers every other June. At the head of the bay, 24 miles from the open sea, are two great cities: Providence and Fall River. In between is an almost bewildering collection of islands, peninsulas, bays, and passages, easy to navigate, lovely to sail.

As in Buzzards Bay, the prevailing summer winds are from the southwest, but they are usually less violent. A typical summer day is likely to include a light northerly in the early morning, then a calm until the early afternoon, when a moderate sou'wester will begin to stir up a few whitecaps. With evening, calm again descends upon the waters of the bay. The swimming is good in many parts of the lower bay—not so good near Providence and Fall River.

While Narragansett Bay took severe beatings from the hurricanes of September 21, 1938, and August 31, 1954 (Hurricane Carol), and also some damage from several other hurricanes, its yacht clubs and fleets have recovered, and the bay is far better equipped than ever before to take another, if it comes. For instance, the Rhode Island Yacht Club, on the Providence River, which has had two clubhouses washed away, is now perched up in the air on "stilts."

There are at least thirty-five good harbors in Rhode Island waters, including Narragansett Bay (a small part of which is in Massachusetts), and we have counted twenty-eight yacht clubs. Boat yards and marinas are well spread out over the bay. At the time of writing there are thirty-eight state summer moorings strategically placed in various harbors, as we shall note in each case. They are painted red and stenciled with the words "State of R.I. Guest Mooring Buoy." They are about 2 feet in diameter, flat on top. A smaller "pick up" buoy is stenciled "150-pound or 250-pound mushroom anchor." Thomas J. Wright, the cooperative Chief of the R.I. Division of Fish and Game, wrote us, "We would be pleased to receive suggestions on the better placement of these buoys on areas that seem to be omitted from our schedule." The Rhode Island Yachting Association is active in sponsoring and stimulating racing, and the Twenty Hundred Club sponsors races by cruising craft to Cuttyhunk and elsewhere.

It is a fine cruising area, as recognized by the Cruising Club of America, one of whose summer-cruise announcements contained these words: "Your Committee, having had so many wonderful reports of cruising in Narragansett Bay, have scheduled the next rendezvous at Bristol, Rhode Island."

There are three important passages running up the bay in a northerly direction: the *West Passage,* starting between the mainland on the west side of the bay and Conanicut Island; the *East Passage,* between Conanicut and Aquidneck islands, with Newport as the usual take-off point; and the *Sakonnet River,* with the much-improved Sakonnet Harbor at its southern end. While Newport and Sakonnet harbors are convenient ports of call for longshore cruisers, we are not forgetting here that they are also starting points for cruising on Narragansett Bay.

In this book we shall follow each of the three above passages northward, stopping at each harbor on the way. The ports are all in Rhode Island, unless otherwise stated. As usual, we are giving the numbers of the largest-scale charts available. Chart 353, however, covers very well the whole bay.

WEST PASSAGE

1. Dutch Island Harbor (236). Among many Rhode Island yachtsmen this is the most popular harbor on the bay, not for its facilities, for there are almost none, but partly because of its lack of them. It is unspoiled, uncrowded even when a yacht-club fleet makes it a rendezvous; the swimming is fine; and except in blows from the north it is fairly well protected. A lighthouse on the southern end of Dutch Island makes it easy to enter at night, and there are no important outlying obstacles after leaving nun 2 to starboard. Supplies are available at Jamestown, a little over ½ miles away. There is a small boat yard with a dock and gas just north of the dilapidated wharf on the east shore. One yachtsman recommends walking over to Mackerel Cove, which, with Dutch Island Harbor, almost divides Conanicut Island. There you will find a splendid swimming beach.

At the time of writing there are, in summer, six state moorings in the harbor. If none is available when you get there, the best anchorage is between the wharf at the northerly end of Fox Hill and the eastern shore of the harbor.

2. Wickford (236). Wickford was formerly Updike's Newtown, named in 1663 and platted in 1707. In contrast to Dutch Island Harbor, it has more facilities for yachtsmen than any port on the bay, including the newly established Wickford Yacht Club. While some may prefer to anchor behind the breakwaters in the outer harbor to obtain more privacy, using perhaps one of the two state moorings in that area, most visitors go into Wickford Cove, where they have much to choose from.

Along the east shore, to port as one enters this cove, is the large marina of Wickford Shipyard, one of the most attractive and best-equipped mari-

Wickford, Narragansett Bay.

nas in New England. Check in at its gas dock for dockage assignment. Besides many slips, gas, Diesel fuel, water, electricity, telephone, ice, hauling and repair work, a laundromat, a swimming pool, and a marine supply store, the shipyard has a fine restaurant. They charge 25 ¢ per foot at the slips. When we were last there, we enjoyed looking over *Tontine,* a handsome 72-foot schooner from the Virgin Islands, tied up dockside. At the southern end of the cove is another first-class establishment, the Wickford Cove Marina, which caters primarily to power boats. There are also at least two boat yards on Mill Cove to the north: Pleasant Street Wharf and Johnson's Boat Yard. Besides all these, there is a town dock, chiefly commercial, that lies across from the Shipyard at the entrance to Wickford Cove. You can tie up here for a two-hour time limit.

For all types of supplies, one can pass westward through the marked channel in Wickford Cove to a public landing located up on the west shore. Here you can tie up temporarily, pick up supplies at nearby Ryan's Market (open Sundays), and stroll among the pleasant shops and quaint old streets of the town.

On our last visit, we had a delightful chat with Ralph Vale, one of the founders and past commodores of the Essex Yacht Club situated on Point Wharf at the entrance to Mill Cove. It is a "fun club," hosting an active sailing program. The clubhouse is housed in an antique oyster house dating back to the 1700s. In 1970, it was being completely refurbished while maintaining much of its original charm. Essex certainly welcomes visiting club yachtsmen, though it has limited facilities for cruising boats, which may, as an alternative, pick up a mooring from Johnson's next door. Mill Cove offers 6-foot depths and good holding ground, and promises a peaceful, scenic anchorage.

Some leading yachtsmen put Wickford at the head of their list of appealing Narragansett Bay harbors, not only because of the many modern facilities and conveniences available, but because Wickford is an interesting community, with many fine old buildings along the principal street leading to the public dock. Gilbert Stuart's birthplace is only a few miles away.

Wickford Coves give perfect shelter, and the surroundings are pleasant and sociable. As many as 850 pleasure craft have been counted here on a summer's day!

3. Allen Harbor (236). This harbor, between Wickford and East Greenwich, was once a shallow cove, but it has been dredged to 8 feet, with perfect shelter and a well-marked channel. It is still used extensively by the Navy, and therefore should be used by yachtsmen as a refuge only in emergencies. The government has now placed a buoy well out from

Calf Pasture, since shoaling has extended further to the east than is indicated on the chart. Stay well offshore!

4. *East Greenwich* (278). This harbor is attractive, and the shelter, bathing, and facilities are all good. But it is on the main line of the Penn-Central Railroad and trains whistle as they go by. It can be uncomfortable in a northeaster. Nevertheless, here is one of the best natural harbors on the bay.

The entrance is made from Warwick Point Light. The channel is well marked and easily entered by day, but it is narrow, and boats drawing more than 6 feet should keep close to the buoys. This is no channel in which to cut buoys.

There is a light on the end of the Shipyard Wharf. In entering at night, head for this light, keeping the flashing white light on the mid-channel buoy on your stern. This will keep you in the channel.

Black can 5 opposite the Norton Shipyard and Marina on the west shore indicates the entrance. There is a bad shoal from this can to Long Point on the port, so keep close to the starboard shore. With many of the moorings already occupied in this harbor, one may be obtained from the shipyard, or at the East Greenwich Yacht Club on the west shore beyond. If no moorings are available, there is ample opportunity to anchor between the shipyard and the club.

There is about 12 feet of water at the shipyard dock and 10 feet at the club. Appropriately, there's a marine store at the yard and a fine bar at the club. The club's charge for an overnight slip averages $4.00, and it's $2.00 for a mooring.

The East Greenwich Yacht Club, established in 1909 and one of the leading boating centers on the bay, is pleased to offer its marina facilities to members of other recognized yacht clubs. In 1970, with 88 per cent of its membership boat owners, its fleet totaled 254 boats, of which many were Sea Sprites, 505s, including 44 Sun Fish. During that year, the club hosted such racing regattas as the Sears, Mallory, and Adams cup. The Atlantic Coast Lightning Championships took place here in 1965. Both Bob Broz, for seventeen years the club's steward, and past commodore Joe Lawton are delightful fellows who can spin yarns all day long about the bay and its 400 miles of coastline.

If you like shore exercise in pleasant surroundings, take a walk in Goddard Park or hike up the long steep hill to the town's main street, where all sorts of supplies can be obtained.

Shallow-draft boats can go nearly to the head of the harbor, which is attractive. But don't proceed beyond Arnold's Boat Shop, where the mud bottom begins to shoal badly. Norton's is the place to go for competent engine, hull, and rigging repair work. In summer, there are four state moorings in Greenwich Bay. In the town are a number of early American houses, including the General James Mitchell Varnum house. There is also the Naval and Military Museum, in the Varnum Armory.

5. *Apponaug Cove* (278). In approaching this cove, make sure to stay well off of "The Brothers," a cluster of dangerous rocks ¾ of a mile due west of lighted buoy "GB." They have often been the nemesis of yachtsmen unfamiliar with Greenwich Bay.

Before entering the channel, you will note the rather expansive Cowesett Shipyard and Marina located on the western shore just southwest of can 3. This place provides full marina and repair service with good water dockside. Just beyond Cowesett's is the Masthead Marina with comparable facilities including a restaurant. Both of these places appear to cater to power boats and have constructed breakwaters to provide greater protection in easterlies.

The cove, which forms the northwestern arm of Greenwich Bay, is navigable through its channel with a depth of 6 feet in 1968. However, the channel is tending to shoal in spots and boats drawing more than 5 feet are advised to proceed with caution. There is a 4-foot tide range here.

The channel leading to the cove begins at nun 2 just off Cedar Tree Point. On Arnold Neck to port, you can pick up a mooring or slip space at Apponaug Harbor Marina. Check in at their gas dock, depth 6 feet, to be assigned a mooring up in the cove. Their charge is 15¢ per foot at the slips; $3.50 for an overnight mooring. Supplies are easily available, taxi service will take you to Apponaug, and the Theodore Francis Airport is merely six minutes away. All types of repair work are on hand; the marina is popular with sailing craft, but one must go to Cowesett for Diesel maintenance and fuel. For better protection in a strong southerly, you can venture further into the cove, avoiding the sandbar extending from the west between cans 5 and 7. The upper channel is lined with tire moorings set out by the town. Since there is little space for anchorage, tie up to these fore and aft. The surroundings are pleasant and quiet, disturbed only by the trains rumbling over the bridge to the west. Charles Dickerson, manager of the marina, is a general factotum and authority on the bay.

6. *Old Warwick Cove* (278). A man who knows the bay says that this is a "nice harbor." The entrance is tricky but has 5 or 6 feet there and inside if you know where to go. A local authority urged hugging the east shore in approaching the entrance. Further in, watch out for a bad shoal, bare at low water, extending 150 yards westward from the west side of the channel to the southeast tip of Horse Neck. Although the latest chart records a 6-foot-deep, 150-foot-wide channel all the way to the turning basis at the cove's head, in 1970 we sounded 4½ feet at m.l.w. along much of this passage. There is, however, a mooring basin with 6 feet in the eastern bight opposite the Warwick Cove Marina halfway up the channel. Earle Steere, the manager at the marina, can offer you gas, ice, a slip or a mooring, and will point out the shopping center nearby. More extensive repair work is performed at the C-Lark Marina toward the head of the cove. This place is snug, and, with the improved dredging, will be found chock-a-block with power boats.

7. Bullock Cove, Providence River (*east shore—278*). Here is a fine harbor whose main channel has unfortunately shoaled-in 1971 to 4½ feet at m.l.w. throughout its entire length. The southern basin, however, gave us a reading at that time of 6 feet. There is private buoyage all the way in. Follow the buoys carefully, since shoaling is taking place and the buoyage has been shifted to mark the best water. Inside on the west shore are the Narragansett Terrace Yacht Club and the Narragansett Terrace Boat Yard. Gas and water are available, and the boat yard does hauling and repair work. Further up to starboard, near the final anchorage basin, is the large new Cove Haven Marina, which we found to be most complete and cooperative. They arrange cookouts for yachtsmen near attractive Haines State Park. Stores, as well as the Crescent Amusement Park, providing fun for the family, are all close at hand. This facility, called the most ambitious boating venture in the East shore of Narragansett Bay, can accommodate boats of 6-foot draft up to 42 feet long.

Bullock Neck is a nice residential area, and the harbor is now one of the snuggest and most attractive on the bay, deep enough for most cruising yachts. Be sure to post a lookout, however, should you enter at low water in a vessel drawing more than 4 feet.

8. Pawtuxet Cove, Providence River (*west shore—278*). Here the chart doesn't tell the story unless, of course, you refer to the latest edition. A prominent 800-yard dike has been constructed from Rock Island to a point just south of the cove's entrance. Come between can 1 and nun 2 heading westward on the range lights. Proceed up the 6-foot dredged channel, pick up the markers to starboard, and make a wide turn around the point, making sure not to hug it too closely. From here the narrow channel behind Washouset Point has shoaled to a 4-foot depth at m.l.w. all the way to the Edgewood Marine on your port and the Pawtuxet Cove Marina further up to starboard. We observed considerable water pollution and a congestion of small craft.

If boats of considerable draft wish to anchor at this harbor, their best bet is to ride in the 100-yard south basin, whose limits are marked by buoys and depth is reported to be 6 feet. Good protection is provided by the dike. This is a very safe anchorage but still open a bit to the south. Should you be an apartment dweller feeling rather homesick, you may get some relief by gazing at a string of apartment buildings rising to the west.

9. Edgewood, Cranston, Providence River (*west shore—278*). While this section of the Providence River above the Pawtuxet River is too wide and exposed to be called a harbor, the presence on this shore of two of the leading yacht clubs on the bay makes this a rewarding port of call for visiting yachts cruising on the bay. From south to north these are the Rhode Island Yacht Club, organized in 1875 and thus one of the oldest yacht clubs in the country, and the Edgewood Yacht Club, organized in 1889 and now sometimes called "the sailingest club on the bay."

The *Rhode Island Yacht Club* is on the north end of Washouset Point on Pawtuxet Neck and easily recognized as the "club on stilts," resting one story up on large steel-and-concrete pillars, high enough, it is hoped, to avoid the fate of its predecessors, swept away by hurricanes. Until very recently, perhaps, this club has stressed social rather than yachting activities. But there are now signs that yachting there is coming back. North from the clubhouse is a long dock. Gulf gas, Diesel fuel, water, ice, etc., are available.

The *Edgewood Yacht Club,* which, though battered, has survived all hurricanes to date, is a short distance to the north. Here a very active sailing program is undertaken, with much stress on Junior activities. There are also races for "Peppy Pappies," formerly called "Tired Fathers," until the fathers said they weren't tired. This busy club is most hospitable to visiting yachtsmen from other yacht clubs, as we know from experience, and if a spare mooring is available, we feel sure a visitor would be accommodated. Four private stakes mark the channel leading to the gas dock, where there is 4½ feet at m.l.w. Various intercollegiate yacht races have been hosted here, and from what we have seen the club carries out well the simply stated objectives of its constitution: "To encourage the sport of yachting, to promote the science of seamanship and navigation, and to provide and maintain a suitable Club House and anchorage for the recreation and use of its members."

Above the Rhode Island and Edgewood Yacht clubs is the Narragansett Yacht Club, protected from the north by Field Point. Here, in the corner, is the Port Edgewood Marina, with berths and moorings, marine supplies, gas, repair facilities, etc. Boats of deep draft can proceed to the anchorage basin at the head of the channel or tie up for supplies at the rather imposing Shipyard Marina, easily identified by its huge blue boat shed.

Since yachtsmen when cruising will generally prefer to stay away from the heart of a big city, we shall end here our voyage up the West Passage of Narragansett Bay and go back to the entrance of the East Passage.

In making your way up the East passage, note that Rose Island Light, just below the new Newport suspension bridge, has been discontinued and is now an abandoned lighthouse. Lighted Bell R12, just off the southwest shore of the island, has replaced it.

East Passage

10. Newport, Aquidneck Island, R.I. (236, 353). One of the principal summer resorts and yachting centers of the Atlantic Coast, Newport is not always a snug or a quiet anchorage although its inner harbor has recently undergone a dramatic restoration. To confuse the waters further, it is a principal naval base and an important commercial center. But the two harbors (inner and outer), divided by city-owned Goat Island, are protected, well marked and lighted, so that Newport is easy of access at all times. Newport is the most practical 'longshore harbor capable of holding a fleet of yachts between Stonington, Connecticut, and Padanaram in Buzzards Bay. Being near the entrance of Narragansett Bay, it is a convenient harbor for those cruising alongshore, as well as a good take-off point for bay cruising.

Most yachts anchor in Brenton Cove, the bight in the southern part of Newport Harbor, but it can be rough there in a northeaster and sometimes in a northwester. Though less convenient for supplies than the main harbor, it is noncommercial and the water is clean. The quietest spot is near the head of the cove; there are nine state guest moorings on the south shore near the point at the entrance of the small inner cove. Just pick up any one that is vacant. There are no landing or other facilities here. For that purpose an anchorage off the Ida Lewis Yacht Club is the best bet.

The Ida Lewis Yacht Club, where cruising yachts are most likely to stop, also has guest moorings and, in addition, launch service is provided. There is no gas, nor are there dining facilities. This club is located in the eastern part of Brenton Cove and occupies the lighthouse, kept at one time by Ida Lewis, where she made such a reputation for the rescue of seamen in distress that several rocks were named for her. The eighteen lives she saved are represented by the eighteen stars in the club's burgee. Charles "Ted" Nelson showed us some fascinating Cup Defender memorabilia in his salty dock-master shack. The present club has a 300-foot

John T. Hopf

Newport Harbor and Narragansett Bay. Brenton Cove lies in left center of the photograph.

gangway to the shore. There is a landing float on the west side, and the club is hospitable to visiting yachtsmen from other recognized yacht clubs, as we have always found. This is a club that is primarily interested in sailing, and the water is deep nearby. In June, during even-numbered years, Brenton Cove and vicinity is the rendezvous for the Bermuda Race fleet, and there, on the eve of the race, is to be seen one of the finest gatherings of cruising yachts to be witnessed anywhere in the United States. On odd-numbered years, the Annapolis-Newport Race now ends at Newport and the races for the America's Cup now take place off Newport. During all of these major events Newport is the hub of the yachting universe, and the Ida Lewis Yacht Club is in the middle of that hub. For the rest of the season the yachts seen in Brenton Cove are apt to be relatively few in number compared to those seen in earlier days or now moored in such ports as Padanaram or Marblehead.

For those who carry their cruisers on trailers and would like to start or end a cruise at Newport, there is a fine, concrete launching ramp in King Park, adjoining the Ida Lewis Yacht Club.

The other yacht club in Newport is the Newport Yacht Club, organized in 1890, and now located on Long Wharf, the town dock in the northeast corner of the harbor. The facilities here were vastly improved in 1970 by the addition of thirty-eight floating slips and a permanent breakwater south of the club. For cruising yachtsmen from other recognized yacht clubs, there are a limited number of slips and moorings, with launch service, available. Showers and a bar are located in the attractive clubhouse. Moored off the docks is a large Turnabout fleet. J. T. O'Connell, ship chandlery, located on Long Wharf, is the place to go for all types of marine supplies.

The harbor's water front facing the Newport Yacht Club has undergone a dramatic, faithfully styled restoration, recapturing much of the Colonial charm of old Newport. Running from north to south, the following new construction can be viewed: Long Wharf Mall, with its many shops and the Newport Chamber of Commerce office, which caters to visiting yachtsmen; the Newport Harbor Treadway Inn, including a swimming pool and the Blue Porpoise Tavern built on the exact site of its predecessor; and historic Bowen's Wharf, where there are charming shops like the Chandlery, China Trade Antiques, boutiques, and an old blacksmith shop.

Jim Kirby, owner of the Treadway Inn, told us in 1971 of plans to install sixty slips along his water front for use by overnight guests or those dining at the Blue Porpoise, from which the schooner *Black Pearl* may be seen. The inn rents Javelin daysailers and offers launch service to its guests to and from Ida Lewis Yacht Club.

Gas, repairs, hauling, and other facilities are obtained along the commercial water front on the east side of the harbor. The Newport Shipyard just south of Commercial Wharf is highly regarded for hauling, repair work, etc., but does not sell gas or Diesel fuel. These are obtainable at the Mathinos and Son Shipyard on Commercial Wharf, where berths are available. Christies, just south of Newport Shipyard, also has berths, with electricity, water, showers, toilets, and a telephone. Christies is said to have an excellent restaurant. Port O'Call, managed by Peter Dunning, is well equipped to handle transients, has a liquor store, and a mechanic considered to be one of the best—Gordon Murphy. When we were last there, Port O'Call was welcoming Nicolette Milnes-Walker on her arrival from England after a forty-five-day solo voyage in a 30-foot sloop.

We prefer the Williams & Manchester Shipyard, the reason being that it obviously caters to sailing craft including the "Twelves" during the Cup Races. This handsome marina equipped with excellent docks is the first one you will reach on leaving the Ida Lewis Yacht Club and entering the main harbor. You will find almost everything you require, including The Pier, claimed to be one of the best harborside restaurants around.

Looking to the west, one can easily observe the result of Goat Island's recent face-lifting. The large brick building, resembling a fancy grain elevator, is the Sheraton Islander Inn, not connected with the Goat Island Marina, whose headquarters is housed in a prominent concrete building just to the south. This expansive marina offers sheltered dockage with 150 slips providing water and electricity. To be assigned a slip, put in at the gas dock facing the inner harbor, where fuel, minor repair services, ice, a laundromat, and marine supplies are available. Large power cruisers are usually tied up at the outer docks while sailing craft are assigned dockage on the north side of the marina building. The minimum dockage fee including water and electricity is $10.00 daily. Efficient John Flynn, the marina's manager, knows his way around Newport and boats. For many years he was manager of Newport Shipyard and cares about giving good service.

Next to the Inn is the Aquidneck Tennis Club. The Marina Pub is a recommended and conveniently located bar and restaurant. Car rentals and taxis to Newport are on stand-by.

H.M.S. Rose, a replica of the Revolutionary War British frigate, has left Newport for a permanent station in Boston Harbor. However, Goat Island Marina remains the home port of the *Bill of Rights,* a recently built replica of a 125-foot gaff-topsail schooner of the 1850s. She is being used for commercially scheduled Windjamming cruises in southern New England and Chesapeake Bay waters. Her builder, seventy-two-year-old

Harvey Gamage, is considered by his fellow natives down East to be the last of the great builders of wooden ships. Concerning *Bill of Rights* he has said, "The last time I see this ship is when it's put its tail to me and is disappearing down the harbor. I won't ever see it again, but I will know it is a good ship, because I built it."

Authorities say that there are three Newports: the *Historic Newport,* symbolized by Thames Street along the eastern shore of the harbor; the *Social Newport,* where once the "Four Hundred" held court; and the *Navy Newport,* still evidenced by the number of sailors in the streets. To this we would add the *Yachting Newport,* which reaches its peaks intermittently when the fleets come in. All are interesting in different ways. When you are there, take a look at the Old Stone Mill in Touro Park, made memorable by Longfellow's "Skeleton in Armor":

> There for my lady's bower
> Built I the lofty tower.

While historians dispute the accuracy of the story that it was built by a Viking nearly a thousand years ago, no one knows who did build it, and no plaque or inscription describes its origin.

Like Glen Cove, Long Island, Newport is reminiscent of the bygone days of great estates, when palatial steam yachts rode at anchor. Many of the estates have since been sold to schools or other institutions and, to understate the situation, yachts are smaller now.

11. *Jamestown, Conanicut Island* (236, 353). While this is an open anchorage on the west side of the East Passage, the presence of the hospitable Conanicut Yacht Club, a short distance north of the ferry dock, and just south of Bryer Point, is an incentive to drop anchor off the club and hope for a reasonably calm night, since the holding ground is rather poor and the water is comparatively shallow. The white stakes mark the 6-foot depths, while there is 5 feet off the end of the pier. Conanicut has a clubhouse with a 220-foot pier and is glad to welcome visiting yachtsmen from other recognized yacht clubs. In approaching Jamestown Harbor from the south, be sure to give The Dumplings a very wide berth as you swing gradually around to port heading in. This spot is a poor place to be in an easterly blow.

South of the ferry, on the eastern shore leading toward Bull Point and inside of some islands or outlying rocks are the piers of the Wharton Shipyard, which takes care of yachts and provides guest moorings, if available, and gas, water, and repairs. The holding ground is said to be satisfactory here. Go in to the Wharton dock on either side of the small island north of Old Salt Works Beach. The Dumpling Association has a private dock just north of this beach. If you want to learn anything about the history of this part of the island, see Charles Wharton; he knows about a good many things besides boats.

To the west between Southwest Point and Short Point, boatmen have found Mackerel Cove a most inviting place in which to venture. The entire rockbound shoreline is privately owned and unspoiled. A pebbly swimming beach stretches across the head of the cove, and although it is public, no one is permitted to build fires or to picnic there. Yachtsmen will find this harbor devoid of any facilities, a fact that adds to its charm, and are advised to navigate slowly, reducing their boats' wash to a minimum. Although the holding ground is good, don't get caught here in a strong southerly.

While you are at Jamestown, get someone to drive you to the southern end of Conanicut Island at Beavertail Point, the site of the third-oldest lighthouse erected on the Atlantic Coast. The view looking down from the cliffs is impressive.

The Jamestown high-level bridge across the West Passage has brought Conanicut Island and Jamestown in the line of traffic from the New York area to Newport and Cape Cod. The island and the community are very much worth knowing. Perhaps one of the state moorings or one of Charles Wharton's will relieve you of any worry that you might be dragging anchor if you decide to pay Jamestown a visit.

12. Coasters Harbor and Coddington Cove (236, 353). Just above Newport, these are very much Navy, and visiting yachts are not encouraged. Navy requirements have precedence. The Navy is also active in Melville.

13. Potter Cove, Prudence Island, Narragansett Bay (278, 353). Here is an excellent anchorage protected from virtually all winds, on the northeasterly end of Prudence Island. Red-and-white markers line both sides of the channel. Many yachtsmen confuse this harbor with the other Potter Cove located on the eastern shore of Conanicut Island. But there is no comparison. Our leading authority on this harbor was once a professional clam digger, who "hung out" there or in the cove on the other side of the island most of the time. Here is how he feels about it:

One of the reasons Potter's Cove is so well thought of is that there's absolutely nothing there but a landlocked anchorage. There is a well up at the farm that has good water. Don't fail to fill a jug or two while there. There is no "most convenient wharf for visiting yachtsmen." If you want to go ashore, you either row or swim. The "best place to obtain a meal" is in your own galley, and if you are looking for a hotel, crawl into your bunk and forget it. Never go to sleep on a strange craft.

Follow the buoys in entering and anchor anywhere. It is crowded on weekends but restful and quiet through the week. There is good clam digging. The mosquitoes are terrible, but other places are worse.

The nearest source of gas, supplies, and repairs is at Bristol, about 3 miles away by water. Potter Cove is worth visiting, but be sure your screens are working, and don't pick a weekend. A visitor to this harbor in August of 1966 wrote that "the mosquitoes had either departed by the time we got there or their numbers and hunger have been exaggerated." Potter Cove now has six state moorings. Use a dinghy if you want to land at the only dock on the southwest shore.

Prudence Island is about 6 miles long and is without a town.

14. Bristol (278, 353). The anchorage here is large and exposed for some distance to the southwest and south. However, under the conditions usually prevailing in summer it is one of the most satisfactory ports on the bay for an overnight stop and large enough to hold a club fleet without crowding. The hospitality of the Bristol Yacht Club, the many facilities available in the harbor, the reactivation of the famous Herreshoff yacht yards—now controlled by the Pearson Corporation—the many fine old houses all combine to give Bristol an especial appeal to cruising yachtsmen.

The Bristol Yacht Club moved in 1955 to its present commodious headquarters on Popasquash Neck along the west side of the harbor near its northern end. The club has come a long way since the days when dues were 5¢ a month and those in arrears for six months' dues were liable to expulsion.

On our last stop here, Fleet Captain Seth Paull filled us in on a bit of its history. His grandfather, Commodore William Trotter, founded the club in 1877 as The Neptune Boat Club of Bristol, with a fleet of six-oared shells. Its laudatory purpose was "for the encouragement of boating, other athletic exercises and social enjoyment, and for the promotion of physical and mental culture." Halsey Herreshoff is presently one of the yacht club's most distinguished members.

It is now rated among the leading clubs on the bay and, as such, hosted in 1970 the National Ensign Championship and the Atlantic Coast 110 Championship. When we were there, it boasted an active Junior Sailing Program of seventy boys and girls. Members of other recognized yacht clubs are made welcome, and a snack bar and barroom are available.

There are three, orange-colored state moorings off the club, but if these are not available, ask the launchman for a possibly vacant club mooring. Launch service runs from 8 A.M. to 8:30 P.M. Gas, water, and ice can be drawn at the club dock. If the marine store is closed next door, you can purchase boat gear from the steward.

Just north of the club lies the Bristol Marine Co., offering hauling service and full repair work. New Bristol and Sailstar class auxiliaries are fitted out here.

The offices and boat yards of the Pearson Corporation, including the famous Herreshoff yards and those of a marina named Hawkins and Fales, are on the east shore. There also is the public landing, about halfway up the harbor. Public moorings are available here, and visiting yachts, we were told, may use these overnight without charge. There are a launching ramp and parking area, a public telephone, and other conveniences. If you wish to have a good look at some of the latest fiberglass designs, drop in at Hawkins and Fales' yard. They are one of the largest distributors of Pearson Yachts, and they'll be happy to roll out the red carpet for visiting yachtsmen. Repairs, hauling, and other services are available at one or more of the yards.

We were advised by a local authority to warn visiting yachts to keep well off the Castle Island light, as there are some uncharted rocks with only 6 feet at low water a short distance to the west of the light.

15. *Warren and Barrington Rivers* (278, 353). This anchorage, about 2 miles up the Warren River, is practically landlocked. The approach is narrow and tortuous, but well buoyed and easy to negotiate under power. Some yachts often find a pleasant anchorage in northerly and westerly winds in the middle of Smith Cove away from the river's current. Upriver to starboard, just before you turn into the Barrington River, is the late Bill Dyer's "Anchorage, Inc.," where the famous "Dyer dinks" are made. Be sure to pay this interesting place a visit, whether or not you are contemplating a new dinghy; you may get some ideas, as we did.

Most yachts continue into Barrington River to the attractive Barrington Yacht Club, located below the bridge to Barrington on the west shore of Tyler Point. Just before reaching the club, you will pass the new Barrington Marina on the point's southern tip. This is the yacht club's facility, providing slip space for twenty-five boats belonging to members and transients. Red range markers on both ends of the clubhouse help you determine the limits of the dredged channel. There is 6 feet of water at the dock of this active club, and since a 3- to 4-knot current runs in the river, it is preferable to pick up one of their moorings if available. Gas, Diesel fuel, water, ice, launch service, a snack bar, and a swimming beach are available to members of recognized clubs that offer reciprocal privileges. The Stanley Boat Yard is nearby with very competent repair service, and a ship store that many consider to be one of the best stocked marine emporiums on the coast. Supplies can be bought in Warren across the bridge, or in Barrington.

One of the outstanding clubs on Narragansett Bay, the Barrington Yacht Club is the headquarters of a fine-looking fleet of cruising yachts, as well as the home of many one-design racing boats. It boasts one of the larger Blue Jay and 420 fleets in the country.

We shall now go back to the entrance of the third passage up Narragansett Bay—the Sakonnet River and Mount Hope Bay.

THE SAKONNET RIVER AND MOUNT HOPE BAY

The Sakonnet River is the third and most easterly of the three passages leading northward up Narragansett Bay. Some bay yachtsmen call it the most beautiful of the three, especially in the fall, when the leaves are turning color.

16. Sakonnet Harbor. This harbor is one of the best examples on the New England coast of what man has done to turn a rather poor harbor into a good one. The harbor has been dredged to 8 feet, the dangerous rock in the middle removed, and the breakwater extended to 800 feet in length, thus giving the harbor some of the protection from northwesterlies that was sorely needed. However, the harbor is still small, and the holding ground is said to be poor. Therefore, it is well to pick up a mooring if one is available. There are two state moorings in the harbor and there is a guest mooring available from the yacht club.

The Sakonnet Yacht Club, organized by John Alden, Edward Brayton, and others, is near the head of the harbor and has a long pier on the east side with 5 feet at m.l.w. at its outer end. Few facilities may be found at this club. The Harbor Master lives several doors north of the club. At the fishermen's dock near the end of Breakwater Point on the west side, gas, water, and ice are obtainable. The Fo'c'sle serves good meals and used to sell chowder "to take out." There is a store nearby.

In approaching Sakonnet Harbor, keep well off Sakonnet Point and watch for long lines of fish weirs, sometimes poorly marked. The best plan is to pick up whistle SR, head from there to red bell 2A, and from there to the breakwater marked by a light at its outer end. Be sure to keep well off the harbor's eastern shore. The charts indicate that the lighthouse tower off Sakonnet Point is abandoned. Three bells and a whistler, less appealing but less expensive, now guide yachtsmen into the Sakonnet River.

17. Sachuest Cove (353). Behind (north of) Flint Point, on the western side of the entrance to the Sakonnet River, is an anchorage that is better than any to be found in Sakonnet Harbor from the point of view of accessibility, room, and privacy. Except in winds from north to east it offers good shelter and has been highly recommended by several yachtsmen as having excellent holding ground.

18. Fogland Harbor (353). This is also easy of access and roomy. If you don't need supplies, you may prefer it to Sakonnet. It is open from north-west to north-northeast, but the holding ground is good.

A yachtsman advises: "In entering the harbor, follow the channel north in Sakonnet River until 100 yards past the point. Then turn and go straight into the middle of the bight. Swing south to a line between the point and two flat-topped modern bungalows on the east shore. There is 12 feet of water here at low tide. If you row ashore and phone from a nearby farmhouse, the garage at Tiverton will send down a taxi for the 4-mile trip to Tiverton. Dinner at the Stone Bridge Inn there is well worth the trip."

19. Tiverton (353). Between the old Stone Bridge, which used to connect Almy Point on Aquidneck Island with the mainland, and the new Tiverton fixed bridge, is a section of the Sakonnet River that has become an active yachting center. The channel span of the Stone Bridge has been removed and the tide rushes through. Go through this bridge and obtain an anchorage or dockage at Tiverton on the east shore. Above, the new bridge, with a vertical clearance of 57 to 70 feet, gives access to Mount Hope Bay and the mill city of Fall River in Massachusetts.

The homey Tiverton Yacht Club has a dock on the eastern water front, though its clubhouse is across the main street, a three-story house with a cupola. The club is very active in small one-design class racing, in which older members, known as the "Dashing Daddies," also participate. As the house rules of the club state, "Privileges of the club will be extended to visiting yachtsmen at all times."

Gas is available at several places along the water front, including the dock at the Stone Bridge Boat Yard just above that bridge on the west shore. The Standish Boat Yard further to the north does hauling and repair work, supplies marine charts, hardware, water, gas, ice, Diesel fuel, compass adjustment, a laundromat, and has grocery and other stores nearby. Jack Brimicombe, who obviously caters to cruising yachtsmen, has moorings at $2.00 a night, slips at 15¢ per foot. There's 10 feet off his dock.

The Pirate Cove Marina, directed by the appropriately named Thomas

Kidd, is across the river from Standish, protected behind a stone breakwater. The facilities are newer here, you'll lie away from the current, but the basin is often crowded with local craft. The small but tidy Sakonnet Marina may also be found on the west shore just north of the swing bridge.

We do not suggest anchoring in Tiverton Harbor, for the river current runs from 4 to 5 knots at times between the bridges.

Tiverton, originally the home of the Pocasset Indians, is an interesting place for a visit, though too near Fall River, we imagine, for good swimming. The Stone Bridge Inn has "atmosphere" and serves excellent meals. Yachtsmen will enjoy its Regatta Room, with its mural of "Candy Boats" racing in the Basin, and its cocktail lounge.

20. Kickamuit River, Mt. Hope Bay (353). There is an attractive anchorage, though too large to be snug, in the river to the east of Bristol Neck. Keep close to the red nuns in the narrow entrance channel, as there are outlying rocks along the shore. Your best shelter can be found along the eastern shore beyond black can 1. The small community of Coggeshall on the point is residential, and there are no facilities or supplies. These can be obtained in Fall River. Two state moorings are reported located off the Kicamuit River.

21. Cole River, Mass., Mt. Hope Bay (353). This anchorage is not snug, being wide open to the south until you get into the narrow part of the river, where it is marshy and too shallow for cruising boats. The modest Swansea Marina is on the east shore of the wide part of the river, at South Swansea on Gardners Neck. There, gasoline, water, ice, electricity, repairs, showers, rest rooms, etc., are available. There is a reported 4 feet of water at one pump, 6 at the other. The yard has marine railways, crank case service, and some marine hardware. Supplies are available not far away. We found the best anchorage in the deep water area southwest of the marina.

With Cole River we end our cruise on the Sakonnet River and Mount Hope Bay. There are yacht clubs and docks on the Taunton River, but most of those cruising Narragansett Bay will not want to go that far—unless, of course, they live there.

Our "cruise" on Narragansett Bay ends here and we now go back to Sakonnet Point and head eastward from there toward Buzzards Bay.

Westport, Mass. (237). There are two Westports, Westport Harbor at Acoaxet and Westport Point upriver. The yacht club and the facilities are at the latter Westport. The entrance is a bit tricky, and there is a 3-

or 4-knot current. A local authority advises as follows: "Pick up the bell southeast of Twomile Rock and stand toward the Knubble (a conspicuous high rock) until Dogfish Ledge is abeam to port. Then head for nun 4 off Halfmile Rock and leave it close to starboard. After that swing around the Knubble and follow the buoys." Don't attempt to enter in strong southerly winds, when the sea breaks on the bar at the entrance. This hidden entrance made Westport a perfect hideout for rumrunners during prohibition days.

The dock that appears to port opposite nun 10 is not a public wharf, as it seems to be, but privately owned. Just beyond, about opposite can 11, is a dock and boathouse that looks like a yacht club but isn't. Instead, it belongs to an octagenarian, Richard K. Hawes, who likes to watch the yachts come and go. He calls his lookout "Cockeast Boathouse." While the tide is strong in the lower harbor and the dockage, facilities, and best anchorages are off Westport Point, if you do prefer to anchor below, pick a spot just above can 11 and about southwest of nun 12. This spot offers one advantage. Supplies are difficult to obtain up the harbor. But here at Acoaxet, you'll find a small general store located within a stone's throw of the water tank marked on the chart and standing visibly to the south.

Most cruising men will prefer to go on further to Tripps Boat Yard or to the nearby Westport Yacht Club on the south shore on Horseneck Point south of can 19. This long-established and reliable yard is now run by Mrs. Fred Tripp and her four sons. In producing the popular "Compleat Angler," a line of trim 22-foot fiberglass fishing boats, they proudly claim to be "builders for those who care a little more." Tripp usually has available a slip, dockage, or a spare mooring. It also supplies gas, Diesel fuel, water, ice, electricity, marine hardware, toilets, and a lift, and offers complete repair work. There's a public wharf, used chiefly by fisherman, at the end of Westport Point.

On one of our visits, we picked up a deep-water mooring at the yacht club next door and came in on the launch to have a friendly chat with Commodore Emile Durand. "Visitors love this place," he exclaimed enthusiastically, and from what we saw of the general area we could understand the reasons for his remark. The club, which offers reciprocal club privileges, has a snack bar, showers, and a nice sandy beach, and runs a jitney service to town. Mr. Durand suggested that we take a nature walk down the road to the west leading into the Cherry & Webb Conservation Area. Here we found a secluded bird sanctuary, wonderfully shaped pieces of driftwood, and a dune affording us a fine panoramic view of the coast and harbor channel.

A yachtsman familiar with Westport wrote us: "Good meals can be obtained at Moby Dick Wharf Restaurant during the summer months at the south end of the bridge. Specialties of the house include delicious quahaug chowder and native lobsters caught daily by its own fleet. The Westport Market, where milk and groceries can be obtained, is ⅓ mile north of the bridge in the village. Excellent surf swimming is found on Horse Neck Beach on the seaward side of the neck that forms the harbor." The eastern half of this beach is state-owned and is open to the public for swimming.

Overshadowing the restaurant is a large plant with a sign on top reading "Prelude Corporation." As one of the first offshore lobstering concerns in the world, its development has been rather remarkable.

William Whipple, a young Methodist minister, began lobstering on his own in Westport, a few years ago, to help himself through graduate school. Being an enterprising fellow, he came to believe that by trap fishing far offshore in deep water he could reap a lobster harvest far more bountiful than through customary, inshore lobstering methods. He soon proved his point by returning to port with a record one-day catch of 2250 pounds. The previous record had been 1600 pounds.

Sumner A. Towne, Jr., interested in knowing how all this happened, interviewed Whipple and wrote an article about him in the September, 1971, issue of *Yankee Magazine*. We excerpt a small part of this article for the enlightenment of our readers.

After some 300 years, the inshore lobster fishing industry of New England is in trouble. Where once there was an abundance of good-sized lobsters for the taking, now lobstermen are often reduced to taking last year's short lobster as this year's chicken lobster (1–1½ pounds). At the same time, however, 130 miles offshore, there is a virtually untapped supply of lobster in the 2–8 pound range. Marine scientists estimate that this offshore fishery can sustain a harvest of 15 to 50 million pounds annually!

While most lobstermen now fish their pots in 20–40 feet of water, Bill Whipple fishes *his* pots at 2,000 feet! Prelude is tapping a heretofore untouched supply of the sea's most prized crustacean and providing the answer to the dwindling coastal supply.

Mr. Towne asked Mr. Whipple why he happened to pick Westport as a base, and here is his answer.

Talks with people all up and down the coast convinced me that the type of lobstering grounds I sought would be most accessible from Westport. I found, for example, that from about mid-June to October, fishermen here willing to make the effort to fish Cox's Ledge about 20 miles out of Westport did phenomenally well compared with those fishing inshore. In terms of daily catch, they were taking lobster at a rate of about 5 to 1—though most did not fish the Ledge daily. So, in 1961, I came here, bringing with me a trap peculiar to the Marblehead area where I grew up. This trap was good at inshore fishing, but it really came into its own on Cox's Ledge. It caught manyfold more lobsters than a conventional trap would.

Now Prelude has gone public, is growing like Topsy, and has two sizable fishing boats named the *Wily Fox* and the *Pat-San-Marie*. Who says good old New England ingenuity is dead?

CHAPTER VII

Buzzards Bay, the Elizabeth Islands, and the Cape Cod Canal

As a cruising ground, Buzzards Bay has much to recommend it. Calms are few, for the southwest wind blows up the bay nearly every afternoon, sometimes strongly enough to become a reefing breeze. Fogs are few, seldom as "choking thick" as the down-east specimens, and usually of short duration. The summer sun will usually burn off the fog before noon. Aids to navigation are frequent, large, and noisy. There is a lane of lighted buoys from Penikese to the canal. There is plenty of company, for the bay is scoured daily by hundreds of yachts—outboards, Beetle Cats, power cruisers, and some of the largest, fastest, and handsomest ocean racers on the east coast. Add the possibility of meeting a square-rigged topsail schooner and a replica of a down-east coaster with a gaff topsail set from hoops aloft. Harbors in the bay range from the busy fishing port of New Bedford to yachty Padanaram and picturesque Cuttyhunk. But no harbor in this area—within easy reach of Boston, New York, and Providence—is deserted.

Tidal Currents. An almost indispensable guide to tidal currents in Buzzards Bay, Nantucket and Vineyard sounds, and through the "holes" between the Elizabeth Islands is *Eldridge Tide and Pilot Book,* published by Robert E. White on Commercial Wharf in Boston. By means of a series of current diagrams, one for each hour of the tide, the book comes as close to predicting tidal conditions as the mind of man can do it. *The Tidal Current Charts, Narragansett Bay to Nantucket Sound* (consisting of two sets of charts at $2.00) are very useful and may be obtained from National Ocean Survey sales agents or from the National Ocean Survey, Distribution Division (C44), Washington, D.C. 20235.

The problem centers around the difference in water level between Buzzards Bay and Vineyard Sound. Whenever the water is higher in the bay, the current will flow southeastward into the sound, and *vice versa.* Because the times of high water are radically different in the bay, Vineyard Sound and Nantucket Sound, the tidal currents, while predictable, are irregular.

Because the tidal currents run with inspiring velocity, particularly in the "holes," careful attention should be paid to their direction. Note that if one must buck the tide, it is better to do so in Buzzards Bay than in Vineyard Sound.

Included annually in *Eldridge* is a letter the original publisher wrote to skippers and mates navigating Vineyard Sound, pointing out that vessels entering Vineyard Sound from the south will experience a strong set to the northwest on both flood and ebb, thus giving the shores of Cuttyhunk and Nashawena the title of "The Graveyard," because of the number of vessels wrecked there. The letter is interesting not only for its information but for the pleasant and personal touch it imparts to an otherwise arid volume of tables and factual information.

Around the Cape or Through the Canal? As he approaches the Texas Tower at the entrance to Buzzards Bay, the eastward-bound skipper must decide whether to sail up Buzzards Bay and pass through the Cape Cod Canal or to sail up Vineyard Sound, east through Nantucket Sound, and then up the outside of the Cape.

The route through the canal is shorter. On a voyage from Woods Hole to Gloucester, the canal saves 36 miles. There are several excellent harbors in Buzzards Bay and beyond the canal in Massachusetts Bay. The route is through protected waters all the way; and, except between the eastern end of the canal and Plymouth, buoys are noisy and close together. The waters of Buzzards Bay and Cape Cod Bay are crowded with commercial craft, fishermen, fine yachts, and big steamers. Should you decide on this course, see page 221 for specific advice on the canal.

The route through the sounds and around the Cape, however, is a good deal more challenging. Once committed to this route, one must be prepared to keep going. From West Chop to Pollock Rip the course lies among shoals and through tide rips. From there one faces open ocean and apparently endless beach with no practical shelter whatever before Provincetown, 45 miles away.

But there is something about the long, seemingly endless dunes of the Cape that has a peculiar fascination to many yachtsmen. What appears to be a point, which you never seem to pass, keeps always ahead of you as you go on for mile after mile. The gradual, convex curve of the Cape gives this illusion. Were it not for the famous lighthouses, Chatham, Nauset, and Cape Cod (or Highland), Race Point, Wood End, and Long Point, you might wonder if you were holding your own.

Until the Cape Cod Canal was opened in 1914 the route around the Cape was crowded with sailing vessels and steamers. Whalers, fishermen, and square-rigged cargo vessels ran down the line of light ships or lay at anchor in Vineyard Haven or Menemsha Bight awaiting a fair wind. Almost every winter gale caught several vessels on the dangerous shoals, parted their ground tackle, and drove them ashore. Coast Guardsmen at life-saving stations manned surfboats to the rescue with courage, strength, and skill now legendary. The great five- and six-masted coal schooners of the first quarter of this century were the last; now only an occasional tanker or fisherman and an infrequent yacht make the passage. However, anyone who undertakes the lonely voyage can take a good deal of satisfaction in having made successfully a difficult passage.

Harbors on the Buzzards Bay Mainland, Mass.

Padanaram, South Dartmouth (252). We are now back on the northwest shore of Buzzards Bay, opposite the Elizabeth Islands. Padanaram is the next good mainland harbor going east after Westport.

On the chart it is called Apponaganset Bay; the town is South Dartmouth; and yet to all yachtsmen and many others, it is known as Padanaram. The only recognition the chart gives to that name is at Padanaram Breakwater. Authorities differ as to how the name "Padanaram" came to be applied to that port. One explanation, told to an interested cruising man by a member of the New Bedford Yacht Club, is as follows:

A man named Laban once lived in South Dartmouth. He thought that if he ran water over a mill wheel, he would get enough power to raise the water up again with something over for other purposes. He built a mill to test the idea, which was dubbed "Laban's Folly." Then, as the Biblical Laban lived in Padanaram, the locality was unofficially given the name. The biblical reference is Genesis 28:1, 2, which reads:

"And Isaac called Jacob and blessed him, and charged him, and said unto him, Thou shalt not take a wife of the daughters of Canaan. Arise, go to Padan-aram, to the house of Bethuel thy mother's father; and take thee a wife from thence of the daughters of Laban thy mother's brother."

A student of local history discounts the story, placing the first use of the name for this community much earlier than Laban's Folly, and says that the term "Padanaram" was first applied to Howland's house, there almost a century before. Anyway, we'll join everybody else and call it Padanaram. Padan-aram was one of the original names of Mesopotamia and lay between the Tigris and Euphrates rivers in Assyria.

There is an excellent and lively anchorage in the Apponaganset River off the South Dartmouth headquarters of the New Bedford Yacht Club, at the head of the harbor to starboard. Heading toward Padanaram from the south, your initial landfall will be a prominent radar installation on Round Hill Point off of which rise Dumpling Rocks. Strangers approaching the harbor from the west should make the sandspit red flashing bell and then proceed to West Passage lighted buoy 9, which is in a northerly direction and is a lighted gong. They are then able to lay a course directly from there to the Padanaram breakwater off Ricketsons Point. This gives an excellent entrance in either darkness or fog. It gives better than 18-foot draft right to the breakwater, eliminating all possibility of getting into any trouble with the numerous rocks in that part of the bay.

A breakwater at Ricketsons Point with a flashing red light on its western end protects the anchorage from the east except in abnormally high tides. Only south and southeast gales and hurricanes cause any trouble at the anchorage, and the breakwater breaks all but the worst of these seas. For a quiet spot, especially desirable for one entering after sundown, swerve in toward shore to starboard immediately after passing the breakwater and anchor just inside the breakwater. It is quiet and calm, and there is no disturbance from the town and automobiles, or from the numerous craft plying about in the large fleet usually anchored in the inner reaches of the harbor. Also the water is cleaner here, and an early morning dip will be enjoyed.

There are landing facilities at the club, however, and it is more convenient. Depth at the main dock is 7 to 10 feet with 4 feet at its newer dock to the south. Visiting yachtsmen must register at the clubhouse to be granted reciprocal guest privileges. Two club tenders run until sundown. It is often possible to obtain a mooring from the steward at a small charge, but to be on the safe side, we suggest phoning ahead for a reservation. He'll issue you a guest card good for seventy-two hours. Gas, ice, and water are available at the dock from 8 A.M. to sunset. Stores, where all kinds of supplies may be purchased, are only a short walk from the clubhouse. A cab can take you to a laundromat located 3 miles away toward New Bedford.

The New Bedford Yacht Club, founded in 1877 and originally located on Popes Island in New Bedford Harbor, was hit hard by Hurricane Carol in 1954. The fine old clubhouse survived, and its shore property offers a protective bulkhead, a cement boat-launching ramp, and extensive dockage. Its facilities are available to members of other recognized yacht clubs.

There is much yachting life in the harbor, the New Bedford Yacht Club starting many boats each Wednesday and Saturday in July and August. In the latter month, the club holds a three-day regatta. There are several dinner-dances held throughout the season at the clubhouse, at which all visiting yachtsmen are welcome. During recent years the New York Yacht Club has paid Padanaram squadron visits during its annual cruise in late July or early August. New Bedford's racing tradition is epitomized in its annual Whaler's Race around the whistler off No Mans Land, thence either way around Block Island, and homeward to Padanaram.

The village boasts no hotel. Good food may be savored nearby at The Sail Loft and at Margie's.

Padanaram is only a short run by automobile or bus from New Bedford, and is much to be preferred to that port. There are two marine yards located on the Apponaganset River. One is the Concordia Company, which is famous for Concordia yawls and Beetle Cats and is located directly north on property adjoining the yacht club. Here you may obtain marine services. They also have a marine railway that can handle boats up to 50 feet in length. There is 6 or 7 feet of water at the ways at low tide. Mechanical service and riggers are available. On adjoining property is a shop called "The Packet," which has a good supply of government charts, sports clothes, and many other things of interest to the yachting set, including new postal service. Mr. Kim White, its owner, is a good source for local information. Norman Fortier, one of the country's finest marine photographers, occupies a fascinating studio adjacent to The Packet. Many a skipper has arranged here to have Fortier "shoot" his vessel hard on the wind off Padanaram. Next door is Manchester Yacht Sails, Inc., an excellent sail loft. You will find them very obliging when it comes to either repairs or new canvas.

Davis and Tripp, located close to the bridge, has gas, Diesel fuel, water, ice, etc. They also have dockage space with electricity, nearby rest rooms, telephone, etc.

Up the river above the drawbridge lies Marshall Marine, famous for building the Marshall Cats.

Yachts over 50 feet in length requiring yard facilities will find several in New Bedford and Fairhaven.

New Bedford and Fairhaven (252). Once famous as a whaling port, New Bedford later became an important textile center. It also has managed over the years to get in the way of at least two devastating hurricanes, one in September, 1944, which finished off the clubhouse of the New Bedford Yacht Club on the Fairhaven Bridge, and another, Hurricane Carol, on August 31, 1954, which badly damaged some of the harbor's boat yards and dock—to say nothing of its fleet.

Finally, New Bedford-Fairhaven and the federal government decided to take action in preventing such future storm devastation, and in 1965 a huge $18 million hurricane dike was completed. This 4600-foot barrier, located at the mouth of the Acushnet River, runs west from Ft. Phoenix to the southern tip of Palmer Island, thence all the way to the western shore. At the location of the present channel, there are two gates, one on each side of a 150-foot opening. These massive hinged gates may be swung shut to close off the harbor in case of storms. In entering through these gates, we spotted a high green light to port and a red to starboard. The current through this opening reaches a maximum of 2.4 knots and the tide has a tendency to set you to the east as you pass through. A diaphragm horn has been installed on the west gate, sounding one blast every ten seconds for a two-second blast. This beautifully constructed barrier, having a maximum clearance of only 2 inches between all its rocks, has now helped to make New Bedford a major harbor of refuge for cruising yachtsmen.

The former yacht club station on Popes Island is now a small marina, known as the Outdoorsman, which specializes in fishing tackle, marine equipment, etc. They have docking facilities for cruising yachts and also supply gas, Diesel fuel, water, ice, etc. There's just 5 feet dockside here with no hauling or repair work conducted. The John S. Dunn Marine Service and Supply are on the west shore of the harbor a short distance south of the bridge. They also supply gas, Diesel fuel, water, ice, marine hardware, etc. This is primarily a fishing dock but they also service yachts.

On the Fairhaven shore close to nun 12 is the Fairhaven Marina, equipped with new dockage and added services such as a laundromat and showers. Gas, Diesel fuel, water, ice, a marine store and other facilities are available, and a slip or mooring can be obtained. This yard's main function is hauling, repairs, and storage, and they are said to be able to take care of yachts up to 135 feet in length and 16-foot draft. D. N. Kelley & Sons has deep water at its yard further north but offers comparatively limited facilities. It is only a ten-minute walk to town or, if you prefer, Fairhaven Marina can arrange to deliver you supplies.

Padanaram has taken the place of New Bedford as the important yachting center of the vicinity, and what was once a branch station of the New Bedford Yacht Club is now the headquarters of that outstanding club. There is no station in New Bedford.

C.E. Beckman still has its well-equipped marine hardware store in New Bedford.

If you can find transportation, an interesting trip to take is to the battleship U.S.S. *Massachusetts,* which is now the official war memorial of the state. It is now moored just above the new highway bridge on the Fall River side and welcomes visitors aboard.

In 1959, a plaque honoring Captain Joshua Slocum was dedicated at Fairhaven's Poverty Point. For it was here on the bank of the Acushnet River that Slocum had rebuilt and launched in 1894 his 36-foot cutter,

Spray, in which he became the first man to circumnavigate the world alone.

New Bedford and Fairhaven have many attractions for yachtsmen, this center being the best for nautical supplies between Boston and Narragansett Bay. The Whaling Museum in New Bedford and the Rogers Unitarian Church in Fairhaven are especially worth visits. There is steamer connection with Woods Hole, Martha's Vineyard, and Nantucket, and bus connections with Providence, Boston, and other points.

In 1924 there were only two of the old whaling vessels left: *Charles W. Morgan* and *Wanderer,* built in Mattapoisett in 1878. Today only the former remains, lovingly preserved in the sand by the Marine Historical Association, Inc., at Mystic Seaport, Mystic, Connecticut, a place that every lover of boats should visit.

As for *Wanderer,* she set out from New Bedford in August, 1924, on her last whaling voyage. On the night of the twenty-sixth she anchored in lower Buzzards Bay. That night the tail end of a West Indies hurricane came up the coast. While her captain was ashore, she dragged anchor, drifted across the lower bay, and was completely wrecked on the reef southwest of Cuttyhunk Island. There are at least two excellent models of her, one at the New York Historical Society, 170 Central Park West, New York City, the gift of George A. Zabriskie in 1939, and another in the H.H. Kynett Collection at Mystic Seaport.

Mattapoisett (252). Large and easy to enter, with few outlying obstacles, Mattapoisett Harbor serves as a popular rendezvous for club fleets, particularly for that of the New York Yacht Club, which meets there from time to time. Its disadvantage from a cruising man's viewpoint is its size and the fact that it is wide open to the southeast. Nevertheless, in ordinary summer weather it is usually satisfactory, with plenty of room for everyone and depths about right for all concerned. Good anchorage is obtainable right up to the town wharf with the amber light. Even the *Shenandoah,* a beautiful 120-foot topsail rigged schooner, makes Mattapoisett a regular port of call.

But the harbor has surprisingly limited dock space. Mattapoisett Boat Yard has a yard and short dock located not far beyond the lighthouse on the northeast shore. Moorings are provided for visiting yachts. There is 5 feet of water at their float at low tide and the yard does engine servicing and repairs and has a marine railway. Gas and water are on tap, and there is a launch for transporting passengers, towing, etc.

Adjoining the boat yard is the Mattapoisett Yacht Club, small, most unpretentious, and hospitable to visiting yachtsmen from other yacht clubs. Here is the most convenient stop to take on gas and water, but no ice is on hand.

A small public dock offering a 4-foot depth at mean low water is located just above nun 8 at the northern end of the harbor, where fuel, ice, and supplies can be picked up. There are four piers, with many boats tied up between them. The model of a swordfish on a pole rises above one of the piers, and from what we have seen we'd call this a fishermen's mecca. A fine concrete launching ramp makes it possible to launch boats from trailers, and there is plenty of parking space for trailers and cars. The town puts out guest moorings in summer.

There is an inn about 100 yards from the town wharf called the Holiday Inn, famous for its buffet. The stores also are not far from the wharf.

Mattapoisett meant to the Indians "Place of Rest," a name that did not seem particularly appropriate when we visited the town docks early on a Sunday morning in August. Later, the town became a shipbuilding, whaling, and salt-manufacturing port. Many of the New Bedford whaling vessels were built here. Its famous tradition of master boat building is still being carried on today at Allan Vaitses Associates Yard on Harbor Road. More than one hundred boats of almost every type of construction known to the modern boating world have been built by Vaitses, whose yard is noted for tackling difficult designs and for working with a variety of materials, both old and new.

Marion (Sippican) (251). Though settled in 1679, Marion was named for a famous Revolutionary hero, Francis Marion, the "Swamp Fox," about whom the "Song of Marion's Men" was written.*

Here is one of the best all-round yacht harbors on the coast. To the east of the entrance is Bird Island Lighthouse—no longer used—and to the west is Blake Point, marked Converse Point on the chart, occupied by summer homes and marked by a tall flagpole. This western shore should be given a wide berth, as there are many outlying rocks. The red nun at the entrance off Ram Island, though close to the westerly shore, must be left to starboard, as its color if not its location would indicate. The black can and the little island beyond are then left to port. At night it is important to note that there are no range lights in the harbor. Like Mattapoisett, Marion can easily be entered under sail.

The harbor's popularity, especially on weekends, affords limited space for anchoring. But by anchoring to the north of Little Island (which is just west of can 9) in 9 feet, good protection is obtained from all winds. Other possible anchorages are in the good water to the south of Allens Point or further to the north along this point's western shore. These two areas, however, are apt to be rough in strong southerlies.

* As reported in *Massachusetts*—American Guide Series (Houghton Mifflin Co.).

It is more convenient, of course, off the Beverly Yacht Club or Barden's Boat Yard on the west shore beyond. This club used to have its clubhouse on Butler Point but lost it in the hurricane of 1938. A new clubhouse was erected at Barden's Yard next to the Town Dock. But Hurricane Carol dealt the club another severe blow. The club has fully recovered and is now well established in a clubhouse converted from a former residence and located just to the south of Barden's Boat Yard and the town dock. There is a pier in front. The club has launch service, provides showers, meals, and a bar in a delightful colonial building. Members of other recognized yacht clubs granting reciprocal privileges are welcomed. Although there are no facilities for cruising boats, the launchman may be fortunate in spotting a vacant mooring for you. Many yachts stop overnight in summer before or after passing through the Cape Cod Canal. It is neither too near nor too far from the canal entrance, and is ideal for an overnight stop.

Bill Coulson runs Barden's Boat Yard to the north of the yacht club and has everything from ship models to ship supplies. He is also Harbor Master at the time of writing. See him for a possible mooring but be reminded that there are only three guest moorings in the entire harbor. Gas, water, ice, and marine supplies are to be had at the stone pier, where there is 4½ feet at m.l.w. You may reserve a mooring from him in advance by phoning. For prompt service and repairs, Bill Coulson and his men are unexcelled, as we know from our own experience. Both Barden's and Burr Brothers close down tighter than a drum on Sunday afternoons at 4 P.M.

After Fessenden Blanchard's death in 1963, his friends wished to express their affection through an appropriate memorial. After contact with the officers of the Cruising Club of America, of which he was a member, it was decided to establish through voluntary contributions a "Blanchard Memorial Guest Mooring" for member yachtsmen putting into Marion Harbor. Therefore, in the spring of 1965, a 600-pound mushroom anchor was set out in 10 feet of water located well to the southeast of the Beverly Yacht Club, where we hope it will be for many years to come. It can be identified by the blue-and-white burgee of the Cruising Club. See the club's launchman for its use.

Near the head of the harbor is Burr Brothers. There is 4 feet at mean low water in the channel leading to Burr's, and about the same depth at the dock. The Burrs have a sail loft, repair and hauling facilities, and sell outboards. They also have the Sippican Marina with a number of slips.

Supplies are conveniently available on the shore road near Barden's. "Petersen's Ice Cream," which started in 1921, is near at hand, and the ice cream is as good as ever. Across the road from the town dock is Jenkins (closed on Mondays), which serves excellent light meals, and provides a gift shop and dairy products; almost next door is a grocery store with an ice-vending machine outside. The post office is up the street. The Colonial Coach on nearby Route 6 serves good drinks and food. They will pick you up and return you to the harbor at no charge.

Here, too, is the homeport of the lovely green hull, two-master *Tabor Boy;* the training ship of Tabor Academy, whose trim campus can be seen just above Barden's. Many homes of Boston summer residents are on wooded slopes on both shores. Some of the finest sailing on the coast is near at hand, and many of the best harbors are within a day's sail. The town has a large summer weekend population, as it is accessible from Boston or New York via New Bedford or Providence.

Marion was the home of Captain Benjamin S. Briggs, master of the doomed half-brig, *Mary Celeste,* whose complete disappearance of crew off the Azores in 1872 still remains the world's greatest sea mystery.

Wareham (251). Once a whaling and shipbuilding port, Wareham has now become an important cranberry center, though on the Wareham River the number of boats being built is probably greater than ever before. These are the products of the Cape Cod Shipbuilding Company, well known for such small sailboats as the Raven, Mercury, and Bull's Eye.

While somewhat off the main track toward the Cape Cod Canal, Wareham River offers several possible anchorages or tie-ups for yachts drawing under 6 feet. One of these is under the partial lee of Long Beach Point, and the other in the narrow part of the river off Wareham Neck below the bridge. The latter is convenient to the town of Wareham and supplies, but it takes quite a jaunt upriver to get there. Long Beach Point, much of which is under water at high tide, is about 1½ miles from nun 4 off Great Hill and an equal distance to the docks up at Wareham.

The buoyed channel to Wareham is crooked and twisting, with the most difficult part at Quahaug Bar, where depths cannot always be counted on. The mean range of the tide here is 4 feet. Going up-channel, hug can 21 close to port, don't be lured into Broad Marsh River no matter how inviting looking, and keep nun 32 well to starboard further up. Warr's Marine Railway, located on the port shore just above nun 30, has 4½ feet at its main dock at low water. Here you have access to moorings, slips, electricity, gas, Diesel fuel, water, showers, ice, and all types of repair and marine supply service. Since a 3-knot current runs along this upper part of the narrow channel, we were definitely advised not to attempt anchoring. At the wharves at Wareham depths are from 5 to 11 feet, according to the *Coast Pilot,* and 9 feet according to the chart. The

Coast Pilot advises strangers to obtain local information about channel depths before attempting to navigate the river.

Onset (251). There are two anchorages here: (1) off the Onset Town Wharf at the end of the channel, and (2) off Point Independence, the later place being smaller and less noisy. It is designated as a special anchorage not requiring riding lights. Of the approaches to them, and the facilities available, a local authority writes as follows:

> When approaching from the Cape Cod Canal or from Buzzards Bay, turn westerly into the 150-foot Onset Bay Channel, keeping about 75 feet to the southwest of flashing white light 11 on a steel-pile dolphin. The Onset Bay Channel has a minimum depth of 11 to 13 feet to Wickets Island and to the 200-foot Onset Town Wharf. There is 8 to 15 feet in the large anchorage basin. The channel is well marked with nine black and eight red buoys. Coming into the inner harbor at night, use the high wide arc light on the town wharf as a range light, after making the turns at Wickets Island. There is good anchorage space and excellent holding ground. Both the Onset and Point Independence anchorages are well sheltered and offer safe anchorage. The Harbor Master is at the town wharf.

In 1971 the State Division of Waterways announced plans to spread the perimeter of the Onset Town anchorage. The state will dredge an area from the entrance of Sunset Cove to near the town pier and from the mouth of East River to the bridge over the river.

The proximity of the business section offers an unusual convenience for purchasing supplies of every kind and having repairs made by competent and experienced mechanics. Water is furnished pleasure craft without charge on application to the Harbor Master at the town wharf. He is on duty there from May to October. To insure greater comforts for yachtsmen, speed regulations will be strictly enforced in the vicinity of both anchorage basins. There is 13 feet at m.l.w. along the face of the town wharf, where boats are permitted to tie up for one hour to stock up on provisions.

Craft drawing less than 7 feet can also use the Point Independence anchorage basin. Swing northeasterly after passing red buoy 10, giving both Onset Island to starboard and Wickets Island to port a good berth until off the large marine railway on the mainland. Then, veer west to an anchorage.

Expect to fight a violent cross current going at ninety degrees to the channel entering Onset. A correspondent writes that the "best anchorage is off the Point Independence Yacht Club dock. The club people are obliging and will supply gas and water and order ice for you. A good yard with a good mechanic is near the club." The club usually has guest moorings but only about 4 feet at its docks. The Onset Bay Marina, the yard referred to, has gas, Diesel fuel, water, ice, electricity, a railway, laundromat, shuttle service, and 6 feet at its slips. In 1971, this marina underwent an expansion program through the construction of forty-seven additional floating slips, and a new restaurant and cocktail lounge.

Mooring facilities are usually available at this marina on the starboard side of the harbor. A note in a yearbook of the Cruising Club of America reads:

> The anchorage is excellent and protected for small craft but should not be used by vessels drawing more than 7 feet. Facilities for supplies are inconvenient, but responsible custody for boats as well as excellent repairs may be obtained.

Repairs can be had at both Onset and Point Independence. Gas is not available at the town wharf. Containers for rubbish and garbage can be found there, and all yachtsmen are asked to cooperate to keep Onset Bay and adjacent waters free of pollution. Complete information of interest to yachtsmen and tourists can be obtained from the Onset Bay Chamber of Commerce. Onset is not an exclusive place, but everyone we have found there, while cruising, is very friendly.

Through the Canal (251). The skipper who has chosen the route through the canal should first consult the tide tables in *Eldridge Tide and Pilot Book* for the time the current turns eastward in the canal. For an ordinary auxiliary to buck the tide is possible, but to do so makes for a slow and tedious trip. By planning stops at one of the attractive harbors in Buzzards Bay, one should be able to count on a quick passage with a fair tide. Onset, Monument Beach, or Pocasset are good shelters close to the west end of the canal. The boat basin at the east end is a satisfactory if not an enthralling shelter.

The canal is supervised by the U.S. Army Engineers. They have laid down rules that are published in *Coast Pilot 2,* page 51, 1966 edition. They may be summarized for yachts as follows:

1. There are traffic lights at Wings Neck at the west end and at the Sandwich control station at the east end. They concern primarily vessels over 65 feet in length; but if the light is red, you may be hailed from a patrol boat or from the shore at Sandwich or Buzzards Bay and given spe-

The Cape Cod Canal, Onset, and Cape Cod Bay.

cific directions.

2. All vessels are required to make a complete transit of the canal without stopping. Anchoring except in case of emergency is not permitted. If you are forced to anchor, get as close to the shore as possible and await the arrival of a towboat, which will shortly turn up to assist you. If you have a radio, call WUA-21, Cape Cod Canal Office, on 2350 kc. Listen on this frequency if you have no transmitter.

3. The normal position of the railroad bridge is up, but it is lowered for trains. If it is down, stop or turn and stem the tide at the designated points. When the bridge is about to be lowered, the operator will sound two blasts of the horn. When it is about to be raised, he will sound one blast. When the bridge is down in thick weather, or if a vessel is approaching and the span cannot be raised, the operator will sound four blasts.

4. Excessive speed causing big wakes is forbidden. Minimum running time at slack water between Sandwich Observation Station and Buzzards Bay Administration Building is forty-five minutes.

5. Vessels travelling with the current have the right of way over those travelling against it.

6. No oil or refuse may be thrown overboard.

7. No fishing from boats or skin-diving is permitted.

8. Auxiliaries must use power. Sailing vessels without power must be towed.

Ordinarily, passage through the canal is a simple affair. The channel is wide enough so that vessels can pass easily, and the current runs straight through.

Boat Basin at Sandwich. This is a convenient if not particularly attractive anchorage at which to await a fair tide bound west or at which to spend a night after a late afternoon passage of the canal bound east. It is secure, easy of access, and 8 to 10 feet deep at low water. Holding ground is good. There is a small marina at the southwest corner with a number of slips, some of which may be available for visitors. It is forbidden by canal regulations to tie up to the Army Engineers' float. Gasoline is available at two floats on the south side. There is an asphalt launching ramp near the marina.

The only real concern here is overcrowding and consequent lack of room to swing. Rafting-up could be rough on topsides in the event of much traffic in the canal, as the wash of passing vessels occasionally works in.

There is a restaurant on the shore, not open in 1971, and a telephone booth at the marina office. There are no supplies available nearer than Sandwich, 2 miles away.

As the next deep-water harbor bound east is Plymouth or Provincetown, this anchorage may be convenient.

Phinneys Harbor, Monument Beach, Mass. (251). We shall now continue to "cruise" along the shores of Buzzards Bay, from east of the Canal entrance southward to Cuttyhunk.

Beating into the prevalent Buzzard Bay sou'wester, many a skipper has cursed the tempestuous seas that build up along the western stretch of the Cape Cod Canal known as Hog Island Channel. Such a nightmarish experience can be largely avoided by heeding the advice of the distinguished yachtsmen John Parkinson, Jr., who has spent much of his lifetime slicing through Cape Cod waters. In his book *The Bay and the Sound,* with photographs by Norman Fortier, he offers this guidance:

> Immediately after you come abreast of Mashnee Island, swing hard-left out of the Canal and skirt the south shore of the Island where the chart shows 9 feet; avoid the buoyed rock on the southeast corner of the Island and you will find yourself in the old Canal channel, which will provide you with a smooth exit in the lee of Wings Neck.*

Phinneys Harbor is another possible port for an overnight stop preparatory to going through the Cape Cod Canal. However, it is not nearly so satisfactory as the Port Independence anchorage at Onset, for it is large, and most of it is open to the southwest except in the southeast corner, where it is open for about a mile and a half to northwesters. This corner, however, is the best place to anchor, if you can get in without hitting a shoal spot on either side of the narrow passage of deep water. Here is located the Monument Beach Anchorage, a long pier with gas, ice, water, and moorings. It is owned by the town but leased to an operator, and a snack bar is at the shore end. There is reported to be at least 6 feet of water at the end.

On weekends or summer evenings the pier and shore front swarm with people garbed in a wide variety of apparel, few of them interested in the peace and quiet sometimes desired by cruising men. A quieter anchorage, well protected from northwesters, but not from the south, is in the old Cape Cod Canal channel just south of the neck of land leading to what used to be *Mashnee Island,* but which the abandonment of the former channel converted into the end of a peninsula. Here is plenty of water if

* From *The Bay and the Sound,* by John Parkinson, Jr., and Norman Fortier (Little, Brown and Company, 1968).

you can keep on the straight and narrow path. You will be some distance from landing and other facilities, but you will find it more private here than at the "Anchorage."

Mr. Barlow's yard is located on the east side of the entrance to Pocasset River. The anchorage is crowded but "deep," as Cape Cod understands the term—better than a fathom at low water. A correspondent familiar with the yard describes Mr. Barlow as a good workman, "last of the real Cape Codders on the Cape," and adds that his prices are reasonable "if you don't mind waiting till he feels like it." Having viewed the summer scene on the Cape, the writer's sympathies are strongly with Mr. Barlow.

Pocasset, Mass. (251). There are several snug and secure anchorages in the bay between Wings Neck and Scraggy Neck around Bassetts Island. Any one of these makes good shelter should one have to lie over to wait for a fair tide through the canal. In the event of a heavy blow or a hurricane, you can scarcely do better than to hole up in one of these anchorages. With two anchors down and plenty of scope, one cannot be safer anywhere in Buzzards Bay.

Pocasset Harbor. This anchorage lies between Bassetts Island and Wings Neck. Simply follow the shore of Wings Neck right into the entrance, leaving nun 2 to starboard and favoring the Wings Neck shore slightly as a bar makes out from Bassetts Island about one-third of the way across. If you are running for the entrance before a powerful sou'wester, don't get "pooped." The late Mr. Blanchard gave this advice with authority. When the tide runs out against a sou'wester funneled into the entrance, the tide rip can be dangerous to an outboard cruiser, at least, and mighty unpleasant. Rather than come out through such a tide rip in a small craft, it would be better to make a detour around Bassett Island and come out by way of Cataumet. As we shall see, there is a channel between Red Brook Harbor and Hospital Cove, Cataumet.

Anchor in the bight of Bassetts Island or take one of the guest moorings put out by Parker's yard in Red Brook Harbor. This berth is clean, quiet, and uncluttered. Although on weekends it attracts a good many yachts from Buzzards Bay ports, most of them are seeking peace and quiet.

There is little point in landing on Bassetts Island, as it is private property, and it is said to be infested with wood ticks and poison ivy.

"The Buzzards" is the name of a yacht club located on Wings Neck in the cove to port just inside of the narrow entrance to the inner harbor. This is a small club with no facilities except a dock and, we have heard, a telephone. It is reported "by sources that we believe to be reliable" that the women members didn't think that the club name was sufficiently dignified or glamorous; they were out-talked and out-voted. The name remains.

In 1971 a very attractive feature of this anchorage was a visit by two local boys to collect our trash and garbage. Instead of seeking payment for this, they offered for sale some of their mother's home-made blueberry tarts, which found a ready market. This happy situation may be too good to continue, but everything possible should be done to encourage these enterprising young men.

Barlow's Landing. This is a possible anchorage for shoal-draft boats. There is a store and a small yard here.

Hen Cove. This, too, is a possible anchorage for shoal-draft boats, but it is large and not very attractive. There are numerous summer homes around the shore, but no store within easy reach and no landing.

Red Brook Harbor. This harbor is a little more difficult of access than others in the neighborhood but is secure and snug, if inclined to be crowded. Simply round the nun north of Bassetts Island, giving it a generous berth, pass close to nun 12, and anchor wherever you can find room. A black buoy with reflectors is locally maintained off the 5-foot spot inside the nun. Several guest moorings are maintained by the two boat yards, Parker's and Kingman's, and there are two marinas with slips providing the usual facilities. Gas, Diesel oil, water, and ice are available at both places, and stores are but a short walk away.

The Chart Room on one of the wharves is a restaurant-lounge very well spoken of.

Hospital Cove. This is a perfectly protected anchorage in the bight north of Scraggy Neck. For one not desperately in need of boat yard facilities, it is a quiet alternative to Red Brook Harbor. Anchor south of the outer island, which looks like a peninsula on the chart.

A yachtsman who has poked his way into many harbors writes:

I drew 5½ feet and entered at dead low tide (purposely), using a lead and creeping. We could see from the bow where the sand shoals ran and by accepting helpful advice from natives (members of the crew), we stuck once; but I put an anchor out to what looked to me like the center of the little harbor and pulled the boat right over with no trouble (sand and mud bottom). For any boat no longer than mine, this makes an ideal harbor to be ranked with Hadley and Quissett for

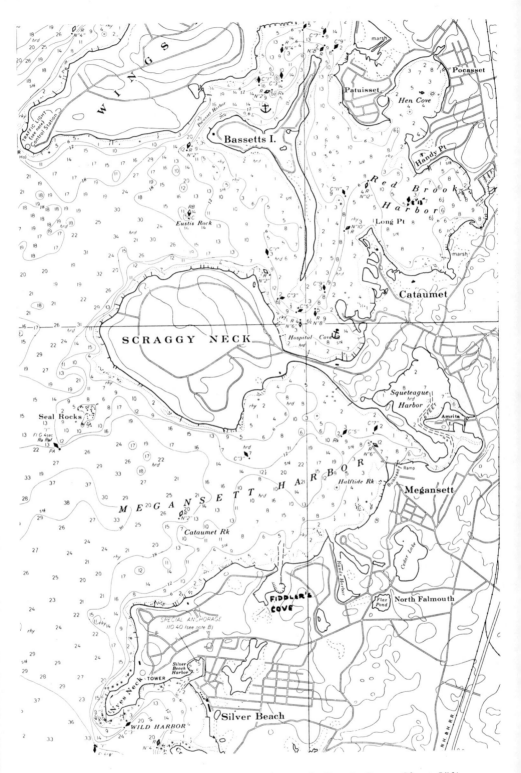

Anchorages along the east shore of Buzzards Bay (refer to Chart 251).

swimming, quiet, etc. The local people will help in getting supplies. Also it is ideal if just going into or leaving the Canal. I strongly advise looking into this harbor. Mine was one of the largest boats ever in there, so they told me, but I won't miss the place again if I can help it.

The narrow channel between nun 8 and can 11 appears to be very dangerous from the chart. However inspection from a skiff with a sounding lead showed it to be wider than it appears and clearly marked. With the use of a little more than ordinary caution, no sober skipper should have serious difficulty in following it. If the wind is strong from the southwest and the ebb tide is running, it is an alternative preferable to the approach north of Bassetts Island.

Megansett and Fiddler's Cove (251). In ordinary weather Megansett Harbor is entirely satisfactory although large and subject to some motion from a sea running up the Bay. There is better protection off the Megansett Yacht Club behind the jetty at the head of the harbor. The town wharf is used by the club, which maintains a guest mooring in the cove. There is no gas at the float, but this can be obtained at Fiddler's Cove. In a hard northwester the anchorage can be uncomfortable. One correspondent recommends following the dredged channel into Squeteague Harbor. Another writes:

> The channel is only marked toward the end, and by red floating wooden poles either painted black at the top or left red. These are hard to see, especially at night, and to the unwary boatman, appear more of a hazard than the shoal water.

While the author is confident that a skillful and alert skipper can take his yacht into Squeteague, to approach the entrance with a brisk northwester astern requires a confidence bred of extensive local knowledge.

On the southern shore of Megansett Harbor is *Rand's Harbor,* which looks like an inverted Y on the chart. A local resident writes:

"The entrance is virtually impossible at low tide and features a large poorly-marked rock in dead center. The rock is not on the chart."

Fiddler's Cove, west of Rand's Harbor, has been dredged out of a marsh in recent years. A channel with a depth of 5 feet at low water is marked with four pairs of red and black stakes. Depth inside is about the same as in the channel. The western part of the harbor is occupied by moored boats. Inquire for a vacant mooring at the marina or anchor.

The basin has a good 5 feet, running up the curved channel to port. This is to be lined with rocks. The starboard or western shore is a sandy beach.

The marina on the eastern part of the harbor has slips with water and electricity for visitors. Gas, Diesel oil, water, ice, laundry service, and groceries are available here. The hospitable Balentines are in charge.

Silver Beach, Wild Harbor, Mass. (251). In the northeast corner of Wild Harbor is snug and often-crowded Silver Beach Harbor. To enter, pass between a pair of privately maintained white and orange buoys outside the jetty and come in cautiously. The dredged channel is subject to silting. As there is no room to anchor, tie up to the bulkhead to starboard and inquire of the Harbor Master for a mooring or slip. The Wild Harbor Yacht Club sponsors an active racing program and plans a clubhouse in the near future.

No gas or water is available here, but there is a small store nearby.

If no berth is available in Silver Beach Harbor, a shoal-draft boat can anchor north of Crow Point.

West Falmouth, Mass. (249, 260). This harbor, well marked by a lighted bell, a can, and a nun outside, and protected by a breakwater, is easy to enter and is well protected for boats drawing 6 feet or less. Enter carefully and anchor at the edge of the channel about 150 yards inside the breakwater. The tide runs about 1 knot here but is not a serious problem. Shoal-draft vessels may continue up the channel, well buoyed with the privately maintained cans and nuns on a miniature scale, to the basin, where chart 260 shows 6 feet. There is a wharf here where a telephone and gas are available. From here it is a short walk to a well-equipped store.

This is a clean and quiet harbor with attractive estates on the shores and no commercial interests except the unobtrusive gasoline wharf at the head of the inner harbor. The lovely summer morning the writer spent in West Falmouth was made lively by schooling mackerel, diving terns, and vigorous activity in Beetle Cats by the younger members of the Chappaquoit Yacht Club.

Quissett (Quamquissett), Mass. (249). Marked by a lighted bell outside and distinguished by a large standpipe on the hill behind it, Quissett is easy to find by day or night. It is a secure and convenient anchorage. The entrance is clearly marked by cans and nuns. Despite their confusing appearance, there is no difficulty in proceeding directly from one to the next, as they are numbered on the chart.

Entrance to the inner harbor is marked by privately maintained buoys, the only serious problem being two half-tide rocks, which are clearly marked on the chart, and which almost always show. In the inner harbor is a Cruising Club of America mooring clearly marked and several guest moorings maintained by the Quissett Harbor Boat Yard. This small but well-equipped yard can make ordinary repairs, and provides gas, ice, and water at its small wharf. There is ample depth (15 feet reported) at this wharf.

There is a telephone at the head of the wharf and a bin for disposal of trash. However, there is no store nearer than Woods Hole, 2 miles away.

If the inner harbor is crowded, as it usually is, there are several guest moorings in the outer harbor. This is adequately protected in anything but a very heavy southwesterly. In the event of such a blow, one could move up into the cove to the south and be comfortable and secure.

In 1970 an inspection of the sediment in Quissett Harbor revealed a mercury content of 0.8–0.9 parts per million and greater than 0.3 p.p.m. in the water. The Food and Drug Administration declares unfit for human consumption anything with greater than 0.5 p.p.m. The only discoverable source of this pollution is anti-fouling paint on the numerous yachts anchored here. An effort is being made at Quissett to ban the use of anti-fouling paints containing mercury.

Woods Hole, Mass. (348). Woods Hole is a large but secure harbor as well as the most northerly passage between Buzzards Bay and Vineyard Sound. The tidal current runs very hard through the passage. *Eldridge Tide and Pilot Book* has a table showing clearly the times at which it turns.

In negotiating this passage, chart 348 is almost a necessity. It shows the buoyage clearly and on a large scale. A local scientist who sails a cat-boat in these waters writes:

We have a 8-20 daytime groundings in the Hole each season. These are mainly due to the skipper's not carrying a chart of Woods Hole on board. Confusion usually results because of this. A glance at the chart clearly shows the correct passing of marks. I have interrupted many a sail to haul some idiot off those rocks. It's incredible, but they come through with Texaco cruise guides and road maps.

Entering from Buzzards Bay, one passes close to the red flashing buoy and the two big nuns. Thence one can leave the beacons on Devils Foot Island and Grassy Island to port and enter Woods Hole Harbor or leave can 3 to starboard and continue through Broadway into Vineyard Sound.

Woods Hole looking east toward Vineyard Sound.

Many vessels have negotiated this turn successfully only to strike Middle Ledge after passing the can as the tide set them heavily to starboard inside the black beacon to the east of the can.

Entering from Vineyard Sound, one may pass either side of Great Ledge; the channel to the west is to be preferred, especially at night. One may then run up Great Harbor on the range of green lights. Again the critical point is can 3 on Middle Ledge. The tide runs very hard here and can set a vessel either way very rapidly.

Because of the heavy tidal currents, it is well to plan your passage at slack water or with a favorable current, but vessels under sail or power negotiate the passage against the current frequently. Do not fear the place, but treat it with considerable respect.

George C. Whitely writes in the April, 1971, issue of *Yachting* at the conclusion of an article on Woods Hole:

> One dollar invested in C & G S chart 348 is insurance for a safe passage through Woods Hole provided the chart is studied *before* the transit and not after a boat has been wrecked, as it was by one unhappy skipper last summer.

There are three anchorages at Woods Hole: Great Harbor, Eel Pond, and Little Harbor.

1. Great Harbor. This is easy of access, large, and secure, but it can be uncomfortably choppy in a southerly blow. Anchor well up near the head of the harbor on the westerly side in a shoal-draft boat. Others will find deep water in the middle. Stay well clear of the large spherical moorings. Big vessels may lie here and require extensive swinging room. The Woods Hole Yacht Club maintains guest moorings and a float with about 5 feet at low water off a stone pier.

2. Eel Pond is a completely landlocked anchorage behind a drawbridge that carries the main stream of traffic through the town. It was opened, in 1971, between 6 A.M. and 9 P.M. on two long and two short blasts of the horn except from 7:45 to 8:30 A.M., from 11:45 A.M. to 12:45 P.M., and from 4:30 to 5:15 P.M. If you arrive at one of these critical times, tie up to the wharf on the starboard side of the gut.

Inside, to port, is the wharf and boat yard of Harbor Master Sumner Hilton. He has rental moorings, gas, Diesel fuel, water, and marina supplies. His yard can make repairs to hull, spars, or engine.

3. Little Harbor. Except in a heavy southerly, this is a good anchorage. However, there are three heavy Coast Guard moorings here, which are frequently occupied by large vessels, and there are no facilities for yachtsmen. There is a public landing on the western shore.

Woods Hole can provide most of what the visiting yachtsman may require. Gas, Diesel oil, water, and ice are available at the Woods Hole Fueling Station on the north side of the steamer wharf. Louis' Fruit Store close to the drawbridge sells fruit and groceries.

Three famous institutions make Woods Hole a center for study of the oceans and marine life: Woods Hole Oceanographic Institution, Marine Biological Laboratory, and United States Fish and Wildlife Service, now known as Bureau of Commercial Fisheries. The latter maintains an aquarium and a number of exhibits of commercial fishing methods that are well worth a visit. The harbor is busy with Coast Guard vessels, steamers, and research vessels, including a huge catamaran.

Buses from Boston and Providence connect at Woods Hole with steamers for Martha's Vineyard and Nantucket.

Hadley Harbor (348). This is one of the most secure and attractive harbors on the New England coast. There is no problem about getting in. The channel is clearly marked with a nun and a can at the entrance. Leave the beacon inside to starboard and just keep your bowsprit out of the bushes. The passage is clear. The wind seems to draw steadily down the channel, and the tide is not formidable. There should be no trouble in beating right up into the inner harbor. One may anchor off the boathouse or farther out, but the owners ask that a passage be left open around the north side of the harbor for the convenience of vessels bringing supplies to the Island.

Naushon Island is owned by the Naushon Trust and has been in the Forbes family for a great many years. They have built on the island but have preserved most of it in its natural state. It is inhabited by deer, sheep, and many species of birds. In order to keep it unspoiled, the trust asks that no visitors come ashore except on Bulls Island, where a float is provided in summer. Picnics, fires under careful control, and dogs are allowed here. Bring your own fuel. Because the island has been so carefully protected, one may sit in one's cockpit at sunset and watch deer come unafraid to the shore to browse.

Hadley Harbor, like Cuttyhunk, a beautiful and protected anchorage close to centers of population, is likely to be crowded, especially on Friday and Saturday nights. Unless you arrive early, you may have to anchor in the outer harbor to have swinging room. In the event of a heavy squall or a sudden wind shift, the effect on those rafted up or anchored on short scope could be confusing in the extreme.

Yachtsmen unable to find a berth in the inner harbor have sometimes anchored in the bight of Goats Neck. Note that this cove is shallow and rocky. The 12-foot contour does not even go inside it.

Quicks Hole (249). This passage affords good shelter in most summer weather. Anchor close under the beach on the Nashawena side. This beach is soft white sand and delightful for swimming. The island is bare and grassy, inhabited mainly by sheep. Therefore, one should bring ashore neither dog nor gun and should not go inland. There are said to be flounders on the sand bottom and striped bass out in the tide between North Rock and South Rock. This is such a beautiful and unspoiled place that it is often crowded, particularly on summer weekends.

One should remember that all of the Elizabeth Islands except Cutty-hunk and Penikese are privately owned by people who are trying to keep them in their original wild state. With a few disgraceful exceptions, yachtsmen honor this public-spirited intention, confine their visits to the beaches, and help to save for all of us a few small islands of solitude un-trampled by the feet of megalopolis.

Robinsons Hole (249). This channel between Naushon and Pasque is narrow, beset with boulders, and scoured by a swift tide. It is an interest-ing passage in fair weather but a poor anchorage. Both shores are pri-vately owned. Yachtsmen are requested not to land here.

Penikese Island, Mass. (249). This island was the site of one of the first marine biology laboratories in the world. Louis Agassiz and a group of students established it and worked on the island for a number of years.

Later it became a leper colony. One can still see evidence of the hospi-tal and some of the buildings.

Finally it was taken over as a bird sanctuary and is now a nesting place for gulls and terns. Each species keeps to its own end of the island.

The waters around Penikese are starred with ledges and bars. Visitors are urged to keep away.

Canapitsit Channel (297). This channel, between Cuttyhunk and Nash-awena islands, affords an entry into Vineyard Sound, but it is narrow and the tide runs hard. The bottom is rock, and the buoys sometimes drag out of position. Also, in strong southerly winds the sea breaks at its southern end. It should be attempted by strangers only with the greatest caution. In 1971 the remains of a yacht lay on the southern end of Nashawena. Reportedly she had come across from Menemsha in the fog and tried to enter Canapitsit without careful identification of the buoys or regard to the state of the tide. She stove a hole in her bow and sank at once. The crew got ashore safely; the yacht was later raised and stripped, and the hull was abandoned.

Cuttyhunk (263). The anchorage in Cuttyhunk Pond is secure, easy of access by day or night, and of ample depth for most cruising boats. On weekends, especially July 4 and Labor Day, it is likely to be very crowded.

Entrance is clear from the chart. From the bell, pass between the beacon to port and the light on the jetty to starboard. Stay in the middle of the channel, being careful of a sand spit on the starboard hand about halfway in. The end of it is abrupt. The color of the water is sufficient guide.

The dredged mooring basin is more or less square. The northeastern side to starboard on entering, is not at all bold. Keep 100 yards from high-water mark. The southwest side is bounded roughly by a line from a lone pile (which carries a sign explaining where to land) to a low modern house to the northwest. The southeast side is bounded by a line along the ends of the wharves. Outside the dredged basin there is about 3 feet of water.

There are four wharves. The first on entering is the steamer wharf, where the ferry *Alert*, from New Bedford, lands. Gasoline is available here. The next is the old Coast Guard wharf. The next is the marina with slips for visitors. Electricity and water are available. Inquire here about use of rental moorings. The next is the fish dock, occupied largely by commercial fishermen and charter fishing boats. Note that in proceeding to or from either of the two latter wharves, one *must* leave the lone pile to port generously. More yachts ground here than anywhere else in Cuttyhunk. The following paragraph and sketch contributed by a local summer resident may clarify the extent of the danger.

Visitors keep running aground. And they do it every day in summer. And, of course, in exactly the same place—or two places. Our windows look over the harbor and never a day goes past that a glance out doesn't spot a keel sailboat heeling awkwardly in the mud just beyond the south corner of the dredged basin. Usually they get there by trying to go from the fish dock to the basin, or vice versa, without due regard for the north-south line that marks the dredged area. I will attempt a crude drawing and attach it to this letter, and you can see for yourself. The second spot for habitual groundings is just inside (to the southeast) of a line running from the old Coast Guard dock to the marina. Anything inside that line is fit only for small outboards except for a few feet out from the slips along the easternmost finger pier.

At the head of the harbor in the shoal water is the Cuttyhunk Yacht Club. It has an active program for juniors but no facilities for visitors.

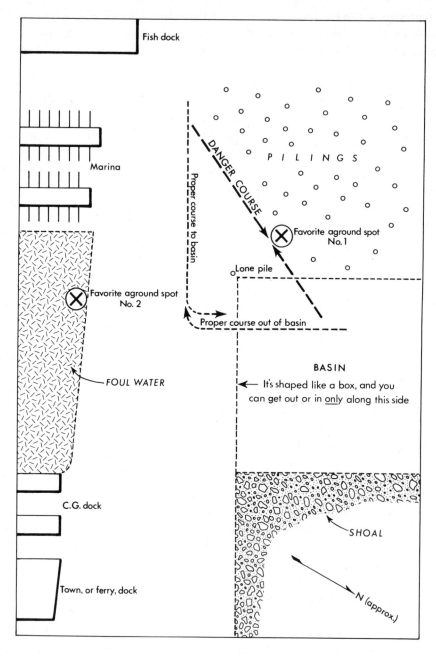

Fish dock

Marina

Proper course to basin

DANGER COURSE

PILINGS

Favorite aground spot No. 1

Lone pile

Proper course out of basin

Favorite aground spot No. 2

FOUL WATER

BASIN

It's shaped like a box, and you can get out or in **only** along this side

C.G. dock

Town, or ferry, dock

SHOAL

N (approx.)

Cuttyhunk Harbor

Land according to instructions on the lone pile and walk up the hill. Turn right at the second group of telephone booths to Thompson's general store. Here are the usual staple supplies and a friendly atmosphere shared by fishermen, summer people, and visitors. Continue up the road for a magnificent view of Gay Head and Vineyard Sound.

The view from the top of the island is superb, including the whole coast from the bridges of the canal to the beaches below Westport and to the eastward from No-mans Land to the south shore of the Cape. It is best to approach the top of the island by the paved road, as all the land is privately owned and the owners are not enthusiastic about trespassers as a result of several unhappy experiences. A town meeting in 1971 halted a growing trend with an ordinance prohibiting sleeping or camping on beaches after 10 P.M.

Cuttyhunk subsists chiefly on fishing, lobstering, and charter parties. The local people are friendly and pleasant but see so many visitors come and go, asking the same questions, that they are a bit reserved. Nevertheless, a sincere search for help or information is likely to be successful at the fish dock. Allen Wilder, Harbor Master, is an official and reliable source of information.

Roman Catholic services are held Sunday mornings in the Cuttyhunk Church, and Protestant services on Sunday evenings. Aside from sociability around the telephone booths and the marina, there is little night life on the island.

Meals and rooms can be obtained at the Bosworth House and meals at the Allen House.

Norman Gingrass operates the Island Air Service. He has a float plane and can land you in New Bedford in less than ten minutes or in Boston in less than half an hour. He is available for charter to any destination within range.

An interesting reminder of old times is the remains of a railway on the starboard hand as you enter the anchorage. Before the pond was dredged and the channel cut, there was water enough in the pond for big catboats, but not in the channel. So in threatening weather the boats were floated on to a cradle on a car and hauled over the sand spit.

Bartholomew Gosnold, memorialized by a tower on West End Point, was the first recorded European visitor to Cuttyhunk, visiting the island in 1602 with the intention of establishing a colony. The project failed, but Gosnold returned to England with a load of sassafras, an infusion of the bark being much esteemed as a medicine. Mrs. Louise Haskell has written of him and of later explorers in *The Story of Cuttyhunk.*

The road to the summit of the island, lined with well-constructed stone walls, appears rather surprising in its present context. It was built,

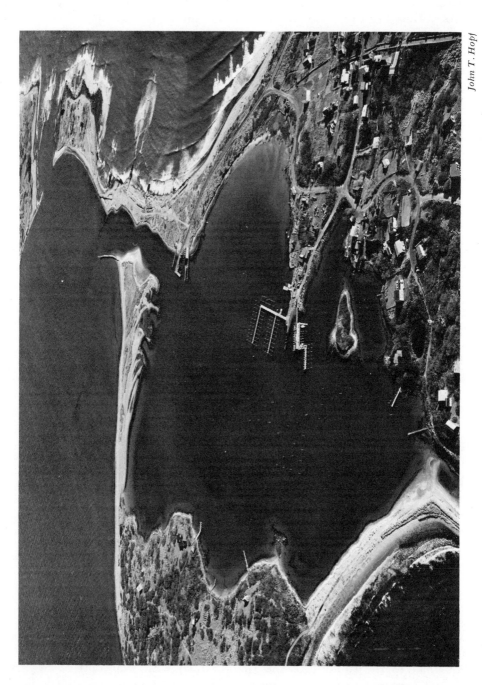

Cuttyhunk Pond. Note how clearly its edges are defined. The dredged area looks dark in this photograph.

however, by the late William M. Wood of the American Woolen Company as the approach to an elaborate mansion he intended to build. The mansion never materialized.

The following paragraph, contributed by a local summer resident of Cuttyhunk and an experienced yachtsman, reflects one of the current problems raised by the popularity of this delightful place.

Remember, please, that all the land on Cuttyhunk is private. . . . We are hospitable to visitors, but their movements are indeed restricted. Access to the West End (the undeveloped part of the island) is via the *paved* road running around the eastern and southern sides of the island. Where the paved road abruptly ends (adjacent to the cemetery), there is a large sign listing conditions under which visitors may walk over the West End land. On my own land—to illustrate the problem —I attempted to limit trespassers by a sign at my driveway entrance indicating a "Private Way." Someone tore the sign off the steel post. . . . I am afraid the time has passed when open hospitality can be offered visitors at Cuttyhunk or elsewhere.

Cuttyhunk, situated as it is within an easy day's sail of popular yachting centers, is a very fragile place. It has a character of its own, an island quality, composed of moors, wild deer, wild roses, ducks, rabbits, commercial fishing, and the surrounding sea. But it cannot maintain this character unless visitors respect it with unusual care. It was the impression of the writer in 1971 that both visitors and local people were trying hard to do this, but it will be increasingly difficult in years to come.

CHAPTER VIII

Vineyard and Nantucket Sounds, and the Voyage Around Cape Cod

General Conditions: The area covered by this chapter is almost all sand. The water is shoal, and the tides run hard; but fog is comparatively rare, the buoys are large, lighted, noisy, and close together except up the outside of the Cape. The winds are usually southerly and quite reliable, sometimes on a hot summer afternoon working up to a reefing breeze.

The water is pleasantly warm for swimming, and fishing is excellent. Harbors are generally kept dredged so that a yacht drawing 5 feet can use most of them—with caution.

Ashore you will find great variety. There are fishing villages like Menemsha and Stage Harbor where the emphasis is on fish, and summer people drop into the background; and there are busy summer resorts like Hyannis and Falmouth where the short-pants set congregates with all the impedimenta of a "trip to the Cape." This usually includes a portable radio. At almost every town you will find some sort of marina where you can fill your tanks and procure the necessities of life.

This is an active exciting place to cruise if you like company afloat and a good time ashore.

Vineyard and Nantucket Sounds

The passage up Vineyard Sound is easy in clear weather. In thick weather, bear in mind George W. Eldridge's letter to skippers and mates published annually in the *Eldridge Tide and Pilot Book*. The gist of it is that the first of the flood tide, instead of setting northeast up the sound, sets north toward the shores of Nashawena and Pasque. A vessel bucking an ebb tide that runs out of the sound is also set to the north. In the event of a foul tide and a head wind, one must resort to power in Vineyard Sound or lie over in Menemsha, Quick's Hole, or Tarpaulin Cove. The tide off West Chop runs at 2 knots frequently and attains even greater velocities at moon tides.

Nantucket Sound, with a fair wind and tide, represents no problem, with good visibility. It is only about 30 miles from West Chop to Mono-moy, and with a 1 or 2 knot tide running under you, it should be no more than a half day's sail. The land on both sides is so low that it soon drops out of sight from the deck of a small yacht, leaving water towers peering over the horizon at odd intervals. One runs compass courses from bell to whistle to gong, surrounded by unseen shoals and moved by un-predictable currents. It is a weird sensation for the navigator unaccus-tomed to it. In the event of a head tide, light airs, or poor visibility, there are a number of picturesque little harbors on the south side of the Cape for shoal-draft yachts. Woods Hole, Falmouth, Hyannis, and Stage Har-bor are deep-water harbors, as the term is understood on the Cape. The harbors on Martha's Vineyard and Nantucket are good stopping places as well as worth-while objectives in themselves.

If you must navigate this channel in thick weather, do so with extreme caution. The following account of the loss of a well-found yawl under the command of an experienced skipper should emphasize the possible dan-gers. Read it with chart 1209 before you, and bear in mind that it was written in the thirties, when Handkerchief Shoal and Stone Horse Shoal were marked by lightships with powerful horns. The nun mentioned has now been replaced by a bell.

The yawl left Nantucket on a clear day with clear weather reported ahead. The Handkerchief Lightship south of Handkerchief Shoal to the southwest of Monomoy was picked up without difficulty in clear weather. From there the course is NE by E ½ E to the Stone Horse Lightship with its diaphone, 5 miles away and about ⅝ mile off the Monomoy beach. The wind was light southwest, almost dead astern.

According to the current tables there would be slack water on that day (August 5, 1938) at the time when the yawl might expect to arrive at Stone Horse. Then a flood tide would have carried her on her way. To allow for a possible set toward the shore during the last of the ebb, the skipper headed half a point to the eastward of the course to Stone Horse toward the flashing white bell 9. This buoy is nearly 1 mile off Monomoy and more than ½ mile outside nun 12 which marks the edge of the shoal southeast of Monomoy. So it seemed as if the margin of safety were sufficient, especially with slack water supposed to be due.

After a mile or two of the five-mile course had been completed, the fog came in thick and from then on the lead was in constant use. The sound of the horn on Handkerchief continued to come down clearly on the following wind. But still no sound was heard either of the dia-phone on Stone Horse to leeward, or the bell. In fact, neither the dia-phone nor the bell ever was heard, even from less than a mile away.

When the log indicated that the bell should have been picked up or Stone Horse heard, the skipper decided to anchor until he could determine his position.

As the vessel swung toward the shore for heading into the wind, she struck. All efforts to get her off failed, for despite the prediction of the current table, a strong northwesterly ebb continued for two hours to drive the yawl more firmly into the sand. Being a keel boat, she heeled far over on her side. Waves and current combined to fill her gradually with sand and water.

A rift in the fog soon disclosed the fact that the boat had struck on the shoal off Monomoy Point near nun 12. Despite the efforts of the nearby Coast Guard, the yawl, being embedded in the sand, could not be hauled off and was a total loss.

The Coast Guard reported that fishing craft had gone ashore almost every day for a week at the same place and for the same reasons.

What are the lessons to be drawn for cruising men from this experience? The opinions expressed by the skipper of the lost yawl can be summed up as follows:

1. Off Monomoy, the direction, velocity, and time of change of the current are unpredictable. This is confirmed by the experience of the Coast Guard. In this case, the tide continued to ebb two hours after predicted slack water. Instead of ebbing in a westerly direction as expected, the direction of the current was rotary, swinging around Monomoy in a clockwise direction, being northwesterly off the point.

(*Note.* The *Coast Pilot* reports that the average velocity of the current at Stone Horse Shoal Lightship at strength of flood is about 2 knots and at strength of ebb 1¾ knots. The greatest observed velocity was 3⁶/₁₀ knots. Flood current there sets about NE ½ E and ebb about SW by W ½ W. Such a direction would not have set the yawl on Monomoy Point, but a northwesterly current with the strength indicated above might and evidently did.)

2. Don't rely on hearing fog signals against the wind.

3. Don't sail through this area in thick weather on a dead reckoning basis, though you may have no trouble even in a fog with an accurate radio direction finder, fathometer, and other modern improvements.

To the above authors would like to add this warning: If you want to go through what are considered by many the most dangerous waters on the New England coast, pick your weather. If caught off Monomoy in fog, anchor and await favorable conditions.

Cruising men have contributed several other suggestions about the navigation of Nantucket Sound.

Fog is much more frequent in Nantucket Sound than it is at Race Point or even outside Pollock Rip. Southerly breezes are likely to bring it in, and although it may burn off in the middle of a hot day, only a change of wind to a northerly quadrant will dry it up.

Winds are subject to sudden changes in direction and velocity. A strong breeze kicks up a short, sharp chop, not very high, but enough to swamp a tender or soak down the sun bathers in short order. When the breeze drops, however, the sea subsides quickly.

In warm summer weather the southwest breeze may continue day and night, but outside Pollock Rip it usually dies away in the late afternoon. Yachts often sail right out of the wind in coming out of Pollock Rip.

There is an intricate short cut between Handkerchief Shoal and Mono-moy that may save a small boat many miles in a passage from one of the south shore harbors. It is to be attempted only on a clear day with a moderate breeze or with local knowledge, as it is not well marked.

Menemsha, Martha's Vineyard, Mass. (264). This is the first shelter available to a vessel bound east up Vineyard Sound. Coasting schooners used to anchor outside in Menemsha Bight waiting for a fair tide up the sound, but it is an uneasy anchorage for a small boat.

Make the bell off the jetty and run in, lying either in the basin just outside or continuing into the pond. Conditions in the basin have been much expanded if not improved in recent years. Now there are marina slips nearly all the way around the shore except on the east side where the original wharf and the picturesque fish houses still stand. Anchoring in the basin is impossible and auxiliaries are not permitted to be along-side among the power boats. Consult Harbor Master Philip Le Vesseur about a slip.

Gas, Diesel oil, water, and ice are available at the wharf in the basin. There is a store, Dutcher's, carrying marine hardware and fishing gear a short distance up the road and a grocery store about ¼ mile away at the wharf on the pond.

Menemsha Basin is a center for sport fishing activity on the shoals to the southwest of Martha's Vineyard. Large motor yachts with high flying bridges and long outriggers crowd the harbor and the gasoline wharf at night and early in the morning, their enthusiasm making for an early start even by the casual cruising man.

Anchoring in Menemsha Pond is discouraged. The entrance is constantly shoaling up, and although frequently dredged, may not be exactly as the chart indicates. It would be well to check on conditions in the channel before entering. Also, because the pond is being used experimentally for the rearing of shellfish, use of the head is prohibited. Unless you have a holding tank, your head will be sealed when you enter. However, the pond is a beautiful, quiet, and picturesque anchorage. It is said to be a pleasant walk from the west side of the pond to the colored sand cliffs of Gay Head, where there is an inspiring view over the waters to the south and west. The surf here after a storm is worth the trip.

Tarpaulin Cove, Mass. (249). This delightful anchorage on the eastern side of Naushon Island is much frequented by picnic parties on weekends, but during the week there seems to be plenty of room. The best place to anchor is off the southwest end of the beach under the light. Chart and lead are safe guides, as the water shoals gradually.

The beach is of fine soft sand, delightful for swimming, although there is little shelter from the sun on a hot day. Late in the afternoon, however, many of the visitors depart and on a quiet evening the beach and anchorage are peaceful and sometimes almost deserted. A correspondent suggests: "Repeated nights spent at Tarpaulin Cove have taught me that the stern anchor, enabling one to lie with the swell regardless of the wind, makes life much more pleasant when the steamer wash swells come in, as they always do during the night."

Camping ashore is forbidden, but fires below high-water mark are permitted.

Naushon abounds in sheep, deer, and ducks, which the owners are trying to preserve. Therefore, no dogs or guns should be brought ashore, and visitors are asked not to venture inland from the beach.

Mr. David Forbes of the Naushon Trust writes:

At Tarpaulin Cove all driftwood has long since been burned up. Most people now bring self-contained fires which burn briquettes. As these do not send off sparks into the woods, and as they are carried off after the picnic, any words of encouragement for that type of fire would be welcome. Fires burning wood or paper should be attempted, if at all, only when the wind is offshore.

A correspondent adds:

I adventured along the entire rim of the cove to enjoy one of the most pleasant moments of our cruise—outstaring a beautiful fawn nestled in a groove of beech trees and at only a 30-foot distance.

John T. Hopf

Menemsha Bight and the entrance to Menemsha Pond.

Each spring, members of the Naushon Trust invite college students to the island to shear those elusive sheep. This has become quite a tradition and might answer many a yachtsman's question concerning who tends that flock!

Lake Tashmoo, Martha's Vineyard, Mass. (347). This is a quiet and attractive anchorage for shoal-draft yachts drawing not more than 4½ feet. The entrance is between two stone jetties a short distance southwest of West Chop.

Be sure to keep away from the west jetty. A sand bank has built out from it very nearly to the middle of the channel. Particularly if coming from the south, swing well clear of the west jetty and favor the east jetty.

Inside the jetties is the shoalest part of the entrance where the channel lies between a can and a nun. Go very close to the can. Then swing back to mid-channel, as marked by buoys. If you make it by the first can and nun, you are safely in. If you ground, you will find the bottom to be sand. Someone will no doubt quickly respond to your signals of distress. As there is only a little more than a foot of tide here, you may well need help to get clear.

The anchorage inside is quiet, perfectly sheltered, and most attractive.

Vineyard Haven, Mass. (347). This is a large and busy harbor, visited frequently by steamers from Woods Hole and Hyannis, and is the commercial center for the island. The ideal place for a cruising boat in Vineyard Haven is behind the breakwater on a mooring, but the chances of achieving this ideal are dim, as the place is crowded with local boats. The town maintains guest moorings for visitors across from the breakwater, and there are two marinas, the Coastwise Wharf Company and the Pilot House, operated by Machine and Marine Service, Inc., on the southeast side of the harbor. If you anchor, be sure to leave the steamer channel clear. One look at *Uncatena* coming by the breakwater with a bone in her teeth will convince you of the seriousness of this advice. Tom Haley is Harbor Master and can advise you in all marine matters.

All supplies and facilities, such as gas, Diesel oil, water, ice, showers, and laundromat are available at the marinas. The Black Dog Tavern on the Coastwise Wharf is said to be excellent, serving "very upper-level home-style cooking." No reservations are accepted. Go early. A short walk up the street is the town, where the usual grocery stores can be found. About ¾ of a mile up South Main Street is John's Fish Market, an excellent source of fresh local fish and information.

The Martha's Vineyard Shipyard, on the southeast shore of the inner harbor, has several marine railways and docks and is well equipped to

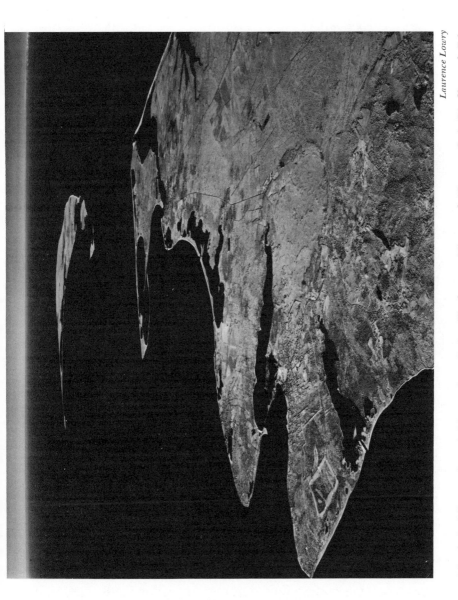

Laurence Lowry

Martha's Vineyard and Nantucket. Lake Tashmoo, Vineyard Haven, Oak Bluffs, and Edgartown can be clearly distinguished.

make repairs. They also have a first-class store for marine supplies and gadgets. This yard has a fine reputation. Another boat yard, which is much smaller but also does first-class work, is located at the end of the short westerly arm of Lagoon Pond. It is run by Erford Burt. If you want Burt to do some work, call him up and get him to pilot you in. Burt specializes in smaller boats.

Those who seek a quieter anchorage than Vineyard Haven harbor may want to lie in the Lagoon behind the drawbridge to the east of the breakwater. A 10-foot channel has been dredged, and the draw is manned from 9 A.M. to 5 P.M. except on Sundays. At other times a phone call to the Highway Department brings quick action. There was, in 1971, a "loosely enforced" prohibition against the use of the head in the Lagoon, Lake Tashmoo, and Vineyard Haven harbor. It is the writer's guess that it is likely to be taken more seriously in the future.

Vineyard Haven is a good spot from which to visit the northwestern part of the island. Automobiles and bicycles can be had in the village. In the old days, when known as Holmes Hole, the harbor sheltered many coasters bound inward or outward around the Cape. Now it is used only by steamers, fishing vessels, and yachts. The Vineyard Haven Yacht Club is an active racing organization and has a small pier and station but no regular launch service, well north (outside) of the breakwater.

Vineyard Haven was famous for a long time as the home of Captain George W. ("Yours for a Fair Tide") Eldridge, son of the Captain George Eldridge of Chatham who made the first accurate large-scale charts of important fishing grounds.

The story goes that in the early seventies the elder George was publishing a book well known to mariners of that time, the *Compass Test. Eldridge Tide and Pilot Book,* referred to in Chapter II, continues the story:

> He told his son, George W., who was at the time in poor health, that if he would go to Vineyard Haven and take charge of selling the book there he might have the gross receipts. This offer was accepted and George began his work. As the ships came into the harbor he would go out to them in his sailboat and offer his book for sale. While engaged in this work he was constantly being asked by mariners as to what time the tide TURNED to run east or west in the Sound. This set him to thinking whether or not some sort of a table might be prepared which would give mariners this important information. So with this in mind he began making observations, and one day, while in the famous ship chandlery store of Charles Holmes, he picked up one of the Holmes business cards and made the first rough draft of a current table on the back of it. This was in August of 1874. Shortly after, with the help of

his father, he worked out the tables for the places, other than Vineyard Sound, which were of the most importance, and in 1875 the first "Tide Book" was published. It did not take long for mariners to realize the help which this sort of a work could be to them, and it soon became an almost indispensable book to all who sailed the Atlantic Coast from New York East. From time to time the Captain added important information for seamen, one of the most important things being the explanation of the action of the currents which caused so many vessels to founder in the "Graveyard." The book has even been referred to as the Mariners' Bible, so constantly is it used and so helpful has it been in making navigation safer.

One Saturday night in July the writer beat up Vineyard Haven harbor and anchored in the southerly part of the harbor long after dark. Sunday morning he was startled to find himself lying close under the quarter of a nineteenth-century topsail schooner, Captain Robert S. Douglas' *Shenandoah*. Built by Harvey Gamage in 1964 in South Bristol, Maine, for the passenger trade, she had some difficulty weathering the Coast Guard regulations. Since then she has been a great addition to waters formerly crowded with coasting schooners, fishermen, whalers, and naval vessels, all under sail.

Oak Bluffs, Martha's Vineyard, Mass. (346). The harbor at Oak Bluffs, 2 miles eastward of Vineyard Haven, is formed by Lake Anthony, entered by a cut in the beach. Two jetties, with a light on the northerly one, protect the entrance. The entrance is somewhat narrow for craft without a motor, but it is possible to approach the jetties closely on either side. There is a depth of 7 or 8 feet in the pond, which is usually crowded in July and August.

A local yachtsman adds:

In late 1967 the town spent a "bundle" and bulkheaded about a third of the circumference of this more or less round area and created on the southwest side a series of slips perpendicular to the bulkhead with floating docks in between. They have water and electricity, and there are now two gas docks in the harbor that have other supplies. Of course, this is right in the town, the main street starting about 100 feet from the dockage.

The jam in there has been so huge in mid-summer, with several excursion boats docking from mainland ports and disgorging 500 to 700 tourists at a crack, that in 1970 steel bulkheading was carried all the way along the south side of the harbor to the jetty, and tourist docking will now be in that area, allowing even more boats to tie up to the southwest side. There is now bulkheading and hard surface walk or driveway around over half of the circle.

Edgartown, Mass. (346). In clear weather Edgartown is easy to make, as the east side of Middle Flats, the principal danger, is clearly marked with a bell, a nun, and a flashing buoy. The Chappaquiddick shore to port is, for these waters, comparatively bold. After passing the light at the entrance, favor the western shore. The best anchorage for deeper draft vessels lies beyond can 9 toward the Chappaquiddick shore. There is shoal water behind can 7, as the chart suggests. Frequently visitors go ashore here, seeing "big" boats lying at anchor.

Pick up one of the boat yard moorings maintained by Esterbrook & Norton if you can. There is a modest charge, but it is well worth it, as the holding ground is said to be poor. A launch man is quoted, "If you make it through the first night, you're probably all right." A summer squall can raise havoc among large and expensive yachts lying to small anchors on short scope.

Yachtsmen who crave isolation and at the same time want to get out of the current as much as possible can proceed into Katama Bay and anchor in 8 or 9 feet in the northern part of the bay, near Chappaquiddick Island, or else northwest of Katama Point on the other side, depending on the wind. The tide runs vigorously through the harbor. A local yachtsman comments:

My comments on this are somewhat unreliable, since a good storm can always open the Katama end of the harbor again. However, for the past several years we have been able to drive directly to Chappaquiddick Island by jeep across the dunes at the head of Katama Bay where the opening closed up several years ago. Everybody thought this would be the end of the current situation in Edgartown Harbor proper, but it wasn't. So much water comes out of Katama Bay, Pocha Pond, and other areas, all of which has to get through the small slot at the nor'east end, that there is about the same tidal condition as there was before.

The Edgartown Yacht Club welcomes all cruising men and maintains a launch service until 10 P.M., which visitors are urged to use. However, the pressure for the use of other club facilities is so great that they can be extended only to members of recognized yacht clubs who are introduced by members of the Edgartown Yacht Club.

The yacht club has no place at which yachts can lie alongside, and no

Edgartown Harbor.

longer dispenses gas, Diesel oil, water, or ice. These can be obtained at the yard of Esterbrook & Norton, prominent on the starboard hand as you enter the harbor. All kinds of repairs to hull, spars, and engine can be made here, and boats up to 35-feet long or 6-foot draft can be hauled on the yard's ingenious elevator. The store on the wharf carries all kinds of yachting gear and marine hardware.

The town has the usual grocery stores, including a combination food and liquor store, which is open into the evening, about 200 yards up the street from the yacht club. An A&P and an excellent fish market, Lowry's, are a long twenty-minute walk to the west on the tar road. The walk alone is worth the trip, for the first part is through shady streets lined with the eighteenth- and nineteenth-century mansions of Edgartown whalers, traders, privateers, and ship builders. The second half of the trip reflects the income tax, the automobile civilization, and the twentieth-century influence of suburbia.

Old buildings and narrow streets give Edgartown an antique flavor somewhat modified by boutiques, gift shops, and modern restaurants. The summer population has a heavy accent on youth, some quite picturesquely dressed and adorned, but, to the casual visitor at least, very pleasantly disposed. Their grandparents, living in the antebellum yachting tradition, are almost equally evident.

First settled in 1642, the town, when incorporated in 1671, was named for Edgar, the son of James II. In the eighteenth and nineteenth centuries, Edgartown was a successful whaling port. Men ashore were active in refining whale oil and making candles, while the women turned out socks, mittens, and wigs. In the Edgartown Cemetery there are headstones dating as far back as 1670, many with curious epitaphs.

Nantucket, Mass. (1209) (343). The trip to Nantucket in ordinary summer weather is a pleasant variation on long-shore cruising. The island is far enough offshore to have an atmosphere of its own despite frequent visits of large steamers bearing heavy cargoes of tourists. Its history, dating from the Vikings' visit about A.D. 1000 (if we accept Pohl's deduction) to the decline of its whaling industry at the time of the Civil War, is a romantic and exciting one. Populated by what Herman Melville calls "fighting Quakers," it was the home port of a hardy, enterprising, audacious people who sailed wherever there was water to float their square-ended vessels. Many a South Sea Island native knew of Nantucket before he ever heard of Boston, New York, or London. Names of Nantucket skippers and vessels still cling to Pacific islands.

The prudent navigator will ordinarily run down the line of lighted buoys from West Chop to Cross Rip. On Cross Rip there is a buoy with a

John T. Hopf

Nantucket Harbor. The large marina is clearly visible. The steamer wharf is identified by a large freight shed. The yacht club is situated between it and the small beach just beyond. The anchorage area lies between the marina and Brant Point.

horn that sounds rather like a distant fog signal's bleat and quite unlike a whistle buoy's groan. In clear weather one can safely cut this buoy by leaving nun 4 close to port, particularly as it may save a considerable beat if the wind is out to the south. However, the navigator will note that Tuckernuck Shoal has a great bulge, marked by can 3. This must be left to starboard and the Tuckernuck bell approached on a course to the south of southeast. In thick weather it would seem the better part of wisdom to leave Cross Rip buoy to starboard. Do not try to judge the depth of the water by its color. Very often, to be sure, a shoal will show yellow, especially on a sunny day. But tidal streams carrying sand in suspension show just as yellow to the inexperienced eye of the visitor.

Be prepared for a rapid change in weather conditions in approaching the island. Often a pleasant sailing breeze will increase to a reefing breeze, and a short sea will get up rapidly. The writer approached Cross Rip with a gentle WNW air under full sail but shortly afterward found himself charging into Nantucket Harbor, single-reefed and soaking wet with the dinghy half full of water. Local residents were quite unmoved. This happens all the time, they say.

Nantucket is a low island and even on a clear day is invisible from the deck of a yacht at a distance of 7 or 8 miles. The first you will see of the island is a bulky water tank to the west of the town. Then radio masts take shape, a church tower, and at last the low line of land.

Entrance is easy. The bell off the dredged channel is an excellent mark. If the weather is thick, beware of steamers. There are a great number converging here in the course of a summer day. A radar reflector is a useful defense measure. The dredged channel is well marked. There are a number of guest moorings put out by the town and some put out by the yacht club. The yacht club launch makes regular trips on the hour and half-hour until 9:30 P.M. There is a nominal charge for its use.

The anchorage is well protected except in heavy east and northeast winds, when the sea gets a 5-mile sweep from the head of the harbor. In the event of a northeaster, creep up as far as your draft will permit toward the basin at the head of the harbor or take shelter under Pocomo Head: it would make excellent protection. The late Mr. Blanchard, a former author of this *Guide,* wrote this about a northeaster in Nantucket:

> In a September gale Nantucket can be very bad. Once, in such a gale, one of the authors was lucky enough to have a shoal-draft auxiliary sloop and managed early enough to get up into Polpis Harbor to the east of the bay leading to Head Harbor. It blew from 60 to 70 mph for 24 hours. We rode it out in Polpis, but in Nantucket Harbor yachts were strewn along the western shore.

If you prefer to be nearer town than the anchorage, approach the Nantucket Boat Basin, a marina surrounded by yellow-topped piles. Go to the south side near the gas pump. You will be hailed through a bull horn by the official in charge. If there is room inside, an attendant will impale your slip assignment on a pole and pass it to you from the float. You may then enter the stockade and proceed to your slip. Each stall is equipped with water tap, electric plug, telephone jack, and an elaborate fire extinguishing system. There are toilet facilities and showers on the wharf and a large restaurant.

Gas, water, Diesel oil, and ice are available here.

The area around the heads of the wharves has been restored. Old buildings have been reconstructed and new ones built, all in the Nantucket architectural tradition of weathered shingle and white trim. Even the A&P conforms. The streets are cobbled. Obviously not planned as part of the restoration are crowds of people, many dressed in the most modern styles, thronging the gift shops, boutiques, and restaurants.

Island Marine maintains a boat yard south of Commercial Wharf where ordinary repairs can be made.

There is frequent airplane connection with "the States," via Executive Airlines and Air New England.

Nantucket offers something for almost every taste. There are, of course, the usual food, clothing, and hardware stores. Then there are a great many little shops purveying all manner of craft work and souvenirs, some of them beautifully executed. There are excellent restaurants, among the best being The Mad Hatter, Captain Tobey's, and the Languedoc.

The Whaling Museum, to which anyone can direct you, is worth several hours of time for anyone interested in American maritime history. In the basement are excellent representations of the different trades involved in fitting out for a whaling voyage. Tools actually used by riggers, coopers, shipwrights, and sailmakers and samples of their workmanship are displayed. Upstairs there is a whaleboat completely fitted out and ready to lower. Pictures, charts, and whaling gear are attractively displayed with excellent explanatory placards. The writer and his crew found this museum in itself worth the whole trip.

Parts of town retain the variety and individuality of old Nantucket. The mansions built by Coffins, Macys, and Starbucks still stand among shingled cottages and brick houses.

Nantucket beyond the town bears its own characteristic atmosphere. Rent a bicycle at one of the many water front shops and ride over to Surf Side. Outside the town, on the moors, you feel the bleak offshore quality of the place despite the cars whizzing by your left ear. Scrubby pines, waving grass, thickets of bayberry and beach plum remind you that this is no continent but an island, which, if not actually afloat, at least stands up to ocean winds and ocean seas. The great South Beach confirms this. A steep sandy beach faces you with savage shoals offshore and a blank horizon. There is a refreshment stand, a lifeguard's tower, and perhaps a throng of bathers, but walk a half mile east or west along the beach and you are at sea.

Continue eastward to Siasconset, an attractive town of gray cottages and roses, on to Sankaty Head, and return to town by the back road.

Lengthy as this account is, the writer cannot forbear to include the following extract from the *Sailor's Magazine* of November, 1848. The article is entitled "A Cruise Along Shore in the Seventeenth Century":

I shall never forget that homeward passage. It was late in November, and we judged ourselves seven leagues southeast of Nantucket. The old man was below, on his beam ends, with a cruel rheumatism, when the wind, which had been blowing hard from the north, hauled to the east. The mate, whose name was Salter, had no thought of running under circumstances so unfavorable, and went below.

"Captain Phillips," said he, "the wind has canted to the eastward, but it is awful foggy—so thick that you can't see across the deck."

"Sound!" said the old man, "and pass the lead below."

They did so, and after a glance at it, he turned to the mate, and said, "Shake out all the reefs, keep her northwest two hours, then sound again, and let me see the lead."

"Yes sir," said the mate, and he passed up the companion-way, not particularly pleased with the prospect.

In two hours, soundings were again had, and the lead passed to the skipper.

"Five fathoms, with sand, and a cracking breeze," said Salter.

"Don't you mean seven fathoms, Mr. Salter?" asked the old man, scraping the sand with the nail of his right-fore finger.

"There might have been *about* seven sir," said the mate, "I allowed pretty largely for the drift: but it is best to be the safe side."

"Right, Mr. Salter, right. I am glad to find you so particular. We are close in with the land, and can't be too careful. You may keep her northwest, half west; I don't expect you can *see* much, but if you don't *hear* anything in the course of fifteen minutes, let me know it.—An open ear for breakers, Mr. Salter! We must be cautious—very cautious, sir."

The mate, although a fellow of considerable grit, was somewhat staggered at the last orders. He, however, nodded a respectful assent, and made his way to the forward part of the vessel. The wind had freshened, and the *Little Mary* (as the schooner was called) was doing her prettiest. Salter leaned over the larboard bow, and was pondering upon the folly of running before a gale of wind through a fog, to make the land, with no other guide than a few particles of gray sand, in which he had no more confidence than he would have had in a piece of drift seaweed.

Eight or nine minutes only had passed, when the roar of breakers struck the ear of the mate. "Luff, Luff, and shake her!" cried he. The schooner was brought to the wind in an instant. The foam from the receding waves was visible under her lee; but in a moment the dark line of Seconset head, in the southwest, told the mate that everything was right.

"We are clear of the scrape, so far," growled Salter; but I don't think a handful of sand is a thing to run by in a time like this. I'll *know* if there *is* any difference between the bottom here, and the last we had, Sam, heave the lead, while I keep her steady."

The lead came up, and the mate declared not only the bottom, but the depth of the water to be the same. "I think," continued he, "all the sand within forty miles of this spot is alike. Sam, pass me some of that which the cook brought on board to clean his things with, while we were lying in Seconset. There," said he, comparing the two, "there is no difference, even in this, except what the water makes"; and he proceeded to prove his position by putting fresh tallow on the lead, and covering it with the sand which had been brought from the uplands of Seconset.

"Sam," said Salter, "you may wet that lead. I'll try it on the old man."

The lead was washed in the sea for a moment, and the mate took it below chuckling at the thought of snaring the old veteran.

"Captain Phillips," said he, with counterfeit anxiety, "the fifteen minutes are gone—it blows spitefully in flaws, and spits thick."

"Mr. Salter," returned the old man, raising himself in his berth to take the lead, "north west, half west, should have brought you within ear-shot of the breakers some minutes ago. I am afraid you have not kept her straight."

He raised the lead, and the first glance at the soundings seemed to shake his very soul—but the flush on his high, pale forehead passed away in an instant. Ordering the skylight to be removed, he placed the lead in a better position, and riveted his clear blue eye upon it for a full minute, when he turned to the mate, with the utmost coolness, and said, "Mr. Salter, I am glad to say that there has been no fault in your steering; the schooner *has* run north west, half west, as straight as a gun-barrel; at the same time I am very sorry to tell you that Nantucket is sunk, and that we are just over Seconset ridge!"

The South Shore of Cape Cod—Falmouth to
Stage Harbor, Chatham (259)

At this point, as we proceed eastward along the south shore of the Cape, it seems well to point out that the cruising yachtsman will not enjoy this attractive part of the Cape if he has a Maine-coast complex and takes running aground too seriously. A sandbar in a shallow bay on the Cape, protected from heavy seas, is a different proposition from a half-tide ledge in Maine with a deep-sea roll crashing over it. Sometimes all you have to do is to jump overboard in water of just the right temperature and push off from a sandbar. Or else shove off with an oar. Seldom does the boat suffer any real harm. And there are many compensations to offset the occasional waits for the tide to turn—one of which is the delightful swimming. There is a special charm about the Cape that attracts congenial people, including summer visitors from all parts of America.

This is one of the areas where shoal draft is an asset. For if, or when, your boat does rest on the bottom while you enjoy a swim, it is much pleasanter, for the meal which follows, if your ship remains reasonably upright.

While, except for Woods Hole, there is not one deep-water, *natural* harbor along this low-lying sandy coast, due to breakwaters and dredging there are several excellent man-made harbors deep enough for yachts drawing up to 6 feet, or more in some cases. There are also a number of others suitable for boats drawing 3 to 4 feet. It is important to bear in mind that the dredged channels into most of these harbors are subject to constant change, according to whether or not the dredgers have kept ahead of the shoaling storms. There are presently several more harbors with adequate water for long-legged craft than mentioned in our previous edition. Many others have plenty of water inside, but are shoal enough at the mouth so they should be entered only on (rising) half-tide.

It is well, therefore, before undertaking a cruise along these shores to check up by telephone in advance to get the latest information. A local Harbor Master, boat yard, or yacht club can usually tell you what the story is.

When cruising in Nantucket Sound, it is very helpful to make use of the *Eldridge Tide and Pilot Book* so as to take advantage of the currents, which run 1 to 1½ knots between Point Gammon and Succonesset Point, up to 3.3 knots off West Chop, and more in Muskeeget Channel.

Falmouth, Mass. (249, 260). Falmouth, one of the best equipped ports on the coast, provides all the services a yachtsman might require. However, it is not renowned for scenic beauty or attractive atmosphere. Many prefer to get provisions, pick up crew, effect necessary repairs, or purchase equipment in Falmouth and move along to a more picturesque anchorage in Hadley Harbor or Cotuit.

Entrance is not complicated. Make bell 16 and run for the green light on the western jetty. Anchorage is difficult because of the heavy traffic and the small size of the harbor. However, Falmouth is lined with marinas, so there should be no problem about finding a place to tie up. Several of these have railways or hoists and can take care of all kinds of repairs to hull, spars, rigging, and engines. Cape Cod Marine Service, operated by the MacDougall brothers, is said to be excellent for repairs to electronic equipment.

There is a supermarket near the southeast corner of the harbor, and the town has numerous attractive restaurants and motels. Bus and airplane service to Boston, Providence, and New York makes Falmouth a good place at which to change crews. Mr. Milton Steele is the Harbor Master. He is likely to know of slips available.

Green Pond, Mass. (260). Like other artificial harbors along the south shore of the Cape, Green Pond has an outer buoy, nun 14, and a jetty with a light on it. The channel is marked with locally maintained buoys, which should be respected. Moorings are usually available, and there are a number of slips with water and power connections at Bill Fischer's yard in the northeast corner of the harbor. If you have to anchor, favor the western part of the basin. The yard is equipped to make general repairs to hull, spars, engines, and sails. It has a well-supplied marine store. There is a telephone booth near the landing.

Although it is small and may be crowded on weekends, Green Pond is a quiet and attractive anchorage.

Menauhant, Eel Pond, Childs River, Mass. (259). Chart 259 gives an inhospitable impression of this harbor, but it is a pretty place and usually peaceful. The entrance is well marked by a flashing bell, two nuns, and a can. In 1971 there was a reported depth of 5 feet in the entrance and 5 to 6 feet in the privately buoyed channel that leads up the Childs River to the confluence of the Childs and Seapit. Beyond here, local authorities say, the 5- to 6-foot depth continues to the Edwards Boat Yard just below the bridge. "Keep in the middle," they say. Here there are slips available and fuel and water. Ice can be purchased about a mile "up the road." There is a telephone booth at the yard. Ordinary repairs to engine, hull, and rigging can be made here.

Menauhant Yacht Club on the west shore as you enter is a private organization for local residents and their children. It has no facilities for visitors.

A privately buoyed channel leads into Waquoit Bay through the Seapit River.

Waquoit Bay, Mass. (259). Like other harbors along this part of the Cape, Waquoit Bay is essentially a large shallow pond shut off from Nantucket Sound by a barren beach. A gap in the beach has been dredged and jettied. Entrance between the jetties is clearly indicated by a beacon on the western and a light on the eastern one. Inside, after can 3 and nun 4, the bay opens up, and there is actually more water at the head than there is on the way in. The channel is clearly indicated by local buoys. There is a grocery store on Putnam Avenue near the head of the bay beyond an open field. The Waquoit Bay Yacht Club has only 2 feet of water at its float at low tide and no facilities for visitors. However, there are many private moorings in the bay, to one of which Harbor Master Peck may be able to direct you. In any case, there is ample room to anchor. The holding ground is good, the fishing at the entrance is often sporty. The swimming is warm and clean, and the surroundings are delightful.

Popponesset Bay, Mass. (259). The chart indicates that this broad and shallow bay is available to little more than Sailfish. However, the Notice to Mariners of 18 August, 1971, mentions seventeen buoys in the bay and at its entrance for the guidance of strangers and refers to a marina on Daniels Island with a ramp, berthage, and moorings. It sounds like a good place to explore in an outboard but can be of little value to any but the most shoal-draft yachts.

A depth of 2 feet at low water was reported in the entrance in October, 1971.

Cotuit and Osterville, Mass. (259). A fascinating network of channels connects Cotuit Bay with West Bay, North Bay, and Prince Cove. Most of these have depth enough to accommodate a vessel of 5-foot draft piloted by a cautious skipper who doesn't mind touching the sand. A depth of 4 feet at low water was reported in the entrance channel in 1971. All these channels are marked with local buoys not shown on chart 259, so the skipper must look sharp. Nevertheless, it is possible to enter either west or east of Dead Neck and to circumnavigate Osterville Grand Island either *via* the bridge east of Little Island or *via* the Seapuit River.

The Cotuit Yacht Club, merely a landing without a clubhouse, is situated on the northwest side of Cotuit Bay. There are no facilities or stores here.

One can continue into North Bay and then up into Prince Cove *via* a very narrow channel. In 1971 local authorities promised at least 4 feet in it. A dredging project scheduled for 1971 promises 8 feet in the channel north of Osterville Grand Island.

The Oyster Harbor Yacht Club stands on Osterville Grand Island on the cove at the entrance to the narrows. There are two boat yards near the bridge in the town of Osterville. On the east side is the Crosby Yacht Building & Storage Co. This is a well-equipped marina with a broad range of facilities, including showers, a snack bar, and a marine hardware store where charts and government publications are available. This yard can haul any yacht that can get to it and is equipped for all kinds of repairs. Just to the south is the yard of Chester A. Crosby. The Crosby family has been building sound wooden boats here for well over a century. Horace S. Crosby and his brother Worthington built *Little Eva,* traditionally recognized as the first "Crosby Cat." These famous vessels, used as commercial fishing boats in Nantucket Sound before the days of gasoline engines, were wide, flat boats with a centerboard, square stern, and an outboard rudder. The sail plan consisted simply of a huge gaff-headed mainsail hoisted on a short heavy mast stepped as far forward as possible and often existing without visible means of support from standing rigging. The boom was longer than the boat and the gaff nearly as long. They were fine able boats for the conditions they were designed to meet, although more than a mite hard-headed off the wind in a breeze. Recently a number of replicas have been built and at least one fiberglass model is being marketed—not, however, by the Crosby yard.

Hyannis Port, Mass. (258). In ordinary southwest summer weather this is a well-protected anchorage, cool and clean, with good holding ground. The yacht club is hospitable to members of other clubs. Gas and water are available on the wharf and a public telephone is close by. A small store provides papers, ice cream, and sundries. More substantial fare can be ordered by telephone from stores in Hyannis.

Hyannis, Mass. (258). Hyannis is the only deep-water harbor between Chatham and Falmouth. It provides all facilities for supply and repair and is a good place at which to leave or pick up crew members, as there is air and bus service to Boston, Providence, and New York. Steamers run to Martha's Vineyard and connect with those for Nantucket and Woods Hole.

Entrance is simple, but it is a lengthy business. Outside the breakwater are numerous rocks and shoals, marked and unmarked. Out here, too, a brisk afternoon southwester blowing against an ebb tide can kick up a short breaking chop, unpleasant in any boat and possibly dangerous in a small open boat.

After passing the breakwater, leave nun 6 to starboard and proceed directly from buoy to buoy. The channel is narrow but about 12 feet deep and easy to follow. There is considerable traffic.

Between Dunbar Point and Harbor Bluff is an anchorage off the Hyannis Yacht Club. Guest moorings may be available. Anchorage is also possible in Lewis Bay, although it is not snug. One can, however, snug up under the weather shore.

If you persevere and go all the way into Hyannis, you will find a large marina to starboard with slips in which to tie up and all facilities, including showers and a marine hardware store. All kinds of repairs can be made here as well. Across the harbor is Klimm's yard, presided over by the pleasant and hospitable owner. Most ordinary repairs can be carried out here, and a few slips may be available. We advise against anchoring because of the heavy traffic of steamers and excursion boats with no more than just enough room to turn.

Up the street from Klimm's yard and a large restaurant is the town of Hyannis. It consists principally of one long, long main street lined with smart clothing stores, a Howard Johnson restaurant, various notion and pottery establishments, and, indeed, everything but a grocery store. After a long trek to the westward, the hungry mariner will find an enormous brick-and-glass supermarket, providing for all his needs. On his journey along this hot cement-paved sidewalk, he will see every type of summer costume, every kind of vacation-bound automobile, every aspect of the summer trade on Cape Cod. It is a far cry indeed from a down-east general store with its confused aroma of oil-clothes, codline, and cheese.

About a mile out of town is a great shopping center with every conceivable type of store from Sears and Filene's to a boutique and a restaurant. Hyannis indeed has much to recommend it.

Parker's River, South Yarmouth, Mass. (258). A new marina, called Gateway Isles Marina, has been artificially dredged through the beach, and a very complete setup has been installed. Gasoline and Diesel oil are available. A restaurant is nearby. The entrance, which will be kept open only by persistent dredging, will at present admit boats drawing 5 feet on the tide, but a call to the marina before coming in is in order. There is a long entrance channel, the better part of a mile. The approach from the sound is easy, since the marina is located directly adjacent to the drive-in theater, readily seen from offshore.

The marina was occupied by power boats in 1971, suggesting that deeper-draft sailing craft cannot easily enter.

Bass River, Mass. (258). The channel and the river have been kept dredged to about 6 feet in 1971. The proper course from the gong outside is marked by privately maintained buoys.

If you can get in, there are two places to go for slips or other facilities: to Ship Shops on the west shore a short distance above the marshy island, or—if you can go under the fixed bridge of Route 28 with 15-feet vertical clearance—to the Bass River Marina. Most sailing craft patronize ship Shops. The marina is easily located by its great storage shed for "in-and-out" storage of small yachts. By means of a powerful fork lift, a boat can be lifted out of water, trundled into the building, and placed in a rack. There are several tiers of racks, so a great many boats can be accommodated. A phone call will get your boat launched and ready to go by the time you have parked your car.

On June 9, 1951, Bass River became one of the most widely talked about ports on the New England coast, at least among readers of the *Saturday Evening Post*. On that date the *Post* published an article by Morton H. Hunt called "The Secret of the Vanished Explorer." In the article Hunt told of the studies and explorations of a schoolteacher-become-archaeologist named Frederick J. Pohl, which led Pohl to believe that Follins Pond, 6 miles upriver, was the site of the Vinland of Leif Ericson and of his Viking encampment in A.D. 1003. Descriptions in ancient Norse sagas seemed to point to the south of the Cape, with Bass River as a likely possibility. But how was Dr. Pohl to find evidence in support of his theory?

He and his wife went to Bass River, and, first near the shore of Follins Pond and later at points on the river, they discovered mooring holes of the type used by the Vikings, drilled in several rocks. The Vikings used to put spikes in such holes at an angle that would enable them to put ropes around the spikes to hold their craft without danger of the ropes' slipping off. Dr. Pohl became convinced that these holes were not the drill holes used for blasting, but could be nothing else but holes drilled by the Vikings. He told his story to Hunt. Hunt wrote the article and started a controversy. Some archaeologists raised objections to his theory, while others came to his support.

One of the criticisms pointed to the shoal water. How could a Viking ship have got that far? But Dr. Pohl adduced evidence to show that the sea level 1000 years ago was 2 or 3 feet higher than it is today. In 1952 Dr. Pohl wrote *The Lost Discovery,* in which he traced in detail the travels of the Vikings in North America, backing his conclusions with most convincing evidence. Unlike many historians, Dr. Pohl took the trouble to visit the places he described.

Admiral Morison, in his scholarly and colorful *European Discovery of America, Northern Voyages* (1971), locates the Viking colony at L'Anse aux Meadows on the northeast peninsula of Newfoundland. He scorns all efforts to locate it in New England. He writes:

> These [mooring holes] were made by the English natives of New England to receive iron eye-bolts through which to reeve a line to a boat mooring or fish trap. I could have shown him some made for me! It is true that Scandinavians then, as now, liked to moor fore and aft, both to an anchor and to a ring-bolt or tree ashore. But in New England there were plenty of stout trees near shore and no need to drill holes in granite rocks.

Allen Harbor, Harwich Port, Mass. (257). There is about 7 feet of water in the channel into Allen Harbor. The harbor itself is completely landlocked, very crowded, and devoted mostly to power boats. It does have excellent facilities however. There are many well-equipped slips, about ninety belonging to the Allen Harbor Yacht Club, fifty to the Allen Harbor Marine Service, and sixteen to the town of Harwich. Most of these are seasonally rented, although Allen Harbor Marine Service is most hospitable and will if at all possible take care of any transients. Allen Harbor Marine Service is operated by Rupert Nichols and is a very well-run operation, with gasoline, Diesel oil, outboard and inboard mechanics, and ship carpenters available during the season seven days a week. There is a very nice gift and marine store here. The harbor is about ten minutes' walk from a shopping center where groceries and other supplies are available.

Wychmere Harbor, Harwich Port, Mass. (258). Entrance to this tight little harbor is made clear by the drawing on page 265. The dredged channel is straight and has been marked at times by local buoys not shown on the chart. However, a direct course from one can to the next should keep you on the straight and narrow path. Inside the harbor, the best water is said to favor the port side—about 5 feet at low water.

The Stone Horse Yacht Club is prominent on the east side of the entrance, and just beyond it is the Harwich Port Boat Works, just inside the entrance to starboard. Gas and some marine supplies are available. As it is difficult to find swinging room in Wychmere, ask here about available slips or moorings. The Stone Horse Yacht Club has six guest moor-

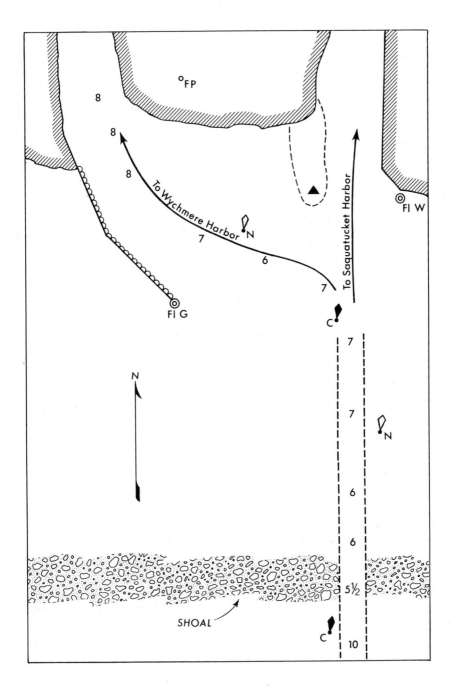

Wychmere Harbor

ings marked by posts with white tops. Ordinary repairs can be made at the Boat Works, and almost any vessel small enough to use the harbor can be hauled. A local yachtsman writes: "Stop at Thompson's Clam Bar on the west side of the harbor for a delicious meal."

A famous Harwich man was Captain Jonathan Walker, who was captured in 1844 while transporting to Nassau in the West Indies some runaway slaves who had appealed to him for help. The captain's right hand was branded S.S. (slave stealer), and he was pilloried on the public highway and put in jail for eleven months in Florida. When Captain Walker got back to New England he told his story. John Greenleaf Whittier heard it and wrote a poem about the branded hand.

Saquatucket, Mass. (257). Of this recently constructed harbor a local yachtsman writes:

> Sharing the entrance to Wychmere Harbor from the sound is a new artificial harbor called Saquatucket Harbor. In its second season of operation (1971), Saquatucket Harbor has about one hundred slips, some of which are reserved for transients. Entrance to the harbor is buoyed and is directly ahead of the outer channel markers, which do not show on the charts. The sketch chart shows the entrance as of summer of 1971. There is a 3½ foot rise and fall of tide, and if you are coming in from the west, the current will be fair all the way down the sound if you arrive at Wychmere Harbor somewhere in the vicinity of high tide. Of course, the reverse is true when returning to the west. Leave Wychmere Harbor at high tide, and if you make 5 knots through the water, you can count on about 2 knots more of fair current all the way up the sound, particularly from Hyannis westward.

Saquatucket is small and likely to be crowded. Anchorage is impossible, and there are no moorings. One must tie up in a slip. Therefore, the port is used more heavily by motor yachts than by cruising auxiliaries. Fuel, water, groceries, and ice are easily available. Showers, laundry machines, and a public telephone are located at the landing. Coast Guard storm warnings are displayed from the marina. A watchman is on duty at all times.

A call or note to the Harbor Master at Harwich, Massachusetts 02645, is a wise move when one is planning a stop at Saquatucket.

Stage Harbor, Chatham, Mass. (257). Chatham is less submerged by the flood of summer visitors than most ports on the south shore of the Cape. There are still commercial fishing vessels based here. They are reminiscent of the husky cat boats used in the days of sail—broad, shallow, with square stern and stubby bow. They are heavily powered and employed in dragging for quohogs and scallops as well as in fishing. In the outer harbor there are a fish wharf and a small boat yard. The yacht club is not dominant. Such yachting as is based here is largely day sailing in small boats. There are increasing numbers of cruising yachts reported, but nothing like the pressure that builds up at Cuttyhunk or Hadley's Harbor on a summer weekend.

Chatham is off the path of cruising yachts "doing" Nantucket Sound, most of whom find it far to leeward when bound either for Nantucket or Woods Hole, and to get out through Pollock Rip calls for a 12-mile beat around Handkerchief Shoal against the prevailing southwest wind. There is a channel between Handkerchief Shoal and Monomoy, which a local authority regards as perfectly practicable. In this author's opinion, a stranger should view it with great caution.

Entrance to Stage Harbor from Chatham Roads is clearly marked by a black and white lighted bell, a can and nun at the entrance to the dredged channel through Harding Beach, and a flasher opposite the jetty. Shoaling to 6 feet is reported in the channel from the entrance to nun 8. On a southwest breeze a steep, confused chop is likely to build up outside the jetty because the south shore of the Cape and the shoals of Monomoy act like the sides of a funnel.

While this may occasion surprise and distress on running in before the wind, it can be frightening to the skipper beating out against it. The worst of it, however, is near the channel entrance. A mile or more outside, the sea is not nearly so bad.

The principal anchorage at Chatham is in the basin east of nun 12 off the wharves. There is said to be a depth of 10 feet here. A quiet and possibly less frequented anchorage is southeast of nun 6 in what used to be the entrance channel before the cut was made through Harding Beach. There is a small marina in the Mitchell River just below the bridge, and next to it the Mitchell River Marina maintains several guest moorings and slips for transient yachts. About 6 feet can be carried to the bridge at low water. The channel is marked with local buoys.

Gas, Diesel oil, water, and ice can be obtained at the Old Mill Boat Yard in the outer harbor or at the bridge. The bridge has a vertical clearance of 8 feet. Yachts that can pass under it will find quiet clean anchorage in Mill Pond and can even penetrate to Little Mill Pond, where there is a town wharf close to the shopping center of Chatham. The trip is worth while in the dinghy anyway, and affords a pleasant way to visit the store.

In the event of accident to hull, spars, or rigging, the most convenient yard for repairs is the Old Mill Boat Yard, operated by Tom Ennis, on the north shore of the outer harbor. He has a railway that can haul yachts up to about a 3½-foot draft and can perform ordinary repairs. In addition, at the Mitchell River Marina, run by the obliging Bruce McCluskey, is a crane capable of hauling small boats or lifting a spar.

If you give the town office a day's notice, the bridge can be opened so a masted vessel can enter the Mill Pond. This is a major project, because there are no gates to stop road traffic, and the bridge must be raised by hand. Two trucks are sent down, one parked across the road on each side of the bridge, and the span is then cranked up. Above the bridge is the Mill Pond Boat Yard, which can handle repairs but is principally devoted to storage and occasional construction. It is operated by Robert Napier, a descendant of the inspired mathematician who conceived the first table of logarithms. The owner is F. Spaulding Dunbar, a yacht designer and excellent source of local information. You may be fortunate enough to see a wooden yacht under construction in this yard.

Repairs to electronic equipment can be made at Chatham Marine Electronics Laboratory.

There is a great deal to see and do in Chatham. There are the well-known Chatham Murals painted by Mrs. Carol Wight and now housed in a barn. There is the Railroad Museum in the no-longer-used railroad station. There is the view of the open Atlantic from Chatham Light. A summer theater is operated by Ohio University. Some people might enjoy boating on Pleasant Bay and Chatham Harbor, the large body of shallow water between the Chatham–South Orleans shore and Nauset Beach.

Harold Claflin Harbor Master of Chatham, reports that there is no channel south of Morris Island. A sandbar runs from Monomoy Island to Morris Island with a few inches of water over it at low water. Currents are strong, and this area should be avoided. No buoys are located here.

Mr. Claflin also warns mariners that no person regardless of his experience should attempt to use the passage into Chatham Harbor between Monomoy Beach and the southern tip of Nauset Beach. It is an area subject to shifting shoals and heavy breaking seas. Although he maintains some buoys here, they cannot be shifted to conform with changes in the channel for several days after a storm because of sea conditions. We strongly recommend that all yachtsmen heed his advice.

In front of Chatham Lighthouse on a bluff is a sign reading:

> About nine miles SE of this place are the shoals of Pollock Rip which turned the *Mayflower* back to Provincetown Harbor and caused

the Pilgrim Fathers to settle in Plymouth instead of on the Jersey Coast, their original destination.

It might be noted also that the shoals off nearby Nantucket turned Henry Hudson back from Cape Cod and in the direction of the river that bears his name.

How those shoals made history!

Monomoy Point, really an island, extends south from the town of Chatham about 6 miles and includes about 3500 acres. It is presently in the possession of the Fish and Wildlife Service of the Department of the Interior, with the exception of a small area that is privately owned in the vicinity of the abandoned lighthouse. This unspoiled and beautiful expanse of dunes is a habitat of much wildlife, and a stop for migratory birds.

Another attraction on the Cape, especially when one is weathered in, is the Cape Cod National Seashore. This comprises a sizable portion of the total area of Cape Cod, from Chatham to Provincetown, and will preserve the natural beauty of the dune land. Many interesting exhibits and restored historical sites are on display. To take advantage of this project, enter the Seashore at Eastham, where the Visitor's Center is established.

Monomoy and Beyond

Cape Cod is the most conspicuous outpost of the mainland on the New England coast. Geologically, it is unusual, and there is nothing like it anywhere on the coast of the United States. It is a narrow glacial peninsula, constantly being modified through the action of wind and sea, but based on a rock and pre-glacial clay foundation that is called by geologists one of the ancient drainage divides of the country. Much of it is terminal moraine, with its few large rocks brought by the glacier from far to the north and scattered around the Cape, conspicuous in the sandy soil.

The first part of the Cape to be seen by the early voyagers from overseas was its Great Beach, running from Provincetown on the north to the southern tip—a long and narrow spit of sand and marsh known as Monomoy Island. Between Monomoy and Nantucket and beyond to the southward are some of the most dangerous waters on our Atlantic Coast—with shoals, variable currents, and frequent fogs that have challenged the courage and seamanship of cruising men since the days of Bartholomew Gosnold and Samuel de Champlain. As we have seen, these shoals affected the whole history of the Yankee coast.

While Bartholomew Gosnold, the English explorer, gave the Cape its present name in 1602, there is little doubt that other Europeans had sighted the Cape in the preceding century, and the Norsemen may have been there six centuries earlier.

From then until now, the sea continued to take its toll, and the timbers of thousands of wrecks lie buried in the sands of the Outer Beach.

One of the Cape's occupations that has passed away is "moon-cussing": cursing at the moon when it comes out from behind a bank of clouds in time to show the beach to a ship that had sailed too close to the shore. According to a story related by Dr. Morison, a certain Reverend Mr. Lewis of Wellfleet saw through the window of his church a vessel going ashore. The congregation was nearer to the door but apparently had their backs turned to the sea. Stopping his sermon, the pastor descended the pulpit stairs and with a shout of "Start fair" led his congregation pell-mell out of the meeting-house door.

Ralph Waldo Emerson wrote in 1854: "Went to Orleans Monday, to Nauset Light on the back of Cape Cod. The keeper Collins told us that he found obstinate resistance on the Cape to the project of building a lighthouse on this coast as it would injure the wrecking business."

Sometimes life saving and the plundering of wrecks were combined. But, compared to the splendid record of heroism of Cape Codders in saving shipwrecked men and women, the unsavory cases of moon-cussing were few indeed.

Edward Rowe Snow, author of *Romance of Boston Bay, Storms and Shipwrecks of New England,* and other books, was taking a crowd of school children through an old house on Outer Brewster. There he found an old book; as it happened, a rare first edition. He took it to the Boston Public Library and there someone noticed certain letters were pricked with a pin. She listed the letters pricked, cracked the code, and got a lot of bearings on Nauset Beach.

Snow rushed down and dug here and there without result and gave up. His brother, a radar expert, rigged up a device like a mine detector to detect the presence of metal in the ground. They tried it, got a click, dug 8 feet down, and pulled out an iron box of gold coins worth $2700. The whole place is now sanded over several feet deep again. Alton Hall Blackington told the yarn at a lecture in Concord, Massachusetts, and showed movies of the whole business.

This may suggest an addition to your cruising equipment.

Before attempting Pollock Rip Channel, consult the *Eldridge Tide and Pilot Book* on the time of the fair current and plan to have it in your favor. If bound east, especially if there is a sea running outside, prepare

The topsail schooner *Shenandoah* heading into a stiff breeze off Vineyard Haven. This vessel is characteristic of a type used in the nineteenth century as privateers, revenue cutters, and cargo carriers where speed was important.

for a rough passage, for a strong current meeting the sea roll can produce a rough and even dangerous rip. One can anchor and await slack water if the situation looks too dangerous to proceed; but once committed to the channel with a fair tide, retreat can be difficult.

Beyond Monomoy the navigator faces 35 miles of practically unbroken beach to Peaked Hill Bar at the tip of the Cape and another long 10 miles to the first shelter at Provincetown. In an easterly storm, this beach can be a dangerous lee shore, but on an ordinary summer day, the trip is a pleasant sail. The bottom shoals gradually toward the shore, so that a sounding determines one's distance from the beach, a very hard thing to judge by eye. The beach is deserted for the most part—an occasional dune buggy breaking the monotony. At intervals, roads penetrate the dunes from towns on the other side, and there will be a flowering of beach umbrellas and a few bathers, but these are soon left astern. Progress is marked by an occasional tower, tank, or flagpole, by the light at Nauset, and by the great tower and radio mast at Highland Light. Offshore beyond the 20-fathom curve is a line of lighted whistles. Approaching darkness poses no great problem, for with the radio-direction station, and powerful beam at Highland Light, and the whistle off Peaked Hill Bar, one's position off the tip of the Cape is easily determined. From here, one can take off for Cape Ann, the Maine coast, or points east, or one can work around to Provincetown.

The approach to Provincetown can be long and slow, for the tide runs hard—up to 2 knots—and there can be an unpleasant rip off Race Point where the flood runs south, swinging around to the southeast between Race Point and Wood End. The ebb runs in the opposite direction.

Beware of Peaked Hill Bar and of Shank Painter Bar. The tendency is to close with the beach in anticipation of the next point, and it is almost impossible to judge accurately one's distance from a featureless beach. Rely on soundings and the line of buoys offshore.

There is considerable activity by draggers out of Provincetown. Some of them are very big, and they proceed with speed and determination.

Steamers bound in and out of Boston are no problem for a yacht bound for Provincetown, but anyone heading north of Race Point should display a radar reflector and keep a sharp look-out, particularly at night. These vessels travel at high speeds and are unwieldy to steer. Under conditions of limited visibility one can be run down with very little time to maneuver. The route around the Cape is interesting in its length and loneliness, especially when one remembers the *Mayflower* turning back from Pollock Rip's "shoals and roaring breakers." Along this beach moved the homeward-bound clippers and whalers in the 1850s, and later in the century racing fishermen and the fleets of four-, five-, and six-masted coal schooners, winged out and heavily loaded, bound east and beating westward in ballast through the shoals. The beaches, then patrolled by Coast Guardsmen, battered wrecks into the sand, from which they occasionally emerge. If one has never made this trip, it is worth doing at least once.

CHAPTER IX

Cape Cod Canal, Massachusetts, to Cape Elizabeth, Maine

General Conditions: On this part of the New England coast, harbors are often widely separated, shallow, and difficult of access. In making a passage either way between Cape Cod and Cape Elizabeth the hardboiled "stick and string" sailor will do well to swallow his pride and start his engine when the wind falls light. It is one thing to be becalmed in Penobscot Bay within 3 miles of many good harbors and with the Camden Hills and the islands of Vinalhaven to admire. It is quite another to roll in the wash of innumerable motor cruisers and sport fishermen off a low, sandy coast with the nearest harbor 15 miles away.

Between Cape Cod and Cape Ann there is a heavy summer population, and Boston suburbs occupy harbors from Scituate to Manchester. Cape Ann is a high, rocky peninsula in this expanse of beach with several good deep-water harbors, but beyond Cape Ann the coast reverts to sand. The Merrimac and Piscataqua Rivers make shelters at Newburyport and Portsmouth, although the former has a formidable bar. Isles of Shoals and Cape Porpoise are also good shelters. For a large yacht there is nothing else short of Portland. Many cruising men bound for the more remote and interesting lands to the eastward sail direct from Cape Cod or Cape Ann to Seguin or Monhegan. For the smaller yacht, however, there are several interesting and well-protected anchorages at which to break the cruise.

Barnstable, Mass. (339). The first shelter east of the canal, Barnstable is a good harbor for a shoal-draft boat. Approach with caution, however. Although efforts are made to keep the channel dredged to a depth of 8 feet, it may silt up. Avoid the neighborhood in an on-shore blow and go up to Wellfleet.

After crossing the bar and rounding Beach Point Light, follow the buoys in. There are more after can 7 that may not be shown on the chart because they must be frequently shifted. In 1971 nun 10 was the last. After this was a green flashing light on a pole, and then a series of brush

274

stakes leading into a tight little bottle of a harbor, which is to be dredged to 8 feet in 1971.

On the starboard side are several private wharves and a cranberry freezer. On the port side is the town landing. One may tie up here for as long as half an hour, but it is not intended as an overnight berth. Next to it is a good launching ramp, and then the well-appointed store of Millway Marina. This establishment specializes in the sale and good health of outboard motors. Gas is available here.

Across the harbor is Barnstable Marine Service, selling gas, Diesel oil, ice, and water. Slips are kept clear for transients. Nearby is a restaurant provided with a bar.

It is a short walk—perhaps a half mile—to the stores in Barnstable.

The principal objections to Barnstable are the bar outside and the small and congested nature of the harbor.

Sesuit, Mass. (381). Another small harbor with a shifting bar, Sesuit is used mostly by fishermen and power yachts. The bar was reported to have only a foot or two over it in 1971, but it was scheduled for dredging to 6 feet.

Inside is the Sesuit Marina with slips for transients and perfect protection. Stores are quite a walk (2 to 3 miles) from the landing, but it is usually possible to arrange a ride.

Wellfleet, Mass. (581). The *only* harbor available for a deep-draft auxiliary in the whole inner sweep of Cape Cod except for Provincetown, Wellfleet is a good place to know about.

The entrance is clearly marked by lighted buoys, and the channel, though narrow in places, is easy to follow. In 1971 the controlling depth was reported as 10 feet, and more dredging was contemplated. Inside Billingsgate Island, the entrance is well protected, so that one does not have to cross a dangerous bar with a breaking sea.

The anchorage is sheltered by a breakwater with a flashing light on the end of it. After passing this, follow the can and two nuns up to the wharves. On the inner wharf next to the launching ramp is the office of the Harbor Master. He can inform you of vacant moorings or of slips or tie-up space available. Large vessels and commercial fishermen often lie on the inside of the first wharf, but the outside is reserved for those buying gas or stopping to load or unload. Anchorage in 10 feet or more is possible in the dredged basin.

Inside the long spit above the wharves is an extensive marina with eighty-five slips for cruising boats and one hundred for smaller craft. Local buoys mark the channel. There is a depth of at least 5 feet in the marina, and dredging is planned for the winter of 1971. Gas, water, and electrical service are available. Diesel oil in reasonable quantities is delivered by tank truck.

Across the parking lot from the landing is Wellfleet Marine. This establishment sells fishing gear and marine supplies, gas, oil, and ice. One can inquire here about vacant moorings. In the summer it is a very busy place indeed. One would do well to get one's business attended to early in the morning.

In the event of accident to hull, spars, or engine, call Bay Sails 349-3840. With a truck, a small traveling crane, and a cradle on a low-bed trailer, they can haul any boat up to 30 feet on the launching ramp. They can also locate a diver to do the work under water if hauling is not practicable.

A fish market and a restaurant are on the road behind Wellfleet Marine. One may call a taxi to go up town to the grocery store, but it is not a long walk, and it is all downhill coming back.

Buses run to Hyannis, connecting with bus and plane transportation to Boston and elsewhere.

The Pilgrims, exploring for a place to settle near Wellfleet, were driven off by Indians in 1620 and moved on to Plymouth.

The lower spar of the flagpole in front of the Town Hall was made from the main boom of the Boston fishing schooner *Quannapowitt,* wrecked on the outside shore of the Cape in November 1913. It is an impressive spar!

A number of interesting excursions are available for a lay day at Wellfleet. Ask the Harbor Master for a brochure on the region supplied by the town.

Provincetown, Mass. (580). Governor Bradford of the Plymouth Colony described Provincetown in 1620 as "an harboure wherein a hundred saile of ships may safely ride." Three hundred and fifty years later, the recommendation is still sound, but in other respects the Pilgrim governor would find Provincetown vastly changed.

The leading mark for the harbor is the Pilgrim Monument, 255-feet high. It can be seen from the east end of the canal and from Plymouth on a clear day. As you approach, you will raise the dunes and the yellow, sandy shore. The Coast Guard station, Race Point Light, and Wood End Light are prominent marks.

Although it is possible to round Race Point and Wood End inside the string of orange-and-white buoys established for the naval trial course, it is well for the navigator to keep near them and to watch his fathometer, for it is very easy to crowd in too close to the beach at Shank Painter Bar.

After rounding the bell off Long Point, run for the southern end of the new breakwater under construction in 1971. This facility provides a safe and reasonably smooth anchorage off two wharves. For those who wish to be alongside, there are marina facilities at the southern wharf. Gas, Diesel fuel, water, and ice were available here in 1971. There may be limited landing facilities for dinghies here as well, although we were told to haul our skiff up on the beach to the north of the northerly wharf. This wharf is devoted to Coast Guard, party-boat, and fishing interests. Except in cases of dire emergency, there is no place here for yachts. Tank trucks deliver Diesel oil for fishermen, and there is a water pipe to the end of the wharf, but it is a busy place, cluttered with trucks, big draggers, and heavy gear.

The main street of Provincetown is unique. It is lined with little shops purveying a wide variety of souvenirs, antiques, and expressions of art, both ancient and modern, of varying degrees of excellence. There are many restaurants, varying from "establishment"-type, serving elegant dinners, to coffee shops and garish fried-clam and hot-dog counters. Grocery stores are few and quite expensive. The streets are crowded in the evening with representatives of the "mod" scene dressed in varied and unusual garb and wondrously bewhiskered, moving to the pervasive rhythms of "rangy-dangy" music.

The Historical Association, the Art Museum, and of course the Pilgrim Monument, are open to visitors. As a contrast to the town, visit the dunes and the outer beach to swim, surf, or fish. W.S. Carter cruising in 1858 in a chartered fishing sloop describes the dunes and beach in these words:

As the Professor desired to examine a beach four or five miles distant, on which the Atlantic rolls its waves unchecked by any land nearer than the "far-off bright azores," we hired a wagon, a span of horses, and a queer little urchin of a driver, to conduct us thither over the sand-hills. In a few minutes we had left behind us the single street of the village and merged into a desert of white sand, that looked as if it had been rolled into high waves by a raging tempest, and then suddenly arrested and fixed before it had time to subside to a level. Here and there in the dells and hollows were patches of vegetation, alders, huckleberry-bushes, low pitch-pines, scrub-oaks, and clumps of wild roses, glowing with the brilliant hues which the sea air gives to flowers. But outside of the village there were no houses, fences, paths, or any traces whatever of man or beast. It was a wilderness, as it was when it first met the eyes of the Mayflower pilgrims. The horses that tugged us onward had the muscles of their rumps unusually developed from working always fetlock deep in sand.

At length we gained the shore and stood by the sea. A prodigious multitude of terns flew up at our approach, and wheeled around in the air clanging their wild and piercing cries. No other signs of life were visible, save a few white sails far away on the horizon. Signs of death were around us in the shape of fragments of wrecks thrown high on the beach by storms. I picked up a piece of bamboo which perhaps had floated from some vessel returning from India or China, or the isles of the East.

Provincetown is a good place from which to take a departure for the Maine coast or Nova Scotia or for the voyage around the Cape. It provides an interesting variation in a cruise east from the canal. Bound west for the canal against the southwest wind, one may be tempted to reach across to Provincetown from Cape Ann; but if the wind continues southwest, you will face a dead beat of many miles to the canal. The shoal waters of Cape Cod Bay can kick up a violent short sea, which makes for a most unpleasant passage. It is preferable to hug the western shore of Cape Cod Bay, where the wind draws off the land and the water is likely to be smooth.

Plymouth, Mass. (245). Plymouth Bay provides the only deep-draft shelter between Scituate and the canal, so is a popular refuge for cruising yachtsmen. Most vessels follow the well-buoyed channel south from Duxbury Pier Light to the dredged anchorage basin at Plymouth. However, this can be a tedious trip for a low-powered auxiliary motoring against the tide. If just seeking shelter for the night, one can anchor under Clark's Island or behind the Nummet to the westward of Duxbury Pier Light.

After leaving Manomet, yachts bound east will have no difficulty in picking out the light on the prominent knob of the Gurnet. Those bound west on a hazy day will be surprised at the interminable length of Duxbury Beach. The nun on High Pines Ledge is difficult to locate in the afternoon sun. There is a clump of pine trees on the shore roughly abreast the ledge from which, no doubt, it is named.

Note that the tide runs as much as a half knot northwesterly parallel to the shore outside Duxbury Beach.

In taking bearings on the high monuments back of Plymouth and Duxbury, note that the highest and most northerly one is on Captain's Hill in South Duxbury and is *not* the monument shown in Plymouth.

A local resident of extensive yachting experience writes:

Formerly the basin at Plymouth was small and crowded. Now, however, there is a 60-acre area behind a 1000-yard breakwater with a depth of 10 to 12 feet. There is good water to the town and state piers. For going alongside the yacht club and Plymouth Marine floats you will have to do it on the tide. There are ample gas, Diesel, water, ice, and repair facilities. All necessaries can be procured at stores in the town. There is good service to Boston and the Cape. The inner harbor is patrolled by the Harbor Master, who does a good job keeping speeds down. The outer channel, which is narrow, is not made any more attractive by the big and heavy fishing party boats that charge out in the morning and in at night.

Plymouth Cordage Co. and Plymouth Marine Railway maintain several guest moorings. Consult the Harbor Master on the wharf at the north end of the anchorage if you do not find him patrolling the anchorage.

Plymouth Marine Railways in the southwest corner of the anchorage is a well-equipped yard capable of hauling vessels up to 65-feet long drawing up to 8 feet. The yard maintains showers for visitors and a well-supplied marine hardware store. Access for deep-draft vessels is limited to high water, however.

There are excellent restaurants and grocery stores not far from the yard.

Prominent on the west shore of the harbor is *Mayflower II,* a replica of a seventeenth-century vessel of the same type as that on which the Pilgrims crossed the Atlantic in the fall of 1620. If she looks a bit high and cranky, it is because her 'tween decks were raised up a foot so tourists would not bump their heads on the deck beams. She was designed by George Baker after extensive research into seventeenth-century shipbuilding practices and built in England in 1957. She was sailed across the Atlantic in the summer of that year by Captain Alan Villiers in fifty-three days. The *National Geographic Magazine* for November, 1957, carried the story of the voyage. Exhibits and wax figures aboard help you to imagine what life was like in 1620 with 102 passengers and about 25 seamen on a winter crossing of the Atlantic. Alongside lies a reproduction of the shallop used to explore the coast of the Cape in search of a place to settle. A visit to the *Mayflower II* is well worth the modest price of a ticket.

In Plymouth there are other museums and exhibits of colonial life, the most elaborate being "Plimoth Plantation," a reconstruction of the Pilgrim settlement as it was in 1627. Guides costumed as Pilgrims explain the tools and household equipment of the early inhabitants and go on to discuss the customs, laws, religion, and economy of the village. It is well worth a half day's thoughtful attention.

Duxbury, Mass. (245). Follow the same course as though going to Plymouth as far as Duxbury Pier Light where the dredged channel to Duxbury turns northward. This channel has been dredged to a depth of 8 feet but it is reported to have filled in some. The basin at Duxbury may also be a little shallower than the 9 feet to which it was dredged.

Although the anchorage may be crowded during July and August, the hospitable Duxbury Yacht Club often can provide moorings for visitors. Duxbury Marine Railway, Bayside Marine, and Long Point Marine provide some tie-up facilities and fuel, ice, and water. Winsor's offers meals and accommodations. There is a well-equipped grocery store in town.

Two Rock Channel running northeast from nun 12 is a quiet anchorage on a summer night although far from facilities. The flats prevent any great sea from building up.

Green Harbor, Mass. (245). This is a narrow channel running up behind Brant Rock. In 1971 it was dredged to a depth of 6 feet. It is subject to shoaling, especially at the entrance, and should be viewed as an adventure for a coming tide. In a heavy sea or conditions of doubtful visibility either Scituate or Plymouth is to be preferred.

North River, New Inlet, Mass. (1207). This harbor, about 2 miles south of Scituate, took its present form when the great storm of November, 1898, broke through the beach into the North River and created the "New Inlet" by which the North and South rivers reach the sea. Previously, the channel was about 3 miles to the south through Humarock Beach near Rexhaume on the South River. The entrance is now just north of the prominent Fourth Cliff, the most southerly of a series of four cliffs starting at Scituate. A bell buoy and five nuns are guides through the entrance, where the tidal current can be strong.

The entrance has been dredged to a depth of about 12 feet at low water. Under ordinary circumstances there is no difficulty about entering, but if it is rough, particularly in an easterly, the bar can be dangerous, especially on an ebb tide.

Make the white bell at the entrance and follow the line of nuns closely. Note that you must keep the sand spit close aboard on your starboard hand after passing the last nun.

The river has a special kind of charm in which its historical background plays a part. From the banks of the North River, chiefly during the eighteenth and early nineteenth centuries, were launched over 1000 ships that carried the reputation of North River ship builders all over the world. At one time twenty-three shipyards operated on the river, eleven of them visible from the Hanover bridge, all 7 or 8 miles from the sea. Plaques along the riverbank tell where some of the principal yards were located. How those men of the past got their ships down the shallow river and over the bar is one of the most interesting stories in New England shipbuilding history.

It is possible to go upstream with a fair tide, following the stakes with pointers on the sides of the channel. Those to starboard are maintained by Scituate and those to port by Marshfield. They are damaged by ice and careless fishermen, but most of them are on station.

At the first highway bridge you will have to anchor. It is a drawbridge, but operates only on twenty-four-hours notice. Call P.J. O'Rourke at 947-9001 or 947-2574. Just above this bridge is Mary's Boat Livery, a source of gas, water, ice, and local information.

If you follow the 4-foot channel of Herring River past the abandoned wharf of the Boston Sand & Gravel Co., you find the modern active Simms Yacht Yard. Here is a crane with an estimated capacity of twenty-five tons, an acre of paved storage space, a big building for inside storage, a wharf and float, and slips for fifty-two yachts. Mr. Simms once owned a yard on the north shore of the Neponset River. He was evicted to make room for the Southeast Expressway and moved his yard to Florida. He returned and bought the Driftway Marina from Mr. Allan Wheeler.

While groceries, etc., are not close to the North River, they are not far away, and arrangements can undoubtedly be made to get them—or get to them—either through Mary's or the Simms.

While the scenery is attractive, particularly along the upper part of the North River, where the marshes give way to high ground, the views are pleasing rather than spectacular. But put up your screens.

Other possible anchorages are near the north shore of the North River just inside the entrance to the west, or in the South River, if you don't draw too much. The Humarock Boat and Marine Co. has a dock at Humarock in 6 feet of water, and supplies gas, ice, and water.

While North River is not a great yachting center and must be entered with great caution, it is an interesting place to explore and is surprisingly quiet and beautiful for a place so near Boston.

Scituate, Mass. (244). Scituate is the first good deep-water harbor located near the route east and west after you leave the canal. With two stone breakwaters and considerable dredging, it is excellent protection. In a heavy easterly, the bar might be dangerous, but this is seldom the case in summer.

The entrance is obvious from the chart. Inside are three yacht clubs.

Hail the float of the Scituate Harbor Yacht Club and ask for Larry Osier. He will sell you gas, fill your water tank, answer your questions, and direct you to a vacant mooring. Showers are available for visitors, and meals are served. Three blasts of the horn will summon the club launch.

Diesel fuel is available at the Scituate Lobster Co. There is a yard on the east side of the harbor that can make repairs.

The town was attacked in the War of 1812 by the British. The story of how the attack was repulsed was told to the late Farnham Smith in 1879 by the two old ladies who as girls had been the heroines of the affair. *The Boston Evening Transcript* printed Mr. Smith's account, as follows:

Rebecca . . . proceeds to tell us how happily their childhood was passed down by the lighthouse; that they all had to help work in those days, and when the war came they had hard work to make both ends meet, food, especially, was so high, and a meal was only got by long hard work; how mad the people got when they heard of vessels being burned by the British, especially if the vessels had grain or flour on board. That here in Scituate the men formed themselves into a guard to look out for the British ships, warn the people of their approach, and if possible protect their property; how one day when two of our ships were in the harbor laden with precious flour, two British ships appeared, and the guard, not knowing they were then off the coast, had gone inland to help harvest grain, or something, she forgot just what. Rebecca looked out from the window and saw the boats being lowered to come into the harbor, and knew their object was to set fire to the American ships. What could she do to save them? Something *must* be done, so she called Abby and asked her advice. There was no time to lose. Couldn't they make believe the guard were coming—how? "Why, by playing on the fife and drum behind the barn out of sight of the 'Britishers.'" Fortunately both girls—in their teens then—were able to play, and fife and drum were in the house, and with a determination to do their duty they began; Rebecca played the fife, Abby beat the drum, the men in the boats heard the sound, looked about, stopped rowing, fearful of running into danger; then to the joy and relief of the girls, they saw the signal hoisted for the boats to return to the vessel. Tired as they were they give "Britishers" a parting tune, "Yankee Doodle."

Mr. Smith received from each lady a personal note. The letters are now in the possession of Eric Parkman Smith of Concord, Massachusetts:

Abbie the Drummer one of the American army of two in the War of 1812, Drove from our shore two

British barges, saved two Vessels laden with Flour
from Capture, and, even from prison with fife and,
Drum, Abbie Bates.

age, 82, Scituate Harbor, Mass.

Rebecca W. Bates, born 1793 aged 86 years—one
of the American army of two in the war of 1812 who
with her Sister aged 15 years saved two large
vessels laden with flour and their Crew from im-
prisonment with fife and drum from being taken by
the British off Scituate Harbor Mass.

Rebecca the fifer.

The Salvage of the *Etrusco*

On the evening of March 16, 1956, in a howling northeast snowstorm,
the 7000-ton *Etrusco,* trying to make Boston Harbor, ran ashore on Cedar
Point outside Scituate. She had neither cargo nor ballast so could not be
lightened.

Unable to get her off, her owners sold her to Global Shipping Co. of
Panama for a reported $125,000, a fraction of her value. Global obtained
the services of Admiral Curtis, USN retired, who had been responsible
for much of the salvage work at Pearl Harbor.

The Admiral found *Etrusco* hard aground, sitting on her bottom on a
stony beach only 100 yards from high-water mark. The insurance companies declared her a "total loss." Everyone who knew anything about it
said she would stay there until she rusted away. However, the Admiral
employed dynamite and bulldozers to dig a channel around her and
astern to deep water. He ran heavy anchors out astern, then cables led to
Etrusco's winches. A few days after Thanksgiving a high run of tides was
expected, and a great effort was to be made with tugs and kedges to get
her off.

On the day before Thanksgiving with an easterly breeze piling the
water on the South shore, *Etrusco* began to move in her berth. Hastily,
tugs were called, steam got on the winches, pumps started, and just before high water the vessel ground over the boulders, lifted and bumped a
bit, and floated into the channel Admiral Curtis had prepared for her.
She was carefully maneuvered into deep water and towed safely to Boston. A pile of scrap became a ship again, a challenge met and mastered.

Cohasset, Mass. (244). To one headed across Massachusetts Bay to Marblehead or Gloucester, or into one of the harbors near Boston, Cohasset
is a convenient stopping place, especially if there are strong head winds.

But don't be alarmed at the array of outlying rocks between famous Minots Light, the marker for Cohasset, and the entrance channel. Samuel de Champlain seems to have come nearly to grief on these rocks about 370 years ago, but even though that great explorer has had plenty of successors in this respect, some of whom weren't so lucky, the cruising man of today, with chart 244, should be able to keep out of trouble by following one of the courses outlined below.

1. *The regular middle course,* always to be followed at night, is as follows: going north, lay a course north by west from red bell 2A off Scituate to Davis Ledge black bell 1 (can in winter) to the east of Minots. This will clear Bates Rock. After leaving the Davis Ledge bell to port, change your course so as to leave Minots Light to port, continuing in a W by N direction until you reach a point just west of the two entrance buoys, black-lighted buoy 1 and black bell buoy 1 (there from June to October). Then head SW ½ S, leaving West Shag Rock to starboard, nun 4 to starboard and can 1 to port. Head for the Sutton Hole Light. Leave black can 3 to port off Windmill Point. Pass between the light and the can and follow the channel in, leaving all lights to starboard and cans to port. Don't enter within an hour of low tide if you draw 5 feet or more, as it is fairly shoal, even in the channel, between Sutton Hole and White Head.

A Cohasset yachtsman suggests: After passing black bell 1, line up the red range lights in Cohasset Harbor and run in by nun 4, leaving it to starboard. Then head for the flashing white light. You will find can 1 a little to starboard. Leave it to port and run for the white light until the red lights line up again. Then run in as above.

2. *The eastern course,* according to the Commodore, is "one which, like matrimony, should only be entered upon 'discreetly, advisedly, soberly, and in the fear of God,'" and also in clear weather. Before reaching the Davis Ledge bell on the course from the south swing in a westerly direction between black can 1 off West Willies and red nun 2 E L off Enos Ledge. Then leave black can 3 to port and head for the Sutton Hole Light and proceed as before. There is plenty of water and plenty of room if you observe the buoys.

3. *The western course* is found by passing between black can 1 CR off Chittenden Rock and red nun 4 off Buckthorn Rock. Pass either side of the conspicuous Barrel Rock Beacon, leaving red run 6 off Sutton Rocks to starboard, and head between the Sutton Hole Light and black can 3. Then proceed as before.

The breakwater extending north from Bassing Beach and the dredging of a good-sized mooring basin have greatly improved Cohasset as a harbor for boats drawing less than 6 feet, though yachts with 5 feet or more, as we said, should proceed with considerable caution, and avoid entering at low tide.

The many outlying rocks off Cohasset are said to break up the seas in strong onshore winds and thus minimize the breakers across the channel entrance—a difficulty that sometimes plagues yachtsmen entering other South Shore harbors.

The Cohasset Yacht Club, which is hospitable to visitors from other yacht clubs, is located—as the chart indicates—on the north shore of the inner harbor around the Bryant Point beacon. The chart indicates 8 feet of water at the outer docks. Usually a spare club mooring is available for visiting yachts. If you can't get one, anchor wherever there is room to swing. Cohasset is very crowded. This may not be easy!

Further up the harbor are two town landings, one (shown on the chart) on the south shore just beyond the entrance to the cove at the western end of the harbor. Hugo's "The Lighthouse," a good eating place, is just to the east of this landing. Gas, water, and ice are obtainable at what used to be Stover's Dock, but is now The Old Salt House, adjoining the public dock.

There is a boat yard—the Cohasset Boat and Storage Co., run by Jeff Dean—just outside of the dam on the south end of the harbor. To the east of this is an area known as Government Island (called Gulf Island on the chart), belonging to the town, which is the highest point of land near the harbor. Here are two circular granite platforms that served as the test assembly platform in the construction of Minots Light many years ago. At the easterly corner of the "island" is the headquarters of a sailing-instruction school for children who do their sailing in 10-foot Sprites.

Cohasset has many beautiful estates and an attractive year-round colony, many of whose members commute to Boston. On half a dozen weekend nights during the summer, the Cohasset Yacht Club holds dances for members and guests. There is a first-class golf club between Cohasset and Hingham. The beaches are all private except for the town beach. That is for residents only. Minots Light is now unwatched, so you probably cannot climb it. But try to imagine what it is like when great waves break on the 114-foot tower and shoot up above the Light. This has actually happened. If you want local color and anecdotes, read Edward Rowe Snow's *History of Minot's Light*. A romantic significance is attached locally to the flashes of this Light—one-four-three, meaning "I love you."

Hull and Allerton, Mass. (246). The chief asset of Hull is its convenience as an anchorage near the entrance of Boston Harbor, though the new state marina west of Fort Warren on Georges Island (referred to later) is equally convenient and more satisfactory in many ways. In order to get to the anchorage at Hull—or to Hingham beyond—it is necessary to pass through what is locally known as Hull Gut (Nantasket Gut on the chart). To minimize the effect of an adverse 3- or 4-knot current, hug the eastern bank closely; it shelves off steeply as the turn is made. But don't go too close to that bank before the turn, as there are many outlying rocks between Point Allerton and Windmill Point. Due to the lighted buoys in Nantasket Roads and the light on Windmill Point, Hull Harbor is easy to get into after dark.

One possible but not very good anchorage, open for some distance from southeast to southwest, is in the bight west of the steamboat wharf. A much better plan is to go further into Hull Bay to the long dock of the Bayside Yacht Club in Allerton on the east shore of the bay. It is just north of Strawberry Hill with its tank and standpipe. There is a depth of 6 feet at the dock, where gas, water, ice, rest rooms, showers, electricity, and marine supplies are obtainable. An overnight tie-up or mooring is a possibility. The Miller Boat Yard, ½ mile away, does repair work and has a marine railway. A short distance across the peninsula is famous Nantasket Beach, one of the finest beaches on the coast. Stores are not far away.

Allerton Harbor, where the Hull Yacht Club is located, is another possibility if you can feel your way in between the shoals, or have a local pilot. There are no charted markers, but some private buoys mark the approach.

Hingham, Mass. (246). The best plan if you wish a quiet night with good protection and attractive surroundings is to proceed about 3 miles beyond Hull to the anchorage off the Hingham Yacht Club, which occupies the former steamboat pier at Crow Point. There is plenty of water at low tide, if you follow the well-charted and buoyed channel to the club pier, conspicuous on the point. Beyond nun 4 range lights mark the channel at night to the club wharf.

A fleet of yachts is moored here and, except in strong northeasterly winds, anchorage (in mud bottom) is good anywhere from the eastern side of the channel opposite the wharf to the islands beyond in the deep area indicated on the chart. In northerly blows one can find complete protection from all winds by leaving Ragged Island to starboard and running in between Langlee Island and Sarah Island (wrongly called "Sailor" on the chart). The late Mr. Blanchard, who lived in Hingham during the summer for many years, told the story that the three islands just inside the yacht club were named for a Hingham girl known as "Ragged Sarah Langlee," who later became Madame Derby, from whom

Derby Academy got its name. Be careful to give the two black cans a fair berth before turning easterly between Langlee Island and Sarah Island. Sometimes these cans set in, so that a line between them does not clear the rock, which does not quite show at low water. Except for convenience in landing, the latter anchorage is often to be preferred, but not on weekends, when it is a favorite rendezvous for assorted craft from Boston.

Due to recent dredging, a good 6-foot anchorage is now available between the Hingham Yacht Club and Ragged Island. There are two large mooring areas adjacent to the old steamboat wharf with depths of 7 to 8 feet. The channel to Sarah Island has been widened to 170 feet, and Hingham Harbor has now been declared by the Commonwealth a "Harbor of Refuge." "Since the dredging," says a local authority, "the catches of striped bass and smelt have been heavy."

Gas, water, ice, launch service, and usually moorings can be obtained from the club. Although it is about a mile from Hingham Village and the nearest railroad station, supplies will usually be delivered if you telephone Hingham from the clubhouse. There is a grocery store a short way down the Hingham Road.

A narrow crooked channel extends from the easterly end of the islands to a town landing and a small basin. It is buoyed but has so silted in that on a low course tide there is scarcely 2 feet at the float. Robert W. Bouvé has a small yard on the west shore of the inner harbor and holds the position of Harbor Master. He sells gas and marine supplies.

Hingham is a fine old New England town, with much historic interest. It was once a customs port, and many schooners hailed from there. Some were built on the shores of the harbor. The Old Ship Church on Main Street is the oldest church still in continuous use for worship in the United States. Hingham Bay has long been famous for its smelts.

There is an anchorage east of World's End on the Weir River that is popular among those who like to poke into unusual places—too popular, it is said, on weekends. This is in the abandoned section of the steamboat channel in the Weir River between World's End and Planters Hill south of nun 6.

Boston Harbor, Mass. (246) (248). Boston Harbor is not a very attractive place for a cruising party. Despite earnest efforts on the part of the city and the Metropolitan District Commission, and the several suburban communities bordering on it, the harbor is dirty, surrounded by unattractive industries, churned by big fishermen, tugs, and steamers. There seems little place here for the casual cruiser and little that is attractive to look at.

Nevertheless, a great many yachts lie in one part or another of Boston

Harbor. There are yacht yards, marinas, mooring areas, yacht clubs, and large ship chandleries. Some of the outer islands are quite attractive and a pleasant day may be spent sailing up the harbor looking at the steamers, tugs, fishermen, and naval vessels. The sheer size and bulk of an aircraft carrier is awe-inspiring to anyone who may be a little doubtful of his ability to sail a 50-foot schooner. The U.S.S. *Constitution* lies afloat at the Navy Yard in Charlestown, a reminder of another century.

South of the Coast Guard wharf and the huge Quincy Market building is a wharf where a number of yachts lie. A replica of Joshua Slocum's *Spray* sails parties from here and there are several fishing party boats. In 1971 a replica of *HMS Rose,* a British sloop of war that patrolled Narragansett Bay during the Revolution, was berthed here. One might land, inspect her, and walk down to the aquarium, a really imaginative presentation of sea life.

However, Boston has a long way to go yet. You will probably not care to push up through the grime into the Charles River or Dorchester Bay, but spread your wings and get out. Beware of steamers as you go. They travel a lot faster than the roll of foam under the bow suggests, and they cannot get out of your way at "slow" speeds in a narrow channel.

A valued correspondent adds:

> From my own point of view, I think the principal risk and constant anxiety in a yachting cruise from the entrance to Boston Harbor to the Mystic River Bridge are the hazards of the motor yachtsmen and Sunday small-boat fishermen. They number in the hundreds on weekends and treat the channels like the traffic lanes on the local urban "through-ways." If you are not swamped by some Chris Craft going wide open, the risk of collision with some careening outboard is ever present with the hapless sailboat helmsman. The chop at the confluence of Hull Gut and the Nantasket Channel when the wind is against the tide is simply unimaginable to a tyro!

The following notes on some of the more attractive islands in Boston Harbor were written by the same correspondent, a resident of Hingham who spends much of his time sailing in this region.

Notes on Boston Harbor

In the summer of 1966 I landed on Outer Brewster, Great Brewster, Little Brewster, and Georges Island. I think they are worth the cautious effort to get there. The mode of transportation was an 18-foot "Cuddy Rhodes" fiberglass sailboat with a plywood dinghy in tow.

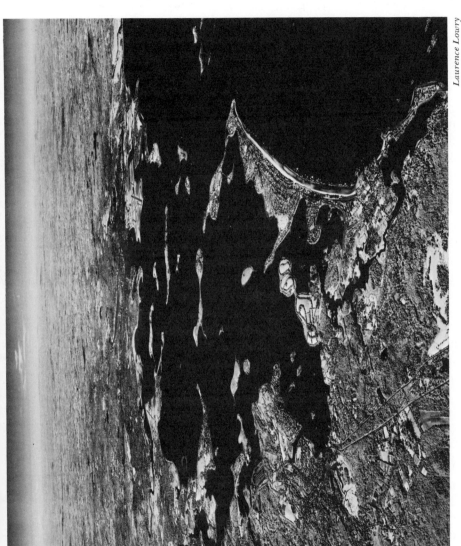

Laurence Lowry

Boston Harbor. A high-altitude infra-red photograph.

A copy of *Tidal Current Charts, Boston Harbor,* Third Edition, saves a lot of vexation from beating against adverse currents in light airs.

Fort Warren on Georges Island is now a State Park. The dock is maintained in tolerable repair, and historic Fort Warren is quite interesting as well as affording a grand view of the entrance to Boston Harbor. The best anchorage is next the shore of Georges Island just north of the pier. The ebb tide sweeps north between Georges and Gallups Island, but a reverse eddy goes south next the Georges Island shore, which is very bold north of the dock.

Boston Light, on Little Brewster Island, is now a national historic landmark, and visitors are cordially received despite rumors to the contrary. We were invited to moor on the white nun buoy maintained by the Coast Guard off the dock on the west end of the Island. The tide runs strongly between Little and Great Brewster Island. The two islands become one at low water. An exhibit of lighthouse mechanism is open to the public inside the tower of Boston Light, but the public is not admitted to the light at the top of the tower.

Great Brewster Island is best approached at the dilapidated pier on the west side. The height at the north end is now a seagull rookery. There are two abandoned 16-inch naval gun emplacements, each at the heights at the north and south ends of the island. There is good anchorage near the abandoned pier. The view is grand from the heights at the north end of the Island.

Outer Brewster is best approached from the north shore, which is very bold. There is a small cove and rocky beach about midway east along the north shore. The abandoned barracks thereon housed the men who tended the submarine nets in World War II.

The north end of the island is rather free of human rubbish and is almost as agreeable to the casual visitor as the offshore islands of Maine.

Marblehead, Mass. (241). Approaching Marblehead from the sea, the skipper picks up first the tall stack and three short stacks of the Salem Harbor power station, a good mark for which to head. Next he will raise the skeleton tower of Marblehead Light. Audible aids, such as Newcomb Ledge whistle to the eastward, Tinkers Island gong, and Pig Rocks lighted bell, simplify the approach in thick weather. There have been extensive changes in buoyage recently. Be sure to have the latest chart.

On rounding Marblehead Neck and heading up the harbor the skipper from less populous places will be impressed by the forest of spars ahead. Some of the vessels are still in the old yachting tradition, with spotless paint, shining varnish, well-polished brass, and colors snapping in the breeze. There are also scores of smaller boats of many classes, mostly molded of fiberglass with wire halyards ringing on metal masts.

The first goal is the Marblehead Transportation Company, a long float with several gangways on the west side of the harbor. Dan Goodwin or his wife "Sunny" may be able to point out to you a vacant mooring. Mr. O.P. Millmore at the Marblehead Rental Boat Company next to the Transportation Company also may be able to provide a mooring. He also runs a water taxi and responds to four long blasts of the horn as well as to calls on channels 11 and 13 on CB radio. Do not pick up a mooring without consulting one of these authorities. It may be only a diminutive mushroom. Anchoring in Marblehead is difficult, for the water is deep and the swinging room limited. There is a persistent rumor that the bottom is carpeted with champagne bottles, pickle jars, tin cans, and other wreckage of a century of yachting and that no anchor made by man will hold here. There may be something in it, for a friend of the author's went on an inadvertent midnight cruise when his anchor line was cut by something on the bottom. A couple of fathoms of chain next to the anchor is a wise precaution anywhere. Anchor if you must, but put out as much scope as you can and plan to get out if the wind comes out of the northeast. If it is necessary to leave your boat in Marblehead, be sure to have a clear understanding with someone ashore. In the past, yachts have been boarded and saved from going ashore. Those who saved the vessels have sometimes found the owners less than grateful.

Launch service is provided by the Eastern Yacht Club and the Boston Yacht Club. Summon the former with three blasts of the horn and the latter with two long and one short. Both clubs monitor CB radio. Hoist a T flag and turn on spreader lights to make yourself easier to find.

The first stop ashore is at the Transportation Company, source of stove fuel, ice, and marine supplies, as well as gas, water, and Diesel fuel. Walk up-town through narrow eighteenth-century streets lined with ancient houses, picket fences, and rose gardens. On the main street either Penni's or Marblehead Supermarket can supply your needs and give you a ride back to the shore with your groceries. You will find numerous art-supply shops, as well as the usual suburban shopping facilities. There is frequent bus service to Boston.

Boston, Eastern, and Corinthian yacht clubs extend hospitality to visitors from other clubs. Make your wants known to the steward. Coats and ties are expected in the dining room. A visit to these clubs gives an idea of what pre-income-tax yachting was like in the days of steam yachts, 90-foot sloops with jackyard topsails, and schooners with two topmasts and steam launches in davits.

In nearby Swampscott are two excellent dining spots, the General Glover Inn and Hawthorne-by-the-Sea. The meal is well worth the ten-minute taxi ride. Coats and ties are required, and reservations are suggested. Nearest hotel accommodations are at Preston Beach Inn in Swampscott or the Hawthorne Motor Inn in Salem. Both are likely to be crowded. Reservations should be made well in advance.

If you are in need of the services of a boat yard, there are several choices. The Marblehead Yacht Yard, locally known as Graves', is north of the Transportation Company on the west side of the harbor. The 12-meter *Easterner* was built here in 1959 and the *Nefertiti* in 1963. The yard can handle any yacht on the coast. On the northern point of the harbor behind old Fort Sewall is Little Harbor Yacht Yard, operated by Ted Hood. Another possibility is Cloutman's, located on the western shore near the Marblehead Harbor Yacht Club. Fred E. Hood, Wilson and Silsby, Norman Cressy, and Bruce Dyson are some of the well-known sailmakers in town.

Marblehead, whose first settler in 1629 is reputed to have lived in a hogshead on Peach's Point, a promontory to the northward of the main harbor, was set off as a separate town from neighboring Salem in 1649. The town itself is a combination of the quaint and the modern. There are good hotels and restaurants on its northwest shore or within its boundaries. Marblehead has two shopping centers, one a few hundred yards up State Street from the town landing and the Boston Yacht Club and the other ½ mile farther away centering around the Boston and Maine Railroad Station and stretching along Atlantic Avenue. A motion picture theater is located in the latter area, and the town also boasts an excellent summer theater with Broadway and Hollywood performers at the Marblehead High School auditorium.

It is impossible to step ashore on the town side of the harbor without finding yourself in streets right out of the seventeenth or eighteenth century. There are lovely Colonial and Georgian mansions at Bank and Washington squares and elsewhere throughout the town, with the Lee Mansion (Marblehead Historical Society) and the King Hooper Mansion (Marblehead Arts Association) the most famous, and open to the public for a small fee.

In addition, there are many less pretentious, dating from the time when this town was one of America's leading fishing and overseas trading ports. Josiah Cressy, master of the famous clipper *Flying Cloud,* was a Marblehead native, as were General John Glover, who commanded the amphibious regiment that rowed Washington across the Delaware; Elbridge Gerry, a signer of the Declaration of Independence and Vice President of the United States under President Madison; Captain James

Marblehead, Manchester, and the South Shore of Cape Ann.

Mugford, Revolutionary War hero; and Captain Nicholas Broughton, who commanded the first American naval vessel, the schooner *Hannah*.

The town lays claim to being the birthplace of the American Navy. The homes of these distinguished settlers still survive, although most are not open to the public except on special occasions. The original of the famous painting, "The Spirit of '76" hangs in Abbot Hall, where the town offices are located, and whose red-brick tower may be seen for many miles at sea. The old Town House at the lower center of town (head of State Street); St. Michael's Church, oldest Episcopal edifice in New England; the Old North Church, with a Bulfinch tower; the Eagle House, locale of the best seller, *The Hearth and the Eagle,* and Burial Hill, one of several cemeteries containing stones with quaint epitaphs, are other interesting sights.

Flanking the entrance of Marblehead Harbor, which was the home port of the America's Cup defenders *Mayflower, Puritan,* and *Volunteer, Nefertiti,* and many other historic racing yachts, are two interesting parks. On the starboard hand entering the port is old Fort Sewall, now a town park, whose guns saved the *Constitution* during the War of 1812 when "Old Ironsides" was pursued by a superior British force. At Lighthouse Point is Chandler Hovey Park, given by a former commodore of the Eastern Yacht Club, which provides a superb yachting grandstand during the yachting season and especially during Marblehead Race Week.

No discussion of Marblehead would be complete without mention of Race Week, usually the last week in July but now expanded by several days. By day astronomical numbers of boats race in many classes and over many courses. At night they all moor in Marblehead somehow, along with a much-augmented fleet of visitors. The evenings are spent in socializing. It is the biggest assembly of sailing craft to be met with anywhere in the world, and no place for the casual cruising man.

In 1965 and again in 1966 the federal government offered to build a breakwater at Marblehead to protect the harbor from northeasters. The town was to put up $357,000 and the government $2,600,000. However, the Town Meeting turned down the proposition in several successive votes. The principal argument against the breakwater was that it would make possible and profitable the construction of marinas at which hundreds of power boats could berth. Not only would the concentration of power cruisers with their noisome fumes and irritating wakes be increased, but it would also narrow the entrance, increase the tidal current, and interfere with the race courses, which have been traditional for generations.

The Marblehead Town Meeting voted a resounding *NO*.

Manchester, Mass. (240). This is a popular and well-protected yachting center, and consequently it is likely to be crowded. In 1968 extensive dredging opened up a channel 10 feet deep all the way from buoys 6 and 7 into the main basin. In 1971 extensive changes in buoyage were made and a new chart was published. Be sure you have this chart.

Although the pairs of red and black buoys are set about 175 feet apart, this indicated width is adequate for vessels drawing 5 feet or less, and Manchester has many of these. The deep dredging is chiefly 100 feet wide. For the outer 500 feet of its length, money having run out, it is only 50 feet wide.

Vessels drawing more than 7 feet are advised not to try to come inside when the time is closer than two hours to the time of low tide. There is a 7-foot area extending for a distance of about 800 feet from the first pair of red and black buoys (numbers 6 and 7) out toward the entrance buoy (number 5 black), which lies in 15 feet of water. Particular attention is called to spring tides, which can run as much as 2 feet lower than mean low.

When the time is right, steer 60 degrees magnetic from the entrance buoy (can 5) to can 7 in the first pair of buoys. Favor the black side, passing only about 20 feet away from can 7, because the deep channel is only 50 feet wide here and for the next 500 feet of distance. From can 7 go on to can 9, still favoring the black side. Can 9 is about 1200 feet away from can 7. After passing can 9, moored boats will keep you in the deep channel, which is here 100 feet wide.

Because in 1970 there were 539 moorings in Manchester Harbor, there is no chance of finding an anchorage. Inquire for a mooring of Carl Magee at the Manchester Yacht Club on the western shore as you enter, or at the float of Manchester Marine. A number of moorings are available for visitors at a nominal charge. Dockage is available at Manchester Marine.

Power boats may continue under the railroad bridge to the inner basin. Gas, oil and mechanical service are available at The Marina, a division of Manchester Marine.

The Town of Manchester, which strikes a suburban note, can be reached from landings in the northeast corner of the harbor, and here can be procured all kinds of supplies. The Historical Society across the street from the library is well worth a visit.

Manchester Marine can perform all kinds of repair work and maintains a supply of rope, marine hardware, and government charts in the supply room. Gas, Diesel oil, water, ice, and stove fuel can be bought at the float. Next to Manchester Marine is the yard of Sturgis Crocker, son of the late well-known marine architect Samuel S. Crocker. Many fine yachts were built here, but in recent years the yard has been devoted largely to storage and repair work.

Manchester is a pretty harbor with a variety of handsome yachts to look at. Sail in and out, even if you don't plan to spend the night.

Gloucester, Mass. (233). This is a well-protected harbor and easy of access at any time, with lights on Eastern Point breakwater and Ten Pound Island. In heavy weather, enter west of Round Rock. Notice on the western shore a bell on Norman's Woe, where Henry Wadsworth Longfellow wrecked the schooner *Hesperus* in verse. The wreck the poem describes was actually on the ledges off Cape Ann, but the romance of the name Norman's Woe was irresistible to the poet.

Gloucester is interesting as the scene of some of the earliest settlements on this coast. English fishermen were operating successfully from here before the Pilgrims landed at Plymouth. Here were drying stages and camps ashore for the crew who cured the fish. As there was always a rush in the spring for the best sites, it is probable that at an early date fishermen wintered here. Later, recognizing the economic possibilities of the salt-fish trade, Gloucester became one of the leading Massachusetts ports and the headquarters of the Atlantic fishery. With the growth of railroads, Boston became the center for the fresh-fish market, but for many years, through the early part of the century, the long main booms of Gloucester schooners swung past Eastern Point to fish on the Grand Banks. *Captains Courageous* took place on one of these vessels.

As a memorial to the fishermen who have been lost from Gloucester there has been erected, on the boulevard on the west side of the harbor, a stirring bronze statue of a fisherman at the wheel of a schooner. It is well worth seeing. To realize what fishing under sail was like, read James B. Connolly's *Out of Gloucester*.

There are three anchorages at Gloucester.

Rocky Neck. This anchorage in Smith's Cove behind Rocky Neck is perfectly protected and convenient to supplies and repair facilities. Moorings and slips are available at Bickford's about half way up the west shore. Rocky Neck Yacht & Vessel or Beacon Marine can make any kind of repair. There is a small snack shop and variety store and several restaurants on the west side of the cove and a grocery store near the eastern end of the causeway.

However, the berth is not in the least attractive. The water is dirty with oil and refuse. Fishing party boats come and go early in the morning and late at night. The atmosphere of the city surrounds it and the odor of Diesel oil permeates it. If you need the facilities offered, Rocky

Laurence Lowry

Cape Ann, looking north, with Gloucester Harbor in the center. The Isles of Shoals, Cape Porpoise, and Cape Elizabeth are just visible to the north.

Neck is the best place on Cape Ann to get them. In the event of a real storm, it is excellent refuge. Otherwise, yachts avoid it.

Gloucester Harbor. There is no good yacht anchorage here, but Burnham & Thomas and Reed's Marina near the head of the harbor provide dockage and the usual supplies. For repairs, go to Brown's Gloucester Yacht Yard, especially for engine problems, or try one of the yards in Smith Cove. The Building Center on the west side of the harbor carries a complete line of marine hardware and supplies as well as charts and government publications, and it is close to stores. The float may be used for short tie-ups. The proprietor of the Building Center, Mr. Charles Heberle, is an experienced cruising man and is glad to advise visiting yachtsmen.

Eastern Point. Except in heavy westerly weather, this anchorage behind the breakwater at Eastern Point is the best in Gloucester. The scene is dominated by the large and active Eastern Point Yacht Club. It maintains several guest moorings in the outer part of the anchorage and a float in the angle between the breakwater and the shore. There is about 4 feet of water at the float at low tide and a rock to the south of it, with about 3 feet over it at low water. In approaching, do *not* keep off to the south to round up, but come straight in, dead slow.

There is a water hose on the float. The telephone is on the far side of the club by the lower entrance. Grocery stores in Gloucester will deliver supplies to the float. Consult with the steward about this. There is no gas or Diesel oil here, no repair facility, and no store near by. The club serves meals in rather formal style; visitors are requested to wear coats and ties. The facilities of the club are available to members of other yacht clubs. Consult the attendant at the desk.

For the vessel in cruising trim ready to start east or west, this is a cool, quiet, and clean place from which to leave, only mildly disturbed by the wakes of fishermen rounding the breakwater early in the morning.

Sandy Bay (243). This is a triangular bay between Straitsmouth and Andrews Point, more or less protected by an unfinished breakwater and the ledges outside it. The original idea was to provide a large and easily accessible harbor of refuge for the Navy, but the project remains unfinished, with most of the breakwater submerged. According to the *Coast Pilot,* "it extends 1200 yards northward from Avery Ledge, then 830 yards northwestward toward Andrews Point." It is buoyed and can be avoided easily. There are three small harbors bordering Sandy Bay: Rockport, Granite Company Cove, and Pigeon Cove.

Rockport, Mass. (243). This is a selfconsciously picturesque little harbor protected by a breakwater. In anything but an easterly it is a snug spot. However, it is heavily overcrowded, particularly on weekends. Boats are moored fore and aft and rafted together in calm weather. Anchoring is forbidden. In an effort to discourage the excessive motorboat traffic, the town voted that no gasoline or Diesel oil was to be sold from the wharves. The fishermen lug gas down the street in cans, and the big party boats are fueled by tank trucks, which station themselves on the town wharf at an early hour in the morning.

Entrance is clear from the chart. Do not sail into Rockport. Even the most stubborn stick-and-string sailors will find it impossible to maneuver among the closely tiered vessels. Lie alongside a wharf or the town float briefly, leaving someone aboard to tend lines, and seek out Harbor Master Lesch. He will suggest a mooring or a place to lie alongside if one is available.

An alternative to entering Rockport harbor is to anchor off the beach just north of Bearskin Neck, the point that forms the northern side of the harbor. There is a town mooring here for visitors. The holding ground is said to be good. On a quiet summer night it is preferable in many ways to the crowded harbor, from which the fishing parties leave early in the morning.

Neither this anchorage nor Rockport harbor is any place to be in a heavy easterly. Go around to Annisquam or Gloucester if a real blow is expected.

Land at the yacht club float. It is crowded, to be sure, but you can squeeze in. The gate at the entrance to the club is open all night, although the building is usually closed early in the evening. There is a place to dump refuse on the wharf and a pay telephone at the head of the wharf.

Ashore, Rockport is an active tourist town in the summer. Bearskin Neck, rather selfconsciously "olde," is crowded with little shops selling antiques, novelties, and craft work. One of the most interesting of these is operated by Eric Ronnberg, a former square-rig sailor and an accomplished rigger, a profession from which he has long been retired. The atmosphere is "arty," but is a great deal more sophisticated than that of Provincetown.

There are several good restaurants and shore dinner places both on the Neck and on the main street. The usual suburban grocery stores and drug stores are easily found.

A quaint town of old houses and winding streets, Rockport has a year-round population of 3500. Settled in the late 1600s, it was a part of Gloucester until 1840. During the War of 1812, a British man-of-war bombarded the settlement, lobbing one cannon ball into the steeple of the Congregational Church, where it still remains. In the latter half of the 1800s, Rockport was famous for its granite quarries, and the stone for many a public building and the paving blocks of streets in many an eastern city came from Rockport—hewn out of the quarries by Finnish and Swedish quarrymen.

Just west of T-wharf is an old stone pier surmounted by a red fishhouse. Paintings and drawings of it have appeared in countless exhibitions, and it is known to artists as Rockport's "Motif Number One."

Rockport attracts to it in the summer bus loads and car loads of visitors. Dressed in the most unconventional attire, they crowd the sidewalks and stores. They spill out into the streets. One frustrated resident writes a letter in which he declares that a helicopter is necessary to get from one place to another. The student of sociology need simply visit Rockport and take his degree. To the yachtsman Rockport is a good shelter, but it is a crowded harbor and a very busy town.

Granite Company Cove, Mass. (243). This is a possible anchorage behind a breakwater of "grout" (quarry waste) just north of Rockport. It is likely to be crowded, is not nearly so interesting or picturesque as Rockport, and is exposed to a heavy surge in easterly weather. The bottom is rough and the holding ground a little chancy.

A correspondent adds:

> A yacht should pass to the north of a rock at the entrance because there are 4-foot spots south of it. There is deep water at the landing where many years ago three- and four-masters would lie alongside and take on half their cargo. Then they would anchor off and be loaded by lighters.

Pigeon Cove, Mass. (243). Pigeon Cove is a small and well-protected cove behind high breakwaters of "grout," waste rocks from nearby quarries. It is less picturesque and less crowded than Rockport, partly because a drop forge plant opens every day at 7 A.M. with a tattoo from a steam trip-hammer.

There is no trouble in entering. Favor the northeast shore. There are no facilities for yachtsmen, no gas, and no water. There is a good market and a small variety store.

Lanes Cove, Mass. (243). This is a small shelter with a foul bottom and a poor chance to lie alongside, but it is a possibility, if one must wait for the tide up the Annisquam River. A local authority writes:

"If it's too hubbly to enter Annisquam, go around to Eastern Point. I've seen it breaking over the breakwater at Lane's when it was OK to go up river."

There is a small grocery store at Lanesville. Buses run to Annisquam and Gloucester.

Hodgkins Cove, Mass. (233). This is no place for a yacht except in an emergency. There is about 20 feet of water. The cove is open to northwest winds. On a hill overlooking the cove is the mansion of General Butler, renowned as the military governor of New Orleans during the Civil War. This is said to be the only estate in Massachusetts with a deed granting ownership to low-water mark.

Annisquam, Mass. (233). This harbor at the entrance to the Annisquam River offers many advantages, particularly to the west-bound skipper. In foggy weather, especially if the sun seems to be shining above the fog, a scale-up north of Cape Ann is almost certain when it is still thick off Thacher's. Also, you are likely to find a breeze drawing down off the Cape Ann hills when it is calm outside. However, in a real easterly or northeaster, the corner between Cape Ann and the Ipswich River is a real trap. With the heavy traffic by Gloucester fishermen passing to and from the offshore banks, the whistle off Cape Ann could be a dangerous place for a small yacht.

There is a bar across the mouth of the Annisquam River; but because of the constant traffic, it is kept dredged and buoyed so that in ordinary summer weather it presents no problem. The tide runs vigorously in and out of the river, but although it can kick up a nasty short chop on the bar, it is no serious problem even to a low-powered auxiliary.

The yacht entering the river will find the edges of the dredged channel very abrupt. Children stand waist-deep in the shoal water almost close enough to touch the passing vessels. It is possible to anchor opposite Lobster Cove on the edge of the channel, but the bottom is soft sand and the holding ground poor. The constant traffic is disturbing as well.

Lobster Cove is the preferred anchorage, but it is likely to be crowded. Go close to can 13, leave it to port, and proceed up the channel to the float of the Annisquam Market, successor to Chard and Wilkinson's, well known to an earlier generation of yachtsmen. Alongside this float one can fit out for a cruise down east with groceries, canned and frozen food, gas, Diesel oil, stove fuel, ice, and marine supplies. There is a telephone, a newspaper and magazine rack and a snack bar in the store. Chowders are a speciality of the house.

From across the bridge over Lobster Cove, buses run to Gloucester, which has rail connection with Boston. There are inns and guest houses nearby.

The Annisquam Yacht Club stands on the point at the mouth of Lobster Cove. It is an active and hospitable club but has no facilities for cruising yachts.

Annisquam is a good place from which to leave for the eastward. A direct course can be laid from the mouth of the river for Portsmouth, the Isles of Shoals, or Seguin. However, once outside the river and the shelter of Cape Ann, you are at sea and must be prepared for what comes. There is little shelter short of Gosport Harbor at the Isles of Shoals.

Annisquam River and Canal, Mass. (233). This passage provides a quick and smooth alternative to what can be a long beat around Thacher's. Especially in the fog, the passage outside can be quite an adventure. Nevertheless, the passage through the canal should not be made without preparation.

Study chart 233 carefully. Note that the channel is buoyed on the basis of entering from Ipswich Bay. The flood tide enters at the ends of the canal and meets north of the railroad bridge. An ebb tide can stir up quite a bobble off the bar at Annisquam, and an ebb tide against the southwest wind in Gloucester harbor can cause a confused chop in the shoal water off the sea wall at the southern entrance.

If traveling with the tide, do not approach a drawbridge until it opens. There is little room to turn, and your reverse gear may not be strong enough to hold you off the bridge. No yacht manuevers well while moving backward.

In approaching a bridge, even after it is open, move cautiously and keep to starboard as much as possible. Thoughtless yachtsmen sometimes come through the bridges at excessive speed. Yet one must move fast enough to have positive control, for the spans are narrow, especially the railroad bridge. If a train is coming, the bridge will be closed and marine traffic must wait.

The channel is dredged through sand and mud, which shifts from time to time, but the buoyage seems reliable, and with ordinary care a cautious skipper can keep off the bottom. The chief peril comes from excessive traffic. On weekends the canal has a good deal in common with the Southeast Expressway. Do not set sail with a fair wind and count on your status as a sailing vessel for protection. The writer encountered one sloop under a spinnaker at the Route 128 bridge. He appeared to have a busy time ahead of him.

Neither end of the canal affords reliable shelter. Lobster Cove is likely to be crowded, and the outer harbor at Gloucester is unprotected and disturbed by passing fishermen. Many yachtsmen prefer to spend the night behind the breakwater at Eastern Point or even at Marblehead or Manchester.

Gateway Marina, Rust Island, Mass. (233). On Little River just north of the high fixed bridge is the Gateway Marina. A buoyed channel with a depth of 5 feet at mean low water leads to the wharf. Yachts up to 40 feet can be at the float overnight. Gas, water, ice, and mixed gas for outboard motors are available. There is a snack bar and a cocktail lounge.

Note on Leaving Cape Ann Bound East

As the hills of Cape Ann drop astern, the eastward-bound skipper finds himself literally at sea. He must cross 65 miles of open ocean to Cape Elizabeth and the islands of Casco Bay. Sheltered harbors are comparatively few. The Isles of Shoals, Portsmouth, York, and Cape Porpoise are the only ones easy of access in a deep-draft boat. In a heavy easterly the whole coast becomes a dangerous lee shore.

Landmarks are few and are not easily recognized by the stranger in hazy weather. One headland, cupola, or water tower shown on the chart looks much like another. None of the harbors is easy to make after dark, and on a foggy night he who would try to reach shelter would be bold to the point of foolhardiness. Fishermen from Gloucester and Portland drag on Jeffreys Ledge and other offshore banks. Not only are they a menace, but tankers and super-tankers from Portland are likely to be passing.

The wise skipper will be prepared to spend a night or two at sea and will have his compass compensated, his electronic gear in working order, and an effective radar reflector in the rigging.

On the other hand, if the weather is at all clear, the Isles of Shoals, Mt. Agamenticus, the Nubble, and Boon Island, far from the course as they may be, are unmistakable landmarks. To the navigator who has once seen them, the Wentworth Hotel at Portsmouth, Little Boars Head, Cape Porpoise, and the tower at Fortune's Rocks will be familiar. The R.D.F. stations at Eastern Point and Portland Lightship are helpful guides. The buoys, while few, are well offshore and noisy. White Island Light, York whistle, Cape Porpoise whistle, and Portland Lightship are about 20 miles apart. Boon Island's fog signal is a valuable check on progress if the weather is thick.

You may be tested and should be ready, but you will probably have a grand slide down east before a summer southwester with a sunset behind the White Mountains.

Essex, Mass. (243). Do not attempt the bar in rough weather. There is said to be a 5-foot channel which is buoyed as far as Conomo Point, but as the channel frequently shifts, the buoys are not charted. Above Conomo there are local markers indicating the channel between sand flats and mud banks. Four feet can be carried to the town. Here there is a boat yard, which hauls and stores yachts for the winter. There are grocery stores, and gas and ice are available. The most prominent feature of this town is the array of shore dinner places along the road.

Essex is working hard to build up its clam resources. Restricted digging, fences to keep out predators, and seeding have yielded good results.

Since Colonial times Essex has been a shipbuilding center. Here grew real white oak, "blue as a whetstun and tougher'n a b'iled owl." Chebacco boats, pinkies, sloops, and finally the big, fast Gloucester fishing schooners were launched into the Essex River. More recently, big draggers were built here.

Anyone interested in the history and technique of building wooden vessels should read Dana Story's *The Building of a Wooden Ship, Frame-Up!* and *Hail Columbia*. But now the yard has turned to winter storage, the smell of sawdust and tar has given way to the subtle effluvium of "clams to go," and Essex launches from a ramp every Sunday a large fleet of outboard motorboats. The river is loud with the sound of motors, choked with their fumes, and coated with their leavings.

Plum Island Sound, Mass. (213). For the shoal-draft cruiser, this is an ideal place to explore. Most of the shore is salt marsh or sand dune and much of it, including almost all of Plum Island and some of the western shore, is maintained by the U.S. Fish and Wildlife Service as a refuge. Water birds, particularly, are abundant. Many different species breed here or visit the island on their migrations.

No very satisfactory directions for entering Plum Island Sound can be given, because the bar is constantly changing and the buoys are moved in an effort to keep pace. One local authority states flatly that if you follow the buoys, you are sure to go aground. Another adds that at half-tide or better you can cross the bar anywhere, even where the buoys are. You have to go by the color of the water and the way the seas lump up over the shoal spots. The bottom is all sand except for one ledge off the end of Plum Island.

Several rivers run into the sound. The Ipswich River is said to be staked out; but as there is almost no water in it at low water and the Town of Ipswich is apparently not going to dredge it, outboard skiffs are about the only traffic on it. Fox Creek is now silted up so as to be virtually no longer navigable.

Laurence Lowry

Plum Island Sound and the entrance to the Merrimac River. The jetties are nearly indistinguishable in this high-altitude infra-red photograph.

The Rowley River is said to be pretty, but is navigable only on the tide.

The Parker River has about 2½ feet at low water, a buoyed channel, and an anchorage basin with about 10 feet at the bridge over Route 1A. Here are two marinas. Below the bridge is Fernald's Marine, with a launching ramp and a motor repair shop. Gas and marine supplies are available at this float. Above the bridge is the Parker River Marina, with a store, a Travelift, a small railway, and extensive floats. A marine hardware store is at the head of the float and a snack shop is near by. Gas is available. One can call a taxi for bus connections at Newburyport.

There is a passage through a drawbridge from Plum Island into the Merrimac River good only on the top half of the tide. The bridge is manned only at high water. The passage is buoyed. Take the eastern side of the drawbridge. Take a slow turn to port around Woodbridge Island, which just shows at high water, and through the cut in the breakwater. This structure was built of stone and topped off with wood when the main channel of the Merrimac River ran through what is now the northern end of Plum Island. The wooden part is in ruins. Then run straight for a marker on the Salisbury shore as indicated on chart 213.

The Puritan judge Samuel Sewall reflected upon the natural wealth and beauty of Plum Island Sound in these terms in about 1650:

> And as long as Plum Island shall faithfully keep the commanded post, notwithstanding all the hectoring words and hard blows of the proud and boisterous ocean; as long as any salmon or sturgeon shall swim in the streams of Merrimac, or any perch or pickerel in Crane Pond; as long as the sea-fowl shall know the time of their coming, and not neglect seasonably to visit the places of their acquaintance; as long as any cattle shall be fed with the grass growing in the meadows which do humbly bow down themselves before Turkey Hill; as long as any sheep shall walk upon Old Town Hill, and shall from thence pleasantly look down upon the river Parker and the fruitful marshes lying beneath; as long as any free and harmless doves shall find a white oak or other tree within the township to perch or feed or build a careless nest upon, and shall voluntarily present themselves to perform the office of gleaners after barley harvest; as long as nature shall not grow old and dote, but shall constantly remember to give the rows of Indian corn their education by pairs: so long shall Christians be born there, and being first made meet, shall from thence be translated, to be made partakers of the Inheritance of the saints in light.

Newburyport, Mass. (213). This historic town, once one of Massachusetts' leading trading and shipping centers, is now devoted principally to yachting and party boating. The harbor is formed by the narrow mouth of the Merrimac River, most of which runs into the Atlantic through the narrow passage between the jetties north of Plum Island. As the silt-laden water dissipates into the ocean, the silt settles. Consequently a bar has built up just outside the jetties. A channel 12 feet deep and 400 feet wide was dredged through the bar in 1970. Nevertheless, with an easterly wind and an ebb tide, the bar can still be a dangerous place. The Coast Guard, State of Massachusetts, and City of Newburyport have joined in establishing a white diamond bar guide advisory sign at the Coast Guard Station Merrimac River boathouse, which has one flashing light installed. This light will be flashing when the bar condition has *2 feet breaking seas or greater*. The light will be extinguished when a lesser sea condition exists. The Coast Guard does not guarantee that the bar is safe if the light is not flashing. The bar can be dangerous at any time. When the warning-sign light flashes, none but experienced boatsmen should attempt a bar crossing.

Copies of the Merrimack River Bar Guide may be found at the following locations: all marinas and sporting goods stores in the city of Newburyport, Coast Guard Station Merrimac River, or by writing to the Commander, First Coast Guard District (b), John F. Kennedy Federal Building, Government Center, Boston, Massachusetts 02203.

One Newburyport yachtsman with whom the writer discussed the bar laughed at any notion of danger and claimed that he took his large motor-sailer over the bar whenever it was convenient. However, he pointed out a sport fisherman nearby with a lofty house and flying bridge. She had broached and rolled over on the bar the previous fall, and he admitted that with an ebb tide it could be "pretty hairy." But it is always O.K. on the flood," he insisted.

A good place to stop is Powers Yacht Yard just below the bridge. Here are moorings at a nominal fee and berths alongside, with gas, water, and electrical connections. Powers carries a large assortment of marine hardware, has a railway capable of hauling any vessel that can get into Newburyport, and is equipped to make all kinds of repairs to hull, spars, rigging, or engine. Sails can be sent to Thomas' sail loft in Gloucester.

Farther up the river, just below the bridge, is the wharf of Ed Berube, which caters especially to sport fishermen. All kinds of gear are available. Charter boats, guides, and free advice are readily available in Mr. Berube's hospitable coffee shop. A tuna tournament that runs from Labor Day to Labor Day is a subject of constant conversation. Last year's winning fish weighed 714 pounds. At Berube's the writer was told that striped bass are abundant in the river. Mr. Berube is an accomplished mechanic and has proved more than willing to be of help in time of need.

It is possible, although perilous, to carry 6 feet of draft inside Plum Island on the high water. It is also possible to push upstream all the way to Haverhill. There are some very pretty stretches of river, but the water is dirty and is spread rather thinly in some places.

Newburyport people have developed a well-deserved reputation for ingenuity. In 1928 when local clam flats were found to be polluted, Newburyport built a chlorinating plant for clams. The costs were assessed on towns bordering the river that contributed to the pollution. In 1961 Massachusetts took over the plant and charged shellfish owners by the bushel. Clams dug in Chelsea Creek are said to be rendered pure and healthful after a dip in Newburyport chlorine.

Philip and James Corbin, two other enterprising residents, purchased the steamer *Sabino,* which for many years operated in Casco Bay. They have completely "restored" her. She has an Almy coal-fired water-tube boiler and a 110 h.p. 2-cylinder Paine compound engine. She will make 7 or 8 knots in smooth water. The Corbins use her party-boating up the Merrimac. With a whistle that Corbin says will "wake up everybody within 10 miles," she is a picturesque addition to the Newburyport scene.

Interesting and original as these Newburyport projects are, it will be hard in any century to top the record of "Lord" Timothy Dexter, merchant, author, and self-styled nobleman, who flourished in Newburyport's days as a prosperous trading center. One of those men who couldn't fail at anything, he shipped a load of warming pans to the West Indies. Contrary to the gloomy predictions of the more conservative merchants of Newburyport, he made a handsome profit. The warming pans were in great demand to dip molasses out of vats into hogsheads. A load of fur mittens in the same port netted a handsome profit when his ship encountered a Russian making up a cargo for home with iron and flax to trade.

This eccentric gentleman wanted to be called "Lord" Timothy Dexter in defiance of the Constitution, and he offered to pave the mainstreet of Newburyport in return for the handle to his name. Newburyport turned him down, but Danvers said that at that price he could call himself anything he wanted, and he moved to that town.

In his declining years he published a book, *A Pickle for the Knowing Ones*. The spelling and punctuation in the first edition were so unusual that he was much criticized. The second edition appeared with several pages of assorted punctuation and the advice, "Reader may pepper and salt to taste."

Almost any citizen of Newburyport can direct you to Timothy Dexter's house and add more legends to the sample above. The late John P. Marquand, himself a citizen of Newburyport, wrote a delightful book on his unusual fellow-citizen.

Another authority is quoted as having said, "The story of Timothy Dexter is the story of Newburyport rum inside a fool."

Hampton, N.H. (1206 insert). The Notice to Mariners dated September 8, 1971, claimed a controlling depth of 8 feet over the bar at Hampton up to the highway bridge. An attendant at Smith's Marina was doubtful about anyone's entering at low water with a draft over 4 feet. The channel is constantly undergoing changes, but the heavy traffic in party boats and motor yachts indicates that it is navigable in reasonable weather.

Enter between the jetties and under the drawbridge. Beware of rocks under the arch of the bridge marked with an arrow. Follow the line of nuns above the bridge past Smith & Gilmore's, which is for party boats only, to George Smith's marina. There is 7 feet in the anchorage area. Smith has a number of slips, but they are rented by the season, and none is reserved for transients. You may be lucky enough to find one vacant for the night. It is recommended that you telephone ahead.

Smith has a launching ramp, a Travelift, and a marine store. Gas, fuel oil, water, ice, and fishing supplies are available. Nearby are a grocery store and a restaurant.

Hampton is devoted to shoal-draft motorboating and fishing. Ashore, it is a summer community jammed on a thin line of dune between the beach and Route 1A.

Rye, N.H. (211). Entrance to this snug little hole in the beach is clear from the chart. It is well protected except in a heavy easterly and has been dredged to depths of 8 to 10 feet. There is 8 feet at the state wharf at low water.

Consult John Widdon, Harbor Master, on the state pier at the head of the harbor for a mooring. Anchoring is difficult in this crowded harbor.

At the state pier are a launching ramp and an outdoor telephone. Restaurants are nearby on the south shore of the harbor, Rye Harbor Restaurant and Ray's having been recommended to the writer. There is a grocery store about a mile to the south on the state road. On the wharf is Rye Harbor Bait and Tackle shop, where fishing supplies, coffee, and doughnuts are available early and late.

The wharf south of the state pier is for commercial fishermen. Lobsters are available here as well as fuel.

Rye is busy and crowded, but it offers good shelter for a small boat caught off this barren coast in unfavorable circumstances.

Portsmouth, N.H. (211). Portsmouth is a city at the entrance to the Piscataqua River. There is commercial traffic in steamers carrying oil, gypsum, and wire. There is a Navy Yard at Kittery devoted largely to submarines, and the Coast Guard has stationed two big cutters in Hart Cove just above Fort Point. Therefore, the prudent skipper will keep his radar reflector in evidence and maintain a sharp lookout in approaching the mouth of the river. There are four anchorages used by yachts in the neighborhood of Portsmouth.

Little Harbor. This is a harbor favored by cruising yachtsmen because it is close to the route along shore. The entrance to the harbor is clearly marked by a flashing red light on the northern jetty and a can off the southern one. The prominent white Wentworth Hotel at the head of the harbor can be seen from a great distance offshore. It is reported that in heavy southeast gales the sea breaks in the entrance, an unlikely event in summer weather. There is a good quiet anchorage just inside the southern breakwater to the south of the channel and out of the current. Beware, however, of a small hump of sand covered with eel grass marked as a 3-foot spot on chart 211.

The Wentworth Hotel can provide rooms and meals ashore, and taxi transportation can be arranged to Portsmouth, whence buses run to Portland and Boston.

Above the hotel is a drawbridge, manned during the summer months, and a 6-foot dredged channel, which forks at a black-and-white can a quarter of a mile above the bridge. Of the southwest fork a local resident writes:

> Sagamore Creek has been dredged all the way up past Mike's Marina to Sagamore Bridge (Route 1A). Sagamore Creek and Mike's Marina are sheltered from all perils of the sea. This marina has Diesel oil, gaso-

line, water, ice, repair service, and dock space available. It is a quiet area. It is within walking distance of Route 1A, where Ladd's Restaurant and ice cream place is located. Also a local grocery store is located at the end of Sagamore Bridge.

The right-hand channel, trending to the north, is also dredged to 6 feet and leads into the Piscataqua River at Goat Island. It is obstructed by a fixed bridge with a vertical clearance of 14 feet. The channel leading west at can 5 is far more intricate and is obstructed by two bridges, the first with a clearance of only 10 feet. If you can get under the bridges and over the shoals, however, you can tie up at "Fishermans Pier" for dinner.

Pepperell Cove. This is a convenient anchorage on a quiet night, but in the event of any southerly weather there can be some motion at the anchorage. "Also, there is a water-ski club there, which will provide entertainment during the evening," writes a correspondent. In front of Frank Frisbee's well-equipped store is the town wharf, where marine supplies, water, and ice, but no Diesel oil, may be purchased. The store closes at 6 P.M.; but if you are in distress, call on Mr. Frisbee in his small house next to the store. He is most accommodating. The Kittery Point Yacht Club is located on the ground floor of a small building at the head of the wharf. It maintains several guest moorings but has no other facilities for visitors. On the second floor of the building, however, Mr. Frisbee runs Capt. Simeon's Galley, a small restaurant and snack bar reported to be of high quality. One can sit out on the pleasant verandah, dine on lobster, and supervise the water front activities. There is no comparable eating place in the neighborhood. By taxi one can journey to Valle's Steak House in Kittery and dine in air-conditioned ease while watching tourists and trucks whiz by on Route 95. Warren's Lobster House is also located in Kittery at the head of the bridge to Badgers Island. It is justly renowned for its excellent seafood.

Portsmouth Yacht Club and Harts Cove

This hospitable yacht club is located not in Harts Cove but in the next cove, west of Salamander Point. The shoal water drops off abruptly into the deep, tide-scoured channel of the river and makes anchoring difficult. However, a mooring may be available. The club has a snack bar open at strategic times and dispenses gas, Diesel oil, and water at the float. Launch service is available here, and the launch will take you down to an anchorage in Hart's Cove east of Salamander Point but cannot hear your signal down there. Hart's Cove is a good anchorage but is cluttered with moorings and somewhat obstructed by the Coast Guard pier, where two large cutters lie.

Back Channel. Although this is a long way from open water, in any kind of bad weather it is the most comfortable and secure anchorage that the river affords. Pass Pepperell Cove and the high land west of it. Leave nun 6 and the beacon on Hick's Rocks to starboard, can 3 to port, and follow the deep, narrow channel to Dion's Yacht Yard on the northern shore. Inquire here for a mooring or space to lie alongside, as anchoring is difficult in the narrow channel. The yard is most obliging and is equipped to make extensive repairs on yachts up to eighty tons.

A short distance above Dion's lives Ted Brown, an experienced commercial seaman and yachtsman and a skillful compass adjuster.

The interested explorer can continue under the highway and railroad bridges far up the Piscataqua into rural New Hampshire. Great Bay and its three tributary rivers make attractive areas to explore in a shoal-draft boat. Bruno & Stillman at Newington have a yard now devoted to building Friendship sloops in fiberglass, a very profitable and convenient contradiction in terms.

Isles of Shoals, N.H. (211). This group of islands affords the first taste of "down east" for the eastbound yachtsman. Well offshore, unfrequented except by fishermen and the residents at the Star Island Hotel, the archipelago has a bleak, rugged appearance.

It was first inhabited by fishing companies from England in the early seventeenth century. To the Isles of Shoals came the distressed Pilgrims from Plymouth in 1621, and to those islands they sent the godless Thomas Morton of Merrymount, who corrupted Indians by destroying the Pilgrim monopoly on the fur trade and interfered with the Kingdom of God in the Wilderness by dancing, singing, and wild weekend parties.

Gosport Harbor. There are no facilties for yachtsmen—no marina, no place to lie alongside, no gas, ice, water, or provisions. Yet to many yachtsmen this is an attractive spot. It has the bleak offshore quality of Matinicus and the islands off Jonesport. There is a stark and elemental simplicity about the place, reminding the summer sailor that not many months ago the gales and seas of the North Atlantic Ocean were piling in on the weather side. A heavy gale badly damaged the breakwater in the winter of 1971–72. It had not been rebuilt in 1973.

A frequent visitor to Gosport Harbor between Star and Smuttynose islands writes:

One can find soft bottom between Cedar and Star islands if lucky. There are some patches of sand in that area. The best place is about midway from the point on the northeast corner of Star and the shore of Cedar Island.

This is a poor anchorage in a northwester. The bottom has kelp and large boulders. If caught there, one can go out through Malaga Gut (between Malaga and Appledore)—hold close to the Smuttynose shore —around the eastern end of Smuttynose, and anchor in the lee of the breakwater between Smuttynose and Cedar Islands.

In a real northeaster the best thing to do is leave the place and go for Pepperrell Cove or "scud for 'Squam."

Poor anchoring practice becomes quite evident here when a northwester holds into the night. There is a lot of shouting, starting of engines, and re-anchoring. On the Fourth of July or Labor Day, there will be fifty or sixty yachts at anchor here.

If you do not go far enough up into the cove between Star and Cedar island and thus anchor on the ridge marked 21 and 27 on chart 211, your anchor will land on what appears to be smooth ledge and will drag until it strikes better holding ground close to Smuttynose or on the edge of the deep water. Should the weather be calm when you anchor and then breeze up in the night, life can become quite exciting.

The Oceanic Hotel on Star Island is owned and operated by the Star Island Corporation. Throughout most of the summer there are various conventions of Unitarians and Congregationalists in progress, but the cruising man is always welcome ashore for a meal or for conversation. The staff of the hotel will gladly explain the significance of various monuments. The candlelight services in the chapel are particularly beautiful.

In case of emergency, the hotel will provide small quantities of galley supplies. Meals are available if there is space available in the dining room. Do not ask for a bath or shower as water is a scarce item, especially in a dry summer.

The last week in June is usually the week designated for high-school age young people. Star Island is a swinging place at that time!

In tying up to the Star Island float, keep clear of the buoyed swimming area.

You are urged not to bring trash ashore to dump, because the island produces daily all the trash it can cope with.

Because of the large number of nesting gulls and small children, you are asked not to walk your dog on Star Island.

A husky Diesel vessel, *Viking,* makes daily trips to Portsmouth.

Appledore Island. For many years fishing was the main business of the island. Then in 1839 Thomas B. Laighton, disappointed in a New Hampshire election, asked for and obtained the position of lightkeeper on White Island, swearing never to set foot on the mainland again. His son, Oscar, and his daughter, Celia, have become almost legendary at the Shoals. In 1847 the family moved to Appledore, where the elder Laighton established a hotel, the famous Appledore House. This was one of New Hampshire's first summer hotels, and, probably because of the unique hospitality of the Laighton family, it became very popular. Some years later a competitor built a hotel on Star Island, The Oceanic, which stands today. In due course Celia married a visitor to the islands, Levi Thaxter, and became well known as a poet of the sentimental school popular in the early days of this century. In 1914 the Appledore House burned. The Laightons all died but Oscar, who wrote his memoirs in 1929 at the age of ninety and finally passed away April 4, 1939, in his hundredth year.

During World War II, Appledore was a Coast Guard base. In 1966 it was occupied by a few cottagers and by acres of breast-high poison ivy.

In 1971, under the vigorous leadership of Professor John M. Kingsbury, Cornell University, in cooperation with the University of New Hampshire and the State University of New York, started construction of an oceanographic laboratory on Appledore. Designed for instruction and research in marine sciences, this facility will house approximately one hundred students and teachers.

Early in the spring Professor Kingsbury obtained clearance from the University authorities and sufficient funding to begin. With characteristic energy and enthusiasm he at once raised a corps of volunteers, acquired necessary supplies, a backhoe, a jeep, and a dump truck, built a barge, pitched tents and set up a six-week summer course. During and following the course, work proceeded apace. When the writer visited Appledore in late July, Dr. Kingsbury was on the mainland seeking support and materials, but progress had been good. By 1972 there should be facilities for a larger group of students and more extensive research.

Appledore was selected as an ideal site because of its unpolluted water and the undisturbed nature of the island and its neighbor, Duck Island. The courses here are supplemented by experience in the Piscataqua River at Odiorne's Point and at Great Bay.

One project involved switching eggs between Black-backed Gulls and Herring Gulls so that each brought up the other's chicks. The expectation is that in 1972 and 1973 the mixed families will interbreed, producing a hybrid whose characteristics will be of great interest.

Appledore Island supports nesting colonies of several kinds of shore and marine birds, including the northernmost nesting colony of snowy egrets in North America and the southernmost nesting colony of guillemots. Portions of the island, therefore, are off-limits without escort. Dogs are prohibited from landing at either Appledore or Star island.

Dr. Kingsbury writes, "Yachtsmen may visit the facilities during the summer months when they are occupied. A self-guiding tour of portions of the island and the buildings is planned."

In the writer's opinion a visit to this project is inspiring. Here are real scholars at work—the gull project is about the only one I could comprehend—at work not only with their minds but with their hands and their creative imaginations. There is the exalting feeling of being among pioneers who are really making things happen both physically and scientifically.

The most significant way in which to assure the success of this venture of incalculable value is by financial contribution through Professor Kingsbury at Cornell.

Smuttynose Island. Smuttynose is interesting because of old Captain Haley. In the early days of the nineteenth century he had a mill and a ropewalk on the little island. He made a practice of keeping a lighted lamp in the window. One February night in 1813 a Spanish vessel, *Sagunto,* went ashore on the eastern side of the island, and in the morning sixteen bodies were recovered. Three of the men had survived the wreck but died trying to reach Captain Haley's light. The Spaniards were buried in a small enclosure still visible on Smuttynose and easily identified by one of Captain Haley's millstones.

In 1820 the captain, while digging rocks for a well, found a cache of silver bars. He used the fortune thus realized to build the breakwater from Smuttynose around to Star Island. In the 1850s, not counting the guests at the Appledore House, there were about 1000 people living on the islands—mostly fishermen.

In March 1873 one Louis Wagner, hearing that Smuttynose was deserted except for three women, and believing that there was money hidden in the house, rowed out from Portsmouth at night, killed two of the women with an axe, and rowed back. The grisly story is recounted by Lyman V. Rutledge in a pamphlet entitled *Moonlight Murder on Smuttynose.* The island is owned today by Thaxter descendants.

Lunging Island, or Londoners. On this island, west of Star Island, formerly owned by Oscar Laighton, the present owner, Rev. Frank B. Crandall of Salem, Massachusetts, maintains a summer home. The cottage is kept supplied with food and clothing throughout the year for the relief of people marooned or shipwrecked on the island.

Mr. Crandall, one of the individual owners of a part of the Shoals, has generously contributed the following.

The Isles of Shoals, as an abode of white men, is older than Plymouth. From 1615 on, it was a fishing base of British companies. My island was the base of the London Company. The name "Lunging" is said to be a sailor's corruption of "London." The other name, "Londoners," confirms this tradition. So my island has this bit of historic interest that it is the first "London" in the New World. The venerable Oscar Laighton used to tell me that the first general store at the Isles of Shoals was located on my island, as it was one place where a landing was possible in almost any weather. The old foundations still remain. My island also happens to be the location of the somewhat famous "Honeymoon Cottage," so named because various notables in the past, such as Professor Forbes of Harvard, had their honeymoons in this secluded and idyllic spot.

The year before I was called to the colors as an Army chaplain in World War II, we discovered the evidence of a considerable excavation at the dead-low water line when we arrived in late May to do some gardening work. The excavation was nearly filled in with sand but a ring of boulders around the edge indicated that it was not the result of a sea action or tide force.

Later I learned that a company of divers, equipped with some really scientific metal finders, working on the radar principle, had come out to explore for bronze or treasure in our waters. Their report was that they located a quantity of bronze in the deep mud of Gosport harbor, probably bronze cannon from some of the old pirate craft sunk in the harbor. In two places they located a cache of gold, buried cleverly in the sand at a point somewhat below low water. One of these was at the spot where they dug on my beach within the harbor but were frustrated by finding that so much sand had washed in that 11 feet down the sea water pushed in through the sand faster than their pumps could take it out. They gave up the quest for the bronze also because of the accumulation of mud on the bottom. They were not equipped to go through this depth. In both cases they realized that it was an engineering operation and were not inclined to make the necessary investment.

More recently the islands came to the attention of yachtsmen in an article in the December, 1954, issue of *Yachting* entitled "Overboard in Hurricane Carol" by Myra Mathers. She tells how the 41-foot cutter

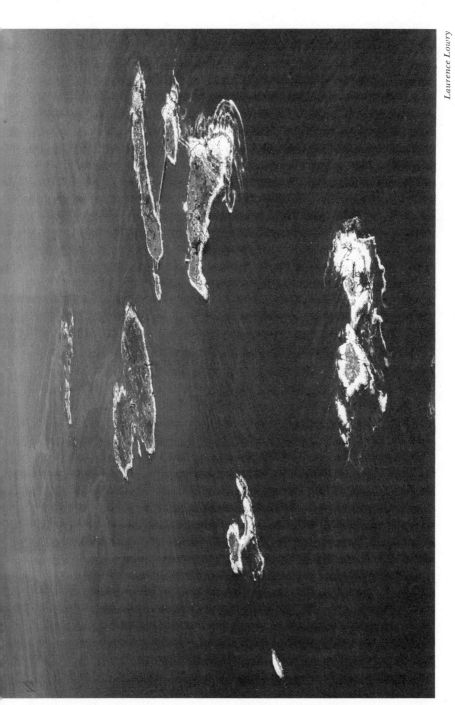

The Isles of Shoals. The anchorage between Star and Cedar Islands is easily seen. This photograph was taken before the Cornell laboratory was established on Appledore Island.

Pendragon, anchored between Star and Cedar Islands, dragged as seas swept over the breakwater and finally had to go to sea. Here the crew fought the hurricane. At one time a member of the crew was lost overboard but was fortunately rescued.

York, Me. (211). A part of the 8-mile York River, this harbor is the only good shelter for deep-draft yachts between Portsmouth and Cape Porpoise. It is a completely landlocked basin in which a goodly fleet of yachts and fishing craft rode out hurricanes Carol and Edna in 1954 with only superficial damage to a few boats.

Those who consider York a difficult harbor to enter should remember that for many years coasting schooners used to enter the river under sail to load bricks at a brickyard above the town.

The entrance is obvious from the chart. The only serious danger is that in rounding the inner nun and heading up the harbor, one will cut the gravel point on the east side too closely. Swing well clear of the nun and stay in the middle of the channel.

The tide in the York River approaches awe-inspiring velocities at full strength. One can buck it all right, even with a low-powered auxiliary, but the eddies swirl one about alarmingly. However, there is considerable mooring area out of the tide to the west where guest moorings are usually available.

Those who like to lie alongside can find wharf space at Donnell's, plainly marked on the north side of the anchorage, at a moderate fee that includes electricity. York Harbor Marine Service can also provide dock space and electricity after 6 P.M. at a moderate charge.

Capt'n Dan's is a simple outdoor restaurant serving "lobster in the rough," hamburgers, hot dogs, and simple lunches. Customers can tie up here if there is room or tie dinghies to the back of the float.

The post office, a grocery store, and several art and antique shops are located on the main street about 1/4 mile up the road from Donnell's.

On the east side of the harbor is the float of the Agamenticus Yacht Club. Visitors are welcome to land and walk across to the beach. The club provides launch service and a guest mooring. On Stage Neck behind the float stood the Marshall House, for years an outstanding landmark of gracious summer living. Wide lawns, a cool veranda, a fleet of rocking chairs, a good dining room, and a sound bar were its principal features. In 1971 it was purchased by a local group that proposed to demolish it. If plans go awry, it will still be standing when this is published.

On the west side of the harbor entrance stands York Harbor Marine Service, Inc. This is a complete boat yard, offering repair service or storage for almost any size yacht. The yard maintains several guest moorings, but if you plan to leave your boat unattended, it would be well to rent a mooring from the yard. Their men will watch it during your absence. Berthage alongside for yachts up to 70 feet is available. Gas, water, ice, and Diesel oil can be bought at the float. There is an excellent marine hardware store connected with the yard. Grant Whipple is the manager.

Up the bank from the yard is Dockside Dining Room, operated by David Roeder. Here one can enjoy a meal ashore either indoors or out with a view of the harbor.

Nearby is the York Harbor Guest Quarters, a comfortable berth ashore for those who have had enough of it afloat. It is run by the hospitable David Lusty and his wife, Harriette, who are the original entrepreneurs of the whole development on Harris Island and experienced salt-water people. Mr. Lusty is also harbor master and a member of the chamber of commerce.

National Rental cars are available at the Guest Quarters.

South of York Harbor 1¼ miles is York Village, a year-round community of charm and historic interest. The Old Gaol Museum and the Perkins House, where the Treaty of Portsmouth between Russia and Japan was negotiated, are worth visiting on a weather-bound day in port. In the center of the village is the York Hospital.

A bathing beach and an 18-hole golf course are both easily reached from the anchorage. The beach is directly across the roadway from the club wharf. The golf course can be reached in the dinghy ½ mile up the river at the York Country Club.

Cape Neddick Harbor, Me. (211). This is a "foul bight," 1¼ miles north of Cape Neddick Lighthouse, to be avoided except in a pinch or in calm weather. It is exposed from east through south. The entrance is well marked, but rocks inside are unmarked. Despite these drawbacks Cape Neddick Harbor would make a haven for a small boat beating west against the prevailing southwester, especially if the wind were strong. The distance from Cape Porpoise makes this harbor a good place to know about, but it is *not* recommended. The beat around Cape Neddick to York is often a tiresome "go" at the end of a long day.

A shallow boat, by using the lead, can go a short distance up to the north end of the harbor and find fair shelter. There is 5 feet at low water at the head of the harbor, protected from all directions except southeast.

For a shoal-draft boat a correspondent suggests a small cove at the southwest of the harbor behind a reef that runs out about 100 yards from the southwest tip of the entrance. The reef breaks up the swells from the southeast. Enter with great care, as there is a ledge a little to the west of the middle. There is no dock, but there is a landing place on the south side where one can leave a dinghy. A road runs from this landing to York Beach, a little more than ½ mile away.

Perkins Cove, Me. (1205). This obscure and shallow harbor is impossible in any kind of a blow, but for a shoal-draft boat it is a picturesque and sheltered anchorage in moderate weather. By virtue of occasional dredging, there may be 5 feet of water in the channel at low water.

To enter, make the black-and-white bell outside, pass between the can and the nun, and, favoring the western shore, proceed cautiously up the channel. Beware of the handsome and busy party boat *Finest-kind*. The shallowest place is abreast a set of ways before you get to the drawbridge. There is a wharf here where gas and water are available. If blowing your horn vigorously gets no action on the bridge from harbor master Kenneth Young or from the local boys, land at the dock and open the hand-operated bridge yourself.

Inside, there are three wharves. The first is used by the local fishermen, the second is for visitors and is provided with electrical outlets. The third is for fishing party boats.

The anchorage is crowded with boats moored fore and aft, but there is room to turn, and you will probably find one of the guest moorings vacant.

Ashore there is an art colony, a restaurant, Barnacle Bill's, and several museums. There are restaurants, grocery stores, drug stores and garages less than a mile away in Ogunquit.

Wells, Me. (1205). This harbor, dredged out of the marsh at the mouth of the Webhannet River with high hopes and at great expense, is something of a disappointment to the skipper of a deep-draft yacht. Very soon after the completion of the dredging and the jetties, it began to silt up. In 1971 the controlling depth in the channel was only about 4 feet. However, the dredging continues and the channel shifts, so enter with great care.

Pass between the red flasher on the northern jetty and the green light on the southern one. At low water boats drawing 3 feet or more should hug the right side of the channel from nun 4 to the pier. Harbor master Abbott reports a sandbar building up on the left side of the channel at marker #5.

One is welcome to tie up at the public float while buying gas. Those wishing to remain longer may secure to the pier. There is a guest mooring marked by a yellow buoy and a red styrofoam pick-up just off the float.

On the east side of the harbor is another public float with access to the beach area. There is a launching ramp here.

The future of this operation looked uncertain in 1971. In the files are elaborate plans for the construction of motels, a boardwalk, amusement facilities, and all the gaudy background of a down-east Atlantic City. However, the capital does not appear to be immediately available, and the difficulty of keeping the sand dredged out of the channel is giving some people cold feet.

The whole project makes an interesting study in ecology, for the character of the swampy estuary was radically changed. The effects on bird life, fish, clams, plants, and people are much debated. Meanwhile the dredging goes on, the sand keeps washing away from the beaches, and more reports are filed. If your boat can get in, Wells is an interesting place to investigate, but the shallow entrance is no place to be in a storm or even a moderate sea.

Kennebunkport, Me. (1205 insert). This harbor, although too shoal for most ocean-racing types, is excellent protection for those of lighter draft. It is marked by a lighted bell a mile off shore and by a light on the end of the easterly jetty. In 1971 the controlling depth in the channel at low water was about 5 feet. Boats of this draft should enter with extreme caution at low water. The channel is well marked. Keep to the right (eastward) of the lobster boats moored in the river. Beware of a rock wall, submerged at high water, just off the River Club floats. Each end of this menace is marked by a granite monument.

There are two yacht clubs on the river, both on the east side. The first is the Kennebunk River Club, and the second, above Chick's Marina, is the Arundel Yacht Club. The latter has limited dock space for overnight visitors, and both are most hospitable.

Kennebunkport has two well-equipped boat yards: Ocean Industries and Reed's. The future of the former was in doubt in 1971, but both yards seemed crowded. Either can haul any boat that can get to it.

On the east side of the river are three marinas: Chick's, Portside, and Arundel. Chick's sells gas, Diesel oil, ice, marine hardware, and charts. A visitor reported that the owner, Booth Chick, was very eager to be of service. One wishing to tie up here overnight should telephone ahead for dock space. In 1971 the number was 967-2782.

At the bridge is an active shopping center with restaurants and stores of all kinds.

The Kennebunk Playhouse is actively producing good drama with a capable summer company—an inspiring change from the movies.

The late Kenneth Roberts has made Kennebunkport famous under the old name, Arundel, in his books of the Revolution and the War of 1812.

Arundel, Rabble in Arms, Northwest Passage, and *Lively Lady* are the best known.

Booth Tarkington was also a summer resident, entertaining friends aboard a "retired" lumber schooner, *Regina,* alongside a Kennebunkport boat house just above the River Club.

There is a museum of antique trolley cars in Kennebunkport for those cruising men who seek this form of stimulation. It is quite a complete collection.

Cape Porpoise, Me. (1205 insert). This is the only harbor for deep-draft yachts between Portsmouth and Portland with the possible exception of York. It is well marked with a powerful lighted whistle offshore, Old Prince bell, and Goat Island Light. Day beacons and buoys with reflectors make entrance at night no great problem, although one foggy night in October the writer made the whistle, sadly moaning and wetly glowing through the murk, and stood off shore, not caring to try the entrance.

Under reasonable conditions, however, one can leave Old Prince to starboard, pass between the can and the nun, between the red beacon off Goat Island and the white beacon of Folly Island, leave can 5 to port, and head for the town wharf on Bickford's Island. Anchor wherever there is swinging room, but don't try hard to get up the harbor for anchorage near the wharf, which may be crowded, public, and uncomfortable.

Cape Porpoise is renowned for the astronomical number of lobster traps set near the entrance. One yachtsman reports a boy tending traps with a wheelbarrow on the flats, and another was told that, with snowshoes, one could cross the harbor on the buoys. The writer asked if the entrance was an especially profitable place in which to set traps.

"No", was the answer, "but we expect it will be, and we want to be ready." In fairness, it must be added that the conversation took place early in July just before the shedders begin to come in.

Gas, Diesel oil, and water are available at the town wharf. There is a good 8 feet alongside the middle, although it is shallower at the northern end. Draggers lying alongside in winter occasionally dump overboard rocks brought up in their nets. If any considerable number of these pile up, the depth would be much reduced. *Beware of two steel I beams projecting over the wharf for lowering bait barrels.* These will foul a yacht's spreaders and can cause considerable damage.

On the wharf is a public telephone, a "snack shack," and Spicer's Galley, a pleasant restaurant that serves good meals at moderate prices.

Up the road about a mile is the village of Cape Porpoise, with a post office, gas station, and grocery store.

Cape Porpoise is a fishing harbor, as the fast, able lobster boats suggest. The bait barrels on the wharf, the float crowded with punts, the men standing around in rubber boots all indicate a community with its mind on the sea rather than summer people. The plastic dinghy, its owner in Bermuda shorts inquiring for stove alcohol, strikes a jarring note. Nevertheless, on almost any summer night a half dozen yachts anchor here.

Note on Tides. Between Boon Island and Cape Elizabeth there seems to be a current setting to the westward on both flood and ebb. The following note has been received from a correspondent:

Too much caution cannot be used when proceeding from Cape Porpoise to Portland Harbor in a fog, especially during spring tides with an easterly wind. Last summer, when lying at Wood Island waiting for a fog to clear, we saw a large schooner under a competent skipper almost bring up dead on Wood Island. The schooner had left Portland Harbor and laid out a course for Boon Island. The following day, when proceeding from Wood Island to Casco Bay, we saw a schooner high and dry on Shooting Rocks. It had come up in the fog the day before from Cape Porpoise and was putting into Portland Harbor. When these courses are laid out on the chart, it is hard to believe that such things can happen, but unfortunately these are facts of incidents that occurred in August, 1936.

This note has been corroborated by other correspondents since 1936. The writer himself once experienced this set of tide in a dramatic manner. The careful navigator will head for Portland Lightship and stay well offshore in thick weather.

Wood Island, Biddeford Pool, Me. (1205). Tucked in behind Fletcher Neck, this harbor is well protected, but it is no substitute for Cape Porpoise in heavy weather, and it is much more difficult to make in the fog.

One may enter either side of Wood Island, although in poor visibility local people prefer to go north of the island, leaving it to port. Make the black-and-white whistle outside, run for bell 3A or can 1, give Negro Island—the grassy island west of Wood Island—a good berth, leave Halftide Rock to port, and anchor outside the entrance to the gut on the western shore. If the visibility is good enough to see nun 2 on Danbury Reef, pass between it and the beacon on Washman Rock, leave Gooseberry Island and the beacon on Philip Rock to port, and enter as above.

Those drawing less than 6 feet can go through the gut into Biddeford Pool. The pool has been dredged to 6 feet, but is likely to silt up around the edges. The Biddeford Pool Yacht Club maintains a guest mooring in the pool, painted a brilliant red with GUEST in black letters.

There are two wharves on the east side. The first belongs to Mrs. John Oddy's Guest House and the second is the yacht club. Gas, water, and Diesel oil are available here. Mr. Andrew Lindsay is in charge. He is a seaman of wide experience and sound judgment and is glad to help visitors in any way he can.

A short walk up the road to the east is a well-equipped grocery store and snack bar. Crowley's near the wharf sells fish, lobsters, and block ice, an increasingly rare commodity on the coast.

Mrs. Oddy may be able to provide a room and serves meals to yachtsmen on reasonable advance notice.

Repairs can be made at Rumery's Boat Yard in Biddeford. The Saco River is well buoyed out.

Bus connections can be made at Biddeford for Boston and Portland. One gets to Biddeford by taxi.

Prouts Neck, Me. (231). Not a particularly snug anchorage, this is a good spot on a quiet night, particularly if one has friends ashore. A lighted bell marks the dredged channel up the Scarboro River. Anchor east of it, out of the current.

The yacht club lies behind a small jetty on the westerly side of the Neck. There is a float with about 3 feet at low water where water and limited supplies of gas are available. The club welcomes visitors, especially in sailing yachts. It provides a 500-pound guest mooring, to which the steward will guide you, and launch service from 0900 to 1700.

About half a mile up the road to the north is a store and the famous Black Point Inn, with an excellent cocktail lounge and dining room. Coats and ties are required, and a reservation is necessary.

There are a seasonal post office and a gift shop a short walk from the club.

The Prouts Neck Association has a beach club for bathing, which is a ten-minute walk from the club. Sandwiches are available for lunch, and bath house and beach privileges can be arranged there.

At Prouts Neck lived Winslow Homer. His studio is open to interested visitors from 10 to 4 during the summer. Almost any resident can direct you to it. The Marginal Way, a cliff walk, surrounds the Neck. The observant yachtsman familiar with Homer's work can identify places from which he painted some of his pictures.

Richmond Island, Me. (231). This harbor is formed by a breakwater running southeast from Cape Elizabeth to Richmond Island. One can lie on either side of the breakwater; the *Coast Pilot* seems to favor the western side. Nevertheless, the rocky cove on the east, Seal Cove, is highly recommended by some yachtsmen familiar with it. Anchor close to Richmond Island in the angle of the breakwater. If entering north of the ledges under Cape Elizabeth, be sure to leave can 1 to port.

CHAPTER X

Portland to Rockland

From gray sea fog, from icy drift,
From peril and from pain
The home-bound fisher greets thy lights
O hundred-harbored Maine!

Casco Bay, Me. (315). At Cape Elizabeth the eastward-bound mariner finds a dramatic change in the coastline. Here the trend of the coast turns from north-and-a-little-east to east-and-a-little-north. The long stretches of beach give way to a succession of deep estuaries studded with rocky islands running off to ledges and offshore banks. Small, well-protected harbors are frequent. Whatever the wind, from almost anywhere between Cape Elizabeth and Schoodic Point there is a choice of several good shelters to leeward. As one goes eastward, civilization grows less pervasive. Uninhabited islands and small fishing communities become more frequent. While no one will go hungry on the coast, one does well to stock up on gasoline, stove fuel, and canned goods at Boothbay Harbor, Rockland, or Southwest Harbor.

At any mainland town in the bay, fresh milk, and ordinary groceries are available. Fishing communities usually support a lobster car with a gasoline pump. Don't plan to lie alongside for long, as a yacht intereferes with business—buying lobsters. Restaurants and hotels are less frequent. One had best plan to eat aboard.

As a general principle, assume that the northeast and southwest ends of islands make out. The northwest and southeast sides are generally bold.

In seeking anchorages, favor those protected from the south. There is always a roll making into the bay from this direction. The strongest winds in summer are southwest, south, or southeast. Most of the bay is protected from the occasional northwesters anyway.

Beware of mosquitoes. They are large, voracious, and numerous beyond belief in Casco Bay. Screens and bug bombs are necessities.

Extensive repairs to hull and spars can best be made at Handy Boat Service next to the Portland Yacht Club. The next large yard to the eastward is at Boothbay Harbor. Almost every fishing community has a mechanic, many of them experts on marine engines.

Fog is more frequent and more lasting on the Maine coast and shuts down with little warning. A well-compensated compass, a radar reflector, and large-scale charts are absolute necessities east of Cape Elizabeth.

While many yachtsmen cross Casco Bay in half a day from Cape Elizabeth to Seguin in pursuit of adventure further east, it is possible to spend a very pleasant week among the coves and islands of this attractive cruising ground. Bound west, a stop at Cape Small, Jewell's Island, or Portland Yacht Club is often a pleasant and convenient break in a long push to windward.

Casco Bay can be explored easily by the weekend sailor. Base on Handy Boat Service at Falmouth or on one of the marinas at South Freeport. Your boat will be cared for during the week, and you can drive from Boston in two to three hours. There is frequent plane service to Portland, so summer weekends can be stretched to two solid days or even more.

Portland, Me. (315). Unless driven in by stress of weather, avoid this harbor. It is large, commercial, dirty, and without good landing places for yachts. Its waters are constantly agitated by ferries, fishermen, and large steamers. Tankers go right through the main harbor to the oil wharves in South Portland. Almost anything you need in the city can be obtained by taxi or telephone from the Portland Yacht Club or Handy Boat Service at Falmouth Foreside.

If you do choose to visit Portland, however, lie on the east side. The following notes were contributed by a 1971 visitor.

Across the harbor from the Portland water front and just beyond several large oil storage tanks is the newly established Centerboard Yacht Club. Fresh water is available at the end of the float where there is 5 feet at low water. Showers and telephone are available at the club house. Blue and white styrofoam blocks mark several guest moorings which are available for visiting yachts (free for one night, $2 per night for the next six nights). Block ice is available across the harbor at Merchants Wharf, the site of the old Portland Yacht Club. On Union wharf there is a chandlery operated seven days a week by Charlie Day.

Little Diamond Island, Me. (315). On this well-populated island, connected with Portland by ferry service, is the marina of Ted Rand. He maintains guest moorings, and at his wharf one can buy gasoline, Diesel fuel, water, ice, groceries, and lobsters. While not one of the most picturesque anchorages, it is a convenient place from which to start a cruise in Casco Bay.

Falmouth Foreside, Me. (315). This large and rather exposed anchorage is between Clapboard Island and the mainland where chart 315 shows "SE Gable." A strong afternoon southwester may raise a chop here; but when the breeze dies in the late afternoon, the chop dies with it.

Before anchoring, hail the float at Handy's Boat Service or the Portland Yacht Club. There may well be a guest mooring available. Launch service is provided on a blast of the horn.

Handy Boat Service is now operated by Mr. Merle Hallett. It is a complete yard offering gasoline, Diesel fuel, water, ice, and stove fuel. There are several berths with plug-in electric service. There is a twenty-ton travelift on the north side of the wharf and a six-ton lift on the south. Repairs to hull, spars, engines, shafts, propellers, and sails can be handled here. Showers and heads for yachtsmen are at the head of the wharf, and there is also a small restaurant with take-out service from a window at the back. The Riodale Shop offers gifts and marine hardware. Transportation can be arranged to a nearby shopping center for groceries, other supplies, and laundromat service. Several yachts are available for charter from Handy's, and one can leave one's yacht here in care of the yard if a week's work must interrupt a cruise.

The Portland Yacht Club is most hospitable to cruising men from other yacht clubs. The steward is likely to know of a vacant mooring. The club maintains a "Bring Your Own" bar and a restaurant where light lunches are available from 12 to 2 and from 6 to 9.

Early in August the Portland Yacht Club sponsors the Monhegan Race for ocean-racing yachts. The course runs from Clapboard Island to Cape Porpoise whistle to Manana whistle and return. The Manana Race for smaller yachts is run at the same time to Portland Lightship, Manana whistle and return. The weekend of the races is a gala occasion, the anchorage crowded with some of the best-known yachts on the east coast.

A correspondent adds:

Portland Yacht Club is one of the nation's oldest and boasts a coffee table given to the club in 1869 made from the wheel of *America*. The handles on the spokes are all worn on one side, suggesting that she had a considerable drag to port.

South Freeport, Me. (315). This quite large and perfectly protected harbor lies nearly at the head of Casco Bay. It is the center for considerable summer activity on the mainland and nearby Bustins Island. The chief landmark for the harbor is an imitation of a medieval castle tower on the shore to the west of the habor.

The tide runs strongly in the entrance to the harbor and through the anchorage, so follow the buoys carefully and avoid being set to one side or the other, even on the short run between the inner cans. Although local boats cut Pound O'Tea Island, the preferred channel leaves it to starboard.

This lovely protected harbor, formed by the Harraseeket River, has become a major boating center. More than 300 boats ride at anchor here in summer. The Harraseeket Yacht Club offers a fine junior sailing program and annually conducts a popular offshore race for sailing auxilliaries.

Two adjacent marine facilities serve this busy harbor, each managed by a team of brothers. Ring's Marine Service is run by Tom and Thornton Ring. Walton and Jerry Baker operate Harraseeket Marine Service. Both facilities dispense gas, Diesel fuel, ice, and water at their service floats. Both offer guest moorings for overnight stays or longer periods.

Harraseeket Marine Service occupies property formerly owned by South Freeport Yacht Basin, Inc., on both sides of the South Freeport town landing. A major expansion program has more than doubled their winter storage capacity. Dredging has added extensive water-front area for slips, and a self-propelled marine hoist can haul boats up to 55 feet and 25 tons. The Bakers maintain a repair shop, and their staff includes a naval architect experienced in design, repair, and survey work. They have a fleet of outboard boats and small sailboats for daily or weekly rental. A fine little gift shop will interest the ladies while the men shop for charts, marine hardware, and supplies. Showers, heads, and a telephone booth are on the wharf. A small restaurant is planned.

The South Freeport Post Office lies just at the top of the hill above the town landing. A quarter mile further, Herschel Maxell keeps his M&S Market open seven days a week. A short taxi ride away, in Freeport, L.L. Bean's famous camping-supply store stays open twenty-four hours a day, every day, and is well worth a visit.

The Rings maintain a string of floats with rental slips and guest moorings. They service outboard motors and have outdoor winter storage space. Their store offers marine supplies and hardware and L.P. gas refills along with a great deal of energy and enthusiasm for a growing business.

The Ring brothers started by offering mooring service and have steadily expanded. They acquired a lease on shore property, built their own pile driver and used it to build a wharf. They have built floats and the buildings ashore themselves. Thornton, a recent graduate of Norwich, and Tom, a student at Maine Maritime Academy, are energetic, imaginative, and most obliging.

The Harraseeket Yacht Club has a float and small clubhouse on the west shore of the harbor. The club is most hospitable to visitors. There is keen racing in Lightnings, Blue Jays, and Turnabouts, and a considerable fleet of cruising yachts.

Although far from the direct route east, South Freeport is an attractive place to spend a night between days spent among the islands in the western part of Casco Bay.

A local yachtsman adds:

> The yacht club sponsors an excellent sailing program in which fifty to sixty children participate each year. The program is conducted by a professional sailing instructor assisted by two junior instructors.
>
> Guest moorings are available at the club. Come in to the floats and ask for Ken Laughlin, harbor master and fleet captain.
>
> Water is available at the float and a telephone at the clubhouse.

The Norman castle on the western shore is not another relic of pre-Pilgrim occupation but was part of a summer hotel built by Amos F. Gerald, a trolley-car magnate, in 1903 as an inducement for people to ride on his cars. He had built or promoted a dozen such railways in Maine and was known as "the Electric Railroad King." In 1914 the wooden hotel burned, leaving only the tower.

Jewell Island, Me., (315). Between the northern point of this island and a small island to the west of it is a well-protected anchorage. This harbor is the nearest to the direct route across the bay, and to the westward-bound yachtsman it means losing the least possible distance to windward in return for a quiet night. The cove is often crowded on summer weekends.

From the west, make the bell off Cliff Island and follow the shore of Jewell Island, keeping far enough offshore to avoid the ledges south of the old wharf. This structure is now so decayed as to be unsafe. Picnic parties still use its pilings as moorings, but one certainly should not try to land on it. Continue off the west shore of Jewell Island and the west shore of the little island with the house on it. This island makes off a long way to the northeast. Do not turn in until you can see the big square boulder on West Brown Cow. If it is hazy, you will have to go by the lobster traps, the fathometer, and a good look-out.

Run up the middle of the cove, favoring the bold eastern shore. There is about 10 feet of water abreast the house on the little island and a little above it. There are several pilings in the mud toward the head of the cove. The first of these is covered at high water and the other is dry at low water. Stay well to the north of them.

From the east, make the nun on Drunkard Ledge and run up toward black-and-white bell "BS" until the southeast point of Cliff Island shows by the end of Jewell. Continue until past the end of Jewell and then turn into the cove. Coming from the east in thick weather proceed with great caution, for the east side of Jewell Island is beset with ledges, and the tide runs in no very predictable manner. One might do better to try one of the shelters up Broad Sound.

From the anchorage at Jewell Island, walk across the northern point to the Punchbowl. At low tide the water is trapped here and tempered somewhat by the sun. There is a nice beach, too. From the southern end of this cove, next to a large white rose bush, runs a well-defined trail, once a Jeep road, to the look-out towers at the southern end of the island. From the concrete towers on a clear day one can see all of Casco Bay, a view well worth the walk and climb. These towers were built during World War II as part of a coast defense battery to protect Portland. Bring a flashlight and explore the tunnels in the gun positions beyond the towers, but beware of open manholes.

The southern end of the island is steep, and in some places there are caves and cliffs of rather loose, rotten rock. It is overgrown with juniper, wild roses, raspberry bushes, and other prickly vegetation, so don't try it in short pants.

Mr. W.S. Carter and several friends visited Jewell Island in a fishing sloop in 1858. He wrote:

> As cooked by the Pilot, we pronounced the haddock excellent; and after dinner we raised the anchor, hoisted sail, and cruised idly among the islands till near sunset, when we put into a delicious little cove— narrow, deep, and shady—on Jewell's Island. As we glided in, an old fisherman who resided on the island came alongside in his dory to have a little chat, and gave us a magnificent lobster, which went immediately into the pot for supper. After coming to anchor, we all went ashore in our boat, except the Pilot, who was detained on board by his duties as cook, to explore the island, witness the sunset, and get milk, eggs, and butter from a farmhouse near our landing-place.
>
> The island, which lies about ten miles east of Portland, seemed to be fertile and well cultivated. The farmhouse was built on elevated ground and the view of the sunset and of the island-studded bay was superb. Fresh and sweet were the eggs and milk and butter with which we returned to our sloop and very jolly the supper we had in the little cabin. The evening was pleasantly cool, and the Assyrian, remarking

that boiled lobster was not wholesome unless well qualified with something acid, availed himself of the Pilot's steaming teakettle and brewed a pitcher of hot lemonade with a strong infusion of whiskey which he administered to each of us in proper doses, as a sure preventive against any ill effects from our supper.

Great Chebeague Island (315). One fairly good anchorage is off the "Lobster Beach" west of the northeastern end of the island. There is a picturesque group of fishermen's shacks on the beach, but it's a bit rough for bathing. There is a better bathing beach on the east side of the island near its northeast end, which is known as Hamilton Beach. A path leads southeast from the "Lobster Beach" to the island's main road.

If seeking supplies or communications, anchor off the stone wharf, but watch the depth, as it is shallow there.

The social center for this part of the island is at Riddle's store at the head of the wharf and at the Hillcrest Hotel, up a hill a couple of hundred yards from the store. The hotel, an ancient hostelry, is well spoken of. It is the only hotel on the island. A sporty nine-hole golf course is close by the stone wharf. There is a public telephone on the wharf, and water, oil, and gasoline are available. The post office is nearby to the south. The store is open from 8 A.M. to 5:30 P.M. Monday through Saturday, and from 10:30 A.M. to 12:30 P.M. on Sunday. Taxi service is available there.

A ferry, the *Polly Lin,* runs frequently to Cousins Island, the quickest access to the mainland and transportation. Another ferry takes automobiles back and forth to Cousins Island but can land at Chebeague at high tide only. The Casco Bay Line steamer to and from Portland calls at Chandler Cove at the island's western end four times a day.

At Rose's Point, on the eastern shore near the island's center and behind Crow Island, there is a small boat yard with only 2 feet of water at low tide.

Chebeague Island, the largest in Casco Bay, like many attractive Maine vacation spots, now harbors retired families who are winterizing their summer cottages and living there the year round.

South Harpswell, Potts Harbor, Me. (315). This is a large harbor and at high water it gives the impression of being rather unprotected. However, when the tide goes and the ledges bare out, it is doubtful if a dangerous or even unpleasant sea would make into the anchorage.

From the west, enter between Upper Flag Island and Horse Island. From the east, follow the chain of buoys from Merriconeag Sound. Note that the channel lies *close* to the east of cans 1A and 3.

On the west shore of the harbor is Dolphin Marina, operated by Mel Saxton. Gas and Diesel oil are available at his float. There is a restaurant nearby, and a marine supply store. Ice can be provided with a little advance notice.

On the east shore is a wharf where gas and water are available.

Harpswell Harbor, West Harpswell, Me. (315). A short distance up Merriconeag Sound on the western side is Harpswell Harbor, well protected and of ample depth. The harbor is notable principally for the Merriconeag Yachting Association, whose wharf, float, and buildings are prominent on the west shore. The association maintains a guest mooring and launch service. A steward is on duty during the day and can direct you to shower or telephone.

Mackerel Cove, Bailey Island, Me. (315). This is one of the principal harbors of Casco Bay. It is easy of access under almost any conditions with a lighted gong outside and a diminutive flasher at the entrance. The most prominent landmarks are two Coast Artillery observation towers on the southern end of Bailey Island. They are not indicated on chart 315.

The only wharf open to the public is at Dockside Motor Inn Restaurant and Marina at the head of the harbor on its west side. Stewart Place is the owner and the best source of local information. Here one may obtain meals, fresh water, gasoline, Diesel oil, lobsters, and clams. Mr. Place has an artesian well said to be the best in the neighborhood. Groceries are available at a nearby store.

Merrill's Wharf on the west side of the cove is the steamer landing and a source of local knowledge. "Sonny" Bailey, who may be found here, has an excellent reputation as a mechanic.

Around the corner in the cove on Merriconeag Sound at the head of Mackerel Cove is Skilling's boat yard, which is capable of hauling most yachts and of making repairs to hull, spars, or engines.

Mackerel Cove is the headquarters of an annual Tuna Tournament, which attracts a number of charter boats each summer. If you are rigged for tuna yourself, you can usually get a local fisherman to go with you as a guide.

Quahog Bay, Me. (315). This is a lovely spot to spend a day, especially if you have children aboard. Enter either from Ridley Cove north of Yarmouth Island or from the south. Avoid the ledges north of Pole Island and south of Center Island. An easterly course, leading to a point between Snow's Island and the point south of it, carried the writer safely in. Anchor either north or south of Snow's Island. The holding ground is good, the protection excellent. The swimming has none of the numbing, breathless quality of the offshore islands. There are flounders to be caught, and there are beautiful protected coves to explore with an outboard or sailing dinghy. Although there have been ugly rumors of an impending development, in 1971 there were only a few scattered cottages on the western shore.

Cundy's Harbor, Me. (315). This is a small harbor, well protected in anything but a heavy easterly, and devoted mostly to local lobstering and to summer cottages rather than the "transient trade." There is a store where limited supplies are available, but there is no gas, water, or Diesel oil on the wharves. Local fishermen lug their gas in cans.

The Basin, Me. (315). This is an attractive anchorage off the eastern side of the New Meadows River and a favorite with many. A frequent visitor warns that one should keep to the *outside* of the bends on entering, where the tide scours the channel. Also he warns of a rock almost in the middle of the anchorage. Although this is shown on the chart, it has picked up yachts in the past.

Sebasco, Me. (315). Here is a good anchorage behind Harbor Island and its outlying ledges, although on a heavy southerly it might be uncomfortable. In entering, keep in the middle. Both shores are studded with ledges, the ones on Harbor Island making out much farther than one might expect from looking at the chart. One of the outer rocks has a locally maintained spindle on it. It is difficult to find at high water, but when you do find it, give it a good berth.

Sebasco Lodge, the prominent hotel on the eastern shore, maintains guest moorings. These are heavy white spars. The ones in front of the float on the east side are more convenient, but if there is any chop running in the harbor, one can be secure and comfortable on one of the western ones. They are 5000-pound granite blocks. Consult the harbor master.

Although Sebasco is far from the direct course across Casco Bay, one who takes the time to run up the bay will find a float with 6 feet at mean low water. Gasoline is piped to it. Water is available in an emergency. Just up the shore from the float is a snack bar open from 10 A.M. to 11:30 P.M. at which anything short of a full-course dinner is available. The hotel will supply the latter. Adjacent to the snack bar is a comfortable lounge for visiting cruisers, with a telephone booth, laundromat, and luxurious showers opening off it.

One could lie here a week without exhausting the possibilities for entertainment and diversion, all of which are available to visitors by arrangement. Off the float lies a fleet of Tech. dinghies for sailing around the harbor. Ashore there are a swimming pool, a nine-hole golf course, tennis courts, and bowling alleys. Movies and dances, both square and otherwise, are frequently scheduled.

If you are in need of supplies, consult the harbor master. The hotel sends a station wagon to Bath to meet guests known to be arriving on buses.

Alvin Brewer has a small boat shop at Sebasco and can take care of ordinary repairs.

If possible, leave Sebasco on the first of the ebb, keep to the eastern shore down to Cape Small, and get a fine lift to windward from the tide. It runs briskly down the New Meadows River and faster than that out of the Kennebec (see note on the entrance to the Kennebec). Across Sheepscot Bay the ebb tide sets to the south or southeast and is less important to the eastward-bound yacht.

Small Point Harbor, Me. (315). The chief advantage to Small Point Harbor is its proximity to the direct route east. As a harbor it is poor because wide open to the southwest, whence comes an annoying roll. However, on an ordinary summer night it is perfectly satisfactory. The best anchorage is north and east of Goose Rock. It is shoal in here, but should be all right for most yachts.

In the event of bad weather, work south through the gut behind Goose Rock at half tide or better, and anchor in the pond behind Haskell Hill. This passage is narrow and obstructed by a bar between Goose Rock and the shore. Local knowledge is helpful in negotiating it. The writer has a fat pile of correspondence on this passage, varying from the sternest advice not to try it without local knowledge to lighthearted directions to follow the line of lobster traps and favor the eastern shore. After a careful weighing of the evidence and two trips into the pond himself, the writer advises the skipper of a boat equipped with an engine and not drawing more than 5 feet to go ahead and try it, dead slow, at half tide or better with a man on the bowsprit. You will see bottom before you touch. Once across the bar behind Goose Rock, favor the eastern shore and anchor when the narrow part begins to open out. You will lie to the tide here but will be secure in any weather.

Looking at Cape Small Harbor from the air, the late Mr. Blanchard wrote that it has a rather tricky entrance channel obscure on the chart. The main channel runs close to the northern end of the little island north of Mill Point and the harbor entrance. It then follows the easterly shore of the island until the middle of the island is reached, when it cuts diagonally across toward the mainland to the east, following this shore closely into the deep and narrow inner passage shown on the chart. The anchorage inside is wonderful.

There is a restaurant on the beach at the head of the harbor to serve the camp ground on Hermit Island. One may inquire here about supplies, but none were easily available at our last visit.

The most voracious breed of mosquitoes ever developed has its headquarters here. Only experienced hands can distinguish them from gulls.

Other Anchorages in Casco Bay. The writer has not visited any of the following or has just sailed in and out. They might well be worth further investigation.

1. *Chandler Cove.* While this might be all right in a winter northeaster, it is usually rolly in a southerly and affords poor protection. Pull up under Long Island, or better yet, go over to the cove in Jewell's Island.

2. *High Head,* near the head of Harpswell Sound, has a newly established and vigorous yacht club with guest moorings. Stay close to the High Head shore on entering.

3. *Winnegance Bay* This is good shelter, especially at the head in Brigham's Cove. The Eastern Yacht Club used to rendezvous here.

4. *Orr's Island.* There is a long, narrow cove in the northern end of the island, perfectly protected. One correspondent writes of it: "Stream two anchors to keep in the narrow channel Excellent lobsters and clams can be bought at the Orr's Island Bridge. No difficulty in entering if you follow the chart."

There is an anchorage at Will's Strait by the bridge, and there is an anchorage and a good store in Lowell's Cove to the north. Gasoline can be bought at the latter. The cove on the south of the east side of the bridge looks snug indeed. Several sloops over 30 feet long were lying well up in here in August 1960.

These and the innumerable other secluded coves and island anchorages we leave to the skipper to explore for himself.

The Mouth of the Kennebec River (314). Once around Cape Small and clear of Fuller Rock with its flashing beacon, the skipper must decide whether to go inside Seguin or outside. Even a careful study of the chart will not reveal the dangers associated with the inside passage. Bear in

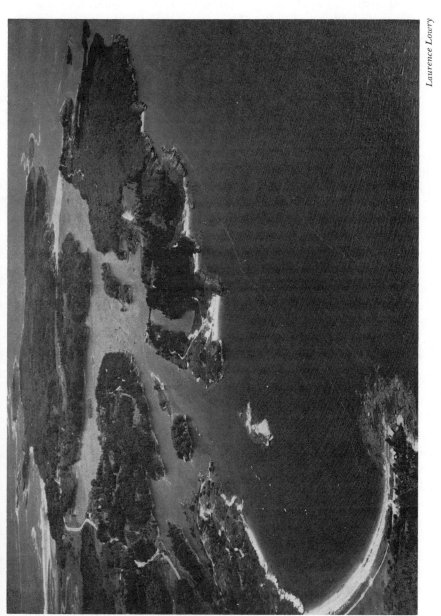

Cape Small and its harbor.

mind, however, that the full force of the Kennebec River runs out through a very narrow opening obstructed by Pond Island, a bar, and numerous ledges and rocky shoals. With a strong breeze anywhere in the southerly quadrant, this situation can raise a really dangerous sea between Jackknife Ledge and bell I. The writer has talked with two yachtsmen who were in real danger of losing their boats in this short stretch off the mouth of the Kennebec. Local people are very respectful of this place and warn strangers away from it in bad weather.

One correspondent writes: "The only time we didn't completely take your advice was between Seguin Island and the Kennebec River, where we almost came to grief in the chop and breakers. We had no power and the wind died."

Several other correspondents have felt that our warnings about this area have been too severe. We quote two letters from experienced cruising men.

> I think that you are much too severe about the Kennebec entrance and the passage back of Seguin. Only a couple of times do I recall going outside, once in light weather to take advantage of the flood tide to the eastward, which by the way was a bad hunch, as we found the flood setting to the *westward*. The second time there was a tremendous sea outside, and I imagine it was pretty choppy in the entrance. Otherwise, I have never seen anything to bother about. With a head wind it may be better to take a long hitch outside. An ebb tide from the river often kills a southerly breeze and leaves a slop that makes for slow going.

> I feel that I must come to the aid of the Kennebec or you will have every yachtsman passing by so far outside that I won't be able to see another sail for the rest of my life, much less expect to find one at Popham Beach. To be sure I was dismasted early one morning in a heavy blow off Seguin while returning from Digby, but in fairness to the Kennebec I should say that my judgment and the rig were at fault rather than the river. I have passed inside from Small Point to the Cuckolds, except in fog, when it is distinctly advisable to stay outside Seguin, for the last twenty summers in all sorts of weather and with no power. I think that your solemn warnings about the district should be somewhat modified.

The ebb tide may well set a yacht down on Seguin Ledges in the short run across the mouth of the river. Also, there are unpredictable magnetic disturbances, which seem to center on Ellingwood Rock. Why should one confront these perils and uncertainties when it is so easy to run from Fuller Rock to the bell off Seguin to the Cuckolds with the great diaphone on Seguin to keep one oriented? The only danger here is Tom Rock.

Mr. W.S. Carter, previously quoted in the accounts of Provincetown and Jewell Island, passing Seguin in an easterly gale in 1858, wrote:

We made sail at once in the direction of Boothbay, but in the course of a couple of hours the wind rose to a gale. The sea grew very rough, and almost every minute a wave would break over our vessel and, sweeping along the deck, deluge the cockpit with water. We closed the cabin to keep it dry, and, gathering at the stern, watched the sea, not without anxiety. The air was so thick with mist that we could see nothing but the raging waves around us, and could not tell where we were going, though the sloop was plunging along at a fearful rate, her bows almost continually under water and her mast opening wide cracks at every tug of the sails. There was considerable danger of the mast's going overboard. In that case we should have been completely at the mercy of the waves, on a coast every inch of which was rock-bound, so that, if our vessel struck, she would be pounded to pieces in ten minutes.

We drove madly along, the grim old Pilot at the helm, and the anxious Skipper, arrayed in oil-skin to shed the wet, clinging to the mast and keeping a sharp lookout ahead. Suddenly the mist rose and rolled away before a sweeping blast, and then we saw Seguin lighthouse, and knew where we were. It was a superb and terrible sight—these wild reefs with the waves foaming and flashing over them, directly in our course. It was growing late, and the gale was on the increase. The sea was white with foam on the surface, but the great waves, as they came leaping and roaring at us, had a black and angry look not pleasant to behold. Our aged Pilot, as he sat clutching the helm, his hat drawn tightly over his brows to keep it from blowing off, glanced uneasily from time to time at the laboring and groaning mast, whose wide seams were alternately opening and shutting, but he said nothing. He had weathered many a harder gale, though never in so poor a craft. The Assyrian, clinging to the cover of the cabin for support, and with strong symptoms of seasickness in his face, at length broke out as a whooping billow swept over us, soaking him from head to foot:

"I say, Skipper, this is coming rather strong. Can't we put in somewhere?"

The Skipper had been for some minutes watching a large schooner about a mile ahead of us, and coming aft, said that it was hardly possible to weather Cape Newagin in such a storm, even if our mast held, about which he had great doubts. The schooner ahead of us was running for shelter into Sheepscut Bay, where there was an excellent harbor, and we could easily follow her in. The Pilot, after an emphatic reference to "that damned old stick," as he called the mast, assented to this opinion, and our course was accordingly changed to the northward.

Following the lead of the schooner for several miles, we reached about nightfall a beautiful and perfectly sheltered harbor, which the Skipper called sometimes Southport and sometimes Abenacook.

For a lighter view of this desperate passage we add the following yarn. The source is unknown to the writer.

An old gentleman, who had been fishing all his life and who had wrung more water out of the cuffs of his pants than most of us have ever sailed over, made a little money in the summer taking summer boarders sailing in his sloop.

One day it breezed up SW near Seguin and got pretty choppy. Spray was flying and she began to take water into the cockpit. The passengers were frightened, and finally one said, "Cap'n, we think you ought to offer prayer for our safety."

"I don't b'lieve that'll be necessary," answered the skipper, easing her over a sea.

"Well, we feel that it is your duty as captain of this boat to ask for Divine help and guidance in this emergency."

"All right," answered the skipper, "I'll do what I can if it'll ease you any." So with both hands on the tiller and the passengers kneeling around him, the captain prayed,

"Lord, I never have interfered in your affairs and you have always used me right. But these people have asked me to speak with you. Now I know we'll get in all right, but if you would like to make these people feel a lot better, you can go ahead and calm the waters. But just remember, Lord, this isn't the Sea of Galilee. This is the North Atlantic Ocean."

The writer passed inside Seguin between the island and Ellingwood Rock in the summer of 1971 with the full ebb tide running out against a brisk southwest wind. We anticipated a real shaking up but found conditions perfectly manageable.

Our considered advice to those passing Seguin is to go inside unless a considerable sea is running or visibility is bad.

Popham Beach, Me. (314). Entering the Kennebec is an adventure at any stage of the tide except dead slack water, and that represents an unstable equilibrium between the current of the river and the coming tide. Without a fair wind or a fair tide, entrance is practically impossible for a low-powered auxiliary.

Still, the effort is worth while. Anchor off the Coast Guard wharf in the cove on the west side of the river. This cove silts up badly, so enter with caution. If a bad blow is in prospect, continue up the river and anchor off Parker Flats, an anchorage once much used by coasters waiting for the tide.

The fort at Popham, built during the Civil War to protect Bath from Southern raiders, has been termed Maine's sincerest compliment to the Confederate Navy. It is an interesting place to visit.

A swim on the beach, especially on the ebb tide, is pleasant.

The Sabino peninsula appears in the early history of our country several times. In 1582 one David Ingram was interviewed by Sir Humphrey Gilbert, then interested in establishing a colony in New England. Ingram had been with Hawkins at the battle of San Juan d'Ulloa near Vera Cruz in 1568. Having been very roughly handled in the battle, Hawkins had neither vessels nor stores sufficient to take his entire expedition to England. Ingram preferred to be set ashore rather than attempt the passage. He walked all the way to St. John, New Brunswick, where he was picked up by a French vessel and taken home. The stenographic account of his conversation with Gilbert, printed in Hakluyt's first edition and reprinted in Ida Sedgwick Proper's *Monhegan, Cradle of New England,* contains the following:

> Taking me into his canoe, we paddled across eastward from the place which he called Sabino to a peninsula which he called Pemcuit [Pemaquid] and where we rested over that night. When the morning broke, I saw not far to seaward, a great island that was backed like a whale.

Although Hakluyt dropped Ingram's account from later editions as "a tissue of lies," there can be little doubt that he visited Sabino, Pemaquid, and New Harbor, and that he saw Monhegan.

In 1605 Champlain visited Sabino twice, once ascending the Kennebec and descending the Sasanoa and Sheepscot. He named Seguin "La Tortue" because of its resemblance to a tortoise.

In 1605 Waymouth and Rosier were on the coast (see Georges Harbor, page 386). They kidnapped five Indians who, with Rosier, recommended to Gorges and Popham of the Plymouth colony a site on the St. George River for a permanent colony. But in 1606 Martin Pring visited the coast and wrote what must have been a glowing account of the Kennebec. Unfortunately Pring's account is lost, but we know that it caused Gorges and Popham to send to Sabino in the spring of 1607 two ships and 120 men led by Ralegh Gilbert, Sir Humphrey's son, and old John Popham, who was eighty years old.

The colony was well equipped and provisioned. It was going to a site well known. The natives were friendly and anxious to trade. The economic basis of the colony, salt cod, furs, and spar timber, was sound. The expedition was well financed, well manned, and well led. During the summer a number of houses were built and the *Virginia*, the first vessel built in New England, was launched and sent out to explore Penobscot and Casco bays. The winter was hard but far from intolerable in spite of the loss by fire of a storehouse. Old John Popham died, to be sure, but young in heart as he was, it is not surprising, in view of his age. Even in Maine a man of eighty can succumb. In the spring a vessel arrived from England with more men and supplies but with the sad news that Ralegh Gilbert's half brother had died. Gilbert decided to return to England to take care of his inheritance. Popham was dead. Without leadership the colony disintegrated, some returning to England and others going south to Jamestown in the *Virginia*. It seems ironic that the English colony with the best chance of survival did not last, while Jamestown, badly led, badly manned, starved and diseased, and with no strong economic resources, survived and eventually prospered.

Apparently the colony was not a complete failure, however, for Humphrey Damerill, one of the colonists, soon after established a store and fishing station at Damariscove. To Damariscove came the distressed Pilgrims in 1621 and received open-handed help.

Seguin Island, Me. (314). This is one of the most dramatic islands on the coast—high, bare, and with steep cliffs on its western side. On the southern peak stands one of the most powerful landfall lights on the coast, clearly visible from Monhegan, nearly 25 miles away.

On the northeast side there is a cove with a heavy Coast Guard mooring providing a safe place to tie up. The bottom is rocky and is sometimes covered with drifting kelp. Land at the boathouse and walk up the long tramway to the top of the island. If the keepers are not too busy, they may show you around the light—an experience not to be missed. On a clear day from the tower, 180 feet above the sea, a large part of the coast is spread out before you. The White Mountains may be visible far to the west. The high land of Cape Elizabeth and many of the offshore islands of Casco Bay will show over the western horizon. Cape Small and the broken country in the mouth of the Kennebec will be at your feet. To the east the Cuckolds shows clearly off Newagen, and the long, low humps of Damariscove reach out southward. Far to the east Monhegan looms over the horizon, and the Camden Hills overlooking Penobscot Bay bound the view down the coast.

Before you leave, walk out on the northern knoll. Gulls and terns nest in the grass and on the cliffs. Bayberries, blueberries, and thistles grow in clumps in the tall grass. You can look down into the sheltered cove onto the deck of your yacht and back to the light tower overlooking the whole scene. Painters, photographers, and poets may well be inspired by this place; and to anyone a visit to Seguin will be a memorable experience.

Harmon Harbor, Me. (314). The next shelter, going east, after Cape Small Point, with the doubtful exceptions of Seguin Island, Popham Beach, and the mouth of the Kennebec River, is this long, narrow cove making northward on the western side of the river 1½ miles above Griffith Head. The *Coast Pilot* has a complete description.

An experienced cruising man, who visited this spot in the summer of 1953, contributes the following:

> Enter close along the western shore to avoid a ledge that makes out from the eastern point and is marked by a red buoy. This ledge dries out and makes good shelter. There is apt to be a little surge, when a swell is running in the river, for a couple of hours around high water when the ledge is covered. There is good water well up the harbor; but don't go up beyond a low point that makes out from the east shore near the head unless you have a shoal-draft boat. Better check depths with the chart.
>
> There are a few farms and summer cottages, and a few local boats on moorings, but no shore facilities. The "prominent hotel" referred to in the *Coast Pilot* was still there but evidently not operating. You can land in the upper part of the harbor and walk across to Five Islands, less than a mile by road (though several by water), where a general store, etc., are located. A nice, quiet harbor, very handy for a coming-or-going layover.

A recent visit to this quiet spot found it essentially unchanged, although a number of small boats were moored in the upper part of the harbor.

Five Islands, Me. (314). The *Coast Pilot* gives an adequate description of this handy harbor on the west side of the river. There is a rock (8 feet over it at low tide) in the middle of the eastern entrance, marked by a horizontally striped buoy that can be passed close on either side. There are two other entrances, one from the northeast and the other from the south, the former being preferable, but both to be avoided by strangers. Some parts of the anchorage are rolly on a southerly, which makes in through the southerly entrance. The holding ground is good in the entire harbor except near the eastern dry ledges. Two guest moorings are maintained by the Five Islands Yacht Club marked "F I Y C Guest."

There is a town landing on the west shore with 10 feet at low water. Provisions, gas, and ice may be obtained here. Lobsters and clams can be purchased from the Thebadeaus on the wharf.

Many older cruising men well remember Five Islands as the home port of the big Friendship sloop *Sky Pilot,* sailed for many years by the late Rev. Nehemiah Boynton and his family. She was built in 1909 by Jean McClain at Round Pond and was used by the Boyntons until World War II. She sank, then, in Townsend Gut. Frank L. Sample, Jr., raised her, refitted her, ballasted her with 9000 axe heads, and sold her to Richard Swanson of Rockport, Massachusetts. She was renamed *Jolly Buccaneer* and was one of the most beautiful and picturesque in the fleet at the annual homecoming of the Friendship Sloop Society.

She was sold in 1966 to a group who used her to smuggle narcotics from Cuba. She was captured and attached by the government and sank at her wharf. She is a total loss.

Because the locale of the story is off the mouth of the Sheepscot River, this is as good a place as any to insert a yarn spun to the authors by Rev. Edward Boynton of Essex, Connecticutt, a son of the late Dr. Boynton.

You see, it was this way:

One day last summer [1945] Al Gould came over in his sloop *Curlew* and was seated on my porch at Five Islands and we were talking of those matters of important and mutual interest which always come to mind when sailor friends of many years get together, where they can look at the rocks and the skies and the running waters of the Maine coast. He said: "Did you ever hear about Captain John Snow of Rockland and the time he moved the old house from Phippsburg on the Kennebec around outside and up to Rockport?" I had never heard about that time, and even if I had, I would have shamelessly feigned ignorance. For *any* story which Al tells is worth repeating. And this was no exception! So he went on:

"There was a summer fellow up at Rockport who bought a beautiful lot of land on the shore a few years ago. Down in Phippsburg he saw an old colonial house which he thought would look well on his place on Beauchamp Point in Rockport. So he went to Captain John Snow, who is in the towage and lighterage business in Rockland and an expert in salvage and all maritime affairs, and asked him to go and look at the house and see whether he thought he could move it around for him.

"John went and looked at it, and thought he could. 'How much will it be to move it?' the man asked John. 'Well,' replied the captain, 'for a long time I have wanted one of those car floats they have in New York Harbor for my business down here. I know where there is one, second-hand, which can be bought cheap. I'll go and get it; move the house; set it up down to Rockport. When I've got it set up, you come down and look at it. If the job is satisfactory, you pay for the float and it belongs to me; and if you don't like the job, you can keep the car float and we'll forget all about any charge.' So the deal was made. John got the float, skidded the house in Phippsburg down onto it; towed it around outside and up Penobscot Bay; skidded it ashore and into place. Then the owner came down to look at it. The job was perfect. Not even a crack in the plaster.

"One day in Rockport I met John," Al continued, "and asked him about it. John did not have much to say, as he is a very modest man. 'Wasn't there any particularly interesting thing on the way down?' I asked. 'Well,' said John, 'there was one. The fog shut in thick when we got out by Popham. I had the tug out ahead, and she was blowing one long and two short. And to make sure, I had a man up in the cupola of the house with a fish horn, and he was blowing one long and two short too. When we got about off Seguin and were about to make the turn, I heard a jangle of engine bells close aboard to starboard through the fog. A moment afterwards the white hull of a steam yacht broke out of the fog. She had her engines going full speed astern with a jingle. You see, her skipper had got a glint in the fog and saw the house looming up dead ahead and thought he was right in on the beach, though there was not less than forty fathoms all around.' "

Hendricks Harbor, Me. (314). The local name for this snug little anchorage is Cosy (or Cozy) Harbor. The entrance is easier than it appears from the chart. It is well to leave the red beacon at least 20 yards to starboard. Pass close to the south of the can and about 10 yards south of the diminutive inner beacon. The channel is narrow here but deep. Inside is a completely landlocked harbor. Hail the float on the east side or inquire of anyone on a boat for a vacant mooring. If one is unavailable, anchor wherever there is swinging room, but do not go to the north of the yacht club flagpole, as the harbor is shoal toward the head. The bottom is sticky mud.

If you sail in, you will find it awkward to land alongside the yacht club float in the usual southwester, as the front of the float lies so far around to the south that one's sails will swing far out over the float. However, with spring lines it can be done. Water is piped to this float.

There is a store at the head of the float operated by Mr. E. W. Pratt. He sells ordinary groceries, lobsters, and gas, and he has a public telephone, a lunch counter, and bowling alley in the store. The establishment is usually open well into the evening.

C. E. Pinkham's general store is ½ mile up the road (turn left at the main road), at the service of those who need anything Mr. Pratt cannot supply.

The Southport Yacht Club stands on a knoll to the north of the landing. This is a small but active club with a busy program for juniors. There is usually a crowd of children sailing around the harbor in Turnabouts or racing in the river under adult supervision. Anyone connected with the club will be most hospitable to cruising men.

The story is told of a certain lady who, having visited this section of Maine for many years, finally purchased a year-round cottage. Announcing the fact with enthusiasm one day to the local storekeeper, she added, "But you've certainly got some queer people around here." "Yes we have," replied the storekeeper, "but they'll all be gone by Labor Day."

Note on the Inside Passage from Boothbay Harbor to Bath. Strangers with no more than 8 feet draft can, with the aid of chart 230, continue through Townsend Gut and Goose Rock Passage to the Kennebec River and Bath. This entire inside passage from Boothbay Harbor to Bath, though narrow, crooked, and with strong tidal currents, is one of the most delightful trips on the coast. Roughly, the route is about 11 miles, and it is well worth the time required, especially if the weather at sea is uncomfortable. But larger yachts should take a pilot, procurable at either end.

The Sasanoa River, leading from the Sheepscot River to the Kennebec River north of Georgetown and Arrowsic Islands, can be made under sail with a breeze from east around to southwest, and is more fun that way than under power. But one would do well to use the top half of the flood tide, when the current is not quite so swift. Note that at the strength of the current in the narrow places the buoys are often run under for short periods.

The tide is not easily predictable in this passage, but works on the following general principle:

Hockamock Bay is a large body of water, so the flooding tide cannot fill it by the time of high water at Boothbay Harbor. Consequently, for nearly three hours after high water, the tide continues to run up the Sasanoa River from the Sheepscot River and down the Sasanoa River from the Kennebec River, of course with diminishing force, depending on the wind, the height of the tide, and doubtless many more obscure forces. When the level of water in Hockamock Bay approximates that in the Kennebec and Sheepscot rivers, there is a brief period of slack water. Then the tide begins to run out of Hockamock Bay and so continues until about three hours after low water on the coast.

The Sasanoa River is not a pipe line and there is a lot of friction delaying the flow of water, particularly at Boiler Rock and the two Hell Gates. Consequently, the time of slack water at any spot on the river is difficult to estimate. However, the best move is to start from Boothbay Harbor about two hours before high water there. This would give something like slack water approaching Hockamock Bay and a fair current to the Kennebec River and down to Fort Popham.

Particular warning should be given of the two Hell Gates, particularly of the ledge above the Lower Hell Gate. An auxiliary cannot buck the tide through here, although a motor cruiser probably could do it. Coming down with the tide, one might think one was entering Niagara Gorge, but keep the power going and the clear channel will appear as you get closer. It is not a difficult place to negotiate, but is very awesome, especially for the first time. Captain Wade of the *Balmy Days* (Boothbay Harbor-Monhegan and return) says that this is a really dangerous place for a small boat. Since the Westport bridge was built, the tide runs harder than ever.

Aside from being a handy passage to the Kennebec River, this is a beautiful trip. There are dozens of secluded anchorages in the ragged shores. The water is ideal for swimming. Clamming and fishing are possible in some places. But rig your mosquito defenses early.

A daring correspondent writes:

> For variety I approached Wiscasset *via* Goose Rocks Passage, Knubble Bay, Montsweag Bay, and the Back River, to be confronted with a new fixed bridge (built 1950) across Back River in Cosweagan Narrows, with vertical clearance at M.H.W. said to be about 8 feet. The horizontal clearance is about twice that and dams the current into a wall of water at a 7-knot clip at strength. I wouldn't turn back, and just got through with the mast down with a 1-knot margin against the stream. Carrying a flood tide all the way to the bridge, the bridge so

effectively dams the river that it was found to flowing south under the bridge. We were probably the first, and perhaps the last, to try this stunt.

Robinhood, Me. (314, 230). This quiet cove in the Sasanoa River is just below Knubble Bay. The entrance is clear from the chart, but is complicated by a powerful tidal current at Boiler Rock. The buoy is often towed under, and entrance against the tide is almost impossible without power. The tide at Goose Rocks Passage looks worse than it is. Favor the bold southern shore on approaching the cove and take advantage of back eddies under the shore.

Once in out of the tide, the skipper will find a large, well-protected harbor off a good marina. Robinhood is a small Maine village still largely "undeveloped" by summer interests.

The Kennebec Yacht Building Co. will take care of ordinary repairs. Through the Hyde Windlass Co. at Bath heavier jobs on shafts and engines can be handled. The yard has a twenty-five-ton travelift, which can handle almost any yacht. The yard operates the Robinhood Marina. Here there is usually a vacant mooring or a berth alongside. Gas, water, ice, and Diesel oil are available. An adequate general store is just up the bank. For more elaborate supplies, take a taxi to Bath, only 8 miles away. Buses to Portland and Boston stop at Bath.

Up the cove near the abandoned coasting schooner is a beautiful and secluded anchorage.

A local correspondent writes:

Riggsville was originally founded and populated by the Riggs family. They built most of the old houses in this area. They were well-known merchants and traders and seemed to have conducted their business with more than their share of Yankee ingenuity and cleverness. . . . The vessel grounded in the cove is a large Dering five-master, which was towed here and abandoned in the '20's. Opposite the schooner is the summer residence of the late William Zorach, internationally known sculptor. Near the water is one of his statues, a bronze replica of one of his aluminum statues in the Radio City Music Hall in New York.

Wiscasset, Me. (314). For one interested in old houses and shaded streets, this is one of the most attractive towns in Maine. The houses were built in the days when Wiscasset throve on shipbuilding and sea-borne trade. At one time the government considered building a Navy yard at Wiscasset.

The trip up the river on the tide is well worth while, but difficult without power. It is 14 miles from the entrance of the Sheepscot to Wiscasset.

The anchorage is south of the wharf just off the swimming club pier and float, where a southerly breeze gets quite a rake. There are two guest moorings.

Yachts up to 30 feet can dock at the town landing (a few hundred yards south of the derelict schooners) for supplies, which are available at any one of the several excellent stores; gas, water, and 110-volt current are available at the yacht club. Haggett's Garage will make engine repairs. "Nick" Roth's small boat yard is on the bend of the river east of Wiscasset. There is launching ramp for boats up to 18 feet by the public landing.

The best place to spend the night ashore and get a meal is either the Wiscasset Inn or The Ledges. Information relating to points of interest to visiting yachtsmen may be obtained at the Wiscasset library.

The Old Jail is now an interesting historical museum. Artists should not miss the collection at the Maine Art Gallery. The Nickels-Sortwell House is the architectural attraction at Wiscasset.

The Central Maine Power Co. operates an electric power plant just south of Wiscasset. Large tankers bring fuel about once a month. It is worth coming a long way to see Captain Eliot Winslow, the local pilot from Boothbay, work one of these enormous vessels around the tight bend just below the town. It must be done on the top of the tide, too, so any miscalculation would have almost disastrous results.

In addition to its lovely old residences and beautifully shaded streets, Wiscasset is notable for the hulks of two four-masted schooners rotting slowly away on the shore just south of Route 1. They are the *Hesper* and the *Luther P. Little*. Dick Vennerbeck tells their story in the *Maine Coast Fisherman* of July, 1950:

> With their appearance of great age it is surprising to learn that they were built not so very long ago at the time of the First World War. For some time during and after the war they sailed out of Boston in the coastal trade; but about 1930, their usefulness diminished, they became the property of the Federal Government, and were tied up in Portland. At that time they were sold to a Mr. Winter at the U.S. Marshal's sale. How the *Hesper* and the *Luther P. Little* came to rest in Wiscasset is involved with the story of the old Wiscasset narrow gauge railroad, since it was to serve this railroad that they were brought from Portland by Mr. Winter.
>
> As early as 1836 it was proposed that a rail line be built from Wis-

casset to Canada in order to make Wiscasset the winter port of the St. Lawrence. Had this plan been successful, Wiscasset might well have become one of the East's most important seaports, shipping Canadian timber and food. Misfortune dogged the plan for many years, however, until finally in 1892 a two-foot gauge railroad was begun from Wiscasset. The line was to have been extended only as far as the Canadian border at this later time, but even this modified plan proved too difficult for the owners. The track was extended only as far as Albion, near Waterville, Maine. The railroad had varrying fortunes during the 40 years of its existence, but its revenue steadily decreased. In the latter years of its operation the road was owned by Mr. Frank W. Winter, who bought the *Hesper* and the *Luther P. Little*.

Mr. Winter's plan was to use the two schooners as coal carriers for his railroad. When the vessels were towed to Wiscasset one did actually carry a load of coal, but not long afterwards, due to increased competition from other transportation systems, the narrow gauge at Wiscasset was forced to close. With no job to do, and having no prospective buyers, the two schooners were scuttled and left at the wharf where they rest today.

So ended the life of a gallant little railroad, and with it the active careers of the *Hesper* and the *Luther P. Little*. Its right of way and rotting piles may still be seen near the northern end of the Maine Central Railroad station platform.

An atomic power plant has been constructed below Wiscasset.

Ebenecook Harbor, Me. (230). This is a large, well-protected harbor easy of access under almost any conditions. After passing Hendrick's Head Light, unfortunately now without a fog signal, make the bold shore to the north of it. Follow this to Dogfish Head and enter through the deep channel between Dogfish Head and the Green Islands. There are three coves making out of the southern shore.

The westernmost is occupied by Brewer's Boat Yard. To enter this cove, round Dogfish Head, giving the eastern side of it a good berth and leaving nun 2 to *port*. Proceed up the cove, keeping about halfway between the ledges to the east and the land to the west. The ledges are bare except at the top of the tide, but should be given a good berth at high water. At low water they are quite steep. Work up through the anchorage and land at Brewer's float on the eastern side. At low water there is only about 6 feet of water here. Gas, water, ice, and lobsters are for sale at the float. The yard has facilities for all kinds of repairs to hull, spars, and rigging. A telephone call to Mr. Sherman at Campbell-Built Products in

Boothbay Harbor will summon a sailmaker. There are two excellent mechanics at the yard. On the wharf next to the float is a powerful derrick and a travelift, which can handle up to twenty tons. Brewer hauls a great number of boats on it every autumn.

The store at the yard stocks, or can obtain at short notice, almost any marine hardware, paint, or engine room supplies you need. On the rise behind the yard is a small lunch room with picnic tables in an attractive setting.

C. E. Pinkham's general store is about ½ mile up the road. Turn right on coming out of the yard and right again at the first crossroad. The store and post office are on this road at the top of the hill.

Consult anyone on the dock about lying alongside for the night or taking a vacant mooring.

The next cove to the eastward is dominated by the summer home of the late Alfred V. S. Olcott. It is a snug and quiet anchorage. Beware of a rock marked picturesquely by a red cider jug suitably decorated. Leave it to starboard.

The easterly cove, Love's Cove, has a float and house belonging to Captain Eliot Winslow, formerly skipper of U.S.S. *Argo* in World War II, now skipper of an excursion boat of the same name. Captain Winslow is a pilot for this part of the coast, taking tankers to Wiscasset several times during the summer. He is also an accomplished compass adjuster. The anchorage is occupied on the chart by a cable area. A considerable fleet of yachts anchored in this cove in August, 1959, without mishap to anchor or telephone cable.

Anywhere else in Ebenecook Harbor affords good anchorage too. Simply avoid the deep water south and southeast of Green Islands. The cove between the largest of these islands and the western one is a pleasant spot, although the tide runs quite hard. The view across the Sheepscot River at sunset is one of the pleasures of a cruise down east.

Townsend Gut, Me. (314, 230). This is the inside passage from the Sheepscot River and Ebenecook Harbor to Boothbay Harbor. It is much used by all types of vessels, sail and power, and presents no great difficulties. It saves a long beat down the Sheepscot River, particularly if the tide is flooding. From the Boothbay Harbor end of the gut, a tack or two will enable you to fetch Ram Island and be on your way down east.

From Ebenecook Harbor, follow the shore of Cameron's Point, double it, and pass close to the flashing light on its easterly side. Leave nun 4 to *port*. The passage lies between this buoy and the lighted beacon. The ledge extends northerly from the nun to a rock usually bare to the northeastward of the beacon.

Continue up the middle of the channel, avoiding a ledge at the mouth of a little bight on the western shore. Secure anchorage out of the tide may be had in Hodgdon's Cove. As you approach the drawbridge, apply yourself vigorously to the horn. The bridge tenders are alert and the bridge usually opens quickly; but if the tide is with you, don't get committed until you see the bridge in motion. As you pass through, you will be asked for the name of the yacht and of the skipper.

South of the bridge is a small anchorage on each side of the gut. The westerly one, Dekkers Cove, is the bigger and better, but note that the wharf is used by shrimp and whiting draggers and the tug *Alice M. Winslow*. These big vessels must have room to maneuver. There are several private landings that no doubt could be used in an emergency, but the big wharf is likely to be crowded with commercial activity and is not a good place for the casual yachtsman. Lobsters are available at the shore end of the wharf.

After passing Dekkers Cove, keep close to the western shore. There is a shoal spot extending from a small point on the eastern side nearly to the middle of the channel. You will notice the tide running over it. Leave the nun off Juniper Point to port.

If these narrow places make you chew your gum fast or smoke cigarettes in quick succession or shout at your crew, it may calm you to know that Captain Boyd Guild sailed the coaster *Alice Wentworth* through the gut, and more recently he has sailed the three-masted schooner *Victory Chimes* through.

Newagen, Me. (314). The principal attraction of this small harbor is its proximity to the direct route down east. It is not a convenient place at which to get fuel or supplies and may be a little rolly at high tide. If it is thick outside, the fog signal on the Cuckholds makes the fact evident. Nevertheless, it is a favorite with many yachtsmen as a convenient, quiet, clean, and picturesque anchorage.

From the west, make the lighted bell in the Sheepscot River and head for the houses in the harbor. As you approach, you will see the nun outside the entrance. Give it a berth of 50 yards and head for the white cottage on the point on the northerly side of the entrance. Do not head directly for the beacon, because there is a kelp ledge with about a foot of water on it directly between the nun and the beacon. The point under the white house is bold. When 30 to 50 yards from it, head between the beacon and the shore, being sure to leave the beacon to starboard. Inside the beacon about 50 yards is a rock with about 8 feet over it. It has never bothered anyone, although some have seen the kelp and been alarmed.

The bottom is gravelly clay, excellent holding ground. There may well be a mooring available. All the moorings are powerful, as they are used for lobster boats in winter or for yachts between 30 and 40 feet long.

From the east, make the bell off the Cuckolds and head northwest long enough to take you clear of the long shoal running about WNW from the Cuckolds. This breaks in rough weather. When the nun shows to the east of Mark Island, run for it and enter as above.

There is a passage between the Cuckolds and Cape Island with ample depth. Pass close to the white nun mooring used by the Coast Guard. Keep off the northern point of the westerly islet. Then keep south of the two half-tide rocks off the westerly point of Cape Island. Run about WNW or WxN½N to pass south of the nun. The ledge inside the nun extends to the south of the direct line from Cape Island or the Cuckolds to the buoy. Once by the buoy, proceed as above.

Inside the harbor there is a heavy float on the northerly shore off the Newagen Inn. If you have business at the inn, you can tie a skiff to the back of the float, but do not obstruct the front of it, as excursion boats of considerable size land here. The inn can provide rooms and meals, and by arrangement with the office one can use their pool, tennis court, and other facilities.

On a rock at the head of the path from the float is a bronze table reading:

NEWAGEN
The Earliest Locality
Visited and Named by
English Explorers
In the Boothbay Region

Here
Capt. Christopher Levett
And the Indian Sagamores
Menawarmet, Samoset
and Cogawesco
Met for Four Days in
December, 1623

Captain Levett was in New England in 1623 and 1624 to establish the fur trade. He built a house on House Island in Casco Bay, ranged from Boston to Newagen at least, visiting the Isles of Shoals and the coast near York. He had a lengthy discussion with Gorges at Little Harbor near Portsmouth and then disappeared. The purpose of the meeting at Newagen was to explain to the Sagamores that exchange of presents and socializing were all very well, but that he wished to establish a commercial relationship. Apparently nothing came of it.

At the eastern end of the harbor is the town landing with a depth of 3 to 4 feet at low water. There is also a lobster car. In recent years gas was sold here, but not in 1971.

There is a narrow passage out the eastern end of the harbor called the Ark between the high shore of Southport and the first island. It is easily navigable with a draft of 6 feet at half tide or better, but the skipper would do well to investigate it himself in a skiff rather than to rely on written directions. It saves a beat around the nun and Cape Island, where the wind can be soft and the sea rough.

Indicative of the climate on the main coast are these temperatures taken with a laboratory thermometer on a pleasant day in early August with a light southerly breeze: air, 70°; Newagen harbor sea water, 61°; Newagen pool, 67°.

That the land and waters of the Sheepscot have changed little in 175 years is clear from the following account of a cruise written by Jacob Bailey in *The Frontier Missionary*, edited by William S. Bartlett (Boston, 1853).

June 9, 1779. About nine we got underway with a gentle breeze from the south-west, and fell down between Parker's island and Jeremisquam into Sheepscot River. The country hereabouts made a romantic appearance; fine groves of trees, shrubby evergreens, craggy rocks, cultivated fields and human habitations, alternately presented themselves to view, and yielded a profusion of pleasure to the imagination.

As night approached it grew perfectly calm, and we were obliged to anchor in Cape Newaggen harbour, a little to the west of Booth Bay. This is an excellent station for small shipping. The land rises with an easy slope from the water's edge on the north and partly on the east, while the remainder is surrounded with islands on which were erected fishermen's huts. Between these islands you pass into the harbour through very small inlets.

Boothbay Harbor, Me. (230, 314). This is an easy harbor to make, is well protected, and provides all the facilities a cruising man could ask for. The writer has entered it with anticipation and has been more than happy to leave it.

The landmark from the west is the brilliant light on the Cuckolds. However, the fog signal is less effective, being almost inaudible a short distance to the westward. There is a short-range radio beacon, which is very helpful indeed. Run for the bell off the light. If you come on a

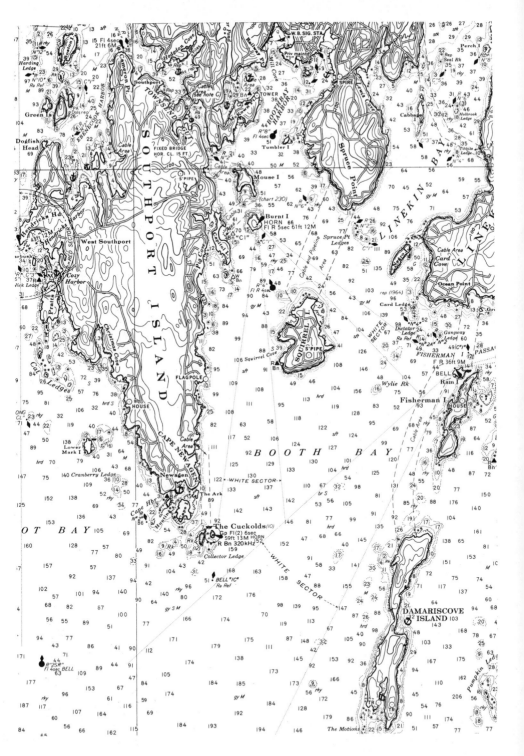

Anchorages in the Boothbay region (refer to Chart 314).

clump of lobster buoys, bear off to the southward, stop, and listen. Once you go by the Cuckolds, the horn is audible for miles.

From the bell, run for Burnt Island light, leaving the flasher off Squirrel Island to starboard. Then make the flasher off Tumbler Island. From the east, make the bell on the Hypocrites Ledge, pass close to Ram Island Light, and head for Burnt Island. Be sure to leave the nuns off Ocean Point to starboard.

In the inner harbor, gas, water, and Diesel oil are available at Pierce's on the east side and at Blake's Gulf wharf on the west side.

On the east side as you enter is Pierce Marine, featuring "in-and-out" storage in a huge gray building behind the wharf. The building was built for the manufacture of fiberglass coffins but due, no doubt, to the healthful and unpolluted atmosphere of the region, it was converted to its present use.

Pierce has a fork lift on the wharf capable of lifting small boats out of water or of stepping a spar in a bigger yacht. He specializes in outboards, sells gas, and operates a motor repair shop and marine supply store where charts and government publications are sold. Mr. and Mrs. Pierce are very helpful and hospitable.

Reed's can make repairs to hull, spars, and engines. He has two railways. Forrest Sherman at Campbell's shop across the street can repair sails. There is a small but adequate grocery store 100 yards north of the yard. Reed's may well have a mooring available. Consult Mr. Jonathan Marsh, the yard foreman.

Fred Blake's on the west side of the harbor offers most of the same facilities, and in addition he has ice, outboard motors, an extensive machine shop, and a marine hardware store. A mechanic is usually available here. Blake also has a crane capable of lifting small boats on to trailers, stepping masts, or raising the stern of a large boat to change a propeller.

Sample's Yacht Yard just west of the inner harbor can haul even very large commercial vessels, does repair work of all kinds, and has several moorings.

Between Samples and the inner harbor lie two interesting vessels fitted out as museums by the enterprising Mr. McEvoy. The steam tug *Seguin,* for many years used out of Belfast for towing and docking big vessels at Searsport and up the Penobscot River, is in herself a unique exhibit. Next to her lies *Sherman Zwicker,* a Nova Scotia fishing schooner used to catch and salt codfish on the Newfoundland banks. She is pretty much in her original state on deck and in cabin and forecastle. The hold has been fitted up with exhibits, film loops, and slide tapes showing what life at sea was like. Mr. McEvoy, also a steam railroad buff, has established a complete railroad museum a short taxi ride from town. He has salvaged and repaired a locomotive and cars from the old narrow gauge Wiscasset, Waterville, Farmington line and supplemented these with many other relics of the old days.

Boothbay Harbor abounds in restaurants, from simple coffee shops to the most elaborate shore dinner palaces serving baked stuffed lobsters with all the fixings, including a paper bib emblazoned with a great red crustacean. There are a movie house and a well-known summer theater. The Rock Tide on the east side provides dinner, dancing, entertainment, and a bar until a late hour, and motel rooms for the night. There is a shopping center just over the hill on the north side of town.

Gift shops of all kinds are numerous.

Although it is rather in the public eye, for a price one can lie alongside Fisherman's Wharf, the wharf on the west side with a float in front of it and a great motel-hotel behind it. From this wharf and Blake's wharf north of it run numerous excursion boats and charter fishing boats. If you have to lie over a day, try Captain Wade's *Balmy Days* to Monhegan or Captain Winslow's *Argo* to Bath. *Liniekin III* offers a boat ride and a clambake on Cabbage Island. Several sailing vessels take parties as well. Inquire at the booth on Fisherman's Wharf.

For those who seek a more peaceful anchorage, the West Harbor behind McKown Point is ideal. Here is the active Boothbay Harbor Yacht Club, which maintains a number of guest moorings. Hail the float and inquire. Meals are available in the club dining room, but no other facilities are provided. There is a public telephone, but no gas and no food store. In the event of really bad weather, retire up the cove to the south behind a big ledge.

On the north side of McKown Point is a Coast Guard base. A radio call to them will be promptly answered. Here also is a research station operated by the Bureau of Commercial Fisheries and another by the state. The latter has several exhibits, including, usually two baby seals.

The pond dammed by a causeway over the hill from the yacht club was once used as an ice pond. Ice was stored in big icehouses on the shore and skidded through chutes into the holds of four-masted schooners. It was shipped to the West Indies and to India before the invention of refrigeration machinery.

In one of the Boothbay barber shops a distinguished member of the Phillips Exeter Academy faculty waited his turn, watching with interest the barber wielding an ancient pair of wooden-handled clippers. When he took the chair the barber asked, "How do you want it cut?"

"Short," answered the pedagogue laconically.

"Don't make no sense. She won't lay down," responded the barber.

"Never has," replied the schoolmaster. When the time came for clippers, the barber started to cut quite a swath. The schoolmaster remarked that his barber at home used scissors principally and clippers only around the edges.

"That's where him and me differs," replied the barber unabashed.

The Penobscot Expedition at Boothbay Harbor

Boothbay Harbor has had two minor brushes with war in addition to sending troops to wars away from home.

In 1779 General McLein of the British Army landed a small garrison at Castine. His commission was to establish a naval base from which British ships could harass American privateersmen and French warships and merchantmen.

Massachusetts, which then included Maine, reacted quickly and organized a large expedition to dislodge him. General Lovell commanded 1200 militiamen; Dudley Saltonstall commanded a "very mixed fleet." Colonel Paul Revere commanded a small band of artillerymen. Esther Forbes in *Paul Revere and the World He Lived In* (Houghton Mifflin Company, Boston, 1942) writes that organizing the expedition "was about like harnessing so many seagulls."

The expedition, with 2000 men and 1200 gallons of rum in 19 armed ships and 21 transports, reached Townsend (Boothbay Harbor) on July 21, 1779. Miss Forbes writes that "The Reverend Mr. Murray entertained the General and his officers in a 'much Genteeler seat than was by most persons expected in that part of the country,' for the coast of Maine was indeed wild enough in those days. Only at Townsend did General Lovell call for a review of his troops and there came off the ships (which were smart enough) and lined up on shore such a collection of 'scare crows' as even the American Revolution in its fourth year rarely brought together."

The Penobscot Expedition ended in disaster, as related under Penobscot Bay, below.

Linekin Bay, Me. (314). This bay opens into the eastern side of Boothbay between Spruce Point and Negro Island. The entrance is obstructed by a half-tide ledge marked by a can and a nun. Do *not* go *between* the buoys. The bay is well protected from the sea and is much used by small boats. Good anchorage is to be found close to the shore almost anywhere. Mackerel abound here in the summer. The building with white doors on the eastern shore is the yard of Paul Luke, renowned as the builder of a number of distinguished wooden yachts and now of aluminum ones.

Negro Island is said to have been named because shipmasters bound from southern ports during the time of the Fugitive Slave Law left escaped Negroes on the island rather than carry them into Boothbay Harbor where they might be recaptured. Anyone leaving on a voyage to Nova Scotia or New Brunswick might pick up the marooned men and carry them to freedom in Canada.

There is a passage east of Negro Island into the harbor off Ocean Point but it is shallow and tortuous. The harbor is wide open to the south and of no use to a cruising boat.

Damariscove, Me. (314). There are two good anchorages here. The best is in the cove on the southern end of the island. From the black-and-white gong on the Motions, run up the middle of the cove, keeping about halfway between the steep shore on the east and the breaking ledges on the west. Just before you come to dry land on the west, bear over to port to avoid a flat ledge making off the eastern shore. On most days when you would want to enter, it will not break, but it would surely trip up a yacht drawing 4 or 5 feet if the tide was down.

Then go back in the middle and anchor off the abandoned Coast Guard wharf in about 10 feet at low water. You will be able to see the bright sandy bottom.

Flounders are caught here in great numbers.

The other anchorage is off the eastern side of the island's narrowest point. A trip-line is a wise precaution here. The beach is stony but a pleasant place to swim or picnic. Picnic parties often anchor off the northern end also. Great numbers of birds nest here, so in the early summer it is a foul and noisy spot.

The island is owned by the Nature Conservancy, and visitors are urged not to disturb any form of wildlife, although the writer has heard no objection to landing and exploring around.

The tower on the eastern ridge was built during World War II so Coast Guardsmen could listen for German submarines charging their batteries at night. Several were heard and attacked by planes from Brunswick.

This island, inhabited by white men for well over 350 years, was at last abandoned in 1959 when the Coast Guard moved to manned moorings in Boothbay Harbor. Late in the sixteenth or early in the seventeenth century English fishermen who came in the summer to fish offshore and dry their catch on the island must have built camps to live in and buildings substantial enough in which to store gear that they did not wish to take home and carry back again. Because the first vessels to arrive in the spring would appropriate the best sites, it seems likely that small parties would remain all winter to protect property and to fish. It is not surprising that we read little of this in published accounts, for most of these men were illiterate; and furthermore, no fisherman, having discovered a good place to fish, is eager to advertise it to others.

In 1608 a Captain Dameril, who was a member of the Gorges and Popham colony at the mouth of the Kennebec, established a store at Damariscove, which became known as Dameril's Isle. The Pilgrims at Plymouth, in distress for food in the spring of 1621, sent Edward Winslow to Damariscove for help. He was generously assisted. Of the settlement Charles K. Bolton writes in *The Real Founders of New England:*

> It is not too much to affirm that Damariscove was, from 1608, let us say, to about 1625, the chief maritime port of New England. Here was the rendezvous for English, French and Dutch ships crossing the Atlantic, and for trade between Damariscove and New Netherland as well as Virginia to the south. Here men bartered with one another and with Indians, drank, gambled, quarreled, and sold indentured servants. In other words, the harbor which a Captain Damerill is assumed to have picked out years before had by the year 1622 become a typical commercial seaport on a miniature scale. In that year thirty ships rode in the harbor during the fishing season.
>
> A century ago the island was covered with a dense growth of evergreens. Now only a few gnarled and picturesque trees cling to the patches of soil, the sheep having made great havoc with vegetation. The northern half of the island, called Wood End, had trees as late as 1870. In some places the land is suitable for tillage. There are two weatherworn houses, a dozen shacks and a few sheep sheds near the head of the harbor. Two hundred yards away lies a fresh-water pond bright in summer with yellow "cow" lilies and a resort for sea gulls in stormy weather. Here Captain Kidd is said to have sunk his treasure, but Dixey Bull the pirate is a more likely aspirant for the honor. Off the shore, two hundred years after Captain John Smith's visit, the American brig *Enterprise* and the British brig *Boxer* fought their famous half-hour battle.

The late Captain Edward A. McFarland of New Harbor used to tell of meeting Joshua Slocum and his fifteen-year-old son aboard the *Spray* in Damariscove after the ship had returned from her round-the-world cruise. The *Spray* went ashore on the ledges east of the entrance, but all hands turned to and got her off without serious damage.

This island is linked with the famous naval battle of the War of 1812 to which Mr. Bolton refers and which is described under New Harbor, below. One of the spars of the defeated *Boxer* is said to have floated ashore on Damariscove Island and to have been used there for many years as a flagpole. But there is some difference of opinion as to its location.

Little River, Me. (314). This is a snug little cove on the west shore of the Damariscotta River behind Reeds Island. The best landmark is a large new house with a white roof. To enter, make the red-and-black gong in the river. Head for the chimney of the house on the point, leaving the red-and-black spindle to port. After you pass the spindle, continue on the same course until within 40 yards of the steep rock on the western shore. Then run up the middle of the cove between the large bare ledge to the east and the shelving western shore. Anchor anywhere inside the ledge where the depth is adequate. There may be a little motion at high water but nothing to bother a salt-water man. In any case, proceed with great caution here and don't try the entrance under any circumstances if there is a heavy sea. It breaks across the whole entrance.

When you do get in, there is a quiet, secure, and lovely anchorage. The writer saw a four-masted schooner in here many years ago.

The large building on Reed's Island is the Ocean Island Inn, which serves shore dinners.

Christmas Cove, Me. (314). This picturesque and landlocked harbor has long been a favorite with cruising men. The origin of its name is confused. Some claim that John Smith lay here on Christmas Day, but the only year he was on the coast was 1614, and his was a summer trip.

The entrance is easy enough from the west. Pass between the nun off Inner Heron Island and the tiny can off Foster Point. Head for the white beacon, but notice that the top of it is painted red, and it is shown as red on the chart. Leave it close to starboard and the black spindle inside to port.

From the east, round Thrumcap and run up the river, favoring the eastern shore so as to avoid the Washbowl, a shelving ledge to the east of Inner Heron. It always breaks. Shoal water extends to the south and east. Continue up the river and enter as above.

Or come through the Thread of Life, less perilous than the name suggests. The entrance is buoyed. The southwest wind blows steadily through it, often quite freshly. The shores are bold, and the middle of the passage is deep. In general, tack when you have two or three pot buoys between you and the shore. Be sure to go *south* of Turnip Island. The writer's entire yachting career was nearly ignominiously ended before it began when his father, sailing the new family sloop on her maiden voyage from East Boothbay to New Harbor, neglected this precaution and saw boulders racing by very close to the keel. The old *Dorothy* was always a lucky vessel.

There are several guest moorings in Christmas Cove marked by white spars with red tops. Land at Coveside Inn and Lodge on the north side of the harbor. Here is a pleasant and efficient hotel and restaurant operated by the Mitchells. At this wharf one can buy gas, Diesel oil, water, ice, stove fuel, and minor supplies. Showers and a public telephone are available. There is a unique gift shop at the head of the wharf.

The principal attraction is the restaurant, however. The atmosphere is quiet, the view over the cove delightful, the prices are reasonable, and the quality of the meals is unsurpassed. The Mitchells themselves supervise the kitchen closely and do all the baking. Anyone who cooks aboard his own vessel in Christmas Cove must indeed have a *cordon bleu* in the galley!

The Mitchells are most accommodating. They will run you up to the store in South Bristol, provide homemade bread, cakes, and pies, meet your guests at the bus station in Damariscotta, receive and hold mail and telephone calls, and dispose of the gurry in your bucket. If there is anything else you want, consult one of the dock boys. There is a 5-mile harbor speed limit, which is likely to be enforced, so the outboard menace is pretty well under control here.

The short walk to the top of the ridge overlooking the harbor and Johns Bay is well worth while. Look over the Thread of Life, across Johns Bay to the fort at Pemaquid Harbor and the light on Pemaquid Point. Far offshore lies Monhegan Island.

There is a casino and swimming pool in the southwest corner of the harbor. Movies are shown several times a week.

Minor repairs can be made by Pete McFarland, who has a small yard up the northern cove. Anything he cannot handle can be done by Harvey Gamage at his yard in South Bristol, or by Goudy & Stevens in East Boothbay.

Christmas Cove has always been popular with yacht clubs. If you happen to anchor in the cove when a rendezvous is in progress with all moorings taken, large numbers of yachts rafted together, and the water vibrating with outboards, flee to Farnum's Cove. The writer spent a busy hour between two and three one morning when a northwest squall swept down on the anchored fleet in Christmas Cove. The commodore went ashore on a ledge, and the whole affair was more fun than a clambake.

South Bristol, Me. (314). This harbor is essentially a passage separating Rutherford's Island from the mainland. The narrowest part of the passage is spanned by a drawbridge at the gut.

West of the bridge is a fairly well-protected anchorage dominated by Harvey Gamage's boat yard. This is probably the largest yard in Maine building wooden vessels. It has earned a fine reputation supplying draggers for the Gloucester, Boston, and New Bedford fleets. Recently the yard has built a number of big sailing vessels, including the schooner *Mary Day* for Captain Hawkins, the square topsail schooner *Shenandoah* for Captain Douglas, the Hudson River sloop *Clearwater,* and the gaff topsail schooner *Bill of Rights.* Almost nowhere else can you see a large wooden vessel being built with sawed frames and heavy 2-inch planking caulked with oakum.

There is a town landing on the southeast side of the harbor.

Under the bridge there is about 5 feet of water at low tide, although shoaling to as little as 2½ feet has been reported. There is a big rock easily visible at half tide on the west side of the bridge. Bound east, head about for the town landing at first and then swing around for the opening to leave the rock to port. The bridge is manned and usually opens promptly, but the tide runs hard and there is little room to maneuver, so wait until the passage is clear. Watch for signals from the bridge, for if someone is coming the other way just as you arrive at the narrow part, there is going to be a collision.

Note that there is a power and telephone cable suspended over the opening at a height of 60 feet.

Despite the complexities described above, at half tide or better there really is little difficulty in negotiating this passage.

East of the bridge is a good anchorage basin, entirely landlocked and perfectly sheltered from every wind. It is much used as a winter mooring area because the swift tide prevents the build-up of heavy ice and helps to keep a boat's bottom clean.

From here a winding passage leads into Johns Bay north of Witch Island.

Gas and Diesel oil can be purchased at Gamage's yard west of the bridge or at a wharf east of the bridge on the north side. It was reported in 1971 that the store at South Bristol had gone out of business, but it is likely that another one will be quickly established.

East Boothbay, Me. (314). This is a better harbor than it appears to be. It is actually exposed only to the east and northeast, yet the river here is so narrow that a dangerous sea seldom builds up in the summer. There is usually a vacant mooring belonging to Goudy & Stevens or Hodgdon Brothers, the two yacht yards. If no mooring is available, anchor just outside the fleet and inside the tidal current.

Land at either of the floats. It is a short walk to the general store and post office. Gas, water, Diesel fuel, and ice are readily available. The nearest bus station is at Wiscasset, a 16-mile taxi ride.

If one is to spend a few days ashore, East Boothbay is an interesting place in which to lie over. Goudy & Stevens, the southern of the two yacht yards, has been building yachts and vessels for a long time. Under Jacob A. Stevens and Wallace Goudy, they built many Alden "Malabar"-type schooners in the 20s and early 30s. During the war they built tugs and small wooden troop-transports. Since then, under "Jim" and "Tunk" Stevens, sons of the founder, the yard has built fishermen, yachts, a steel towboat, a line of fisherman-type power boats and, in the winter of 1966–67, a replica of Commodore Stevens' *America*.

To the north is Hodgdon Brothers yard, also with a long tradition. One of the famous boats built by Hodgdon Brothers is the two-masted schooner *Bowdoin*, veteran of many voyages of exploration into Arctic regions. In the summer of 1954 Donald B. MacMillan, awarded the rank of Rear Admiral as he set out from Boothbay Harbor on June 26, made his thirtieth voyage north in her in his eightieth year. The *Bowdoin* was on the Greenland Patrol during the last war, stationed for a while at the island's northernmost airfield at South Strom fjord. Admiral MacMillan accompanied Admiral Peary on the latter's 1908 expedition, which culminated in the discovery of the North Pole. *Bowdoin* is now permanently berthed at Camden, Maine.

Blue Dolphin, a husky Gloucester-type schooner formerly engaged in oceanographic work in the Arctic often is to be seen at Hodgdon's.

Recently the Hodgdon yard and the yard to the south of Goudy & Stevens, formerly the Rice Brothers Yard and then the Fuller yard, have been bought by the Tillotson Corporation and are now engaged in building Challenger and Caravelle yachts for John Alden, Inc.

Down the road to the south about 2 miles is the small yard of Paul E. Luke, facing Linekin Bay. Luke builds only one or two boats at a time and to the highest standards. He built *Doubloon,* an ocean racer that rolled completely over three times during an Atlantic gale and brought her crew home safely.

Those who don't enjoy climbing around boat yards will perhaps find Andersen's ceramic ware interesting. This shop is on the road to Boothbay Harbor and is notable for the creative forms developed here. On the road to the south is the studio of Earl Barlow, marine artist. Mr. Barlow knows boats. His pictures not only have artistic feeling but are technically correct. The peak halyards of a Friendship sloop or the topsail rigging of a coasting schooner lead clearly to their proper pins.

At the shopping center in Boothbay Harbor at the junction of routes 96 and 27 is a children's book shop run by Mrs. Chipman, formerly in charge of the children's book department at the Harvard Coop in Cambridge. She is a well-known reviewer of children's books, has a large, well-chosen stock, and insists on suiting the book to its reader.

On Lobsterman's Wharf, rendered conspicuous by the deck-house of a wartime troop transport built in East Boothbay, is an excellent restaurant serving lobsters and clams, coffee and pie, in attractive surroundings. Mr. Rogers' establishment has an excellent reputation among yachtsmen, and Mr. Rogers himself is a most friendly and accommodating gentleman.

Damariscotta River, Me. (314). The following account of the river and its attractions was provided by Edward A. Myers, founder of Saltwater Farm, now administrator of the University of Maine's marine laboratory at Wentworth Point, and for many years a resident of Lincoln County.

A man with an occasional liking for quiet water and poking about could do worse than spend some time on the Damariscotta River. As in so many other places, he'd better hurry, because the developers have found the Damariscotta. The long bold shore at the river entrance, uninhabited only a couple of decades ago from Reed's Island to Farnham Point, is now a proliferating line of cabins, with one real beauty—a dock, float, and runway all painted bile green and covered with spotlights that wipe your night vision when you're trying to sail up at night. The river is a 15-mile estuary that can accommodate 25 feet of draft as far as Prentiss Cove, 2 miles below the Damariscotta-Newcastle Bridge, and 10 feet of draft the rest of the way. Give little heed to the *Coast Pilot,* which grimly suggests the need for local knowledge above East Boothbay. Anyone with chart 314 can do it handily. And there are now supplies and dockage at Damariscotta.

If fogged in in Christmas Cove or Little River, creep out to the west shore of the Damariscotta River, which is bold enough to let you see the surf well before running out of water, and follow it north. It may be a beautiful summer's day a mile or so upriver, and there's a pleasant day's sail ahead of you in the bights and coves of the river.

Above East Boothbay and South Bristol (described elsewhere), there is an anchorage at least every mile, and scarcely a place where a fresh breeze can get enough fetch to bother your night's sleep.

1. Meadow Cove. About ½ mile above East Boothbay, work in toward either of the coves divided by the ledge just south of the 27-foot spot on the chart.

2. *The Back Narrows*. Run right up the middle between can 3 and the Boothbay shore. (The overhead cable used to have an authorized clearance of 46 feet; the chart now says 40 feet, but they haven't touched the cable.) Continue to the 13-foot sounding, after which favor the mainland shore for anchoring in the little cove to the west. Those with raw courage, mean low water slack, 3½-feet of draft or less, and a liking for such adventure may make the passage around the north end of Fort Island as follows: Put the beat-up wharf that's at the southwest end of the cove on your stern and head for the opening (on the chart as a rock and a 2-foot spot) on about 58 degrees mag. The leading mark is a dead spruce tree at a little hole in the woods, but it may not always be there. After passing between the two rocks previously referred to, shape around the Fort Island shore, return to soundings, get your heart out of your boots and return it to its usual position, and sail on someplace where you can tell somebody you've done it.

Both Meadow Cove and Back Narrows are good places to await a fair tide through the regular narrows. When entering at Fort Point, leave nun 10 to starboard; give it a modest berth if the tide is running hard. On the flood, you will be set to the east as you pass the nun anyway. This buoy can be pulled under on spring tides and has been timed as out of sight for three or four seconds. There isn't enough room on the chart to tell you this, but the 2-footer marked by the nun is about 50 yards southeast of it; east of that, there is a clear passage right up the east shore, where, on repeated runs, soundings have never been less than 14 feet. This is the route used by the locals if they want to get up through the narrows on the ebb.

3. *Seal Cove*. More than a mile in length, this deep cove is a secluded spot in which to spend the night or to explore with the dinghy. Coming upriver, round Hodgsons Island and head right up the middle between the islands into the passage between the two bits of mainland that form the cove. The overhead power line has an authorized clearance of 40 feet above high water. If your vessel can get under, you can go quite a distance on into the cove and anchor near the 14-foot spot. If not going so far, find good bottom about 100 yards north of the telephone line. When uncovered, the ledges around the 14-foot spot well in are generally covered with seals, young and mature. They are always fun to watch as they slither overboard at your approach. When the ledges are covered, the seals can be found out in the river, usually around the ledges west of Hodgsons Island. Recently somebody found a market for baby seals and was seining them at a great rate for shipment out of state. The seal population is down in the neighborhood, and returning mothers may not return another year.

4. High Head is ⅝ mile to the north on the same shore. It is not identified on the chart, but one can get in behind the head with 5 or 6 feet.
The shore is bold, except for the head of the cove, which is a good place
to gather mussels for a chowder.

5. Carlisle Island is directly across ½ mile of river from High Head.
In entering from the south, watch out for the 2-foot spot near the mainland. It is easier to enter from the north. The island and Carlisle Point
are at present uninhabited. Be sure to have a trip line on the anchor, as
the bottom is rocky and the tidy busy.

On your way up, watch that 3-foot sounding on the shoulder of Pleasant Point. The print is tucked under the shore, but the shoal itself seems
to be able to reach out 50 yards and catch you.

6. Pleasant Cove is around Carlisle Point to the west. As the chart indicates, favor the southerly shore on entering. The bottom is good mud
holding ground. Land on the north shore near the road. A lot more people are using Pleasant Cove, I notice. There are now five moorings where
there used to be just the one for years. No outboard menace yet, and
water skiing not observed. The Boothbay Playhouse, which has summer
stock, is a twenty-minute walk away. Go south on the tar road about a sea
mile to Route 27; then turn right for the playhouse.

7. Clark Cove lies on the east side of the river, about 1 mile northeast
of the Pleasant Cove anchorage. This was once an extremely active spot
with a brickyard, weir, and the wharf of the American Ice Company. Less
than a century ago, vessels cleared from the wharf directly for London,
South America, and such thirsty spots as Savannah, Charleston, and New
Orleans. The kitchen of one of the houses is floored with South Carolina
hard pine, swapped for bricks wanted by the Charleston-born mate of one
of the ice schooners. The few pilings that marked the old ice wharf have
been taken by the ice, which snapped them off well under low water.

At the end of the long wharf is a pump house that used to supply the
lobsters of Saltwater Farm and is now feeding Class-A salt-water to half a
dozen marine biological experiments being conducted in the old lobster
shop. The lobster car on the east side has 3 feet at low water; the float on
the west side has 6 feet. There are two moorings with 800-pound granite
blocks; pick up one if it is unoccupied, but inquire ashore if you plan to
stay on it any length of time.

Clams, quahaugs, oysters, and scallops are planted experimentally on
both sides of the wharf, so the owner respectfully requests that you do
not disturb the laboratory.

On clear northwest days it is possible to see Mount Washington from the Town House on the hilltop, ten minutes' walk from the cove. It makes quite a sight as it rears up 90 miles away.

8. Wadsworth Cove, Poole's Landing, and Salt Marsh Cove are on the west side of the river to the north of Clark Cove. Wadsworth is a cozy spot, although big enough to have held a Cruising Club rendezvous some years ago. When rounding the can to enter, hold on to the westward for a bit; the pair of Cruising Club yachts that didn't were lucky enough to have the *Sunbeam* handy to haul them off the ledge. You may not be so lucky.

9. Poole's Landing, which once enjoyed a steamboat wharf over which feldspar and bricks were loaded, is a good little anchorage in a northerly, and is within a mile of a 321-foot hill that commands a good view of the surrounding land and water.

10. Salt Marsh Cove drains out pretty dry, but there is plenty of water and good bottom at its entrance. On Kelsey Point opposite begins the back nine of the Wawenock Golf Club, which is about ½ mile east through the brush. The back nine is still on the architect's board, however, and only the most tenacious golfers should attempt to make their way from the river bank to the front nine. If you must play golf, the best place to land is Clark Cove.

11. Lowes Cove across the river from Wadsworth now has four or five moorings at its entrance, and they hold the various research craft of the University of Maine's Graduate Department of Oceanography. The cove drains out but is sometimes worth a dinghy exploration at high water to its very head if you'd like to see the complete spectrum of spring brook, marsh, wetland, mud flat, shingle, and granite transition from the land to navigable water. Two-thirds of the way in, there is an abandoned brickyard, one of eighteen that flourished on the river in the days when Back Bay Boston needed Maine brick. Interesting to conjure how the old-timers worked brick schooners in and out of such a bight.

Lowes Cove's north shore is formed by Wentworth Point, a gift of 130 acres to the University of Maine from the late Ira C. Darling. There is well over a mile of shoreline on the property. The oceanographic faculty there now numbers ten, and the summer population of students, graduate assistants, and staff is usually over fifty. There are more than thirty marine research projects underway, including a sea grant on oysters, mussels, crabs, and scallops, and one on the thermal effects of nuclear power plants, funded by the Maine Yankee Atomic Power Company.

In the Spring of 1972 only one-half of the pier is in being, the other and usable half awaiting a loosening of the legislative purse strings. Aquacultural experiments will be conducted the year round in a building currently scheduled for completion at the head of the pier. Interested visitors are encouraged—by appointment if time allows—and should allow time for a tour of the laboratories, which are ½ mile from the pier and the float, which has 6 feet at low water. Picnicking, camping, and hunting are understandably prohibited.

12. *Dodge Lower Cove.* Follow the chart and notice that the red spindle on Glidden Ledge is not at the westernmost edge. After coming up with the spindle, hold to the channel along the westerly shore until the ledges are abeam to starboard; then lay your course for can 13. (This amendment is suggested because two men, both of Damariscotta, came up through at night, held to the westerly shore, and found a ledge. The fact that it was well above the ledges and actually part of the shore just shows how careful you have to be in the writing.)

Dodge Lower Cove has a shingle beach and a tidal island where a deer can occasionally be started. On the way up, notice the broken ground between the Fitch Points below Glidden Ledge on the east shore. This is apparently a seal whelping area—if that's what seals do—and your boat's arrival will usually send twelve or twenty seals splashing into the water.

Continuing upriver, one passes Wiley Point on the east shore, the landing place of a punitive expedition sent from Boston by Governor Andros of Massachusetts around the turn of the eighteenth century. The splenetic governor sent the task force to punish the wrong Indians, in this case the peaceful Wawenocks. The latter rose to the occasion, however, and massacred most of the force in what is now a suburban development of Damariscotta seen as one turns can 13.

13. *Prentiss Cove,* 1 mile above Wiley Point, is a good place to stop for a swim. The tidal flats tend to warm the water. Pull in just north of the uninhabited island there.

Unless it's the top of the tide, run the buoys carefully from here to the head of navigation. Be sure to locate can 13 and head for it, as it always appears to be east of where the chart says it should be. You cannot lay a course from N14 to C15 unless your boat is amphibious. Favor the west shore a bit, give the long Goose Rocks a berth, and when you are well up with Hall Point, lay for C15.

Between C17 and N18, opposite the Riverside Boat Yard, there are a number of moorings set down by the yard or by local yachtsmen. There are generally no lobster or crab pots this far upriver, so the small buoys you see in this area are moorings, most of them on fairly long pennants because of the tide. *Caveat,* power boats.

14. Damariscotta and Newcastle. These twin villages lie on each side of the fixed bridge over the Damariscotta River. Both have post offices; the larger trading center is at Damariscotta, on the east side; the bus station (Bangor, Boston, Rockland) is right in the center of town at a drugstore.

After passing N18, favor the Newcastle side of the river until up with the small-boat anchorage north of Jack's Point. Then cross the river to the pier, with 6 feet of water on either side of its floats. The tide sets from east to west across the end of the pier, and some allowance should be made for it in landing. It would be possible, by a combination of carelessness and bad luck, to be carried up under the bridge by a flood tide (which overruns the book by about an hour), the last such mishap being recorded in 1918. There is a quiet back eddy on the western side of the pier.

The pier provides Gulf gasoline, piped fresh water, ice, showers, and five moorings, as well as the predictable amenities of a water front restaurant and bar seven days a week during the summer and six days from Labor Day into November (the exception is Tuesday). Chasse's Marina is above the bridge, but maintains five moorings below; Nick Chasse is willing to send to the pier for your outboard if you need service; you may also rent a small outboard for the trip to the oyster shell heaps and Salt Bay.

Gay's, the Yellowfront, and the First National, all on the main street, will deliver to the pier. The Old Maine Shop is the local chart agency. The state liquor store and laundromat are half a block off Main Street, and on the way, if you'd like to escape reality, you can pick up *The New York Times* or the *Wall Street Journal* at Clark's. The Damariscotta Information Bureau is at the head of Main Street; just opposite is the Chapman House, restored as a museum of local and county history. Striped bass are to be caught in the river, either from a boat or from the bridge, the largest recent catch being thirty-five pounds. Bob Gilliam's fresh-fish market is at the head of the pier. If the pier is crowded, there is a long float for dinghies alongside the launching ramp at the Damariscotta town parking lot, just east of the gulch where the ancient coaster *Lois M. Candage* is dying by inches.

Anchorage, in the unlikely event there are no moorings available, is in the channel in good mud bottom. If you are lucky with a patent anchor, you may bring up a bit of brain coral dumped there by sailing vessels returning in ballast from alewife voyages to the West Indies. Hang a bucket over the stern to help lying with the tide, but don't forget to take it in in the morning.

Below the red-brick Congregational Church on the Newcastle side are the bedding logs of a shipyard where the *Wild Rover* was constructed over a century ago. This ship rescued a Japanese castaway from the China Coast, returned him to Boston, and sponsored his religious education at Amherst. He returned to his home country to establish the first Christian college in Japan. The great-grandson of *Wild Rover's* owner attended the centenary of Doshisha University and found a bas relief of the ship over the doorway of the college's oldest building.

A mile north of the Twin Villages, on both sides of the river, are enormous mounds of oyster shells left by feasting Indians many centuries ago. One estimate places the Newcastle shell heap at twelve million bushels. They are indicated on chart 314 at Glidden Point. Go up in the dinghy to be there at slack water, at that point about eighty-five minutes after the book tide at Portland, unless you like to run the rapids under the highway bridge on the way out. Kayakers seem to like it at the full ebb, but you will find it just a nice paddle at slack water.

(Here Mr. Myers' account ends.)

McFarlands Cove, Me. (314). This is a delightful secluded anchorage on the west side of Johns Bay northward and northwestward of Davis Point. A steep hill about 150 feet high rises from its western shore. Anchor about halfway between Witch Island and the shore to the westward in 3 to 4 fathoms. Watch out for the rock (awash at low water) 200 feet off the northwest point of Davis Point.

There are no supplies here, the nearest being at the South Bristol bridge, less than a mile to the southwest.

Pemaquid Harbor, Me. (314). From the south, enter close to the east shore of John's Island. The ledge to starboard is really a small island and always shows. Swing to the east and pass halfway between the wharf in front of the restored stone tower of Old Fort William Henry and Beaver Island. Anchor east of Beaver Island out of the tide. This cove shoals up quite far out from the shore but affords good anchorage. However, if you find it rolly here, go up the Pemaquid River beyond the shore dinner wharf, cross the bar above the nun buoy, and anchor in a perfectly protected basin behind the ledges. This is something of a gunk-holing operation, but there is a channel. If you wish to compromise, anchor in the tide off the wharf. However, excursion boats use the float frequently so allow them room.

This harbor was one of the first places on the coast occupied by white men; and before that, it was one of the principal Indian settlements. In 1605 Waymouth found a large Indian town here. He kidnapped one of its leaders, Skidwarres, who was returned in 1607 by Gilbert on his expedition to establish a colony at the mouth of the Kennebec. Samoset, the chief who welcomed the Englishmen to Plymouth, lived here and at New Harbor.

The English established themselves at Pemaquid early in the seventeenth century about the same time the French occupied Castine. Raids and counter-raids succeeded each other through that century, interrupted by Indian attacks and by pirates. Until the French finally abandoned their ambitions in Maine in the middle of the eighteenth century, Pemaquid was the British outpost.

On the night of September 4, 1813, the British brig *Boxer* lay off the fort and sailed out to be defeated by the American *Enterprise* the next day.

Inside the tower of the old fort is an interesting exhibit of artifacts recovered from the harbor and the site of the old fort. In the summer of 1965 Mrs. Helen Blakemore Camp commenced archaeological exploration of the area west of the old clam factory and shore dinner wharf. There is now a museum displaying many of the relics uncovered, and the work is still in progress.

The village of Pemaquid Beach just behind the stone tower has a small store. It is a pleasant walk across to New Harbor. Meals, snacks, and shore dinners are available either at Gilbert's lobster pound on the wharf or one of the many motels nearby.

There are two beaches close to the anchorage, a rarity on this rocky coast. The larger is south of the village facing south to John's Bay and the open sea. The breakers can be big enough here to tumble a swimmer about, but seldom is swimming dangerous. The other beach faces west toward John's Island. It is well protected and the water is warmer than at the other beach.

Pemaquid Point, Me. (314). Pemaquid Point is forked with a wide-open rocky cove between the two parts. The eastern promontory is a high ledge of dark rock with a conspicuous dike of white granite running its length. There is an automatic light on the top of this dike and a state park nearby. The rocks are likely to be black with tourists watching the spectacular surf. The western point is longer than the eastern one and of low shelving rock. From it a ledge runs off more than a mile to a red-and-black can buoy. In really heavy weather such as occurs after a hurricane or a prolonged northeast gale, the sea breaks all the way from the point to a rock outside the can. In ordinary summer weather, however, it is perfectly safe to leave the unlighted gong off the point close to port bound east.

On an ordinary summer day the wind is quite likely to be soft between the gong and the light and for some little distance east. It is often quicker and more comfortable, particularly if bound west under sail, to stand well offshore. The breeze seems to pick up along the east shore of the point once you are well by the light, so anyone bound up Muscongus Bay from the west can weigh the advantages of slopping through the soft spot to pick up the fresher breeze under the shore. On a rough day, beware of Pumpkin Cove Ledge, an unmarked rock with about 20 feet of water a mile northeast of the light.

Mackerel often are plentiful off Pemaquid Point, and the writer has many times jigged up a codfish on the edge of the ridge between the gong and the can.

Pemaquid Point has had its tragedies. The *Angel Gabriel* struck near the location of the present lighthouse in the August hurricane of 1635; five lives and the possessions of a hundred passengers were lost. In the storm of September 16 and 17, 1903, the coaster *Sadie and Lillie* and the fishing schooner *George F. Edmunds* were lost. The crew of one of these was saved by a man's swimming ashore through the breakers with a lead line and hauling the others through the surf one by one. Vessels were sometimes lost by skippers' neglecting the western point and turning the corner after passing the light.

Muscongus Bay, Me. (313). This is one of the most beautiful and least publicized parts of the coast west of Mt. Desert. Many yachtsmen cross directly from Pemaquid Point to Old Man whistle and go on to the Penobscot or follow the inside course from Pemaquid Point to the bell off Eastern Egg Rock and thence through Davis Strait to Port Clyde.

For anyone bound from New Harbor to Port Clyde, it is not necessary to go out to the Eastern Egg Rock Bell and up through Davis Straits. Leave Haddock Island close to port, Franklin Island to starboard, and Gangway Ledge to starboard. Then pass between Barter Island to the north and Thompson Island to the south. Hug the Barter Island shore as close as 50 yards until you come to the southeast point.

Then leave Old Horse Ledge Beacon to port, Hooper Rocks N6 to port, and black can C3 to *starboard*. This route is the shortest possible between New Harbor and Port Clyde—with good shelter at both places.

However one with a little more time to spend will do well to explore Muscongus Sound, the villages of New Harbor, Round Pond, and Friendship, and to look in at some of the quiet and little-frequented coves mentioned at the end of our account of the bay.

The presence of Franklin Island Light, deserted quarries, and well-buoyed channels to Waldoboro and Thomaston remind the cruiser casually crossing the bay that fifty to one hundred years ago here was the scene of much commercial activity. Schooners as well as a few square-riggers were built at Thomaston and Waldoboro. The *Governor Ames,* first six-master ever built and a huge vessel, was launched at Waldoboro with all her spars stepped, rigging set up, and sails bent. She was taken down on the tide at once and finished fitting out at Round Pond.

How so small a river floated so big a vessel is a source of wonder today. Sloops and small schooners were built at Bremen on Bremen Long Island, at Friendship, Round Pond, New Harbor, and wherever a good stand of oak and pine was near the water. Considerable lobstering and inshore fishing was done from dories and sloops. There were quarries at Round Pond and Tenants Harbor, and fortunes were made by Muscongus Bay men hauling ice, lime, coal, wood, salt, granite, molasses, rum, and fish. Many of the solid old houses at Round Pond, Wiscasset, Damariscotta, Waldoboro, and Thomaston were built by skippers and owners of ocean-going vessels. As recently as thirty years ago, the writer remembers, a passing schooner on the horizon was not uncommon. In 1938 several of us boarded the three-master *Thomas H. Lawrence* off Pemaquid Point with a cargo of pilings to keep the New York World's Fair out of Flushing mud. Since then I can remember having seen only two commercial sailing vessels on the coast—except for party boats.

New Harbor, Me. (313). This little harbor is usually crowded with fishermen, but it is well worth a visit for those who want to see a Maine fishing village intent on fishing.

New Harbor is one of the few small Maine harbors still active in the lobster and fishing industry. Consequently, it is apt to be noisy in the early morning, particularly when mackerel or herring are running. However, there is much compensation in watching the men at work and listening to their accounts of how the job is done. Some of them are glad to take visitors out with them to haul a line of traps. There are few places more typical of the unspoiled Maine village.

The harbor is well protected except in a heavy easterly. Even then, the ledge at the entrance breaks up any dangerous sea.

On approaching from the westward, follow the bold shore of Pemaquid Point to Yellow Head. This is high and quite yellow. The rock lies in layers about 2 feet thick and breaks off in rectangular chunks. It is easily recognized. Note that the chart shows a half-tide rock right in front of Yellow Head. This often breaks, but it is stretching a point to call it a half-tide rock. Stand offshore to clear the dry ledges and run up to make the red lighted bell off the entrance if the weather is thick.

The only tricky thing about New Harbor is that nun 4 appears to be too far to the south. It isn't. Respect it. Leave the black spindle inside the nun to port and anchor anywhere inside it. A southwest wind usually draws westerly out of New Harbor. Because the harbor is often crowded, it is worthwhile to hail the second gasoline float on the northern shore and inquire for a mooring. A dredging project in 1966 gives 8 feet of water to Gilbert's and a 6-foot channel to the head of the harbor.

The first wharf on the north side is an abandoned steamboat wharf, now the property of the Gosnold Arms, an inn behind the big hedge above the wharf. The next two are private wharves, but the next belongs to the Small Brothers of Portland. They buy and ship lobsters and sell gas. There is a small store on the wharf. The next wharf is private, but the next belongs to Manly Gilbert, since boyhood a resident of New Harbor and an authority on local matters. He, too, buys lobsters and sells gas and fish. There is a good, clean restaurant on his wharf that is highly recommended.

The only well-supplied grocery store is Reilly's on the hill by the church about a mile away. At Hanna's Garage is Merritt Brackett, a master mechanic. Here, too, one may get a taxi to Damariscotta, the nearest bus station.

There are several good places to get a meal ashore or spend the night. Two are the Gosnold Arms on the north side of the harbor and the Thompson House on the south. To reach the latter, land on the stony beach on the south side, follow a path through the field to the road. Turn right on the road and climb a short steep hill. The Thompson House is on the left just over the hill.

There are many attractions nearby. The view from Pemaquid Point, comprising the whole coast from Seguin to Monhegan and nearly to Port Clyde, is well worth the hour's walk. If there has been a heavy southerly or southeasterly, the surf there is a thrilling sight.

There are two good beaches. One is Pemaquid Beach, about a mile to the west of the hill. Leave the garage to port and bear left on entering Pemaquid Beach, a village about a mile west of New Harbor on Johns Bay. Or walk about a mile east from the harbor on the road that runs along the north side to Long Cove. Here is a sand spit, bare at low tide. Although small, it is an attractive little beach and nearer than Pemaquid. At low tide after a southerly breeze the water is warmer here than anywhere else.

One John Brown was a landowner in New Harbor in 1625, and as of that date increased his estate by the purchase of Muscongus Island. He must have been pretty well established by that time. A stone marker to the west on the road along the north side of the harbor relates the story of his deed to the property.

Mr. Harold Castner of Damariscotta, an authority on local history, writes of this transaction:

> John Brown and his son-in-law John Pierce bought the entire John Brown Tract in 1625 for 50 beaver skins and the very first deed in America was executed, which is recorded in Wiscasset even now. . . . Because of the phraseology of that deed it has been used ever since in America; and Abraham Shurt, the chief magistrate who did it, has been called "The Father of American Conveyances."

One could not close an account on New Harbor without relating an incident that occurred many years ago at Penniman's Store on the hill.

A local workman, well known for his conservative approach to financial matters, drove up to the gasoline pump at the store. The proprietor's son, a youngster of some fourteen summers, promptly appeared and grasped the pump hose.

"Shall I fill her up?" piped the boy.

"No, no, just one gallon," quickly replied the owner of the car.

"What you tryin' to do, Gilbert, wean 'er?" was the prompt and fitting rejoinder.

The *Enterprise* and the *Boxer*

Because the surrender in this famous battle was "at a point some four or five miles east from Pemaquid Point, four miles southwest of East Egg Rock at the mouth of the Georges River and about seven miles west northwest of Monhegan," it is appropriate to mention it here.

The full story of the action between the British *Boxer* and the American *Enterprise* off Pemaquid Point on September 5, 1813, is a commentary on the economic, political, and military background of both nations at that confusing juncture in their histories.

In the spring of 1813 a Mr. Tappan of Portland headed a syndicate to buy woolen cloth for the American Army. The army desperately needed the cloth for uniforms and blankets so was not overly particular about where it came from. Tappan found a supply in St. John, N.B., part of the British dominions with which his country was at war. Nevertheless, it was cloth and was available if the syndicate would see to its delivery at Bath. So the Tappan syndicate chartered the neutral Swedish brig *Margaretta* and sent her to St. John for the cloth. The British were willing to sell the cloth to anyone, even their enemies, because they were badly impoverished by the heavy expenses of the Napoleonic wars and wanted money more than they wanted the American Army to go without blankets. Consequently *Margaretta* loaded British cloth in St. John for Bath while H.M.S. *Boxer* was fitting out in the same harbor to cruise against U.S.S. *Enterprise* and American privateers.

As both vessels were ready to leave at about the same time, Tappan suggested to Captain Blyth of *Boxer* that in exchange for a draft of £100 on a London bank he convoy *Margaretta* to Bath as, loaded with British goods and bound for an American port, she was susceptible to capture by privateers from either country. Blyth accepted and left St. John in company with the neutral Swedish brig, under charter to his enemy, loaded with British cloth to warm his enemy's army!

Off West Quoddy Head in the fog he even took *Margaretta* in tow.

The comic-opera quality of the whole incident is emphasized by a capture *Boxer* made off Campobello, a small boat with a picnic party led by the wife of the American commanding officer at Eastport. Blyth released the ladies and the American officer sent him a gracious letter of appreciation.

On September 4, early in the morning, *Boxer* and *Margaretta* were off Monhegan. A small boat came off to her asking for medical help, as a fisherman on the island had been hurt. *Boxer's* surgeon went ashore with the fisherman, accompanied by two midshipmen and a British Army Lieutenant who was taking the cruise on *Boxer* for his health. They carried fowling pieces with the intention of shooting pigeons.

At eleven o'clock that morning, *Enterprise,* under Lieutenant Burrows, was sweeping out of Portland in a flat calm. A light southerly air came in during the afternoon. As *Boxer* and *Margaretta* parted company near Seguin about 3 P.M., Blyth fired a few guns after his convoy, "should any idle folks be looking on."

Enterprise, slowly crossing Casco Bay, heard the firing but in the haze could see nothing. *Boxer* turned east and lay that night behind John's Island in Pemaquid Harbor. *Enterprise,* almost becalmed, jogged eastward during the night. Dawn found her off Pumpkin Rock with a light northerly air.

Burrows saw *Boxer's* spars over John's Island, recognized her, and hauled on the wind. About seven o'clock *Boxer* made sail and stood down John's Bay, firing three guns as a signal to the party ashore on Monhegan. About eight-thirty, off Pemaquid Point, *Boxer* broke out her colors and fired a gun. Burrows, to leeward in the light northerly air, figured that the wind would come southerly later in the day and kept offshore.

At eleven both vessels lay becalmed about 5 miles west of Monhegan. The pigeon-shooting party appeared in a rowboat, heading for *Boxer.* The breeze came in S.S.W., however; both brigs stood off to the southeast on the starboard tack, and the rowboat returned to Monhegan.

Burrows was now to windward and found that his vessel was faster than *Boxer* on any point of sailing. Accordingly, at three o'clock, he put his helm up, ran down to *Boxer,* and, broadside to broadside, both vessels fired away. Captain Blyth was killed at the first broadside. Burrows was mortally wounded by a musket ball very soon after but lay propped up on deck and encouraged his officers. Lieutenant McCall took command.

Enterprise's main braces were shot away and the sails on her mainmast swung aback. But McCall set foresail and jib, ranged ahead of *Boxer,* and swung across her bow, coming so close that both vessels prepared to board. However, they did not strike. As *Enterprise* crossed *Boxer's* bow, McCall himself sighted a long nine that had been moved aft to the port quarter and struck *Boxer's* main topmast just above the cap of the lower mast. Her main topmast and topgallant carried away and dragged overside to leeward.

McCall then took in foresail and jib, luffed across *Boxer's* bows, and raked her with four broadsides.

Enterprise ceased fire and called, "Have you struck?"

Boxer replied, "We will never strike to any damned shingle jack!"

Enterprise repeated the question and received an affirmative answer.

"Then haul down your colors," hailed *Enterprise.*

"We can't. They're nailed aloft," was the answer.

Enterprise withheld her fire while the colors were lowered.

Both vessels returned to Portland. Before the funerals of the two captains were held, a Mr. Kinsman representing Mr. Tappan, asked McCall for permission to examine Captain Blyth's effects. McCall refused and Kinsman explained the "deal" Tappan had had with Blyth. McCall, realizing the embarrassment to Tappan and to Blyth's family, not to mention the confused international repercussions, found the draft for £100 in Blyth's pocket signed by Tappan and permitted Kinsman to exchange it for $500 in specie.

An armed sloop was sent to capture the party on Monhegan, and a magnificent funeral was conducted for both captains in Portland.

As evidence of the good sportsmanship with which the whole affair was conducted, I quote a paragraph from Captain Sherwood Picking's *Sea Fight off Monhegan:*

—the two crews fought with equal bravery. James, historian of the British Navy, who rarely has a good word to say of Americans, is forced to the damaging admission that "—upon the whole, the action of the *Boxer* and the *Enterprise* was a very creditable affair to the Americans." On the American part this equality of courage was freely admitted. At a naval dinner given in New York shortly after the battle, one of the toasts offered was, "to the crew of the *Boxer*: enemies by law, but by gallantry, brothers."

Many a yacht race is fought with more acerbity than this important naval engagement.

The ensign of the *Boxer* is among the trophies of the Naval Academy at Annapolis, and the tattered folds of the *Enterprise* are close by those of the *Bonhomme Richard* in the National Museum, Washington, D.C.

The sternboard of the *Boxer,* about 10 feet long, beautifully painted, hangs on the south wall of the George B. Wendell Collection in Mystic Seaport, Mystic, Connecticut. There is a local tradition about Boothbay that a long spar buried in the grass at the north end of Damariscove Island is the *Boxer's* maintopmast. Rumor has it that the spar floated ashore at Damariscove and was erected at the north end of the island as a flagpole, where it stood for many years toward the end of the last century.

The source for this very circumstantial account is Captain Sherwood Picking's *Sea Fight off Monhegan,* published in 1941 by the Marchigonne Press in Portland. Captain Picking, a Portland man himself, was a naval officer, a seaman, and a yachtsman. He had access not only to McCall's report of the battle and to the British Admiralty's minutes of the court-martial conducted later but to letters and memoirs of many of the participants. The account is admirably documented and most interestingly written. Captain Picking was, unfortunately, killed in an airplane crash in 1941 while on his way to England to serve as a liaison officer with the British Navy.

Round Pond, Me. (313). Round Pond is a quiet, well-protected harbor tucked away up Muscongus Sound. The entrance is perfectly clear from the chart, but one must thread one's way carefully through a maze of lobster traps. Anchor anywhere in the middle of the harbor unless you expect a heavy easterly. Then get as far up under the northeast point as possible.

Land at the town wharf or at the small boat yard operated by Bruce Cunningham. Neither float has more than 4 feet at low water, so approach cautiously. Gas and lobsters are available.

Mr. Cunningham can haul, store, or repair any yacht up to 40 feet. He is highly recommended as a craftsman and has attracted considerable attention by his design and construction of the "Padebco" power boats.

"Padebco," a combination of the names of his children, Paul and Deborah, is not a class or stock type but a tradition of quality and originality. In 1966 he launched *We Two,* his twenty-fifth, and largest, hull. Rumor has it that he may try a sailing yacht. Consult Mr. Cunningham about repairs to hull, spars, or engine.

On the knoll overlooking the yard is the Anchor Inn, an excellent shore-dinner place. There is a grocery store to the right on the main road above the inn. Besides groceries, the owner sells a mackerel lure here that has the reputation of being infallible. If you don't catch mackerel on it, there are no mackerel around. It will infallibly catch something, though. The writer has seen it catch pollack, lobster traps, and even a sea gull.

During the last century, Round Pond was a busy commercial port, shipping granite, building boats and vessels, and engaged in overseas trade. Captain Joshua Slocum put in here after leaving Gloucester on his famous trip around the world in *Spray.*

Muscongus Bar, Me. (313). This boulder-strewn bar between Muscongus Island and Hog Island can be crossed at half tide or better with a draft of 4 or 5 feet by crossing close to a bush stake on the southern part of the bar. This is the shoalest place, but there are no boulders here. At this place there is about a foot of water at a "low dreen" tide, so half tide would provide better than 4 feet. This crossing can save considerable time for one bound east from Round Pond.

For a picnic ashore and a swim, try the beach on the north end of Muscongus Island, but anchor well off, at least 100 yards, as the beach shelves very gradually and there are boulders near the southern end.

Muscongus, Me. (313). This is a bight in the west shore of Muscongus Sound above Round Pond. In ordinary weather it is well protected. The cove is dominated by the marina of Mr. and Mrs. Nelson Webber. Their float has about 4 feet at low water. They sell gas, oil, and water. There is a pay phone and a head on the wharf. Lobsters, clams, and crab meat can be obtained with a little advance notice. Guest moorings are available at a nominal fee. Ordinary repairs can be effected and help can be called from Bruce Cunningham's Yard in Round Pond for anything Mr. Webber cannot handle. A paved launching ramp is next to Webber's wharf. There is no grocery store at Muscongus.

Mr. Webber has an enviable reputation as a builder of dories, skiffs, and lobster boats. One may be under construction in the barn when you call.

Friendship, Me. (313). This is a busy town devoted almost entirely to lobstering. Seven dealers buy from about 150 fishermen. It is easy to enter by day or by night. From the west simply run up the bay from Harbor Island, making short runs from one bold point to the next on the west sides of Black, Cranberry, and Friendship islands. Lobster traps will tell you when you are getting into shoal water. From the east, entrance is a little more complicated, the most difficult problem being to find can 1 off Morse's Island in thick weather. A direct course from nun 2 goes too close to the ledges off Gay Island, and following the shore of Morse Island can lead too far west. Also, the tide runs hard through this passage. The narrow gut west of Garrison Island is quite deep and wide enough to beat through.

The best anchorage is on the south side of Friendship Harbor east of the black beacon with a square white reflector. Do not disregard the 5-foot sounding on chart 313 northeast of the wharves off a prominent shell heap. This is a ledge that has occasionally tripped up a yacht.

Land at Al Roberts's wharf, the farthest west on the northeast side of the harbor. Tie your skiff to the back of his float or to a ladder on the wharf. Do not obstruct the front of the float. It interferes with the business of the day, which is buying lobsters.

Besides buying lobsters, Al sells gas, has a water hose, and also maintains a small store on the wharf, in which he sells fishermen's supplies.

Al and his wife, Betty, are most hospitable and friendly people. They are ready with advice and quick to offer help. Consult them in any emergency.

There is a grocery store and a hardware store about a mile from the shore. It is a pleasant walk.

In the event of damage to hull, spars, or engine, call Winfield Lash at Lash Brothers Yard in Hatchet Cove.

On most summer nights, Friendship is a peaceful and idyllic anchorage, but Wednesday preceding the last weekend in July, it becomes very active indeed until the following Sunday noon. On this weekend is held the annual regatta of the Friendship Sloop Society.

Friendship Sloops and the Friendship Sloop Society

During the latter part of the nineteenth century the Muscongus Bay sloop was evolved for fishing and hauling lobster traps in Muscongus Bay. Seldom over 28 feet long, either lapstreak or carvel planked and usually built with a centerboard, she was well adapted for working among the ledges and up the rivers. In the eighties the need for bigger, faster fishing schooners for the Boston and Gloucester fleets led to the development of the clipper fisherman. This model was adapted in smaller scale to the Gloucester sloops that fished inshore. Muscongus Bay build-

Carlton Simmons

A recent Friendship Sloop Society regatta.

A Friendship sloop photographed in her working rig in the early years of the century.

ers combined characteristics of these new sloops with those of the boats their fathers had developed to produce what came to be known as the Friendship Sloop.

Wilbur A. Morse of Friendship probably built more Friendship Sloops than any other one man. For most of the first two decades of the century he ran a yard on the north shore of the harbor in which half a dozen sloops might be under construction at the same time. He had a basic model, now owned by Winfield Lash, which he modified according to the needs and desires of the purchaser.

These sloops were admirably adapted to their use. They varied in length from about 22 feet to over 45 feet, the latter being used for off-shore trawling and handlining and for carrying freight. They had high, sharp clipper bows with hollow water lines to keep the crew relatively dry. Aft, they were wide and low to the water to provide ample working space and to facilitate lifting traps and fish aboard. The cockpit floor was usually of loose boards so water could drain into the bilge and be pumped out. The stern was a rounded transom, neatly tucked up. The run was quite flat. This, combined with a large sail plan and ample ballast of beach rocks, made a stiff and fast boat.

The mast was well forward so she could be used to haul traps among the ledges under mainsail alone. Yet with a staysail and jib set on her long bowsprit, she could slash through a chop with real authority. Auxiliary power consisted of a long oar and a thole pin on the lee side. A man could steer with one hand and give his sloop steerage way in a calm with the other. In light summer weather the larger sloops often carried tremendous gaff-and-jib topsails over a sail plan generously conceived to begin with. In winter, topmasts were struck and smaller, heavier lower sails were bent.

Construction was inexpensive. A finished sloop ready to take to sea, except for ballast, which could be picked up in any rocky cove, cost between $600 and $1000.

Of course many besides Wilbur Morse built Friendship Sloops and adapted them to their own needs. Other members of the Morse family, as well as Carters, McClains, and many more, contributed to the evolution of the type.

With the advent of gasoline engines, sloops became obsolete for fishing and the Morse yard turned to building draggers. Some of the sloops had been used as yachts, but summer sailors were afraid of the topsails and large mainsails so cut them down to make them easier to handle. Then they complained that Friendship Sloops were slow and clumsy, and yachtsmen moved on to the Bermuda mainsail and Genoa jib. Very few Friendship Sloops were built until after 1960.

THE FRIENDSHIP SLOOP SOCIETY

In the fall of 1960 Bernard MacKenzie entered his old Morse-built sloop *Voyager* in a Boston Power Squadron race. It blew hard that day, and *Voyager,* cut down as she was, had the breeze she needed to stand up and win, while more modern types lay down and suffered. MacKenzie, much impressed, went to Friendship, and with the help of Herald Jones, the Lash Brothers, Carlton Simmons, the Roberts, and Earl Banner of the *Boston Globe,* established the Friendship Sloop Society to preserve and perpetuate the type. With this purpose in mind about fifteen sloops gathered at Friendship in 1961 to hold a regatta. Since then a considerable number of new sloops has been built, many by the Lash Brothers in Friendship, but also by other builders up and down the coast. Recently two builders have developed fiberglass sloops. Bruno & Stillman in Newfields, New Hampshire, are building a 30-footer designed especially for them. She carries a topsail and jib topsail and has been "raised up" in her topsides to give headroom below. Jarvis Newman of Southwest Harbor, Maine, used *Old Baldy,* built by James Rockefeller, as a "plug." She is only 25 feet long, but rigged with a gaff topsail she is a fast and beautiful little vessel.

On the Tuesday or Wednesday before the last full weekend in July, gaff-headed sails begin to show up off Pemaquid Point and Monhegan. Al Roberts, Cannoneer to the Society, unlimbers his huge brass cannon, half-size replica of an 1812 naval gun, and salutes each sloop as she comes up the harbor. One by one they round the point of Friendship Island or slip by Garrison Island until as many as half a hundred line both shores. Spectator craft, Coast Guard vessels, and innumerable outboards crowd in. On Thursday, Friday, and Saturday they race and rejoice. By Sunday night, only the lobster boats and one or two lingering sloops are left.

Almost the only point on which the members of the society fail to find friendly agreement is a definition of a Friendship Sloop. From their most recent book, *Enduring Friendships,* we quote:

A Friendship Sloop is a gaff-rigged sloop with a fisherman look about her. A Friendship Sloop is a beautiful fusion of form and function. A Friendship Sloop is a state of mind composed of independence, tradition, resourcefulness, and a most fortuitous combination of geography and language in the name Friendship.

THE FRIENDSHIP MUSEUM

Under the leadership of Mr. and Mrs. Roberts the Friendship Museum has been incorporated to preserve records and relics of the old days in

Friendship. The town gave the museum the old brick schoolhouse and generous people have contributed tools, pictures, artifacts, and records. Mrs. Carrie McFarland, daughter of Jonah Morse, brother and shop superintendent for Wilbur, runs the museum. She attended the school in which the museum is housed, she knew the men who used the tools, she knows the vessels in the pictures. Nowhere is there a more communicative and better-informed curator. A visit to the museum is well worth while.

Harbor Island, Me. (313). This is a well-protected harbor little used by yachts. The dangers are unmarked but not difficult to avoid.

The north ends of both Harbor and Hall's islands are shoal. If entering from the west, keep far enough off the Harbor Island point to see the south end of Davis Island (grassy) over the north end of Hall's Island. When Franklin Island Light shows over the grassy southern end of Hall's, run up for it until well by the first trees on Hall's Island. From there follow the Hall's Island shore closely. You can go as far up as the fishermen's camps on Hall's Island and anchor in 4 fathoms with mud bottom.

A Muscongus Bay resident comments: "Use the entering ranges mentioned in the *Guide* but do so with caution, as they bring you close to shoal areas. These areas are well delineated by the pot-buoys, however, and water unoccupied by these is probably quite safe.

If entering from the east, give the north point of Hall's Island a very good berth at high water and a generous berth at low water. Continue across the harbor to pick up the Franklin Island range as noted above.

There is no permanent settlement here. Fishermen camp on Hall's Island in the summer for the lobstering. There is an old stone house on Harbor Island now used as a summer home. It is a short walk across to the west side of the island where there are some impressive cliffs and caves.

Harbor Island is clean, quiet, well-sheltered and right on the direct course from Port Clyde to New Harbor, Pemaquid, and the west, via the Thompson-Barter Passage. Also, it is a good base from which to explore the beautiful islands of Muscongus Bay.

Georges Harbor, Me. (313). This anchorage lies between Allen, Benner, and Davis islands.

The snuggest anchorage is between Allen and Benner islands close under the Allen Island shore. The writer once saw a coaster made fast to trees lying here loading pulp wood through a chute. In entering from the south, hug the Allen Island shore to avoid a ledge in mid-channel. The entrance from the north is wide open. As the tide runs vigorously, it is well to take a stern line ashore to prevent rolling on the ebb.

One of the owners of Allen Island writes, "Don't smoke or light fires on Allen" and goes on to describe his property as a tinderbox. Indeed it is. When one considers that the heel of a pipe or a flipped match could transform a lovely island forest into a smoking rock pile in a few hours, one realizes that it is impossible to be too careful with fire. One of the aphorisms of cruising is that if you own a boat, you own all the islands. Down east this is almost literally true. Owners of islands, whether in residence or not, are generally glad to have visitors enjoy their property.

Rosier and Waymouth Visit Allen Island in 1605

The granite cross on the shore of Allen Island overlooking the harbor was set up in 1905 to celebrate the 300th anniversary of George Waymouth's visit. An account of that visit and its connection with early efforts at colonization is extracted from a research paper written in 1962. Anyone seeking the full account with the academic paraphernalia of supporting references may communicate with the writer.

In 1605, the year of Champlain's second Maine cruise, George Waymouth in *Archangel* sailed from Plymouth, England, under the orders of Lord Thomas Arundel and Ferdinando Gorges with the mission of locating a site for a permanent colony in New England.

His Maine landfall was Monhegan. Like other visitors before and after he found plenty of codfish, wood, water, and wild roses, but a wretched anchorage. From the anchorage, writes James Rosier, historian of the expedition,

> we might discern the mainland from the west-southwest to the east-northeast, and a great way, (as it then seemed and we afterward found it) up into the main we might discern very high mountains, though the main seemed but low land . . .

These mountains were the Camden Hills. Proponents of the White Mountains do not realize how dimly the White Mountains are visible on the clearest days and how boldly the Camden Hills stand up on any but the haziest days.

Finding Monhegan to be as uneasy an achorage as it is to this day,

> we weighed anchor about twelve o'clock, and came to the other islands more adjoining to the main, and in the road directly with the mountains, about three leagues from the island where we had anchored.

North of Allen Island, possibly in the same spot where Champlain had spent a night in 1604,

> he found a convenient harbor; which it pleased God to send us far beyond our expectation, in a most safe berth defended from all winds, in an excellent depth of water for ships of any burthen in six, seven, eight, nine, and ten fathoms, upon a clay ooze, very tough.

The new anchorage was unquestionably Georges Harbor north of Allen Island and protected by Burnt, Davis, Allen, and Benner islands. Waymouth named it Pentecost Harbor. Rosier describes the scene in delightful and delighted language. He describes scenes of aboriginal picnics and mentions the "cranes" we see today, called Great Blue Herons by the ornithologists, but still "blue cranes" by the fishermen.

The crew, led by Captain Waymouth, turned to energetically to put together a small boat they had brought with them, the boat later referred to as the "light horseman." They dug a well and sank a barrel in it, sent a boat's crew fishing for cod, haddock, and "thorneback" (which may be dogfish), explored the islands, cut firewood, and made several spare spars. They picked up great blue mussels with pearls in them and marveled at "the shells all glittering with mother of Pearle." Meanwhile, they lived like kings on lobsters, flounders, lumpfish, and strawberries. Of American strawberries one of England's noted doctors of the time wrote, "God could have made, but never did make a better Berry." They found even the spruce gum as sweet as frankincense. What an Eden it was that they had found! And Rosier describes it with the ecstasy of one set down in Paradise.

Then natives appeared with brilliantly painted faces, dressed in skins. Of course they had seen Europeans before, and friendly relations were at once established. Knives, rings, tobacco pipes, peacock feathers were offered, and the Indians responded with beaver skins. One afternoon all hands had a lobster bake on the shore and lay around afterward smoking tobacco through the broken large claws of lobsters. Rosier writes of his Indian friends:

> They all seemed very civil and merry: shewing tokens of much thankfulness, for those things which we gave them. We found them then (as after) a people of exceeding good invention, quick understanding, and ready capacity.

He admired their women and little children:

They [the women] were very well favored in proportion of countenance, though colored black, low of stature, and fat, bareheaded as the men, wearing their hair long; they had two little male children of a year and a half old as we judged, very fat and of good countenances, which they love tenderly.

The savages had good table manners, he records, and showed proper respect for Christian services:

. . . they behaved themselves very civilly, neither laughing nor talking all the time, and at supper fed not like men of rude education, neither would they eat or drink more than seemed to content nature; they desired pease to carry ashore to their women, which we gave them with fish and bread, and lent them pewter dishes which they carefully brought again.

On June 3 they visited the Indian camp at New Harbor, going in their "light-horseman," surrounded by a fleet of canoes. Although they feared treachery at first, the trip turned out to be a great success, with trading and feasting. But the worm at the bud of this rose shows in a sentence of Rosier's: "Thus because we found the place answerable to the intent of our discovery, namely, fit for any nation to inhabit, we used the people with as great kindness as we could devise, or found them capable of."

One day five or six Englishmen jumped two Indians with whom they were sitting around ashore eating peas. They had a hard time to subdue the Indians, but they did it at last and tied them up below with three others. Rosier shows little regret and no guilt at this betrayal of trust. He writes:

. . . we would have been very loth to have done them any hurt, which of necessity we would have been constrained to have done if we had attempted them in a multitude, which we must and would, rather than have wanted them, being a matter of great importance for the full accomplishment of our voyage.

Having seized five Indians and two canoes and having set up a cross on the shore, Waymouth left Pentecost Harbor behind.

After pausing on Cashe's Ledge to catch some more codfish, they returned to England to report their success and prepare a new expedition.

The captured Indians soon regained their good dispositions. They shared everything they had with one another, were friendly and merry. When they had acquired some command of English, they described with appropriate gesture and enthusiasm their method of killing, cutting up, and eating whales. Rosier lists their names as Tahanedo, Amoret, Skicowaros, Maneddo, and Saffacomoit.

When Waymouth arrived in England, Gorges and his associate, Popham, were delighted with the report. The Indians were well treated, questioned, and found to be truthful, friendly, intelligent, and naturally enthusiastic about their country. These, of course, have always been characteristics of Maine men.

We know that Tahanedo, *alias* Nahanada, was taken back to Pemaquid by Pring in 1606, and that Skicowaros, or Skidwarres, returned in *Mary and John* in 1607 as a guide for the Kennebec expedition. Maneddo probably died in Spain, for there is no record of his return to England after his capture by the Spanish with Challons in 1606. Saffacomoit, returned from Spain after Challons' disastrous voyage, was sent home by Gorges in 1614 with Captain Hobson and apparently died soon after. The remaining Indian, called by Rosier "Amoret," was really Tisquantum, as this is the name Gorges gives him. He was sent home by Captain John Smith in 1614 when Smith visited Monhegan and then coasted south to Cape Cod. Tisquantum was left on the Cape, as his home had been at Plymouth. But before he could get to Plymouth, a Captain Hunt, who had been left in Maine by Smith to complete a cargo, stopped at the Cape. Tisquantum, who had been well treated by Smith's party, came aboard Hunt's vessel with sixteen other Indians. They were at once clapped under hatches; and Hunt sailed for Málaga, where he sold them as slaves. However, the Spanish recognized that they would not make good slaves, and they were released and taken care of by some monks near Málaga. An English vessel, loading wine at Málaga for thirsty Newfoundland fishermen, took Tisquantum to Newfoundland, where he met Captain Mason, the Governor. He introduced him to Captain Dermer, who was much interested in New England and wanted to start a colony. He took Tisquantum back to England to talk with Gorges again, and then to Monhegan and south to the Cape. Here at last Tisquantum was free to go home. He returned to Plymouth in the fall of 1620 just ahead of the Pilgrims, to find his village wiped out by disease. He spent the winter with the Wampanoags on the Cape and in the spring stepped out of the woods with his friend Samoset to greet the Pilgrims with his famous words, "Welcome, Englishmen"—the only man in the world acquainted with Indian ways and English people, the only man in the world who could have saved the Plymouth plantation.

Other Anchorages in Muscongus Bay.

For the information of the leisurely cruiser, there are a number of attractive out-of-the-way anchorages in this bay, some of them of no value as
shelter in a storm and most of them inaccessible from the mainland and
without supplies.

Marsh Harbor. This lies between Louds Island and Marsh Island.
The anchorage is at the northeast end of the passage close to Marsh Island and off a small beach that faces south. It is good shelter on a quiet
night and a good place to picnic.

Greenland Cove. This lies at the north end of Muscongus Sound and
is completely sheltered. Anchor under the lee of Ram Island in a southerly.

Louds Island East Cove. Here is a sweet anchorage off a beach; but it
is rather open to the southeast, where chart 313 shows 9 feet at the northeast corner of the island. Enter cautiously. For shoal-draft boats only.

Louds (Muscongus) Island (Loudville). The landing for the island is a
wharf in a cove nearly bare at low water northwest of the north end of
Marsh Island. A few fishing boats are usually moored off the cove in summer.

Of chief interest in this island are the many stories, most of them exaggerated, to the effect that at the time of the Civil War, Louds (Muscongus) refused the draft and became independent territory. In order to get
the record straight for cruisers in these waters, a local authority furnishes
the following article:

Muscongus or Louds Island was formerly known as Samoset's Island.
The noted Indian chief, Samoset, is said to have had his headquarters
here and to be buried in the early Indian cemetery on the northern
end of the island.

Most of the inhabitants—now 17 families—are fishermen, and there
are some good farms.

Alexander Gould was probably the first white settler, coming to the
island in 1650. William Loud, an English naval officer, settled there in
the middle of the eighteenth century. One son, Roberts, stayed on the
island. The Louds who now live there are his descendants. The Carters
are of Scottish descent and have long been active in island affairs.

The Polands are of English ancestry. Lemard Poland, who came from Massachusetts, is said to be the only man from the island who saw service in the Revolution.

The political history of the island is unique. It is classified as a part of Lincoln County and has always been true to the United States *when properly approached.* The people pay taxes to the State. For many years they had no voting privileges. At the time of Lincoln's first election they voted with Bristol. Due to a controversy the vote was thrown out.

Up to that time, taxes had been paid to the Town of Bristol. The only local expense was for support of the school, which was met by receipts from fishing privileges bought by New London fishermen. After the loss of voting privileges, the islanders, on advice of several lawyers, refused to pay taxes to the town, saying, "We are willing to support the United States but refuse to help Bristol."

When a draft of soldiers for the Civil War was made, the island was included with Bristol, and by some accident an unequally large percentage fell to the islanders. The men refused to honor the draft. They sent a lawyer to Augusta to learn their rights and were told that Bristol had no right to draft them. They then made a proportional draft and bought substitutes. No citizen enlisted.

Some years ago, a law passed at Augusta, with regard to unorganized territories, provided that residents of such places obtain a certificate from the State Assessor to whom they pay taxes. They then pay poll taxes in the nearest town. In the case of Loudville this is Bristol. The citizens now may vote in state and national elections under these conditions, either by coming to the mainland or by absentee ballot. All legal business such as certificates of birth, death, or marriage and licenses are obtained by the islanders from the Town of Bristol.

The families now living on the island for the most part are descendants of the early settlers and the names Poland, Loud, and Carter are common.

Hog Island. North of Muscongus Island lies Hog Island, "330 acres of untouched wilderness," probably the only mature and unspoiled forest the cruising man will find. The story of the establishment of this island as a sanctuary begins in 1910 when Mabel Loomis Todd, on a cruise in Muscongus Bay, learned of the imminent destruction of Hog Island's forest by a lumber company. She bought the island at once except for the peninsula at the north end where a hotel stood, and it was untouched for decades.

Then in 1935 Dr. James Todd, no relation to Mabel Loomis Todd, bought the peninsula on the north end and gave it to the National Audubon Society. In 1936 a summer camp was started here to instruct adults in natural history and methods of teaching it in schools, camps, and Audubon Societies throughout the country. Carl D. Bucheister was the first director and assembled a faculty of leading authorities on birds, marine life, plants, and insects. In 1958, Mr. Bartram Cadbury succeeded Mr. Bucheister as director and continues his good work. In 1960 Mrs. Bingham, the owner of Mabel Loomis Todd's part of the island, gave her part to the Audubon Society. Henceforth the entire island will be maintained as The Todd Wildlife Sanctuary. No management practices are contemplated as yet except the clearing of hurricane blow-downs.

Anchor in the cove at the north end of the island off the floats. Work south enough to get out of the tide, but move cautiously, as the cove shoals up rapidly. If you are interested in the program of the camp, go ashore during visiting hours (9–11 A.M. and 2:30–5 P.M. in 1966). A guide is usually available to show visitors around the northern end of the island. There is a path to the southern end along the shore and through the woods. In the evenings there are often lectures on their special interests by members of the staff. Visitors are welcome at these, but should not land until after 7 o'clock, as the camp is at dinner. For more information, consult Mr. Cadbury, the Director, or write The National Audubon Society, 1130 Fifth Avenue, New York City.

No supplies are available, although "Bun" Zahn has a lobster pound and float to which gas is piped behind Oar Island near the beached coaster *Cora Cressy*. This vessel was once in the coasting trade. She was bought by Levaggi, the famous restaurateur of Boston, and tied up to a Boston pier for use as a floating night club. This proved unprofitable, so she was sold to Mr. Zahn and towed to Bremen about 1936. He started to drill holes in her to use her as a floating lobster pound, but she was so heavily constructed that he couldn't make enough holes to provide sufficient circulation to keep the lobsters alive. She now forms one side of his pound and seems unlikely ever to move from her present berth. Gas is available here.

Cranberry Island. There is a good summer anchorage in the northeast cove between Cranberry and Friendship islands. Anchor among the lobster boats or just outside. There are no supplies, but there is a small settlement of fishermen who come in the summer for the lobstering.

Otter Island. There is a deep, narrow cove in the southern end of the island that makes a good anchorage on an ordinary summer night. The west shore of the cove is very bold. There is room for a handy sloop to round to and anchor. Across the ridge to the west is a pleasant beach. The island is heavily wooded, but a passable trail leads from the ridge east of the anchorage down the length of the island. Blue herons nest near the middle on the east side. There is a house on the north end.

Oar Island. There is an anchorage north of the island off the Lusty Lobster plant. Gasoline and, of course, lobsters are available here and also at Zahn's lobster pound behind Oar Island, where the hulk of the five-master *Cora F. Cressy* lies. There are launching ramps at Waldoboro and Dutch Neck. There is a store at Medomak.

Burnt Island. This large and heavily wooded island has now been abandoned by the Coast Guard. However, the substantial wharf on the west side and the observation tower on top of the island still stand. One can anchor off the wharf, although it is rather an uneasy berth. The cable area on chart 313 appears to fill the entire area, but the old cable, if it is still there, actually comes ashore on the south side of the cove south of the wharf. Look sharp and you will probably see it and can avoid anchoring on top of it. If you do hook it with an anchor, you can probably haul it up enough with a winch to get clear, and of course it is no longer in use.

An alternate anchorage is in the cove north of the bar between Burnt and Little Burnt. This is ordinarily a quieter anchorage. On his way to establish the colony at the mouth of the Kennebec Raleigh Gilbert lay here in 1607 for one night but soon moved over to Georges Harbor, a procedure that the writer heartily recommends. In mid-July Little Burnt is a good place to pick raspherries.

Monhegan Island, Me. (313). This is a foreign country to the cruising man bound east from Falmouth Foreside, Sebasco, Boothbay Harbor, and "civilized" mainland ports. High, rocky, unprotected, and alone, Monhegan lies 9 miles to the south and east of Pemaquid in an atmosphere all its own.

In approaching from the west, make for the middle of the island until the light green shape of Manana is distinguishable from the dark green of Monhegan. Run in to the north of Manana, being respectful of a black can marking a half-tide rock northwest of Manana. Leave this can to *starboard;* that is, go to the *north* of it. The shores of Manana, Smuttynose (which closes the north end of the harbor), and Monhegan are quite bold and the water is very clear. Enter between Smuttynose and Monhegan, and hail the wharf for a mooring. If no one is on the wharf, pick up a vacant mooring, but don't go far away without being sure the owner will

Augustus D. Phillips

Monhegan Harbor looking north. The corner of Manana shows on the left. A quieter anchorage than one in the harbor can be found inside the islet appearing over the steamer wharf.

not soon return.

It is possible, of course, to pass south of Manana and run down into the harbor. If there is much wind and sea, this can be exciting, especially as there is scant room to round to among the moorings. One yachtsman caught in this predicament had to run right out the northern entrance and round to outside. If there is little wind, it is likely to be soft to the south and southwest of Manana. The breeze draws nicely through the harbor and up the Monhegan shore, so the northern entrance is preferable. One can spend a most uncomfortable half-hour slopping around in the tide and chop to the south. In thick weather the horn and radio beacon on Manana make approach from the west simple enough. From the east one loses the horn near the cliffs, but there are several bells, gongs, and whistles.

The tide runs quite hard in and out of the St. George River and will set you north on the flood and south on the ebb. Two wrecks on the southern end of Monhegan are reminders of this.

A yacht can lie alongside the wharf at Monhegan, but this has disadvantages. The tide runs hard by the front of the wharf and is likely to set one off to the westward. Unless there is someone on the wharf to catch a line—and there often is—making fast to a piling calls for an agile hand on the foredeck. And once made fast, you will soon have to move for the mail boat from Port Clyde or the *Balmy Days,* an excursion boat that runs daily from Boothbay Harbor. One can slide in on the north side of the wharf and tie up with long lines to allow for the tide. The only "out" about this is that others do the same and tramp back and forth across one's boat, scrub off topside paint, and bump interminably alongside.

Overlooking the harbor is the Island Inn, an old-fashioned resort hotel with wide veranda, long steps, and a fancy cupola. Rooms and meals are obtainable here.

Climb the steep little dirt road by the inn and look back over the harbor. The bleak, treeless bulk of Manana, the restless harbor, the fishhouses at your feet suggest Newfoundland, Labrador, or the islands west and north of Scotland.

At the crossroads beyond, turn left and climb the hill to the lighthouse, now unwatched. Pass north of the buildings and follow a path through the woods to the east. The ledges jab through the thin soil, and old twisty trees cling to the rocky ridge of the island, and even down in the valley where the woods are tall and quiet, one can hear the surf on the shore. In a few minutes you will come out on the 120-foot cliff at Whitehead, from which, on a clear day, you can see Matinicus Rock, Isle au Haut, the Camden Hills, and the islands at the entrance to Penobscot Bay.

Don't climb down the cliffs. It is perfectly possible, but the rock is "rotten" and a chunk of it may break off in your hand or under your foot. There have been a number of tragic accidents here in recent years in which someone has fallen overboard and others have drowned attempting a rescue. The water off the cliffs is deep and there is always a sea running here. The "suds" around the rocks consist of so much air and so little water that it is too thin to support a swimmer but too wet to breathe.

Continue around the island to the south. Notice the dead trees behind Burnt Head, killed one winter when an easterly gale piled *solid green water* over the cliff.

On the southern end of the island lie two wrecks. The larger is that of the tug *D.T. Sheridan,* which went ashore in heavy snow early one February morning in 1950. She was bound east, towing a barge, and in due course made Manana Whistle. She laid a course to clear the south end of Monhegan and was running on the fathometer. A strong flood tide set her so far to the north that she struck the Washerwoman, a rock on the southern extremity of the island. The shore was so steep that the fathometer gave no warning. The barge was cast off and later picked up. Efforts to get the tug off failed, and a gale broke her in two and scattered her all over the southern end of the island. Even now the wreckage is impressive. The other wreck is a little white yawl that struck in the same place under almost identical circumstances on a foggy morning in June, 1956. Little is left of her now.

After leaving the wrecks, follow the path up the hill, by several quaint cottages with carefully tended gardens, and continue down the road by the Monhegan House and the Trailing Yew to the Monhegan Store. Here is a generous variety of canned goods, meat, fruit, and frozen foods. There is a pay phone here and another on the porch of the Monhegan House. The post office is on the road just before you turn left up the hill.

Many of the summer inhabitants of Monhegan are artists, a fact said to account for unusual costumes, hats, beards, and footgear. The best-known artist to frequent Monhegan was Rockwell Kent, whose view of Manana in winter hangs in the Metropolitan Museum of Art in New York.

You may be fortunate enough to meet one of the year-round Monhegan residents. They are rugged and sensible people. On January 1 they load up their fast, able power boats with traps and bait and go lobstering in the deep water around the island. Fog, snow, heavy winter winds, and those biting winter northwesters that make the sea smoke with vapor—all this they endure to haul and bait and set again. But the lobsters are plentiful and hard in winter and the price is high. On June 1 they take up again, and there is no lobstering around Monhegan for six months.

They believe that they can catch all the lobsters there are while the price is high. In the summer they go trawling, or seining, or they take jobs "ashore."

Go ashore on Manana and visit the fog signal station and the radio beacon. Perhaps one of the Coast Guard crew will show you the Viking runes carved in the rock about 1000 A.D. by visiting Norsemen. There is some disagreement over the authenticity of these runes, but many eminent authorities believe they are genuine. Then stop in on Ray Phillips, the so-called "hermit," who lives in a camp on the east side. A college graduate with his own view of life, he is a most interesting conversationalist, despite his fearsome beard.

If you plan to spend the night at Monhegan, board the *Balmy Days* when she comes in from Boothbay and ask Captain Wade's permission to use his mooring close under the eastern shore of Inner Duck Rocks, locally called Nigh Duck. Captain Wade uses this himself during the hours his passengers are roaming the island, but it is usually vacant at night. It is a powerful mooring, and the spot is far quieter than Monhegan Harbor. Don't worry about swinging into the ledge unless your boat is over 50 feet long and the wind comes off hard northeast.

If you like codfish, run off to the bell on Gull Rock Shoal and head due east until the lighthouse drops into the trees. The writer has done well here.

Monhegan is historic ground, as a plaque near the schoolhouse will testify. From about 1610 on it was the base for English fishermen on the coast. In 1614 Captain John Smith of Pocahontas fame tried to organize an expedition to New England. As there seemed to be no prospect of loot, gold mines, or a northwest passage, he got no backers. However, when he began to hint at the possibility of an Eldorado in Maine, and when he guaranteed to bring home a load of fish in case the gold was not easy to get at, he was swamped with investors.

He arrived in May, 1614, set his crew to fishing at once, and built a small boat. In this he and a few chosen friends explored the coast from the Penobscot River to Cape Cod, making an excellent chart. They returned to Monhegan to find one ship loaded with cod and the other nearly so. Smith sailed for Spain with the loaded vessel, sold the codfish there to a population who had had enough of herring and sardines, and returned to England with a very handsome profit.

The next year Smith sailed with a fleet of seventeen sail, intending to plant a permanent colony in Maine; but storms, privateers, and pirates broke up the expedition.

A correspondent, steeped in the lore of the coast, contributes the following:

Be sure to mention old John Smith, who spent the summer of 1614 at Monhegan, gave the name to New England at that time, cruised all summer in a small boat from Mt. Desert to Cape Cod, and left the finest chart of the coast that had been done up to that time. As a chart of Penobscot Bay you could almost navigate by it today; it covers all of the coast and islands. I can almost see the place where my house is located on it. But the strange thing about this chart is that, although it is so remarkably complete, it has no record of Castine Harbor at all. He evidently went down the bay at a time of fog or haze, and missed Castine altogether. It is not a prominent entrance from the outside, anyway.

Note on Approaching the Coast from Nova Scotia. Matinicus Rock is a better point to head for than Monhegan in coming to the Maine Coast from Nova Scotia. While the light on Monhegan is excellent, fog conditions make the approach to Matinicus preferable.

Matinicus has a powerful horn audible from the east and south. Monhegan's fog horn, situated on Manana Island to the west of the southern part of the larger island, is frequently inaudible from the east. Monhegan's east shore is high bold cliffs, while Matinicus Rock is a small place with a horn that can be heard long before a vessel, under normal conditions, could strike the shore.

Fog along the Maine coast tends to pile up on the windward side of the islands; it is often clear on the leeward side. For example, in approaching Monhegan Island in the fog from the east, head a mile or two off the southern end for the lighted whistle to the southwest of the island, so as to open up the Manana fog signal. Avoid Gull Rock Shoal marked by a bell, where the sea breaks in heavy weather.

The authors found that, on approaching Monhegan Island in fog from the eastward, the breakers were plainly heard on the northern part of the easterly shore well before the cliffs were visible. They were not audible on the southern part of the shore until after the cliffs hove into sight.

Port Clyde, Me. (313). This is a large and convenient harbor, well sheltered and easy of access but not very inspiring ashore. It was once much used by coasters and mackerel seiners.

From the west, leave Gig Rock bell and the Sisters to starboard and the nun off Hooper Island to port. Can 3 on the northern end of Hart Bar must be left to *starboard*. It is not a mark for the entrance to Port Clyde but for passage along shore. From here, run up the harbor, leaving nuns to starboard and cans to port. Marshall Point Light is so situated that by keeping it fine on your starboard bow you can run in from Davis Strait, picking up the buoys as you come along.

From the east, a course from Mosquito Island bell to Marshall Point Light clears all dangers except to the deepest yachts.

On a quiet night, anchor off the wharves. If it looks rolly there, move over under the Hooper Island shore. If really heavy weather is expected, go through the passage north of Raspberry Island and anchor north of Hooper Island. Anchorage off the fish plant at the entrance to the inside passage is possible, but it is likely to be a noisy berth and troubled by tide.

There are three wharves at Port Clyde. The southern one is the ferry wharf for the Monhegan boat. The second has a lobster car and gas pump. The third is a town wharf. This is the place to land.

There is a good store at the head of the middle wharf and a restaurant, Driftwood, is just up the hill. Here also are a gift shop, a small variety store, a garage, and a post office. There used to be a sardine factory on the cove to the east of the landing, but it burned in 1971. It is a pleasant walk to Marshall Point. A LORAN station was established there in 1971.

Damage to hull, spars, or engine can be repaired by Lehtinen's yard in Tenants Harbor.

The passage back of Raspberry Island can be negotiated at almost any tide by anyone drawing less than 6 feet. Enter between the fish-packing wharf and Raspberry Island, keeping well to the eastward to avoid a kelp ledge in mid-channel. Continue around the bend, favoring the outside or starboard side. Just beyond a dammed-up cove is a ledge that usually shows. In 1970 it had an iron spike in the top. Leave this to starboard and continue in the middle. Coming in from the river, stay between the rock with the iron in it and two ledges off the end of Raspberry Island. This is a convenient way to get from the upper part of Muscongus Bay to the eastward, particularly for one in need of fuel or supplies.

On a flat ledge about 20 yards south of the silver oil tanks at the head of the ferry wharf are deep grooves gouged by rocks driven along by the glacier during the ice age.

St. George River, Me. (313). This broad and beautiful river was selected by Waymouth and Rosier in 1605 as the best place at which to establish a permanent English colony in Maine. Rosier wrote:

"I will not prefer it before our river Thames, because it is England's richest treasure," and then added that he wished that the Thames had all the desirable features of the St. George. He left for England with this sentence of regret:

". . . the river . . . did so ravish us with all variety of pleasantness, as we could not tell what to commend, but only admired: . . . and we all

concluded . . . that we should never see the like river in every degree
equal until it pleased God we beheld the same again."

The river is remarkably free of navigational hazards, the most dangerous being an unmarked ledge west of Hooper Island in the mouth of the
river. Keep well on the western side of the river to avoid this. Other dangers are marked.

Pleasant Point Gut, Me. (313). This gut forms a bottle-tight anchorage
between Gay Island and the mainland. Entrance is easy. In running up
the river, be very generous to the half-tide ledge to the west of Hooper Island. It extends far out into the river. Favor the western shore. The lobster traps around it are very helpful. Leave the can outside the gut to *starboard*. It is placed for vessels entering the river. Favor the northern
shore. Ledges make out northward from Flea Island at high water, but at
low water everything is exposed. Once inside, continue close to the mainland shore among the anchored lobster boats. There is an extensive mud
flat behind Flea Island, on which the writer spent an ignominious hour
or two. Deep-draft boats can anchor in the bight of the northern shore
just inside Flea Island. Those of shoal draft can go on up the harbor. Just
south of the wharf is a half-tide rock. The rest of the harbor is soft bottom.

At half tide or better a boat drawing 4 feet can easily go through behind Gay Island into Davis Cove and Friendship Harbor, but the channel is tortuous. Directions for it are picturesque but confusing. Take a
local pilot for best results. Roland Stimson, the harbor master, is a good
one to ask.

There is a wharf with a gas pump and a lobster car on the north shore.
At the head of the wharf is a small store selling fishermen's supplies,
candy, and tobacco, but no food. The nearest grocery store is 4 miles up
the road. Next to the wharf is a lobster pound, now abandoned because
the lobsters somehow found a way out unknown to the owner.

Pleasant Point Gut is much used for winter moorings. It is perfectly
protected and the swift tide prevents the formation of really heavy ice. In
the event of really heavy weather, there is no better place to hole up.

Turkey Cove and Maplejuice Cove are secure and unfrequented anchorages. On the shore of Maplejuice Cove is the farm where Andrew
Wyeth did much of his best-known work. The house is being restored
and is intended as a center for Wyeth memorabilia.

Thomaston, Me. One can go all the way to Thomaston on a flood tide,
but the town from the water is not very inspiring. There used to be great
shipyards at Thomaston, where 1000-ton schooners were launched with

every spar in place, sails bent, and rigging set up. Later, draggers and yachts were built in great numbers. In recent years, with the popularity of fiberglass construction, the yards have suffered. Fiberglass hulls are sometimes finished out here, but there has been little construction recently.

Thomaston affords all the necessities and many of the luxuries of life, but it is as well visited by car as by boat.

Tenants Harbor, Me. (313). Well protected and close to the route down east toward Penobscot Bay and Mt. Desert, Tenants Harbor is popular with cruising men. With a lighted bell at the entrance and shores free of dangers, it is easy to make at any time. The bell on the buoy has an unusually deep and rich tone.

Anchorage is good anywhere near the head of the harbor. Beware of a 2-foot spot shown on chart 313 off the southern shore.

On the north shore is the small but well-appointed Lehtinen's boat yard, capable of all ordinary repairs. West of it is the establishment of Jim and Mary Ann Brown, Spindrift Cruises. Besides providing a complete and personally supervised charter service, the Browns sell gas, oil, ice, and marine supplies, including charts. They provide minor repair service for motors and rigging and are most helpful in providing for your needs, whatever they may be. There is a tide gauge at the corner of their float indicating the depth alongside at any time. It is about 4½ feet at low water.

The town landing is the next wharf to the west and is used extensively and almost exclusively by fishermen.

Up the road less than a quarter of a mile from the landing is a good grocery store. A garage, an ice cream and variety store, and a laundromat are to be found on the main street west of the grocery store. There is a telephone booth on the corner.

If you are just stopping for the night and not in need of fuel and provisions, you will find quiet and protected anchorage in Long Cove.

Alternate Courses:
Muscle Ridge Channel or Two-Bush Channel

The navigator may be in doubt whether to work his way through the islands and ledges of the Muscle Ridges or to take the longer and easier course outside.

Bound East. In most cases, especially if the tide is fair, the best course is inside. The run from Mosquito Island to Whitehead is less than 6

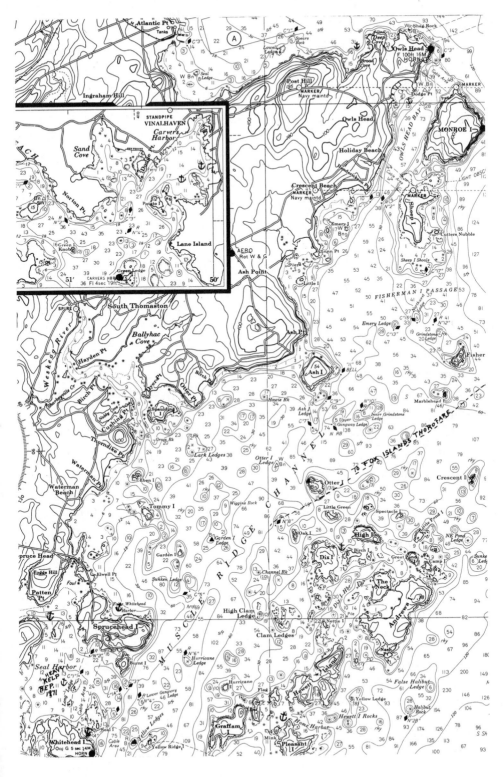

Anchorages in the Muscle Ridge Channel (refer to Chart 310).

miles, a good deal shorter than the run to Two-Bush. If you change your mind on the way, Tenants Harbor is close to leeward. At Whitehead you can run on up the channel if the tide is fair or wait out a foul tide in Seal Harbor. If the weather is thick, you may have some trouble making Whitehead because the sound of the fog signal does not seem to carry well against the wind. However, before you can get into any trouble, you will be able to hear it. There is a bell on Southeast Breaker and a good horn on Two-Bush.

The course up the channel is easy, even in thick weather. However, on most days there will be a scale-up in the channel. The islands to the south seem to dry up the fog and stimulate the wind. The tide runs hard but pretty much along the course. One can usually get an echo with the horn off the high land at Sprucehead. The fathometer provides a safe way to prevent wandering to either side of the channel. There are several shelters easily available should the tide turn. Best of all, perhaps, the sea is smooth and the traffic is not likely to be dangerous.

Outside, the breeze may be lighter, the sea rougher, the runs between buoys longer, and the traffic perilous indeed. A 100,000-ton tanker cannot maneuver with agility. The tide seems to run to the west with greater strength and for a longer time than it runs east. The only possible shelter on the outside course is Home Harbor, and that is difficult in the fog.

Bound West. With the wind northwest, particularly if it is early in the day, the inside passage is much to be preferred, for it keeps one to windward, and the northerly is likely to hold longer and blow harder under the land than it does offshore. However, if it gets to be mid-morning, the outside course may be a good gamble, for the wind may very well shift southerly within a few hours, and distance down the bay becomes distance to windward. If the northwester holds long enough to get you by the Two-bush gong, you can probably fetch right into Port Clyde on the southerly. If the wind does not shift, Monhegan or Georges Harbor is a realistic shelter.

If the wind is southerly, the beat down the Muscle Ridges with a fair tide is pretty and provides an active day for all hands on sheets and backstays. The wind will be fresher under the islands than it will outside. However, the beat down the bay has its pleasures too, and one who likes being to windward can be happy off Two Bush, where he can fetch a long way to the westward. The beat from Whitehead around Mosquito Bell can be a long pull.

If it is thick and calm, you might as well motor outside where the buoys are loud and the navigation easy. Be sure to hang up a radar reflector.

At night the outside route is to be preferred, for the lighted buoys are a great help. The only drawback is the occasional presence of super-tankers, which must be treated with the greatest respect.

Shelters Between Whitehead and Rockland

Whitehead Island. There is a rocky cove behind Whitehead Light off the wharf formerly used by the life-saving station. The chart shows moorings there, but they have now been removed. The holding ground is good, but a trip-line on the anchor is a wise precaution, as the bottom is rocky.

Whitehead is a manned lighthouse. Perhaps the keeper can show you where a predecessor set irons in the rock for machinery to operate the fog signal by wave action. It is reported to have worked pretty well until a storm carried it away.

Seal Harbor. This was formerly much used by coasters waiting for a good chance. Enter between can 1A and can 3. A preferred anchorage used to be northwest of can 1 behind Long Ledge. However, a correspondent reported in the summer of 1971 that the bottom here was foul with kelp and grass, through which his thirty-five-pound plow anchor could not penetrate. The anchorage behind the jetty at Sprucehead is rough and crowded. The best place to anchor is north of the unnamed island in the northeast corner of Seal Harbor. Good holding ground and perfect shelter help to compensate for distance from the direct route and lack of supplies. There is a store at Sprucehead.

Dix Island. The place labelled Dix Island Harbor is a secure anchorage though not a snug one. Entrance is among unmarked ledges, but most of them show at high water, and all of them are evident at low water. A preferable anchorage for a small yacht is in the cove between Dix Island and Birch Island north of the bar. Enter either side of Oak Island, follow the north shore of Dix Island, and anchor northwest of the tip of Birch Island.

Dix Island is a good place to explore. It was the site of a big quarry once, with schooners and barges loading at the wharf and gangs of stone-cutters living ashore. Now it is all overgrown and the pits are full of water. There may be some congenial fishermen from Rockland camped here with their families for the summer.

False Whitehead Harbor. This is a quiet cove. There is no problem in entering except for the possible presence of old weir stakes.

Home Harbor. This is a handy little place to know about, as it is well to windward in the prevailing southwester. It is between Pleasant and Hewett islands (the latter misspelled *Hewell* on the chart) just inside Two Bush Island. From Home Harbor it is easy to get around Two Bush and then fetch well down the coast. It is also a good place from which to take off for Matinicus. There are no supplies or facilities of any kind, but in past years there has been a settlement of fishermen who come out with their families from Rockland for the summer lobstering.

To enter from the east, go either side of Yellow Ledge, which is high, bold, and really yellow. Be sure to pick up Hewett Island Rocks and then follow the Hewett Island shore, giving the Pleasant Island Shore a good berth off the high bluff. Anchor north of the fishing boats near the weir, where chart 322 shows 16 feet. To get out of the tide, creep with the lead as far south as possible. There is some scour of tide, but it is not uncomfortable.

To enter from Muscle Ridge Channel run for the small prominent house on Flag Island until you lose Whitehead Light. Then go right up the middle of a hole west of Flag Island. Keep in the middle and look out for a cross tide. You will see bottom, but the writer has carried 5 feet through at low water. When you are through the narrow passage, follow the shore around to the east until well clear of ledges to the south. This is a real piece of gunk-holing, but it is done frequently by the fishermen.

Rockland, Me. (209, 310). Rockland is useful as a base of supplies and as a place to pick up or leave guests, but its picturesque qualities are limited.

It is an easy harbor to make under almost any conditions, with a lighthouse and horn on the end of the breakwater. Beware, however, of big fishermen and island steamers that may be running for the same mark as you are.

In an easterly, anchor in the lee of the breakwater if not in need of supplies. Otherwise, make nun 2 and follow the dredged channel southwesterly to the yacht anchorage. Move very carefully here. The channel is reported to have shoaled up badly. Two red range lights on the public landing will lead one in at night. There are several guest moorings off the landing. The Rockland Yacht Club is located in the Chamber of Commerce building at the head of the wharf. Donald Webb is in charge.

The next wharf to the north is the Maine Deck Marina, owned by Virginia Larson. There is ample space here to be alongside and ice, gas, water, electrical outlets, and propane gas are available. On the wharf or close by are a laundromat, restaurant, and launching ramp. Grocery orders may be telephoned from here, and taxis are available for transportation to bus station or airport.

In Lermond Cove behind Crockett Point, marked by a radio tower, is the wharf of the Maine State Ferry service from which "steamers" run to North Haven, Vinalhaven, and Matinicus. If you can go no further east than Rockland, spend a day on these boats and see at least something of Penobscot Bay.

Next to the ferry wharf is the wharf of Horatio Knight, offering gas, Diesel fuel, and the safest berth in Rockland in a real blow.

Ashore, the city of Rockland provides almost anything the cruising man may require. Department stores, grocery, drug, liquor, and hardware stores are a short walk from the wharf. The Thorndike Hotel can provide beds ashore, and meals and cocktails. There is a movie theater not far away. Charts, government publications, and books of local interest are available at Huston-Tuttle's on Main Street. Rockland Boat Shop and Hunter Machine Shop sell marine supplies. Skin divers may have air bottles filled within twenty-four hours by Morris Gordon & Son.

The harbor master is Leroy Benner. He can be reached by telephone at National Sea Products or through the police station.

Repairs of all kinds can be carried out in Rockland. Consult the harbor master or Donald Webb at the chamber of commerce.

Rockland, despite its many advantages, is not an attractive place in which to spend vacation days. The harbor is large, shoal, and likely to be rough. Despite the installation of a sewage treatment plant, the water is likely to be dirty and filmed with oil. Big fishermen and ferries agitate the waters frequently. Rather than lie in the harbor itself, one can withdraw to Broad Cove on the northern side of Owls Head and there find peace and quiet and a magnificent view of the Camden Hills.

CHAPTER XI

Rockland to Schoodic Point

Penobscot Bay, Me. (1203). This bay is the goal of many cruising men. The bays are broken up by hundreds of islands and inlets. The shores are usually bold and of clean pink or yellowish granite. The islands are overgrown with dark spruce trees interspersed with fields of grass and raspberry bushes. Among the rocks are smooth, sandy beaches.

The harbors are many and vary from "live" yachting centers like Camden to uninhabited coves like Buckle Harbor and Webb Cove. The fishing is good almost anywhere. The local people are friendly and willing to help the stranger.

The weather is variable and interesting. It may be thick fog all day with nothing to be seen but an occasional buoy and the loom of spruce trees. Or it may "scale up" into a smoky sou'wester with a chop running up the bays and even the nearby shores a hazy blue-green. The next day it may come off a slashing northwester with the puffs off the hills and islands turning the water green and white, and with every tree standing out clearly. On such a day the mountains of Mt. Desert, Blue Hill, or Camden are sharp-cut against the horizon. Whatever the weather, there is always a sheltered harbor to run for at night.

Not only are the waters and the land of Penobscot Bay attractive, but there is an historic and economic background to this region, with which few yachtsmen are acquainted. One of the authoritative books on the region, and "required reading," *Sailing Days on the Penobscot,* by George S. Wasson and Lincoln Colcord (published by the Marine Research Society of Salem, Massachusetts), states that in one year in the middle of the last century 3500 sailing vessels cleared from Bangor.

Scores of shipyards were launching schooners, brigs, barks, and ships by the hundreds for both the domestic and foreign trades; the whole region was given up to shipbuilding and operation as a primary industry. On almost any summer day the upper part of Penobscot Bay near Belfast was literally white with sailing ships, many of them schooners built in the region and engaged in the lucrative lumber trade, with Bangor as the port of loading. In the decade 1870 to 1880 Bangor was the largest port of export for lumber in the world.

This condition changed completely in the succeeding fifty years. In 1930 Bangor was importing lumber for building purposes. In August, 1932, the writer sailed close to a Russian steamer off Dark Harbor loaded high with logs being delivered to Bangor from Vladivostok, to be used in the paper mills.

The country about Castine is rich in historical lore, especially as regards the French occupation before the coming of the English. With the outbreak of the American Revolution, the British moved in on Castine, building Fort George, which now stands above the harbor and is used by the town as a baseball ground.

The largest naval engagement of the Revolution was fought off Castine. The Penobscot Expedition, consisting of forty sail of vessels, had been fitted out by Massachusetts in an effort to recapture the town. General Lovell had charge of the troops; Commodore Saltonstall headed up the fleet; and Paul Revere, the Boston silversmith, commanded the artillery.

The fleet anchored outside, off Dice's Head. Troops were landed, the fort was invested, and some one hundred American militia were lost scaling the high bluff of Dice's Head. But the Army and the Navy could not agree. A colonel tried to persuade Saltonstall to enter the Bagaduce River and finish off two British sloops, so that the soldiers could attack with less opposition. In reply Saltonstall "hove up his long chin and said, 'You seem to be dam' knowing about the matter. I am not going to risk my shipping in that dam' hole.'"

After three weeks, a British fleet under Sir John Collyer, consisting of seven men-of-war headed by a couple of 74s, appeared coming up the Eastern Bay from New York. The American fleet got under way and fled; every American vessel was beached and burned during the afternoon and night of August 13, 1779, all the way from Turtle Head to Bangor. The men took to the woods and walked back to Massachusetts. The keels and timbers of several of these ships can still be seen at extreme low tide, around Sandy Point Bay and above Winterport on the Penobscot. (See further account of this expedition under Boothbay Harbor, above.)

The British occupied Castine again in the War of 1812, and the proceeds of the customs collected there at that time were used to found Dalhousie University in Halifax, now the largest and most important institution of higher learning in the Maritime Provinces.

A walk around Castine is well worth while; the town has been fitted out with a set of remarkably full and accurate historical signs, which meet the eye on every hand. The Wilson Museum there is also worth seeing. A visit to the Penobscot Marine Museum at Searsport, just across the bay from Castine, is strongly recommended.

The following notes may be of interest to yachtsmen entering Penobscot Bay for the first time:

Need for Careful Navigating. "Penobscot Bay is a region of rocks and ledges, and extreme caution is necessary in navigating." In Muscle Ridge Channel and in all the thoroughfares the chart must be constantly watched. Most of these waters have been surveyed with wire drags, and the charts are excellent.

Fog. Don't worry about it. The frequency of fog and its dangers are vastly overrated. No one likes it. Dangerous situations can arise quickly. Carelessness brings its punishment swiftly. But for generations people have navigated Penobscot Bay in the fog and never before with such good equipment as we have today.

In general, the principles of navigating in the fog are applied common sense. Granted a reliable compass, a watch, an engine or a fair wind, a sounding lead or fathometer, and a chart, one simply lays a course, takes one's departure, and writes the time in the log. The fog shuts down. The world consists of the crests of two waves and the trough between. A lookout is posted to watch, listen, and blow the horn. A reliable helmsman keeps his eyes on the compass and devotes his attention to nothing else. The skipper stands aft, watch in hand, alert for what may befall. Everything has some meaning. A lobster trap will suggest shoal water and will indicate the direction and force of the tide. Gulls screaming will indicate the presence of an island or ledge. The smell of spruce trees, the swash of water on the shore, the distant hoot of a horn, or the muffled tinkle of a bell—all are to be fitted into the pattern.

As time runs out and the mark is near, it is well to stop and listen for a bit. Or take a sounding. Something will turn up. If it doesn't, make a square, timing each side and recording each course. As a last resource, anchor. But fully half the time the fog will scale up in the course of the run, giving you first a wider view of the water and then a dim view of the nearest land. Or you may sail right out of the fog as you would step out of a door.

I remember hunting around for Kimball Island one foggy afternoon and being startled by the sight of Isle au Haut right over me. In seconds the whole northern end of the island was sparkling in bright sun, while behind, still shrouding Kimball Head, was the heavy white mass of the fog.

The odds are against fog, but if it does shut in, make a start, be extra careful in your navigation and extra watchful for unforeseen error, and you will probably "make" all right. Lay your courses for bells, whistles, bold shores, or the lee sides of islands.

Swimming. In Penobscot Bay, curb your enthusiasm to swim. Sharks are rare, but especially in good herring years they seem to frequent Penobscot Bay. The year 1960 may have been exceptional, but in that summer two white sharks were killed off Rockport, a mako shark was killed of North Haven, a 1000-pound mako was killed two miles outside Isle au Haut Thoroughfare, and another was brought into Bar Harbor. Mackerel sharks were in and out of weirs all up and down the shore, and the writer saw one big fellow off Monhegan. Halves of porpoises and parts of seals were picked up in the bay, and Basil met his sad end.

Basil was a pet seal, the personal friend of Harry Goodridge of Rockport. The following account is told as I heard it from Captain Williams of Bremen, who knows Mr. Goodridge. Its authenticity is above suspicion.

Basil was adopted by Mr. Goodridge when he was but a pup and grew up to be very friendly. He enjoyed riding on the stern of Mr. Goodridge's power boat. He came ashore and visited the house, often sleeping in a doghouse in the yard. He enjoyed riding in the cab of the truck. Once Harry took him to a fresh-water pond. Basil enjoyed it so much that it was three hours before he was ready to go home.

In late July, 1960, Basil was riding on the stern of the boat when Harry sighted a shark in the lower part of the bay. He tried in vain to harpoon the creature, gave up at length, and headed home with Basil still on the stern. Harry noticed that Basil was restless, so he bailed some water over him and even stopped and caught him a few mackerel.

Just outside Rockport he had occasion to cut a wide circle, and in the wake he heard a splash. Basil was gone. He returned to the spot at once and saw a mist of blood in the water. The shark appeared for another pass and Harry got an iron into him.

For an hour and a half he fought the shark, at last got a line on his tail, and towed him into Rockport. He hooked his truck to the shark and hauled him up the street to his home, where he measured the brute. He was 11 feet long. Then he took the shark to a fish factory and weighed him in at over 1000 pounds. Within were found the remains of Basil and two other seals.

Somehow this yarn damped the author's ardor for swimming in the open waters of the bay.

Islands. Don't miss landing on an uninhabited island. If possible, bring a bucket of lobsters and something to go with them. If you anchor off the lee side and explore the shore in the dinghy, you will probably find a little beach to land on. You may startle some crows off the seaweed as you land. The rocks are usually steep, clean granite and the water so clear that you can see bottom in two fathoms. Build your fire on the lee side close to high-water mark. While you wait for the lobsters to boil, take a swim, or put on a mask and explore the ledges close to the shore. After the lobsters are dispatched, put out the fire thoroughly and strike inland. You will find thick spruce brush. The blowdowns are usually grown up to raspberry or blackberry bushes. In mid-July or late August the sun-warmed berries are food for the gods—but don't go berrying in short pants!

On the seaward end of the island, if it is seldom visited, you may find the messy nests of gulls and shags with eggs or young birds in early July. Eiders and terns are less common but they do nest on Maine islands. Work back along the shore. You may find a lobster buoy or net float among the debris at high-water mark—or a bait box or a watch; you never know. A blue heron may fly up as you round a point.

There are caves in some islands and cliffs, great smooth ledges, or rough beaches. Ospreys often nest in trees near the shore. Climbing the tree is doubtful procedure. The birds resent your intrusion, the trees are often dead and the branches brittle, and the nest is so big and rough that you can't climb out around the edge anyway. Better not molest the local residents.

When you are ready to leave, check the fire again to be sure it is cold. Whether you return aboard loaded with plunder or not, your trip ashore will be one of the pleasantest parts of the cruise to remember during a long, dreary February.

Lobstering. You will see lobster traps wherever the water is shoal and the bottom is rocky. A clump of lobster traps will often indicate a shoal or a ledge in the middle of a bay or will define the edge of a channel. If you come on lobster traps in the fog, proceed with great care unless you are sure of your location.

In the summer lobsters are more active, particularly in the warmer, shallower waters where they shed their shells and grow new ones. A "shedder's" shell feels like thin cardboard. Shedders are cheaper and have less meat in proportion to the size of the shell, but probably no less per pound. Opinion is divided. Some people abhor them; others prefer them.

About 6500 lobster licenses are issued annually. To get a lobster license you must have been a resident of Maine for three years or be a veteran and a resident for one year. You must also pay $10. A strong case has been made for increasing the fee to $50 or $100 to provide funds for research and to drive out the "moonlighters." About 2000 of the 6500 license holders are year-round fishermen.

Diving for lobsters is against the law. They can be taken only in conventional traps. These are wooden crates about 2 by 3 feet, built either of spruce bows and laths or of oak frames and laths. They are ballasted with flat rocks or cement, and baited with herring, alewives, redfish, or whatever comes to hand. The bait is salted and allowed to age a little to work the oil out of it and make it attractive to a lobster a little way off. On a warm still day it makes itself known.

The trap is baited and dropped overboard in shoal water. A ¼-inch nylon line leads from the trap to a bottle, called a toggle, and on to the buoy. Each man paints his buoys a characteristic color. The toggle is attached to help float the line so that weed and other debris doesn't collect on it and drag the buoy under in the tidal current. Sometimes several traps are set in tandem with a buoy at each end of the line. This buoy will probably be a gallon jug in a cage of laths with a flag on top. With a winch geared to the engine, a man can haul the string of traps so that he has one trap on the davit, another halfway up, and the third on the bottom. In the days of hauling from a dory or sloop, a man could haul only one trap at a time, and that was hard work. In a sloop the trick was to pick up the buoy and sail gently off with it, thus towing the trap to the surface. Then it was necessary only to haul it alongside, not to lift it from the bottom.

Under sail one very seldom fouls a trap but under power it is well to avoid crossing between the toggle and the buoy. The line is likely to lie slack just below the surface and may be sucked in by your propeller. Half a dozen turns of nylon line hauled tight and twisted hard around your shaft can present a very difficult problem. If you have to cut the line, try to save the buoy and tie it on again. Your thoughtfulness will be appreciated.

A lobsterman is an independent *entrepreneur* with a considerable investment at stake. He may fish 200 to 300 traps, although some far exceed that figure. A trap, line, and buoys cost between $10 and $15. His boat with the necessary electronic depth sounder and radio telephone will cost between $3000 and $5000. Then he must have a shore privilege and some sort of fish house. He must buy bait, gasoline, and replacements. He may well have $10,000 tied up in his business. A single winter gale can wipe him out. Do you wonder that lobsters are expensive?

Although there have been violent disagreements among lobstermen, sometimes amounting to "trap wars," in general they respect each other's gear and watch out for each other's safety. Poachers are dealt with roughly. Nothing could make a yachtsman so unwelcome in a fishing community as to be seen hauling traps. A resident of Maine who is both a lobsterman and a yachtsman has this to say on the subject:

I have heard a good deal in legislative hearings and elsewhere of hauling traps by yachtsmen, and I don't believe it. In the first place it's hard work to haul by hand and it's wet and dirty if you're not dressed for it. In the second place most of the dinghys you see behind yachts couldn't take a trap aboard without tipping over. In the third place, if you haul from the yacht itself, it's practically impossible to get a trap aboard without scraping it up the side and taking aboard a quantity of mud, kelp, bait drainings, and all the rest of it. When you consider that the average haul in the summer of 1966 was about a quarter of a pound per trap, the odds against getting something to eat out of a trap make the procedure pretty ridiculous. I doubt that it's much done.

With over 200 traps to pull, a lobsterman is on the water a good part of the day. Wherever you are in Maine, if you look or listen carefully, you are likely to find someone tending traps. A distress signal will bring almost instant help. A flare, a series of shots, or steady blowing of the horn will bring one of these men, who are always watching out for one another and for you, too. You will find them able and helpful people.

You can best repay their help by giving of your friendship in return. A drink in your cockpit and a carton of cigarettes will be much appreciated. Anything else you care to do will probably be appreciated too. These men are not "quaint characters" but are often well-informed, intelligent, and independent businessmen engaged in a hazardous occupation that sometimes demands all the courage, endurance, and intelligence a man can call upon. Many of them have wrung more water out of their socks than most summer sailors ever see.

Penobscot Bay

Suggested Courses. To one bound east, there are four good routes:

Eggemoggin Reach. This long, sheltered channel lies between Deer Isle and the mainland and is spanned by the 85-foot Deer Isle–Sedgewick Bridge. The course runs about southeast, making a good reach either way in the prevailing southwest breeze.

There are several good harbors along the reach. One could anchor almost anywhere along the shore.

From Devils Head at the southeast end of the reach, cross Jericho Bay, pass through Casco Passage between Swans Island on the south and John and Black Island on the north, cross Blue Hill Bay and Bass Harbor Bar, and sail up the Western Way to Mt. Desert.

The Thoroughfares. This route crosses West Penobscot Bay to Stand-in-Point, goes through Fox Islands Thoroughfare by the town of North Haven, and crosses East Penobscot Bay to Mark Island. Then it goes south of Deer Isle, and through well-buoyed passages among the islands and ledges to Jericho Bay and York Narrows. Thence it is an easy run across Blue Hill Bay to Bass Harbor Bar and Mt. Desert.

Merchants Row. Instead of entering the maze of islands between Isle au Haut and Deer Isle at Mark Island, one can make the Brown Cow Whistle and thread one's way through spruce-covered islands and bold granite ledges to Jericho Bay and York Narrows. The usual route is north of Merchants Island and south of McGlatherys, between Colby Pup and Colby Ledge, and up the bay. It is prettier if rather more complicated to go between George Head Island and John Island, north of St. Helena, Bare and Coombs islands, between Spruce and Devil Island, north of Saddleback to the bell, and thence to York Narrows. These routes, by far the most interesting, are often clear of fog when it lies thick in the Eastern Bay, and there is usually a good breeze drawing down off Isle au Haut.

Outside. Another alternative is to go through the islands south of Vinalhaven, past Otter and Brimstone islands, outside Saddleback Ledge to the bell off Roaring Bull south of Isle au Haut. Thence it is a long pull offshore to Great Duck, passing south of Long Island. The run from Great Duck up the Western Way in the late afternoon with the light on the Mt. Desert Hills is a memory to treasure. The outside course is best on a clear day, for the region south of Vinalhaven is a frightful place in the fog, especially if a big sea is running.

Rockport, Me. (209, 310). Located 6 miles by water north of Rockland, this is a good anchorage, sheltered from all but heavy southerly and southwesterly winds, and easy of access. The best landmark is Indian Island, with the white light structure. The light is now discontinued, but there is a flashing white-lighted beacon (ten seconds) at the south end of Lowell Rock.

The harbor is perfectly clear except for the stone pier on Porterfield Ledge marked by a beacon. There is a weir on the west shore. Anchor well up in the harbor near the mouth of Goose River.

The public landing is at the head of the harbor on the east side of Goose River with 3 feet or less at low water. Here also is the yard of Rockport Marine, Inc., operated by Lucian Allen. It was on Mr. Allen's travelift that James Rockefeller launched his Friendship sloops. They were built near the top of Bald Mountain, hauled to the yard on a low-bed trailer by oxen, and launched by machine. The centuries mix picturesquely.

Mr. and Mrs. Allen run an attractive restaurant, The Sail Loft, close to the landing. The pleasant atmosphere is exceeded only by the quality of the food.

Supplies are available just up the hill from the landing on the main street. There is a post office here, and there is a bus stop, where connections can be made for Rockland, Portland, and Boston.

Repairs can be made at Rockport Marine or nearby in Camden. Henry Bohndell, a sailmaker and rigger of wide reputation, lives in Rockport.

Jay Hanna lives on the hill on the east side of the harbor. His principal occupation is building models and making ship carvings. Six of his models are in the Smithsonian Institution. The schooners *Mary Day* and *Bill of Rights* carry trail boards carved in his shop. His work is a beautiful example of what a real craftsman can accomplish with skill and study. A visit to his shop is an inspiration.

The Penobscot Boat Works, founded by Carl D. Lane and now operated by his son Robert, occupies a shed and wharf on the west shore. They build yachts on commercial lines. The problem here, Mr. Lane says, is that a commercial boat is built with a large capacity to haul cargo. If she is used as a yacht, she must be heavily ballasted in order to get her to her proper lines. Therefore, the yachtsman buys a great deal of space he doesn't need and loads it with heavy and expensive ballast, thus requiring heavy and expensive power. Mr. Lane has developed vessels that look like their commercial counterparts but are more lightly built and are designed for the weights to be carried. Some of his products are most attractive.

The wharf below the weir belongs to Howard Kimball, an unfailing source of lobsters.

If you are interested in skin-diving or shark fishing, look up Harry Goodridge. An account of his encounter with a 1000-pound white shark is to be found on page 411.

Rockport is active in the cruise business. Two vessels hail from here. The 81-foot staysail schooner *Joseph W. Hawkins* is commanded by Donald Hawkins, nephew of *Mary Day's* skipper. She was built as the yacht *Ladona,* used for years as a scallop dragger under the name *Jane Doré,* and rescued from oblivion by Captain Douglas, owner of *Shenandoah*. *Timberwind,* the former 70-foot pilot schooner at Portland, also sails, under Captain Bill Alexander. In addition, the Camden fleet, seeking an anchorage near home for the last night of their week's cruise, often makes Rockport on Friday night. The scene is picturesque if not always peaceful.

If there is a southerly chop running up the bay, Rockport can be uncomfortable on the ebb tide, but it is seldom dangerous in the summer. For well over a century vessels lay here winter and summer, loading lime, ice, lumber, and lobsters. Ruins of the old lime kilns are still visible on the west side of the harbor, and Rockport ice was said to be so clear you could read a book through it. Half a million tons a year were shipped to the southern states and the West Indies before the invention of mechanical refrigeration.

Camden, Me. (209, 310). Entrance to Camden is facilitated in fog or in darkness by the lighted beacon and bell on the Graves. From here, head for the light and the fog bell on Curtis Island and make the black can inside. There is a black-and-white can in range with the west side of Curtis Island and the black can 3. From here a channel dredged to 10 feet in 1960 runs up the harbor. It is marked by red and black trawl buoys.

Anchoring is allowed in the outer harbor only. The yacht club has guest moorings and a launch service. The town of Camden also maintains three guest moorings off the northerly shore, in 15 feet. These are spar moorings, consisting of ton-and-a-half granite blocks, and marked "Camden Guest 1, 2, and 3." If in doubt about moorings, consult yacht club steward Bud Chater, who will also hold mail and messages for yachtsmen.

The inner harbor is full of private moorings, so anchoring is not permitted there. However, the public dock has two floats: No. 1 is for on-and-off loading, No. 2 for tie-ups of about an hour for shopping trips ashore. There is also a granite dock, usable at high water, and there is a town-owned spar mooring, which may be used for periods up to twelve hours. The floats have 20 feet at low water.

The harbor master is Rusty Robbins, often to be found at the town wharf.

On the site of the old steamer wharf is an asphalt launching ramp. On the west side of the harbor is the hospitable yacht club. Farther up the harbor are wharves selling gasoline, Diesel fuel, ice, marine hardware, and ship chandlery. The most interesting of these is Lok Marina, invented and developed by the late Dr. Raymond Tibbetts. On the harbor is a solid deep-water wharf and float. In the northerly corner is a lock capable of lifting a 42-foot boat drawing up to four feet. It is lifted into a basin whose water level is somewhat above the level of the street. Here one may tie up at finger floats, perfectly protected, convenient to stores, showers, toilets, electrical outlets, indeed all the luxuries of life ashore. Of course with the luxuries go all those things we go to sea to escape. For those who wish to leave their boats, who must haul out, or who seek dockside service, Lok Marina is convenient.

The idea was conceived by the ingenious Dr. Tibbetts about 1952 in the course of a trip abroad. Before he invented the marina he had done very well with crystal microphones for hearing aids. He is credited with inventions ranging from electric refrigerators, hydraulic airplane controls, and a skate sharpener, to a hot-air balloon, which, bearing a cat triumphantly aloft on a windy day, bilged on the cupola of a livery stable and burned it down. The Camden post office now occupies the site.

On the south shore of the inner harbor is the Camden Yacht Clubhouse, presented to the town by the late Cyrus H.K. Curtis, Philadelphia publisher, who long had a summer home here. Negro Island, at the west side of the entrance, was renamed Curtis Island in his honor. His steam yacht *Lyndonia* was a familiar sight along these shores for many years.

Renamed *Southern Seas,* she was lost in the Pacific in a typhoon off Okinawa in 1945. Built in 1922 by Mr. Curtis and later converted to Diesel power, she was bought in 1940 by Pan American Airways and used off the east coast of Australia. After Pearl Harbor the Navy took her over, removed her luxury fittings, and turned her into a nautical wayside inn for unattached stragglers in the war zone. Virtually every correspondent covering the Pacific war west of Pearl Harbor lived aboard her at one time or another.

Emmet Crozier writes of her in the *New York Herald Tribune* of November 5, 1945:

So she went down in a typhoon. A strange end for the staid old *Lyndonia*—her *de luxe* plumbing forty fathoms down in green sea water off Okinawa and giant crabs scuttling over teakwood planks. But those last years were good years, crammed with excitement and usefulness. The strange plunge in the raging, tempest-tossed waters of the China Sea was better than rotting away at a pier in Philadelphia.

On the east shore is Wayfarer Marine, managed by Graham Barlow. Here are all the usual and necessary supplies and facilities for repair, hauling, dockage, and winter storage. Electronic gear can be repaired here also.

The town offers all the usual stores and several good restaurants. Charts and government publications are available in The Village Shop. Through buses run east and west to Bangor, Portland, and Boston.

Camden has a well-deserved reputation for fine yacht-building. The late Elmer Collamore was a one-man yard. He rebuilt John Alden's old *Malabar II*, putting in new backbone, frames, planking, and deck, but using the old ballast keel, spars, and even the old interior cabinet work. When he finished, she started right off on a transatlantic voyage. He also built *Heritage*, a 28-foot replica of a Rockport stone-sloop. She is a piece of cabinet work from truck to keel.

Jim Rockefeller in a "yard" near the top of Bald Mountain built several Friendship sloops of the *Pemaquid* type. One of these, *Old Baldy*, was used as a "plug" for Jarvis Newman's fiberglass sloops built at Southwest Harbor. Rockefeller also completely rebuilt the 36-foot Friendship *Sazerac*. He built power boats and gunning boats, and now has established The Great Eastern Flying Boat Company.

Malcolm Brewer, formerly the superintendant at Camden Shipbuilding and Drydock, has built several beautiful yachts modeled on coasting-schooner lines designed by Murray Peterson as well as a Friendship sloop, *Patience*.

Geerd Hendel, well-known designer, has an office in Camden.

Another project originating in Camden is the Windjammer or Schooner Cruise. Back in the late 30s Captain Frank Swift bought the little coaster *Clinton* and fitted her out to carry summer people on weekly cruises among the islands between Camden and Mt. Desert. With only a skipper, mate, and cook aboard, the passengers did most of the work and lived in rather primitive conditions. But they had a good time and the idea caught on. At one time Captain Swift owned not only the *Clinton* but *Annie K. Kimball, Lois M. Candage, Eva S. Cullison* from the Chesapeake, *Endeavor, Enterprise, Mattie, Mercantile,* and *Stephen Tabor*. There may have been others I have forgotten. Before long, the ever-tightening Coast Guard regulations and the ever-increasing age of the vessels made them impossible to support. Captain Swift sold out. Now Les Bex owns *Mattie* and *Mercantile* and has added *Mistress*. Captain Young's *Stephen Tabor*, over one hundred years old, is the oldest vessel actually being used under American registry. Captain Jim Sharp sails the big *Adventure*, built as a Gloucester fishing schooner, and Captain Boyd Guild goes out of Rockland in the three-master *Victory Chimes*. Captain Havilah Hawkins, formerly owner of *Alice S. Wentworth*, had a new schooner, *Mary Day*, built up Harvey Gamage in South Bristol. To the south of Cape Cod the topsail schooner *Shenandoah* and the coaster *Bill of Rights* preserve the tradition. All of these vessels operate under sail alone, except for such help as they get in calm weather from a yawl boat with a powerful Diesel engine lashed under the stern. Were it not for these vessels and for the others sailing out of Rockport, there would be no sailing vessels on the coast to remind us of what the old-timers were like.

In the literary line, Camden excels, too. On the shore behind Lok Marina are the offices of *Down East,* a monthly magazine devoted to the most colorful aspects of coastal, inland, and mountain Maine. The magazine's brilliant color photographs brighten some of the year's darkest days. *National Fisherman* on the main street is the breath of life to those suffocating in suburbia in the winter months. It is primarily a trade paper for fishermen but carries news of coastal towns, the homely recollections of Captain Perc Sane, and advertisements as fascinating as the news. These two, with the *Maine Times* published weekly in Topsham, help us to keep in touch.

If you have to be fogbound some time, arrange to have it happen in Camden. The shady streets are lined by beautiful old houses built by shipmasters and merchants when Penobscot Bay granite, lime, fish, ice, and lumber were well known in the world's ports. Often when it is thick in Camden Harbor, the sun will be shining warmly on the tops of the mountains.

The trail up Mt. Battie starts from the end of Megunticook Street. It is a brisk twenty-minute climb with a rewarding view—if you don't mind discovering when you arrive breathless at the top that others have driven up in automobiles. Mt. Megunticook, the highest of the Camden Hills, is more challenging, but it is overgrown on the top, so the view from the summit is obstructed. However, Ocean View Lookout and Bald Rock on the sides of Megunticook afford magnificent prospects of the coast. On a clear day one can see from Monhegan to Mt. Desert and north to Blue Hill.

Don't miss the opportunity to visit Admiral Donald B. MacMillan's *Bowdoin,* built by Hodgdon Brothers in East Boothbay in the early 20s for arctic exploration. Admiral MacMillan, a member of Peary's expedition to the North Pole, and a seaman, explorer, scientist, and educator in the broadest senses of the words, took the vessel north twenty-six times. At last she was given to Mystic Seaport in 1959. That institution, unable to maintain her properly, returned her to Maine in 1968 in the care of the Schooner Bowdoin Association, composed of former members of *Bowdoin's* crews. Jim Sharp leased her from the association. She is being fitted out as a museum of arctic lore, but several times a year sets her sails and cruises the coast.

From Camden to Upper Penobscot Bay

It is not necessary to go around the whistle off Robinson Rock. Many yachts of moderate draft cross Job Island bar. Take a southeast course about 600 yards north of Little Bermuda, a grassy island between Lime Island and Job Island. There is said to be more than the advertised 5 feet on the bar, but the writer's advice is to pick a rising tide and to move very slowly.

Less terrifying is the passage south of Lasell Island. From Camden, head well up toward the high part of the island, giving Goose Rocks a very generous berth. There are said to be many seals on this rock, but if you come close enough to see them on the course for Lasell Island, you will have other things than seals to think about. Two half-tide rocks extend well to the northeast of Goose Rocks. After you pass south of Lasell Island, follow the shore for a bit before heading across for can 3 to avoid the rock north of Mouse Island.

If bound for Pulpit Harbor, pass north of Goose Island and leave can 1A to starboard.

Gilkey Harbor, Islesboro, Me. (310). This is a large harbor, not snug, but secure enough and with magnificent views of the Camden Hills. In the early days of the century it was a popular summer resort with "cottages" in the grand manner. The harbor was often crowded with large and luxurious yachts. The writer remembers having seen J. P. Morgan's famous *Corsair* at anchor here.

The easiest entrance is from the south between Job Island and the Ensign Islands. A lighted bell to port and a nun off Minot Ledge to starboard mark the passage. Entrance from the north presents no problems, but the most interesting passage is east of Job Island, and for anyone coming from the eastward it saves either crossing Job Island bar or going down around Lasell Island. The tricky part of this entrance is the long sandbar making out from Middle Island. The passage is buoyed out with red and black balls maintained by the yacht club. They have proved entirely reliable. Come out the northern end close to little grassy Tumbledown Dick and anchor around the point in Ames Cove off the Tarratine Yacht Club. Move carefully in here, for there is only about 3 feet at the float at low water and 5 feet in the anchorage.

Water is piped to the float, and there is usually someone around to welcome the visitor. There is a telephone at the club, and Pendleton's store will deliver groceries to the wharf in response to a call. It has been possible to obtain lunches at the club.

The Islesboro Inn on the point north of the Club has several guest moorings and a wharf with water and electricity. There is 6 feet of water at the wharf. Showers and laundry machines are also available. The inn has a dining room, cocktail lounge, and overnight accommodations. Cruising parties are welcome.

Across the harbor in Cradle Cove is the Dark Harbor Boat Yard, with guest moorings, gas, ice, water, Diesel fuel, marine supplies, and dockage with electric power. There is 10 feet of water here at low tide. Ordinary repairs can be made here.

Dark Harbor itself, a picturesque cove on the east side of Isleboro, has been dammed and is not navigable.

Crow Cove is a quiet and secure anchorage except in a heavy westerly. It is not easy to land here, because of the flats.

The ferry from Lincolnville Beach lands at Grindle Point.

Western Penobscot Bay to Bangor

A Belfast resident, Donald Lewis, who has cruised the Western Bay for years writes the following pages on the trip from Camden to Bangor. Charts 310 and 311 cover this area.

Leaving Camden and heading roughly northeast, you find the land on the west a bold shore with few sheltered anchorages but with Bald Rock and Mounts Battie and Megunticook, all over 1000 feet high, furnishing a backdrop. On the east is a chain of islands extending south from the tip of Isleboro: Job, Lime, Lasell, Saddle, and Mark. All are privately owned, and landing parties are discouraged. However, there is a good anchorage off the stony beach at the northwest end of Lasell sheltered from anything but a northwester. Shelter from this quarter is close by in Gilkey Harbor.

Lincolnville Beach, Me. (310). Five miles above Camden is Lincolnville Beach, where a fine landing float has been installed. There is 3 to 8 feet of water at the float, and a guest mooring is often available. Two of the finest shore-dinner establishments on the coast are located here: The Lincolnville Lobster Pound and The Beach Inn. The float is located on the north side of the ferry slip, and a five-minute walk takes you to the village and restaurants.

The ferry, *Governor Muskie,* leaves from here to carry passengers and cars to Gilkey Harbor, Isleboro, 2½ miles across the bay. Practically hourly service is maintained during the summer months, and three or four trips a day the year around.

In heavy winds from northeast through east, Lincolnville Beach anchorage would be uncomfortable, but in ordinary summer weather it offers a rare chance to step from your boat into a first-class shore-dinner restaurant. There is also a small garage, as well as a post office, an antique shop, a grocery store, Penobscot Indian Trading Post, and U.S. Route 1, coupled with a beach best at high water. This is a good place to try when the crew and guests (especially the ladies), long for some shore activity.

Continuing up the bay, you come to Spruce Head and Great Spruce Head (not to be confused with Spruce Head Island in the Muscle Ridges nor again with Great Spruce Head Island, which is not more than 7 miles distant in a straight line, in East Penobscot Bay). Lighted bell number 9 is a buoy that is religiously made by all commercial traffic passing up and down Penobscot Bay. If you have no radar, you may avoid an unpleasant rendezvous with a super-tanker by hugging the shore, which is bold here. From number 9 it is nearly a straight run to Fort Point or Searsport bound up the bay, and a straight line leads southerly from number 9 to Owls Head.

This correspondent, in a 25-footer and in a dense fog, mistook the bow wave of a Spanish freighter, bound down the bay, for breakers on the shore, and, in avoiding the supposed breakers, passed actually under the bow of the freighter.

The large house opposite number 9 has a beautifully toned bell on the porch, which is often rung in answer to salutes from passing boats.

Saturday Cove, Me. (310), is exposed to the east and dominated by the summer home of Horace Hildreth, former governor of Maine and U.S. Ambassador to Pakistan.

Bayside, Me. (311). If you follow the mainland shore northward from Saturday Cove you will come to the popular summer colony of Bayside. Here is located the Northport Yacht Club, a good wharf and a float with 6 feet at low water. A guest mooring is available, for the use of which you should see Mr. Al Keith, who lives near the wharf and is the most accommodating type of ingenious Yankee. He is, among other things, the harbor master. There is a very well organized and popular summer sailing program here for the young people.

The anchorage looks exposed, and it is to the east, but the usual summer southwester blows from over the land, making a fine lee, and you will imagine yourself moored off the shore of a large lake, because there is no ground swell, and unless the wind is dead on shore, Bayside is a most attractive place.

Belfast, Me. (311). The city of Belfast, 3 miles to the northwest, at the head of Belfast Bay, is the trading center of Waldo County. Present facilities include a city float and wharf, neither ideal, but usable. The float is aground at low water, and the wharf is better used at some other stage of the tide. There is a gas pump at the float. C.A. Paul maintains a machine shop.

Once foul with oil, sewage, and the refuse from chicken-processing plants, Belfast Harbor was usually shunned by yachtsmen. Now the Harbor Committee writes, "Both poultry companies and the City of Belfast itself have new sewage treatment facilities . . . Marina facilities are also in operation." The best anchorage is above the tugboats, on the west side, good holding ground, 10 to 20 feet of water, and completely sheltered. There is a guest mooring off the municipal wharf. The business section starts at the head of the wharf. By 1973 the pollution stands to be largely eliminated.

The dock of the Eastern Maine Towage Company is home for a fleet of two boats. The steam tug *Clyde B. Holmes* and one of the Diesel tugs service traffic docking at Searsport, Bucksport, and Bangor. Other Diesel tugs tow outside, often going as far as South Carolina or the Great Lakes. The owners, officers, and crews are fine, friendly men and in a pinch will let you tie alongside.

The old *Seguin,* built in 1884, and the last survivor of the tow boats that used to haul the ice and lumber schooners up and down the Maine rivers, is now a part of a marine museum at Boothbay Harbor.

To have the privilege of riding a steam tug as this correspondent does on occasion, defying a thick black night, and inhaling the odor of oil and steam, and hearing the jingle from the pilot house calling for full speed ahead, is worth a great deal to those of us who grew up in the age of steam.

Searsport, Me. (311). Searsport has a float, behind a log jetty, which can be used with impunity only at half tide or better. The harbor is wide open to the afternoon southerly. There is, however, the Penobscot Marine Museum, the purpose of which is to preserve the treasures of the age of sail and steam in these waters. For the yachtsman who likes such things as marine museums, the one at Searsport is a must. East of Searsport Village is Macks Point, the second-busiest seaport in the state of Maine. But this port is entirely commercial, and a small boat would have difficulty finding a place to land at the big piers.

The threat of oil refineries in this region has been defeated. There is complete shelter and good holding ground in Stockton Harbor.

Penobscot River, Me. (310). The Penobscot River has been extolled in many books and articles. Its entrance is at Fort Point, and it is navigable for 24 miles to the city of Bangor. With a fair tide and a good southwest breeze, by starting at low-water slack, you can carry a favorable current to Bangor. Coming up the Western Bay enter between Fort Point Ledge and the light. The currents are strong here. The customary route leads west to the nun near Odom's Ledge, although the *Coast Pilot* gives other directions.

After passing the ledge, the Waldo-Hancock Bridge comes into view. This is one of the most beautiful suspension bridges in the country, with a vertical clearance of 135 feet and a horizontal clearance of 750 feet, and with 10 fathoms or more of water from shore to shore. The tide runs hard here, and currents are tricky, with the ebb tide the more powerful.

Bucksport, Me. (310). Fort Knox lies on the western bank opposite the town of Bucksport. Bucksport has a new wharf and float with 6 feet at low water. This wharf is handy to the main street, where any needed supplies can be purchased. It should be possible to pick up a vacant mooring here. At long last, here is a chance to go ashore here on the Penobscot River!

The trip east of Verona Island is possible, best on a rising tide, and adds variety to the trip up and down the river. There is a vertical clearance of 17 feet under the Verona Island bridge at high water. Peary's boat, the *Roosevelt,* was built at Verona Island. Until 1932 all Route 1 traffic was ferried across the Penobscot from a point just above the Fort to the city of Bucksport. You can see the remains of the old landing on the Prospect side as you go by.

In continuing up the river, keep over to the paper-mill side and watch for the two cans, which may be nearly towed under in the current. The channel around Frankfort Flats is not difficult for small boats. Just follow the buoys. Keep out of Marsh River.

Winterport. The Winterport Marina and Boat Yard offers the only boating facilities on the river worthy of note. Hauling up to twenty tons, storage, stores, fuel, and ice are available. Moorings and floats are here. Bear in mind that this is the only place to fuel nearer than Castine. Bangor has no fueling facilities. The boat yard is owned by Lieutenant Commander Raymond E. Dillon, U.S.N. (Ret.), and he will personally tend to your wants.

Above Winterport you have left ocean water behind. You cannot see below the surface. The *Coast Pilot* has good directions from here to Bangor, Crosby Narrows is beautiful, as is the entire river.

Bangor. Land at the public floats just above the first bridge. The floats are small, crowded, inaccessible to sailing yachts, but with 8 feet off the face of the float at low water. Bangor has poor holding ground in the basin opposite the city. The river is dirty and smelly. The Bangor House is a famous establishment. There are many garages and shops. Bangor is the second-largest city in Maine and has many cultural advantages, but for the river traveller it leaves much to be desired in the way of accommodations.

The float is in a state of poor repair, with broken planks. There are no moorings worthy of the name. There are no facilities. On asking where to find the Harbor Master, the writer was told to ask a policeman, although it was the concensus that the Harbor Master lived in Brewer, across the river. It is indeed sad to find a neglected water front where once the sailing fleets of the world congregated. Even now, Bangor has a Power Squadron unit as well as the Coast Guard Auxiliary. The best thing on the float is the authoritative sign warning the guest to live up to regulations. Enough said!

Don't anchor in the river overnight. Pick up a mooring at Winterport. There is a mooring, sometimes available, at Gondola Cove, a mile or so below the Waldo-Hancock Bridge on the western shore. Tankers run the river at any stage of the tide and at any time of day or night. When they finish discharging, down the river they go. If, in an emergency, you have to anchor at night in the river, get over to the edge of the channel, and be certain that you have a darned bright anchor light. Not to care for these details is to invite certain disaster. In spite of this rather pessimistic account, the trip up the river is well worth taking. You will likely have a northerly in the morning and a southerly in the afternoon. George Wasson's *Sailing Days on the Penobscot* is required reading in these waters.

Notes on Western Penobscot Bay and the River

Tidal currents are strong, and when they are opposed to the wind, the bay can become "feather white" and the river choppy. The Western Bay is free of any obstructions away from the shores, making sailing here a beautiful experience. Whatever way the wind is, you can sail long courses without a change of course. Fogs are frequent in the mornings and sometimes last all day. Don't try sailing the river in a fog. Usually it scales up by mid-morning, but it is thick while it lasts. Half a dozen cruise schooners, the delight of camera fans, inhabit the bay. Where else can you find two or three old coasters, and the black trailing smoke of a steam tugboat?

West Penobscot Bay and the Penobscot River are good cruising grounds for those who like to go ashore frequently and want something to do when they get ashore. This whole area is becoming very boating-conscious. Youngs in Belfast is the best source of lobsters. Call them up and they will deliver. Lobster trap buoys are not the problem in this part of the bay that they are farther down the bay.

In approaching the river from Castine, stay well off the eastern shore to avoid an offshore half-tide boulder about halfway up from Castine to the entrance of the river. This shows on the chart.

The Penobscot River and Belfast Bay are scheduled to benefit from the anti-pollution program, and there is no doubt that in the foreseeable future this area of the coast will again come into its own as a cruising territory.

(Here Mr. Lewis's account ends.)

Castine, Me. (311). Commodore Saltonstall, in command of the expedition to take Castine from the British in 1778, referred to it as that "dam' tide hole" and refused to take his fleet in to attack the fort. While the tide runs no less hard today, the writer found no difficulty. The light on Dice's Head and the bell in the mouth of the river make the entrance clear enough.

Push up the Bagaduce beyond the Maine State Maritime Academy's vessel, formerly *Ancon,* command ship at the Normandy beachhead, to the hospitable wharf of the Castine Yacht Club east of the commercial wharves. Visitors are warmly welcomed. One may tie up here, telephone, shower, or walk uptown for supplies at Ken's Market or Macomber's Market. Do not lie at the float for more than one hour. Inquire of the sailing master for available moorings. If none is available, do not anchor in the river. It is deep, tide-scoured, and with poor holding ground. Cross over and lie behind Hospital Island, Holbrook Island, or in Smith Cove, as described below.

The next wharf west of the yacht club belongs to Alonzo Eaton and Sons. Mr. Eaton runs a small boat yard, builds "Castine Class" day sailors —beautifully constructed little sloops—can take care of any ordinary repairs, and sells gas, Diesel oil, and marine hardware. Mr. Eaton has long been recognized as a leading authority on Penobscot Bay. The next wharf west of Mr. Eaton's was formerly owned by Mr. Dennett but now is being rebuilt under new ownership with the intent of preserving the historical character of the Castine water front.

Between Dennett's and the town wharf (which provides only hourly, or, at most, overnight, dockages) you will see the remains of the Acadia Wharf, which burned in a disastrous fire in the autumn of 1970.

The Maine Maritime Academy ties up its vessel, *State of Maine* next to the town wharf. The vessel is open to inspection, and the recreation facilities of the academy—pool, ping-pong, and bowling—are open to the public every evening at a small fee. The academy trains officers for the

Merchant Marine, part of the curriculum consisting of a winter cruise on the vessel. The old buildings of the Castine Academy have been taken over by the new school.

Castine was a settlement of great importance in Colonial days, for it marked the western limit of French occupation, subject to raid and massacre by the British. Pemaquid was the British outpost, subject to reciprocal raid and massacre by the French. During the Revolution the British established a naval base at Castine. Commodore Saltonstall was sent with a fleet and army—the artillery under the command of Paul Revere—to reduce it. The British commander acted with resolution and energy, withdrawing into his fort, covering what vessels he had, and digging a canal across the neck to get his vessels out. But reenforcements came before the Americans made any serious attack, and the American fleet fled up the Penobscot River. By morning all were destroyed. Paul Revere, in a towering rage, walked back to Boston and demanded a courtmartial to clear his reputation. The story is told vividly in Esther Forbes's *Paul Revere and the World He Lived In*. Again during the Civil War, Castine was fortified and garrisoned, but no hostile Confederate action developed. The old British fort on the top of the hill has been restored. A number of earthworks around the shore have been cleaned up and labeled. There is a most interesting museum, to which any local resident can direct you.

Castine has both Roman Catholic and Protestant churches, the most distinguished architecturally being the Unitarian, with its Bulfinch tower, Paul Revere bell, and original box pews.

There is a fine Community Hospital ready to help in case of emergency.

Anchorages at Castine are all on the south side of the Bagaduce River:

Hospital Island. Smaller boats can lie close to the east of Hospital Island. This is near the town and pretty well out of the tide. This anchorage is newly congested with the considerable moored racing fleet of the Maine Maritime Academy.

Smith Cove. Big vessels and cruise schooners anchor in the mouth of Smith Cove, where 3 to 4 fathoms can be found more or less out of the tide.

Smith Cove, No. 2. A more interesting anchorage is at the head of Smith Cove close to the bold spruce-covered headland southeast of Sheep Island. This is the prettiest and best-protected anchorage in the neighborhood. Beware the middle ground of the cove, marked by a locally maintained red buoy on the southwest side of Lawrence Bay before you round Sheep Island, leaving it well to port on entering.

Holbrook Island. One of the finest harbors for a yacht to spend a night in is the gut to southward of Holbrook Island. This is a deep channel with bold water on either side. Sail in past Goose Falls on the south, once the site of one of the most famous tide mills on the Maine coast. Around the next point on the south, which is absolutely bold, is a deep cove that makes a perfect anchorage. If an attempt is made to go farther in, around (Ram) Island and out by Nautilus Rock, extreme caution should be used in locating the rock in the middle of the channel just beyond the anchorage.

A project has been undertaken to dam Goose Falls, drain Goose Pond behind it *via* a channel cut to the head of Weir Cove on the south side of Cape Rosier, and develop an open-pit copper mine in the bed of the pond. Samples have been taken assuring the developers that the ore is rich enough to make the project pay. Ore will be concentrated on the site and tailings dumped in the bay by barge. Concentrate will be trucked to refineries.

When the mine is exhausted, the water will be allowed to return again, and the scene can try to revert to a wild state. The life of the project is estimated as "five to ten years." Reclamation started in 1971.

Weir Cove, Cape Rosier, Me. (311). This is a quiet anchorage on an ordinary summer night, but it would be rough in a heavy southerly. In entering from the southwest, leave Buck Island to starboard, giving the mainland a generous berth. The chart does not show all the ledges here, but if you keep clear of shaded areas, you will be all right. After passing Buck Island, head straight up the cove and anchor just south of a small island with a house on it connected to the mainland by a footbridge.

There are several private floats on the west side of the cove. One may land at F.F. Clifford's float off his boarding house, Cedar Cottage. This is the only wharf on the west side and is just above the small island. From here it is a pleasant walk north on the road to a country store where ordinary groceries are available.

Weir Cove is usually a placid and unfrequented anchorage, but should the weather look ugly, go into Horseshoe Cove, Orcutt's Harbor, or Bucks Harbor.

Horseshoe Cove, Me. (311). This is an easy harbor to enter for the second time, but the writer got cold feet the first time he entered on finding himself rushing up a narrowing inlet studded with ledges before a smoky sou'wester with a green crew adorning the foredeck. However, it is such a good place when you are in and it is really so easy to make that it is well worth the few nervous moments you may have at the start. Seal Cove Boat Yard maintains aids to navigation in this cove.

The first marks at the entrance are Dog Island to port and a privately maintained beacon on a ledge making out south from Howard's Point, the eastern point of the cove. This is on station from June 1 to September 15, or later. Continue up the cove, favoring the eastern shore. Pass a wharf and float with several boats moored off it and continue up the eastern shore. Keep Eagle Island Light to the east of Dog Island. Near another clump of moorings you will see a red cask on an iron pole on the southern end of Cowpens Ledge. Pass between the beacon and the black spars, keeping away from the beacon and close to the spars. Run up the cove, parallel to the ledge, *keeping at least 75 yards west of it.* About halfway up the ledge there is a rock awash at low water, which extends somewhat to the westward. As you converge with the high shore to the west, you will see several moorings. All but the outer one belong to the Seal Cove Boat Yard. Take one of these and prepare to spend the night in quiet comfort. Nothing can touch you here, as has been amply demonstrated in recent hurricanes.

If you are in need of any sort of repair work to engine, hull, spars, or sails, row further up the cove to J.H. Vaughan's Seal Cove Boat Yard. He will gladly care for your needs. If no one is around, apply yourself to the "crank and cuss" telephone at the west end of the big shed. It connects with Mr. Vaughan's house. Despite the somewhat confused appearance of this yard, good work is done here.

Mr. Vaughan is an ingenious and enterprising man. He pioneered the strip-and-glue construction with Farnham Butler at Mt. Desert Yacht Yard and built at his own yard the prototype of the AC/26. He builds and sells the highly successful "Shark" cruiser, and has developed a basic hull design from a Carver's Harbor peapod. Leaving her double-ended on the waterline, he broadened her out above to hold her up under power and found her fast and able with a 15-hp outboard. Intrigued by the design, he drew out the lines to make a 26-foot hull adapted to inboard power. Any sort of variation, from lobster boat to cabin cruiser, is possible.

There is another 1½ miles of wild, unspoiled cove beyond the yard, with 2 feet of water as far as the "lower falls," which drop 4 feet to tide water at low tide but can be shot as rapids one-and-one-half hours before and one hour after the flood.

Take the dinghy, with oars or outboard, and run up the creek about one and one-half hours before flood. You will have an utterly wild 2-mile

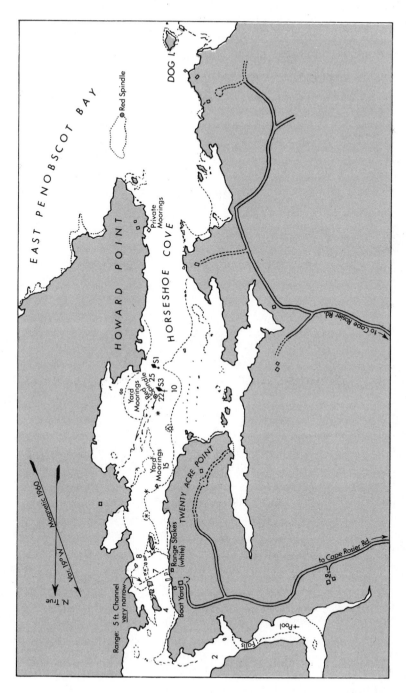

Principal aids and obstructions, Horseshoe Cove, E. Penobscot Bay, Maine. From air photo, 1" to 400'. Note: observe channel marks. It is not recommended to go beyond 15 ft. anchorage without local pilot except in tender.

prowl between clean granite shores with the trees almost overhead, and the fun of shooting small rapids. Have a warm swim on the rocks of the little lake at the head. Then follow the tide out about an hour after flood.

Orcutt Harbor, Me. (311). This harbor between Bucks Harbor and Horseshoe Cove is not as snug as either of its neighbors but is a quiet and attractive anchorage. It would be well for the stranger to move carefully in here. The upper part of the harbor is studded with ledges.

There are three small boat yards here. All three do hauling, storage, and maintenance work. Steve Bridges is renowned locally as a mechanic and is equipped to do welding. Robert and Gordon Condon build small boats, both sail and power. The third yard, Gerald Gray's, is primarily hauling and storage.

It is a short walk from this attractive anchorage to the four corners at South Brooksville where most supplies can be purchased.

Note on Sequence of Harbors

Having proceeded up the west side of Penobscot Bay and ascended the River to Bangor, we now continue down the Western Bay, dealing with the anchorages on North Haven and Vinalhaven Islands and going off to Matinicus. We then work up the Eastern Bay, describing Isle au Haut, Deer Isle, and Eggemoggin Reach.

Barred Island, Me. (310). There is a quiet and snug anchorage in the midst of the archipelago between Butter and Great Sprucehead islands. Enter from the northwest, passing between the high peak of the northernmost island and a privately maintained beacon off a ledge on the southern side of the entrance. Follow the shore of the peaked island, giving it 150 yards berth, and swing to starboard, keeping about halfway between the big island to port and the smaller one to starboard. Ledges make out from both islands, and there is a 5-foot spot to be avoided. This is usually well marked with lobster buoys. Proceed with care and keep a good eye out for bottom.

Once up to the middle of the big island, you are in about 3 fathoms, with mud, clay, and gravel bottom. Anchor anywhere short of the bar.

The big island is inhabited in summer by the Schauffler family. Their house is on the southern end of the island but out of sight of the anchorage. They are glad to have you explore the island but are justly concerned about fire. Light no fires ashore and do not smoke in the woods.

Great Sprucehead Island, Me. (310). This island is owned by the Porter family and is the source of many of Eliot K. Porter's magnificent photographs in *Summer Island,* published by the Sierra Club. There is fair anchorage off the Porter's float, but of course the island is private property and one should not land without permission.

Butter Island, Me. (310). There is an anchorage off the beach on the north side of the island, but be sure your anchor is well set. There have been reports of weed and kelp on the bottom.

The beach is quite smooth for a Maine beach, and the water temperate if not warm. It is a short climb to the grassy peak of the island, which affords a grand view of Upper Penobscot Bay.

There used to be a town, Dirigo, on Butter Island, with a post office, summer hotel, and other evidences of civilization. Gradually it shrunk and at length was abandoned, and one winter the whole village was removed. Only cellar holes remain.

The western slope of the island may still abound with wild raspberries in late July. Don't go for them in short pants. If you hear a boiling sound near your feet, run as fast as you can for the shore. Yellow jackets in defense of hearth and household gods show no mercy. Butter Island, like others in Penobscot Bay, is privately owned. The owner is glad to have cruising men visit it but requests that they build no fires and leave it cleaner than they found it.

Pulpit Harbor, Me. (310). This harbor is one of the best and one of the most popular on the coast. The principal difficulty is finding it. There is no buoy outside. To one running north off the shore of North Haven in the late afternoon, it is almost invisible, especially toward low water. Before you get to Egg Rock and after you pass a prominent point with a cove behind it, look carefully along the shore. Pulpit Rock is a large boulder on the northern end of a ledge running apparently parallel to the shore. Just beyond it, to the north, is a red barn with white trim and a little beyond that a huge yellow mansion high on the hill. If you get that far, stand inshore and start working back to the south. Going this way there is no problem, because the ledge on which Pulpit Rock stands is not parallel to the shore but makes off to the north. Follow the shore and you will soon find yourself inside, wondering how you could ever have missed that tremendous Pulpit Rock.

Inside there is a large harbor with several small coves making off it. The first one on the south side just inside the entrance is Minister's Creek, sometimes called Cabot's Cove. The Cabots own both shores and

View from Pulpit Harbor looking west beyond Pulpit Rock to West Penobscot Bay and Mt. Megunticook. The dot over the vessel is an osprey from the nest on the Rock.

keep their fleet here. The cove is narrow, hence swinging room is restricted. However, in a heavy westerly or southerly it is very well protected.

Most yachts anchor in the mouth of the cove making up to the northeast. There is plenty of room here, perfectly good protection, and a landing with public telephone. In approaching this anchorage, keep well away from the north shore, especially the point fringed with birch trees and occupied by a large summer house. There are no guest moorings for visitors.

There are no stores at Pulpit Harbor and no gasoline or water hoses. However, it is a pleasant forty-five-minute walk through beautiful Maine country to the village of North Haven, where you can buy all you can carry back. In an emergency one could telephone from the landing to Waterman's store in North Haven or to Brown's boat yard.

There may be an osprey's nest on Pulpit Rock again this year. For many years it was occupied, some say for 300 years, although old inhabitants deny it. If the ospreys have been induced to return, do not land on the rock or molest them in any way.

The view of the Camden Hills from Pulpit Harbor against a calm summer sunset is one of the memories that will last long after the color photos are faded and torn. In that presence you can turn to your shipmates and say truly, "We have arrived."

Fox Islands Thorofare, Me. (235, 310). This passage between North Haven and Vinalhaven Island is not difficult to navigate and has numerous quiet anchorages. The entrance is marked by a square stone monument on Fiddler Ledge off Stand-in Point. This is a prominent mark indeed.

In the fog the bell and gong outside the Thorofare make it an easy entrance to find. Set your course to pass between the buoys and you will surely make one or the other. But beware of heavy traffic here. One August morning the writer encountered a lobster boat, a sloop, and a big motor sailer all making the bell simultaneously in peasoup fog. Sardine carriers use the Thorofare extensively because it is the shortest route from the westward to the sardine factories at Stonington, Southwest Harbor, Jonesport, and Lubec. These are fast, heavy vessels, often powered with high-speed Diesels that are very noisy. Their cargoes are highly perishable, and they navigate by clock and compass. Despite rules of the road and radar, when you hear one coming, make as much noise as possible and give her all the room you can.

After passing the Fiddler, run in for Brown's Head Light. Although this is conspicuously white against the green hillside behind it, in the fog it is hard to find, as the sound of the horn does not carry well to windward. Run by the spectacular Sugar Loaves and keep up the middle of the Thorofare, checking buoy and beacon as you pass.

Although you can anchor under the shore almost anywhere in the Thorofare, the best anchorages are east of the town. The first is Perry Cove, a snug little cove making westward out of Seal Harbor. This is a quiet spot and likely to remain so, as the surrounding shores are privately owned. Seal Cove is good as long as you keep out of the deep hole in the middle and avoid the shoal and rocky west shore above Perry Cove. Waterman Cove north of Iron Point is well protected, and the head of Carver Cove behind Widow Island is as quiet an anchorage as one could desire. At none of these places are there public landings or any shore facilities at all.

On many trips through this passage the writer has noticed that the fog seldom shuts in north of Calderwood Neck. Bound west from Deer Island Thorofare or Isle au Haut, you will almost always get a scale-up under this shore.

Notice Goose Rock Light, one of Maine's most picturesque.

North Haven, Me. (235, 310). This anchorage on the north side of the Thorofare is a convenient place to stop as it is directly on the route east and west. Anchor anywhere off the town and clear of the steamer wharf, easily identified by a small house high in the air over the slip.

The yacht club on the second wharf west of the steamer wharf has maintained guest moorings in the past marked with orange buoys. One may land at the club wharf, but remember that the buildings along the shore side of the wharf are private residences. East of the steamer wharf are the landings for Waterman's general store and Brown's boat yard. Gas and water are available here. The post office is across the street. To the east along the main road is a community building in which there are often movies or dances during the summer. In the basement is a snack shop.

When your shopping is finished, it is well to move along to one of the anchorages mentioned previously and leave the North Haven fleet to roll in the wash of skylarking outboards and passing sardiners.

A story is told of a distinguished Harvard professor, long a summer resident of North Haven. Two fishermen were watching him sail in a small boat in the Thorofare. The professor was having a good deal of trouble keeping clear of anchored yachts. Said one to the other, "Old Professor —— *knows* an awful lot, but he don't *re-al-ize* nothin'."

The sign on the shore advising of the presence of a water pipe crossing the Thorofare should be taken literally. The writer anchored in a state of excitement one day and fouled it. Gentle twitching, brute strength, and deep diving failed to dislodge the anchor. A passing fisherman tried his hand with no better success. Finally exercising a "kill or cure or break the water pipe" philosophy, he let out the entire scope of the line and calling on every ounce of horsepower his boat possessed, described huge circles around the anchor at high speed. Just before we got seasick from our own wash, the anchor broke the surface. We hastily gathered in the line and departed, leaving the pipe intact, I am told.

This pipe was laid under unusual circumstances. The residents on the south side of the Thorofare live too far from Vinalhaven to be on town water. In dry summers, they eyed the North Haven standpipe with longing. At last, money was raised to lay a water pipe under the Thorofare. Several mainland contractors and one North Haven resident bid on the job. The latter's bid was much the lowest. The committee raised grave doubts as to whether the job could be done at the bid price, and asked the local man how he proposed to do it so much more cheaply than experienced contractors who owned barges, derricks, and heavy equipment. He refused to tell, but the contract was awarded him, as it appeared that he knew what he was doing.

During the winter he laid the pipe across the Thorofare on the ice and made up the connections. Then he sawed a trench in the ice and lowered the pipe safely to the bottom.

One of the hardest tasks for the yachtsman coming from the west, unable to go farther east than North Haven, is to turn back at that point. To the east and north of North Haven lies the eastern Paradise: Isle au Haut, Eggemoggin Reach, Blue Hill Bay, and the waters about Mt. Desert. Not until he has pushed the prow of his boat to the head of Somes Sound or dropped anchor in Northeast Harbor can any yachtsman say he has seen the best of the coast of Maine. But West Penobscot Bay is a good start, and will only increase his determination to return down east another year.

Vinalhaven Island, Me. (310). This large island is so cut up with inlets, channels, and ponds, that one is seldom more than a short distance from the water. Vinalhaven was settled before the Revolution and has had an eventful history involving lumber, fish, and granite, with occasional excursions into privateering. This story is told in *Fish Scales and Stone Chips,* by Sidney L. Winslow. The chapters on the granite boom are most interesting. The pillars for the Cathedral of St. John the Divine in New York were quarried in Vinalhaven. It was intended that each pillar should be cut from one piece of granite. After three had broken on the lathe or in transport, the idea was abandoned and the pillars were made in sections. But the broken pieces of the huge monoliths still lie in a Vinalhaven quarry. The old granite quarries on Hurricane Island are conspicuous. Fifty years ago a thousand men were working in them, and it was a wild place; Hurricane Island granite was known everywhere. The waters around Vinalhaven abound in unusual tales, too.

The full-rigged ship *Hualco,* 1086 tons, had been launched in Belfast in 1856, just as the 1857 depression was coming on. She lay at anchor in Belfast harbor for six months, unable to get a charter. Then she sailed, ostensibly for New Orleans, but no one knew her business. She was heavily insured.

She sailed from Belfast one morning, and ran down the Eastern Bay with all sail set before a northwest breeze. Approaching Saddleback Shoal, the story goes, the helmsman, a young fellow who had just been fishing off Saddleback, protested to the Captain. "You are heading right for Saddleback Shoal, Captain!" "Mind your business, damn you, and I'll mind mine!" roared the Captain, who evidently had an insurance job to do.

The *Hualco* struck the needlepoint of Saddleback Shoal going about 8 knots, knocked her bottom out, went over the shoal, and sank in twenty minutes in deep water. Within half an hour the crew, all natives of Belfast, were in the longboat heading for home, and the ship had disappeared.

More recently the mail boat from Rockland to Vinalhaven was lost. One February day in 1946 she left Vinalhaven for Rockland. Apparently her forward hatches were not tightly secured, for when a heavy northwest squall struck, she took water over the bow and filled her foc'sle and forehold. Down by the bow, she could not be steered; and as the squall developed into a full gale, she filled and sank, leaving three men adrift on a raft in subzero cold. They made Leadbetter's Island at last and attracted the attention of people on Vinalhaven and so were rescued.

Little do we realize as we run up the bay before a 20-knot southwester what double the velocity and winter cold can do to Penobscot Bay. Every winter Maine men are lost at sea.

Vinalhaven is a week's cruise in itself. Hoping not to dim the joy of such a cruise, the editor lists a few shelters on Vinalhaven. Let us start from the western end of Fox Islands Thorofare and circumnavigate the island.

Crockett's Cove. A possible anchorage on the way into Fox Islands Thorofare is in Crockett's Cove, just eastward of Crockett's Point, the southeastern point at the entrance of the Thorofare on Vinalhaven Island. A mooring is occasionally available. There is 6 feet of water at the float at low tide.

The following advice is taken from the yearbook of the Cruising Club of America:

> Stand for the end of Crockett's Point with North Haven Monument (square stone beacon off Crabtree Point) astern. Keep a distance of about 100 feet off Crockett's Point and head for a small red house on the opposite side of the cove until the center of the cove is opened, then head straight up the center until abeam of the float on the port hand. Least depth entering: 18 feet at low water. There is excellent holding ground.

The nearest supplies are at North Haven, 3½ miles away. There is no telephone connection at the cove.

The Basin. This is a dramatic spot and well worth a visit. But anchor outside. All correspondents and advisers with whom the writer has talked warn against going inside. A large proportion of yachts trying this passage fail to make it successfully.

Cedar Island. There is a snug little anchorage between Cedar and Lairey's islands. Enter from the south and proceed cautiously. The writer found Irving Johnson's old *Yankee* in here once, but another time he found bottom startlingly close. Lairey's Island is clean, smooth, white granite and affords what Samuel Johnson in his *Journey to the Hebrides* called "wild and noble prospects."

Hurricane Island. This account of the Outward Bound School was contributed by Mr. Peter O. Willauer, the director.

The island, formerly the scene of a profitable granite quarry, is now the site of the Hurricane Island Outward Bound School.

The first Outward Bound School was established at Aberdovey in Wales in 1941 to help reduce the alarming loss of young British sailors on merchant ships following sinkings by German U boats. Lawrence Holt, head of the Blue Funnel Line, had noted that while younger and physically better-equipped men succumbed, the older and more experienced officers survived. He reasoned that success in meeting severe challenge depends more on attitude than on physical prowess. He turned to Dr. Kurt Hahn, headmaster and founder of the Gordonstoun School, who had succeeded in putting physical challenge into his curriculum as a means of developing character in his students. Together, Mr. Holt and Dr. Hahn organized the first four-week course for young seamen, "Outward Bound," for the fleet and for life. The Aberdovey Sea School more than fulfilled the hopes of its founders in developing an individual's initiative, resourcefulness, and individuality. It was apparent by the end of the war that supervised exposure to a series of testing and hostile situations was indeed a successful approach to the difficult transition from youth to manhood. The idea spread rapidly and there are now twenty-nine Outward Bound Schools throughout the world, including six in the United States, the one at Hurricane Island being the first Outward Bound Sea School in the Western Hemisphere.

In the standard courses run consecutively from May through October, over one hundred young men, aged sixteen and one-half through twenty-three, are exposed to increasingly severe challenges for twenty-six days at Hurricane Island. Half are on full scholarship, assuring a variety of cultural and economic backgrounds. The students are divided into watches of twelve, each with two instructors: a senior watch officer and his assistant. The watch officers are men who know themselves and understand youth and must be skilled in the variety of activities at the school. The watch officers are assisted by specialists in seamanship and navigation, ecology, rock climbing, fire fighting, first aid, and drownproofing. This latter is a sub-surface floating and bobbing-for-air technique that enables a man to stay afloat almost indefinitely. The specialists in these various techniques are men of extraordinary experience that assures a high standard of instruction and safety.

The Hurricane Island program is not limited to young men. Courses, varying somewhat in length and design to accommodate the specific group, are offered for girls and adult men and women, school administrators, graduate and undergraduate students (with credit available), and community and youth workers, to name a few. During the 1971 season, over 168 adults climbed, sailed, and ran along with their juniors.

One of the most important components of an Outward Bound School is its Rescue Services. There is always a watch of twelve students on duty at the island. They monitor the Citizen's Band Radio (KEK-2392 channels, four during the day and eleven at night), 2182 on radiotelephone, and are also in telephone communication with the Coast Guard and the hospital in Rockland. The school is well equipped to perform search and rescue services in the Penobscot Bay area as well as fire-fighting aid and emergency medical care. Three power boats (*MV Hurricane, Reliance, and Vigilant*) are completely outfitted with radar, radiotelephone, C.B. radio, fire-fighting equipment, diving gear, and first aid materials. A doctor is usually in residence on the island.

The school also has fourteen 30-foot, open, ketch-rigged whaleboats. These wooden strip-built craft are light enough and long enough to be rowed by twelve men, but also go well to windward under sail. Early training includes a capsizing and righting drill, and the whaleboats, full of water and with twelve men on board, still have 6 inches of freeboard due to the 32 cubic feet of styrofoam flotation. Basic instruction in these boats emphasizes navigation, sail-handling, and above all, safety. The instructors are on board during the training cruises, but by the final expedition the students handle the whaleboats alone. They take long cruises under a variety of conditions including fog and night running, and you may see them as far east as Cutler. All water-borne activities are patrolled by one of the school's three power boats, and the many hours spent on the water in training for group independence afloat provide plenty of action for the Duty Watch's Search and Rescue Unit.

About halfway through the course and after several ecology lessons, the students are each placed on an individual uninhabited island for four days and three nights. Equipped with a line and hook, sleeping bag, eight matches, a 9-foot square plastic sheet, an Hibachi stove fashioned from a #10 can, a first aid kit, two quarts of water, a knife, and a journal, every student has his hours of self-appraisal, of seeing himself in unique perspective. With a little ingenuity, one can eat well on the Maine islands, but who has ever been really alone for three days? The solo is a test of the mind and the spirit, of each individual against himself and against the raw components of his environment. If you come across one of these students on solo, he would prefer to be left alone!

By all means pick up the guest mooring off the old granite wharf next to the large mess hall on the east side of the island, or anchor, being careful to avoid the half-tide ledges just east of the anchorage. A member of the Duty Watch is available at the Rescue Station on the main pier to show visitors around.

(Here Mr. Willauer's account ends.)

A local authority claims that the ball bearing was invented on Hurricane Island. A derrick was being built to handle heavy blocks of granite. The boom had to turn in order to swing the blocks off the wharf to the holds of vessels alongside. The ingenious foreman had the plate at the base of the derrick grooved to form a raceway, set several iron cannon balls in the groove, clapped a similar plate on top, and erected the spar on the upper plate. When the cannon balls were well slushed with grease, the derrick operated with great ease and precision.

There is much abandoned and rusted machinery on the island, including the remains of huge stationary steam engines. There is also considerable beautifully fashioned cut stone abandoned near the wharf. The scenery is magnificent, and the view from the cliff overlooking the southern end of the island is particularly superb. Should you want a good idea of what Hurricane Island must have been like when the quarries were running, read Ruth Moore's *Speak to the Winds*.

Old Harbor, Me. (310). This cove behind Green Island affords little protection from the south and has a rocky bottom. There is a lobster shipping plant here that holds lobsters in great wooden tanks with a carefully controlled water supply. The lobsters are shipped in crates in refrigerated trucks to Boston and points west.

Carvers Harbor, Me. (332). When anyone says he is going to Vinalhaven, he usually means Carvers Harbor. It is one of the few places on the coast, like Cape Porpoise and New Harbor, where commercial fishing has not been eclipsed by tourism.

The waters to the southwest, south, and southeast of Carvers Harbor are extremely dangerous. The tide runs swiftly between rugged and unmarked ledges and the whole area is wide open to the sweep of the North Atlantic. If one gets ashore in this area, one might well lose his boat.

However, the entrance to Vinalhaven is well marked. Note the white sector in Heron Neck Light, which leads one by James and Willies Ledge. The lighthouse has a powerful horn replacing the former siren. But even the horn is reported unreliable at certain spots. Use great caution in approaching it in thick fog. Once inside the cordon of ledges, follow Heron Neck and Green Island around to the east, pass between Folly Rocks and Green Island, and run up the harbor by the lighted beacon on Green Ledge.

From Deer Island Thorofare or anywhere up East Penobscot Bay, first make Triangle Ledge. This is not always easy, especially in the afternoon with the sun in your eyes. The buoy appears to be very small indeed and seems a long way off shore. Then simply follow the string of nuns around to the south and southwest by Point Ledge beacon and in to Green Ledge light. Against the very considerable tidal current, this can be a slow process, especially in the late afternoon.

In clear weather there is no very serious problem, but a boat without power in the fog can have a miserable time out there where no buoy has any noise-making machinery and the tide runs very hard.

From the southeast one would make Saddleback Ledge, and leave Diamond Rock to port. It is a very large rock standing well above high water. Then pass between nun 2 and Carvers Island and leave nun 4,

Augustus D. Phillips

Carvers Harbor, Vinalhaven. Winter Harbor, East Penobscot Bay, Deer Island Thorofare, and Blue Hill are visible at the top of the picture.

Point Ledge, and Green Island Ledge to starboard. This is extremely perilous in the fog.

Inside Green Ledge the channel is clearly marked. Be sure to give nun 4 a good berth to avoid the half-tide rock between it and Green Ledge. Round Potato Island and anchor in the cove to the east and opposite the wharves in the town.

The main street of the town, with post office, restaurants, stores, and a movie house with street telephone opposite, runs around the head of the harbor. Just west of the Williams Yard is the town landing, with a large parking area. A channel with 6 feet at low tide has been dredged to this point.

Along the main street to the west is the Gulf Wharf, operated by James L. Calderwood, who sells gasoline, water, and Diesel fuel. Ice can be had at Bickford's Fish Wharf. There is a boat yard run by Quinn and Hopkins farther up the harbor, which can haul and repair most yachts. The Islander, close to the main street, provides rooms and excellent meals. A few houses take "roomers."

Recently a visiting yachtsman at Carvers Harbor remarked to one of the fishermen in the harbor that the noise of the electric plant seemed a bit annoying. The reply was, "It's damned annoying when you don't hear it."

There is no yacht club at Carvers Harbor and no provision for tying up boats for any length of time. The business of Vinalhaven is lobsters and fish. If you obstruct a wharf any longer than necessary, you may become unpopular.

If one has any leisure time at Carvers Harbor, one should walk up the hill to the standpipe. It is possible to climb the ladder of this tank (keeping on the inside of the ladder) and on a clear day obtain a splendid view around the southern and western horizon from Isle au Haut to the Camden Hills. The top of the tank is reported to be open, so be careful!

For many years Vinalhaven derived much prosperity from the many granite quarries in the neighborhood. This stone was shipped in barges to Boston, New York, and Philadelphia. Much of it was for paving blocks in New York, but it had other uses. The huge pillars on three sides of the altar of the choir of the Cathedral of St. John the Divine in New York, each more than 54 feet in height and weighing approximately 120 tons, came from Vinalhaven. Likewise, the massive stone eagles adorning the post office in Buffalo, the granite of the State Capitol in Albany, Grant's Tomb, the Philadelphia Mint, and several large government buildings in Washington and Annapolis all came from Vinalhaven. One could spend an interesting day roaming over the quarries of this section, especially on nearby Hurricane Island.

On the main street at Vinalhaven is a granite eagle said to have adorned Pennsylvania Station in New York. The local resident who discussed it with me was very doubtful that it had come from Vinalhaven in the first place. A dedication ceremony was to have been held on Labor Day 1966. The same resident doubted that the ceremony would be unduly crowded. The eagle is unquestionably a most evil-tempered fowl who is determined to take no backwash. He fiercely turns his back on the harbor to face the monoxide fumes to which he is accustomed.

About a mile and a half from the harbor is an air strip with air taxi service to Rockland, where one can connect with planes to Boston and Bar Harbor.

A new community hospital has been established in Vinalhaven. Medical help is quickly available here through the clinic.

Now Vinalhaven is a fish town. The people who live here are busy catching, selling, packing, and shipping fish as well as building fishing boats. Like New Harbor, this is a modern, unspoiled Maine town. It has not gone to sleep on its memories of the 1880s, but its people are vigorously making a living with the best facilities our century has to offer. The big, comfortable, able boats are powered with the best and most reliable engines. They have power winches, fathometers, radio direction finders, and short wave radios. Their owners are alert, intelligent, energetic people, untouched by the sometimes patronizing attitude of summer visitors.

There are two active fish wharves at Vinalhaven. In the one next to Calderwood's, Burnham & Morrill, fish is processed and sent to Machias, where it is canned as fish flakes. At Bickford's, herring are frozen in very cold brine and shipped frozen to the West Coast, where they are used very successfully as tuna bait. The frozen herring are most lifelike and stay on the hook without falling apart.

The eastern shore of Vinalhaven is a paradise for the skipper who likes to explore the unfrequented rocky points, coves, and islands of Maine. From Sheep Island north to Coombs Hill the coast is broken and studded with ledges. Move very cautiously in here. The 1965 *Coast Pilot* says on page 95, "Arey Cove and Roberts Harbor are much obstructed by rocks and ledges, and are unsafe for strangers."

The islands to the southeast of Vinalhaven are generally grassy with few, if any, trees. The rocks are black and sharp and the whole area is full of unmarked ledges. The tide runs hard. However, on a clear day some of the islands are very dramatic places to visit.

Vinalhaven Island, Eastern Side

On the eastern side of Vinalhaven is an amazing body of inland water, just inside Coombs Hill and Bluff Head. One entrance is between Hen

Islands and Penobscot Island. Favor the Hen Islands shore in order to avoid the ledges in the middle of the passage which are submerged at high tide. The other entrance is between Bluff Head and the Hen Islands. Bluff Head is bold except for a ledge on its northwest corner which is usually visible. To enter this way, it is necessary to steer very close to the Bluff Head shore, particularly near the southern end of Bluff Head Island, in order to avoid a long ledge which runs out southeasterly from the Hen Islands.

Winter Harbor. Continue up the harbor with a close eye on the chart and a good hand on the foredeck. Contrary to an earlier edition of this work, the 2-foot spot most assuredly *does* exist, as does also another ledge, unmarked on the chart, where the water appears deepest between the 2-foot spot and the ledge to the southeast, bare at low water.

The adventurous cruiser can sneak into the little cove south of Starboard Rock. This offers good holding ground and perfect protection. However, it is a good idea to explore in the dinghy before entering. A little stream runs into this cove, and between the tide and the current from the stream the mud bars shift from time to time.

In the writer's opinion (his boat draws 5½ feet) the following letter suggests a chancy but most interesting adventure:

1. From Starboard Rock follow close along northern shore. Give point at creek moderate berth. Bear toward islet west of creek.

2. From islet, southwesterly, leaving mid-channel ledge *close* to port.

3. From high point of ledge, west by south, favoring southerly side of channel.

4. From NW point of Long Island head for bridge on Calderwood Neck until quarry derrick passes out of sight.

5. Turn gradually to port passing between ledge and point where chart shows 15 feet.

6. Run WSW ½ W for high ledge off cove on starboard hand (in direction of derrick). Leave ledge close to starboard.

7. Veer to mid-channel and anchor SSW of ledge where chart shows 10 feet.

8. Pass north of old weir, holding to mid-channel. Anchor between old weir and old quarry derrick.

The section in this *Guide* on Fox Islands Thorofare deals with shelters between Calderwood's Neck and Brown's Head.

We now take the reader offshore to the Green Islands and Matinicus.

Green Islands, Me. (322). These two low, grassy islands lie east of Metinic and south of the Northern Triangles. Little Green, the westernmost of the two, appears to be uninhabited, although there are a few shacks on it. Large Green has a cove on the northern side with several large winter moorings described as "piles" on the chart. Pass a line to one. On any day you might be likely to visit, the mooring should hold you.

Residents of the island are lobstermen who come out from Sprucehead or Rockland for the summer's fishing. Unfortunately, some visitors to the island have wantonly damaged houses and fishing gear. You may get a cool reception, but it is important to stop in at one of the houses and make clear your purposes before exploring around.

The middle of the island is grass, eaten quite smooth by sheep. All around the shore is a windrow of driftwood composed of odd boards, pulpwood, and the drifting detritus of modern civilization. In among it all, though, you may find a treasure.

The island is a nesting place for gulls, terns, petrels, and other sea birds. Be careful not to disturb them or tread on their eggs.

There isn't much on Green Island; and in the fog, the whole area is very dangerous, with the perils badly marked. However, on a warm summer day it is a pleasant place from which to contemplate the Camden Hills.

It is a short run to Matinicus or Home Harbor for the night.

Matinicus, Me. (322). The islands in this group are well worth a special trip, but the region should be approached with caution. There are no really snug harbors, supplies are limited, unmarked dangers are frequent, and tides are swift. In fog or storm the careless or inexperienced can get into real trouble.

Matinicus is low and cannot be seen from the deck of a small boat at 10 miles. Just set your course from Vinalhaven, Two Bush, or Isle au Haut and you will raise the islands.

In clear weather there is little difficulty in making Matinicus from the north. From Bay Ledge Whistle or the black-and-white bell south of it, leave the can on Zephyr Rock well to starboard to clear Zephyr Ledges. Leave No Mans Land to starboard and head for West Black Ledge until you are past the Barrel. This is a high rock and breaks except in the very quietest weather at high water. Give the red-and-black bell on Harbor Ledge a good berth and run in north of Wheaton Island.

In thick weather the job is not so easy. The tide runs about NNW on the flood around No Mans Land and SSE on the ebb. Further north, it runs more NW and SE. A shoal-draft boat on a quiet day can make the lighted bell 5 MI north of Matinicus, pass between Two Bush Island and

Matinicus, run off to Two Bush Ledge, leave Beach Ledges nun to star-board, and follow the shore in. In a larger boat or in rough weather, from bell 5 MI pass *close* northward of No Mans Land, run up toward the Barrel until you hear it break, and then make the bell and run in. The ledges to the east of the island stand up quite prominently at low water and break heavily. They are easy to hear in the fog and in most cases are quite bold. The radio beacon on Matinicus Rock may be some help too. Nevertheless, it is wild country in bad weather. The cautious mariner will pick his chance to visit these dramatic islands.

Inside Wheaton Island you will find the inner harbor to starboard be-hind the breakwater. This is a shallow cove obstructed by a big ledge, and it is crowded with local craft. The only place for a visitor is to port in the cove between Wheaton Island and Matinicus. You may be able to find a vacant mooring in here by inquiring of one of the fishermen, but don't just pick one up and go ashore. Seiners often use Matinicus for a base and come and go at all hours of the day and night. They are big ves-sels up to 75 or 80 feet long that take a lot of swinging room, and their crews may be understandably impatient at two in the morning.

The many lobster boats that appear to be moored on short scope at the head (SW part) of the cove under Wheaton Island are actually made fast to two heavy cables that run right across the cove. These cables do not lie right on the bottom and could prove very embarrassing in anchoring or weighing. Anchor, then, to the north of the lobster boats. A trip line is a wise precaution, as the bottom is rocky.

Do not count on buying gas here except in an emergency. It has to be carried off in cans.

Row up the inner harbor and land at the stone wharf. You will have to climb a ladder, for there is no float. At the head of the wharf are the post office and a telephone booth, which connects with Rockland *via* micro-wave radio. The store is just beyond the post office, a pleasant general store that carries almost everything anyone in an island town might re-quire.

It is a pleasant walk up the dirt road beyond the store to the top of the island. The western and southern shores are bleak and stony beaches backed by grass, scrub, and wild rosebushes. There are a few summer cot-tages along the shore. From the north end of the island on a clear day the view of the outlying islands of Penobscot Bay backed by the Camden Hills is well worth the walk.

Matinicus in many ways is the most interesting island on the Maine Coast. Its population of one hundred, engaged in fishing and lobstering, is of the highest quality; its well-kept wharves and fish houses, its large and handsome boats, all speak of high standards. The water front in the harbor is most picturesque, with ancient wharves, fish houses, and fishing gear strewn about in apparent confusion but actual efficiency. A native of Matinicus is proud of his island's history, a longer history than that of any community on the mainland. John Smith sent fishing schooners to Matinicus from Jamestown in Virginia.

On the island today there are a church and a school over one hundred years old, for children from grades one through eight. During a recent winter, the teacher went on strike to protest what he felt to be outrageous conditions for learning in the schoolhouse. The Department of Eduation in Augusta sent out another teacher. There was a brief confrontation before the building. The striking teacher asked, "Are you going to cross my picket line?" The strikebreaker replied in the affirmative, went in and rang the bell, and school recommenced. It was a scale model of similar confrontations in New York, Boston, and other large systems.

Matinicus, like many isolated communities, is undergoing profound changes caused by the pressures of the rest of the world. At least 60 percent of the island is now owned by summer people. Cottages are springing up. A generating plant provides electricity for the island, and telephone service is clear and regular. Prices of food and supplies from ashore keep going up. Lobster prices don't keep up with them. The herring have not been plentiful. The inshore fishing grounds, where trawling and handlining used to be profitable, are nearly fished out and are infested with dogfish. Foreign imports depress fish and lobster prices. Young people are leaving the island, first to go to high school and then to find careers ashore. This writer, in talking with a few residents, felt a sense of desperation, an unusual desire to close ranks against the outside. For instance, there is no float. The mail boat, when it comes at low water, must land passengers on the beach from a dory. Gas is difficult to buy. The fishermen-owners of shore property on the harbor are holding it tightly, refusing to admit outsiders lest the familiar scene be changed.

Of course every inhabitant of the island cannot be thus categorized, and many of the people we met were most hospitable and helpful. Yet here is an island town with its own fragile atmosphere and character, unable to resist the pressure of a pragmatic machine age. Unlike Cuttyhunk, Matinicus is not recognized and appreciated for this, and the inevitable is happening too rapidly.

Still, to the cruising man, Matinicus is unique. The fog sifts through the spruce trees, the dark weed swings in the tide, the distant surf on the ledges underlies every sound. The gentle motion in the harbor is never quite lost. Especially at night you feel you are far offshore, just on the edge of a life beyond your own.

Criehaven, Ragged Island, Me. (322). The anchorage behind the breakwater on the northwest side of the island is small and shoal and should not be attempted except in reasonably settled weather. If caught in a northwester, go over to Matinicus or around Ragged Island to Seal Cove.

Approach to the harbor at Criehaven is not difficult with the nun on Harbor Ledge and the light on the breakwater. Harbor Ledge usually breaks and should be located by the careful navigator. It appears from the chart that a direct course from the nun to the light will lead unduly close to the ledge.

Enter cautiously and anchor or lie alongside a lobster boat temporarily. Go ashore and inquire for a mooring. Picking one up at random is a little dangerous because the buoys are just like lobster buoys. If you can't get a mooring, anchor in about 2 fathoms just inside the breakwater. The best water appears to be on the northern side of the harbor. The water is very clear, so you will surely see bottom before you hit anything.

Criehaven used to be a year-round town busy with lobstering, trawling, and handlining. There was a church, as well as a school, a store, a post office, a lobster buyer who sold gas and marine supplies, and daily communication with Rockland in the summer *via* mail boat. Now the island is inhabited only in summer by lobstermen from Rockland, who go to Matinicus for supplies. None of the above-named symbols of civilization are apparent. Much of the southern part of the island has been bought up by outsiders who wish to keep it in its present state.

Walk across the narrow isthmus to Camp Cove and follow the trail down the eastern part of the island. It is badly overgrown and you may get lost, but you can't be very seriously lost. You can hear the surf on the shore from anywhere on the island. The southern end is a bare heath with a view south, east, and west to unbroken horizon, notched only by the twin towers of Matinicus Rock.

Ragged Island was called Racketash by the Indians. White men mispronounced it "Ragged Arse," and so it was called for years. Our respectable government, unwilling to print such words on a chart, now labels it Ragged Island.

Matinicus Rock, Me. (322). The short trip from Matinicus or Criehaven to the rock on a calm day is well worth the time. There is a heavy mooring on the western side and a skidway on which to land. However, if there is any sea running, do not attempt to land in a light cockleshell of a yacht tender.

When you get ashore, you will be met by one of the crew of the light station, who will ask you to sign a release for you and your party. If it is a convenient time, perhaps you will be allowed up in the tower, from which on a clear day there is a magnificent view of the Matinicus group, the islands of Penobscot Bay, Isle au Haut, Mt. Desert, and the Camden Hills. As you stand there 45 feet above the ground and 90 feet above high water, reflect that in winter storms, solid water has broken the quarter-inch plate glass of the lantern, washed over the whole island, destroyed the engine houses and boathouse, driven the keepers into the old stone house for protection, and tumbled the great boulders about the shore.

Among frequent visitors to the rock are ornithologists interested in the unusual bird life. Arctic terns nest in the grassy meadow on the northwest part of the island. Leach's petrels, guillemots, and the rare Atlantic puffins nest among the boulders. There is a small camp occupied by Audubon Society parties during the nesting season. In response to an inquiry about bird life on the rock, the writer received the following letter from Mr. Carl W. Bucheister, President of the National Audubon Society.

Now in connection with your description of Matinicus Rock, may I urge you to recommend to your readers that the rare Atlantic puffin, which in summer is found nesting only on that rock within the United States, can actually best be seen by cruising around the island. I know from many visits to the rock that one can approach the puffins on the water quite closely, and also see them perching on the island itself to better advantage from a boat.

I ask that you make this recommendation in your text because the constantly increasing numbers of visitors to Matinicus Rock in the summertime constitute a real threat to the Arctic terns, puffins, and Leach's petrels. Many individuals who know nothing about birds and their habits walk right into the tern colonies, causing the adults to fly up, leaving eggs and young. Frequently visitors, completely innocently, walk on eggs and young. Often I have seen visitors stand for hours in the area of big boulders of rocks under which the puffins nest, and they keep the birds from returning to their young with food. The Leach's petrels nest in burrows in the turf between the rocks, and people walking on these turf areas cave in the nesting burrows. This, as you will understand, causes the death of the adult and/or young in the burrow.

At the urging of the Society, the U.S. Coast Guard, in cooperation with the Bureau of Sport Fisheries & Wildlife of the Department of the Interior, has put up signs on the rock with legends asking people not to go beyond certain points.

Our Society can have no objection to a person landing on Matinicus Rock in order to see the lighthouse. We are concerned, as is the Coast Guard and the Bureau of Sport Fisheries & Wildlife, over people going right in to the areas where the birds nest.

Seal Island and Wooden Ball Island Me. (322). Seal Island was formerly used as a target for naval gunnery practice but is now attacked by aircraft only. No bombing exercises will be conducted after 5 P.M., on Sundays, or in bad weather. Vessels in the danger zone will be "buzzed" in warning before exercises are held. No live ammunition will be used. These conditions, of course, are subject to change. See the most recent edition of the *Coast Pilot*.

There is no good landing place on Seal Island and very little reason to seek one.

Beware of Malcolm Ledge between Seal and Wooden Ball islands. It is unmarked and is bare at low water.

Wooden Ball, so named, perhaps, for the eminence on the northeast end, is a barren white rock, tinged faintly green with grass and, at the writer's last visit, supervised by a few lonely and scraggy sheep. Another visitor reported a group of plastic lawn chairs outside one of the camps near the middle of the island.

There are several coves on the southeast side of the island, but only in the quietest weather could one land. Beware of a 1-foot spot off the northeast end of the island. It is unmarked and often does not break.

Isle au Haut, Me. (310, 308). No Maine cruise can ignore Isle au Haut. High, wooded, and touched only on the edges by the twentieth century, it is one of the most dramatic and attractive of Maine islands.

Provide for all your needs before visiting Isle au Haut. In 1971 supplies were very limited and may not be available at all in later years. You will enjoy the island much more if you do not have to be concerned with these matters.

Isle au Haut was named by Champlain in 1604 and means, of course, High Island. The pronunciation of the name, however, is not as obvious as its meaning. On the lobster cars in Stonington you will hear it called "Aisle au Holt" by fishermen, and so it was written in early deeds. Summer people, masters of high school French, favor "Eel-a-Ho." One fisherman, in an effort to please, called it "Eely-Oley." The late Dr. Howard Sprague, who lived for many summers near Point Lookout, contributed the following authoritative information.

I have just been looking over my 1961 edition of the *Cruising Guide* and want to give you some definitive information about the naming of Isle au Haut based on some research I did a couple of years ago in Houghton Library. I wanted to find out what name appeared in Champlain's original accounts and on his early maps. (I suppose one calls them "maps" rather than "charts.") The corruption Isle *au* Haut comes from the carry-over of the accenting of the "e" in *Isle* in Isle Haulte and its transformation into a separate and meaningless extra word "au." This was pointed out some years ago by Mrs. Bowditch. The "au" is meaningless in this context. Champlain called it the "high island" and the translation of Isle au Haut would, of course, be "The island of high."

On page 86 of volume I of *The Voyages and Explorations of Samuel de Champlain,* translated by Bourne-Allerton Book Co. in 1922, it says "and nearly in the middle of the sea there is another island which is so high and striking that I named it Isle Haute."

These spellings of Haute and Haulte appear in the original French accounts.

The earliest Champlain map, of which I have a Xerox copy, shows the island with a key reference letter F and the key shows the spelling *Ille haulte.* Mount Desert is *Ille des mont desertz.* This map has the title "Carte Geographique De La Nouvelle Franse Faiette Par Le Sieur De Champlain Saint Tongor's Capitaine Ordinaire Pour Le Roy En La Marine" (all capital letters), published in 1612.

Nowhere in Champlain's accounts have I found the corruption *Isle au Hault.* Mrs. Sprague tells me the accenting or stressing of the final "e" is common in Southern France and Canada and the development of this "au" must have come about from the pronunciation by those who were ignorant of French.

Much of the island is now part of Acadia National Park. In 1878 or 1879 Mr. Ernest W. Bowditch of Boston first visited the island. In 1880, with some of his friends, he formed the Isle au Haut Company and bought a house at Point Lookout. No women, no children, no dogs were the cardinal rules. Since then the rules have been relaxed. At the time of his death, Mr. Bowditch owned almost half the island.

In 1945 and 1946, his children gave most of this land to Acadia National Park. It is preserved nearly in its wild state, modified only be several trails and a road for fire-control purposes down the west side of the Island.

The navigation of this area in the fog is chancy business. The tide runs hard and there are few bells and whistles. One Isle au Haut fisherman with wry understatement adds, "and them spar buoys are awful dam' quiet."

Head Harbor. Coming up from seaward, this is the first anchorage at Isle au Haut. It is wide open to the south, and Roaring Bull Ledge, despite its whistle, is a dangerous obstruction. The bottom in the harbor is rocky and there is a weir. After several days of a winter northeaster, bore tides have been reported in Head Harbor that make it untenable, but these almost never occur in the summer, and anchorage in the cove at the head of the harbor is entirely satisfactory on a summer night.

There used to be a little village here, and several substantial houses still stand, but the place is largely deserted now, and there will probably be no one to disturb you.

There is a jeep road around the island that passes by the head of the harbor. It is a pleasant walk to Duck Harbor to the westward and a good climb up Duck Mountain on a trail leaving the left-hand side of the road. It is marked by red plastic ribbons on trees and bushes and by yellow blazes.

Duck Harbor on the southwest corner of the island is small, shoal, and beautiful. There is room for no more than two or three yachts to anchor, and recent visitors report that it has silted up considerably. To enter, make The Brandies, a big ledge that is always exposed and that has a great square boulder on top of it. Go up the bay until you can see right up the harbor and then head in. Be sure to identify Duck Harbor Ledge as you pass. Anchor abreast the big black rock on the southern side.

The road to Head Harbor goes by the north side of Duck Harbor and the trail up Duck Harbor Mountain makes off it. The road goes the other way, north, to Moore Harbor and the Thorofare.

At the head of Duck Harbor is an old graveyard. Students of *Sailing Days on the Penobscot* will be interested in some of the names recorded there.

Recently Duck Harbor has been used as a camp ground by groups of young people from the mainland. It is all part of Acadia Park, so this is not unreasonable, but one cruising man reported their presence as very disturbing. Two moorings are often available here.

Moore Harbor. This harbor does not appear to be so well protected as others on Isle au Haut, but it is perfectly good under summer conditions and is actually a lot better than it looks. Enter close to Moore Head on a course about east magnetic to avoid Rock T and a long ledge off Trial Point. Go south of the weir, avoiding the prominent ledge in the middle of the harbor, and anchor east of the weir. In 1970 there was a vacant mooring in here. There is no settlement here and there are no supplies.

Seal Trap. This is an interesting bit of gunk-holing to try on a rising tide in a shoal-draft boat. The swimming inside is reported to be warmer than elsewhere. One correspondent suggests that the name has nothing to do with seals but is a corruption of the French *ciel,* meaning sky or heaven. A bit of one or the other is trapped here between the wooded shores.

Isle au Haut Thorofare. This well-protected anchorage is the principal shelter at Isle au Haut and in ordinary weather presents no serious difficulties. Note that Kimball Rock always breaks and at low tide is a very prominent mark. Be sure to make the can at Marsh Cove Ledges. Then run for Robinson Point Light, leave the beacon to port, and run up the middle of the passage. Anchor out of the tide on the Kimball Island shore, but beware of ledges and boulders on this shore. Also notice that Moxie Island makes off to the northeast a little, drops off to deep water, and then shoals up to a flat ledge with about 3 feet at low water. When the nun on the northern end of the dredged channel appears between the can and the nun on the southern end, you are about in the channel. When the two nuns line up, you are almost on the rock. These ranges are good only until the Coast Guard changes the buoyage. There is a snug little pocket just halfway between can 5 and the fish house on Moxie Island. There is room for only one boat to swing here in 7 or 8 feet at low water.

Land at the southernmost wharf where the new power house is located and walk north along the road. You come soon to a path up to the church, where services are held regularly in summer. It is all an island church should be.

You will pass the post office, presided over for many years by Mrs. Rich. Beyond this is a library and community center built by the "autumn people" for those who stay the winter. Just beyond this was a store in 1971, but it may not survive. The year-round population has fallen off, enrollment in the school is down to two scholars, and many of the summer people bring in their own supplies from Stonington.

There is a dredged channel through the mussel bar at the north end of the harbor. There appeared to be about 6 feet of water in it at ordinary low water in 1970. Simply follow the buoys, but at the northern end bear a little to the west to avoid Eustis's Rock, named for good reason for the late Mr. Augustus Eustis, for many years a devoted summer resident.

The Thorofare used to be a busy place, as *Sailing Days on the Penobscot* attests. There was a considerable settlement of lobstermen and handliners. The mackerel fleet often lay here in the summer. Coasters and trading vessels frequently stopped, and throngs of blueberry pickers, known as "plummers," came down from Deer Isle. Now, with fast motorboats, there is no need to live near the fishing. Summer people have bought up much of the land not owned by Acadia Park, and the island is inhabited in winter only by a few people who like living there.

Point Lookout. Although it is rather exposed to the northwest, this is a beautiful anchorage with lovely views of Isle au Haut, the Camden Hills, and the islands to the north.

Entering from the west in the fog, expect a scale-up north of Kimball Island. Keep well off the shore because the ledges shown on the chart appear to make off Kimball Island even farther than the chart suggests. From the north, respect the beacon off Flake Island and give the northern end of the island a generous berth.

Off the granite wharf is a mooring maintained by Mr. Frederick Eustis and labelled GUEST. Other moorings may be available. Hail the wharf. If not, anchorage anywhere between the wharf and the ledges off Flake Island is entirely satisfactory.

Land at the float north of the granite wharf. Water is piped to this wharf, but there are no other supplies here. The entire point is now private property, held by a community consisting mostly of doctors who value their privacy. You are, of course, welcome to walk along the road to the left as you come off the wharf. It soon works back to the right, and at the place where it joins the tar road a trail leads up Champlain Mountain to the highest point on the island. However, the summit is now overgrown with high brush and trees, so there is no view.

To the right on the tar road is the Thorofare and the small store.

Burnt Island Thorofare. This narrow and tortuous channel is not difficult at half tide or less, when the dangers are exposed, but at high water it is considerably more difficult. Entering from the west, make the shore of Burnt Island at a stony beach near the west end, and hug this shore until you are up to the peak of the island in order to pass north of the half-tide rock shown between the figures 12 and 16 on chart 308. Then line up the northeast corner of a wharf on Isle au Haut with the south corner of the house behind it. When just west of a line between the wharf on Burnt Island and the wharf on Isle au Haut, drop the hook and snug down to enjoy a beautiful and secluded anchorage. One cruising man on attaining this goal was moved to quote the following devout prayer of thanksgiving:

> Lord, we thank thee that thy Grace
> Has brought us to this pleasant place,
> And most earnestly we pray
> That other folk will stay away.

To continue to the eastward, head for the big rock blocking the opening. When less than 100 yards from it, turn south and round the south end of it. If the tide is high and the ledge is covered, edge up to it very cautiously until you see it. It is dangerous to proceed without locating this mark. Once by this ledge, proceed to the eastward, favoring the Isle au Haut shore heavily. Move slowly and watch for bottom.

Pell Island Passage. If Burnt Island Thorofare sounds too tricky or if it is blowing hard so that moving slowly is impossible, pass between Pell Island and Burnt Island. From the west, go close to the north of Mouse Island and head for the beach on the southwest end of Wheat Island. When about 100 yards off it, swing to the north and follow the Wheat Island shore. Keep away from Pell Island. Keep an eye for Channel Rock to the eastward. It is unmarked but usually shows and always breaks. Still, at high water on a quiet day it could be a menace.

East Side of Isle au Haut. There is excellent protection in anything but a northeast gale behind York Island. There is an old wharf on the island and a good well. Entrance is complex and the ledges are said to be covered with kelp. Proceed with care on a rising tide. From an earlier *Guide,* we add, do not go between Dolliver Island and Rabbits Ear. Enter between the two rocks southwest of Rabbits Ear.

Great Spoon Island, easily identified by its shape, is now a bird refuge owned by the Audubon Society. In July there are flocks of guillemots, and sea ducks around the island. Several ravens preside over the scene.

Black Horse and *White Horse* are as radically different as their names suggest. There must be an interesting geological explanation to their differences and their propinquity.

The region to the east of Isle au Haut is no place to be in rough or thick weather. The ledges are unmarked, the tide runs swiftly, and the offshore seas pile in here unobstructed. They seem to crest up wherever you look and break tremendously on half-tide ledges. If the Isle au Haut shore is obscured, it is easy to get confused out here.

Isle au Haut to Stonington. This part of Maine is excelled by none and equaled only by the country between Mistake Island and Jonesport. Here are bold shores, deep channels, and uninhabited islands covered with spruce, balsam, and sweet fern. The shores are smooth, clean granite ledges, easy to walk on and delightful to swim from. Among the ledges are hidden sandy beaches. Many of the islands have been used to run

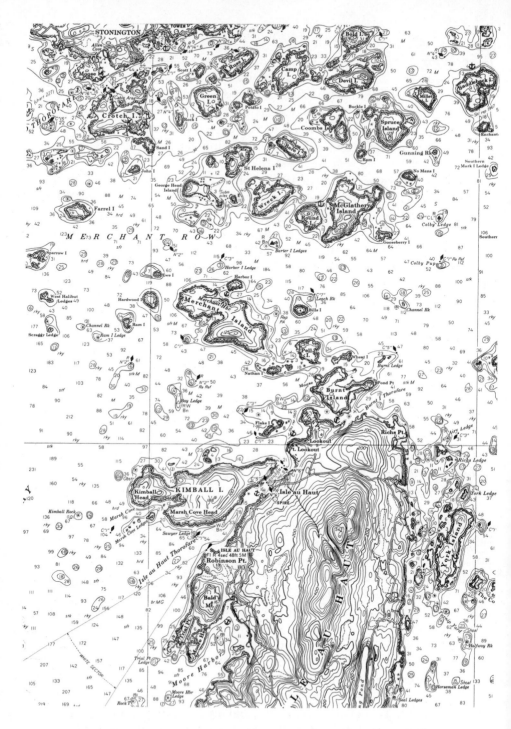

Anchorages between Isle au Haut and Stonington (refer to Chart 308).

sheep and are criss-crossed with deeply worn sheep runs. Don't follow these into the woods unless you enjoy walking like a sheep. The fishing is usually good. There are a few clams still, and when the herring or mackerel are running and the weirs are fishing, one may get a chance to watch the fishermen pump one out and get a few really fresh fish. Lobstermen fish this region extensively and are most friendly and stimulating people if they are approached with the esteem and respect that they deserve.

There are so many beautiful coves among these islands that it would swell this book to undue proportions to include all of them. Also the writers would incur the undying enmity of yachtsmen who want to meet here only those who have the interest and enterprise to explore for themselves.

We might, however, make a few casual suggestions. Merchants Island has a good harbor and was inhabited in Revolutionary times. There is a cove between McGlathery and Round Island. Enter it from the north. The grave of Peter Eaton overlooks the harbor and is all that remains of a once-busy community. Hearing that the island was to be "pulped" in 1954, Martin R. Haase, a summer resident of South Brooksville, whose *Diablesse* is often seen in these waters, organized Friends of Nature to purchase and preserve it in a wild state. He writes:

> We let nature maintain the island and are happy to have people enjoy it properly by appreciating its beauty. Incidentally, we pay about $150 a year taxes on the island and would gratefully accept contributions (tax deductible) from those who like the island to be preserved in its wilderness state.

Look in at the cove north of Spruce Island. There is a summer place on Devils Island and a good anchorage north of it. Anchor north of Saddleback and enjoy a swim on the southern beach. It is shark-proof. There is no better place for a bucket of lobsters and a bottle of beer. There is an *uncharted* and unmarked rock between Enchanted Island and Saddleback between the 12- and 18-foot soundings. The cruise schooners often put on a clambake in the cove southwest of Russ Island.

It was on one of these islands that I stood with a lobsterman looking into the thick fog. As the sun broke through, I observed hopefully, "It's clear overhead."

"Yes," he answered deliberately, "but the hell of it is, Roge, we ain't bound that way."

Stonington, Me. (309, 227). Approach is easy from east or west along the well-marked channel of Deer Island Thorofare. The tides run east and west, the buoys are close together, and most of the islands and ledges are bold. From the south the approach is a little more difficult. Come up either side of Rock Island and leave can 1 to port. Anchor under Green Head or farther east off the wharves. The bottom is stiff clay.

Land at Colwell's or Atlantic Hardware. Gas, water, and Diesel oil are available here, as well as some marine supplies. Bartlett's Market is less than 100 yards up the road. There is a liquor store, and there are various other stores and a post office on the main street. One of the best restaurants in the region is several miles away by taxi at Bridge End, the southern end of the bridge over Eggemoggin Reach.

Repairs to hull, spars, or engine can be handled at The Moose Island yard. The Billings brothers at this yard built one of the last commercial schooners in Maine, the *Enterprise,* in the late 30s. The yard is now the best place for repairs between Boothbay and Southwest Harbor.

Clarence Hale, an obliging and skillful sailmaker, lives just north of the bridge.

Stonington used to be a busy town. Groundfish, lobsters, and herring were bought and shipped out. Pulpwood and cordwood went out and coal came in. In 1938 the writer saw the huge four-masted schooner *Theoline* discharging coal into half a dozen little bay schooners for distribution to the islands. But granite was Stonington's principal product. At Webb Cove, Crotch Island, St. Helena, George Head, and other islands there are still piles of grout (imperfect blocks of granite) alongside which schooners and barges loaded stone for buildings in Boston, New York, and Philadelphia. One of these that comes to mind was the old *Annie Reuben.* Here foremast was stepped far forward and her mainmast far aft to give her a big main hatch and room for long lengths of stone. It gave her also a tremendous foresail without reducing her mainsail a great deal. A member of her crew whom I met on one of the islands told me he ate breakfast in her foc's'le at dawn under Charlestown bridge in Boston and ate dinner at dark under Green Head, Stonington. She was flying light, winged out before a smoky sou'wester. He said she sailed in company with a steamer eastward from Cape Ann until the steamer swung off to go into Portland. I last saw her in the coal dock beside the subway tracks in the Charles River basin. As I sculled around her stern in a fragile single shell, a down-easter leaning on the rail said in unmistakeable accents, "When she goes, she'll go fast." He was referring not to her speed through the water but to her heavy cargoes of coal and stone.

Now the granite quarries are closed; Perini is shipping out a little grout in trucks, but Crotch Island has been sold, and rumor hints it is to be "developed." The sardine factory seldom runs. No steamers land. No schooners anchor in Green Head Cove. On the wharf where I saw *Theo-*

Air view looking southeast with Stonington in the foreground.

line discharging coal, a group of "sports" in Hawaiian shirts drink beer and fish for mackerel in desultory fashion. The wharf where the old *Webster* lay, a red-bearded Hercules discharging her deck load of pulp logs, is deserted. The "mod squad" in an incongruous variety of clothes and haircuts treads the streets that Charlie Barr and his America's Cup crew of Deer Islanders once trod.

If you have finished your business, better make sail and beat down the Bay toward Isle au Haut to more enlivening scenes.

Webb Cove, Me. (227, 308). Should the weather look threatening, retreat to the head of Webb Cove. It is a secluded and beautiful place and perfectly protected. The holding ground is excellent.

Sylvester Cove, Deer Isle, Me. (310). This cove, south of Dunham's Point, and open to the west when the tide is high, is not much to look at on the chart, but is a good anchorage in this beautiful region. Pigeon Island Reef makes a natural breakwater. The reef at the entrance is marked by a red spar buoy. Anchor in among the fleet. There is a landing float on the north side of the cove maintained by the Deer Isle Yacht Club, and a 250-pound mushroom mooring available for visitors. Minor supplies can be had at a store about a mile from the anchorage. The Camden Hills are seen to great advantage at sunset on a clear night. There is an interesting summer colony at Dunham's Point.

In a brisk southwester it can be uncomfortable, but after the tide is halfway out, the reef provides good shelter.

Northwest Harbor, Deer Isle, Me. (310). As the best shelter between Bucks Harbor on the north and Pulpit Harbor or Stonington on the south, this long inlet, shallow at the upper end, is worth noting. The inner harbor is an extensive mud flat at low tide. The anchorage, sheltered from all but northwesterly winds, is in mid-harbor below the small wharf on the northeast side.

In the days of sail Northwest Harbor had a rope walk and sail loft. Many vessels wintered here and fitted out in the spring. Now it is quiet and deserted except for an eagle that the author observed one night presiding over gulls, ospreys, and a few cottages tucked away among the trees.

At the head of the harbor is the village of Deer Isle, where ordinary supplies are available.

Eggemoggin Reach, Me. (308, 311). When it is thick or rough down the bay, retreat to Eggemoggin Reach. This is a long sheltered passage between Deer Isle and Little Deer Isle on the southwest and the mainland on the northeast. It is seldom foggy, for the warmth of the land dries up the fog. There are snug and attractive harbors at each end—Bucks Harbor on the west and Naskeag on the east. There are a marina and restaurant under the bridge, good protection at Center Harbor and also in the Benjamin River. Dangers are clearly marked and easily avoided. The tide does not run hard except at the east end between Torrey Castle and Devil's Head. It floods in at both ends, meets about at the bridge, and flows out the way it came.

There is likely to be an extensive soft spot in the mouth of the Benjamin River. Better stay well over to the southern side. Also, near the flasher at the west end the wind is likely to give out.

Best of all, you can reach through here bound west. To be sure, you will have a beat down the Western Bay the next day—but the wind might shift.

Bucks Harbor, Me. (311). Called Buck Harbor on the chart, this snug harbor at the western end of the reach is easy of access under almost any condition. It is not always so easy to get out. The writer has spent many hours stewing in the hot morning calms near the flasher. The southwest wind seems slow to get up into this distant corner of the bay.

Anchor off the yacht club but avoid the area south of the buoy. A ledge runs from it to Harbor Island. A quieter anchorage is in the cove to the east.

Land at the yacht club and walk less than a quarter of a mile to the four corners, which is the heart of South Brooksville. A mile down the road to the left is the yard of mechanic Steve Bridges, mentioned under Orcutt Harbor. To your right is the post office and Condon's Garage— another source of help for the ailing engine. Straight ahead is the remarkable store of the remarkable Eddie Noessel. He runs a down-east cross between a country store and a supermarket. He stocks the finest of S.S. Pierce groceries and is renowned for his skill as a meat cutter. He has his finger on the public pulse. One winter, contemplating his empty freezer cabinet, it occurred to him to fill it with snowballs. He accordingly laid in a large stock of snowballs put up by the dozen in cellophane bags. In July they found a ready market at 69¢ a bag. "People said I was crazy," remarked Eddie, "but they keep coming back for more." One winter there was very little snow. During the subsequent summer, customers noted a decline in the quality of the product, a certain iciness, suggesting frozen slush. Eddie explained to the writer that the snow was so cold and dry that it wouldn't pack into snowballs, so he had to shovel it into a box and set it behind the stove to warm up a bit. Some of it got overdone, but none burned.

Mr. Noessel's store was formerly owned by Ray C. Gray, a man much beloved by a former generation of yachtsmen. He was renowned for his delicious homemade ice cream. When President Roosevelt passed through Eggemoggin Reach in a cruiser on his way home from signing the Atlantic Charter in 1941, he sent a boat ashore for a supply of Mr. Gray's ice cream.

"If I'd have known who those sailors were getting it for, I'd have given it to them," I heard him say the next day. Mr. Roosevelt, of course, was an experienced cruising man, and Mr. Gray was almost the only Democrat in the county.

Gas, water, ice, Diesel fuel, and stove fuel are available at the granite wharf operated by Clifford Leach in the northeast corner of the harbor.

The yacht club is most hospitable to members of other clubs. There is an active racing program in small boats, an occasional dance, a tennis court, and a pleasant clubhouse.

Repairs to hull, spars, rigging, or engine can be effected by J.H. Vaughan at Seal Cove Boatyard in Horseshoe Cove. Clarence Hale has a sail loft nearby in Sargentville.

Walk up the road beyond the post office to Caterpillar Hill and Winche Mountain for a grand view of Penobscot Bay.

Billings Cove, Sargentville, Me. (307). This cove is open to the southeast but in ordinary weather is a quiet anchorage. Land at the wharf on the east side and walk up the road to the four corners. Turn left and continue for a mile or more to the old schoolhouse, now used by Clarence Hale and his son Donald as a sail loft. Mr. Hale is an excellent workman and a most accommodating gentleman. He has been to sea in coasters and sloops and has made sails for a number of the cruise schooners, among them Boyd Guild's *Victory Chimes*. His son has learned the art by working with his father. The loft is well worth a visit.

Benjamin River, Me. (307). This is one of those places, like Burnt Island Thorofare, that is much easier at half tide or less, when the dangers are exposed. On entering, favor the eastern shore a little, as both shores consist of flats studded with boulders, but the channel is not quite in the middle. From the big field with the church at the head of it, marked *spire* on chart 307, a long bar makes out with a big boulder almost on the end of it. A locally maintained spindle has been sighted here, but don't count on it. Give the whole concern a generous berth to starboard. Anchorage is off the east shore near the buildings of the Benjamin River Boatyard. This yard was bought from Frank Day and his son when Webbers Cove Boatyard in East Blue Hill gave up storage and repairs to build fiberglass lobster-boat hulls. The Days planned to build a new shed and to continue to build boats.

No supplies are easily available here.

The afternoon southwester is often very light off the mouth of the Benjamin River. The alert skipper will keep to the Deer Isle shore.

Center Harbor, Brooklin, Me. (308). This is a convenient harbor on the north shore of the reach just east of the Benjamin River. The chart makes clear the approach from the westward. Anchor about abreast the cove in Chatto Island if there is room. The bottom is mud. If the wind comes hard northwest, this anchorage can become uneasy, but it would be easy to run over under the lee of the eastern Torry Island.

One can approach Chatto Island nun 2 from the east by passing between the eastern Torry Island and High Head. By doing so, one can save more than a mile and avoid going out into the tide around Torry Castle. It is an easier passage in the fog also.

At Center Harbor there is a small boat yard run by Joel White. A customer of the yard who stores his boat there—hence a qualified authority —told the writer that Mr. White's yard is, in his opinion, "the best yard anywhere, bar none." That is high praise! Mr. White and his crew do beautiful work. The yard recently completed a replica of a 1900 pulling boat for Mystic Seaport, and has built yawl boats for cruise schooners as well as auxiliary yachts.

The yard can handle any type of repair work to hull, spars, or engine. Clarence Hale in Sargentville will repair sails or rigging. Marine hardware and gas are available at the yard float, and water at the yacht club float.

About half a mile up the road from the yard is The Brooklin General Store, owned by Mr. Al Ormondroyd, a very accommodating gentleman who will deliver purchases to the float if business is not too pressing.

The Center Harbor Yacht Club is on the north shore near the harbor entrance. There is about 4 feet of water at the float at low water. This is a hospitable club with an active program. Water is piped to the float.

Naskeag, Me. (308). A gravel bar divides this harbor into an eastern and western part. Most boats lie in the eastern part, which is easily entered from the east. The passage between the two anchorages is extremely narrow and should not be attempted at low tide without local knowledge. The western half of the harbor is rather well filled with ledges; caution is advised. The Triangles do not show, even at low water.

The village is on the north side, but there is no dock. There is a public beach approached by a road running north.

Hog Island is an attractive island with a few small beaches. Devils

Head at its southern end affords a good view to the eastward.

A good anchorage is north of the middle of Hog Island.

Southeast Harbor, Deer Isle, Me. (308). Note that the entire harbor is shown on chart 308; the entrance and eastern part are shown on chart 227. This is an excellent harbor and most convenient for boats using Deer Island Thorofare or Eggemoggin Reach.

A correspondent sends in the following:

> If one is looking for extreme privacy, a way can be found south of Stinson's Neck (via Southeast Harbor and on) into Long Cove, in the very heart of the island. Here, completely surrounded by land, is a pool with a depth in the middle variously estimated at from 20 to 30 fathoms. But the channel in had best be negotiated at the top of the tide.

The anchorage is described as Hawley's Deep Hole, with a depth of 102 feet. Don't enter here unless prepared for adventure. There are many boulders.

Swans Island, Me. (308). This big irregular island has four good harbors on it and a ferry connection with the mainland from Mackerel Cove to Bass Harbor on Mt. Desert. Land for summer cottages is becoming increasingly valuable.

Mackerel Cove. There is no difficulty in entering, as the dangers are well marked. However, there are two confusing places. One is the deep passage south of Orono Island. Note that nun 4 is *south* of the rock it marks and must be left to *port*. Then beware of the 3-foot spot to the northeast. The other bad spot is the long ledge outside Roderick Head. This is completely submerged at high water, extends far out into the harbor to the eastward and the top, which uncovers first as the tide goes, is on the western side. If you seek shelter in the snug cove east of Roderick Head, be very careful of this menace.

The ferry lands behind can 3 and there is a post office there, and a store and a restaurant. Do not crowd the ferry wharf, as the vessel needs room to maneuver.

Buckle Harbor. This is a secure anchorage between Buckle Island and Swans Island. Pass between can 5 and can 7 and favor the Buckle Island shore. There is a house on Buckle Island occupied by summer people. It is difficult to get ashore on Swans Island because of the extensive mud flats.

Seal Cove. This is a good shelter with good holding ground but it is tricky to enter because there appear to be boulders on the shoal spots. Favor the western shore and watch for clumps of rockweed on the bottom. Avoid them. The shores are mud, starred with ledges.

There is little point in going ashore.

Burnt Coat Harbor. When Champlain sailed west from Passamaquoddy in 1604, he named Swan's Island Brûle-Côte, translated freely as Burnt Hill. The name, garbled by the centuries, still clings to Burnt Coat Harbor.

In making this harbor from the west in thick weather, be very cautious, for the tide in Jericho Bay seems to run in different directions at different times. From Saddleback bell to Halibut Rocks, the tide may set on the ebb anywhere from SSE to WNW. If the breeze is light, you may be badly set. Under Marshall Island there is usually a scale-up and a good draft of breeze, and the tide in Toothacher Bay seems to run pretty much along the course to the channel bell off Hockamock Head. The light and horn make entrance from the bell easy.

Run up the harbor and anchor to the southward of the wharves if you are in need of fuel or supplies, but do not plan to lie there overnight unless you are sure your anchor is well set. Many yachtsmen have dragged here and found their anchors heavily fouled with kelp and weed. Move to the north of Harbor Island.

On the wharf at Swan's Island one can buy gas, and limited marine supplies at the store of M.B. Sprague. Follow the road up the hill to the tar road where the post office stands. To the right about half a mile is the store. To the left it is an easy walk to the light at Hockomock Head.

Colonel James Swan, for whom the island was named, was born in Scotland, emigrated to Boston at the age of eleven, and became a clerk in the office of Thaxter and Son. He wrote a book on the African slave trade, assisted at the Boston Tea Party, was wounded at Bunker Hill, and advanced in the Continental Army to become a major in the cavalry. He became secretary to the Massachusetts Board of War and adjutant-general of the state. He speculated in land in Virginia and Kentucky and became a wealthy man. In 1784 he bought Burnt Coat Island, gave it his name, established sawmills, encouraged settlers, and was on his way to establishing a feudal empire. However, he happened to be in France at the time of the French Revolution and devoted his energies to saving his friends, among them Marie Antoinette. He loaded their property aboard a vessel in charge of Stephen Clough of Wiscasset. At the last minute, however, the aristocrats, including the Queen, were arrested and guillotined. Captain Clough brought the furnishings and clothes to Wiscasset, where some of them still may be seen. Colonel Swan was accused of owing a debt of two million francs, which he denied, and he was jailed. Being a man of principle, he refused to pay, although he could have raised the money. He was released in 1830 by Louis Philippe and died very soon after.

The island, bereft of its squire, grew in a more democratic way and became prosperous through the sale of lumber, fish, and finally lobsters. Now there is a growing income from summer people. The island has a population of 500 in the winter and 5000 in the summer.

If you are leaving bound east, do not hesitate to use the narrow eastern entrance. Simply leave the two black cans close to starboard and favor the Swan's Island shore slightly after you pass can 3.

Passages from Jericho Bay to Blue Hill Bay

Casco Passage and York Narrows. These are the most commonly used passages north of Swan's Island. One would use Casco Passage going to and from Eggemoggin Reach and York Narrows in connection with Deer Island Thorofare. Both are deep enough for most yachts and clearly marked with buoys. The tide runs pretty hard to the east on the flood and west on the ebb. Approach to Casco Passage from the west is marked only by a nun, but York Narrows has a lighted bell. At the eastern end, the two passages join at can 1 and the black-and-white bell outside it. On the ordinary southwest breeze one can usually fetch through Casco Passage. York Narrows is wide enough to beat through. There is excellent shelter at Buckle Harbor and Mackerel Cove on the south and between Black and Opechee islands on the north.

Pond Island Passage. This is an easy and well-buoyed passage north of Pond Island. It might be more favorable than Casco Passage if one were bound east on an ebb tide.

Outside. Go down Toothacher Bay, between John Island and Swan's Island and east of the Sisters, Black Island, and Great Gott. This route has the advantage of avoiding Bass Harbor Bar and of a dramatic approach to the hills of Mt. Desert, but it is not recommended in thick weather. Note that the ebb tide sets to the southeast out of Blue Hill Bay, making real dangers of the Drums, Horseshoe Ledge, and South Bunker Ledge. Watch the way the tide sets by pot buoys.

As a commentary on the run of tide, consider the course of a skiff lost in a brisk southerly and thick fog somewhere south of Drum Island. It turned up twenty-four hours later bobbing around under a wharf in Bass Harbor—a journey of 6 miles across Bass Harbor Bar.

Lunt Harbor, Frenchboro, Long Island, Me. (308). Protected from everything but heavy northeasters, this is a very attractive harbor little frequented by yachts. With a bell to the west and a gong to the northeast, entrance is easy. Outside the ferry wharf is a large winter mooring, ordinarily unoccupied in the summer.

To land, row up the harbor through the shoal water and go ashore on one of the wharves on the east side. There are no stores on the island. Gas and Diesel fuel may be available in an emergency. The car ferry from Swan's Island and Bass Harbor lands at the granite wharf.

There is a tar road running along the shore with dirt roads running off into the woods. These make easy and pleasant walking to the south and east sides of the island. Deer, pheasant, and beaver have been released on the island by the State Game Commission.

The population of the island, like that of Matinicus and Isle au Haut, is dwindling, but it has had a recent increase. In the fall of 1969 the Department of Education in Augusta declared that there were so few children on the island that no teacher would be sent to teach such a small school. The children would have to board on Mt. Desert for the winter. The people of Frenchboro at once set about increasing the number of children on the island by taking into their homes fifteen state wards. This swelled the school to the required number, a teacher was sent, and the arrangement worked out well. All but a very few of the children adjusted happily to island life and to their new families.

Anyone who drops in here should read what *Sailing Days on the Penobscot* has to say about Outer Long Island. Some fifty years ago Lunt Harbor had a bad reputation along the coast as a rendezvous for pirates and rough characters. The offshore fishing fleet is reported to have put in there often for a wild night ashore, but now one will find there the usual Maine fishermen quite ready and willing to be cordial and helpful to visiting yachtsmen.

Regarding the island a correspondent writes:

The most important thing I know of about Outer Long Island is that on the southwest side there is a bog of several acres in extent, which in early August is completely filled with blossoms of Pogonia! Now, Pogonia is one of our relatively rare New England orchids, with a lovely purple or mauve color, a very delicate and beautiful flower.

When I find a single blossom near some inland lake, I rejoice. I'll never forget the first time I came around the point there and saw several acres of solid Pogonia in bloom. It took me quite a while to believe what I saw.

The foregoing paragraph was written in 1936. In 1970 they were still blooming. Enjoy them where they are. They will not stand transplanting.

Blue Hill Bay, Me. (307). This long deep bay is bounded on the west by the mountains of Mt. Desert and on the north by Blue Hill. Swan's Placentia, Black, and Gott's islands protect it from the open Atlantic on the south. Its shores are bold, for the most part heavily wooded, and sparsely inhabited. Its harbors, though few, are clean and well protected. Often when it is thick outside, Blue Hill Bay will be only hazy.

The best way to get a quick look at the bay is to enter on a coming tide through Flye Island Narrows and run up the bay west of Long Island to Blue Hill. The next day, cross north of Long Island, beat down through Bartlett Narrows, go west of Hardwood Island toward Tinker Island; and if you have an ebb tide with you and the wind to the west a bit, you should be able to fetch Lopaus Point and Bass Harbor Bar. The views of the Mt. Desert hills from the west are magnificent. Should the breeze die or the tide turn foul, there are numerous coves in which to seek shelter.

Allen Cove, Me. (307). This is a big open cove well protected from west, south and east with good holding ground. It is surrounded by farms and hayfields. The Northeast Harbor fleet often uses it as a rendezvous on club cruises. There is no landing place and nothing ashore for which to land.

Blue Hill Harbor, Me. (307). Entrance is clear from the chart. Simply leave all cans to port and sail right in, giving the nun off Sculpin Point a fair berth. The Kollegewidgwok Yacht Club maintains several guest moorings marked with white cans. If none is available, hail the float and inquire, but at low water approach with caution. The area bounded by nun 2, can 7, and the club float is good anchorage. Although it appears open to the southeast, in Hurricane Carol in 1954 winds of 80 miles an hour hit on the top of the tide when Sculpin Point was awash, yet no boats were lost. Still, one can push up the harbor beyond can 7 and nun 8 and anchor off the old steamer wharf. With a shoal-draft boat or the dinghy you can go all the way to the village on the tide.

Blue Hill. The yacht club landing is to the right of the small boats in the harbor.

The yacht club is open from June 15 to September 15, and a steward is in attendance from July 4 to Labor Day. It is a station of The Cruising Club of America. There is a telephone at the club, and one can order groceries delivered from Blue Hill. The steward can be consulted concerning repairs to hull, spars, or engines. Clarence Hale in Sargentville is an expert sailmaker and rigger. Captain Walter K. Carter is a compass adjuster of wide reputation living nearby.

It is about a 2-mile walk to Blue Hill, most of it along a rather uninspiring tar road. However, the village is quite interesting. There is a blacksmith on the main street, an artist in black iron. Further up the street are the Cranberry House and Blue Hill Inn, most attractive places to dine. Beyond the inn is the well-known Rowantrees Pottery, started by two ladies in the 1930s as an educational venture. The manganese deposits found on the slopes of Blue Hill are used to make the lavender and black glaze characteristic of Rowantrees products. Two other potteries in town have developed from the original establishment and now are healthy competitors.

The Blue Hill Historical Society has acquired the Jonathan Fisher house and keeps it open to the public in the summer. The Reverend Fisher was an eighteenth-century graduate of Harvard who took his bride to Blue Hill and served there as a very active minister for the rest of his long life. His biography has been written by his descendent, Mary Ellen Chase. Her own autobiography, *Windswept,* tells of her early life in and near Blue Hill.

Also in Blue Hill are the Kniesel Hall Music School and a golf course.

Blue Hill itself, 560 feet high, dominates every view of the town. If you want to climb it because it's there, take Route 15 north from the town for about a mile and turn right on a road to the east, which in 1970 bore a sign "Mountain Shop." The trail leaves the left (north) side of the road at a yellow sign, "Trail to Lookout Tower." It is a steep trail through the woods and up the shoulder of the mountain. About halfway up, it is joined by an old jeep road. This is the easier and longer way; but a short, steep path cuts off to the right.

Near the top, the blueberries are magnificent. The view from the tower on a clear day stretches from Rockland to the Mt. Desert hills and south to Isle au Haut and the islands down the bay.

If it is a dry time, there may be a watchman on duty keeping an eye open for forest fires and helping to triangulate them.

The Gazetteer of Maine states,

The name Blue Hill comes from a commanding elevation of land near the center of the town. It was formerly covered with trees—

principally evergreens—which, at a distance, gave a very dark blue tint —whence its name.

East Blue Hill, Me. (307). This is a small cove open to the southeast. Its principal attraction is Webber's Cove Boat Yard. For many years this yard had an enviable reputation as a builder of fine wooden yachts and fishing vessels. Now it has turned to the construction of a stock fiberglass powerboat hull that can be finished as a lobster boat, a party boat, a sport fisherman, a cruiser, or whatever the owner wants.

Morgan Bay is beautiful, well protected, and, once you are well inside, free of dangers.

Union River Bay is well protected and affords magnificent views of hills and shores. One can anchor on the east side in Mill Cove or on the west side in Patterns Bay.

Mt. Desert Narrows. It is no longer possible for masted vessels of much draft to pass from Blue Hill Bay into Frenchman's Bay under the bridge at Mt. Desert Narrows. Since the late eighteenth century a drawbridge has spanned the narrows. However, in 1957 a fixed bridge with a clearance of 25 feet above high water was built, and Mr. K.K. Thompson, bridge keeper and descendant of Cornelius Thompson, who built the first bridge on this site, was retired.

Prettymarsh, Me. (307). This is a large harbor, but it affords good protection, for one can anchor under whatever shore is to windward. Somes Cove offers very good shelter in a heavy southwesterly. There was a large white mooring in the western part of the harbor in 1969 that had every appearance of a guest mooring.

The shores are privately owned. There are no facilities whatever, and even the road out is not easy to find.

Prettymarsh is clean and quiet, and affords a delightful place in which to be alone.

Bartlett Narrows (307). This is a deep and easily negotiated passage of surpassing beauty. There is good shelter in Great Cove. Many projects have been proposed for this island, but the last time the writer was there, the island appeared to be uninhabited.

There are several shelters on the west side of Mt. Desert Island. The best is probably the cove north of the bar behind Moose Island. Seal Cove, Goose Cove, and Duck Cove all have small settlements of summer people and are pleasant places from which to view the sunset on a summer evening. Do not count on them for protection in a storm or for extensive supplies.

Bass Harbor (307). A large, wide-open harbor between Lopaus Point and Bass Harbor Head, this has been comparatively little used by yachts despite its being very close to the course east and west across Blue Hill Bay. There are much more scenic and better-protected shelters at Southwest Harbor, Northeast Harbor, Seal Harbor, and Somes Sound.

However, Bass Harbor is beginning to be favored by some yachtsmen because of the increasing congestion in the other harbors and because of serious efforts to improve facilities at Bass Harbor. Under the leadership of Robert Hinckley of Southwest Harbor, Mr. and Mrs. Bauer have established a base on the site of an old boat shop at the first wharf on the eastern side of the harbor. They provide guest moorings, gas, Diesel fuel, water, ice, and marine supplies. Ashore are the attractive Deck House Restaurant and a motel. There is a store nearby. Repairs of all kinds can be made, and the Bauers are making every effort to welcome cruising men.

The upper part of the harbor is well protected and has been dredged to 10 feet. The town, devoted to sardine factories, lobstering, and boat-building, is far more simple and less "summery" than the sophisticated resorts of Northeast Harbor and Bar Harbor.

The ferry to Swan's Island runs from a wharf at Bass Harbor.

Bass Harbor Bar (306). The rocky bar, strewn with boulders, can be crossed under ordinary conditions anywhere north of the middle, but the best water is close to the channel can. In the fog, it is possible to go close enough to Bass Harbor Head to pick up the sound of the fog bell.

The tide runs hard across the bar and reverses the usual rule for Maine passages. It floods west into Blue Hill Bay and ebbs east. With the tide ebbing south in the Western Way and flooding north, it seems likely you will have to buck it one place or the other unless you can hit slack water and have the best of both tides. Bound west, one may do well to avoid the bar altogether and use the ebb tide to beat down to Burnt Coat Harbor, thus getting well to windward. Bound east, it is much more important to have a fair tide through the Thorofares and in the Western Way than it is across the bar.

Bound east from Bass Harbor for Petit Manan and the Bay of Fundy you would do well to start on the ebb, have a fair tide across the bar, be set to windward as you cross Frenchman's Bay, and have the full strength of the powerful flood beyond Schoodic, where it really counts.

When the wind is blowing hard against the tide, the rip on the bar can become very unpleasant and even dangerous for a small boat. Under these circumstances, wait in Bass Harbor or go out around Placentia and Gott's islands. A hard southerly and an ebb tide in the Western Way can build up a dangerous rip between the nun and the can.

Under most conditions, however, there is no problem in crossing the bar, finding the gong on Long Ledge, and running up the Western Way. The first real view of the hills as you come by Long Ledge on a summer afternoon is one you will long remember.

Mt. Desert Island, Me. (306, 307). Mt. Desert Island is the culmination of many a cruise. After a day among the granite and spruce islands to the westward, to round Long Ledge and see the panorama of the Mt. Desert hills in the afternoon sun is breathtaking. As you sail up the Western Way, they grow higher, more distinct, and more impressive until you tuck into Northeast Harbor at night with the hills rising steeply around you.

The island was rediscovered in 1604 by Champlain on his cruise westward from St. Croix Island. He named it *L'isle des Monts Désert,* the island of the barren mountains. To be logical, one should pronounce the name of the island in French, with the accent on the last syllable, or in English with the accent on the first syllable. But to mix the two and call it Mt. De*sert* suggests the last course at a banquet. There is nothing logical about the English pronunciation of foreign words, however, so do as you like. Most local people refer to their home as Mt. *Des*ert, in spite of the late President Eliot of Harvard.

The island affords excellent anchorages, better than adequate shore facilities, and good communication. There are miles of sailing in protected waters with superb mountain views. The trip up Somes Sound is an example of this. Here is the only fiord on the Atlantic coast of the United States. The mountains drop sharply into the sea just as they do in Norway. And at the head, the mountains give way to a lovely valley with a snug harbor at the foot of it.

Do not neglect the trails. Most of the island is now part of Acadia National Park. The park maintains trails and carriage roads and publishes a map, available at the stationery store on the west side of the main street in Northeast Harbor or through the Mt. Desert Chamber of Commerce. The trails are, on the whole, well marked, but some of them are very rugged indeed, leading up over almost vertical ledges by means of iron ladders set into the rock. A good day's walk is from Northeast Harbor, by the Asticou Inn, and up the trail toward Jordan Pond. Swing left up the south shoulder of Jordan Mountain. The trail soon comes out on bare

Mt. Desert Rock with the Mt. Desert Hills and Frenchman Bay in the background.

Augustus D. Phillips

ledge, so that as you climb, you gain changing views of Sargent, Pemetic, Jordan Pond, and the islands to the south. From the top of Jordan on a clear day one can see Mt. Desert Rock to the south and Mt. Katahdin to the north.

Cross over to the top of Sargent Mountain, stopping for a quick dip in Sargent Pond. Then return down the south side of Sargent to the Jordan Pond trail. The writers have seldom made this trip without seeing deer in the woods and a variety of birds, including ravens and eagles, on the upper slopes.

One might vary the trip by stopping at the Jordan Pond House at the south end of the pond, widely renowned for delicious popovers.

Do not leave Mt. Desert without hiring a car and driving to the top of Cadillac (locally, Green) Mountain at sunset. From Rockland to beyond Petit Manan the coast lies at your feet, fading in outline as the lights wink on.

History is all around you here, too. Champlain writes of seeing the island in 1604. The Jesuits visited the island in 1613 and settled at the foot of the field on Fernald's Point. Here they found a spring between high and low water that runs freely today. East of Bass Harbor Head is Ship Harbor, dry at low water, where an American privateer is said to have escaped a British warship during the Revolution. In Somes Sound at the foot of Acadia Mountain is a brook where French naval vessels used to fill water casks. Whether Norsemen actually lay alongside the cliffs of Flying Mountain and fought the Indians coming down the sound in canoes is doubtful, but the scene is not hard to imagine. Indians, Frenchmen, and Englishmen; fishermen, seamen, pirates, farmers have rowed and sailed these waters for centuries. Only recently has it become a "Vacationland." Still in the recollection of many are the days of steam yachts and great schooners at Seal Harbor, fifty-room "cottages" with formal gardens, stables, and battalions of servants at Bar Harbor, and ladies of leisure with parasols and flowered sun hats enjoying it all. A minor theme was the plain living and high thinking of President Eliot of Harvard and a number of his modest and distinguished colleagues. Characteristic of him is the story told of one of his journeys from Rockland to Northeast Harbor on the steamer *J. T. Morse:*

As the President was leaning on the rail contemplating the unfolding beauties of Blue Hill Bay, a member of the crew stood beside him a moment and said, "We've been talking about who was the smartest man that travels on this boat. We concluded it was you, but what we don't know is —if you're so smart, why ain't you rich?" To which Mr. Eliot responded with a characteristic blend of wisdom, modesty, and wit, "I guess I never had time."

Visit the Sawtelle Museum on Cranberry Island for more detailed information on the island's history.

For more modern developments, visit the Jackson Laboratory south of Bar Harbor where continuing work is done on hereditary aspects of cancer. The College of the Atlantic, a new institution in Bar Harbor, is doing advanced ecological studies. The Maine Sea Coast Missionary Society's *Sunbeam* is based on Northeast Harbor and is busy helping people in isolated communities to live richer and better lives. There is a great deal to see and do on Mt. Desert, and a summer is not time enough in which to do it.

Southwest Harbor, Me. (307). This harbor is commercially the most important on the island, with a sardine factory, a fish wharf, a lobster buyer, four boat yards, and the Coast Guard base. However, these enterprises do not in any way render the harbor unpleasant.

Southwest Harbor is easy to make under any conditions from east or west. In anything except an easterly or southeasterly storm it is well protected and the holding ground is good. For convenience we will describe the two anchorages separately.

1. Manset. The most convenient anchorage is off the Henry R. Hinckley yard, unmistakably labeled. The yard maintains guest moorings. Here one has an unobstructed view up Somes Sound and across the Great Harbor of Mt. Desert to the mountains back of Northeast Harbor. At the float, at which the depth of water is indicated by a tide gauge, one can obtain water, ice, gas, Diesel oil, briquets, alcohol, and some ship chandlery. What is not available here can be bought at the yard. The yard can make any kind of repair. In the shed is an excellent shower and toilet for visiting yachtsmen, especially those just back from down east.

The only objection to Hinckley's is that it is usually crowded. The yard float is the base for an extensive charter operation, so that on Fridays and Saturdays, especially, the float may be stacked four deep on each side with yachts fitting out or returning. This means hauling hoses, boxes, and grocery bags over the life rails and under the booms of those lying inside you, and, friendly and anxious to help as they are, interfering with the activities of yard personnel. Unless you have a major job to be done, it is much better to lie on a mooring and bring supplies aboard by skiff. There are less congested places to buy gas at the next wharf, Willis', or across the harbor at Harvard Beal's.

The Moorings, next to the yard, is a good place for a drink and a meal ashore. About a mile and a half to the east on the shore road is the Sea

Wall Restaurant, also said to be an attractive place to dine.

The nearest store is to the west on the shore road and up the hill to the left at the first corner. Here the two Smith ladies have established a small but complete grocery with extras like homemade bread and doughnuts, locally picked blueberries and raspberries, and locally grown vegetables. The ladies are most helpful in finding what you need in the crowded store; and if business is not too demanding, one of them may give you a ride back to the wharf.

Hinckley has a reputation for building fast and able fiberglass yachts. Ask permission to walk through his shop and see the process.

Just west of the road to the store is the shop of Jarvis Newman, an imaginative entrepreneur in fiberglass. He has developed a yacht tender, available either with a centerboard or without, that is steady, rows well, tows well, and is unsinkable. These are nicely finished in varnished mahogany in his shop. He also developed a fiberglass Friendship Sloop by using as a "plug" for his molds the hull of *Old Baldy,* a 25-foot Friendship built by James Rockefeller of Camden to the lines of Abdon Carter's famous *Pemaquid.* A number of these sloops have been finished very attractively, rigged, and equipped with power. One has been fitted with a topmast and makes a fast and attractive little yacht. Mr. Newman does most of the work himself and is more than willing to discuss it. He and Ralph Stanley completely rebuilt the ancient sloop, *The Venturer.*

2. Southwest Harbor. The town is at the head of the harbor. There is good anchorage off Harvard Beal's fish and lobster wharf or off the Southwest Boat Corporation wharf. There may be a vacant mooring available here.

This is a busy place with excursion boats and fishermen constantly coming and going. However, it quiets down at night. Gas, Diesel fuel, water, ice, and, of course, lobsters are available at Harvard Beal's wharf.

Repairs of all kinds can be made and some marine supplies can be purchased at Southwest Boat Corporation now run by the able "Junior" Miller. This yard can haul and repair any vessel on the coast. A lot of heavy commercial work on seiners, draggers, and sardine carriers is done here as well as yacht work.

It is quite a walk up town, but the chances of getting a ride are better than even. In town there are grocery stores, drug stores, a movie theater, a laundromat, and a restaurant.

A taxi can be hired to go to the airport at Trenton or to connect with the bus at Bar Harbor for Ellsworth, Portland, and Boston. A correspondent adds the following notes regarding nearby attractions:

The Great Harbor of Mt. Desert looking east from Southwest Harbor across the entrance to Somes Sound and out the Eastern way. Northeast Harbor and Seal Harbor are just above the middle of the picture.

The best mountain accessible from "Southwest" is, of course, Western; but unless you are a confirmed hiker and know the way to it, take a car. The others are Dog (renamed Saint Sauveur), Robinson (Acadia), and Flying Mountain. These may be reached by anchoring in Valley Cove (a good place to picnic, if one must picnic!); or Norwood Cove, where it is simpler to ask directions of the first person you see. There are two lakes: Long Pond and Echo Lake; the latter is fine for those who like fresh-water swimming. Jesuit Springs in Fernald's Cove is worth looking at. This is a fresh-water spring below the high-tide mark, famous for its clear and sweet water. As soon as the tide has gone out halfway, the water is fresh, and the spring may be distinguished on the beach. The Jesuits, who settled on the point above it, used the spring in the seventeenth century. On a clear day one would do well to take a car from Southwest Harbor to the south end of Long Pond and climb some of the trails on Western Mountain.

A channel has been dredged up the north side of the harbor to the town wharf. There is no room here to anchor, but the trip in the dinghy will save more than half of the walk from Beal's.

Somes Sound, Me. (306). The sail from Northeast or Southwest Harbor up this fiord is a truly inspiring experience. Plan to have a fair tide through the narrows. As you approach, you will see to the west a long field on Fernald's Point. At the foot of it is Jesuit Spring, referred to above, where the first settlers got water in 1613. Leave can 7 to port and keep in the middle.

Valley Cove is the first indentation on the west side. Here the mountains rise almost sheer from deep water, leaving only a narrow strip of beach at the foot of the cliff. Acadia Park maintains four heavy moorings here for visitors. Except in heavy weather, it is a good place to spend an afternoon and evening. There is a trail from the beach across the foot of the slide and up the sound to Man o' War Brook, where it branches, one branch going up Robinson Mountain and the other across to Echo Lake. The latter makes a pleasant walk with a welcome swim in fresh water at the end of it. Robinson Mountain is a steep but short climb affording a good view of the sound.

Then one can sail on up the sound by Hall's Quarry to where the mountains step back a little from the water and the entrance to Somes Harbor appears to the west of Bar Island.

The entrance to this cove is narrow and marked by buoys. Bar Island is part of Acadia National Park, and can be used for picnics. Anchor off the middle of Sheep Island, in 15 feet, or pick up the guest moorings off

Somes Sound. This is an infra-red photograph.

Sheep Island and behind Bar Island.

Somesville, Mt. Desert Post Office, is at the west side of Somes Harbor.

There is a village landing with 4 feet at low water, on the west shore of Somes Sound. From there it is only a short walk to the post office and village. Supplies are available at Fernald's Store and Higgins' Store. The Mt. Desert Yacht Yard, which takes charge of many of the local yachts in these parts, is located to the east, on the eastern shore of the head of Somes Sound. It is well equipped to handle yachts up to 60 feet. Its moorings are always available to visiting yachtsmen, and it is the best source of local information. Consult Mr. E. Farnham Butler, the proprietor. He is an authority on marine matters on the island and has generously contributed much of the data here presented.

The Mount Desert Yacht Yard has pioneered the modern strip construction, building light displacement, reverse sheer yachts by nailing and glueing together inch-square strips of cedar. There should be at anchor off the yard one of the *Controversy*-type yachts. Ask Mr. Butler to discuss the ingenuity with which these yachts have been planned. They have an enviable record.

Northeast Harbor, Me. (306). From the water, Northeast Harbor is attractive indeed. It is easy of access, perfectly protected, and surrounded by spectacular views. The light and fog bell on Bear Island make entrance easy at night or in thick weather. Be careful to avoid a ledge just off the entrance between nun 2 and can 1. There is a notorious dead spot off Sargent Head. Keep to the eastward as much as possible to avoid it.

Seek a berth on the east side of the harbor, as there is considerable motor boat traffic to and from the wharves and the marina at the foot of Sea Street. The town maintains a number of guest moorings distinguished, in 1971, by orange tops. A marina with the usual facilities is there if you want it; it has slips for transients. Snug down and contemplate the calm waters, the large number of magnificent yachts, the gracious cottages, and the lovely hills. Ignore the churning power boats, the automobiles snarling along scenic Peabody Drive, and the vast parking lot.

Anything you need ashore is quickly obtained. The Clifton Dock on the west side of the harbor near the entrance provides gas, Diesel fuel, water, ice, stove fuel, and some marine supplies. An order may be telephoned to the Pine Tree Market from here.

However, if you wish to go up-town, land at the float moored to the southernmost wharf in the cove. On the wharf is a big green box containing trash barrels into which you can dump your bucket. There are several telephone booths on the wharf. The harbor master, Lew Damon,

Laurence Lowry

Northeast Harbor. The marina at the head of the cove on the left has been considerably enlarged.

has an office on the sidewalk to the right.

On a small eminence overlooking the parking lot is a red building devoted to the interests of visiting yachtsmen. There are showers and toilets at a modest fee, lots of periodical literature if you have to wait, and a pleasant attendant to answer questions. Bring your own soap and towels. On foggy days when everyone wants to lay over and clean up, one does well to come in early and avoid the rush.

Turn your back on the shore and walk up Sea Street. You come at once to Flick Flye's restaurant, where lobsters are the specialty—live or cooked. Ice is available here as well.

Within 200 yards you come out on the main street. To your left is a garage where you can rent a car or get a taxi to connect with the bus at Bar Harbor. To the right are the post office, a laundromat, and the hardware store of F.T. Brown, which carries a good inventory of marine hardware as well as charts and government publications. Across the street is a movie theater, and behind it is a liquor store. The Pine Tree Market is a well-stocked grocery with party items as well as staples. They will usually deliver you and your order to the wharf. Farther down the main street are various clothing and novelty shops reminiscent of Camden, Bermuda, and Nassau. A stationery store sells maps of the island as well as papers and paperbacks. There is a drug store and near the end of the street is the Towne House, a restaurant serving good meals. After shopping along the main street of Northeast Harbor, you ought not to need a store again for a week.

There is a new medical center at Northeast Harbor.

It is a good walk on a well-traveled trail to the Jordan Pond House. The trail starts behind the Asticou Inn at the head of the harbor.

On the east side of the harbor, almost exactly opposite the foot of Sea Street, is the Asticou Terraces Dock, the approach to the Asticou Terraces, a unique memorial park left to the town by the late Joseph H. Curtis of Boston. The trip ashore, with a short walk to the top of Asticou Hill, is one of the most rewarding side jaunts of a cruise to Maine. Take it at sunset, or by moonlight. At the top is Thuya Lodge, the old Curtis house, containing the noted Curtis collection of botanical books, open 10 A.M. to 6 P.M. daily. A famous botanical collection has recently been transplanted to the Terraces. At the Asticou Inn, Charles Savage has developed a beautiful Japanese garden.

The Northeast Harbor Fleet has its clubhouse and dock at Gilpatrick's Cove, just west of Northeast Harbor. Don't try to get to the club by water! The anchorage is small and very poor. Cruising yachts are extended a cordial invitation to join the fleet's numerous special races and cruises.

The road skirting the eastern shore of the harbor has been named "Peabody Drive" in honor of the late Dr. Francis Greenwood Peabody of Harvard University, who, throughout a long life, cruised these waters. Once, when asked his occupation, Dr. Peabody replied, "I stay ashore winters"—a sentiment which cruising men will appreciate.

The authors are indebted to the late Mr. W. Rodman Peabody of Boston, son of Dr. Peabody, for the following story concerning President Eliot of Harvard University.

There is a crop of interesting stories about President Eliot, who, you may know, was a very skillful sailor and who sailed the Maine coast with a good deal of regularity from the end of the 1860s to the time of his death. For many years after his first wife died his summer home was a little sloop called the *Sunshine* and his headquarters were at Calf Island in Frenchman Bay.

President Eliot was, as you may guess, an imperturbable person even when fate was against him. I remember once as a small boy sailing from Bar Harbor to Northeast Harbor with my father, who was preaching at Northeast Harbor. We lunched with President Eliot and then started home for Bar Harbor. You may recall that at the mouth of Northeast Harbor there is a ledge with a high rock at each end. It is now protected by red and black buoys, so that there are two entrances to the harbor. In those days the ledge was unbuoyed.

As the President walked with us to the float, my father asked him for the bearings of the ledge which was directly in front of his house and dead to windward. He immediately got in his rowboat and said: "I will sail you out until you are clear and then row home."

We got under way in a stiff southwester and were swinging to it well when we came up with a crash. The boat stopped, slid off, hit again, and went free. The President, who was steering, without a gesture of concern, then turned the wheel over to my father and said: "Those were the two high points of the ledge. If you will take a careful bearing, you will always know their exact location in the future. Good-by. You preached a good sermon." Without another word he hauled in his painter and rowed away.

Seal Harbor, Me. (306). This harbor offers adequate protection on an ordinary summer night. There will be just enough motion to rock you to sleep. But in a heavy southerly or southeaster, Seal Harbor can be very unpleasant.

Gas and water are available at the town landing. Whether you need supplies or not, take the short and pretty walk to the village. There is a thoroughly adequate store.

The summer homes of Fords and Rockefellers overlook the harbor. The late Mr. John D. Rockefeller was glad to make available to horseback riders and hikers the carriage roads and trails on his extensive estate. The family continues this hospitable tradition.

Seal Harbor is the home port of the *Sunbeam,* the Maine Seacoast Mission boat that serves the inhabitants of Maine's most isolated island communities. (See the article about the mission under Bar Harbor, below.)

Great Cranberry Island, Me. (306). Spurling Cove on the north side is a good anchorage in southerly weather. For those passing through, it saves time. The island is not particularly interesting, though the view is superb.

The "Pool," entered from the northeast side, is an excellent anchorage for shoal-draft boats. With a draft of more than 3 feet it is necessary to leave and enter with half tide or more. When entering, follow the southeast side of the channel and, while rounding the little point, keep only a few yards off the beach. Anchor where the fishing boats are moored; there is about 6 feet at mean low water and a soft mud bottom.

Great Cranberry Island has claim to fame as the birthplace on February 22, 1822, of John Gilley, Maine farmer and fisherman, immortalized in "John Gilley" by Charles W. Eliot, available in his *The Durable Satisfactions of Life,* Thomas Y. Crowell & Co., New York, 1910. Everyone sailing these waters should read this short but moving account of the life (and death by drowning) of a native and life-long resident of the islands of Mt. Desert.

Islesford, Little Cranberry Island, Me. (306). This is a great place from which to jump off for down east. Stock up in Manset or Southwest Harbor and sail over to Islesford. Anchor off the wharves and row ashore for a visit to the Sawtelle Museum. This has a number of old charts and many relics of the French days. A walk across the island to the abandoned Coast Guard station, marked "Tower" on the chart, is a refreshing change from the carefully cultivated paths around Northeast Harbor. You are again on a Maine island, with granite ledge, huckleberry, and sweet fern giving way to a stony beach, a view of Bakers Island, and the sea breaking heavily on the offshore ledges.

Get back aboard in time to enjoy the sunset behind the mountains. This is the best place from which to see it.

Plan your start, if you can, to give two hours of ebb tide out of Frenchman Bay and a flood tide beginning to make after you pass Schoodic.

Thus you will quickly pass that desolate tide-ridden stretch between Schoodic and Petit Manan where there is little shelter and where finding what shelter there is could be a nervous experience in thick weather.

The lower part of this bay is wide open to the sea, but there are few dangers, and navigation is easy. There are bold shores and noisy buoys on both sides, with Egg Rock Light's fog signal and whistling buoy in the middle. In the writer's experience the afternoon southwester is likely to be light and fluky off Schooner Head and in the mouth of the bay, but above the Schooner Head and up the steep shore it draws vigorously into Bar Harbor. Winds among the Porcupines are fluky and often very gusty.

The upper part of the bay is well protected by the Porcupines, Ironbound, and Jordan Island, affording a large area of smooth water with few dangers, good harbors, and grand views of the hills.

Some of the more popular shelters are discussed below.

Bar Harbor, Me. (306, 205). There is no trick to getting into this harbor. One may enter either between Bald Porcupine and Sheep Porcupine Islands or from the south through Cromwell Cove and around the end of the breakwater. The *Coast Pilot* 1960 warns that at high water on a smooth day it may be impossible to see the breakwater.

Bar Harbor is a beautiful place to anchor and contemplate the mountains, but it is likely to be rolly in anything southerly. The water is deep and the holding ground poor. However, there are a number of guest moorings available, and one may lie alongside the wharf for a short time. Gasoline, ice, water, and fuel oil are available here, although there is only 3 feet at low water. There is about 6 feet at the marina west of the municipal pier.

There are all kinds of stores at Bar Harbor, including a state liquor store. Hotels, motels, restaurants, and a movie theater are within a short walk of the municipal pier. Buses run to Ellworth and Bangor to connect with through buses to Portland and Boston. Northeast Airlines at Trenton is a short taxi ride away. The Bar Harbor Club provides showers and facilities for visiting yachtsmen. Inquire at the information center on the municipal pier. The Bar Harbor Yacht Club maintains a clubhouse and landing at Hull's Cove. The club welcomes cruising men.

North of the harbor is the conspicuous landing of the *Bluenose,* a steamer ferry making regular trips between Bar Harbor and Yarmouth, N.S. She leaves about 8 A.M. and returns around 9:30 P.M. Her route runs west of Egg Rock and Mt. Desert Rock, then about southeast by east for Yarmouth.

The Roscoe B. Jackson Memorial Laboratory, located about a mile south of Bar Harbor on the Seal Harbor Road, is the largest center of mammalian genetics research in the world. Its scientists carry on fulltime basic research in genetics and diseases in which heredity is a factor, such as cancer, mental illness, muscular dystrophy, neuromuscular defects, and radiation-induced sickness. The laboratory maintains a colony of 500,000 experimental mice of some 60 different inbred strains. About 2,000,000 animals are produced each year, a third used by Jackson Lab scientists, the rest shipped to researchers all over the world. If you're in any of the island harbors, call the laboratory and inquire about their programs for visitors.

During the early part of the century Bar Harbor was a glittering social center. Enormous Victorian cottages on huge estates overlooked Frenchman Bay. Steam yachts and even an occasional square-rigged yacht anchored in the harbor. Social distinctions were very significant.

But with changing times this grandeur faded, and the 1947 fire, which destroyed most of the mansions and much of the town, ended the period dramatically.

Bar Harbor is now quite a different place. Six to seven thousand tourists spend the night in Bar Harbor and nearby campsites almost every night during the summer. They swarm on the shores, stand about on the wharf, and jostle on the streets and in the restaurants. The atmosphere at Bar Harbor today is much more like that of tourist centers to the westward than it is like a Maine town or an old-time "resort."

The National Park facilities attract many campers and hikers. The Park Service makes a great effort to keep the camp grounds neat and clean and to provide programs for interested visitors. Lectures on history and on the birds, animals, and plants of the region are given frequently.

"God's Tugboat." A unique vessel, which may be seen in almost any harbor of the Maine coast, is the Diesel motorship *Sunbeam,* owned and operated by The Maine Sea Coast Missionary Society of Bar Harbor. The *Sunbeam* is easily distinguishable because of the white cross on either side of her bow, denoting the practical Christian service in which she is engaged.

The *Sunbeam* is 65 feet long, powered by a 225 h.p. Diesel engine, and draws 7 feet. The vessel is built of steel, and the bow section is reinforced with extra-heavy steel plate and frames for ice-breaking purposes.

The *Sunbeam* was built in Warren, Rhode Island, in 1964, and is the sixth in the succession of vessels that have served the mission since it was founded in 1905. The mission's work is interdenominational, with the objective of providing Christian leadership and pastoral care along the coast and on the islands of the Maine coast, and to engage in all efforts that are calculated to contribute to the moral and spiritual welfare of the inhabitants. The *Sunbeam* is used as transportation for mission workers, and as a lifeline for isolated families and communities, especially in frigid winter weather. This splendidly equipped small ship symbolizes in its ready and able service the total program of the mission, which comprises Christian work in uncounted practical ways—preaching, teaching, aid to the sick and unfortunate, encouragement of young people, visitation and ministry to the lonely, and much more. The mission has an embrace large enough to take in all members of its widespread parish, regardless of their estate, whether clean and scrubbed or spattered with mud from the flats, yet intimate enough to call each one by name. At present mission workers are stationed either full- or part-time in the following places: Lubec, Jonesport, South Addison, Cherryfield, Milbridge, West Gouldsboro, Swans Island, Frenchboro, Matinicus, Monhegan, Loudville, and Bar Harbor. In addition, services are held either regularly or on a seasonal or itinerant basis in the following: Mason Bay, Cape Split, Wyman, and Islesford. Visitors are always welcome at the mission stations and churches as well as on board the *Sunbeam* and at the headquarters, 24 Ledgelawn Avenue, Bar Harbor, where since 1970, items relating to the history of the mission have been on display in a small museum.

The mission's annual reports and bulletins constitute an offshore saga full of salty incident and color. Any yachtsman interested in keeping in touch with the Maine coast throughout the year would do well to subscribe to the mission and receive its unique publications.

These, plus the newsy monthly *National Fisherman,* published at Camden and more fully described under that harbor, serve to brighten the long months of those who, like the late Dr. Francis Greenwood Peabody of Harvard, "stay ashore winters."

Skillings River, Me. (306). There is a quiet, though fairly large, anchorage far up in Young's Bay. The river is narrow, but there is no difficulty in entering. Southwest of Hyde Point the mussel beds have grown up and extend farther into the channel than the chart shows. No supplies can be obtained, with the possible exception of lobsters at the pound just below the point.

Sullivan, Me. (306). The Sullivan anchorage is exposed to the south. There is a strong tide in the river, and there is a narrow and rocky place that forms rapids. It is not recommended for strangers.

Sullivan is a small village on the north side of the harbor 3½ miles above the entrance. There is a privately owned wharf that bares at extreme low tides.

It was on the western side of Hancock Point that a German submarine landed three spies on a late autumn morning in World War II. As they walked up the road, the sheriff's son noticed them, lightly clad in city clothes. He became suspicious, followed their tracks, and notified the F.B.I. They were located in Bangor and followed until they revealed their "contacts" and then were arrested.

On the eastern side of Hancock Point is a dock with about 6 feet at low water and a guest mooring. It is a pleasant place to spend a night in quiet weather.

Between Hancock Point and Sullivan, the Taunton-Sullivan river flows into Frenchmans Bay and near its outlet, on the side toward Hancock Point, is the former site of Mt. Desert Ferry, the busy terminus of the Maine Central Railroad. Here passengers and freight were transferred to three ferry steamers for points inside the bay and to Bar Harbor and other harbors along the ocean side of Mt. Desert Island. The amount of traffic can be visualized if one remembers that at that time there was only a clay-and-dirt road from the mainland, over a bridge, to the island, and almost everything that went onto and from the island was by boat, either from Mt. Desert Ferry or from Rockland. Mr. Dean K. Worcester describes the scene in the early days of this century as follows, in the *National Fisherman:*

Mount Desert Ferry, of which no trace remains, was a place on the mainland where the railroad track came down alongside deep water, so that the Bar Harbor Express, with its dozen or more sleeping cars, could lie at one side of the dock, while Norumbega lay at the other, rising and falling in the 10' tide.

The train used to arrive about 7 AM and when the passengers and their baggage had been put aboard, Norumbega would shove off for Bar Harbor, nearly an hour's journey. There was a restaurant in the forward deckhouse, where you could have breakfast and at the same time see where you were going. The course lay nearly due south, and since Mount Desert Island's abrupt mountain ranges and valleys, carved by glaciers, also run more or less north and south, their endwise profile as seen from the steamer was particularly dramatic. After having left New York on a hot summer evening, it was a pleasure to watch the island approaching in the clear cool morning light, gently suffused with eggs and bacon and coffee.

At least that's how I remember it, 50-odd years later.

Sorrento, Me. (306). With a magnificent view of Mt. Cadillac across Frenchman Bay, Sorrento is one of the most beautiful harbors on the coast. It offers good shelter, as one can duck behind Dram or Preble Island, depending on the direction of the wind.

In entering Sorrento from the south, favor the westerly side of the entrance between those two islands. The *Coast Pilot* reports reefs extending 100 yards from Preble Island and 50 yards from Dram Island. The entrance from the westward is narrowed by a reef, partly showing at high water, which extends 175 yards from the north side.

There is a summer resort, but no hotel or eating place within 5 or 6 miles. The Sorrento Yacht Club uses the town wharf with a float where there is 6 feet at low water. Stop there for local information. The club maintains at least one visitor's mooring. Water is obtainable at the float. Gasoline can be had in cans from a garage ⅛ mile away, if you have your own cans. Ice is not obtainable. There is a public golf course a mile away. Limited supplies may be obtained 3 miles away at the corner of Route 1. Sorrento is a yachting center for this part of the bay—a quiet, attractive place to visit.

There is a good anchorage in Eastern Point Harbor to the east.

Stave Island, Me. (306). A good but large harbor. In southerly weather, anchor close under the high slopes of Jordan Island. Foss Cove, back of the spar buoy, is small, shoal, and unattractive.

Winter Harbor, Me. (204, 306). Easy of access, deep, and clearly marked, Winter Harbor is an excellent place to spend the night for yachtsmen bound east or west. Bound east, it cuts the run from Mt. Desert to Mistake Island enough to make it an easy day's run even in a modest breeze. Bound west, it postpones until next day what can be a long beat across Frenchman Bay in the chill of a late afternoon.

Entrance from the south is easy with the obvious abandoned lighthouse on Mark Island and the lighted bell off it. From the north, simply follow the bold shore of Grindstone Neck, being certain to leave can 3 and the white beacon to *starboard*. It looks impossible as you approach, but there is plenty of deep water close to the shore. Then leave nun 2 *close* to port and run up the harbor. There are two good anchorages here.

Sand Cove. This is a deep cove on the western side of the harbor under Grindstone Neck. Here is the hospitable and well-appointed Winter Harbor Yacht Club. The club maintains two guest moorings, a float, and a pleasant clubhouse. A steward is in attendance from 8 A.M. to 6 P.M. during the summer. Whatever your needs, discuss them with the steward and receive instant and courteous attention.

You may telephone a grocery order to Winter Harbor Food Service and have it delivered to the club. A tempered salt-water swimming pool, shower, and snack bar, and perhaps even a dinner can be found at the club. The steward is said to blow a horn in answer to fog signals from boats nearby, but perhaps the skipper would do well not to rely on it implicitly. Water and ice are available at the club float.

From the south end of the porch a path leads up the hill to the site of the old Grindstone Inn, a symbol of post-Victorian elegance that burned in 1956. The view across to the Mt. Desert hills remains, however, and is worth the walk. There are a number of cottages along the road on the ridge. With their carefully tended lawns and shrubbery, wide porches, and graveled drives they maintain a dignity and hint at an attitude toward vacations of which but a memory remains.

The Frenchman Bay Lodge located a short distance to the north along the ridge serves excellent meals. It is well to call from the club as early as you can to give adequate notice.

The Fisherman's Inn, located in the village of Winter Harbor, is a pleasant walk from the club and is reported to serve excellent meals and cocktails at a reasonable cost.

Winter Harbor Cove. This small and crowded cove, called the Inner Harbor locally, is much better protected than the anchorage in Sand Cove. Although it is crowded with fishermen, there is usually a mooring available. Land at the float on the east side. It is a short and pleasant walk through an eastern Maine countryside to the "Main Street." Turn left for the store and the telephone booth; right for the post office. Gas, oil, and Diesel fuel are available at Reedy's wharf at the head of the cove with a depth of 2 feet at low water. You will find Winter Harbor a refreshing change from Northeast Harbor.

The cove may be noisy in the early morning with departing fishermen, but you will want to get along anyway.

It was here that I first heard of fishing for herring with piano wire. One man rows a dory or pea-pod quietly up a cove. Another drags over the side a length of piano wire too short to reach bottom. There is a weight on the end of the wire. If herring are in the cove, they will brush against the thin wire and their number can be estimated by the frequency of the jiggles on the wire. If there are enough, the cove is stopped off and seined.

The Grindstone Neck development was laid out about 1892 by the late John Moore, a native of nearby Steuben, who did business in New York and owned the neck and the Schoodic Peninsula. Before his death he presented the latter to the federal government as part of Acadia National Park.

The view of Mt. Desert and the islands of Frenchman Bay on a clear morning from the Winter Harbor entrance, with the sun shining on the cliffs of Cadillac Mountain, is worth going a long way to see.

The easternmost outpost of the Mt. Desert Region, Winter Harbor is one of the most attractive points in this picturesque section of Maine. Bound east, it is the last summer resort settlement until one reaches St. Andrews, N.B.

CHAPTER XII

Schoodic Point to West Quoddy Head

General Conditions. To be headed east by Schoodic whistle before a summer sou'wester with Mt. Desert fading astern and the lonely spike of Petit Manan Light just visible on the port bow is about as close to perfection as a man can expect to come on this imperfect earth.

Astern lie supermarkets, yacht clubs, water skiers, high-charged power cruisers, the pageantry associated with racing and day sailing. Ahead lie cold waters, racing tides, the probability of thick fogs and delightful scale-ups. The islands and most of the mainland shores are uninhabited except for small communities of lobstermen. The long, low, wooded promontories keep one well offshore in rounding them, but between, once east of Petit Manan, are islands, coves, and quiet creeks. You won't go swimming much. The water is fiercely cold. But the fishing is good and there are still clams in some places.

For the experienced navigator with a touch of the explorer, this country is the Promised Land, and for the "cricker" it is a happy hunting ground. The gregarious, the inexperienced navigators, and those who like to dress up and go ashore for dinner at the yacht club every evening will be happier west of Schoodic.

There are a few cautions to bear in mind. Perhaps the first is to be sure that you have proper charts. Charts 303, 304, 305, and 1201 are essential. An accurate compass in which the navigator can have implicit confidence is necessary. Log, lead, and look-out are never to be neglected.

Next, *be careful*. Careless errors may exact their price very quickly on this lonesome coast.

Thirdly, be prepared to stay a while. You may be fogbound or windbound, but be sure that you will have to wait out tides. A tide setting against the wind on this coast can raise a dangerous sea in short order. To beat against a Fundy tide in a light breeze is a losing battle.

Alternate Routes. On this coast there is usually a choice between an inside and an outside passage. From Schoodic one can head well outside Petit Manan, leaving the bell to port in ordinary weather. If a big sea is running, it may be wise to go outside the whistle off Southeast Rock. Or one may go inside, across Petit Manan Bar in smooth weather.

One going inside must be wary of a string of ledges just inside the course, Old Man and the Black Ledges, and of Moulton's Ledge and Stone Horse Ledge just east of them. Petit Manan Bar itself is a dangerous place in rough or thick weather. It is a shallow, boulder-strewn bar across which the tide runs heavily. The buoys, nearly a mile from either shore, are small and hard to find.

The coast between Schoodic Point and the bar looks desolate in the extreme. The harbors are some distance from the course and are either tricky to enter, like Corea, or exposed, like Prospect Harbor. The mouths of Dyer and Gouldsboro Bay are obstructed by ledges and islands. When a heavy sea is running, this is an awesome piece of coast. In thick weather with a strong and unpredictable tide running, it can be a horror. For instance, the tides here appear to change direction during the ebb or flood. I have noticed the ebb tide still running west at the first of the flood to well around to the southwest a few hours later.

Once across the bar, however, one can run up Pigeon Hill Bay or, by using the bold shores, work through the Douglas Islands to a secure and beautiful anchorage behind Trafton Island.

The run offshore, outside Petit Manan Light, is much easier. Although the horn on the light is very hard to hear to the westward, one could scarcely hit any of the dangers outside without hearing the bell or the whistle. Thence the run to Nash Island whistle is not difficult, as the tide affects the course but little. Cape Split is just beyond.

Or one can run outside to Seahorse Rock, the bleak dramatic cliff of Crumple Island, and the powerful horn on Mistake Island. There is good shelter in the Cow Yard or back of Knight Island. The outside route continues outside the Libby Islands, Cross Island, and up Grand Manan Channel to Quoddy Head. Cutler is the best shelter and indeed nearly the only one on this route, and Cutler is easy to make with the help of the whistle outside.

If one has a short enough mast, one may run up Moosabec Reach by Jonesport. The chart claims 39 feet clearance under the bridge at high water. From Jonesport through Roque Island Thorofare, Roque Island Harbor, Foster Channel, Machias Bay, and Cross Island Narrows is a quiet and delightful sail among some of the wildest and most attractive scenery on the coast spoiled only by four unsightly radar towers behind Bucks Harbor and the huge low-frequency radio towers on Thornton Point back of Cross Island. After passing through Cross Island Narrows, one enters the Bay of Fundy dramatically as one passes Old Man and Cape Wash. Cutler is the nearest and best port at which to stop and draw breath before making the crossing to Grand Manan or the run up Lubec Narrows.

Fish Weirs. Among the islands down east where the tide runs hard and the waters are well protected, herring are trapped by means of weirs (pronounced "wares"). A weir consists essentially of a circular fence of brush supported by poles four to six inches thick driven into the mud. The fence has an opening on the side facing the ebb tide. From this opening one or two or sometimes three leaders or wings run off at a broad angle to each other. Each wing extends a few yards inside the weir.

The herring run up the bay with the tide and on the ebb "settle back" between the wings and work into the trap. At low water a day or so later when they have "worked the feed out of them" the fish are seined; and if the haul is good, a carrier is called. This big vessel, perhaps 70 feet long, is equipped with a powerful pump. This sucks the fish out of the seine, scales them, and dumps them into the hold. They are lightly salted and rushed to the factory to be canned as sardines. The scales are sold for "pearl essence," for shirt buttons, for making fire extinguisher foam, and —it is said—for clearing beer.

The weir is usually built in about 7 feet of water. One wing runs into the shore where room enough is left for a dory to squeeze by. The outer end is run into deep water. It is usually safe to go close to the outer wing of a weir. The law requires a white light on the outer end of the outer wing, but his law is not frequently observed.

In the winter, ice freezes around the stakes and sometimes breaks them off. This leaves a dangerous stub submerged at high water. If a weir has been abandoned for some time, such stakes can be a dangerous menace. It is well to mark all weirs on your chart as you see them.

Never miss a chance to watch a carrier pump out a seine. It is exciting to see the men "drying in" the net into dories, forcing the fish into a tight pocket. The pump throws an acre of suds, the fish flip madly on deck, everyone runs around in rubber boots up to his knees in fish. The radio will probably be squawking over it all at full power, and everyone is enjoying the party and getting richer by the minute. The writer saw two men make $15,000 in half a day out of one weir. All kinds of fish are likely to shoot out of the pump, including mackerel and flounder. And fresh herring make a first-class supper.

After the carrier leaves and the excitement subsides, you may hear some good yarns and—if the ladies are not in evidence—some salty singing.

Schoodic Harbor, Me. (305). Known locally as One Squeak, this is not a desirable anchorage. A considerable roll makes in.

Bunker Harbor, Me. (305). Closer than Winter Harbor or Prospect Harbor to the straight course down east, Bunker Harbor is a good shelter and a very pleasant place. Entrance, however, especially for the skipper who is making it for the first time, can be tense.

From Schoodic whistle follow the bold shore of Schoodic Island. The part of the island shown green on chart 305 almost always breaks. Thence make the short run to the lighted bell off Brown Cow. Then follow the shore down to Bunker Harbor and run up the middle. Between the point and the outlying ledge is a shoal with about 7 feet at low water. You may see kelp. Of course, if a heavy sea is running, the entrance is impossible.

If you are coming in from the east, you will see a high pyramidal rock just south of the entrance. This is on the base of the southern point of the harbor and is indicated as a tiny circle on chart 305. The half-tide rock east of it and the ledge colored green on the chart are submerged about half tide. However, they usually break. Halfway between them and the pyramidal rock is about right. If it is high water and you can't see the ledge, give the pyramidal rock a good 50 yards berth. Move slowly and watch for bottom.

Entrance from the north is only for the luckiest of strangers.

On a quiet night, anchorage in the outer harbor is entirely satisfactory, although a slight roll makes in. If conditions are threatening, go into the inner harbor. Stay close to the anchored boats, as the west side of the harbor has a number of ledges. The cove was dredged to 10 feet a few years ago. Inquire for a mooring or a chance to lie alongside a fisherman if you can't find swinging room.

There are two gas wharves with 2 feet at the first and 8 to 10 feet at the second.

It is a pleasant walk of about a mile up the road to Chipman's Grocery and gas station at Birch Harbor if you can stand the cars whizzing by on the way to or from the park at Schoodic Point.

Birch Harbor, Me. (305). Avoid this harbor. It is open to the south and east and most of it dries out at low water.

Prospect Harbor, Me. (305). The approaches to Prospect Harbor are well marked with a whistle, a bell, a gong, and the quick flashing bell off Spruce Point. The ledges off the harbor mouth, Old Woman, Old Man, Big Black Ledge and Little Black Ledge, are all bold and break noisily most of the time. Entrance to the inner harbor is marked by a light without a fog signal and a black-and-white bell. If the weather looks threatening and you draw less than 6 feet, anchor behind the sardine factory and use it for protection. In normal circumstances however, it is pleasanter to be to windward of it. A visitor in 1971 writes that not only was the factory free of objectionable odor but it was a positive advantage.

When the plant is working, the refuse discharged into the harbor makes the finest kind of toll or chum; we caught nine beautiful mackerel in about fifteen minutes. Others were catching enormous numbers.

Be sure your riding light burns brightly, for sometimes big sardiners charge in at night with fish for the factory.

Ashore, the town is spread out along the road by the harbor. It is clean, pleasant, and quiet. Stinson's store between the wharves and the fish plant is open Monday to Friday, but not on weekends.

Corea, Me. (305). This is the best shelter between Schoodic and Petit Manan. If one is making the run east in the fog, this is a good place at which to break the trip. The whistle outside makes it comparatively easy of access. One can work one's way along from Schoodic whistle to the Old Woman to the bell off Cranberry Point to the Corea whistle. From there, run for the western end of Western Island, follow the north shore of Western Island until well up to the eastern end, and not *until then* head for a gray cottage among the trees on a conspicuous yellow ledge. Favor the easterly side of the entrance. The harbor is shallow, about 6 feet at low water, with a mud bottom. In 1965 one of the wharves on the east side was buying ground fish—cod and hake mostly—to be shipped to Machias and canned. The other wharves are used by lobstermen, some of whom tend up to 300 traps. Gasoline and Diesel oil are available.

It is a pleasant walk from the wharves on the east side up the shore to the north. Here a developer has bought land on Gouldsboro Bay and is advertising "homes" in Paul Bunyan Shores. If you weather this hazard, bear to the left and continue to the small country store. Ordinary supplies and local information are available here. Ask about the tracking station on the hill behind the town. You can continue to bear to the left and come back to the west side of the harbor, where there is a remarkably well-appointed ship chandlery run by Don Anderson. Flake ice is available at the large fish wharf on the east side of the harbor.

Corea is a small, pleasant Maine village, still "undeveloped" despite the menace of Paul Bunyan. It has a bleak northern quality about it; it is what I imagine Labrador to be like.

Gouldsboro Bay, Me. (305). This is a large protected body of water that can be entered either through the Western Passage or through Eastern Way. It is far from the direct route but a pleasant place to explore.

At the head of it is Joy Bay, of which a correspondent writes, "Joy Bay is an excellent anchorage but the 5-foot spot in the entrance is really there. We weathered a near hurricane in there."

Supplies can be obtained at Steuben at the head of the bay.

Dyer Bay, Me. (305). Our correspondent adds categorically, "All Dyer Bay is good." One anchorage is at Over Cove on the east shore. It is reported that there is a store here. Gasoline is said to be available across the bay from Over Cove.

Another anchorage is Carrying Place Cove behind Birch Point. Move carefully here. The flats are extensive. No supplies are available.

Kelp is said to be heavy in the southern part of the bay.

Note on Petit Manan, Me. (305). Petit Manan Point makes out in a long bar to Petit Manan Island and continues underwater, as soundings indicate, for a long way offshore. This place can be very dangerous. Fishermen treat it with respect.

The difficulties are produced by three factors. The tide offshore runs east on the flood and west on the ebb and does so with considerably more vigor than it does farther west. Also, however, the tide runs in and out of Pigeon Hill, Pleasant, and Narraguagus bays to the east, and of Dyer and Gouldsboro bays to the west of Petit Manan. Consequently three different tidal currents meet off the light. This confuses the sea and sets one off one's course unpredictably.

The second difficulty is the exposed position of Petit Manan. It is a long way from a secure harbor and open to the full sweep of the Atlantic. In addition, the bottom is very uneven. The chart shows pinnacles rising 150 feet off an apparently smooth bottom. The consequence is that the sea is always rough and can be confused and dangerous. It is particularly dangerous when the ebb tide meets a brisk southerly wind. A cruiser drawing little water and sporting a hurricane deck and flying bridge could get in serious trouble here very quickly. The motion would find weak spots, too, in a sailing yacht's rigging. The safest course is to pass outside the bell under any conditions and to stay outside the whistle if the sea is heavy.

The third problem is fog. Petit Manan holds the record for maximum number of hours of fog-signal operation for any one year between 1950 and 1963—over 2000 hours. When the fog drops over the rough and tide-scoured waters off Petit Manan, the difficulties are vastly increased. No fog signal is very effective to windward. Anyone running east on a foggy afternoon is very unlikely to hear the Petit Manan horn far to windward. As one approaches, it is the part of discretion to shut off the engine—not just put it in neutral—and drift for a few minutes until the boat loses way. Really listen intently for a solid minute at the very least.

In addition to aberrations of the fog signal, remember that the island is low and that one cannot approach it closely from any direction. One would not even see the loom of the shore before striking.

Plan, then, to pass well outside the light and count on hearing the fog signal, the bell buoy, or the whistle *after* passing the island. Once by the light, it is a long haul to the Nash Island whistle, but the tide will set you off your course little, if any, and the Nash Island whistle seems to be one of the best on the coast. Whether it is the particular buoy or has to do with conditions around Nash Island, we don't know, but you can hear it all over the bay. From Nash Island whistle, run for Pot Rock, The Ladle, and Cape Split. The rock east of The Ladle *almost* always breaks.

Petit Manan Bar has been discussed above under Alternate Routes. On no condition should one try this in the fog. The chances of finding those little buoys are dim indeed.

Because it is occasionally pleasant to have the rocks and shoals of the coast peopled by figures of the past, the authors venture to repeat here a story told by the late W. Rodman Peabody of Boston, son of Dr. Francis Greenwood Peabody of Harvard University, regarding Petit Manan Bar. Having to do with the nautical adventures of the late President Eliot of Harvard, this story may be put down as a companion piece to another yarn related by Mr. Peabody and included under Northeast Harbor, above.

I shall always remember another fresh southwest afternoon when, although he was of advanced age, the President had gone cruising with us as far east as Cutler. We were standing across Tit Manan Bar heading for the opening which was marked only by a fisherman's buoy. It was blowing freshly and as we approached the Bar there was a heavy rip. My father, whose boat was one which was characterized by a friend as having "rather long spars for a parson," stood in the companionway watching his whipping topmast with grave concern. Forty years of deference, however, left him tongue-tied. From my position by the main-sheet I recognized that he was praying for the best but without much hope. Obviously the topsail ought to have come in. Not a word came from the President, but I saw him glance at my father, take in the situation and give one long and careful look at the whipping spar and then I thought I saw a slight wink from an almost imperturbable face.

We came through whole and the President remarked casually: "If you don't mind taking the helm now, Frank, I think I will take my afternoon nap." No reference to the sea, the wind or the spars was ever made by either of them, but the younger generation clinging to the weather rail had a thoroughly enjoyable fifteen minutes.

Pigeon Hill Bay, Me. (305). A shoal-draft boat with an adventurous skipper can run up Pigeon Hill Bay and east between Pea and Currant Islands into Narraguagus Bay. The area is a popular region for herring, so beware of fish weirs. They consist of circular fences of brush supported by poles driven in the mud, and at high water they are hard to see. There is no really good anchorage in Pigeon Hill Bay.

Narraguagus Bay, Me. (305). This pleasant bay affords protected sailing, quiet anchorages, and dramatic scenery. It is nearly uninhabited, but the people, either cruising yachtsmen, herring fishermen, or lobstermen, you will enjoy. There are several anchorages here, excluding Douglas Island Harbor, which is no harbor at all so far as a small boat is concerned.

Trafton Island, Me. (305). This is one of the most attractive islands on the coast. The easiest approach is from the east. Round the northeast point and work up the west side of the point by the cliff to a big white rock. Anyone drawing under 6 feet can anchor here.

The island is wooded, but there are open glades in the woods, patches of birch, and thickets of alder. The woods are grown up enough so that walking is not difficult. The south end of the island is covered with huge boulders of white granite that lie in confused masses, making caves and passages among them. There is a rocky beach in the southern cove. At high water on a warm day the swimming on the beach in the northern cove is good and there may still be some clams on the flats. There are two unobtrusive cottages owned by James Rea on Trafton's behind the little island west of the anchorage. The anchorage is quiet and protected. It is supervised during the absence of Mr. Rea by the owners: an osprey, a family of seals, and a supercilious shag. It was much used years ago by coasters waiting for a "good chance" down the bay.

Dyer Island, Me. (305). There are two coves on the west side and one on the east that are picturesque and quiet anchorages for small boats on a calm night. None would be much good in a blow. Apparently Northeast Cove is the best. A correspondent reports 8 feet in the middle and 5 feet near the shores. The bottom is mud. A small ledge makes out from the south side about halfway in. The tide runs about ½ knot through this anchorage. Beware of mosquitoes.

There is a camp for underprivileged children on the island.

Milbridge, Me. (305), is a former shipbuilding town that is now devoted to sardines. It is possible to get up the Narraguagus River to the town but difficult, because of extensive flats and numerous fish weirs. One can tie up at Wyman's sardine factory if it is not inconvenient, but it is not a picturesque berth. Minor supplies are available. Through buses stop at Cherryfield.

Flint Island, Me. (305). One can anchor with safety in Flint Island Narrows. The tide runs vigorously. Flint Island itself is a delightful island, much like Trafton. Notice the cliff on the southwest corner of Shipstern Island. The rock looks strikingly like the stern of an eighteenth-century warship.

Pleasant Bay, Me. (305). This bay exists to be explored. The writer knows nothing of it and has located no correspondent who writes of it.

Cape Split, Me. (305). This harbor is accessible from the sea and easy to make. If coming from the west in thick weather, make for the lighted whistle to the west of Nash Island. After passing the island to starboard, The Ladle offers an easily recognized landmark for the entrance to Cape Split, as the rock to the east almost always breaks. Regarding this rock, a local fisherman writes, "The sunken rock to the east of The Ladle does not always break. If the sea is calm and no roll and high tide, it is just a very dangerous ledge."

Another approach is first to pick up Pot Rock and leave The Ladle to starboard. If coming from the east, note that one cannot run directly from Tibbett Narrows for nun 2 off Wright Point. Bear off to the south and then north. Note that the rocks off the entrance bare at a third from high tide.

Favor the east side of the harbor to avoid an old weir that runs far out into the harbor from the long point on the west shore just south of the wharves. There is good anchorage off the wharves. A quieter berth is to be found in Otter Cove, which indents the east shore of the harbor before you come to the wharves.

Gasoline and simple provisions can be obtained at the well-stocked store of D.H. Look & Sons at the head of the wharf. There is through bus connection at Columbia Falls. One can hire a car at Cape Split to meet this bus.

Local fishermen consider Cape Split "the best harbor between Northeast Harbor and Canada—better than Cutler, where there is said to be an undertow." Be careful if running in in thick weather, for Cape Split fogs are more numerous and denser than fogs almost anywhere else except in Machias Bay.

A correspondent reports having the fog come down on him from above in less than ten minutes after it touched the top of Jordans Delight. A visitor to Cape Split contributed the following note about thirty years ago. It is still pertinent:

> There is a general store near the fishing dock on the east side which has many fine groceries, also rigging and simple boatswain supplies. Letters to be mailed can be left with the storekeeper. There is a spring almost in front of the store.
>
> The country up here is indescribably beautiful: very small fishing villages—excellent harbors; saw only one summer place—at Tibbett Narrows. The natives at Cape Split are very helpful people, who evinced quite an interest in our cruise (which may have been only because we were boys, in a small boat, in September). . . . Their houses are beautifully kept up, with delightful gardens. A walk over to Tibbett Narrows requires about 15 minutes each way and gives a view up Moosabec Reach to Jonesport. Cape Split has an atmosphere about it which I've never experienced before and which I like to think is common to all points to the east of it.

This correspondent recommends that boats drawing 5 or 6 feet anchor well up the harbor among the fishing boats. The harbor shoals up fast to the east of the channel. The tide runs in the channel and there is a slight roll. The holding ground is good, being sticky mud.

The late Mr. Delbert Look of Cape Split was a man of energy and vision. It was he who, back in the thirties, developed the method of transporting lobsters in crates. It had been the practice to dump lobsters into the hold of a smack, which was bulkheaded off and bored with holes to provide circulation. The motion of the vessel killed some lobsters and broke claws off others. However, if the lobsters were crated, there was insufficient circulation of water and they died from lack of oxygen. Mr. Look bought an old schooner, *Verna G.,* lined her hold with cement, and installed powerful pumps so that water could be circulated under pressure. Then he loaded her with crated lobsters and, with pumps running constantly, shipped lobsters to Boston with very low mortality. The method was soon imitated and prevailed until it became cheaper to ship by truck. The wreck of *Verna G.* is rotting on the beach at Cape Split.

During World War II, Delbert's son Oscar was reported missing after Bataan. The father believed firmly that nothing serious had happened to his son and refused to shave his beard in token of it until his son's safe return.

Oscar survives his father and today operates a tremendous lobster pound just above the wharf. The project involves hundreds of thousands of dollars and great risk. The idea is to hold lobsters over a period of low price until the price rises. The difficulty is that lobsters are delicate creatures. If it rains heavily so that the salinity of the water is affected, they will die. If they are fed too much, the food will rot and poison them. If fed too little, they will cannibalize each other. They do not eat with their claws but with very hard "teeth" in the mouth under the proboscis. These teeth can easily grind up another lobster's shell. Of course if the price fails to rise, the whole scheme is a failure. However, it is difficult indeed to make a living in Cape Split. Oscar is buying lobsters and taking this risk in order to do what he can to support the economy of this small town.

The Great Northern Land and Cattle Company has bought 140 acres of land on Cape Split and plans to develop it in two-acre building lots. Purchasers are expected to buy "for what Maine used to be, not for what it has become," so houses are to be more or less traditional in style. A wharf and docking area is planned.

This may never come off, but the writer plans to visit Cape Split again as soon as possible in order to see it as it has been for so many years.

Moosabec Reach, Me. (304). Until 1959 Moosabec Reach was the common way for yachts to go east and west along the coast. With the construction of the Beals Island Bridge with a clearance of 39 feet above high water, only the smaller yachts, sardiners, and old-fashioned gaff-rigged boats can use the reach. The Bridge has speeded up the tide by ½ knot and formed a powerful back eddy on the north side west of the bridge during the ebb tide. Do your calculating on the bridge in advance. If the tide is running with you, it is difficult to change your mind at the last minute. The tide in the reach is said to turn about 1½ hours before high and low water.

The approach to Jonesport from the west is easy. Tibbett (usually called "Tabbott") Narrows is buoyed. The tide runs right along the channel except between Shabbit Island Ledge and Fessenden Ledge. Here there seems to be a cross tide. Allow for it.

Jonesport, Me. (304). Since the following account was written, the *Coast Pilot* reports that an oil wharf and storage area have been built on Sawyer's Cove and a Coast Guard station has been established on the north shore of the reach just west of the bridge. Furthermore, herring have been very scarce in recent years, so the factories may not be as active

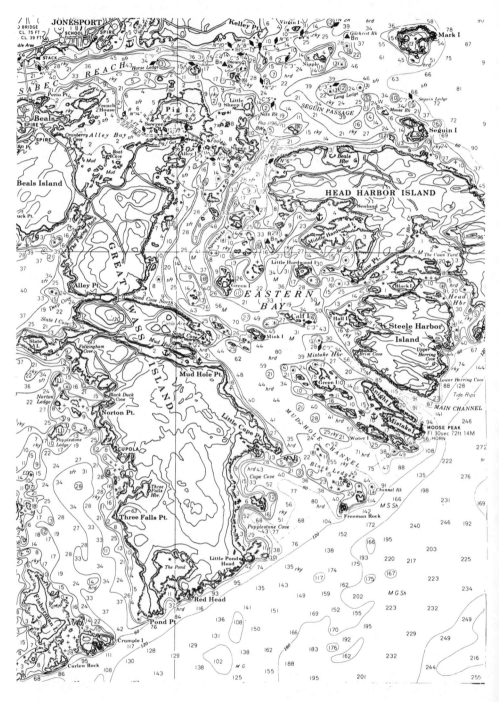

Anchorages between Mistake Island and Jonesport (refer to Chart 304).

as they were. Visitors should proceed with great caution. The writer will be happy to hear any up-to-date information.

Jonesport, Me. (304). This is a sardine-and-lobster town strung along the north side of the reach. The best place for yachts to stop is in Sawyer Cove east of the town. There is often a sardine carrier's mooring vacant here. Do not push far up the cove.

Land at the stairs by the yellow building, which belongs to the Look Lobster Company. There is a store on the wharf that sells fishermen's supplies and gasoline. If you plan to come alongside the wharf, beware of a ledge running parallel to the west shore. On the end of Look's wharf is a red, yellow, and green flashing light. Head for this in such a way that it lines up with the length of the wharf.

There is no ice at Jonesport, and water may be had in an emergency at the Underwood factory just west of the bridge. Groceries are available at D.O. Hall's well-equipped store about ¼ mile to the north. Follow the road at the head of the wharf and inquire. The post office is close to the store.

If you need other supplies or wish a meal ashore, walk into Jonesport about half a mile to the west. Here are excellent stores of all kinds. The Custom House is in the same building as R.H. Rogers' hardware and appliance store.

Huntley's Lodge on Ocean Street serves meals and can accommodate guests for the night. The Ship Ahoy specializes in lobster dishes.

Hans Taubenberger operates a machine shop and repair yard on the water front. He is well spoken of.

Beals, Me. (304). This town is on Beals Island just west of the bridge. Gas, Diesel oil, and supplies are available and there is a post office. The harbor was dredged to 7 feet in 1957 and may have been dredged since. Some yachtsmen report it quieter, cleaner, and pleasanter than Jonesport. Here are several boat shops building various kinds of small boats but specializing in "Jonesport" boats. These are very narrow, sharp boats with a high bow and steep sheer. They have much less flare than boats used farther west. A spray hood or house covers the forward half, and aft is a long narrow cockpit. The stern is cut off square and the run is flat. The propeller is often well forward of the stern to keep it clear of pot warps and is driven by as powerful an automobile engine as the owner can find. One of these boats, "trying her out" wide open, flinging spray for yards to port and starboard, and dragging a huge wake, is a dramatic sight.

Annually about July 4 there is a great celebration at Jonesport of which the main event is a race to determine whose is the fastest lobster boat in Maine. Another feature is a two-man dory race.

In case of emergency, repairs can be made at one of the yards at Beals.

Moosabec Reach, Me., continued (304). East of Jonesport the buoys are close together, and the tide runs with increasing force. At Nova Rocks Light it is truly inspiring. However, the tide follows the channel and provides little difficulty. Keep clear of Gilchrist Rock by following nuns 6, 4, and 2. Then take a course for Roque Island Thorofare. The tide will set you off very little on this course, and Roque Island is quite bold. The entrance to the Thorofare is not obvious at first, but appears as one closes up on it.

Eastern Bay, Me. (304). This is fascinating country to the explorer. One of the most interesting things about it is the contrast between high and low water. The mean tidal difference is 11 to 12 feet. The most interesting way to approach this region from the west is outside, direct from Petit Manan.

When you leave the bell at Petit Manan on a compass course for Seahorse Rock bell, you will see nothing at all ahead. Shortly after you pass Tibbett Rock you will pick up the great white cliff of Crumple Island. Nash Island Light and the stacks at Jonesport will show up inshore. As you approach Seahorse Rock, it will be breaking heavily here and on Seal Ledges. The abandoned Coast Guard station on Great Wass Island only emphasizes the bleak dramatic quality of this country.

Crumple Island and Freeman's Rock are great fissured domes of granite with little or no vegetation, bold shores, and tremendous surf breaking on them. As you round Red Head, if the day is clear, you will pick out four great mushrooms on the hill behind Bucks Harbor. It is not an interplanetary landing site, but a radar station. Moose Peak Light is on the southern end of Mistake Island. From here one can continue to Head Harbor and the Cow Yard, or run up Mudhole Channel.

However, if the visibility is poor, the trip is a lot less fun and harder on the nerves. If there is not a heavy sea running, from the bell off Petit Manan, lay a course to pass between Tibbett Rock and the nun south of it and on to clear Crumple Island. Allow for a tide running across your course for the first part of the run to the nuns. If you don't see either nun, you can tell when you pass between them by the way the water shoals up.

Continue on the course to clear Crumple Island. The tide will be on your starboard quarter on the flood and your port bow on the ebb. Very little if any allowance is necessary, because if you are set to the north, you

will see pot buoys and hear Sea Horse Rock bell; and if you are set to the
south, you will see nothing and hear nothing until you bring Moose Peak
horn out by Red Head. Note that there is a shoal outside Sea Horse
Rock, which you will pick up on the fathometer.

The cliffs are very bold on the end of Curlew Rock, Crumple Island,
and Great Wass Island. There is always a big roll, so you will hear the
surf and notice the backwash off the cliffs before you get too close.

Keep Moose Peak on your port bow and work eastward until it is
abeam. The easiest thing to do is to run up the Main Channel way,
round the northerly end of Knight Island, and anchor in Mistake Island
Harbor. A bold alternative is to try for Head Harbor and the Cow Yard,
but running in on that shore before the wind and sea in a thick fog is not
appealing to many, especially as the eastern shore of Steele Harbor Island
is irregular and fringed with outlying rocks. If the day is not too far advanced, you can follow the sound of the surf on Head Harbor Island to
Black Head. Do not get in too close if the fog is very thick, for while the
cliffs are steep and the water deep close to the shore, there is a fringe of
ledge at the foot of the cliff that makes out in dangerous irregular jags.
From Black Head run for the gong on Little Breaking Ledge. The sea
will be much smoother and the fog might scale up a bit. Thence, run for
the bell off Mark Island and then for the entrance to Roque Island Thorofare. The tide will cause little trouble, for it is more or less parallel to
your course.

In clear weather an alternative is to round Freeman Rock and Channel
Rock, pass northeast of Black Ledges, and run up Mudhole Channel.
There is a snug anchorage behind Mudhole Point behind a weir. If the
tide serves, go right up into The Mudhole (see specific directions). In
clear weather, one can run northeast of Mink Island, west of Green Island and Spectacle Island, between Head Harbor Island and Sheep Island, and out into Seguin Passage. Note that the tide ebbs to the east-
southeast and floods to the west-northwest here. This passage or the
buoyed one to the east of Spectacle Island is beautiful, not too difficult to
navigate at half tide or less when the ledges show, and is much more
likely to provide a breeze than is the trip around Moose Peak. Two
things make it difficult: most of the islands are low and flat, and the fish
weirs obstruct one's view and confuse the scenery. In general, bear in
mind that the outside wing of the weir, usually with a board nailed to
the outer post, is likely to be in deep water. Another helpful hint is that
on the course west of Spectacle Island, once you are by the rocks north of
Green Island, you can run for The Nipple. Of course the navigator
would do well to watch the set of the tide carefully, but the range is a
good one, and The Nipple makes an easily identified mark.

Westward-bound navigators sometimes prefer to beat south through the smooth waters rather than slop about in a big chop offshore with, perhaps, not enough wind. In thick weather, however, the Eastern Bay can be a "horror show" for the stranger. Keep outside the powerful horn on Moose Peak and run for the diaphone at Libby Islands. Bound west, follow the 20-fathom curve to Seahorse Rock and take off from there.

There are numerous shelters in this area, several of which are described below.

Head Harbor, Me. (304). This shelter lies between Head Harbor Island and Steel Harbor Island. It is exposed to the south. In entering, keep in the middle of the channel. The ledges on both sides make out farther than the chart appears to indicate. In heavy southerly weather it breaks all across the entrance. The south point of Man Island is a great black ledge of basalt rock, entirely different from the other rock in the neighborhood.

This is a rocky and uneasy anchorage. Most yachtsmen continue into the Cow Yard.

The Cow Yard, Me. (304). This anchorage is farther in and offers better protection than anything nearby, though on a high tide a bit of a roll comes in. Moor behind the black rock northeast of where the chart shows 8 feet. Use the lead.

Although the chart shows 20 feet all through the anchorage, extensive sounding on the bottom of a moon low tide in 1971 showed no depth greater than 15 feet.

There is an inside route from the Cow Yard to Jonesport, but don't attempt it without a local guide. The Cow Yard is a nice little place and is highly recommended.

Back in the 1930s Mr. Caleb Foote published the following paragraphs in *The New England Yachtsman*. They are as reliable now as they were when they were written.

Head Harbor and the Cow Yard beyond it form one of the nicest places to visit on the coast. There is no settlement save a simple summerhouse built on the point that forms the entrance of the Cow Yard, and one fisherman's shack. To starboard, the meadows alternate with woods and outcroppings of rock on the hills of Head Harbor Island, while the smaller islands to port, too numerous to count, are forest-covered to the water's edge.

In entering, beware of an uncharted 2-foot spot which lies about 60 yards west of Man Island. This rock is on a line from the south point of Man Island W ½ S to the little point in Upper Herring Cove on Steel Harbor Island (see chart 304). The rock off the Steel Harbor shore (almost) always breaks. The aforementioned summerhouse and white flagpole on the point above the 15-foot spot in the harbor are good landmarks.

In a sou'wester Head Harbor is quite exposed, so it is best to go on into the Cow Yard, perfectly protected from any wind. The big black rock in the middle of the entrance always shows. Sail between this and the little island, where the chart shows 8 feet. A fishing boat is moored in 5 feet very close to shore in the northern part of the Cow Yard, and anchorage can be had just outside her in 8 feet. There is a good spring beyond a rock in the meadow 25 feet east of the fisherman's shack.

While you are stopping here, roam over Head Harbor Island. In September the crop of lush, red, mountain cranberries is wonderful to see, while the view from the top of the hills is superb. On a clear day the whole coast from Grand Manan to Mt. Desert lies at your feet. On a calm day at high water, a deep narrow indention on the shore of the 10-foot cove inside Black Ledge on the east side of the island forms a swimming hole unsurpassed anywhere.

Head Harbor is one of the choice spots on the coast; but the bay to the west is full of interesting places. While as you stand on Black Head you look inshore to Roque Island, its sand and its near virgin timber, to the east lie Machias Bay, sparkling in the sunshine, Libby Island Lighthouse, the fine, bold cliffs of Cross Island and the dim outline of Grand Manan.

A visit to the Cow Yard by the writer in August, 1954, corroborated everything Foote writes. Following are a few notes made on that visit:

Land on the beach on the north shore at the highest point of land. Climb through the woods up a steep cliff, bearing to the east, so as to come out in the cut-over section. The going is rough. Ascend to the highest point, described by Foote. The caretaker lives in a cottage on the north shore west of the above-mentioned beach. He can supply fresh water from the spring noted by Foote, and occasionally lobsters.

The temperature here, taken by a laboratory thermometer at 7:45 A.M. on August 9, 1954, was air 60°; water 56°.

The Cow Yard was visited by an experienced cruising man in 1971 and the reports of past years still stand.

Mistake Island Harbor, Me. (304). The best way to get in here is to run up the Main Channel Way northeast of Mistake Island. The wind is likely to be light and fluky in here, and the tide runs hard. There are swirls and eddies off the shore, but nothing violent or dangerous. The cliffs on Steel Harbor Island are high, sheer, and bleak with only grass and gnarled trees near the edge. Knight Island, on the contrary, is heavily wooded and "prettier." *Do not* at any tide go between Knight Island and Mistake Island. This looks tempting at high water.

Round the northeast end of Knight Island. There are ugly ledges along the shore to the southwest, but at half tide they are exposed. Give the shore a good berth. There is a fish weir northwest of Knight Island. Right in front of the weir's mouth is a rock with about 6 feet at low water. One wing makes off to the northeast. Shave this and continue between the weir and Knight Island. Behind the weir, the Coast Guard maintains a spindle on a prominent ledge, which protects their anchorage. A shoal-draft boat can leave this beacon to starboard and work up into the cove where the Coast Guard moorings are located. This is a snug spot indeed, but the skipper who goes in here with a boat drawing more than 4½ feet is courageous. For deeper boats the anchorage is anywhere northwest of this ledge about where chart 304 shows 10 feet. Do not attempt to enter or leave west of Mistake Island. Even the fishermen seldom do this.

Land at the Coast Guard steps on Mistake Island and follow the boardwalk to the light.

The Mudhole, Me. (304). This is a most attractive cove on the east side of Great Wass Island. There is a satisfactory anchorage between the weir in the entrance and the point to the west of it. However, the bottom is likely to be heavily grown up with kelp and weed, so be sure the anchor really has hold of something before you go ashore.

If the tide is well up—say two hours—go on inside. Hang very close to the southern shore, as the big rock in the middle almost blocks the entrance and is submerged at half tide. Inside is a long lovely cove with mud flats at the head but with high rocky banks heavily grown up to spruce, birch, and alder. Kingfishers flash from branch to branch. Great blue herons stand pensively knee-deep. Ospreys dive, and a bald eagle supervises the entire operation.

Row up to the head of a cove where a road crosses. Go north for a pleasant walk to Beals or south to the abandoned Coast Guard station and the bleak southern end of this island.

There are several other interesting places in the Eastern Bay. Northwest of Crow Point there is a good shelter in ordinary weather. North of Middle Hardwood Island is another. Pig Island Gut is navigable at half tide or better and has been dredged and buoyed out. Behind Seguin Island north of Head Harbor Island there is another anchorage. One must move carefully in this region, but it is indescribably beautiful and sufficiently difficult of access so that it is not yet crowded.

Roque Island, Me. (304). Roque Island is both a symbol and a delightful fact. Situated far east of Schoodic and 'Tit Manan, shrouded by Fundy fogs and scoured by icy Fundy tides, it is the goal of many east-coast yachtsmen. To have anchored off the beach at Roque is to be marked as an able salt-water man. Few of the rocking-chair sports get by Schoodic. To clear 'Tit Manan and Moose Peak in a fog choking thick and to make a landfall on the back side of Roque is no feat for a mere church-steeple navigator. Most of the yachts you meet on Lakeman's or Bunker Cove are manned by men whom you can respect.

Equal to the difficulties of getting to Roque are the delights of being there. Roque Island itself and the islands surrounding it are owned by the Gardner family. The Gardners, like the Forbes of Naushon, have owned their island for generations. In 1806 Joseph Peabody and a partner, both of Salem, bought the island and built several vessels near the tidal mill dam at the head of Shorey Cove. In 1864 Peabody's daughter Catherine bought the shares of the other owners and with her husband, John L. Gardner, took title to the entire island. Except for the years 1870 to 1882, when it was owned by Longfellows and Shoreys, it has been in the family ever since. Subsequent generations have added the neighboring islands and have preserved the group as nearly as possible in a natural state. The present owners are glad to have considerate visitors enjoy the islands but ask that they use only the northerly end of the beach and especially that they be very careful with fire. Some years ago a careless visitor gave himself and the owners several very anxious hours before a forest fire was extinguished. When you consider how a fire would change a beautiful wooded island to a smoking ash heap spiked with charred stumps, you surely can forego the pleasure of a cigarette until you get back aboard.

The authors appeal vigorously to all visitors to leave the islands as beautiful as they find them. Do not smoke or light fires ashore.

The island is crossed and criss-crossed with wood roads that make easy and pleasant walking. It is more difficult to walk along the shores, because promontories make out at intervals with no beaches at the foot of the cliff. Bushwhacking is a slow and scratchy business.

Of course the great white beach is the central feature at Roque. The sand is soft and fine and in it are to be found large white clams, the pursuit of which, while not always productive, is excellent exercise. In the middle of a sunny summer day, the water is warm enough for a brief ceremonial dip, but few will stay in very long.

Anchorage off the beach is usually satisfactory on a quiet night, but if there is a sea outside, one may roll a bit. There is a cove on the south end of the beach that offers some protection. However, the two best anchorages are in Bunker Cove at the west end of the Thorofare or at Lakeman's Harbor between Lakeman Island and Roque.

Bunker Cove. Coming from the west, enter between Little Spruce Island and Roque Island. The entrance is not easy to see from the end of Moosabec Reach, but it will open up as you approach. Beware of the 3-foot rock north of Little Spruce Island. It is really there. Anchor just inside the islet with a cap of trees, pulling out of the tide. The best water is close to the cliff. A shoal-draft boat can follow the cliff well up the cove into wild and beautiful surroundings and perfect shelter. In any case, row up the cove as far as you can go, or use the outboard if you must. If you row, you have a chance of seeing an osprey or a kingfisher diving or a great blue heron fishing in the shallows. Once well up in the cove, you will find it easy to believe the story that in the War of 1812 an American privateer fled here at high water, cut away her masts, and lay in the mud. Camouflaged with spruce brush, she was never found by her British pursuers.

The only objection to Bunker Cove is that it may be crowded. If it has been smooth outside, you may even find a stock power cruiser or two. The alternative is to continue through the Thorofare to Lakeman's Harbor.

Roque Island Thorofare. This is a comparatively shallow passage leading to Roque Island Harbor and the beach. There has been a good deal of controversy about a rock in the middle of the passage marked on chart 304 as "Rep." It certainly has been reported and there can be no doubt that yachts have bumped over it. The evidence, however, suggests that these disasters occur only to fairly deep-draft boats at low water. A sardine boat skipper told the writer that there is a bar with about 6 feet between the little island off Roque and Great Spruce Island and that he does not use the passage at extreme low water.

Mr. Orin Leach of West Southport, Maine, sent the writer a fathometer tracing of his passage of the Thorofare at two hours and forty-five minutes after low water. It shows a level hard mud or gravel bottom at 14 feet. About 75 yards to the west of where it begins to deepen, a sharp rock rears up to exactly 14 feet, the same level as the gravel bar. So the rock definitely *is* there, but the part of it that Mr. Leach went over is no shoaler than the controlling depth in the passage.

Coming from the east, the Thorofare can be located by a weir just north of the opening.

Roque Island and its anchorages (refer to Chart 304).

Roque Island Harbor. The most attractive anchorage here, of course, is off the beach. The owner, Mr. Gardner, asks that visitors use the north end of the beach. In spite of the cold water, the swimming is good. For a pleasant climb, go to the north end of the beach and strike back into the woods. You will soon pick up a trail up the hill. This ascends by a series of steps—as a visitor to Roque you are entitled to form your own opinion of how many there are. A few yards above the top step a trail leads to the right and comes out on a ledge at the top of the hill. From here one can see the harbor, the beach, and the country to the south and east.

Note the 7-foot spot between Double Shot and Great Spruce Islands. This often breaks at low water in rough weather.

Lakeman Harbor. Entering Lakeman Harbor, favor the Roque Island shore slightly. The Lakeman Island shore seems to make out more than the chart suggests. Correspondents report that the harbor has shoaled in recent years. Move in cautiously and anchor out in the middle.

For many years there was a colony of fishermen from Jonesport on Lakeman Island. The Carver family maintained a tattered logbook, a photostat of which is now in the possession of the Cruising Club of America, in which visitors registered, wrote comments, and drew sketches. It is a most interesting memorial extending over several generations. It has been reported, however, that the camps on Lakeman's are now deserted and that this pleasant practice has come to an end.

A pleasant trail comes to the shore at a stony beach on the Roque Island side. It is a good walk if you can find it.

Shorey Cove. This is a fine spot in anything southerly, but wide open to the north. The homes of the island's owners are in the southwest corner of Shorey Cove.

The authors of this *Guide* have been cursed on many accounts, the most valid of which is that they have "spoiled" Roque Island with their unbounded enthusiasm for it. We regret it if it be true, but we reply that it cannot be spoiled by considerate and appreciative visitors. It can be spoiled, as any place in the world can be spoiled, by selfish, careless, and lazy devils who litter the shores, pollute the water, burn the woods, and assault the sensitivities of others. We believe that if you are seaman enough to bring a boat to Roque, you are sportsman and gentleman enough to preserve it.

Roque Bluffs Anchorage, Me. (304). This anchorage, exposed to the southeast, is in the bight formed by Shoppee Point and Shoppee Island on the northeast shore of Englishman Bay. There is a small settlement, Roque Bluffs, on the west bank of the small Englishman River at its mouth.

The Watts Brothers, Ralph and Scott, are authorities for this part of the coast. The former, long a boatbuilder, lives in a house on a knoll on the south side of the road on the south side of Shoppee Point. Brother Scott lives further up the road to the northwest on the opposite side.

There are no supplies.

On the north side of the point at the end of the road is a substantial wharf built and maintained by the owners of Roque Island. It is available for use by visiting yachtsmen.

Anchorage off this wharf would be protected only in winds from the northeast quadrant. In heavy weather it is preferable to lie at nearby Roque Island or in Little Kennebec Bay less than 4 miles to the east.

Anyone wishing to travel by land east or west from Roque Bluffs can order a car by telephone from Machias, about 7 miles distant, where there is through bus connection in both directions.

The Brothers, Me. (304). These islands, known locally as Camp Island, are virtually one island running east and west—great high ledges at both ends and low in the middle. They lie about 6 miles northeast of Head Harbor. Sail through the Brothers Island Passage between them and Green Island (known locally as the Green Nubble) to the north.

The owner has built a small house in a field on the northerly side of the westerly height. It's a lonely place but quite beautiful and dramatic. The ledges, especially on the southern side, are covered with a light yellow lichen. At low water the boulder-strewn "beach" in the middle on the northern shore is the world's slipperiest, the rocks being overgrown with dulce and other gelatinous weeds.

After three-quarters tide it is possible, with a small boat, to run over a bar into a deep pool between the two higher parts of the island. Ashore the coverage is mostly grass (there's one spruce tree), and there are many swales of iris.

The owner welcomes visitors and warns newcomers to be careful with cigarettes and matches, since the soil or "mink-dirt" is a kind of peat and inflammable. He informs us that the peat is "the result of a blight of heavy forests along parts of the Maine coast in the fifth and sixth centuries A.D.," at which time The Brothers was wooded. Evidence of sticks and leaves is still distinguishable in the peat. A correspondent reports seeing the peat at the east end afire. Several hours' work failed to extinguish it.

Machias Bay, Me. (304). This is a beautiful and well-protected bay, often clear of fog when the Bay of Fundy outside Cross Island is thick. The shores are generally bold, there are a number of good harbors, and the tide doesn't run hard except through the passages. Libby Islands diaphone makes a good guide in the fog to one entering or leaving. The sensitive cruiser can almost avoid looking at the radar domes back of Bucks Harbor or the desolation wrought on Thornton's Point by a government eager to communicate. The heavy Diesel generators providing power for this installation can be heard all over the bay and sound like a big motorship. To one who hears them for the first time through the fog, the experience could be alarming.

In 1970 there appeared to be a very real possibility that Occidental Oil Company would set up a refinery on the shores of Machias Bay. Tankers weighing 100,000 tons and drawing 50 feet would tie up to a pier to be built on the east side of Stone Island, and the oil would be pumped ashore. Granted radar, tugs, and all the mechanical and electronic aids conceived by the mind of man, surely some day one of those great tankers would go ashore in the fog and tide. The destruction such a spill would cause is incalculable. Fortunately the plan was abandoned as the result of vigorous opposition by conservationists.

However, the fundamental problem of reasonable security for Washington County residents remains. Summer business is scanty, lobsters support few, there has not been a good herring run in years. Pulpwood, clams, and subsistence farming cannot support very many. Oil is not the answer, probably, but an answer must be found.

Foster Island Channel, Me. (304). This channel leads into Machias Bay from Englishman Bay. All the islands look the same, being great domes of black rock covered with grass. Coming west in the late afternoon, squinting into the sun, it is often difficult to make out the passage and identify the buoys. Foster Island has a white house on it and Ram Island is the highest dome.

Beware of a rock north of Scabby Island. It is about 3 feet under water at low tide. The writer talked with a man who sounded it with an oar.

Starboard Cove, Machias Bay, Me. (304). For anyone seeking a quiet overnight anchorage in calm weather not far from the alongshore course, this is a good spot. There is little shelter in northeast or easterly winds. But the convenient cove between Starboard Island and the mainland is perfectly protected by a bar until two hours from high water. Then a sea might roll in from the south, but the ground is so broken in that direction that it would not be dangerous in the summer.

Just inside the point of Starboard Island is an old weir, and there is another across from it. Beware of old stakes. Anchor near the 6-foot spot as far to the south and east as you can get.

There is no gasoline or store at Starboard.

Starboard Creek dries out at low water. It can then be forded by the few summer residents living at Point of Main, whence there is a gorgeous view on a clear day.

Anyone visiting Starboard Cove should not fail to go ashore to the impressive hogback shown on the chart at the northeast shore of the creek. It is heaped high with small pebbles of jasper, "a compact, opaque, often highly colored, cryptocrystalline variety of quartz, commonly, used in decorative carvings." To the layman, jasper is a stone of extraordinary smoothness.

Bucks Harbor, Me. (304). This harbor is easily located by the four great white radar domes on the top of Howard mountain to the southwest of the entrance.

The harbor is open to the east. The preferred anchorage is southwest of Bar Island fairly close in and west of the weir. In September, 1960, there were weirs on both sides of the entrance. At night or in fog, watch for them.

The inner harbor is very shoal. In heavy easterly weather it is possible to go on the tide to the bridge connecting Bucks Neck with the mainland and tie up to it. This is called "Hurricane Anchorage."

Just west of the gravel beach on the south side of the harbor is the wharf and lobster car of Millard Urquhart, Jr. He sells gas and Diesel oil. Water and electricity are available. In his store on the wharf he sells fishermen's supplies. Gas is also available at Roy Sprague's lobster pound in the harbor. About 1 mile northwest is the settlement on the main road at the head of the harbor. Here is Colbeth's General Store, a well-stocked, hospitable place. One can telephone here for transportation to Machias, about 9 miles distant, where there is through bus connection east and west.

Machiasport, Me. (304). A spire and a cupola mark this small settlement on the bank of the Machias River about 4 miles below Machias, the head of navigation and the principal town of the region.

It is best to come up the river on the tide. Above Round Island the tide sets northwest across the flats, so it is important to follow the buoys closely to stay in the narrow channel.

Anchor in the stream off Charles Ingalls' Machiasport Boat Shop. Mr. Ingalls can take care of repair work and is a reliable authority on local matters.

Gasoline can be bought at the sardine factory.

On the west shore of the river at Birch Point are the Picture Rocks, said to have been carved by Indians as they passed in their canoes from Quoddy to the Penobscot to let those arriving later know they had passed Machias on their way to and from the two reservations.

The first naval battle of the Revolution was fought at Sanborn Point. Fort O'Brien, named after one of the participants in the battle, is on the west bank just above the point. The following account of the battle by Richard Hallet appeared in the Boothbay *Register* of October 1 and 8, 1959.

Maine on the Warpath; the Battle of Machias

To Machias goes the honor of Maine's first pitched battle with the British in 1776 [1775]. Little Machias, with its 80 families, its 150 fighting males, and its formidable Jerry O'Brien, who had mauled a King's magistrate four years before heading that faction, was "not so peaceable."

Two months after the battle of Lexington, Captain Ichabod Jones came home to Michias in his trading sloop *Unity*. Her hold was full of bread, pork, fish, and beans, without which his fellow-citizens must have starved; but before he would open his hatches for trading purposes, he tried to get the people to sign a paper binding them to let him take lumber back to Boston; lumber to make barracks for the King's troops. Ichabod was a prosperous merchant, and probably not the greatest patriot alive, but yet perhaps he was not altogether on the King's side either. He was neutral, at a moment when neutrality was dangerous—since he who would not take sides had everybody for his enemy.

Yet perhaps he might have won his point and filled the holds of his two sloops, the *Polly* and the *Unity*, with lumber for Boston—his argument being that lumber was their only money and that if they didn't send lumber they must starve to death—but unluckily for him, the citizens had heard of the battle of Lexington. The shot had been fired that had been heard around the world, and Machias had raised a liberty pole.

Captain Moore of the King's tender *Margaretta* ordered them to take it down. They refused. The *Margaretta* was the British fighting ship, armed with 16 swivels, which had convoyed Captain Jones' sloops to Machias. Captain Jones, the neutral, persuaded his British friend to stay his hand until a town meeting could be held and the people induced to reverse their obstinate stand on the liberty pole.

Next day was Sunday and the town seethed with argument. . . . Benjamin Foster, who owned a saw-mill, and as a youth had been a soldier at Louisburg . . . called on all to follow him who wanted to capture the *Margaretta* and the two sloops of Ichabod. The O'Briens were right at his heels and many others.

It was Sunday: but "the better the day, the better the deed" in the opinion of Ben Foster. The English officers would come to church and these "not so peaceable" sons of Machias could seize them at their devotions.

But the plan miscarried. The day was warm, the church windows were open, and the preacher's servant, London Atus . . . from his perch high in the Negro pew saw a band of armed men of Machias approaching, gave a frightened cry, and jumped out of the window.

The two Joneses and Captain Moore followed him through the same window. Captain Jones hid in the woods, Captain Moore got back aboard the *Margaretta* and sent this message on shore: "That he had express orders to protect Captain Jones . . . and that if the people presumed to stop Captain Jones' vessels, he, Captain Moore, would burn the town."

In the teeth of this threat Foster and his men took possession of the two Jones sloops. But the *Margaretta,* as if stupefied by this transaction, lay out in the stream and withheld her fire.

The patriots of Machias lined the shore opposite the *Margaretta* and called out to her to "surrender to America." That was a new sound in the ears of British captains; and the tender's skipper called back, "Fire and be hanged to you."

The people on shore fired, and the tender returned this fire, still not using her cannon, and, slipping her cable, went down-stream, stayed the night lashed to a small sloop commanded by one Captain Toby; and in the morning, taking Toby out of his sloop for pilot, made all sail to get off, as wind and tide favored.

At this inglorious retreat, the Americans were all on fire to give chase. Forty of them, under command of Captain Jeremiah O'Brien, swarmed aboard Ichabod's sloop *Unity.* A few had guns, for which there was only a round or two of ammunition; the rest brought pitchforks and narrow axes. After they were under way, they built breastworks of pine boards, to screen them from the fire of the enemy.

A more unequal fight there could hardly be, than this between the sloop *Unity,* which had no guns, and the schooner *Margaretta,* which had sixteen, between the handful of undisciplined Americans and the schooner's veteran crew. But the sheer courage of the O'Briens was a blaze of fire in which the British were shriveled up.

Captain Moore hailed the *Unity* and told her plainly to keep off or he would fire. It availed him nothing. He cut the boats from his stern but at best the *Margaretta* was a dull sailor and the *Unity* came up with her. He opened fire half-heartedly with his muskets, and killed one of the *Unity's* men. The two vessels came so close that John O'Brien, brother of Jerry, made a great leap and jumped onto the *Margaretta's* quarterdeck. Seven muskets were fired at him; but he bore a charmed life; and when those seven musketeers charged him with fixed bayonets, he gave a wildcat screech to unnerve them, and jumped into the water.

His brother picked him up; and just then the *Margaretta's* helmsman was shot in the heart, the ship broached to, and Captain O'Brien ran the bowsprit of his sloop through her mainsail. His ammunition was all gone; but twenty of his men boarded the King's ship armed with pitchforks. . . . Captain Moore had already fallen, mortally wounded; and the sight of those oncoming pitchforks was too much for the midshipman Stillingfleet, who was second in command. He "abscombed himself away" in the hold of the ship and gave up. Pitchforks in that short terrific battle were more than bayonets; and in no time at all the Americans were ready to secure their prize.

They had lost two men, but they had taken the *Margaretta* captive. This was on June 12, 1775, and was certainly the first naval contest of the Revolution. Only Lexington and Concord had preceded it; Bunker Hill was still to come.

Two weeks later the Provincial Congress passed a vote of thanks to Captain O'Brien, Captain Foster, and their men for this exploit and gave into their keeping the captured vessel and the two sloops, *Unity* and *Polly*. Captain Ichabod Jones' neutrality had lost him these valuable properties.

Machias, Me. (304). To the yachtsman partial to "cricking," Machias is one of the slickest chances. On the other hand, an experienced local cruiser writes, "My personal advice to a fellow cruising man would be to keep my boat away from Machias except in an emergency. It has historical interest, etc., but it would be best to tie up or anchor at Machiasport or Bucks Harbor and motor to Machias."

There is a highway drawbridge to be passed 2 miles below the town. It will be opened during daylight hours to a signal of three blasts of a whistle. Enter on the last of the flood and not before half tide.

Machias is a town of considerable economic and historical interest. For many years it was a shipping point for long lumber from the forests to the north and west. Several million feet were shipped each year to the West Indies and the New York and Boston markets. Many sailing vessels were tied up at the wharves in the old days, loading and waiting to load lumber.

There is little water traffic into Machias now except boats brought up the river for repairs. The last vessel to carry out a cargo of long lumber was the *Edward Smith,* a three-master, with more than 500,000 feet, mostly spruce dimension, in the autumn of 1940. The last four-master at Machias was the *Spindrift,* launched there in the early 20s.

The father of Dr. Small, a local dentist and an authority on marine and historical matters, owned the last fleet of three- and four-masters of American registry on the Atlantic coast.

Captain Moore of the *Margaretta,* who was mortally wounded in the action described under Machiasport, died in the Burnham Tavern (1770), now maintained in its original condition as a museum by the local D.A.R. chapter. There is a display of Revolutionary relics and records.

Also of interest are the stories of the erection of the first liberty pole, of the organized resistance of the people of Machias to demands of the British in Boston that Machias send lumber to construct barracks at Boston, and of Hannah and Rebecca Weston's bringing supplies of powder and shot 8 miles through the wilderness to assist the patriots. Booklets on the early history of this district are available from the local D.A.R. chapter.

Northwest Harbor, Cross Island. In anything but really heavy weather, there is good shelter just inside Northwest Head off a steep stony beach. The cove is uninhabited, and the surroundings are lovely. A bald eagle circled overhead as we scouted his domain.

Cross Island Narrows, Me. (303). The argument has almost always favored going through the narrows rather than out around Cross Island. It is harder to buck an ebb tide in the Bay of Fundy than it is in Machias Bay, and the wind is likely to leave you slopping around off the cliffs in a confused sea. With a fair tide, you get a fine boost through the narrows, and the breeze will be better inside. In the fog, Machias Bay is often clear when it is thick outside and there is likely to be a scale-up in the narrows. Beating west with a fair tide it might be better to stay outside and get a powerful lift to windward down Grand Manan Channel. However, stand well off the cliffs to avoid a soft spot that often develops there.

Bound east from Foster Channel, look for can 3 at the entrance to the narrows much farther off Cross Island than you expect. You will find it nearly in range of the power house on Thornton's Point. It usually appears more white than black, as the gulls and shags seem to give it special attention.

The usual course is north of Mink Island. However, there may be less tide south of the island. The wind in Northeast Harbor may be fluky, but it seems to draw across the channel very nicely. One can usually fetch through either way.

There is good anchorage in Northeast Harbor. Work as far south as your draft will permit and get out of the tide. Do not let the children row around here in the pram. If they get in the tide near Mink Island, you may have a rescue operation in hand.

The anchorage off the old Coast Guard station, now occupied by a detachment from the Outward Bound School, is less sheltered but perfectly satisfactory.

It is possible to enter from the eastward between Scotch Island and the ledges to the north. The new edition of chart 303 makes it look easier than the old one did. The writer carried 5 feet in here and saw a great deal of real estate under the keel, but he proved that it can be done.

Cross Island is a rough island to walk on. It was cut over before World War II and has grown up through the slash into a tangle. However, a walk along the cliffs on the south side is interesting if you can find your way.

The radio towers on Thornton Point can no longer be ignored. There are twenty-odd of them—we couldn't agree how many. Almost 1000 feet in the air, they spread a net of copper wire so that someone in Washington can talk to someone under water in a submarine in the North Sea. This is an ultra-low-frequency station, so low that it is said to bother the hearing of dogs. No dog is supposed to be able to live within 7 miles of the installation. It is pleasant to remember Thornton Point heavily wooded and to recall the feeling that as one passed through Cross Island Narrows one was way down east in primitive surroundings and a long way from civilization.

On emerging from the narrows and passing the bell, one enters Grand Manan Channel, which is part of the Bay of Fundy. The character of the coast changes abruptly. The shore consists of steep, bold, black cliffs, in places covered with greenish lichen. There are no off-lying islands. The seas roll up from the south, troubled by tides. On several occasions the writer has left the mild sunny waters of Machias Bay with a pleasant southwest breeze, and, in the few minutes it took to traverse Cross Island Narrows, found himself rolling almost becalmed in a confused chop with a graying sky, the feel of fog in the air, and the sea breaking heavily on the forsaken cliffs of the Old Man. It is a short run to Cutler.

Cutler, Me. (303). Cutler is a well-protected harbor, easy of access and very well marked with an offshore whistle, a bell, and a lighthouse. It affords food, fuel, a meal ashore, and a quiet anchorage out of the tide. It is the last such anchorage before the 14-mile stretch of cliff along both sides of Grand Manan Channel. Therefore, you are likely to find other cruising yachts here on almost any summer evening.

In ordinary weather, coming from the west, pass between Cape Wash and the Old Man, keep just off Western Head, and run in north of Little River Island. Notice that Little River Light will not be visible until you round Western Head. The fog signal is seldom heard until you are close in. If the tide is running hard, particularly on the ebb, a rip builds up off Western Head. This rip, combined with several shoal spots near the course from Cape Wash, makes it advisable to run off to the whistle and then run in for the lighthouse in heavy weather. One correspondent found the ebb tide on this course running at 1 knot. Allow generously for it, especially near full and new moon.

From the east the landmark for the harbor is Long Point, distinguished by a big mowed field. A tide rip usually is found off this point too. Notice that in thick weather one can follow the line of 100-foot soundings down the American shore of Grand Manan Channel right to the bell off Cutler harbor. The 100-foot contour turns sharply to the westward after Long Point.

One can enter either side of Little River Island. The preferred entrance is on the north side, but there is often a dead spot off the light and in the northern entrance. Chart 303 shows 10 feet in the southern entrance, a figure that this writer regards as possibly inflated. There may be 6 feet at low water but not a great deal more. Watch for old weir stakes near both shores of the harbor.

Anchor well up the harbor off the landings. In the event of a really heavy easterly, anchor close under Little River Island or go to the head of the harbor on the high water and pass between the two great boulders. A shoal-draft boat can lie here afloat. A deeper one will ground on the mud for an hour or two each side of low water.

Gasoline and Diesel oil are sold at Neil Corbett's wharf just west of the Harborview Restaurant, a white building on piles just west of the small beach on the north side of the harbor. Ice is available frozen in gallon milk cartons if the Little League has not played too recently. Of the water, a correspondent writes:

> Water is now piped to Neil Corbet's wharf. Cutler water, however is extremely hard. If in need of really usable water, get someone to carry you and a few jugs about five minutes' drive up the Machias road, where there's an ever-running roadside spring piped to a spot opposite the old cement plant used for building the naval installation. Really

good water is sometimes hard for a cruising boat to find, and this is excellent.

The best place to land from a skiff is either at Corbett's or on the beach. There is a wharf in front of the long yellow building on the east side of the cove with a set of stairs running down to low water. However, these may be very slippery, and the wharf is not in good repair. From the lobster car next to the stairs you will have to climb a ladder.

Across the road from the yellow building is the little store of Philip and Margaret Geel, well equipped with all the necessities of life and some of the luxuries. Outside is a public telephone and next door is the post office, which is closed at the noon hour.

The Harborview Restaurant is renowned among cruising men for its excellent lobster and superb homemade pies. Year after year we hear that it is about to close up, and annually we give thanks that it has not done so. Some cruising men regard it as an obligation to patronize it. The Harborview, however, had finally closed its doors in July, 1973.

There is no boat yard at Cutler, but engine repairs can be made by George Farris or Rowland Ramsdell. Buses run from Machias to Portland and Boston. In 1971 the nearest place to spend the night ashore was Machias.

If you have to lie over a day or two at Cutler, get in touch with Captain Purcell W. Corbett and plan an expedition to Machias Seal Island, where the variety of offshore bird life is extraordinary (see Appendix), or a fishing trip to some of the offshore banks. If you are fortunate enough to be in Cutler in blueberry season, it will take but a short time to pick a quart of the best wild berries in the state.

Cutler used to be a very prosperous little town, depending on line trawling for ground fish, lobsters, herring, clams, pulpwood, and blueberries. Lately, however, there has been little trawling, the herring runs have been light, and clam flats have been either polluted or badly depleted. There has been some income from the radio base, but summer people, lobsters, and blueberries are now the principal supports of the town.

Grand Manan Channel, Me. (303). This is a deep and tide-scoured channel between sheer cliffs. There are almost no off-lying dangers on either side except Sail Rock and Morton Ledge, and there is a good fog signal at each side of the eastern end. The tide runs from 2 to 3 knots and even faster at times. Therefore, it is scarcely worthwhile beating against it with a gentle breeze. However, as the turn of the tide approaches, back eddies begin to build under both shores, and it is possible to creep along close to the cliffs with a favorable current an hour or two before it turns in the channel.

The time of the moon makes a great deal of difference in the strength of the tidal current and in the duration of slack water. At the time of full moon and new moon, the tide will run at a full 3 knots with no more than a half hour of slack between tides. At first quarter and last quarter, the tide may run no more than half as hard, with as much as an hour to an hour and a quarter of reasonably slack water.

Beware of this stretch of water in a small boat with a heavy southwester against an ebb tide. It can get dangerous quite quickly, and refuges are not as close as they are among the islands to the westward.

In the fog, navigation is fairly simple because of the steep shores and the fog signals, but be alert for sardiners heading for the factories at Eastport and Lubec. They are big, heavy vessels and can move at a rate to inspire caution in any yachtsman.

A radar reflector is a sensible if not a necessary precaution, as these vessels rely heavily on radar to enable them to keep moving at top speed in thick weather. It is vital to them that they get their fish to the factory as fresh as possible.

Be particularly careful of heavy logs and other debris adrift in this channel. The tide seems to keep it on the move.

Indians from Passamaquoddy Bay were accustomed to paddle down Grand Manan Channel on an ebb tide during the morning calm and cut sweet grass behind Little River Head, where it grows abundantly. Then with a spruce tree in the bow and a flood tide under them, they sailed back in the afternoon. A fisherman hauling a trawl one blowy day beheld a spruce tree bearing down on him with a great collar of foam below it, nearly obscuring the bow of the canoe in which it stood. The Indian, unable to go forward without swamping the light craft and unable to bring her to the wind with his sail plan so far forward, hunched in the stern, clutching his paddle and baling for his life. As he flashed past, he waved his bale dish, and with the gift for brief and pithy expression for which his people are noted, shouted, "Too much bush!"

Many a racing yachtsman lugging a spinnaker in a squall may have felt that he was carrying too much bush.

There is no shelter on the Canadian side of the channel and only two possible shelters on the American side: Haycock Harbor and Bailey's Mistake.

Haycock Harbor, Me. (303). This shelter is about 6 miles from West Quoddy Head. The harbor itself is exposed to the south, but there is a small gut leading out of the west side of it opening into a small basin with a few wharves and farmhouses.

The harbor is hard to pick out from offshore, but is marked by a sort of "double shot" headland on its east side. Enter halfway between the "double shot" headland and the one to the west on a northerly course and favor the north and northwest shore until you can see straight up the gut for several hundred yards to where it turns into the basin. Sighting straight up the gut, turn west and place the south end of a small gravel beach dead astern. There is a mess of bad boulders (covered by only 1 foot of water at low tide) before you reach the bar.

If you can clear the boulders, you can make it; but don't forget to allow for the ground swell if any is running. The tide runs strongly over the bar, but there is more water than over the boulders. The only spot inside where there is more than 2 feet of water at low tide is close under the cliffs on the north side. It's a 9-foot hole at low water, but you'll need a bow-and-stern line to keep your keel fitted into it. This is a pleasant and remote little eel rut, where you will not be disturbed by any sounds except the surf on the ledges outside. Those who like to go into small un-marked places should not miss it if the tides are right.

Bailey's Mistake, Me. (303). Marked by a whistle and a can buoy, the harbor is easy to make, but, except on a quiet night, likely to be rolly. Leave the can, the ledges, and an old weir to port. Anchor under the high land on the western side of the harbor where chart 303 shows 16 feet. Beware of old weir stakes.

On the high water, it is possible to penetrate far up into the northwest-ern cove, but this pretty well dries out at low water.

The picturesque name of this harbor refers to an error in judgment on the part of one Captain Bailey, skipper of a four-masted coaster bound for Lubec before the middle of the last century. He miscalculated the tide, perhaps, and instead of rounding West Quoddy Head and running into Quoddy Roads, he rounded Eastern Head and struck the ledges off Balch's Head. The legend goes that he and his crew were so pleased with the town and surroundings when the fog lifted that they built houses from the schooner's cargo and settled there. The Portland *Press Herald* for September 30, 1966, in commenting on this happy ending, observes: "But lumber to Lubec in the 1830's? Who said coals to Newcastle?"

An earlier shipwreck was said to have been behind the first settlement. Captain Congdon, skipper of a privateer in the War of 1812, ran his ves-sel ashore here to prevent her seizure by the British. After the war he re-turned with his bride, settled, and established a profitable lumber mill. He was frozen to death with his two oxen in a blizzard in 1822 on the road to Lubec.

Sail Rock, Me. (303). The easternmost point in the United States, Sail Rock is appropriately named. It is marked by a flashing whistle to the southeast. Here the ebb tide running out of Quoddy Roads meets the tide running southwest down the channel and creates quite a bobble. To approach it in the fog is unnerving, for it sounds like surf breaking on the shore. As you approach, dimly looming through the fog appears a line of breakers. Sailing vessels do well to stand well clear of the rock in light weather, for the tide could set a vessel ashore here.

The moorings shown on chart 303 behind Quoddy Head have been removed.

One often finds a good breeze under Quoddy Head when it is calm outside.

CHAPTER XIII

The Island of Grand Manan

While not a desperate seafaring adventure, the voyage to Grand Manan can be exciting in itself, and it brings with it all the fun of "going foreign." Foreign charts, foreign money, a different cast to the language, different time (Atlantic), Customs formalities, and the Canadian flag at the starboard spreader give the trip glamor, especially if you are going for the first time.

Preparation. No notice need be given to American Customs of your departure. However, it helps to have positive identification for each member of your crew in anticipation of your return. New and expensive foreign items like cameras might be registered, or a bill of sale by an American firm provided. Very seldom, however, is a yacht questioned, and the writer has checked in by telephone on two occasions.

The navigator should have Canadian charts 4340 and 4342. They are much more detailed than H.O. 1057, the best United States chart available. The Canadian Coast Pilot, *Nova Scotia SE Coast and Bay of Fundy,* is very helpful. These can be obtained from the Canadian Hydrographic Service, Department of Mines and Technical Surveys, in Ottowa. Write for the *Catalogue of Nautical Charts, Sailing Directions and Tidal Information,* order specifically what you want, and include payment, with due regard for the exchange rate. This should be done well in advance, as delays are frequent and the materials are indispensable.

The easiest way to make the crossing is to leave Cutler on the first of the flood tide and steer for the bold west shore of the island south of Dark Harbor. The tide will vary in strength with the phase of the moon, but something like 1½ to 2 knots is about right. It isn't very important anyway, because your course converges with a bold shore and you can't very well miss the whole island. If the weather is clear, there is nothing to be concerned about. If it is thick, beware of sardiners, keep the radar reflector in evidence, and watch the clock. When time runs out, look for the cliffs first pretty well up off the water. Often on a sunny day the top will be clearly visible when the fog is thick around the bottom. When you make the shore, follow it up at a reasonable distance offshore. There are occasional irregularities, so don't get in too close. If the fathometer reads over 15 fathoms, you are surely safe.

Dark Harbor. This is an intriguing place, but one which no skipper with a grain of caution should attempt. Between a rocky bar and the cliffs is a lagoon with access to the sea through a gap in the bar. Most of the time the water runs like a brook through the gap and down the outside of the bar. Just before high water, however, the level of the sea outside equals for a few minutes the level of the pond. At this instant in a shoal-draft boat, one might nip in. The same is true, of course, as the tide falls. The writer once saw a yawl inside, but believes that anyone who would attempt the passage would be willing to go over Niagara Falls in a barrel. Dark Harbor is best reached by land.

The principal occupation at Dark Harbor is raking dulse. Dulse is a seaweed that grows just below ordinary low-water mark. On the full moon and the new moon when "low dreen" tides occur, men from the other side of the island come over and inhabit the dulse camps, little shacks on the bar. At low water they rake the weed up, spread it on smooth rocks to dry, and retire to the camps to restore their flagging energies for another tide. It is said to be socially a very stimulating time— exclusively stag.

Dulse when dry is a dark brown or purplish substance, rather leathery, with a strong taste. To the writer it resembles somewhat the tongue of an old shoe rescued from a bait barrel. However, it is much esteemed by many people, especially health-food zealots, who find it rich in important minerals and vitamins. Others declare it "goes good with the beer." It is shipped to Saint John and packed for sale in little plastic envelopes.

North Head Harbor, N.B. (4340, 4342). Continue northward along the west shore of Grand Manan. As you approach the light and fog signal on Long Eddy Point, swing offshore to avoid the bar and the rip that builds up over it. Then follow the north shore of the island. Here there is almost always a scale-up because the fog is dried up in its long trip over the warm land. The tide seems to flood northwesterly by the northern side of the island, but near the turn of the tide it is variable. In the tide swirls around the point, marine life abounds. Phalaropes, gannets, gulls, and terns feed on the fish schooling here. Seals, porpoises, and often whales, are frequently seen. Continue by Ashburton Head, where the British vessel *Lord Ashburton* was lost, and pass Whale Cove. This is a fairly good anchorage in southerly winds, but landing is a little difficult because the government wharf dries out at low water. Pass the lighthouse and fog signal on Swallowtail and make Net Point Bell. From the bell, run into the "made" harbor at North Head, marked by a small red light bulb on the southeast corner of the easterly pier. Inside, tie up to the smallest boat you can find or the one that does not appear to be about to leave. Tying to the wharf itself involves long lines fore and aft to allow for the 17-foot rise of tide.

Ashore are a bank, store, snack shop, and the Custom House. You are required to register your arrival in Canadian waters and obtain a cruising permit. The walk to Swallowtail is very pleasant, through a hayfield, by neat houses and up a steep path through the woods. On a clear northwest day, one can see the New Brunswick coast for a long way to the north and the faint line of the Nova Scotia coast to the east.

There used to be a fish-meal plant in North Head that gave this pleasant place an evil reputation. It has been removed. There remains a fish factory—"factory" in the old Hudson Bay Company sense of the term— where fish are salted for export, but it is in no way objectionable, as all the waste is taken to the fish-meal plant in Black's Harbor.

Anyone interested in the historical background of the island should look up Mr. Elmer Wilcox, director of the Grand Manan Museum and Historical Society.

The Shore Crest Inn, operated by Mr. and Mrs. Lowell Small, can provide meals and rooms ashore with reasonable notice.

A new hospital at North Head was opened in April 1971. There is no boat yard or repair facility, but in case of emergency, call Mr. Herbert Macaulay at his home in Castalia or in the Customs Office at Seal Cove. Not only is he well informed about Grand Manan, but he sells Canadian charts.

Gasoline and Diesel fuel may be obtained in reasonable quantities by calling Arlington Lambert of Imperial Oil Co., or Allison Ingalls of Gulf Oil.

Many yachtsmen bound for Saint John like to stop at North Head, enter Canadian Customs, and on the very last of an ebb tide head directly for Partridge Island at the mouth of the Saint John River. As you converge with the New Brunswick shore, you should hear the horns on Point Lepreau, Tiner Point, and Partridge Island, but be far enough offshore to avoid being sucked into Mace's Bay and shaken up by the rip off Lepreau. Partridge Island has an excellent fog signal and a radio beacon.

Coming west, it is a much easier run to North Head than it is to Head Harbor on Campobello, for not only are there excellent horns on Long Eddy Point and Swallowtail, but there is a good radio beacon on Southwest Head.

In North Head Harbor, the writer was lying alongside a sardiner in a little 28-foot sloop with three boys. It was a black night, thick o' fog. I came on deck in my pajamas about 9:30 to look around before turning in and heard a heavy motor running outside the breakwater and the rush of a bow wave. It came rapidly closer, rushed through the narrow gap. Navigation lights glowed through the fog, the reverse gear roared and ground; the heavy sardiner, still going a good 6 knots, swung, and headed straight for us. I grabbed the boat hook and felt very foolish with it as a head appeared over the bow, now frightfully close, and shouted, "Cut him in half."

More violent reversing churned the water in the little harbor, the great presence swung sideways, and stopped alongside without even squeaking the tire that the fierce character forward dropped over the side as he shouted in a cheerful New Brunswick burr, "Wouldn't cr-rack an egg, skipper-r. We ain't dr-runk, but we ben drr-rinkin'."

I put on my pants and found the rest of the evening most instructive.

The ferry from Saint John and Black's Harbor lands at North Head and brings cars to the island. As one car was being unloaded, hanging from a crane 25 feet above the water between the rail of the ferry and the wharf, a local resident beside me observed, "There's one for sale cheap right now." Its value increased rapidly, however, when it landed safely on the wharf.

At North Head the writer was cautioned not to sail down the eastern side of the island, even with a fair wind and tide. The bottom is very rough and the tide runs hard. Bulkhead Rip is especially dangerous. In the days of sail, fishermen used to anchor there and fish on the flood tide, where the bottom rises from 40 fathoms to 4 in a very short distance. When the tide began to slack, they left at once, for if caught here in the ebb they would cut an anchor line rather than lie there with the heavy ebb tide pouring over the submerged cliff and backing up against a southerly sea.

If you have no time to visit Seal Cove, Grand Harbor, or Southwest Head in your own boat, rent a car at North Head and at least see them by land.

Seal Cove, N.B. (4340, 4342). With an ordinary southerly breeze, Seal Cove is an easy run from Roque Island, Cross Island, or Cutler. The big problem is to make the proper allowance for tide. The writer allowed 1½ knots of tide from Libby Island to the whistle off Southwest Head, starting at about half flood, and came out about right. Another cruising man leaving Cutler Whistle at about half flood found about 1⅓ knots. Obviously the current moderated as slack water approached; and as the tide runs hardest on the Grand Manan shore, that is the place to catch it slack. Should one start at the first of the tide, no doubt a greater allowance would be appropriate. However, one can easily check progress in clear weather by frequent cross bearings, and in thick weather the radio beacon on Southwest Head is very reassuring. If conditions are right, you can hear the horn on Machias Seal Island. Note, however, that magnetic disturbances have been reported in this region. Also the radio beacon either has changed frequency or occasionally wanders off.

Make the whistle off Southwest Head and run up the shore, being sure to stand clear of Buck Rock. It breaks noisily and is easily avoided even in the fog. Round the breakwater at Seal Cove and tie up to the least active vessel you can find. If you arrive during business hours, check in at once with Mr. Herbert Macaulay at the Customs office at the head of the wharf. Gas, water, and Diesel oil are available at the wharf by calling Arlington Lambert of Imperial Oil or Allison Ingalls of Gulf Oil.

Seal Cove is a delightful town, busy in an unhurried way. There is a store that is a pleasant gathering place as well as a source of food and refreshment. The business of the town is fish—principally herring. There is a sardine factory and there are a number of smokehouses. The latter can be identified at once by the vents along the ridgepole sheltered by a little roof above them and by the spicy aroma of driftwood smoke and salt herring. The fish are first heavily salted for a week or less according to taste and then strung on sticks run in through the gills and out the mouth. The sticks are hung on racks in the bottom of the smokehouse over a driftwood fire built on the dirt floor. Day by day they are moved to higher racks until they are finished just under the roof. When the fish come out, they are a beautiful red-gold color. To prepare a smoked herring, cut a strip off the belly, remove the head, and wiggle the fish as if it were swimming. This loosens the flesh from the bone. Open the creature up, remove the two sides of meat, peel off the skin and store in sealed Mason jars. Smoked herring can be eaten "as is" with beer or soaked out and either fried or boiled.

Herring is the economic mainstay of the island and in recent years the herring run has been thin. More visitors have come with the new car ferry, but Grand Manan has had some hard times. One ingenious resident, alongside whom the writer lay in 1968, was doing a profitable business searching for wrecks among the ledges to the southeast of the island. With an electronic device to indicate the presence of metal and with information from draggers who had fouled their gear, he went out and salvaged what he could find by scuba diving. He had just recently found a steamer loaded with copper rods. Only gold could have been more valuable.

The vessels you will see at Grand Manan are heavy Nova Scotia-built craft. The lobstermen and fishermen use a big broad-sterned boat with high bow and low waist, heavily powered and equipped with good electronic gear. Sardine carriers are usually double-ended to render them easier to maneuver in the weirs and are equipped with pumps like great vacuum cleaners to suck the fish out of the seines and scale them. The scales are used for pearl essence, which is used in shirt buttons and fire extinguisher foam, among other things. These vessels are built heavily of knotty spruce and designed to navigate the Bay of Fundy in winter—a rugged assignment.

From Seal Cove it is possible to explore Wood Island and the Kent Islands where Bowdoin College maintains an ornithological and oceanographic station. Also one can run up the east side of the island on the flood tide to Grand Harbor and on to North Head, but the navigator must be very much alert here. These are dangerous waters with very uneven bottom, violent tides, and dense and frequent fog. Some of the channels are dry at low water, the buoys lying high and dry.

If your schedule affords a day ashore, Seal Cove is an excellent place to spend it. Walk south on the tar road through pretty rolling country by snug houses to the point where the road crosses quite a big brook and turns to gravel. Here there is a wood road to the right that leads across to the cliffs. On the way, it becomes a trail and pretty nearly peters out, but it will get you there. The cliffs are breathtaking, especially with the fog blowing up over them and the black water below. The rock is crumbly and breaks off in long vertical slivers, so take no chances on these cliffs. It is not difficult to follow the shore south toward Southwest Head. You will come on the Southern Cross, an easily recognized pinnacle of rock just offshore. You will also find a sign marking the spot where William and Lucas Jones were wrecked in February 1963. After a snowstorm they were raking moss off Haycock Harbor when their outboard motor died. The wind came off northwest and bitter cold. In their open skiff they drifted across the channel and struck close to Southwest Head. Their skiff was destroyed, and they were nearly drowned. However, William managed to scale the cliff and get to the lighthouse through the heavy snow, whence help was sent to his brother. Few men wrecked on these cliffs are so lucky.

It is a long walk back to Seal Cove, but you may be fortunate enough to get a ride.

In addition to its natural charm for the casual visitor, the island is of unique interest to the geologist and historian. Grand Manan comprises two great and widely differing sections, dividing it almost from end to end: the western section identified in 1839 by Dr. Abraham Gesner, provincial geologist, as trap rock, and the eastern as schistose rock. The actual contact of the two sections is visible at Red Point, near Seal Cove, but cannot be seen at Whale Cove at the north, as it is buried under the beach. The formations of the eastern section range in age from twice to many times that of the western. The latter is of the Triassic period, extending from 160 to 185 million years ago, while the eastern section is of the Palaeozoic and Pre-Cambrian eras, extending from 360 to perhaps 1500 million years ago. The western section constitutes the only extensive example of Triassic igneous rock in New Brunswick, and Red Point affords one of the few easily accessible views of these geological formations in contact.

To those who know Grand Manan, it is one of the few unspoiled spots on the continent. It has a simple charm unmatched along the coast.

The amateur sailor with a staunch and well-equipped boat and a competent navigator would add great interest to his cruise by spending a few days at Grand Manan.

CHAPTER XIV

West Quoddy Head to Calais, Maine

General Remarks. The waters described in this chapter are shown in detail on chart 801. Starting at West Quoddy Head and running north, they include Lubec Channel, Cobscook Bay west of Eastport, Friar Roads between Eastport and Campobello Island, Western Passage leading from Eastport north into the mouth of the St. Croix River, Head Harbor Passage along the northwest shore of Campobello Island, the two Letite Passages from the Bay of Fundy into Passamaquoddy Bay, that bay itself with two small tributaries, and finally the St. Croix River as far as Calais. Of this country, Campobello Island, Deer Island, the northern and eastern shores of Passamaquoddy Bay and of the St. Croix River are Canadian territory. It is often clear in the bay when the fog lies thick outside. Although it is all interesting country, the best cruising ground is "the blue Passamaquoddy."

This large protected bay is something quite unexpected to one coming in through Lubec Narrows or Letite Passage out of the cold Fundy fog. It is likely to be warm and sunny with much less fog and tidal current. The shores are high and bold with dramatic cliffs, jutting promontories, and steep beaches. There are few yachts, some sardiners, frequent Canadian ferries, and a great deal of bird life. Besides St. Andrews, there are several pleasant anchorages in the bay.

Tidal Conditions. Anyone navigating the waters to the north and west of Campobello Island should realize that the tides in those waters are controlled by the stream that enters and leaves north of Campobello, rather than by that which enters and leaves through Lubec Narrows. This statement should make clear the information contained in the following paragraph.

The flood south of Campobello Island sets to the northeast. In Quoddy Roads and Lubec Narrows the current starts to run south one and one-half hours before high water and north one and one-half hours before low water. It attains a velocity of from 4 to 8 knots. North of Campobello the flood sets in a southwesterly direction and splits, going south of Moose Island into Cobscook Bay and north through the Western Passage.

Hence, when bound north from Lubec toward Eastport, after passing Treat Island, head over toward Campobello Island on the flood tide. The flood runs southwest along the eastern side of Deer Island. The floods in the Western Passage are stronger than the ebbs, attaining 6 knots during spring tides. There is a strong whirlpool just southwest of the lower point of Deer Island. The current runs for three-fourths of an hour after the tide table shows high and low water. Through Letite Passage the flood sets to the north, and the ebb the reverse. This current meets the current through Head Harbor Passage about halfway between Head Harbor and the White Horse. There is said to be good fishing in the Head Harbor eddy.

An experienced correspondent writes: "Head Harbor Passage develops into a dangerous breaking inlet off the light during and after northeast storms. I have cruised extensively in both oceans and never seen rougher water for a cruising boat."

In proceeding northward through the Western Passage one will find that the tide swirls off Eastport. A small boat going north against the tide should stay close to the west shore. There is a swift current on the ebb around Deer Point making north between Deer and Indian Islands. By going up the west shore one profits by the eddies behind the points. Avoid the old weir off Kendall Head covered at high water. The best general rule for this passage is to hug the American shore on all tides if bound north, the Deer Island shore if bound south.

If forced to make this passage with an overnight stop, Clam Cove on Deer Island is possible, open only to the south, but there are no supplies. Farther up on the west shore is North Harbor, a good anchorage. Anchor southeast of where chart 801 says "40," southeast of the weir.

The waters of the narrow passage between Moose and Deer Islands are frequently white with thousands of gulls and terns snatching fish from the boiling waters.

Quoddy Roads, Me. (801). Quoddy Roads are open southward and eastward. The best anchorage is northward of Quoddy Head, but this is recommended only if you miss your tide.

Lubec Narrows (801). This narrow and shallow channel, now spanned by a bridge with a vertical clearance of 47 feet at a mean high water, can be a real adventure. The tide at full strength runs 6 knots or better. A correspondent writes:

> I would suggest a very strong word of caution to all regarding the tidal current under the Lubec-Campobello bridge. We ran through with the tide behind us and had all we could do to prevent piling up

Lubec Narrows and Passamaquoddy Bay.

on the supporting piers. The eddies on the bay side are fierce, and even the sardine carriers have difficulty getting through.

There are several things to keep carefully in mind if you are planning to enter Passamaquoddy Bay under the bridge.

1) Measure accurately the height of your mast *above the water.*
2) Remember, in the light of the statement above, that the tidal current turns about half an hour to an hour before high water; although the tide is still rising, the current begins to run south under the bridge and the current is slack at this time. The current is slack again at about the time of low water.
3) Consult the chart below and determine the clearance under the bridge with respect to mean low water.
4) Consult the tide table and correct the clearance for the height of the tide on the date in question.
5) If it is going to be a very near thing, note that the curve gives height under the navigation light, which hangs about 18 inches below the underside of the bridge.
6) Check your arithmetic. If the calculations are all correct and if you have forgotten nothing, you will have an uneventful passage. Good luck.

You may have implicit confidence in the chart. Mr. Alan Bemis constructed it, and his account of its construction is printed below.

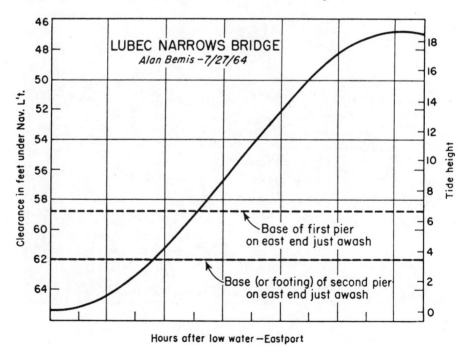

Hours after low water —Eastport

With more fixed bridges crossing our waterways every year (and dynamite hard to come by) it is helpful to know their vertical clearance precisely. Published clearance is usually figured at mean high water, and down Fundy way the stage of the tide makes all the difference. We all need to know our exact mast height too. Height above the water seems to be the only parameter not included in the CCA Measurement Rule so many owners don't know it exactly.

Last July *Cirrus* with Dwight, Helen and Davie Shepler and myself aboard decided to determine some of these half-knowns under the new Lubec Narrows bridge that allows landlubbers to roll on four wheels from Lubec to Campobello Island. Luck made our calibration easy with a 0.0 low tide at Eastport that morning, i.e., mean low water. We ran up a whisker pole on the flag halyard flying 8.4 feet above any more permanent part of the rig and cruised up and down stream under the center span until, as the tide rose, the whisker pole finally struck the green center navigation light.

We kept a log on the time of day, observed various markers awash and such, providing data for the clearance chart submitted herewith. Then departed speedily on the flood to run Cobscook Falls before the puzzled Lubec populace sicked the harbormaster on us.

The published figure is 47 feet at mean high. Our calibration indicates this is the correct figure for clearance under the green navigation light which seemed to hang down about 18 inches below the bridge structure. Please note that there are wide departures from mean high and mean low. The bridge has seven piers, three east of the channel and four west. The pair on either side of the channel carry big steel and timber fenders which throw huge bow waves in the tide and leave turbulence and back eddies below them. Placing your ship in the center of the span is easier going downstream, and will be more exciting as you wonder if Bemis' calibration is correct. (No guarantee made or implied.) However, it is a long way around Campobello Island even with your rig still standing.

Lubec, Me. (801). Lubec is a small town, population 1800, on the northeastern tip of Lubec Neck, a 1½ mile peninsula extending northeast from the mainland toward the New Brunswick island of Campobello. North of the peninsula is Johnson Bay; south of it, Lubec Channel. It is the easternmost town in the United States, of which West Quoddy Head (the easternmost point in the United States) is a part, edging out Eastport, 3 miles to the north, by ¾ of a mile.

A standpipe, 1½ miles west of the town, a church spire, and a stack on the water front are prominent in approaching the town.

The best and most convenient stopping place for yachts is the public

Laurence Lowry

West Quoddy Head Light, the easternmost point in the United States. An infra-red photograph.

marina, north of the town in back of the breakwater. It is expected that this facility will be expanded by the government within the 1971 to 1972 period. Here there is 20 feet of water at high tide and none at low tide. The contract has been negotiated for the completion of the marina, so in 1972 the extension should be added so that there will be 7 to 10 feet of water at low tide. For anchorage, proceed to Johnson Bay to the west of the town, an excellent but large anchorage for small boats. All supplies are available close by the marina. Gasoline and Diesel oil will be delivered by tank truck; water is at Peacock's dock just above the bridge. Groceries may be had at several stores. There are two places to obtain a meal ashore. There are two rooming houses, The Triangle and Stuart's, and a six-unit motel, The Eastland, near the Lubec Airport.

The post office and Customs headquarters are located at the end of the bridge. The bridge has a clearance of 47 feet.

Though distant less than 3 miles by water from Lubec, Eastport has no ferry to Lubec. The only alternative is a 40-mile journey by road. See the account of Lubec Narrows, above, for data on the bridge and the current in the narrows.

There is a 2000-foot air strip 2.4 miles west of Lubec. It is lighted upon request.

Mr. Carroll Peacock and his son, Robert S. Peacock, of the R.J. Peacock Canning Company, are authorities for marine information in this section. They are most hospitable to visiting yachtsmen. Don't pass by Lubec without going through one of the sardine canning factories on which depends much of the prosperity of our easternmost town.

Cobscook Bay, Me. (801). Cobscook is a large bay full of islands and narrow passages, and very pretty. On account of the heavy tides, which in some places attain the force of rapids, it is not much frequented by strangers. But, aside from the falls west of Falls Island, there is nothing that ordinary care cannot overcome.

Note that nun 8 on Birch Point Ledge between Birch Point and Seward Neck usually tows under on every run of tide.

Cobscook Falls, Me. (801). These are reversible falls located just west of Falls Island, where chart 801 reads "67." They run 10 knots at full run and are something to see. Only crazy men like the one who provided these data (and who prefers to remain anonymous) run them at full run. He reports that the safest time for sane folk to pass through is at low slack, because all hazards are well above water. The maximum strength of flood current occurs about two hours before high water at Eastport.

The inward run of tide is much more turbulent than the outrun, due to the rock formation. On the inward run the current flows straight past Falls Island to a large ledge, Roaring Bull, which makes out from the western tip of Falls Island. This forces the current violently over toward the north shore, from which it swirls back south to meet the current coming around the south side of the island. This southbound current carries one's boat off "Government Rock," located just west of figure "57" on chart 801. "Two Hour Rock" is just to the southeast, southwest of figure "21" on the same chart. It uncovers two hours after high water. In the lee of "Roaring Bull" a big whirlpool develops.

On the outward run, however, the current follows a much straighter course.

A more cautious approach is south of Falls Island.

Because of the interest of venturesome cruisers in running the falls, the following is presented from an experienced cruising man who has been running them for many years in a 45-foot yawl:

Water is swift, with plenty of huge haycocks, and tosses one around plenty. Skipper should proceed up the bay on the rising tide from Eastport. As he approaches the falls, he should place himself in the middle of the stream. The detail chart is quite accurate. Stream will carry one around "Roaring Bull," then one must starboard the helm to avoid points of rock to starboard. A large swirl carries one to port after passing "Roaring Bull." Beware of the big whirlpool west of the "Bull." There are no particular difficulties about going out with the tide if one places oneself in the center of the stream above the rapids. Current runs 10 to 12 knots; should not be attempted in dinghies or small boats, which whirlpools suck down. Dennys River is a charming, isolated spot.

An equally experienced authority adds: "I would discourage this. For anyone unaccustomed to these tides, it's fearsome."

Indicative of the attractive anchorages in the bay are the following:

Dennys Bay. On the high tide one can travel quite close to Dennysville. The best anchorage over a low tide is about 1½ miles below the town.

Birch Islands. There is a good, snug spot among these islands where chart 801 reads "9."

Leighton Point Cove. This cove affords a good anchorage below the falls. The shores are uninhabited. Getting in is quite a trick on the full run of tide. The currents off Denbow Point are as strong as in Lubec Narrows. This is known locally as Schooner Cove.

Coffin Point. There is a pretty anchorage southwest of the Point *south* of Falls Island.

Black Head. There is a pretty, quiet anchorage between Black Head and Long Island west of the southern part of Seward Neck. The shores are uninhabited, the protection is excellent, the holding ground is good (though a little kelpy), and the cliffs are high.

Eastport, Me. (801). Between Eastport and Deer Island is a tidal commotion truly frightening to the skipper unprepared for it. It is caused by the tide coming in north of Campobello meeting the tide running up Lubec Narrows. Huge whirlpools 30 feet in diameter and 3 or 4 feet deep spin even big sardiners halfway around. Great boils rush up, making mounds off which a yacht slides sideways. The whole maelstrom is in constant motion, so passage through it, especially in light weather, can be very exciting. With a fair current and with power or a working breeze, there is no great danger to a seagoing yacht, but a small open boat might find it very dangerous indeed. In rough weather or in a storm, it is too furious to approach, and under any weather conditions it is best taken at slack water.

Eastport now has a heavy wharf and breakwater that provides a protected place to tie up out of the tide. The Customs officer is usually to be found here, and yachts returning from Canada should check in. All members of the crew should be provided with positive identification and proof of citizenship, just to be on the safe side.

Gas, water, fuel oil, and sometimes ice are available at the wharf. S.L. Wadsworth & Son, ship chandlers, can supply most of your wants and tell you where to take care of the rest. Among other things they carry United States and Canadian charts. There are stores, restaurants, and a post office up-town.

Eastport is primarily supported by herring, most of which is canned as sardines. Recently, however, herring runs have been small, and Eastport has suffered badly. It has cast longing looks at the oil industry; and although many people quite sincerely oppose it, others wish to bring it in. Consider the plight of a 100,000-ton tanker trying to negotiate the tide between Eastport and Deer Island!

During his administration, Franklin Roosevelt started the Quoddy Project to generate electricity by impounding water in Cobscock Bay at high tide. It was never completed, but is periodically revived and reconsidered.

Just south of Eastport is a fish-meal factory at Prince Cove that spreads a foul effluvium for miles to leeward. It is an unmistakable landmark.

You will notice on the chart the international boundary line running between Eastport and Deer Island, past Lubec, through Lubec Narrows and Quoddy Roads and then down Grand Manan Channel. The story goes that Daniel Webster and Lord Ashburton, having agreed that the boundary line should follow the main stream of the St. Croix River, met to float down the river and establish the axis of the stream. Mr. Webster enjoyed a good dinner and an excellent rum punch. He lay down for a brief nap, which cost us if not Deer Island, certainly Campobello and Grand Manan. Just a very little nudge with an oar may have made the difference between Head Harbor Passage and Lubec Narrows.

They say that the fates of nations are decided as often at the cocktail bar as they are at the council table.

Welshpool, Campobello, N.B. (801). This fishing village, across Friar Roads from Eastport, is on the north side of Friar Bay. There is a summer colony including what was for many years the summer home of the Franklin D. Roosevelt family.

In the summer of 1966 President Johnson and the Prime Minister of Canada met at the Roosevelt house to dedicate a memorial to the memory of President Roosevelt. The Roosevelt estate is now open to the public and is well worth a visit.

The anchorage is rather exposed, but there is a good wharf. The *Canadian Coast Pilot* states that in westerly weather small craft can find good protection alongside this wharf in 12½ feet. There is a black buoy located off the west point.

Harbor de Loutre, Campobello, N.B. (801). Though not so snug or picturesque as Head Harbor on the north end of the island, this anchorage on the northwest side is excellent and well protected. After entering, proceed south, leaving the black-and-red spar buoy to port. Anchor south of the point and weir making out from the west shore, off two houses on the west bank.

Head Harbor, Campobello, N.B. (801). One may enter this delightful anchorage on either side of Head Harbor Island. If it is thick, the simplest entrance is north of the island where the diaphone at East Quoddy Head makes a reliable guide. Note that the channel between the light and the northern end of Head Harbor Island is very narrow. The writer, after making the light in the fog, followed the shore to enter Head Harbor, was confused by soundings of over 100 feet, and found he had inadvertently followed the eastern shore of Head Harbor Island.

There is a clump of spar buoys between the island and the entrance to the harbor. These are all black and are to be left close to port in order to avoid old weirs on both sides of the entrance. Once by the spars, proceed up the middle and pick up one of the large winter moorings inside.

One of them, conspicuous because of a neat pennant and pick-up buoy, belongs to a local party boat. Provide your own pennant and lie on one of the others.

There is no store, no gas, and no float at Head Harbor. Land at the big government wharf and climb a ladder or land on the beach. Just up from the shore on the road leading westward to Wilson's Beach is Head Harbor Haven, the establishment of Mr. McCann. He runs a camp ground where trailer people cruising ashore can find anchorage. He has a telephone that yachtsmen can use for collect calls. He also has a most interesting combination of museum and marine junk yard with many relics from the daily life of commercial sail.

It is a good half hour's walk to Wilson's Beach, where there is a fish-packing plant, a store, and a Custom House. The fish plant will sell shaved ice, and if you are fortunate, the storekeeper will drive you, your ice, and your groceries back to the wharf. If this is your first Canadian port, you would do well to bring your yacht registration along and enter Canada here. It is much easier than at Pugsley Wharf in St. John.

In August the wild raspberries on the north shore of Head Harbor are ambrosial.

The entrance south of Head Harbor Island is perfectly practicable in clear weather. Be sure to leave all black buoys to port.

Wilson's Beach, N.B. (801). Entering the labyrinth that is the government wharf can be a bit scary the first time, especially in a strong wind; but once you make the turn into the basin, all is secure, although you may need to do some fancy steering. Go for the wharf with the gas pump. One of the stores is at the end of that wharf. The ice is free. It is shaved ice, and you get it in bags or pails supplied by you, and, if necessary because of the tide, passed down to you on a line. Shaved ice turns out to be wonderful in a boat. It fills all the spaces left by the old ice, and it holds for a long time.

Entry into Canada definitely should be made here. The Customs House is at the end of and just around the corner to the left of the gas dock. The Customs officer couldn't be nicer; and it is far more convenient to do this business at Wilson's Beach than it is against the Pugsley Terminal Wharf on the east side of St. John Harbor.

There is a good store just up the hill from the wharf.

If you seek a more peaceful anchorage when your business here is done, go round East Quoddy Head and spend the night in Head Harbor.

Jackson Brothers is a family business started by Howard Jackson many years ago and now carried on by two of his grandsons, Keith and Don Jackson, and by their brother-in-law, Vaughn Newman. In an interview with Lyman Owen of the *Maine Coast Fisherman* printed in the August, 1965 edition, Vaughn said:

> In the course of a year all total fish, including all kinds, would run about 3 million pounds . . . some years go as high as 4 million. For instance, last week we sent out six truckloads which averaged 16,000 lbs. a load . . . all haddock. Our average yearly run to Portland would come to about 65 to 70 trips. It has run as high as 112, and in off years might drop to around 40.
>
> Our heavy salted fish, cod and pollock, are trucked to St. John, N. B., for the foreign market, chiefly the West Indies. We also do some light salting for local consumption.

Since along the U.S. east coast line trawling is almost forgotten, it was of great interest to learn the extent of such trawling out of Campobello. We asked Vaughn about the operation there. He said:

> Our trawl boats have to run [their lines] on the high or low water . . . the current is too strong when the tide is running. On the slack of about two hours at high water and the same at low water, our boats are out there ready. They have a buoy line which they put overboard and put out the trawl warp with an anchor at end of it. The trawl is put out in a straight line and then other buoys and trawl warps are let out. The last buoy may be held in the boat and they'll lay on that for the next tide and then start hauling.
>
> When the trawls are brought in, the fish are gutted and the catch is brought right in to the fish house [Jackson's]. They immediately start baiting their trawls for the next set. If they are not going to trawl the next day, they clean their hooks, replacing some of them, and lay their lines in the trawl tubs. Most of our trawlers carry six to eight tubs: a tub will hold 1800' of trawl line, and the hooks run about three to a fathom.

Northwest Harbor, Deer Island, N.B. (801). This is a well-protected and very attractive harbor with high, wooded shores dropping steeply to the water; in places there are impressive cliffs. In clear weather, entrance is easy. Often when it is thick offshore, there will be a scale-up north of Campobello that will carry you all the way to Deer Island. Note that the flood tide runs south around the end of Deer Island. Be sure to give the spar outside the harbor a good berth, as the ledge appears to extend beyond it.

Run up the middle of the harbor. Off the cove on the north shore there is a weir and a big ledge. The writer anchored in front of the ledge on a quiet night and all was well. A later visitor reports the bottom is smooth rock there and suggests going farther up the harbor among the old moorings where the bottom is soft. Beware of old weirs on the south shore. There is one that extends a long way into the harbor just before you get to the mouth of the little cove. There is a small settlement at the head of the harbor, but the nearest store is at Richardson.

In getting out of the harbor, especially in the fog, you may find the tide very confusing. The writer found the first of the ebb setting northeast much earlier than expected.

Lord's Cove, Deer Isle, N.B. (801). Coming from the south, favor the east side of the channel slightly until up to the white ranges and then run in. A visitor in 1971 reported 20 feet at low water where chart 801 shows 3 feet. There is a good store at the head of the harbor and another a short distance away in Richardson. The latter sells marine supplies as well as groceries.

There is no gas or Diesel fuel on the wharf.

From the north, the entrance is clearly indicated on chart 801.

St. Andrews, N.B. (801). Entrance from the east is confusing at high water because Tongue Shoal is submerged and what is marked on the chart as a lighthouse turns out to be a small globe on top of a pole, which looks much like a spar buoy. The buoy in front of it is small and inconspicuous. At low water, the gravel bars running off Navy Island are so high that they look like part of the island. However, once you locate Tongue Shoal, simply follow the line of buoys. The red light on the wharf is simply a red electric bulb of doubtful candlepower on a white pole.

Entrance from the west is clearly marked, but the channel is narrow and the buoys small.

There are four guest moorings consisting of Clorox bottles painted red and clearly labeled GUEST, courtesy of the Kiwanis Club.

The western part of the harbor has been recently dredged and is much improved.

Land at a float on the east side of the long wharf. The Customs office is at the head of the wharf. There is an information booth close to the head of the wharf manned by very helpful people. If St. Andrews is your first Canadian port, you will need a cruising permit. But note that St. Andrews is on Atlantic time and that the office is closed on Sunday.

There is no gas or Diesel oil pumped to the wharf, but if you need enough to make it worth while, call the Irving Oil Co., or Kim Cowan at Imperial Esso and a tank truck will appear. Gas for boat use is colored purple in Canada and is considerably less expensive than automobile fuel.

Water is piped to the wharf and there may be a hose. No ice is available at the wharf but at a sporting goods store on the main street you can buy milk cartons filled with water and frozen.

The town of St. Andrews is essentially one long street with all necessary and many interesting but unnecessary stores. Besides grocery, meat, liquor and drug stores, and restaurants, there is a County Crafts shop famous for handknit sweaters, each in a unique pattern. There are also china shops carrying all manner of delicate and unusual English china.

There is a large hotel overlooking the town and another on the main street. Train, bus, and air connections are easily made from St. Andrews.

Because cruisers from "the States," having come to St. Andrews, may wish to have some of the historical background of this most attractive region, the following footnote is taken from an article in *The New York Times* by Earl M. Benson:

> Among the town's early settlers were Loyalists who came in 1783 in square-rigged vessels from Castine, Me. They thought Castine, on the eastern bank of the Penobscot River, would be in British territory. When they learned that the St. Croix River was to be the boundary line, they sailed farther east to what is now St. Andrews. Some of them even took down their houses in sections and towed them in scows behind the ships. There are still many descendants of these Loyalists living in the town.
>
> These pioneers believed in town-planning. Before building began, the land was surveyed and laid out in squares. The thirteen side-streets, which begin at the water front, were named for King George III and his twelve children.
>
> At the wharf head the visitor will find one of the most rewarding spots in St. Andrews, the County Craft Shop, where the yard is bright with yarns drying in the breeze from the bay. Inside the wide doors are the articles made in local cottages and farmhouses.

There are several shops of interest to the tourist. In one grocery store, established 130 years ago, one can find tempting foods from all parts of the world. Two china shops display sets of Wedgwood, Spode, Chelsea, Royal Doulton and Belleek that are as complete as those in many large cities. Another shop offers the products of various New Brunswick handicrafts—pottery, wooden ware, hand-wrought iron, and home-made jams, jellies, and cheeses.

The story of the building of Greenock Church is a strange one. In the early days there was but one church in the town, the Church of England, and the rector offered his church to the Presbyterians who had no place to worship. At a public meeting a townsman arose and charged the Presbyterians with being "too mean to build a church of their own." This aroused the ire of Christopher Scott, a wealthy sea captain, who came from Greenock, Scotland. He declared that the Presbyterians would have a church like the one in his native town and he would pay for it all himself. He kept his word and the church was built in 1824.

This church, with its Christopher Wren spire, is remarkable for its fine proportions and excellent design. It is unique in that it was constructed without nails or any other metal except that which was used in the locks and door hinges. All woodwork was fastened together by wooden pegs, and today the church appears to be as sturdy as when it was built. Below the steeple clock is a colored bas-relief of a green oak tree, the coat of arms of Greenock. The three-deck pulpit of Honduras mahogany and curly maple, its panels edged with small hand-carved acorns, is a masterpiece.

Fishing is an important local industry. Conley's, Ltd., operates the largest lobster pound in the world (on Deer Island). Each year the company ships tons of live lobsters to all parts of the United States and Canada. Visitors are welcome. Trips can also be arranged with the herring fishermen to go out at daybreak and watch them gather their catch.

Guides will take fishing parties for landlocked salmon and lake trout on Chamcook Lake. Small-mouthed black bass are found in Wheaton Lake and there is good fly-fishing for speckled trout and Atlantic salmon in the Digdeguash River.

There are two golf courses, one a tricky 9-hole and the other an 18-hole course overlooking Passamaquoddy Bay. Greens fees are moderate, and lunches are served at the golf clubhouse.

St. Croix Island, Me. (801). Though there is no harbor here, the island affords an interesting stop on the way upriver. It was on this island that Pierre du Guast (Sieur de Monts) and Champlain and their men celebrated their first Christmas in the New World in 1604.

Of vastly greater historical importance is the fact that this island saw the first European settlement in New England. Here the French first settled in the New World. They remained only one winter, moving on to Nova Scotia, which became a British possession through the Treaty of Utrecht in 1713. Professor W.F. Ganong, who has written the best history of the island, has said, "From the day the keel of her small boat grated on the beach of Dochet [St. Croix] Island, this continent has never been without a population of those races which have made the history of the principal part of America—the French and the English." The island was made a national park in July, 1949.

Anchor about 100 yards west of the white conical building on the west shore. The bell on the structure's west side is not longer used. There is no fog signal. But watch for a ledge, covered at high water, just northwest of this spot. Approach cautiously.

In a ledge at the highest spot on the island is a small metal marker, with the legend "International Boundary." This may have been true once, but today the boundary between the United States and New Brunswick is in the middle of the river to the east. The United States Government owns part of the island, but not all of it. The light is unwatched.

The only historical marker is a metal plaque on a boulder on the northeast side of the island reading as follows:

1604   1904
To Commemorate
The Discovery and Occupation
of this Island by
De Monts and Champlain
Who Naming It
L'Isle Saincte Croix
Founded here 26 June 1604
The French Colony of Acadia
Then the Only Settlement
Of Europeans North of Florida
This Tablet is Erected by
Residents of the St. Croix Valley
1904

The burying ground, where a few skeletons have been unearthed, is in the plateau at the south end of the island. But there are now no traces of it.

Anyone interested in the historical background of this region should read the references to St. Croix Island in *Voyages of Samuel de Champlain* by W.L. Grant (Charles Scribner's Sons, 1907). The island was dis-

Augustus D. Phillips

Saint Croix Island. Sieur de Monts and Champlain spent the winter of 1604–5 in the field at the right end of the island. Artifacts and graves have been discovered here.

covered in 1604 and named by Sieur de Monts "Isle de Saint Croix" (Holy Cross Island) on account of the "cross" formed above the island by the river from the west, Oak Bay from the north, and Warwig Creek from the east. A footnote states that at the celebration of the three-hundredth annivery of its settlement "it was resolved that it be henceforth called Saint Croix Island." The Maine Historical Society has published a well-illustrated volume, *Tercentenary of De Monts' Settlement at Saint Croix Island, June 25, 1904* (Portland, 1905). The French had a hard winter on the island, thirty-five of the original band of seventy-nine dying of scurvy. The survivors left the following summer for Port Royal, N.S., later renamed by the British Annapolis Royal.

There is an excellent account of the settlement, "The French at Saint Croix Island—the First European Settlement in New England," in a pamphlet entitled *French in New England*. See also *Saint Croix—the Sentinel River,* by Guy Murchie (Duell, Sloan and Pearce, New York, 1947).

A fitting conclusion to any reference to St. Croix Island is a few lines written by Henry Milner Rideout for the Tercentenary of St. Croix:

> Into the hill-cleft waterways
> With ceaseless ebb and flow astir,
> Into the sunset blaze
> Craftily steering,
> High on her mast
> They bore the banner of Old France
> To the new Land Acadia, and cast
> Their anchor by this island of the bays
> At the commandment of Pierre du Gast
> And merry, brown Champlain, the King's geographer.

Calais and St. Stephen. One who really loves rivers can go up the picturesque St. Croix on the tide, following the dredged channel. The international bridge here is the principal place for crossing into Canada. Neither town is spectacular.

Chamcook, N.B. (801). A correspondent writes:

Chamcook Harbor, N.B. is an excellent though deserted anchorage. It is large but secure, with excellent holding ground. The entrance to the outer harbor, between two buoys, is very narrow, and the tide runs like a trout brook for a few hundred feet, but there is little current inside.

Entrance to the inner harbor is a gap not over 100 feet wide between two sandbars, just as you pass an ancient factory undergoing renovation, and a new shipyard producing trawlers. We draw 4 feet and entered on the bottom of the tide, using the color of the water as a guide. We used the lead to find a sheltered berth at the head of the inner harbor and spent a couple of pleasant hours toward high water watching the automobiles driving across the sand spit to Ministers Island. It was early evening of a very Canadian Sunday, and competition was keen to see which would be the last car that could possibly make it before high tide covered the road.

This is one of the few really secure small-boat anchorages in Passamaquoddy Bay. *Canadian Coast Pilot* mentions buoys showing passage from outer to inner Chamcook Harbor, but the chart shows none—and there aren't any!

Digdeguash River, N.B. (801). Located in the north part of Passamaquoddy Bay, this is a delightful little anchorage. The government charts do not give the correct depths at the mouth. One can go up on the last half of the flood and have plenty of water to the bridge, now a permanent steel structure. Round to just below and anchor, running out a stern line to the bridge. It would not be too good a place in a heavy southerly unless one were confident of one's ground tackle, as it would be difficult to work out. One can row up through a gorge into a pond, about ¼ mile across, into the northerly end of which the river flows over a waterfall. Walk up the river about ½ mile and find more falls and deep swimming pools. It is nearly perfect. One can get milk at a farmhouse just east of the anchorage. There is no village.

One cruising man got a different impression of this place, as indicated by the following report:

Digdeguash struck us as rather big and bleak and certainly *not* "a delightful little anchorage." Also you have to work through the deuce of an unbuoyed mess to get up to the bridge, and why anchor *right under* U.S.–Canada Route 1, or whatever it is? [It's Canada's 1-A.—*Ed.*] However, we spent a whole day at a perfectly safe anchorage further out and had a swell time visiting the pond in the dink.

Magaguadavic River, N.B. (801). Pronounced "Mack-a-davy," this pretty river makes an interesting day's exploration. Plan to go up on the flood and return on the ebb.

The entrance to the river is wide and deep, but it soon narrows and becomes quite shallow. It is buoyed all the way to St. George, but the buoys are small and inconspicuous.

The principal feature of St. George is a huge pulp mill. It is interesting to follow a log through the course of its reduction from wood to paper but a little depressing and rather smelly.

St. George is a pleasant little Canadian town with the usual stores, post office, telephone, and so on.

Little Letite Passage, Deer Island, N.B. (801). This is a narrow passage from Passamaquoddy Bay running south of McMasters Island into Letite Passage with 14 feet at low water. It is not recommended for strangers.

A correspondent writes as follows about this district:

> I cruised all these waters last summer. Grand and Little Letite Passages are blemished by the new big high-tension line to Deer Island. Do urge all to run Little Letite Passage, which is good fun and perfectly safe on half tide or better. Wonderful climb and view at McMaster Island. Anchor at Red Pebble Beach, west side of island, at the south of Sea Cave.

Another correspondent adds: "Not good fun if the tide is strong."

Letite Passage, Deer Island, N.B. (801). This is the principal deep-water entrance to Passamaquoddy Bay. The tide runs through here with considerable violence, making swirls, eddies, and boils. However, with power or a fair wind, one can run through with a fair tide. There is no difficulty about making the run at slack water. There are good fog signals on Pea Point and Bliss Island. There is a whistle off Mascabin Point.

CHAPTER XV

The Coast of New Brunswick and the Saint John River

General Conditions. The 40 miles between Head Harbor or Letite and Saint John can assume a variety of disguises according to the conditions. Usually in the summer the trip is a featureless grind, started at an inconvenient hour to catch the tide and completed under the tension of entering a harbor obstructed by salmon nets and threatened by ocean steamers. If you are lucky enough to catch a northwest breeze, it is a magnificent sail at an incredible speed by a panorama of cliffs, hills, and forests broken by occasional tiny harbors. But run into a head wind, rain, or a real blow and the trip can be an absolute nightmare, especially when the tide turns against you. Shelters are few and widely spaced. In thick weather or heavy seas, they are hard to find, and with a 3½ knot tide running, one's reckoning is soon only a little better than guesswork.

The 40 miles is divided in half by Point Lepreau and the halves subdivided, the western half at The Wolves and the eastern at Split Rock. The first 10 miles from Letite or Campobello to The Wolves has three big fog signals—East Quoddy Head, Bliss Island, and Pea Point. The whistle at The Wolves is a good mark. There are several harbors in this part of the run and slightly less tide than one finds farther east.

The second 10 miles, from The Wolves to Lepreau, is dominated by the diaphone and whistle buoy at Lepreau. The armchair navigator scanning chart 4334 would assume that little difficulty would be encountered here. The diaphone is positively shattering. The point on which it stands is high and bold. The whistle is well offshore and is big enough and loud enough to be worthy of its position. However, bending over the cabin table on a small boat bound E ¾ S from The Wolves, the situation looks very different—what you can see of it. Many cruising men aver that the fog factory, located on Point Lepreau, turns out a concentrated product experienced at its thickest in this region. Many cruising men who have been by Lepreau frequently have never seen it. The tide runs to the eastward in the first part of the course but soon sets heavily to the north into Mace's Bay. Off the point you will find, even on a still day, a very active tide rip with short breaking seas and vigorous swirling currents. Standing on the plunging bowsprit, choked by fog, blasted by the diaphone blowing from a bearing it should not occupy, looking and listening for an elusive whistle is not quite the same as studying the chart before that comfortable fire at home.

Once well by Lepreau, however, the worst is over. On the course to Split Rock bell the tide will affect you but little and from there to the buoys off Partridge Island you have the powerful horn and the radio beacon to guide you. Of course you must remember that Saint John is a deep-water port frequented by big steamers. You may find them groping for the fairway buoys or anchored awaiting a tide. A radar reflector is a flimsy but a valuable means of defense to be seconded by a powerful foghorn. Also you may run into salmon nets, of which more under Dipper Harbor.

There is a good deal to be said for breaking the run at Dipper Harbor, which is about halfway, at Chance, or Musquash. If the breeze is light or you don't travel very fast under engine, you may arrive at Saint John with the tide running against you. Getting up the river under these conditions is hard work, especially as that is a likely time for steamers to be coming down. A layover assures arrival with a fair tide and plenty of time to go up the falls the same day.

If you do want to try it in one piece, consider starting from North Head Harbor or Whale Cove on the last of the ebb tide. The distance is a little less than that from Head Harbor, and there are no obstructions on the course at all. One can home in on the Partridge Island radio beacon right from Grand Manan. The big horns at Lepreau and Tiner Point will give a check on position as you converge with the shore, but you will be well outside the rip at Lepreau. Going west, the Grand Manan alternative is even more favorable, for the radio beacon on Southwest Head is about in line with Swallowtail. Also note that there are big fog horns on Swallowtail and Long Eddy Point.

Once at Saint John, go up the falls as soon as the tide serves. If you have to wait, the best place is at Pier 3 on the west side. Market Slip is somewhat silted in.

With the falls astern you have before you many miles of pleasant river, lovely coves, farmland and wooded hills, lakes and pretty towns. Dangers are fairly well marked now—no more of black cows to port and brown cows to starboard. The swimming is warm. Fog is nearly unknown. The people you meet are almost without exception hospitable. It is nearly perfect cruising ground. Only those cussed ones among us who don't like lotus as a steady diet yearn to get back to salt-water.

Preparations. The wise skipper will not leave Grand Manan or Passamaquoddy without the basic equipment recommended in Chapter II. Of these a reliable and accurately compensated compass is a *sine qua non*.

One should have Canadian Charts Nos. 4334 (Bay of Fundy, Brier Island to Cape Chignecto), 4314 (Plans of Harbors: Chance, Dipper, Musquash, and Lorneville), 4319 (Saint John Harbor), and 4333 (Point Lepreau to Cape Spencer).

One should also have a copy of *Nova Scotia and Bay of Fundy Pilot, Tables of Hourly Direction and Velocity of the Currents and Time of Slack Water in the Bay of Fundy and Its Approaches,* and the *Bay of Fundy Tide and Current Tables.*

All these may be purchased from the Canadian Hydrographic Service, Surveys and Mapping Branch, Department of Mines and Technical Surveys, Ottawa. Write and ask for a catalogue. With your order, send the exact price of your purchase by International Money Order in Canadian money.

Saint John River Weather

One last comment—the weather in the Saint John River Valley and adjacent area is generally fine in the summer months, a fact that may seem unbelievable after what may often be a long run through dungeon fog to get up the coast to Saint John. Once through the falls, even with the most solid fog condition outside and in the harbor, I have never seen a zero visibility condition in the river proper. There are low ceilings and rain occasionally, as anywhere else in the East, but the weather is generally sunny, warm, and dry. Swimming is superb, as the water is considerably warmer in the river and lakes. The winds prevail from the south and west, with occasionally fresh northwesters when a front has gone by. This makes for ideal sailing along close shores with no sea. Nothing is pleasanter than scudding along among verdant farmlands at 7 knots with not a ripple underneath. The height of the river varies from time to time but only through a foot or so, and I have found the soundings on the charts excellent.

The following accounts of L'Etang Harbor, Finger Bay, and Back Bay were contributed by Mr. Hugh G. Williams of Bremen, Maine.

L'Etang Harbor, N.B. (4313). This is a fascinating complex of harbors, coves, and sheltered but striking passages, with heavily wooded islands and high black cliffs, often riddled with caves. It is still almost completely wild. In one cove, the arrival of a 24-foot sloop from the States actually brought a couple of carsful of sightseers. This body of water includes Bliss Harbor, Letite Harbor, Blacks Harbor, and possibly Back

Bay, as well as many unnamed, uninhabited anchorages. Chart 4313 appears to be an accurate guide, and hazards are few except for countless abandoned weirs. In this area the gunk-holing cruiser will be well advised to reach his anchorage on the bottom of the tide when possible. Otherwise the cockpit conference before supper will be enlivened with the appearance of weir-stake after weir-stake, each one nearer than the last. Trying to anticipate the pattern is an absorbing pastime.

A recent visitor to L'Etang adds:

This is fascinating, as the *Guide* says, and beautiful. In it, at Crazy Point, is the most lovely anchorage on the whole East Coast, beautiful but big enough really only for one boat; two would be crowded; three, impossible. Crazy Point is on the south side of Letang Peninsula.

Crazy Point is named on Chart 4313. Just outside is the anchor symbol. You get to it by driving generally north between Letang Head and McCann Island and then bearing off to the north-east from Letang Head about a mile.

Do not anchor where the anchor symbol is. Enter straight in from the east, going parallel to the shore, and keeping north of the little ledge on the east end of Crazy Point itself. You will find yourself in a deep, narrow, wooded, rocky cove without a house or a human being anywhere in sight. If the tide is low, you can scratch around and get the world's sweetest quahaugs.

Finger Bay (4313) is recommended as a very secure, secluded berth. Anchor just off its mouth. Favor the islands on your starboard hand going in, but not too close. Pick your anchorage with the lead, and remember there is a good 25 feet of tide in these parts. There are a few farms within walking distance of the shore; the dock of an abandoned clam factory makes a good landing place because there is a good gravel road to the main highway between St. George and Back Bay. At any farmhouse with a telephone, supplies may be ordered for delivery right to the old wharf. Call the store of Sylvester Hooper & Sons, 755-3729.

Back Bay (4313) itself appears to be the only protected anchorage with supplies available between Cutler and Saint John. Blacks Harbor is unprotected, busy, and smelly (on an easterly the smell comes to Finger Bay). Head Harbor is without supplies, and the other possibilities are way up in Passamaquoddy. Back Bay is protected by a breakwater built in 1962, and vacant moorings may well be available between it and the government wharf. It's only fair to add that there's a sardine factory here, too; however, the locals point to it as a handy source of fresh water.

An excellent source of local information is Mr. Sylvester Hooper, owner of the store. Gas cans may be filled at the store, but if large amounts of gas are needed, they can easily be delivered by truck from St. George, about 8 miles away. Hooper's store will deliver supplies anywhere between Letite Village and Blacks Harbor, in response to a telephone call.

(Here Mr. Williams's account ends.)

Dipper Harbor, N.B. (4314). This harbor is a very pleasant stopping place on the long road to or from Saint John. It is easy of access, with the diaphone on Lepreau and a bell buoy outside. Running in from the bell, plan to make Fishing Point, which is bold, rather than the east side of the harbor. Just inside the point is a weir and there is another farther in. Keep to the east of these and you will go clear of the ledges off Devine Point. These ledges and another just outside the breakwater are marked by very thin black spar buoys. The light on the end of the breakwater appeared small and feeble to the writer in 1966.

Behind the breakwater is a pleasant surprise. There is a basin dredged to 6 to 8 feet with usually a vacant mooring. If no mooring is available, lie alongside the lobster car or a sardiner if one is tied up at the wharf. If you tie up to the wharf itself, plan on a 20-foot rise of tide.

The wharf is backed with a breakwater on which the Canadian Government recently spent a reputed $250,000, yet in heavy winter gales water still comes over.

There is a small store ¼ mile up the road from the shore. The countryside here is pleasant but quite unlike Maine. The hills are higher and covered with tamarack as well as spruce. Swamps in the valleys are tangled with alders. Farms are less frequent. Narrow black-top roads wind through the hills, hedged in with second-growth forest. The shores are precipitous cliffs varied by open coves, often principally flats at low water. The inhabitants do a little subsistence farming but rely principally on lobsters in the winter and herring or salmon in the summer.

A very pleasant local fisherman, Mr. Cecil Clark, stopped aboard while we lay at the wharf on Sunday afternoon and told us about the salmon fishing. The nets are about 300 feet long and are attached end to end to make a set of sometimes as much as a mile. The top is supported by floats on the surface. The footline is weighted so the net forms a curtain about 3 to 5 fathoms deep. There is a buoy with a flag at each end. It is set across the tide or diagonally along it, usually near the mouth of a river. The Saint John is very popular. The fisherman may patrol along the net in his boat, trying to drive fish in, or he may just tie up to the net and wait. The net drifts with the tide, sometimes fouling another or getting wound up by tidal eddies. The fishing is best when the water is rough, the salmon then coming up, as Mr. Clark said, to play near the surface. Sometimes a single man will get as many as eighty big salmon of twenty pounds or more in a single tide. On many other occasions he may get none. The price is good, as anyone who has tried to buy salmon knows well. The principal danger to the fishery is the increasing pollution of the Saint John River.

If you see a net ahead of you—and you should keep a sharp eye open for them off Saint John—turn and run along it. You will presently find the owner. He will wave you toward the clear water. Even if you doubt the wisdom of his advice, follow it. He knows where he is and where the other nets are. Getting your propeller fouled in a net can be a terrible experience. The water is icy, and there is almost no alternative to going overboard.

A visitor to Dipper Harbor in 1970 found no mooring available, was not enthusiastic about the lobster car, and found no sardiner at the wharf. He adds, "My opinion is that coming to anchor in Chance is better than fooling around in Dipper."

A well informed Saint John yachtsman states categorically, "Dipper is best."

Chance Harbor, N.B. (4314). This harbor has been dredged and except in southeast winds you can anchor right up against the rocks opposite the government wharf; but it may be rolly.

Musquash Harbor, N.B. (4314). Musquash does not appear to afford good protection unless you care to go up the stream into the upper hole on the tide. One St. John yachtsman took a dim view of the whole scene, and another simply remarked "Be careful."

Lorneville, N.B. (4314). This harbor dries out at low water.

Saint John, N.B. (4319). There is no difficulty in finding Saint John. The excellent horn and radio beacon on Partridge Island assisted by the line of buoys making off to the south should make the approach easy. In the fog, particularly, one may become involved in a labyrinth of salmon nets. There is a lengthy account of salmon-fishing operations under Dipper Harbor on page 561. Suffice it to say here that the nets are made of heavy polypropylene twine and can easily disable a yacht if her propeller gets fouled up. Note, however, that the nets are tended by men in small boats. They will wave you off to the safest water with an oar. Follow their directions. They know how their net is lying in the tide, and they are likely to know where other nets are set. The salmon season is open from May 15 to August 15, and the nets are ordinarily set from ebb slack to high water. The fishery is not so lucrative as it used to be, so there are fewer nets being set. In 1973 the fishery was being phased out.

The second hazard off Saint John is the steamer menace. Saint John is a large and busy commercial port, like Halifax, one of Canada's principal ice-free Atlantic outlets. Vessels coming in may be anchored outside awaiting favorable conditions. In this case they are required to ring a bell. Or they may be entering the channel, blowing the whistle and moving cautiously. Bear in mind that at slow speeds a great steamer is not under very good control and certainly is not agile enough to avoid a small yacht. Steamers coming out, once clear of the inner channel, are likely to be moving considerably faster and will be on you very rapidly indeed. About the only possible defensive action is to hang up a radar reflector, blow the horn vigorously and often, and—especially—*hang close to the very edge of the channel.*

A visitor to Saint John in 1971 adds:

On entering Saint John Harbor from Partridge Island it has been common practice in thick weather, which is usually the case, to run up the left side of the channel to the big bell on the end of what used to be the first pier. This is because Customs clearance and falls information is available there without getting mixed up with the complicated docking in the city. The only trouble is that now a new docking arrangement for the Digby Ferry has been constructed down harbor from the bell, and even respecting the left-side buoys on entering, one comes pretty close to the end of this new dock and/or the bow of the huge new ferry serving Digby.

The wise skipper will have cleared Canadian Customs at Grand Manan or Wilson's Beach and can proceed directly up the harbor. However, if the formality has been neglected, it is necessary to do it at Pugsley Wharf, the first wharf on your starboard side on Reed's Point. The only possible alternative is to telephone from the Royal Kennebecasis Yacht Club and have an officer come out. He will do it, but it is a nuisance for him and will cost you the price of his transportation.

Pugsley Terminal Wharf is a menace for a small boat. It is a massive concrete wall against which the harbor chop dashes, complicated by great washes from hurrying tugboats. The Customs house is a blue building on the south end of the wharf. If you cannot tie up here, and you usually cannot, you will have to jump for a ladder and deal with the Customs officer while your wife keeps the yacht out of trouble off the end of the wharf.

If and when you have solved the problem of entry into Canadian waters, you may want a pilot to help you up the falls. If you are lucky, Mr. Ed Hartshorn of Canadian National Railways will have appeared on Pugsley Wharf. He keeps an eye on the channel from his office at the Canadian National grain elevator and, if he can get away, meets visitors. He writes:

> No one who is able to get a yacht to Saint John should be at all frightened of the falls—just respect them. And use good common sense. And do not go looking for thrills. But as we are all sailing for fun, it does take some of the worry out of it if you have some help, and that is where we of the RKYC love to be of any service.

Call Mr. Hartshorn at Canadian National, Mr. Gerry Peer of Akatherm Atlantic, Mr. Russ Macnamara of the Department of Transport, or the Royal Kennebecasis Yacht Club.

If you have business at St. John, or if the tide is not right, tie up at Market Slip on the east side of the river. This is partially filled in, so move very carefully here. All kinds of supplies are available, and repairs to machinery can be made at Saint John Iron Works. Remember, however, that most seafaring here is heavy commercial work and few places are prepared to handle yacht work. Remember, too, in planning your day, that Saint John is on Atlantic time, one hour ahead of Eastern time.

When your needs are taken care of, cross over to West Saint John and tie up between piers 3 and 4. Here is likely to be a big floating crane on a barge, much easier to tie up to than a wharf, which you can step on to at high water, and which will be above your spreaders at low water. This berth is the quietest in Saint John harbor.

As slack water approaches, about two hours twenty-five minutes after high water and three hours fifty minutes after low water, move up the river, keeping more or less in the middle. The state of the current at the bridge before the falls gives a pretty good idea of conditions at the falls. When the tide looks to be as slack as it is going to be—and that is nothing but an uneasy equilibrium between the current of the river and the Fundy tide—go up the middle of the river. Keep close to Split Rock on the starboard side just before the bridge over the falls, and the tide will carry you out into the middle. Avoid the other side of the river, as the remains of old bridges close to the bank are dangerous.

Pass under the middle of the bridge and edge over close to the pulp mill. You will see a great boiling and swirling to starboard. This is the "pot." Keep away from it. Pulp logs are sometimes shot up in the boils with force enough to damage a propeller or start a seam. Often the whole area is covered with suds from detergent used in the mill so if there are pulp logs floating around you can't see them. Move slowly or cut the power altogether and let the tide carry you along until you are in the clear.

Coming down through the falls, follow the same course.

Push on up the river by Boars Head—remarkably well named—to the Royal Kennebecasis Yacht Club at Milledgeville.

Royal Kennebecasis Yacht Club, Milledgeville, N.B. (4344). Round Boar's Head and Ragged Point and continue to the anchorage off the yacht club. Avoid Red Rock, marked by a green flasher on a black pontoon. There is now a breakwater off the club and a marina with berths for transients. A mooring may be available if you would rather lie off.

There is a dinghy float at which to land and a wharf on which gas, water, ice, and Diesel fuel are available. At the club is a telephone and a substantial bar. There is a small marine railway next to the club. There is a good grocery store just up the road. Saint John is a ten-minute taxi ride away; it has all the facilities of a big city. Investigate the situation on buying bonded liquor. If you agree not to broach it until you leave Canada, there may be a considerable saving.

The members of the Royal Kennebecasis Yacht Club are without doubt the friendliest and most hospitable people in the yachting world. They will do anything they can to make your visit pleasant. There are a few amenities that seem minor but that the considerate yachtsman will follow. For instance, you should fly the Canadian flag, the maple-leaf, at your starboard spreader on entering Canadian waters and the United States ensign at the staff astern or on the leech of the mainsail. When you take the American flag in at night, take in the Canadian one too. Bring along an extra club burgee, especially if you belong to a club whose members do not often visit Saint John. Perhaps the gentleman who pilots you up the falls would appreciate it. Anyway, be sure to pay his taxi fare back to the city, and don't let him die of thirst on the way. Always write out Saint John—don't abbreviate it. And remember that Saint Johns is in Newfoundland, not New Brunswick.

We who have been treated so hospitably in Canada await the opportunity to return the hospitality at our own yacht clubs and in our own harbors.

The Royal Kennebecasis Yacht Club is a center for yachting on the river, not only for visitors, but for local people as well. On one occasion the Cruising Club of America, an assemblage of salt-water, stick-and-string gentlemen accustomed to Bermuda and transatlantic passages, visited the club. They proceeded from Massachusetts in a seamanlike manner through all kinds of weather. From Mt. Desert on they had it thick all the way, but being accomplished navigators, they all made it without serious incident, by means of compass, chart, fathometer, R.D.F., and all the best of equipment and judgment. At Saint John a local pilot met them. At just the earliest reasonable time they passed the falls and proceeded triumphantly through the last of a sunny summer day to the peaceful anchorage at Milledgeville. As they were snugging down, a power cruiser came roaring in, flying the American yachting ensign and bearing a nondescript pennant at her bow staff. The owner bumped up to the wharf. A member of the Cruising Club, thinking perhaps the new arrival had been a little late for slack water at the falls asked, "How did you make it coming up the falls?"

"What falls?" inquired the new arrival.

He had come all the way from New York on an oil-company chart; and, without any advance planning or even knowledge of their existence, had hit the falls at exactly slack water.

Mention should be made of **Kennebecasis Bay,** a large body of water extending northeast from the Saint John at Grand Bay. Some of the nicer summer homes of Saint John residents are situated in the communities along the shore, and much of the sailing activity of the various clubs is carried on in this area. Forester Cove at the entrance to the Kennebecasis River is large and deep but gives good protection. Attractive sand beaches can be found on the north end and in the cove at the south end of Long Island.

The Saint John River. After leaving Milledgeville, leave Kennebecasis Island to starboard and push on up the river. The shores are mountainous with beaches at the water's edge backed by forests and farms. Occasionally one passes small towns with ferry slips or little coves where tributaries enter. Beware of bars off these. The waters are protected enough so no sea ever makes up, and a breeze usually draws up from the south. Fog is almost unknown. An occasional salmon leaps, and local yachts add interest to the scene, especially on weekends.

There is not much shelter until you come to Whelpley Cove at the end of Long Reach, although one could anchor almost anywhere under the shore. The writer anchored in a hurry off Oak Point with his broken topmast hanging from the spreaders while the entire Cruising Club of America sped by. One valued friend in a 40-foot yawl with only two men and a woman aboard was jibing an enormous spinnaker with great skill and coolness. He found time in the midst of the evolution to ask if we needed help.

Beyond the dramatic Gorham Bluff, one can follow the chart sharply to the right or proceed north along the river and enter the narrower deeper channel between Pig and Hog islands and get into **Kingston Creek** and Belle Isle Bay, one of the most beautiful and desirable cruising areas on the river.

On the right around Gorham Bluff is **Shamper Cove,** a shoal one with foul bottom. Crossing the head of Shamper Cove and again turning right to the south'ard brings one into **Kingston Creek,** one of my favorite spots. The west side of the cove is bounded by high granite bluffs and, farther in, a steep hillside down which a rocky brook falls with a fine soft music on quiet nights. On the east side the cove is bounded by steep meadows and farmlands, both sides affording fine shelter except in the case of strong winds out of the north. Kingston Creek about ten years ago was navigable for a distance of almost 2 miles, but, due to continued logging operations in the surrounding woods, it is difficult to carry 6 feet more than a mile in. The waterlogged pulpwood has lessened the charted depth considerably, and while we felt our way some distance in carrying 6 feet, an accompanying boat drawing 3 feet struck the foul bottom right next to us. The rest of the cove provides good anchorages along the shores, provides great exploring country, and is quiet and peaceful.

It is reported to be windy in strong southwest weather as the wind funnels through the anchorage.

Belle Isle Bay

From Kingston Creek, exploration of **Belle Isle Bay** is a *must*. It is uncharted except for about a mile at the opening. However, it has bold shores, and from our experience it is navigable for a distance of about 5 miles for drafts of up to 10 feet. Several points make out from the shores and small sandbars can be found off these, but they are clearly identifiable.

When entering Belle Isle Bay, keep right on going north past Shamper Cove (don't try to get into the bay by crossing through Shamper south of Belle Isle) and make a U-turn to the east at the north end of Belle Isle (Hob Island). (See inset on chart 4344.) At that north end is a red-and-black spar and a red spar. Go between them. Then going south there are two black spars. Leave them close-aboard to starboard on your way south into the bay, and, naturally, close aboard to port on your way north past the island and back into the river. This is the opposite of red right returning. From the more southerly of the two black spars you can lay a course of 138 magnetic, which will take you toward a white target painted by a fisherman on the south shore of the bay. Carry that course until you get in the middle and then turn northeast for Ghost Island.

Proceeding up the bay one comes first to a pretty, wooded, unnamed island (Ghost Island), on the east side of which will be found what appears to be a naturally formed obelisk of rock. The island is steep to, and you can tie right up to the trees on most of it, except where the beach lies on the west side. The scenery at this point is grand, with high granite bluffs giving way to thick woodlands and occasional farm areas. Since Jenkins Cove is no longer uninhabited, many visitors now prefer the anchorage at Ghost Island.

Around the next high bluff on the left lies one of the best coves I have ever been in. It is *Jenkins Cove,* named for the family owning and still operating the farm on the north side. The cove is spacious but well protected, with good holding ground. The real surprise, however, is a hidden secondary cove of minute but deep dimension found only after completely entering the main cove. This small cove is ideal and completely sheltered, with steep sides of beautiful granite, birch, and spruce. The Jenkins Farm, besides operating a small country store, has the finest vegetables, berries, and fruits in the area, which is a great pleasure when these things get a little scarce on a cruise.

Brown's Cove just beyond Jenkins Cove is not nearly as scenic and, being a V-shaped cove and open to the south, it does not afford very much protection in strong winds. A little way down the bay on the opposite side is *Erbs Cove,* which we have looked into but never entered. While it appears to be deep, it is another wide-mouth cove with no particular attraction. Another mile up the bay is Long Point, beyond which the depths are in doubt, and local knowledge seems to indicate that 4 feet or less draft may be required for the additional 4 or 5 miles to the end of this beautiful bay.

As you come out of the bay to go on up the river, either course may be used as in entering, but the natural track would be up the Hog Island Channel. The black spar about halfway up the length of Hog Island must be left to starboard and rounded sharply. The channel lies close to the island as will be seen until nearing the north end where it swings over to Pig Island, passing between the island and a red spar as it enters the river proper.

Navigation and Canadian Buoyage

Since we are moving well up the river now, it may be appropriate to have a few remarks on navigation and buoyage from here on. Although what I am about to say has been modified substantially by the efforts of the Canadian authorities in 1959 and 1960, the average cruising man may be somewhat startled by what he sees of navigational aids indicated on the charts, indeed if he sees them at all.

If the river is high, as it sometimes is during the summer months, spars showing on the charts often project above the surface a little, even 6 inches. These sometimes have to be sought out, but with no tide, smooth water, and only a moderate current, you can usually go right up to where you think something should be and look around. What looks like a dead tree stuck in the bottom should not be disregarded. It may replace a spar buoy carried away by the huge log rafts that are towed down the river.

The channels among the islands are relatively easy to follow, in that most of the islands are low and grassy, and the weeds and aquatic plants seem to grow to the surface up to a depth of almost exactly 5 feet. If uncertain, follow the water clear of growth and it will almost always be deep. A great many cattle, sheep, and some hogs graze on the islands in the river and along the grassy shores. However, the old tale that the brown cows will always be to starboard and the black-and-white ones to port when entering just isn't so.

Things indicated as lights with varying characteristics on the chart may be almost invisible by day because of foliage and location. By night, with a few exceptions, these lights will average what appears to be about 25-watts intensity.

Lastly, we mention the matter of birch and spruce stakes with the foliage still attached. These are easy to follow and should be treated like any other buoyage. The depths may vary somewhat from the charts, but I have found that in most periods when we have visited the river, the charted depths are conservative. As mentioned above, the Canadian authorities have taken definite steps to improve the aids in the river and have done a great deal, particularly in the lower portion.

Tennant Cove to Grand Lake

Tennant Cove, just beyond the entrance to Belle Isle Bay, is a poor one, having a bad entrance and being shoal.

Our next run would be up the right side of the river, passing either side of Spoon Island and bearing right to go up the east side of Long Island. Just before coming to the end of this sizable island, one should enter *Washadamoak Creek,* passing along the east side of Lower Musquash Island until the entrance to Washadamoak Lake appears. It is buoyed and, though narrow, can easily be followed, bringing the cruising man into a lovely, long lake with numerous coves and bays and fine cruising country. This lake is now accurately charted.

Many New Brunswick yachtsmen recommend the anchorage at Colwell's wharf up the Lawson River beyond the entrance to the lake.

Beyond the entrance to **Washadamoak Lake** the water deepens and the lake becomes navigable to deep-draft vessels for a considerable distance. An unnamed cove lies about three miles up the lake and is well sheltered from the east and south. A little farther along, one comes upon **Lewes Cove,** which contains a lovely granite bluff and two small wooded islands, Spruce and Birch. It affords protection from all directions and is an excellent spot. About 3 miles beyond is the town of Cambridge with the village of Narrows on the opposite side of the lake. Here limited supplies may be secured. A swing bridge crosses the lake at this point; and, although I have never been through it, I am told the lake is navigable for considerable draft as far as Cody, another 10 miles. Though the scenery is not quite as dramatic as Belle Isle Bay, this lake definitely should not be missed, the hills rising to several hundred feet on either side.

Another anchorage favored by local yachtsmen is **Big Cove** on the southern shore of the lake about 3 miles from the entrance. Go *well* in past the little island and anchor at the end off the last farmhouse to port. Draft of 6 feet is all right, but anchor to starboard and well in.

Gagetown, N.B.

Leaving Washadamoak Lake and going on north, the narrow, deep channel reminds one of the European canals. On leaving Colwell's Creek, one should be careful not to continue to the north of Upper Musquash Island, as a bar obstructs this channel about halfway out to the river. Rounding Killboy Island, turn south and head for the open river, turning north when in the mainstream. Continuing north, we enter Gagetown Creek and tie up at **Gagetown,** where limited supplies and fuel may be had. This is one of the "larger" towns on the river, and about anything can be found if the demand is great enough.

Our plans would now take us south of Gagetown Creek again and on up the river proper to the almost invisible entrance to the **Jemseg River,** where one passes between shores about 75 feet apart to enjoy a 3-mile run up to the highway bridge at the village of Jemseg. This is a new high-level bridge with an 85-foot clearance, replacing the old drawbridge.

After successfully negotiating the bridge, we make for **Grand Lake,** following the marked channel out of the Jemseg River and across Purdy Shoal at the lower end of the lake. This channel is well marked with both stakes and brush; and, with a few obvious places easily identified on the chart excepted, the whole area of Grand Lake is a fine cruising ground with ample depths, sheltered coves and bays, and fine beaches. The water is generally clear and clean enough to drink, and we have often filled our tanks with it. It is suggested that this be done above Grand Point bar.

Grand Lake, N.B.

The lake averages 3 miles in width and is about 25 miles long. In my opinion no trip to the Saint John River should fail to include a run into Grand Lake.

In Grand Lake the first important spot is **Douglas Harbor** on the northwest shore. This is a lovely series of coves shown in a detailed insert on the Canadian chart. Straight up the harbor toward the wharf will be found a long sand spit, which serves as a dandy swimming beach. We usually moor about halfway between this spit and the wharf in about 8 or 9 feet.

The cove on the left as one enters the harbor looks fine, but, though deep inside, has a 1-foot bar across the entrance and must be explored only in dinghies. The cove on the right, opposite, is fine and much more secluded if there are several boats near the wharf area. There is good holding ground all over the harbor, and though it is deep in spots, one can always find a good place to lie.

Mill Cove and **White Cove** on the southeast shore of the lake are perfectly good anchorages, though wide coves and not very snug. The same is true of **Young's Cove** about halfway up the lake, where we have been a couple of times when we wanted to get near the highway from Saint John in order to swap crews. Though we have never used it, the small cove inside Fanjoy Point near the village of Waterborough can also be used for the crew-shift problem. **Cumberland Bay** is a large bay running west-southwest to east-northeast and, having a wide mouth, is likely to be choppy with the prevailing winds.

Entering the northeast arm between Goat Island and Cox Point, there are two coves on the left and one on the right. **Barton Cove,** the latter, is deep, but, again open to the southwest. **Flowers Cove** on the left is interesting and completely snug.

It has been a popular rendezvous site. In the south arm of the cove there is an inner cove that, as in the case of many Canadian lakes, has a sharp, narrow sand spit enclosing a completely protected deep anchorage. However, electric power has come to the new cottages around Flowers Cove and two difficult-to-notice wires now cross the entrance to this charming spot at a height of about 25 feet. One of the boats on the cruise in 1971 took the wires down, knocking out the power to one side of the cove, and was thoughtful enough to yell and scream as we started to proceed into our old haunt with wires unnoticed at about the height of our spreaders. I'm sure there will be others who see the 10-foot sounding inside this neat hole and start in oblivious to the wires, which don't show against the background of the woods. Oddly enough the second cove on the left, which is unnamed, is likewise a fine anchorage. While we did not lie in this one, we looked it over, and a fine snug anchorage in 10 feet of water can be found just beyond the point at the entrance. At **Newcastle Creek** a couple of miles farther up the left side of the lake, there is a small but deep harbor, a large power station, and a small town, the only sign of anything resembling big industry for miles. This is not a good place to lie but can be used for supplies if the charm of Grand Lake extends one's visit.

Into the North Woods

From here we embark on another delightful adventure by following the marked channel around Lead Island and Moray Points into the mouth of the **Salmon River,** a fine north-woods stream in which one can carry 6-foot draft for about 11 miles upriver to the town of Chipman pretty nearly into the deep woods of central New Brunswick.

The banks of the Salmon River are thickly wooded, and when one can make the run upstream under sail as we did, a sense of departure from the conventional cruising atmosphere is most evident. There is the delicious north-woods smell of pine and wild flowers, and the only sound is an occasional bird call, or the scurrying of animals in the woods. There is no sign of civilization except at Camp Wesegum, a Canadian religious camp about halfway to Chipman.

After this peace and solitude we finally made the turn at Davis Turn, and with some surprise saw three bridges, a dam, a busy sawmill, and log booms filling the river. You can tie up to the wharf at the foot of the bridge or to one of the scows tied along the bulkhead. This is a lumber town and railhead with both Canadian Pacific and Canadian National Railroads crossing the river at this point. All kinds of supplies are available in the town, and the people are most friendly and helpful. Our 40-foot cutter was the first masted vessel they'd seen in town, and we had a large number of visitors, adult and youthful, the latter bearing most welcome gifts of fresh blueberries and home-grown lettuce.

A local authority reports that R.K.Y.C. cruises have been going regularly to this town for the last eighty years, sometimes with yachts up to 65 feet.

Another interesting side trip from Grand Lake is described below by

Mr. Love in an excerpt from his account of a cruise in these waters in 1965. The 1934 Sailing Directions to which he refers are printed after his letter.

While on this cruise I had occasion at the time of the Douglas Harbor rendezvous to make an investigation of the chain of lakes which run in a westerly direction from the southwest end of Grand Lake. We had towed a Boston Whaler along as a tender, and I was able to make an extensive run in comparatively little time.

The entrance to this fascinating waterway is at Indian Point 2.3 miles northwestward from the mouth of the Jemseg River and is marked by red and black spar buoys and bush stakes. One must stay close to in rounding Indian Point, and immediately behind it one finds a very small neat cove with about 9 feet of water. At normal river height, 6 feet can be carried in.

Although the 1965 edition of the Sailing Directions for the Saint John River completely overlooks the description of the waterway from this point, I followed those in the 1934 edition and found them to be reasonably accurate with the old channels originally dredged for logging operations about as described. What has happened where these channels come into the lakes I do not know, but I would surmise that 6 feet could still be carried most of the way.

I had a beautiful trip through Maquapit Channel, or thoroughfare, across Maquapit Lake, through French Lake Thoroughfare, across the bottom of French Lake and a short distance up the Portobello River, a distance of about 10 or 11 miles. What the status of the one highway bridge is I don't know but it seemed operable, clearance being about 15 feet closed. This is a real gunkhole trip, but perfectly beautiful.

Indian point.—This point is 2-3 miles northwestward from the head of the Jemseg river, being low and composed of sand and gravel. The entrance to Maquapit thoroughfare is close southward of this point.

Indian point dredge track, so called, is a channel 3,000 feet long and 75 feet wide, dredged to a depth of 9 feet, and trends southwestward from that depth in Grand Lake, and, rounding Indiand point close to, leads into Maquapit thoroughfare.

Buoys.—The northeastern end of this channel is marked by a pair of spar buoys, a red and a black. A black spar indicates the southern side of the channel at Indian point. The channel is also bushed and should be navigated with caution.

Maquapit thoroughfare empties into Grand lake at Indian point and is the outlet of an extensive chain of lakes with connecting streams as follows, Maquapit lake, French lake thoroughfare, French lake, Indian lake and Portobello river. Maquapit thoroughfare, 200 to 300 feet wide, is a deep stream, depths varying from 9 to 19 feet with several sharp bends, leading into Maquapit lake. Good sheltered **anchorage** will be found throughout its length of about 2½ miles.

Maquapit lake, about 5 miles long, has a greatest width of 2½ miles. A dredged channel, 3,600 feet in length with a sharp turn in it 1,200 feet from the upper end of the thoroughfare, leads into the deeper portion of the lake. This channel, 75 feet wide, has been dredged to a depth of 7 feet. A similar dredged channel 2,700 feet long leads from the upper end of the lake into French lake thoroughfare. This channel, 75 feet wide and 7 feet deep, is in two reaches, 2,000 feet and 700 feet long, which meet at a sharp angle.

French lake thoroughfare, similar to Maquapit thoroughfare, is 12 to 24 feet deep and 2 miles long. It is crossed by a highway bridge near the settlement of **Lakeville Corner.** A dredged channel leads from this thoroughfare into French lake. This channel, 2,400 feet long, is 75 feet wide and has a depth of 7 feet. Like the previous dredged channels, it has a sharp bend in it which in this case is 600 feet from its lower end.

French lake is about 2¼ miles long and 1¼ miles wide. There are two islands in the lake, French and Apple, the deepest water being eastward of them; westward of the islands, it is very shoal. Depths vary from 7 to 13 feet over the greater part of the lake.

Bushes mark the sides of all the above channels. However the assistance of a local pilot should be obtained by any stranger wishing to make a trip through these waters.

Note.—A canoe trip of historic interest, one of the favourite water routes of the Indians in the early days, may be had by portaging at Maugerville from the Saint John to the **Portobello river,** a distance of one to two miles. French lake is reached by descending the latter river and thence the various water areas just described provide a through channel to Grand lake. The shores of the latter may be skirted throughout, if so desired, before rejoining the Saint John river at Lower Jemseg. In very dry seasons sufficient water for even canoes may not be found in some parts of the Portobello river.

The low marsh land and numerous ponds surrounding Grand, French and Maquapit lakes are the feeding grounds for large flocks of black ducks, whistlers, teal and other water fowl. Each autumn brings numerous hunters to the vicinity for the annual duck-shooting.

On to Fredericton, N.B.

This is the story of the "Rhine of North America," and obviously I am enthusiastic about it. The Saint John River, of course, continues in a northerly and westerly direction for many miles. It is navigable from where we left it at Lower Jemseg as far as Fredericton with drafts as deep as 6 feet. This latter run I have never made because I have felt other parts of the river and area are more attractive. Fredericton itself is a small city bustling with business activity and a very active chamber of commerce, which puts on a prominent outboard and small-boat regatta every year. For the average cruising man I think there are years of more fascinating cruising to do in the area we have described.

APPENDIX A

Birding Under Sail

by

CHRISTOPHER M. PACKARD
Maine Audubon Society

Intrinsically bound with the sound of the sea is the call of the gull. The sea has a bird-life peculiarly its own. It is constantly changing, whether one cruises along the coast or heads offshore; and it also varies from month to month. Whether one is content merely to admire the freedom and grace of a bird's flight over the open sea, or becomes intrigued in identification and behaviorism, birds can provide added pleasure to any cruise. A yachtsman is in a unique position to observe and enjoy some of the choicest birds of New England. The following paragraphs name some of these and suggest avenues of further exploration.

The most common gull along our coast is the herring gull, which takes unusual pleasure in perching on moored craft. How many a yachtsman has forsworn anything to do with birds after such an early and intimate encounter. However, though at times unwanted companions, they do much to keep our harbors clean. Actually there are a number of different kinds of gulls along our coast. The great black-backed is our largest. A little smaller than the herring gull is the ring-billed, especially plentiful in harbors south of Maine. You may occasionally see gulls with black heads and dark backs; these are probably laughing gulls, which breed west of Penobscot Bay. In late summer the Bonaparte's appear along the coast. Just slightly larger than a tern, we are more apt to see immatures or non-breeding birds already in their winter plumage. The more you look at gulls, the more different kinds there may appear to be. However, gulls have a number of different plumages for different stages of growth. Fortunately the field guides show these, and with their help, you will soon be able to identify a first- or third-year gull with hardly a second glance.

"Mackerel gulls" are the name fishermen use for terns. Graceful, swallowlike, plunging into water after small fish, they are a joy to watch. The common tern is probably the most abundant, until you reach a place like Matinicus where several thousand arctics breed. A third species found in New England is the roseate.

Close relatives to the gulls and terns are the shorebirds. Commencing in late July, you are apt to encounter migrating flocks. Many different species occur at this season, such as the black-bellied plover, ruddy turnstones, dowitchers, sanderling, and semipalmated sandpipers. However, the one which breeds on our rock-bound islands is the spotted sandpiper. This is the one that wanders over the rocks, frequently stopping and teetering. There are shorebirds, however, that are really a yachtsman's speciality. These are the phalarope. Thousands gather in the Bay of Fundy in August, and often large flocks will be seen resting on the water offshore. Both red and northern species occur at this season, truly pelagic shorebirds that the land-bound birder all too seldom sees.

Among the islands from Casco Bay east, you may see some brownish ducks with a flotilla of ducklings. The common eider has been increasing on the Maine coast as a breeding species. As soon as courtship is over and the eggs are hatched, the males usually go off by themselves. However, by late summer small rafts of eiders, both sexes and all ages, will be seen congregating over shoal beds where they feed. Stay clear!

A non-breeding sea duck that may be found occasionally is the scoter. All three species (common, surf, and white-winged) do summer along the coast. Two other species may surprise you. Black ducks (we usually think of them breeding on fresh water) do breed on some offshore islands. They may be seen resting on the ocean, though they do not dive or feed in deep water. The common loon, the bird of Maine's inland lakes, now breeds on islands as far at sea as Matinicus. We think the outboard motoring on inland waters may have been just too much for them to stand.

Superficially similar to the loon is the double-crested cormorant (shag to fishermen). This is the dark-colored bird often seen perching on a nun or can with wings outstretched in a spread-eagle fashion. Colonies nest on islands, sometimes building their nests on the ground, and at other times building in trees. Fishermen long thought the cormorant was a dangerous competitor, but studies seemed to indicate it ate only trash fish. Again the bird is suspect, large numbers of shiny tags having been found in cormorant rookeries; tags used to mark salmon in Maine's restoration program for that fish. Extensive studies will probably again be undertaken to determine this relationship.

Man's interests and those of birds have clashed all too often. The eagle, once seen with regularity along the Maine coast, has within recent years been able to produce less than six young annually in the entire state. The osprey, still nesting on innumerable Maine islands, is also becoming less common. There are more unoccupied nests than occupied. The stately great blue heron, which was a common sight in coves, is no longer producing young in former numbers. It is in cases such as this that bird counts become important. Unless counts are made this summer, we will have nothing with which to compare a summer hence. Yachtsmen are in a unique position to help determine the magnitude of this changing picture of New England seabirds.

At the turn of the century our seabird colonies were threatened by plume hunters. Protection was provided and gradually colonies of terns, eiders, and gulls increased. Today there is again concern due to visits to offshore islands by people seeking recreation. If you visit a bird colony, bear in mind that your presence may be keeping adult birds from incubating eggs or causing the young needless and often fatal exposure. The greatest care must also be observed not to step on eggs or young, which in the case of seabirds are usually protectively colored. On grassy islands where petrels nest, great danger can be caused by walking across the turf and compressing petrel burrows. The situation has reached such proportions that part of Matinicus Rock is being declared "off bounds" during the breeding season by the U. S. Fish and Wildlife Service and U. S. Coast Guard. On Machias Seal Island the Canadian Wildlife Service requests that you keep to paths and the bird blind. If you do visit a seabird colony, please observe discretion.

It is on Matinicus Rock and Machias Seal Island that the puffin nests; a species that birders will travel miles to see. Matinicus marks the southernmost breeding colony on the Atlantic seaboard, and if cruising Penobscot Bay, swing around Matinicus Rock, especially the cliffs on the eastern side. Here you should get wonderful views of puffins in the water, close to your boat. A few pair of razorbills (auk) may also be found at the Rock, but far more will be seen off Cutler and Machias Seal. The third alcid that breeds in New England is the black guillemot. This is a little black bird with conspicuous, white wing patches, which breeds from Pemaquid east. It is a great diver and upon surfacing small eel-like fish may be seen clutched in its beak. Again nature may trick you. By late summer, many guillemots will already be wearing winter coats of white —back to the field guides!

When the fog rolls in we call it "Shearwater weather." It is at such times that we usually get the largest counts of greater and sooty shearwaters. I have come upon a raft of sixty or more sitting on the water off Matinicus in fog. With the breeze blowing and fair weather, the shearwaters are usually on the wing. They may come soaring in close to your boat, and just as suddenly disappear. These are truly pelagic birds, spending much of their lives over the open ocean, and the manner in which they ride the wind currents is a pleasure to see.

Also spending much of their time at sea are petrels. The Leach's breeds on a few of our turf-covered offshore islands in eastern Maine. The Wilson's petrel when encountered in summer off the New England coast is biologically "wintering." It breeds during our winter months in the Southern Hemisphere. Collectively these birds are called "Mother Carey's Chickens," both by Maine coast fishermen and by mariners for generations. If you see small dark birds, fluttering close to the surface and often acting like swallows, check out the petrels.

While it may seem strange to mention land birds in a cruising guide, they will be frequently encountered. At anchor in the coves along the coast, one is treated to a chorus of bird songs in the evening and early morning. The notes of the hermit thrush, white-throated sparrow, black-throated green warbler, and parulas drifting out across the water add to the tranquillity of the hour and setting.

Many land birds migrate across the Gulf of Maine, some traveling as far as from Nova Scotia to Cape Anne or Cape Cod in a direct line. I have encountered hummingbirds and chimney swifts far at sea. Often warblers and other small birds will alight on your yacht, pausing for a short rest. At such times these birds are extremely tame and may even hop over your body or roost on your head! Occasionally, black-backed gulls will pursue these small migrants. The gulls will swoop down on them, forcing them close to the water where they become easy prey. On several occasions I have had migrants seek refuge on my boat from marauding gulls.

The fall migration starts in late July off the New England coast, and reaches its height in late August and early September. At such times you may even encounter butterflies at sea. While I do not recommend taking a butterfly book aboard, do not overlook taking a book on land birds, for you may have an opportunity to identify a surprising number even far offshore.

Never before have so many fine books been available to assist in bird identification. The three most useful are: *Birds of North America* by Robbins, Brunn, and Zim (Golden Press, New York), which illustrates all North American birds in color; the *Audubon Water Bird Guide* by Richard H. Pough (Doubleday & Company), which has excellent colored illustrations and a text that gives details about the habits of seabirds; and *A Field Guide to the Birds* by Roger Tory Peterson (Houghton Mifflin), which has long been a standard identification guide. Any of these is easily stowed aboard. *Birds Islands Down East* by Helen Cruickshank (Macmillan Company) should be read before you set sail. The State Audubon Societies will offer other suggestions of good books, and can provide you with check lists of birds likely to be found in New England waters and along the coast.

The yachtsman who has become proficient in bird identification is in a position to provide extremely valuable information to the State Audubon Societies. These organizations are dependent upon records of seabirds from fishermen or upon their own, all too infrequent, offshore field trips. Concentrations of shearwaters, dates of offshore encounters with land birds, records of migrating waterfowl, etc., are the type of information these Societies are anxious to obtain. Do not underestimate the value of your observations. The following would like to hear from you: The Maine Audubon Society, 22 Elm Street, Portland, 04111; the New Hampshire Audubon Society, 63 N. Main Street, Concord, 03301; the Massachusetts Audubon Society, Drumlin Farm, Lincoln, 01773; and the Rhode Island Audubon Society, 40 Bowen Street, Providence, 02903.

APPENDIX B

Geology of the Maine Coast

by

OLCOTT GATES

Department of Geology, The Johns Hopkins University
and
Maine Geological Survey

The yachtsman sailing the Coast of Maine is enjoying a cruising paradise (barring a little fog now and then) which was 400 million years in the making. The history of these 400 million years is written in the rocks that frame Maine's green islands and bold headlands. The yachtsman cannot help but notice their great variety; and I hope the following description of the geology of the Maine Coast will heighten both his joy in this pleasant land and his interest in its origin.

Let us begin our geological cruise at West Quoddy Head and work westward. One always sees more of the coast beating back, and besides we will be following in the wake of C. T. Jackson, a Boston physician and Maine's first state geologist, who in 1836 sailed in the Revenue Cutter *Crawford* from West Quoddy Head to begin the first systematic study of the geology of Maine.

From West Quoddy Head to the Cow Yard most of the rocks are dark gray, dark geen, black, or dark rusty brown. They are massive and unlayered although commonly highly fractured. These dark massive rocks are termed *gabbro*. Typical examples can be studied on West Quoddy Head, the shore around Cutler harbor, the bold cliff on the east side of Bunker Cove, and Black Head on Head Harbor Island.

A close look at gabbro—preferably with a magnifying glass—will reveal a mass of interlocking crystals, some of which are white or gray and others black or dark green. The white crystals are of *feldspar,* a mineral composed of oxygen atoms tied together by atoms of calcium, sodium, aluminum, and silicon. The dark mineral is *pyroxene,* also composed largely of oxygen atoms but tied together by atoms of magnesium and iron as well as silicon. Feldspar and pyroxene are two very common minerals in the earth's crust.

On the north side of West Quoddy Head or at Balch Head south of Baileys Mistake the dark gabbro can be seen cutting sharply across a sequence of layered rocks; and *dikes* (narrow tabular bodies) of black gabbro cutting other rocks are numerous along this part of the coast. Chemical analysis indicates that gabbro has the same chemical composition as the basalt that makes up typical lava flows. The massiveness and crystallinity of gabbro, its cross-cutting relation to older rocks, and its chemical similarity to basalt all suggest that gabbro is an *igneous* rock, one that formed by the cooling and crystallizing of hot molten rock—*magma*—like the liquid lavas erupted from volcanoes. However, in the case of gabbro, the magma never reached the surface as lava. Instead it intruded rocks below the surface and cooled slowly at depth so that there was time for large crystals to grow.

At a few places, the observant yachtsman will notice that the rocks are layered, built up bed after bed like a pile of books of different thicknesses. Good examples are on the cliffs between Baileys Mistake and Haycock Harbor, beneath and just east of the steep cliff at the northeast end of the beach at Roque Island, and along the shore below the summer cottage at the Cow Yard. Each layer or bed is an accumulation of mud, limey mud, sand, volcanic ash, or large fragments of volcanic rocks (called *breccia*) which long ago settled as sediment on the sea floor, hence their name—*sedimentary* rocks. Most sedimentary rocks, such as sandstone, shale, or limestone, do not contain volcanic materials, but those of the Maine Coast largely do. Some black basaltic lava flows (on the point beyond the fish weir at Roque Island beach, for instance) are also present on this part of the coast. A third type of rock is a glassy one containing scattered white or pink crystals of feldspar. A good example is the reddish rock on the shore of Bucks Harbor in Machias Bay. Such rocks are called *porphyry*. They generally are volcanic igneous rocks which cooled quickly on or near the surface so that only a few crystals had time to form. Some of these porphyries have an intricate swirling banding, like ribbon candy, made by the flow of very sticky and stiff lava.

For the sake of simplicity, the sedimentary rocks with ash and volcanic fragments, the basalt flows, and the porphyries will be collectively termed *volcanics*.

Sailing from the Cow Yard on our next run to Mt. Desert, we pass the now familiar gabbro and volcanics along the shore of Head Harbor Island on the port hand, but to starboard on Steel Harbor Island there is a new rock—massive pink *granite*. The granite continues along the shore of Great Wass Island and the chain of small islands to the bell off Egg Rock; and from here to Casco Bay we shall rarely be out of sight of pink granite. Granite, like gabbro, is an igneous rock that rose as magma from deep in the earth and slowly cooled beneath the earth's surface. Thus like gabbro it is coarsely crystalline; but the minerals are different, hence the pink color rather than the dark colors of gabbro.

Four minerals can be seen in most of the Maine Coast granites, particularly with a magnifying glass: white calcic and sodic feldspar; pink potassium-rich feldspar; *quartz* which looks like glass and is composed of oxygen and silicon; and a black mineral which may be either platey *mica* or fibrous *amphibole,* both of which are made up of oxygen, silicon, magnesium, iron, aluminum, and water.

The most spectacular body of granite on the Maine Coast is that which makes up the mountains of Mt. Desert. This great mass forced its way as magma up through several miles of volcanics. Otter Point is close to the contact between the granite and the host volcanics, and there along the shore line can be seen huge angular blocks of volcanic and sedimentary rocks shattered where they collapsed into the granite magma. On the shores of Bar Harbor and Northeast Harbor are excellent exposures of bedded volcanic and sedimentary rocks; and the Cranberry Islands and Seawall Point are made up primarily of volcanic breccia carrying numerous large fragments of lava and other volcanic rocks spewed out by volcanoes and spread over the sea floor by submarine landslides.

From Mt. Desert to Islesboro the rocks are dominantly granite along with a lesser amount of the volcanics and gabbro that the granites intrude. The shores of Deer Island, Merchant Row, and Isle au Haut are largely granite. The Fox Islands are more complex geologically. Most of North Haven Island, including the shore of Pulpit Harbor, is of dark basaltic lava flows and volcanic breccias. The shore of Fox Island Thorofare displays a spectacular array of red, yellow, and purple porphyries, bedded ash, and coarse breccias full of angular rock fragments torn from the throats of volcanoes by violent eruptions and deposited on the sea floor. Most of Vinalhaven Island is of granite well exposed at Carvers Harbor and in nearby granite quarries.

The Matinicus group of islands is also largely of granite. If fogbound at Criehaven with time to spare, take a walk along the east shore of Ragged Island for about one hundred yards south of Camp Cove to a magnificently exposed contact of granite against bedded rocks. Here is proof that granite is emplaced as a hot liquid. The granite truncates the layers in the bedded sediments along a line as sharp as a pencil line, and small fingers and offshoots of granite extend upward into the host rocks. Clearly, the granite must originally have been a liquid forced into the surrounding rocks. Note that right along the contact and in the offshoots the granite is somewhat finer-grained than elsewhere. The chilling of the magma against the slightly cooler host rocks prevented the growth of large crystals. And the magma must have been hot enough to heat the rocks it intruded, for the latter are very hard and considerably recrystallized.

West of the Fox Islands, the granites continue (the Muscle Ridge is largely in granite) but the rocks the granites intrude are no longer volcanics. The host rocks are now *schists*. We have crossed a contact between volcanics on the east and schists on the west which extends from Owls Head, south of Islesboro, through Castine, Blue Hill, Bartlett's Island, and then inland to the northeast. This zone of schists intruded by granite continues west along the coast to Cape Elizabeth and beyond. Good exposures of schist are on Hooper Island west of Port Clyde, on Pemaquid Point where the schists are laced with sinuous granite dikes, and on the islands of Casco Bay where the north-northeast trend of the islands lines up precisely with the north-northeast trend of the vertical layers in the schist.

Schists are rocks formed by the transformation or metamorphism (hence the term *metamorphic* rock) of older parent rocks, commonly sandstone, shales, and limestones. Although many metamorphic rocks retain the bedding of the parent sedimentary rocks, the original grains of sand, silt, and clay have been completely recrystallized to new minerals, and the rocks have been sheared and very intricately and tightly folded. This recrystallization requires high temperatures and the intricate folding testifies to tremendous pressures. These high temperatures and pressures can only be found deep in the earth's crust; and high-grade metamorphic rocks such as schists probably have at one time been buried to a depth measured in miles.

From West Quoddy Head to Islesboro we have cruised through bays and islands underlain primarily (excluding granite) by gabbro and by volcanic rocks of many kinds. A very few fossils of marine shellfish (brachiopods) found in the volcanics indicate that these rocks date from the Silurian geologic period, some 350 to 3,000 million years ago. Volcanics like these and of approximately the same age extend into New Brunswick to the east and are found near Boston and in the eastern Carolinas to the southwest. Many geologists believe that these volcanic rocks are remnants of a long volcanic island archipelago, much like the present East Indies, which during the Silurian period bordered the North American continent from Georgia into Canada.

The metamorphic schists west of Islesboro represent sedimentary rocks originally deposited on the sea floor which must have been pushed many miles down into the earth's crust to levels where temperatures are high and pressures tremendous. The only earth forces capable of squeezing rocks once at the surface to great depths are those that also raise mountains. Most of the world's present mountain chains, such as the Alps or Himalayas, are composed of thick sequences of sedimentary rocks which have been pushed together as in a vise between major blocks of the earth's crust. Gravity measurements show that high mountain ranges are underlain by masses of light rock—such as sedimentary rocks are—which extend to depths far deeper than the mountains are high. In other words, most of the sedimentary rock has been folded down and forms a root under the mountain range comparable to the underbody of an iceberg. It is in this root that the temperature and pressures are high enough to metamorphose the original sediments into schists.

Our cruise westward from Islesboro through the schists has thus taken us deep into the depths beneath an ancient mountain chain. Similar metamorphic rocks extend from Georgia to Newfoundland, and geologists interpret this belt as the root of a great mountain chain which they call the Appalachian mountain system because the finest, most extensive exposures of this metamorphic belt are in the present-day Appalachian Mountains. The Maine part of the ancient mountain chain is clearly younger than the Silurian volcanics, for they too are folded and fractured, although they were not buried as deeply as the schists. Geologic studies of the Appalachian mountain system suggest that this ancient mountain range was built in different places and different times over a period ranging from 300 million to 200 million years ago.

The masses of granite so numerous along the Maine Coast intrude both the volcanics and the schist, and hence must be younger than the volcanic archipelago or the old Appalachian mountain system. Throughout the world, large intrusions of granite are confined to former mountain systems, and commonly the greater the degree of metamorphism in the root rocks, the more abundant the granite. These facts have led some geologists to the conclusion that the temperatures at the roots of mountain systems may become so high that the rocks not only are metamorphosed but actually melt, and this molten rock is granite magma. The magma thus formed then may work its way upward to cooler levels of the crust beneath the mountains where it crystallizes to granite. Hence it is possible that the granite of Mt. Desert may have begun as a sequence of sedimentary rocks on the sea floor. And today the streams on Mt. Desert and the waves beating against its cliffs are eroding the granite and returning it as sand and clay on the ocean bottom.

Today in the place of the ancient volcanic island archipelago and the old Appalachian mountain range there is the happy configuration of bays and islands that makes the Maine Coast such a good cruising ground. Erosion extending over a period from 200 million to only one million years ago has reduced the former mountain range to a low rolling upland cut by broad valleys in which slow meandering streams flowed southeast to the sea. These valleys were the forerunners of the great bays such as Casco, Penobscot, Blue Hill, Frenchman, and Machias. Above this upland stood a few hills of particularly resistant rocks, the granites of Mt. Desert and Isle au Haut and the metamorphic rocks of Blue Hill and the Camden Hills. Geologists call such erosion remnants *monadnocks*. As erosion gradually removed the weight of overlying rocks, the rocks deep in the roots of the ancient mountains slowly rose so that the volcanics, schists, and granites now at the surface originally were considerably deeper.

Across this rolling upland cut during millions of years of erosion spread the Pleistocene continental ice sheets, possibly as far to the southeast as Georges Shoals. The coast of Maine (during the ice age) must have been much like parts of the present coasts of Greenland and Antarctica. Beginning about one million years ago, there were four separate advances and retreats of the ice; and the intervals when the land was ice-free were probably longer and the weather milder than since retreat of the last ice sheet. In Maine, only the last advance and retreat of the ice has left a record. The advance began about 40 thousand years ago and the last ice disappeared from Maine only about 10 thousand years ago. Ancient man in Eurasia probably followed the arctic game northwards during the last retreat of the ice there.

The glacier, which must have been thousands of feet thick, was armed by innumerable rock fragments imbedded in it and thus was a very effective gigantic file as it moved across the volcanics, schists, and granites. The broad stream valleys were scoured out and deepened to form the present bays; and low hills and knobs were smoothed and polished to make the typical low round Maine island. Close examination of almost any smooth shore-line rocks will show many grooves and striations, generally trending between east and south, made by rocks gripped in the ice at the base of the glacier. The ice was thick enough to bury Mt. Desert and the Camden Hills and locally on the lee slopes (to the southeast) plucked away large blocks of bedrock to form steep cliffs. Valleys, such as those between the mountains on Mt. Desert which once were V-shaped, were scoured out to a U-shape. Somes Sound is the most spectacular example of a scoured-out U-shaped glacial valley east of the Rocky Mountains.

As the glacier melted back, it deposited its load of immense boulders, gravel, sand, and fine rock flour in long, looping, morainal ridges marking the front of any particular ice-lobe, in outwash plains of sand and gravel where streams poured off the ice front, and in patches of bouldery clay scattered randomly over the bedrock. This glacial garbage is a mixture of rock fragments picked up by the ice sheet both locally and hundreds of miles inland. The sand and pebble beaches of Maine are found where the sea has cut into these unconsolidated deposits of gravel, sand, and clay and then has reworked, resorted, and redeposited this material in the wave zone. The beach at Roque Island is perhaps the finest example. The low cliff behind it exposes the glacial bedded sand and clay from which the beach sands are derived. Many of the bars, like those at Bass Harbor Head and Petit Manan, are of glacial debris eroded from the original glacial deposits by the sea and concentrated in bars by tidal currents.

The yachtsman's most intimate contact with deposits arising from the Ice Age is the black sticky mud which makes such good holding ground in Maine's harbors, such a mess of his topsides and deck when the anchor comes aboard, and such extensive and uniquely fragrant mud flats at the head of many coves and bays. Mud like this, commonly with clam shells of a more arctic type than found in Maine today, occurs as far as 100 miles up the Penobscot and Kennebec Rivers at an altitude of more than 100 feet. The same type of black clay occurs in places along the coast up to an altitude of 200 feet. Clearly, the Maine Coast must have been flooded by the sea after the ice retreated to a height of almost 200 feet above present sea level.

The submergence and the rise of the land since was caused by two main factors. The weight of thousands of feet of ice depressed the earth's crust; but at the same time there was enough water stored up in the great continental ice sheets to lower sea level even more, so that during maximum glaciation sea level all over the world was probably as much as 300 feet below what it is today. When the ice melted back, the ocean filled much more rapidly than the earth's crust rose in response to unloading of the ice. Consequently the sea flooded far inland, depositing black and brown mud in protected bays. The black mud on the mudhook was originally deposited there and has since been eroded by waves and streams and residimented on the bottom of Maine's harbors and bays.

Geologists disagree as to whether the sea is still withdrawing from the Maine Coast. If it is doing so, withdrawal is so slow that the Maine Coast will remain a cruising paradise for many future generations of yachtsmen —if we can control the water-skiers and the atom.

APPENDIX C

New York State Pump-out Stations

Here is a selected list of the New York State marinas which, at the time of writing, have pump-out facilities for use by boats equipped with the state's approved marine toilet pollution control devices. Note that this list covers *only* those coastal and inland areas described in this guide and *does not include all* facilities within New York.

A special New York State chart indicating all existing facilities is updated from time to time and may be obtained free by writing the New York State Department of Environmental Conservation, 50 Wolf Road, Albany, N.Y. 12201.

Catskill, N.Y.	Hop-O-Nose Marina
City Island, N.Y.	Consolidated Yachts
	Minneford Boat Yard
Coecles Harbor, N.Y.	Coecles Harbor Marina
Coeymans, N.Y.	Gerry Finke's Marina
Glen Cove, N.Y.	Glen Cove Yacht Service
Hudson, N.Y.	Hudson Power Boat Squadron
Mamaroneck, N.Y.	Nichols Yacht Yard
Mattituck, N.Y.	Mattituck Inlet Boat Basin
New Suffolk, N.Y.	North Fork Shipyard
Port Jefferson, N.Y.	Port Jefferson Marina
Port Washington, N.Y.	Peterson's Shipyard
Sag Harbor, N.Y.	Baron's Cove Marina
Shinnecock Canal, N.Y.	Shinnecock Canal Boat Basin
Staatsburg, N.Y.	Norrie Point Yacht Basin
Tarrytown, N.Y.	Tarrytown, Marina
Threemile Harbor, N.Y.	Threemile Harbor Boat Yard

APPENDIX D

Hospitals

Almost every city along the coasts of New York, Connecticut, Rhode Island, and Massachusetts has a hospital. In Maine however, they are less frequent. Hospitals are located in the following towns and cities:

Kittery	Rockland
York Harbor	Camden
York Village	Belfast
Biddeford	Bangor
Saco	Castine
Portland	Blue Hill
Brunswick	Ellsworth
Bath	Bar Harbor
Boothbay Harbor	Eastport
Damariscotta	Calais

Index

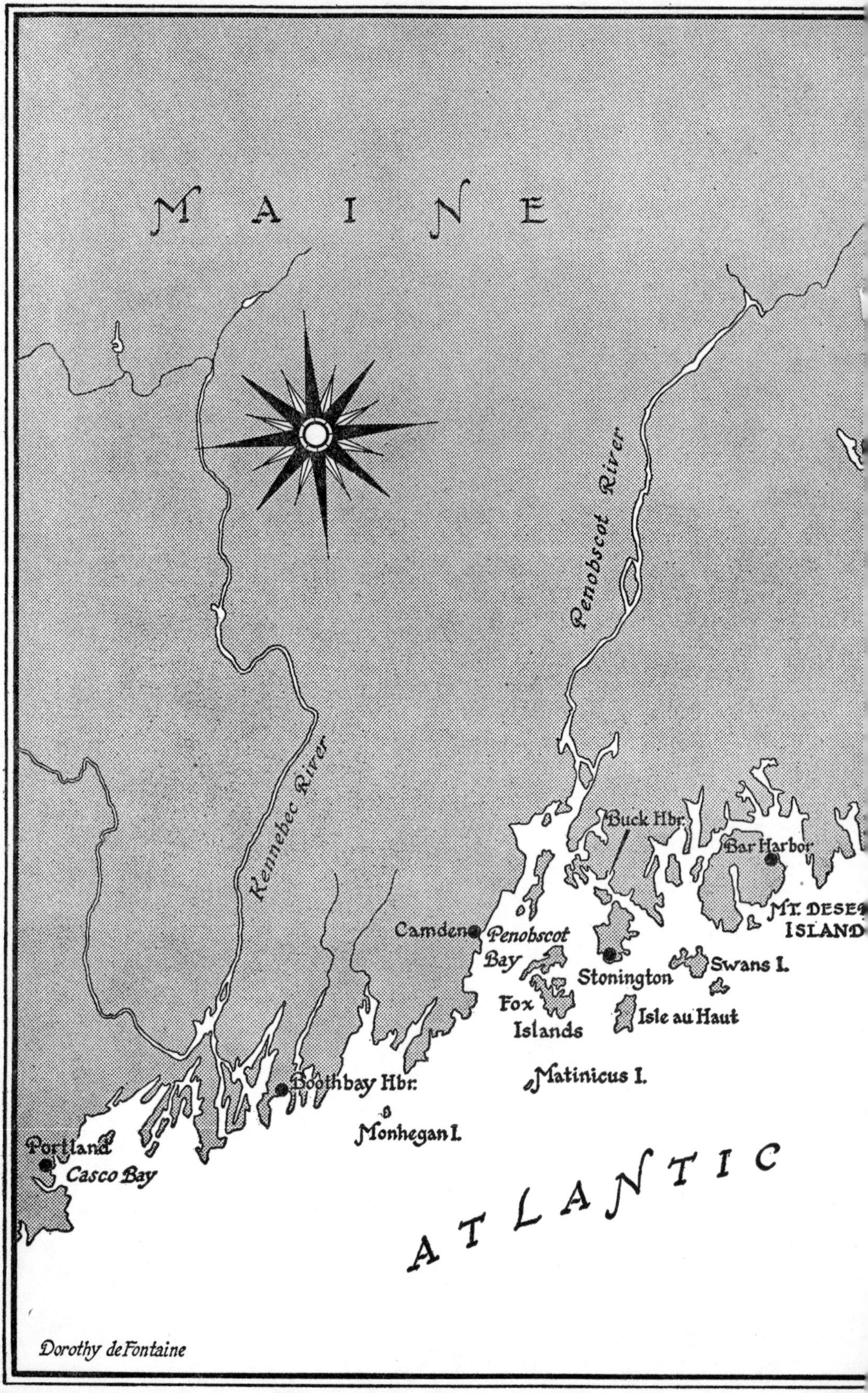

MAINE

Penobscot River

Kennebec River

Buck Hbr.

Bar Harbor

Mt. Desert Island

Camden

Penobscot Bay

Stonington

Swans I.

Fox Islands

Isle au Haut

Matinicus I.

Boothbay Hbr.

Monhegan I.

Portland

Casco Bay

ATLANTIC

Dorothy de Fontaine